STUDY GUIDE

STUDY GUIDE

Richard O. Straub
University of Michigan, Dearborn

to accompany

MYERS' PSYCHOLOGY FOR AP*

David G. Myers

WORTH PUBLISHERS

Study Guide
by Richard O. Straub
to accompany
Myers' Psychology for AP*

© 2011 by Worth Publishers

Printed in the United States of America

ISBN 13: 978-1-4292-5543-1
ISBN 10: 1-4292-5543-9

Second printing 2011

*AP is a trademark registered
and/or owned by the College
Board, which was not involved
in the production of, and does
not endorse, this product.

Worth Publishers

41 Madison Avenue

New York, New York 10010

www.bfwpub.com/highschool

Contents

Preface

This Study Guide is designed for use with *Myers' Psychology for AP** by David G. Myers. It is intended to help you learn material in the textbook, to evaluate your understanding of that material, and then to review any problem areas. Beginning on page ix, "How to Manage Your Time Efficiently and Study More Effectively" provides detailed instructions on how to use the textbook and this Study Guide for maximum benefit. It also offers additional study suggestions based on principles of time management, effective notetaking, evaluation of exam performance, and an effective program for improving your comprehension while studying from textbooks.

This Study Guide offers many useful features. Each unit includes three review tests: In addition to the two Progress Tests that focus on facts and definitions, there is a Psychology Applied test that evaluates your understanding of the text unit's broader conceptual material and its application to real-world situations. This test contains at multiple-choice questions and an essay question. For all three review tests, the correct answers are given, followed by textbook page references (so you can easily go back and reread the material). In addition, complete explanations are given not only of why the answer is correct but also of why the other choices are incorrect.

The unit review is organized by major text section. For each section the fill-in and essay-type questions are organized under their relevant learning objectives.

General Internet Resources

To obtain general information about psychology-related topics, you might want to consult some of the following Web sites. Russ Dewey's Psych Web is an effort to compile a great deal of information for psychology students and teachers, including self-quizzes, lists of psychology journals on the Web, and self-help resources. Psych Web is available at the following site: www.psychwww.com.

Deborah Kelley-Milburn and Michael A. Milburn's "Cyberspace: Resources for Psychologists on the Internet" (*Psychological Science*, [1995, July], Volume 6, 203–211) is another excellent resource. This review provides helpful information on Listservs, Usenet groups, electronic journals and newsletters, databases, grant and job information, and library catalogues.

*AP is a trademark registered and/or owned by the College Board, which was not involved in the production of, and does not endorse, this product.

Both the American Psychological Association (APA) and the American Psychological Society (APS) have Internet services. These services provide not only information about their organizations but also selected articles from their main journals, information about current research in the discipline, and links to other science-related sites on the Internet. Their locations are as follows:

APA: www.apa.org/ and APS: www.psychologicalscience.org

Finally, and perhaps most important, is Psychtalk, a list for students interested in discussion topics and controversies related to psychology. Topics that have been discussed over the past few years include child abuse and the nature-nurture issue. To subscribe, send a message to:

psychtalk-request@fre.fsu.umd.edu

The message should read "subscribe psychtalk (your name)."

Acknowledgments

I would like to thank all the students and instructors who used the college edition of this Study Guide and provided such insightful and useful suggestions. Special thanks are also due to Betty Shapiro Probert for her extraordinary editorial contributions and to Don Probert for his skill and efficiency in the composition of this guide. I would also like to thank Peter Twickler, Jenny Chiu, and Stacey Alexander of Worth Publishers for their dedication and energy in skillfully coordinating various aspects of production. Most important, I want to thank Jeremy, Rebecca, Melissa, and Pam for their enduring love and patience.

Richard O. Straub

How to Manage Your Time Efficiently and Study More Effectively

How effectively do you study? Good study habits make the job of being a college student much easier. Many students, who *could* succeed in college, fail or drop out because they have never learned to manage their time efficiently. Even the best students can usually benefit from an in-depth evaluation of their current study habits.

There are many ways to achieve academic success, of course, but your approach may not be the most effective or efficient. Are you sacrificing your social life or your physical or mental health in order to get A's on your exams? Good study habits result in better grades *and* more time for other activities.

Evaluate Your Current Study Habits

To improve your study habits, you must first have an accurate picture of how you currently spend your time. Begin by putting together a profile of your present living and studying habits. Answer the following questions by writing *yes* or *no* on each line.

_____ 1. Do you usually set up a schedule to budget your time for studying, recreation, and other activities?

_____ 2. Do you often put off studying until time pressures force you to cram?

_____ 3. Do other students seem to study less than you do, but get better grades?

_____ 4. Do you usually spend hours at a time studying one subject, rather than dividing that time between several subjects?

_____ 5. Do you often have trouble remembering what you have just read in a textbook?

_____ 6. Before reading a chapter in a textbook, do you skim through it and read the section headings?

_____ 7. Do you try to predict exam questions from your lecture notes and reading?

_____ 8. Do you usually attempt to paraphrase or summarize what you have just finished reading?

_____ 9. Do you find it difficult to concentrate very long when you study?

_____ 10. Do you often feel that you studied the wrong material for an exam?

Thousands of college students have participated in similar surveys. Students who are fully realizing their academic potential usually respond as follows: (1) yes, (2) no, (3) no, (4) no, (5) no, (6) yes, (7) yes, (8) yes, (9) no, (10) no.

Compare your responses to those of successful students. The greater the discrepancy, the more you could benefit from a program to improve your study habits. The questions are designed to identify areas of weakness. Once you have identified your weaknesses, you will be able to set specific goals for improvement and implement a program for reaching them.

Manage Your Time

Do you often feel frustrated because there isn't enough time to do all the things you must and want to do? Take heart. Even the most productive and successful people feel this way at times. But they establish priorities for their activities and they learn to budget time for each of them. There's much in the saying "If you want something done, ask a busy person to do it." A busy person knows how to get things done.

If you don't now have a system for budgeting your time, develop one. Not only will your academic accomplishments increase, but you will actually find more time in your schedule for other activities. And you won't have to feel guilty about "taking time off," because all your obligations will be covered.

Establish a Baseline

As a first step in preparing to budget your time, keep a diary for a few days to establish a summary, or baseline, of the time you spend in studying, socializing, working, and so on. If you are like many students, much of your "study" time is nonproductive; you may sit at your desk and leaf through a book, but the time is actually wasted. Or you may procrastinate. You are always getting ready to study, but you rarely do.

Besides revealing where you waste time, your diary will give you a realistic picture of how much time you need to allot for meals and other fixed activities. In addition, careful records should indicate the times of the day when you are consistently most productive. A sample time-management diary is shown in Table 1.

Plan the Term

Having established and evaluated your baseline, you are ready to devise a more efficient schedule. Buy a calendar that covers the entire school term and has ample space for each day. Using the course outlines provided by your teachers, enter the dates of all tests, term paper deadlines, and other important academic obligations. If you have any long-range personal plans (concerts, etc.), enter the dates on the calendar as well. Keep your calendar up to date and refer to it often. I recommend carrying it with you at all times.

Develop a Weekly Calendar

Now that you have a general picture of the school term, develop a weekly schedule that includes all of your activities. Aim for a schedule that you can live with for the entire school term. A sample weekly schedule, incorporating the following guidelines, is shown in Table 2.

1. Enter your class times, work hours, and any other fixed obligations first. *Be thorough.* Using information from your time-management diary, allow plenty of time for such things as getting to school, meals, extracurricular activities, and the like.

Table 1   Sample Time-Management Diary

Behavior	Monday Time Completed	Duration Hours: Minutes
Sleep	7:00	7:30
Dressing	7:25	:25
Breakfast	7:45	:20
Walk or bus to school	8:20	:35
Soda or energy drink	9:00	:40
French	10:00	1:00
Socialize	10:15	:15
Video game	10:35	:20
Social networking	11:00	:25
Psychology	12:00	1:00
Lunch	12:25	:25
Study Hall	1:00	:35
Psych. Lab	4:00	3:00
Part-Time Job	5:30	1:30
Walk or bus home	6:10	:40
Dinner	6:45	:35
TV	7:30	:45
Study Psychology	10:00	2:30
Socialize	11:30	1:30
Sleep		

Prepare a similar chart for each day of the week. When you finish an activity, note it on the chart and write down the time it was completed. Then determine its duration by subtracting the time the previous activity was finished from the newly entered time.

2. Set up a study schedule for each of your courses. The study habits survey and your time-management diary will help direct you. The following guidelines should also be useful.

(a) Establish regular study times for each course. The 4 hours needed to study one subject, for example, are most profitable when divided into shorter periods spaced over several days. If you cram your studying into one 4-hour block, what you attempt to learn in the third or fourth hour will interfere with what you studied in the first 2 hours. Newly acquired knowledge is like wet cement. It needs some time to "harden" to become memory.

(b) Alternate subjects. The type of interference just mentioned is greatest between similar topics. Set up a schedule in which you spend time on several *different* courses during each study session. Besides reducing the potential for interference, alternating subjects will help to prevent mental fatigue with one topic.

(c) Set weekly goals to determine the amount of study time you need to do well in each course. This will depend on, among other things, the difficulty of your courses and the effectiveness of your methods. Many

Table 2   Sample Weekly Schedule

Time	Mon.	Tues.	Wed.	Thurs.	Fri.	Sat.
7–8	Dress Eat	Dress Eat	Dress Eat	Dress Eat	Dress Eat	
8–9	Psych.	Study Psych.	Psych.	Study Psych.	Psych.	Dress Eat
9–10	Eng.	Study Eng.	Eng.	Study Eng.	Eng.	Study Eng.
10–11	Study French	Free	Study French	Open Study	Study French	Study History
11–12	French	Study Psychology Lab	French	Open Study	French	Study History
12–1	Lunch	Lunch	Lunch	Lunch	Lunch	Lunch
1–2	History	Psychology Lab	Stats.	Study or Free	Stats.	Free
2–3	History	Psychology Lab	Bio.	Free	Biology	Free
3–4	Free	Psych.	Free	Free	Free	Free
4–5	Job	Job	Job	Job	Job	Free
5–6	Job	Job	Job	Job	Job	Free
6–7	Dinner	Dinner	Dinner	Dinner	Dinner	Dinner
7–8	Study History	Study Biology	Study Biology	Study Biology	Free	Free
8–9	Study English	Study History	Study Psychology	Open Study	Open Study	Free
9–10	Open Study	Open Study	Open Study	Open Study	Free	Free

This is a sample schedule for a student with a 16-credit load and a 10-hour-per-week part-time job. Using this chart as an illustration, make up a weekly schedule, following the guidelines outlined here.

teachers recommend studying at least 1 to 2 hours for each hour in class. If your time-management diary indicates that you presently study less time than that, do not plan to jump immediately to a much higher level. Increase study time from your baseline by setting weekly goals [see (4)] that will gradually bring you up to the desired level. As an initial schedule, for example, you might set aside an amount of study time for each course that matches class time.

(d) Schedule for maximum effectiveness. Tailor your schedule to meet the demands of each course. For the course that emphasizes class notes, schedule time for a daily review soon after the class. This will give you a chance to revise your notes and clean up any hard-to-decipher shorthand while the material is still fresh in your mind. If you are evaluated for class participation (for example, in a language course), allow time for a review just *before* the class meets. Schedule study time for your most difficult (or least motivating) courses during hours when you are the most alert and distractions are fewest.

(e) Schedule open study time. Emergencies, additional obligations, and the like could throw off your

schedule. And you may simply need some extra time periodically for a project or for review in one of your courses. Schedule several hours each week for such purposes.

3. After you have budgeted time for studying, fill in slots for recreation, hobbies, relaxation, household chores, and the like.

4. Set specific goals. Before each study session, make a list of specific goals. The simple note "7–8 PM: study psychology" is too broad to ensure the most effective use of the time. Formulate your daily goals according to what you know you must accomplish during the term. If you have course outlines with advance assignments, set systematic daily goals that will allow you, for example, to cover fourteen chapters before the exam. And be realistic: Can you actually expect to cover a 65-page unit in one session? Divide large tasks into smaller sections; stop at the most logical resting points. When you complete a specific goal, take a 5- or 10-minute break before tackling the next goal.

5. Evaluate how successful or unsuccessful your studying has been on a daily or weekly basis. Did you reach most of your goals? If so, reward yourself immediately. You might even make a list of five to ten rewards to choose from. If you have trouble studying regularly, you may be able to motivate yourself by making such rewards contingent on completing specific goals.

6. Finally, until you have lived with your schedule for several weeks, don't hesitate to revise it. You may need to allow more time for biology, for example, and less for some other course. If you are trying to study regularly for the first time and are feeling burned out, you probably have set your initial goals too high. Don't let failure cause you to despair and abandon the program. Accept your limitations and revise your schedule so that you are studying only 15 to 20 minutes more each evening than you are used to. The point is to *identify a regular schedule with which you can achieve some success.* Time management, like any skill, must be practiced to become effective.

Techniques for Effective Study

Knowing how to put study time to best use is, of course, as important as finding a place for it in your schedule. Here are some suggestions that should enable you to increase your reading comprehension and improve your notetaking. A few study tips are included as well.

Using SQ3R to Increase Reading Comprehension

How do you study from a textbook? If you are like many students, you simply read and reread in a *passive* manner. Studies have shown, however, that most students who simply read a textbook cannot remember more than half the material ten minutes after they have finished. Often, what is retained is the unessential material rather than the important points upon which exam questions will be based.

This Study Guide employs a program known as SQ3R (Survey, Question, Read, Rehearse, and Review) to facilitate, and allow you to assess, your comprehension of the important facts and concepts in *Myers' Psychology for AP**, by David G. Myers.

Research has shown that students using SQ3R achieve significantly greater comprehension of texts than students reading in the more traditional passive manner. Once you have learned this program, you can improve your comprehension of any textbook.

*AP is a trademark registered and/or owned by the College Board, which was not involved in the production of, and does not endorse, this product.

Survey   Before you read a text unit, determine whether the text or the study guide has an outline or list of objectives. *Myers' Psychology for AP** includes an outline and a number of learning objectives for each section of the unit. Read the outline and the objectives (framed as questions), then read the textbook chapter fairly quickly, paying special attention to the major headings and subheadings. This survey will give you an idea of the unit's contents and organization. You will then be able to divide the unit into logical sections in order to formulate specific goals for a more careful reading of the unit.

In this Study Guide, the *Unit Overview* summarizes the major topics of the textbook unit. This section also provides a few suggestions for approaching topics you may find difficult.

Question   You will retain material longer when you have a use for it. Previewing the unit will allow you to generate important questions that the unit will proceed to answer. These questions correspond to "mental files" into which knowledge will be sorted for easy access. The preview questions that appear throughout the text unit can easily be used for this purpose.

As you survey, jot down several additional questions for each unit section. One simple technique is to generate questions by rephrasing a section heading. For example, the "Preoperational Thought" head could be turned into "What is preoperational thought?" Good questions will allow you to focus on the important points in the text. Examples of good questions are those that begin as follows: "List two examples of . . . ." "What is the function of . . .?" "What is the significance of . . .?" Such questions give a purpose to your reading. Similarly, you can formulate questions based on the unit outline.

Read   When you have established "files" for each section of the unit, review your first question, begin reading, and continue until you have discovered its answer. If you come to material that seems to answer an important question you don't have a file for, stop and write down the question.

Using this Study Guide, read the unit one section at a time. First, preview the section by skimming it, noting headings and boldface items. Next, study the appropriate section objectives in the *Unit Review.* Then, as you read the unit section, search for the answer to each objective.

Be sure to read everything. Don't skip photo or art captions, graphs, or marginal notes. In some cases, what may seem vague in reading will be made clear by a simple graph. Keep in mind that test questions are sometimes drawn from illustrations and charts.

Rehearse When you have found the answer to a question, close your eyes and mentally recite the question and its answer. Then *write* the answer next to the question. It is important that you recite an answer in your own words rather than the author's. Don't rely on your short-term memory to repeat the author's words verbatim.

In responding to the objectives, pay close attention to what is called for. If you are asked to identify or list, do just that. If asked to compare, contrast, or do both, you should focus on the similarities (compare) and differences (contrast) between the concepts or theories. Answering the objectives carefully not only will help you to focus your attention on the important concepts of the text but also will provide excellent practice for essay exams.

Rehearsal is an extremely effective study technique, recommended by many learning experts. In addition to increasing reading comprehension, it is useful for review. Trying to explain something in your own words clarifies your knowledge, often by revealing aspects of your answer that are vague or incomplete. If you repeatedly rely upon "I know" in recitation, you really *may not know.*

Rehearsal has the additional advantage of simulating a test, especially one that includes essay questions; the same skills are required in both cases. Too often students study without ever putting the book and notes aside, which makes it easy for them to develop false confidence in their knowledge. When the material is in front of you, you may be able to *recognize* an answer, but will you be able to *recall* it later, when you take a test that does not provide these retrieval cues?

After you have recited and written your answer, continue with your next question. Read, recite, and so on.

Review When you have answered the last question on the material you have designated as a study goal, go back and review. Read over each question and your written answer to it. Your review might also include a brief written summary that integrates all of your questions and answers. This review need not take longer than a few minutes, but it is important. It will help you retain the material longer and will greatly facilitate a final review of each chapter before the exam.

In this Study Guide, the *Unit Review* contains fill-in and brief essay questions for you to complete after you have finished reading the section and have written answers to the objectives. The correct answers are given at the end of the unit. Generally, your answer to a fill-in question should match exactly (as in the case of important terms, theories, or people). In some cases, the answer is not a term or name, so a word close in meaning will suffice. You should answer these questions several times before taking a test, so it's a good idea to mentally fill in the answers until you are ready for a final pretest review. Text page references are provided with each section title, in case you need to reread any of the material.

Also provided to facilitate your review are two *Progress Tests* that include multiple-choice questions and, where appropriate, matching or true–false questions. These tests are *not* to be taken until you have read the unit and completed the *Unit Review.* Correct answers, along with explanations of why each alternative is correct or incorrect, are provided at the end of the unit. The relevant text page numbers for each question are also given. If you miss a question, read these explanations and, if necessary, review the text pages to further understand why. The *Progress Tests* do not test every aspect of a concept, so you should treat an incorrect answer as an indication that you need to review the concept.

Following the two *Progress Tests* is a *Psychology Applied* test, which should be taken just prior to a test. It includes questions that test your ability to analyze, integrate, and apply the concepts in the unit. Each *Psychology Applied* test includes an essay question dealing with a major concept covered in the unit. As with the *Progress Tests*, answers for the *Psychology Applied* test are provided at the end of each unit, along with relevant page numbers.

The core of each unit concludes with *Key Terms.* This requires that you write definitions of all key terms on a separate piece of paper. As with the *Unit Review* learning objectives, it is important that these answers be written from memory, and in your own words. The *Answers* section at the end of the unit gives a definition of each term, sometimes along with an example of its usage and/or a tip to help you remember its meaning.

One final suggestion: Incorporate SQ3R into your time-management calendar. Set specific goals for completing SQ3R with each assigned unit. Keep a record of units completed, and reward yourself for being conscientious. Initially, it takes more time and effort to "read" using SQ3R, but with practice, the steps will become automatic. More important, you will comprehend significantly more material and retain what you have learned longer than passive readers do.

Taking Lecture Notes

Are your class notes as useful as they might be? One way to determine their worth is to compare them with those taken by other good students. Are yours as thorough? Do they provide you with a comprehensible outline of each class? If not, then the following suggestions might increase the effectiveness of your notetaking.

1. Keep a separate notebook for each course. Use $8^1/_2 \times 11$-inch pages. Consider using a ring binder, which would allow you to revise and insert notes while still preserving class order.

2. Take notes in the format of an outline. Use roman numerals for major points, letters for supporting arguments, and so on. Some teachers will make this easy by outlining their points on the board. If the class discussion is not clearly organized, you will probably want to reorganize your notes soon after the class.

3. As you take notes in class, leave a wide margin on one side of each page. Afterward, expand or clarify any shorthand notes while the material is fresh in your mind. Use this time to write important questions in the margin next to notes that answer them. This will facilitate later review and will allow you to anticipate similar test questions.

Evaluate Your Test Performance

How often have you received a grade on a test that did not do justice to the effort you spent preparing for the test? This is a common experience that can leave one feeling bewildered and abused. "What do I have to do to get an A?" "The test was unfair!" "I studied the wrong material!"

The chances of this happening are greatly reduced if you have an effective time-management schedule and use the study techniques described here. But it can happen to the best-prepared student and is most likely to occur on your first exam with a new teacher.

Remember that there are two main reasons for studying. One is to learn for your own general academic development. Many people believe that such knowledge is all that really matters. Of course, it is possible, though unlikely, to be an expert on a topic without achieving commensurate grades, just as one can, occasionally, earn an excellent grade without truly mastering the course material. During a job interview or in the workplace, however, your A in English won't mean much if you can't actually write a clear business letter.

Probably the single best piece of advice to keep in mind when studying for tests is to *try to predict test questions.* This means ignoring the trivia and focusing on the important questions and their answers (with your teacher's emphasis in mind).

A second point is obvious. How well you do on tests is determined by your mastery of *both* class and textbook material. Many students (partly because of poor time management) concentrate too much on one at the expense of the other.

To evaluate how well you are learning the material, analyze the questions you missed on the first test. If your teacher does not review tests during class, you can easily do it yourself. Divide the questions into two categories: those drawn primarily from class and those drawn primarily from the textbook. Determine the percentage of questions you missed in each category. If your errors are evenly distributed and you are satisfied with your grade, you have no problem. If you are weaker in one area, you will need to set future goals for increasing and/or improving your study of that area.

Similarly, note the percentage of test questions drawn from each category. Although tests in most courses cover *both* class notes and the textbook, the relative emphasis of each may vary from teacher to teacher. While your instructors may not be entirely consistent in making up future exams, you may be able to tailor your studying for each course by placing *additional* emphasis on the appropriate area.

Exam evaluation will also point out the types of questions your teacher prefers. Does the test consist primarily of multiple-choice, true–false, or essay questions? You may also discover that a teacher is fond of wording questions in certain ways. For example, a teacher may rely heavily on questions that require you to draw an analogy between a theory or concept and a real-world example. Evaluate both your teacher's style and how well you do with each format. Use this information to guide your future test preparation.

Important aids, not only in studying for tests but also in determining how well prepared you are, are the *Progress* and *Psychology Applied Tests* provided in this Study Guide. If these tests don't include all of the types of questions your teacher typically writes, make up your own practice test questions. Spend extra time testing yourself with question formats that are most difficult for you. There is no better way to evaluate your preparation for an upcoming test than by testing yourself under the conditions most likely to be in effect during the actual test.

A Few Practical Tips

Even the best intentions for studying sometimes fail. Some of these failures occur because students attempt to work under conditions that are simply not conducive to concentrated study. To help ensure the success of your time-management program, here are a few suggestions that should assist you in reducing the possibility of procrastination or distraction.

1. If you have set up a schedule for studying, make your family and friends aware of this commitment, and ask them to honor your quiet study time. Close your door and post a "Do Not Disturb" sign.

2. Set up a place to study that minimizes potential distractions. Use a desk or table, not your bed or an extremely comfortable chair. Keep your desk and the walls around it free from clutter. If you need a place other than your room, find one that meets as many of the above requirements as possible.

3. Do nothing but study in this place. It should become associated with studying so that it "triggers" this activity, just as a mouth-watering aroma elicits an appetite.

4. Never study with the television on or with other distracting noises present. If you must have music in the background in order to mask outside noise, for example, play soft instrumental music. Don't pick vocal selections; your mind will be drawn to the lyrics.

5. Study by yourself. Other students can be distracting or can break the pace at which *your* learning is most efficient. In addition, there is always the possibility that group studying will become a social gathering. Reserve that for its own place in your schedule.

If you continue to have difficulty concentrating for very long, try the following suggestions.

6. Study your most difficult or most challenging subjects first, when you are most alert.

7. Start with relatively short periods of concentrated study, with breaks in between. If your attention starts to wander, get up immediately and take a break. It is better to study effectively for 15 minutes and then take a break than to fritter away 45 minutes out of an hour. Gradually increase the length of study periods, using your attention span as an indicator of successful pacing.

Some Closing Thoughts

I hope that these suggestions help make you more successful academically, and that they enhance the quality of your college life in general. Having the necessary skills makes any job a lot easier and more pleasant. Let me repeat my warning not to attempt to make too drastic a change in your life-style immediately. Good habits require time and self-discipline to develop. Once established, they can last a lifetime.

Psychology's History and Approaches

UNIT OVERVIEW

Psychology's historical development and current activities lead us to define the field as the science of behavior and mental processes. Unit 1 discusses the development of psychology from ancient times until today and the range of behaviors and mental processes being investigated by psychologists in each of the various specialty areas. In addition, it introduces the biopsychosocial approach that integrates the three main levels of analysis followed by psychologists working from the seven major perspectives. Next is an overview of the diverse subfields in which psychologists conduct research and provide professional services.

Unit 1 concludes with a Close-Up explaining how to get your study of psychology off on the right foot by learning (and pledging to follow!) the SQ3R study method. This study method is also discussed in the essay at the beginning of this Study Guide.

NOTE: Answer guidelines for all Unit 1 questions begin on page 9.

UNIT REVIEW

First, skim each section, noting headings and boldface items. After you have read the section, review each objective by answering the fill-in questions that follow it. As you proceed, evaluate your performance by consulting the answers on page 9. Do not continue with the next section until you understand each answer. If you need to, review or reread the section in the textbook before continuing.

What Is Psychology? (pp. 2–7)

Objective 1: Describe the evolution of psychology from its early pioneers to contemporary concerns.

1. Psychological science seeks to answer questions about how people _____ , _____ , and _____ as they do.

2. The Greek philosophers _____ and _____ concluded that the _____ is separate from the _____ and that knowledge is _____ . One of their students, _____ , disagreed, arguing that knowledge grows from the _____ stored in our memories.

3. French philospher _____ believed that _____ _____ flow from the brain through what we call _____ to the muscles, enabling body movements.

4. English philosopher _____ argued that the mind at birth is a blank slate, or _____ _____ . His ideas, together with those of his countryman _____ , helped form _____ , the view that science should rely on _____ and _____ .

5. The first psychological laboratory was founded in 1879 by Wilhelm _____ . His student, _____ , introduced the school of _____ , which explored the basic elements of mind using the method of _____ . This method proved _____ (reliable/unreliable).

6. Under the influence of evolutionary theorist Charles Darwin, psychologist _____ assumed that thinking developed because it was _____ . He founded the school of _____ , which focused on how mental and behavioral processes enable the organism to adapt, survive, and flourish.

7. The first female president of the American Psychological Association was _____ . The first woman to receive a Ph.D. in psychology was _____ .

8. Psychologists who explore thinking and behavior by conducting experiments are called _____ _____ .

Objective 2: Describe the evolution of psychology as defined from the 1920s through today.

9. The historical roots of psychology include the fields of _____ and _____ .

10. Some early psychologists included Ivan Pavlov, who pioneered the study of _____ ; the personality theorist _____ ; and Jean Piaget, who studied _____ .

11. In its earliest years, psychology was defined as the science of _____ life. From the 1920s into the 1960s, psychology in America was redefined as the science of _____ behavior.

12. As a response to Freudian psychology and to _____ , which they considered too mechanistic, pioneers _____ and _____ forged _____ psychology. This new per-

spective emphasized the _____ potential of _____ people.

13. During the 1960s, psychology underwent a _____ revolution as it began to recapture interest in how our _____ processes and retains information. The study of brain activity linked with mental activity is called _____ _____ .

14. The text author defines psychology as the scientific study of _____ and _____ processes.

15. In this definition, "behavior" refers to any action that we can _____ and _____ , and "mental processes" refers to the internal, _____ _____ we _____ from behavior.

16. As a science, psychology is less a set of findings than a way of _____ _____ .

Contemporary Psychology (pp. 8–15)

1. Worldwide, the number of psychologists is _____ (increasing/decreasing). Thanks to international publications and meetings, psychological science is also _____ .

Objective 3: Summarize the nature-nurture debate in psychology, and describe the principle of natural selection.

2. The nature-nurture issue is the controversy over the relative contributions of _____ and _____ .

3. In 1859, naturalist _____ explained species variation by proposing the process of _____ , which works through the principle of _____ _____ . This is the principles that traits contributing to _____ and _____ will most likely be passed on to succeeding generations.

4. Although the debate continues, we will see that _____ works on what _____ endows and that every _____ event is simultaneously a _____ event.

Objective 4: Identify the three main levels of analysis in the biopsychosocial approach, and explain why psychology's varied perspectives are complementary.

5. Each person is a complex _____ that is part of a larger _____ _____ and at the same time composed of smaller systems. For this reason, psychologists work from three main _____ of _____— biological , _____ , and _____-_____— which together form an integrated _____ approach to the study of behavior and mental processes.

6. Psychologists who study how the body and brain enable emotions, memories, and sensory experiences are working from the _____ perspective.

7. Psychologists who study how natural selection influences behavior tendencies are working from the _____ perspective.

8. Psychologists who believe that behavior springs from unconscious drives and conflicts are working from the _____ perspective.

9. Psychologists who study the mechanisms by which observable responses are acquired and changed are working from the _____ perspective.

10. The _____ perspective explores how we encode, process, store, and retrieve information.

11. Psychologists working from the historically important _____ perspective explore how people attempt to fulfill their potential.

12. Psychologists who study how thinking and behavior vary in different situations are working from the _____-_____ perspective.

13. The different perspectives on the big issues _____ (contradict/complement) one another.

Objective 5: Identify some of psychology's subfields, and explain the difference between clinical psychology and psychiatry.

14. The branch of psychology devoted to measuring our abilities, attitudes, and traits is _____ .

15. Psychologists may be involved in conducting _____ _____, which builds psychology's knowledge base, or _____ _____, which seeks solutions to practical problems.

16. Psychologists who study our changing abilities from womb to tomb are _____ psychologists.

17. Educational psychologists study influences on _____ and _____ .

18. Psychologists who investigate our persistent traits are _____ psychologists, where those who explore how we view and affect one another are _____ psycholotgists.

19. Psychologists who help people cope with problems in living are called _____ psychologists. Psychologists who study, assess, and treat troubled people are called _____ psychologists.

20. Medical doctors who provide psychotherapy and treat physical causes of psychological disorders are called _____ .

Close-Up: Tips for Studying Psychology
(pp. 14–15)

Objective 6: Describe several effective study techniques.

1. To master any subject, you must _____ process it.

2. The _____ study method incorporates five steps: a. _____ ,
   b. _____ , c. _____ ,
   d. _____ , and
   e. _____ .

List five additional study tips identified in the text.

a. _____

b. _____

c. _____

d. _____

e. _____

PROGRESS TEST 1

Multiple-Choice Questions

Circle your answers to the following questions and check them with the answers beginning on page 10. If your answer is incorrect, read the explanation for why it is incorrect and then consult the appropriate pages of the text (in parentheses following the correct answer).

1. In its earliest days, psychology was defined as the
   a. science of mental life.
   b. study of conscious and unconscious activity.
   c. science of observable behavior.
   d. science of behavior and mental processes.

2. Who would be most likely to agree with the statement, "Psychology should investigate only behaviors that can be observed"?
   a. Wilhelm Wundt
   b. Sigmund Freud
   c. John B. Watson
   d. William James

3. Today, *psychology* is defined as the
   a. science of mental phenomena.
   b. science of conscious and unconscious activity.
   c. science of behavior.
   d. science of behavior and mental processes.

4. Who introduced the early school of structuralism?
   a. Edward Titchener
   b. Wilhelm Wundt
   c. William James
   d. Mary Whiton Calkins

5. Who wrote the early textbook *Principles of Psychology*?
   a. Wilhelm Wundt   c. Jean Piaget
   b. Ivan Pavlov   d. William James

6. Which of the following exemplifies the issue of the relative importance of nature and nurture on our behavior?
   a. the issue of the relative influence of biology and experience on behavior
   b. the issue of the relative influence of rewards and punishments on behavior
   c. the debate as to the relative importance of heredity and instinct in determining behavior
   d. the debate as to whether mental processes are a legitimate area of scientific study

7. The seventeenth-century philosopher who believed that the mind is blank at birth and that most knowledge comes through sensory experience is
   a. Plato.   c. Descartes.
   b. Aristotle.   d. Locke.

8. Which seventeenth-century philosopher believed that some ideas are innate?
   a. Aristotle   c. Descartes
   b. Plato.   d. Locke.

9. Which psychological perspective emphasizes the interaction of the brain and body in behavior?
   a. biological
   b. cognitive
   c. behavioral
   d. evolutionary

10. A psychologist who explores how Asian and North American definitions of attractiveness differ is working from the _____ perspective.
    a. behavioral   c. cognitive
    b. evolutionary   d. social-cultural

11. A psychologist who conducts experiments solely intended to build psychology's knowledge base is engaged in
    a. basic research.
    b. applied research.
    c. industrial-organizational research.
    d. clinical research.

12. Psychologists who study, assess, and treat troubled people are called
    a. basic researchers.
    b. applied psychologists.
    c. clinical psychologists.
    d. psychiatrists.

13. Today, psychology is a discipline that
   a. connects with a diversity of other fields.
   b. is largely independent of other disciplines.
   c. is focused primarily on basic research.
   d. is focused primarily on applied research.

14. (Close-Up) In order, the sequence of steps in the SQ3R method is
   a. survey, review, question, read, reflect.
   b. review, question, survey, read, reflect.
   c. question, review, survey, read, reflect.
   d. survey, question, read, review, reflect.

15. Psychologists who study how brain activity is linked to memory, perception, and other thought processes are called
   a. humanistic psychologists.
   b. psychiatrists.
   c. clinical psychologists.
   d. cognitive neuroscientists.

Matching Items

Match each psychological perspective, school, and subfield with its definition or description.

Terms

_____ 1. biological perspective
_____ 2. social-cultural perspective
_____ 3. psychiatry
_____ 4. clinical psychology
_____ 5. humanistic perspective
_____ 6. behavioral perspective
_____ 7. industrial-organizational psychology
_____ 8. cognitive perspective
_____ 9. basic research
_____ 10. applied research
_____ 11. evolutionary perspective
_____ 12. psychodynamic perspective
_____ 13. structuralism
_____ 14. functionalism
_____ 15. behaviorism
_____ 16. cognitive neuroscience

Definitions or Descriptions

a. behavior in the workplace

b. how people differ as products of different environments

c. the study of practical problems

d. an early school of psychology that used introspection to explore the contents of the mind

e. the mechanisms by which observable responses are acquired and changed

f. how the body and brain create emotions, memories, and sensations

g. how we encode, process, store, and retrieve information

h. the view that psychology should be an objective science that avoids reference to mental processes

i. how natural selection favors traits that promote the perpetuation of one's genes

j. the study, assessment, and treatment of troubled people

k. brain activity linked with perception, thinking, memory, and language

l. the disguised effects of unfulfilled wishes and childhood traumas

m. adds to psychology's knowledge base

n. an early school of psychology that focused on the adaptive value of thoughts and behaviors

o. the historically significant perspective that emphasized people's potential for growth

p. the medical treatment of psychological disorders

PROGRESS TEST 2

Progress Test 2 should be completed during a final unit review. Answer the following questions after you thoroughly understand the correct answers for the section reviews and Progress Test 1.

Multiple-Choice Questions

1. The first psychology laboratory was established by _____ in the year _____ .
   a. Wundt; 1879   c. Freud; 1900
   b. James; 1890   d. Watson; 1913

2. Who would be most likely to agree with the statement, "Psychology is the science of mental life"?
   a. Wilhelm Wundt
   b. John Watson
   c. Ivan Pavlov
   d. virtually any American psychologist during the 1960s

3. In psychology, *behavior* is best defined as
   a. anything a person says, does, or feels.
   b. any action we can observe and record.
   c. any action, whether observable or not.
   d. anything we can infer from a person's actions.

4. Carl Rogers and Abraham Maslow are most closely associated with
   a. cognitive psychology.
   b. behaviorism.
   c. psychodynamic theory.
   d. humanistic psychology.

5. In defining psychology, the text notes that psychology is most accurately described as a
   a. way of asking and answering questions.
   b. field engaged in solving applied problems.
   c. set of findings related to behavior and mental processes.
   d. nonscientific approach to the study of mental disorders.

6. Two historical roots of psychology are the disciplines of
   a. philosophy and chemistry.
   b. physiology and chemistry.
   c. philosophy and biology.
   d. philosophy and physics.

7. The Greek philosopher who believed that intelligence was inherited was
   a. Aristotle.   c. Descartes.
   b. Plato.   d. Simonides.

8. The way we encode, process, store, and retrieve information is the primary concern of the _____ perspective.
   a. biological   c. social-cultural
   b. evolutionary   d. cognitive

9. Which of the following individuals is also a physician?
   a. clinical psychologist
   b. experimental psychologist
   c. psychiatrist
   d. biological psychologist

10. Dr. Jones' research centers on the relationship between changes in our thinking over the life span and changes in moral reasoning. Dr. Jones is most likely a
    a. clinical psychologist.
    b. personality psychologist.
    c. psychiatrist.
    d. developmental psychologist.

11. Which subfield is most directly concerned with studying human behavior in the workplace?
    a. clinical psychology
    b. personality psychology
    c. industrial-organizational psychology
    d. psychiatry

12. Dr. Ernst explains behavior in terms of different situations. Dr. Ernst is working from the _____ perspective.
    a. behavioral   c. social-cultural
    b. evolutionary   d. cognitive

13. Which perspective emphasizes the learning of observable responses?
    a. behavioral   c. biological
    b. social-cultural   d. cognitive

14. A psychologist who studies how worker productivity might be increased by changing office layout is engaged in _____ research.
    a. applied   c. clinical
    b. basic   d. developmental

15. (Close-Up) A major principle underlying the SQ3R study method is that
    a. people learn and remember material best when they actively process it.
    b. many students overestimate their mastery of text and lecture material.
    c. study time should be spaced over time rather than crammed into one session.
    d. overlearning disrupts efficient retention.

16. The biopsychosocial approach emphasizes the importance of
    a. different levels of analysis in exploring behavior and mental processes.
    b. basic research over pure research.
    c. pure research over basic research.
    d. having a single academic perspective to guide research.

True–False Items

Place a T or an F in the blank next to each statement.

_____ 1. Psychology's three main levels of analysis often contradict each other.

_____ 2. The primary research tool of the first psychologists was the experiment.

_____ 3. The subject matter of psychology has changed over the history of the field.

_____ 4. Every psychological event is simultaneously a biological event.

_____ 5. Today, most psychologists work within the behavioral perspective.

_____ 6. The major perspectives in psychology contradict one another.

_____ 7. (Close-Up) *Spaced practice* promotes better retention than *massed practice*.

_____ 8. (Close-Up) Overlearning hinders retention.

_____ 9. A major goal of psychology is to teach us how to ask important questions and to think critically as we evaluate competing ideas.

_____ 10. The school of structuralism fell from favor in part because the method of introspection was unreliable.

PSYCHOLOGY APPLIED

Answer these questions the day before a test as a final check on your understanding of the unit's terms and concepts.

Multiple-Choice Questions

1. *Psychology* is defined as the "science of behavior and mental processes." Wilhelm Wundt would have omitted which of the following words from this definition?
   a. science of
   b. behavior and
   c. and mental processes
   d. Wundt would have agreed with the definition as stated.

2. Jawan believes that psychologists should go back to using introspection as a research tool. This technique is based on
   a. survey methodology.
   b. experimentation.
   c. self-examination of mental processes.
   d. the study of observable behavior.

3. Dharma's term paper on the history of American psychology notes that
   a. psychology began as the science of mental life.
   b. from the 1920s into the 1960s, psychology was defined as the scientific study of observable behavior.
   c. contemporary psychologists study both overt behavior and covert thoughts.
   d. all of these statements are true.

4. Terrence wants to talk to a professional to help him cope with some academic challenges he's facing. You recommend that he contact a(n)
   a. industrial-organizational psychologist.
   b. developmental psychologist.
   c. counseling psychologist.
   d. psychiatrist.

5. Professor Gutierrez, who believes that human emotions are best understood as being jointly determined by heredity, learning, and the individual's social and cultural contexts, is evidently a proponent of the
   a. psychodynamic perspective.
   b. biopsychosocial approach.
   c. evolutionary perspective.
   d. biological perspective.

6. The philosophical views of John Locke are to those of René Descartes as _____ is to _____ .
   a. nature; nurture
   b. nurture; nature
   c. rationality; irrationality
   d. irrationality; rationality

7. Duiring his presentation on the history of psychology, Sanjay notes that Darwin's theory led most directly to the development of the school of
   a. structuralism.
   b. behaviorism.
   c. functionalism.
   d. humanism.

8. In concluding her report on the "nature-nurture debate in contemporary psychology," Karen notes that
   a. most psychologists believe that nature is a more important influence on the development of most human traits.
   b. most psychologists believe that nurture is more influential.
   c. the issue is more heatedly debated than ever before.
   d. nurture works on what nature endows.

9. Dr. Waung investigates how a person's interpretation of a situation affects his or her reaction. Evidently, Dr. Waung is working from the _____ perspective.
   a. biological   c. cognitive
   b. behavioral   d. social-cultural

10. Dr. Aswad is studying people's enduring inner traits. Dr. Aswad is most likely a(n)
   a. clinical psychologist.
   b. psychiatrist.
   c. personality psychologist.
   d. industrial-organizational psychologist.

11. The psychological perspective that places the MOST emphasis on how observable responses are learned is the _____ perspective.
   a. behavioral   c. social-cultural
   b. cognitive   d. evolutionary

12. During a dinner conversation, a friend says that the cognitive and behavioral perspectives are quite similar. You disagree and point out that the cognitive perspective emphasizes_____ , whereas the behavioral perspective emphasizes _____ .
   a. conscious processes; observable responses
   b. unconscious processes; conscious processes
   c. overt behaviors; covert behaviors
   d. introspection; experimentation

13. Concerning the major psychological perspectives on behavior, the text author suggests that
   a. researchers should work within the framework of only one of the perspectives.
   b. only those perspectives that emphasize objective measurement of behavior are useful.
   c. the different perspectives often complement one another; together, they provide a fuller understanding of behavior than provided by any single perspective.
   d. psychologists should avoid all of these traditional perspectives.

14. (Close-Up) Your roommate announces that her schedule permits her to devote three hours to studying for an upcoming quiz. You advise her to
   a. spend most of her time reading and rereading the text material.
   b. focus primarily on her lecture notes.
   c. space study time over several short sessions.
   d. cram for three hours just before the quiz.

15. (Close-Up) A fraternity brother rationalizes the fact that he spends very little time studying by saying that he "doesn't want to peak too soon and have the test material become stale." You tell him that
   a. he is probably overestimating his knowledge of the material.
   b. if he devotes extra time to studying, his retention of the material will be improved.
   c. the more often students review material, the better their exam scores.
   d. all of these statements are true.

16. The psychological views of William James are to those of Edward Titchener as_____ is to _____ .
   a. nature; nurture
   b. nurture; nature
   c. structuralism; functionalism
   d. functionalism; structuralism

Essay Question

Explain how researchers working from each of psychology's major perspectives might investigate an emotion such as love. (Use the space below to list the points you want to make, and organize them. Then write the essay on a separate piece of paper.)

KEY TERMS

Using your own words, on a separate piece of paper write a brief definition or explanation of each of the following.

1. empiricism
2. structuralism
3. functionalism
4. experimental psychology
5. behaviorism
6. humanistic psychology
7. cognitive neuroscience
8. psychology
9. nature-nurture issue
10. natural selection
11. levels of analysis
12. biopsychosocial approach
13. biological psychology
14. evolutionary psychology
15. psychodynamic psychology
16. behavioral psychology
17. cognitive psychology
18. social-cultural psychology
19. psychometrics
20. basic research
21. developmental psychology
22. educational psychology
23. personality psychology
24. applied research
25. industrial-organizational psychologists
26. human factors psychologists
27. counseling psychology
28. clinical psychology
29. psychiatry
30. SQ3R

ANSWERS

Unit Review

What Is Psychology?

1. think; feel; act
2. Socrates; Plato; mind; body; innate; Aristotle; experiences
3. René Descartes; animal spirits; nerves
4. John Locke; *tabula rasa*; Francis Bacon; empiricism; observation; experimentation
5. Wundt; Edward Titchener; structuralism; introspection; unreliable
6. William James; adaptive; functionalism
7. Mary Calkins; Margaret Floy Washburn
8. experimental psychologists
9. biology; philosophy
10. learning; Sigmund Freud; children
11. mental; observable
12. behaviorism; Carl Rogers; Abraham Maslow; humanistic; growth; healthy
13. cognitive; mind; cognitive neuroscience
14. behavior; mental
15. observe; record; subjective experiences; infer
16. asking and answering questions

Contemporary Psychology

1. increasing; globalizing
2. biology; experience
3. Charles Darwin; evolution; natural selection; reproduction; survival
4. nurture; nature; psychological; biological
5. system; social system; levels; analysis; psychological; social-cultural; biopsychosocial
6. biological
7. evolutionary
8. psychodynamic
9. behavioral
10. cognitive
11. humanistic
12. social-cultural
13. complement
14. psychometrics
15. basic research; applied research

16. developmental

17. teaching; learning

18. personality; social

19. counseling; clinical

20. psychiatrists

Close-Up: Tips for Studying Psychology

1. actively

2. SQ3R; a. survey; b. question; c. read; d. review; e. reflect
   a. Distribute study time.
   b. Learn to think critically.
   c. Listen actively in class.
   d. Overlearn material.
   e. Be a smart test-taker.

Progress Test 1

Multiple-Choice Questions

1. **a.** is the answer. (p. 6)
   b. Psychology has never been defined in terms of conscious and unconscious activity.
   c. From the 1920s into the 1960s, psychology was defined as the scientific study of observable behavior.
   d. Psychology today is defined as the scientific study of behavior and mental processes. In its earliest days, however, psychology focused exclusively on mental phenomena.

2. **c.** is the answer. (p. 6)
   a. Wilhelm Wundt, the founder of the first psychology laboratory, was seeking to measure the simplest mental processes.
   b. Sigmund Freud developed an influential theory of personality that focused on unconscious processes.
   d. William James, author of the early textbook *Principles of Psychology,* was a philosopher and was more interested in mental phenomena than observable behavior.

3. **d.** is the answer. (p. 7)
   a. In its earliest days psychology was defined as the science of mental phenomena.
   b. Psychology has never been defined in terms of conscious and unconscious activity.
   c. From the 1920s into the 1960s, psychology was defined as the scientific study of behavior.

4. **a.** is the answer. (p. 4)

5. **d.** is the answer (p. 6)
   a. Wilhelm Wundt founded the first psychology laboratory.

b. Ivan Pavlov pioneered the study of learning.
c. Jean Piaget was this century's most influential observer of children.

6. **a.** is the answer. Biology and experience are internal and external influences, respectively. (p. 8)
   b. Rewards and punishments are both external influences on behavior.
   c. Heredity and instinct are both internal influences on behavior.
   d. The legitimacy of the study of mental processes does not relate to the internal/external issue.

7. **d.** is the answer. For Locke, the mind at birth was a blank tablet. (p. 3)
   a. Plato assumed that much of intelligence is inherited and therefore present at birth. Moreover, he was a philosopher of ancient Greece.
   b. Aristotle held essentially the same viewpoint as Locke, but he lived in the fourth century B.C.
   c. Descartes believed that knowledge does not depend on experience.

8. **c.** is the answer. (p. 3)
   a. Aristotle was a philosopher in ancient Greece who would have agreed with Locke that knowledge comes from experience.
   b. Plato assumed that character and intelligence are inherited.
   d. Locke believed that the mind is a blank slate at birth.

9. **a.** is the answer. (pp. 10, 11)
   b. The cognitive perspective is concerned with how we encode, process, store, and retrieve information.
   c. The behavioral perspective studies the mechanisms by which observable responses are acquired and changed.
   d. The evolutionary perspective focuses on how the natural selection of traits promoted the survival of genes.

10. **d.** is the answer. (pp. 10, 11)
    a. Behavioral psychologists investigate how learned behaviors are acquired. They generally do not focus on subjective opinions, such as attractiveness.
    b. The evolutionary perspective studies how natural selection favors traits that promote the perpetuation of one's genes.
    c. Cognitive psychologists study the mechanisms of thinking and memory, and generally do not investigate attitudes. Also, because the question specifies that the psychologist is interested in comparing two cultures, d. is the best answer.

11. **a.** is the answer. (p. 13)
    b. & c. Applied and industrial-organizational psychologists tackle practical problems.

d. Clinical psychologists (and researchers) focus on treating troubled people.

12. **c.** is the answer. (p. 13)
    d. Psychiatrists are medical doctors rather than psychologists.

13. **a.** is the answer. (p. 12)
    c. & d. Psychologists are widely involved in *both* basic and applied research.

14. **d.** is the answer. (p. 14)

15. **d.** is the answer. (p. 7)

Matching Items

1. f (p. 10)	7. a (p. 13)	13. d (p. 4)
2. b (p. 10)	8. g (p. 10)	14. n (p. 5)
3. p (p. 13)	9. m (p. 13)	15. h (p. 6)
4. j (p. 13)	10. c (p. 13)	16. k (p. 7)
5. o (p. 10)	11. i (p. 10)	
6. e (p. 10)	12. l (p. 10)	

Progress Test 2

Multiple-Choice Questions

1. **a.** is the answer. (p. 4)

2. **a.** is the answer. (p. 4)
   b. & d. John Watson, like many American psychologists during this time, believed that psychology should focus on the study of observable behavior.
   c. Because he pioneered the study of learning, Pavlov focused on observable behavior and would certainly have *disagreed* with this statement.

3. **b.** is the answer. (p. 7)

4. **d.** is the answer. (p. 6)

5. **a.** is the answer. (p. 7)
   b. Psychology is equally involved in basic research.
   c. Psychology's knowledge base is constantly expanding.
   d. Psychology is the *scientific study* of behavior and mental processes.

6. **c.** is the answer. (p. 6)

7. **b.** is the answer. (p. 2)
   a. Aristotle believed that all knowledge originates with sensory experience.
   c. Descartes was a philosopher of the seventeenth century.
   d. Simonides was a well-known Greek orator.

8. **d.** is the answer. (p. 10)

a. The biological perspective studies the biological bases for a range of psychological phenomena.
b. The evolutionary perspective studies how natural selection favors traits that promote the perpetuation of one's genes.
c. The social-cultural perspective is concerned with variations in behavior across situations and cultures.

9. **c.** is the answer. After earning their M.D. degrees, psychiatrists specialize in the diagnosis and treatment of mental health disorders. (p. 13)
   a., b., & d. These psychologists generally earn a Ph.D. rather than an M.D.

10. **d.** is the answer. The emphasis on change during the life span indicates that Dr. Jones is most likely a developmental psychologist. (p. 13)
    a. Clinical psychologists study, assess, and treat people who are psychologically troubled.
    b. Personality psychologists study our inner traits.
    c. Psychiatrists are medical doctors.

11. **c.** is the answer. (p. 13)
    a. Clinical psychologists study, assess, and treat people with psychological disorders.
    b. & d. Personality psychologists and psychiatrists do not usually study people in work situations.

12. **c.** is the answer. (p. 10)
    a. Psychologists who follow the behavioral perspective emphasize observable, external influences on behavior.
    b. The evolutionary perspective focuses on how natural selection favors traits that promote the perpetuation of one's genes.
    d. The cognitive perspective places emphasis on conscious, rather than unconscious, processes.

13. **a.** is the answer. (p. 10)

14. **a.** is the answer. The research is addressing a practical issue. (p. 13)
    b. Basic research is aimed at contributing to the base of knowledge in a given field, not at resolving particular practical problems.
    c. & d. Clinical and developmental research would focus on issues relating to psychological disorders and life-span changes, respectively.

15. **a.** is the answer. (p. 14)
    b. & c. Although each of these is true, SQ3R is based on the more *general* principle of active learning.
    d. In fact, just the opposite is true.

16. **a.** is the answer. (p. 10)

b. & c. The biopsychosocial approach has nothing to do with the relative importance of basic research and applied research and is equally applicable to both.

d. On the contrary, the biopsychosocial approach is based on the idea that single academic perspectives are often limited.

True–False Items

1. F (p. 10)
2. F (p. 4)
3. T (pp. 4–7)
4. T (p. 9)
5. F (p. 10)
6. F (p. 10)
7. T (p. 14)
8. F (p. 14)
9. T (p. 7)
10. T (p. 4)

Psychology Applied

Multiple-Choice Questions

1. **b.** is the answer. (p. 4)
   a. As the founder of the first psychology laboratory, Wundt certainly based his research on the scientific method.
   c. The earliest psychologists, including Wilhelm Wundt, were concerned with the self-examination of covert thoughts, feelings, and other mental processes.

2. **c.** is the answer. (p. 4)

3. **d.** is the answer. (pp. 4–7)

4. **c.** is the answer. (p. 13)
   a. industrial-organizational psychologists study and advise on behavior in the workplace.
   b. Developmental psychologists investigate behavior and mental processes over the life span.
   d. Psychiatrists are medical doctors who treat medical disorders. There is no indication that Terrence is suffering from a medical disorder.

5. **b.** is the answer. (p. 10)
   a., c., & d. Each of these perspectives is too narrow to apply to Professor Gutierrez's belief. Moreover, the psychodynamic perspective (a.) emphasizes unconscious processes, in which Professor Gutierrez has not expressed a belief.

6. **b.** is the answer. Locke believed that all knowledge comes from experience (nurture). Descartes believed that some ideas are innate (nature). (p. 3)
   c. & d. The text does not discuss the views of these philosophers regarding this issue.

7. **c.** is the answer. Like Darwin, James assumed that thinking, like smelling, developed because it was adaptive. (p. 5)

8. **d.** is the answer. Because both nature and nurture influence most traits and behaviors, the tension surrounding this issue has dissolved. (p. 9)

9. **c.** is the answer. (p. 10)
   a. This perspective emphasizes the influences of physiology on behavior.
   b. This perspective emphasizes environmental influences on observable behavior.
   d. This perspective emphasizes how behavior and thinking vary across situations and cultures.

10. **c.** is the answer. (p. 13)
    a. Clinical psychology is concerned with the study and treatment of psychological disorders.
    b. Psychiatry is the branch of medicine concerned with the physical diagnosis and treatment of psychological disorders.
    d. Industrial-organizational psychologists study behavior in the workplace.

11. **a.** is the answer. (p. 10)

12. **a.** is the answer. (p. 10)
    b. Neither perspective places any special emphasis on unconscious processes.
    c. Neither perspective emphasizes covert behaviors.
    d. Introspection was a research method used by the earliest psychologists, not those working from the cognitive perspective.

13. **c.** is the answer. (p. 10)
    a. The text suggests just the opposite: By studying behavior from several perspectives, psychologists gain a fuller understanding.
    b. & d. Each perspective is useful in that it calls researchers' attention to different aspects of behavior. This is equally true of those perspectives that do not emphasize objective measurement.

14. **c.** is the answer. (p. 15)
    a. To be effective, study must be *active* rather than passive in nature.
    b. Most exams are based on lecture *and* textbook material.
    d. Cramming hinders retention.

15. **d.** is the answer. (p. 15)

16. **d.** is the answer. (pp. 4–5)

Essay Question

A psychologist working from the biological perspective might study the brain circuits and body chemistry that trigger attraction and sexual arousal. A psychologist working from the evolutionary perspective might analyze how love has facilitated the survival of our species. A psychologist working from the psychodynamic perspective might search for evidence that a person's particular emotional feelings are disguised effects of unfulfilled wishes. A psychologist working from the behavioral perspective might study the external stimuli, such as body language, that elicit and reward approach behaviors toward another person. A psychologist working from the cognitive perspective might study how our thought processes, attitudes, and beliefs foster attachment to loved ones. A psychologist working from the humanistic perspective would have explored ways in which love fulfilled the person's growth potential, and a psychologist working from the social-cultural perspective might explore situational influences on attraction and how the development and expression of love vary across cultural groups.

Key Terms

1. **Empiricism** is the view that knowledge comes from experience and that science should rely on observation and experimentation. (p. 3)
2. Introduced by Edward Bradford Titchener, **structuralism** is the early school of psychology that used self-reflection (introspection) to examine the structural elements of the human mind. (p. 4)
3. Introduced by William James, **functionalism** is the early school of psychology that emphasized how behavior and mental processes enable the organism to adapt, survive, and flourish. (p. 5)
4. **Experimental psychology** is the study of thinking and behavior using the experimental method. (p. 6)
5. **Behaviorism** is the view that psychology should focus only on the scientific study of observable behaviors without reference to mental processes. (p. 6)
6. **Humanistic psychology** is the historically significant perspective of psychology that emphasized the growth potential of healthy people. (p. 6)
7. **Cognitive neuroscience** is the study of how brain activity is linked with thought processes such as memory and perception. (p. 7)
8. **Psychology** is the scientific study of behavior and mental processes. (p. 7)
9. The **nature-nurture issue** is the controversy over the relative contributions that genes (nature) and experience (nurture) make to the development of psychological traits and behaviors. (p. 8)
10. **Natural selection** is the principle that those traits of a species that contribute to reproduction and survival are most likely to be passed on to succeeding generations. (p. 8)
11. Psychologists analyze behavior and mental processes from differing complementary views, or **levels of analysis.** (p. 10)
12. The **biopsychosocial approach** is an integrated perspective that focuses on biological, psychological, and social-cultural levels of analysis for a given behavior or mental process. (p. 10)
13. **Biological psychology** studies the links between biological and psychological processes. (p. 10)
14. **Evolutionary psychology** uses principles of natural selection to study thinking and behavior. (p. 10)
15. **Psychodynamic psychology** studies how unconscious drives and conflicts influence behavior and thinking. (p. 10)
16. **Behavioral psychology** focuses on principles of learning in the scientific study of observable behavior. (p. 10)
17. **Cognitive psychology** is the scientific study of thinking, knowing, remembering, and communicating. (p. 10)
18. **Social-cultural psychology** is the study of how situations and culture influence thinking and behavior. (p. 10)
19. **Psychometrics** is the scientific study of the measurement of human abilities, attitudes, and traits. (p. 12)
20. **Basic research** is pure science that aims to increase psychology's scientific knowledge base rather than to solve practical problems. (p. 13)
21. **Developmental psychology** studies physical, cognitive, and social change over the life span. (p. 13)
22. **Educational psychology** studies how psychological processes affect teaching and learning. (p. 13)
23. **Personality psychology** is the study of a person's characteristic pattern of thinking, feeling, and acting. (p. 13)
24. **Applied research** is scientific study that aims to solve practical problems. (p. 13)
25. **Industrial-organizational psychology** applies psychological concepts to optimizing human behavior in the workplace. (p. 13)
26. **Human factors psychology** is the study of how humans and machines interact. (p. 13)

27. **Counseling psychology** is the branch of psychology that helps people cope with challenges in their daily lives. (p. 13)

28. **Clinical psychology** is the branch of psychology concerned with the study, assessment, and treatment of people with psychological disorders. (p. 13)

29. **Psychiatry** is the branch of medicine concerned with the physical diagnosis and treatment of psychological disorders. (p. 13)

30. **SQ3R** is a study method consisting of five steps: *survey, question, read, rehearse,* and *review.* (p. 14)

Research Methods: Thinking Critically With Psychological Science

UNIT OVERVIEW

Unit 2 explains the limits of intuition and common sense in reasoning about behavior and mental processes. To counteract our human tendency toward faulty reasoning, psychologists adopt a scientific attitude that is based on curiosity, skepticism, humility, and critical thinking. Unit 2 also explains how psychologists, using the scientific method, employ the research strategies of description, correlation, and experimentation in order to objectively describe, predict, and explain behavior.

The next section discusses how statistical reasoning is used to help psychologists describe data and to generalize from instances. To describe data, psychologists often rely on measures of central tendency such as the mean, median, and mode, as well as variation measures such as the range and standard deviation. Statistical reasoning also helps psychologists determine when it is safe to generalize from a sample to the larger population.

Unit 2 concludes with a discussion of several questions people often ask about psychology, including whether laboratory experiments are ethical, whether behavior varies with culture and gender, why animal research is relevant, and whether psychology's principles have the potential for misuse.

Unit 2 introduces a number of concepts and issues that will play an important role in later units. Pay particular attention to the strengths and weaknesses of descriptive and correlational research. In addition, make sure that you understand the method of experimentation, especially the importance of control conditions and the difference between independent and dependent variables. Finally, you should be able to discuss three important principles concerning populations and samples, as well as the concept of significance in testing differences.

NOTE: Answer guidelines for all Unit 2 questions begin on page 27.

UNIT REVIEW

First, skim each section, noting headings and boldface items. After you have read the section, review each objective by answering the fill-in questions that follow it. As you proceed, evaluate your performance by consulting the answers beginning on page 27. Do not continue with the next section until you understand each answer. If you need to, review or reread the section in the textbook before continuing.

The Need for Psychological Science
(pp. 19–24)

Objective 1: Define *hindsight bias*, and explain how overconfidence contaminates our everyday judgments.

1. The tendency to perceive an outcome that has occurred as being obvious and predictable is called the _____

   _____ . This phenomenon is

   _____ (rare/common) in

   _____ (children/adults/both children and adults).

2. Our everyday thinking is also limited by _____ in what we think we know.

3. Most people are _____ (better/worse/equally wrong) in predicting their social behavior.

Objective 2: Explain how the scientific attitude encourages critical thinking.

4. The scientific approach is characterized by the attitudes of _____ , _____ , and _____ .

5. Scientific inquiry thus encourages reasoning that examines assumptions, discerns hidden values, evaluates evidence, and assesses conclusions, which is called _____ _____ .

How Do Psychologists Ask and Answer Questions? (pp. 24–37)

Objective 3: Describe how psychological theories guide scientific research.

1. Psychological science uses the _____ _____ to evaluate competing ideas. Psychologists make careful _____ and form _____ , which are _____ based on new _____ .

2. An explanation using an integrated set of principles that organizes and predicts behaviors or events is a _____ . Testable predictions that allow a scientist to evaluate a theory are called _____ . These predictions give direction to _____ .

3. To prevent theoretical biases from influencing scientific observations, research must be reported precisely—using clear _____ _____ of all concepts—so that others can _____ the findings.

4. The test of a useful theory is the extent to which it effectively _____ a range of self-reports and observations and implies clear _____ .

5. Psychologists conduct research using _____ , _____ , and _____ methods.

Objective 4: Compare and contrast case studies, surveys, and naturalistic observation, and explain the importance of random sampling.

6. The research strategy in which one or more individuals is studied in depth to reveal universal principles of behavior is the _____ _____ .

7. Although case studies can suggest _____ for further study, a potential problem with this method is that any given individual may be _____ .

8. The method in which a group of people is questioned about their attitudes or behavior is the _____ . An important factor in the validity of survey research is the order and _____ of questions.

9. We are more likely to overgeneralize and make other mistaken judgments from select samples that are especially _____ .

10. Surveys try to obtain a _____ sample, one that will be representative of the _____ being studied. In such a sample, every person _____ (does/does not) have a chance of being included.

11. Large, representative samples _____ (are/are not) better than small ones.

12. The research method in which people or animals are directly observed in their natural environments is called _____ _____ .

13. Case studies, surveys, and naturalistic observation do not explain behavior; they simply _____ it.

14. Using naturalistic observation, researchers have found that people are more likely to laugh in _____ situations than in _____ situations. Also, using observations of walking speed and the accuracy of public clocks, researchers have concluded that the pace of life _____ (varies/does not vary) from one culture to another.

Objective 5: Describe positive and negative correlations, and explain how correlational measures can aid the process of prediction but not provide evidence of cause-effect relationships.

15. When changes in one factor are accompanied by changes in another, the two factors are said to be _____ , and one is thus able to _____ the other. The statistical expression of this relationship is called a

_____ _____ . A graphical representation of this relationship is called a _____ .

16. If two factors increase or decrease together, they are _____ _____ . If, however, one decreases as the other increases, they are _____ _____ . Another way to state the latter is that the two variables relate _____ .

17. A negative correlation between two variables does not indicate the _____ or _____ of the relationship. Nor does correlation prove _____ ; rather, it merely indicates the possibility of a _____ - _____ relationship.

If your level of test anxiety goes down as your time spent studying for the test goes up, would you say these events are positively or negatively correlated? Explain your reasoning.

18. A correlation between two events or behaviors means only that one event can be _____ from the other.

19. Because two events may both be caused by some other _____ , a correlation does not mean that one _____ the other. For this reason, correlation thus does not enable _____ .

Objective 6: Describe how people form illusory correlations, and explain the human tendency to perceive order in random sequences.

20. A perceived correlation that does not really exist is an _____ _____ .

21. People are more likely to notice and recall events that _____ their beliefs. This error in thinking helps explain many _____ beliefs.

22. Another common tendency is to perceive order in _____ _____ .

23. Patterns and streaks in random sequences occur _____ (more/less) often than people expect, and they _____ (do/do not) appear random.

Objective 7: Explain how experiments help researchers isolate cause and effect, focusing on the characteristics of experimentation that make this possible.

24. To isolate _____ and _____ , researchers _____ control for other _____ .

25. Research studies have found that breast-fed infants _____ (do/do not) grow up with higher intelligence scores than those of infants who are bottle-fed with cow's milk. To study cause-effect relationships, psychologists conduct _____ . Using this method and _____ assigning participants to groups, a researcher _____ the factor of interest while _____ _____ (controlling) other factors.

26. If a behavior changes when an _____ factor is varied, the researcher knows the factor is having an _____ .

27. When neither the participants nor the person collecting the data knows which condition a participant is in, the researcher is making use of the _____ - _____ procedure.

28. Researchers sometimes give certain participants a pseudotreatment, called a _____ , and compare their behavior with that of participants who receive the actual treatment. When merely thinking that one is receiving a treatment produces results, a _____ _____ is said to occur.

29. An experiment must involve at least two conditions: the _____ group, in which people receive the experimental treatment, and the _____ group, in which they do not receive the treatment.

30. To ensure that the two groups are identical, experimenters rely on the _____ _____ of individuals to the experimental conditions.

31. The factor that is being manipulated in an experiment is called the _____ variable. Other factors that may influence the results are called _____ variables. The measurable factor that may change as a result of an experiment's manipulations is called the _____ variable.

32. The aim of an experiment is to _____ a(n) _____ variable, measure the _____ variable, and _____ all other variables.

Explain at least one advantage of the experiment as a research method.

Statistical Reasoning in Everyday Life
(pp. 37–42)

Objective 8: Discuss the importance of statistical principles, and explain how data may be depicted graphically.

1. Researchers use _____ to help them see and interpret their observations.

2. Once researchers have gathered their _____ , they must _____ them. One simple way of visually representing data is to use a _____ _____ . It is important to read the _____ _____ and note the _____ to avoid being misled by misrepresented data.

Objective 9: Describe the three measures of central tendency, and identify the measure most affected by extreme scores.

3. The three measures of central tendency are the _____ , the _____ , and the _____ .

4. The most frequently occurring score in a distribution is called the _____ .

5. The mean is computed as the _____ of all the scores divided by the _____ of scores.

6. The median is the score at the _____ percentile.

7. When a distribution is lopsided, or _____ , the _____ (mean/median/mode) can be biased by a few extreme scores.

Objective 10: Describe two measures of variation.

8. Averages derived from scores with _____ (high/low) variability are more reliable than those with _____ (high/low) variability.

9. The measures of variation include the
   _____ and the
   _____ _____ .

10. The range is computed as the _____
    _____ .

11. The range provides a(n) _____
    (crude/accurate) estimate of variation because it
    _____ (is/is not) influenced by
    extreme scores.

12. The standard deviation is a _____
    (more accurate/less accurate) measure of varia-
    tion than the range. Unlike the range, the
    standard deviation _____
    (does/does not) use information from each score
    in the distribution.

13. The symmetrical, bell-shaped distribution in
    which most scores fall near the
    _____ with fewer and fewer near
    the extremes is called the _____
    _____ .

Objective 11: Identify three principles for making
generalizations from samples.

14. It is safer to generalize from a _____
    sample than from a _____ sample.

15. Averages are more reliable when they are based
    on scores with _____ (high/low)
    variability.

16. Small samples provide a _____
    (more/less) reliable basis for generalizing than
    large samples.

Objective 12: Explain how psychologists decide
whether differences are meaningful.

17. Tests of statistical _____ are used
    to estimate whether observed differences are
    real—that is, to make sure that they are not sim-
    ply the result of _____ variation.
    The differences are probably real if the sample
    averages are _____ and the

difference between them is _____
(relatively small/relatively large).

18. Statistical significance does not necessarily indi-
    cate the importance or _____
    significance of a difference or result.

Frequently Asked Questions About Psychology (pp. 42–46)

Objective 13: Explain the value of simplified laboratory conditions in discovering general principles of
behavior.

1. In laboratory experiments, psychologists' concern
   is not with specific behaviors but with the underlying theoretical _____ .

2. Psychologists conduct experiments on simplified
   behaviors in a laboratory environment to gain
   _____ over the many variables
   present in the "real world." In doing so, they are
   able to test _____
   _____ of behavior that also operate in the real world.

Objective 14: Discuss whether psychological research
can be generalized across cultures and genders.

3. Culture refers to the enduring
   _____ , _____ ,
   _____ , and _____
   shared by a large group of people and passed on
   from one generation to the next.

4. Although specific attitudes and behaviors vary
   across cultures, the underlying _____
   are the same. For instance, throughout the world
   people diagnosed with _____
   exhibit the same _____ malfunc-
   tion. Likewise, similarities between the
   _____ far outweigh differences.

Objective 15: Explain why psychologists study animals, and discuss the ethics of experimentation with both animals and humans.

5. Many psychologists study animals because they are fascinating. More important, they study animals because of the _____ (similarities/differences) between humans and other animals. These studies have led to treatments for human _____ and to a better understanding of human functioning.

6. Some people question whether experiments with animals are _____ . They wonder whether it is right to place the _____ of humans over those of animals.

7. Opposition to animal experimentation also raises the question of what _____ should protect the well-being of animals.

8. The ethical principle that research participants should be told enough about the research to enable them to decide whether they wish to participate is _____

_____ . Another important principle states that participants should be fully

_____ once the research is finished.

Describe the goals of the ethical guidelines for psychological research.

Objective 16: Describe how personal values can influence psychologists' research and its application, and discuss psychology's potential to manipulate people.

9. Psychologists' values _____ (do/ do not) influence their theories, observations, and professional advice.

10. Although psychology _____ (can/cannot) be used to manipulate people, its purpose is to _____ .

PROGRESS TEST 1

Multiple-Choice Questions

Circle your answers to the following questions and check them with the answers beginning on page 28. If your answer is incorrect, read the explanation for why it is incorrect and then consult the appropriate pages of the text (in parentheses following the correct answer).

1. After detailed study of a gunshot wound victim, a psychologist concludes that the brain region destroyed is likely to be important for memory functions. Which type of research did the psychologist use to deduce this?
   a. the case study   c. correlation
   b. a survey   d. experimentation

2. In an experiment to determine the effects of exercise on motivation, exercise is the
   a. control condition.
   b. intervening variable.
   c. independent variable.
   d. dependent variable.

3. To determine the effects of a new drug on memory, one group of people is given a pill that contains the drug. A second group is given a sugar pill that does not contain the drug. This second group constitutes the
   a. random sample.   c. control group.
   b. experimental group. d. test group.

4. Theories are defined as
   a. testable propositions.
   b. factors that may change in response to manipulation.
   c. statistical indexes.
   d. principles that help to organize observations and predict behaviors or events.

5. A psychologist studies the play behavior of young children by watching groups during recess at school. Which type of research is being used?
   a. correlation
   b. case study
   c. experimentation
   d. naturalistic observation

6. To ensure that other researchers can repeat their work, psychologists use
   a. control groups.
   b. random assignment.
   c. double-blind procedures.
   d. operational definitions.

7. The scientific attitude of skepticism is based on the belief that
   a. people are rarely candid in revealing their thoughts.
   b. mental processes can't be studied objectively.
   c. the scientist's intuition about behavior is usually correct.
   d. ideas need to be tested against observable evidence.

8. Which of the following is NOT a basic research technique used by psychologists?
   a. description
   b. replication
   c. experimentation
   d. correlation

9. Psychologists' personal values
   a. have little influence on how their experiments are conducted.
   b. do not influence the interpretation of experimental results because of the use of statistical techniques that guard against subjective bias.
   c. can bias both scientific observation and interpretation of data.
   d. have little influence on investigative methods but a significant effect on interpretation.

10. If shoe size and IQ are negatively correlated, which of the following is true?
   a. People with large feet tend to have high IQs.
   b. People with small feet tend to have high IQs.
   c. People with small feet tend to have low IQs.
   d. IQ is unpredictable based on a person's shoe size.

11. Which of the following would be best for determining whether alcohol impairs memory?
   a. case study   c. survey
   b. naturalistic observation d. experiment

12. Well-done surveys measure attitudes in a representative subset, or _____ , of an entire group, or _____ .
   a. population; random sample
   b. control group; experimental group
   c. experimental group; control group
   d. random sample; population

13. What is the mean of the following distribution of scores: 2, 3, 7, 6, 1, 4, 9, 5, 8, 2?
   a. 5   c. 4.7
   b. 4   d. 3.7

14. What is the median of the following distribution of scores: 1, 3, 7, 7, 2, 8, 4?
   a. 1   c. 3
   b. 2   d. 4

15. What is the mode of the following distribution: 8, 2, 1, 1, 3, 7, 6, 2, 0, 2?
   a. 1   c. 3
   b. 2   d. 7

16. In generalizing from a sample to the population, it is important that
   a. the sample be representative of the population.
   b. the sample be large.
   c. the scores in the sample have low variability.
   d. all of these conditions exist.

17. When a difference between two groups is statistically significant, this means that
   a. the difference is statistically real but of little practical significance.
   b. the difference is probably the result of sampling variation.
   c. the difference is not likely to be due to chance variation.
   d. all of these statements are true.

18. A lopsided set of scores that includes a number of extreme or unusual values is said to be
   a. symmetrical.   c. skewed.
   b. normal.   d. dispersed.

19. Juwan eagerly opened an online trading account, believing that his market savvy would allow him to pick stocks that would make him a rich day trader. This belief best illustrates
   a. a placebo effect.
   b. illusory correlation.
   c. hindsight bias.
   d. overconfidence.

20. Which of the following is the measure of central tendency that would be most affected by a few extreme scores?
   a. mean   c. median
   b. range   d. mode

Matching Items

Match each psychological perspective, school, and subfield with its definition or description.

Terms

_____ 1. culture
_____ 2. median
_____ 3. placebo effect
_____ 4. hindsight bias
_____ 5. mode
_____ 6. range
_____ 7. standard deviation
_____ 8. scatterplot
_____ 9. mean
_____ 10. measures of central tendency
_____ 11. measures of variation
_____ 12. critical thinking
_____ 13. illusory correlation

Definitions or Descriptions

a. the mean, median, and mode
b. the difference between the highest and lowest scores
c. the arithmetic average of a set of scores
d. the range and standard deviation
e. the most frequently occurring score
f. the middle score in a distribution
g. a graphed cluster of dots depicting the values of two variables
h. a measure of variation based on every score
i. shared ideas and behaviors passed from one generation to the next
j. "I-knew-it-all-along" phenomenon
k. reasoning that does not blindly accept arguments
l. experimental results caused by expectations alone
m. false perception of a relationship between two variables

PROGRESS TEST 2

Progress Test 2 should be completed during a final unit review. Answer the following questions after you thoroughly understand the correct answers for the section reviews and Progress Test 1.

Multiple-Choice Questions

1. Which of the following research methods does NOT belong with the others?
   a. case study   c. naturalistic observation
   b. survey   d. experiment

2. To prevent the possibility that a placebo effect or researchers' expectations will influence a study's results, scientists employ
   a. control groups.
   b. experimental groups.
   c. random assignment.
   d. the double-blind procedure.

3. Which statement about the ethics of experimentation with people and animals is FALSE?
   a. Only a small percentage of animal experiments use shock.
   b. Allegations that psychologists routinely subject animals to pain, starvation, and other inhumane conditions have been proven untrue.

c. The American Psychological Association and the British Psychological Society have set strict guidelines for the care and treatment of humans and animals.
   d. More animals are used in psychological research than are killed by humane animal shelters.

4. In an experiment to determine the effects of attention on memory, memory is the
   a. control condition.
   b. intervening variable.
   c. independent variable.
   d. dependent variable.

5. Which of the following is NOT characteristic of a normal curve?
   a. The distribution is bell-shaped and symmetrical.
   b. Most scores fall near the mean.
   c. About 95 percent of all scores fall within one standard deviation on either side of the mean.
   d. The distribution describes many types of psychological data.

6. Which of the following BEST describes the hindsight bias?
   a. Events seem more predictable before they have occurred.
   b. Events seem more predictable after they have occurred.

c. A person's intuition is usually correct.

d. A person's intuition is usually not correct.

7. The procedure designed to ensure that the experimental and control groups do not differ in any way that might affect the experiment's results is called

a. variable controlling.

b. random assignment.

c. representative sampling.

d. stratification.

8. Illusory correlation refers to

a. the perception that two negatively correlated variables are positively correlated.

b. the perception of a correlation where there is none.

c. an insignificant correlation.

d. a correlation that equals −1.0.

9. In generalizing from a sample to the population, it is important that

a. the sample be representative.

b. the sample be nonrandom.

c. the sample not be too large.

d. all of these conditions exist.

10. The strength of the relationship between two vivid events will most likely be

a. significant.

b. positive.

c. negative.

d. overestimated.

11. Which of the following is true, according to the text?

a. Because laboratory experiments are artificial, any principles discovered cannot be applied to everyday behaviors.

b. No psychological theory can be considered a good one until it produces testable predictions.

c. Psychology's theories reflect common sense.

d. Psychology has few ties to other disciplines.

12. Which type of research would allow you to determine whether students' grades accurately predict later income?

a. case study   c. experimentation

b. naturalistic observation   d. correlation

13. In a test of the effects of air pollution, groups of students performed a reaction-time task in a polluted or an unpolluted room. To what condition were students in the unpolluted room exposed?

a. experimental   c. randomly assigned

b. control   d. dependent

14. To study the effects of lighting on mood, Dr. Cooper had students fill out questionnaires in brightly lit or dimly lit rooms. In this study, the independent variable consisted of

a. the number of students assigned to each group.

b. the students' responses to the questionnaire.

c. the room lighting.

d. the subject matter of the questions asked.

15. What is the mode of the following distribution of scores: 2, 2, 4, 4, 4, 14?

a. 2   c. 5

b. 4   d. 6

16. What is the mean of the following distribution of scores: 2, 5, 8, 10, 11, 4, 6, 9, 1, 4?

a. 2   c. 6

b. 10   d. 15

17. What is the median of the following distribution: 10, 7, 5, 11, 8, 6, 9?

a. 6   c. 8

b. 7   d. 9

18. Which of the following is the measure of variation that is most affected by extreme scores?

a. mean   c. mode

b. standard deviation   d. range

19. The set of scores that would likely be most representative of the population from which it was drawn would be a sample with a relatively

a. large standard deviation.

b. small standard deviation.

c. large range.

d. small range.

20. If a difference between two samples is NOT statistically significant, which of the following can be concluded?

a. The difference is probably not a true one.

b. The difference is probably not reliable.

c. The difference could be due to sampling variation.

d. All of these conclusions can be reached.

Matching Items

Match each term with its definition or description.

Terms

_____ **1.** hypothesis
_____ **2.** theory
_____ **3.** independent variable
_____ **4.** dependent variable
_____ **5.** experimental group
_____ **6.** control group
_____ **7.** case study
_____ **8.** survey
_____ **9.** replication
_____ **10.** random assignment
_____ **11.** experiment
_____ **12.** double-blind

Definitions or Descriptions

a. an in-depth observational study of one person
b. the variable being manipulated in an experiment
c. the variable being measured in an experiment
d. the "treatment-absent" group in an experiment
e. testable proposition
f. repeating an experiment to see whether the same results are obtained
g. the process in which research participants are selected by chance for different groups in an experiment
h. an explanation using an integrated set of principles that organizes observations and predicts behaviors or events
i. the research strategy in which the effects of one or more variables on behavior are tested
j. the "treatment-present" group in an experiment
k. the research strategy in which a representative sample of individuals is questioned
l. experimental procedure in which neither the research participant nor the experimenter knows which condition the participant is in

PSYCHOLOGY APPLIED

Answer these questions the day before a test as a final check on your understanding of the unit's terms and concepts.

Multiple-Choice Questions

1. You decide to test your belief that boys drink more soft drinks than girls by finding out whether boys consume more soft drinks per day in the cafeteria than girls do. Your belief is a(n) _____ , and your research prediction is a(n) _____ .

   a. hypothesis; theory
   b. theory; hypothesis
   c. independent variable; dependent variable
   d. dependent variable; independent variable

2. Your friend is conducting a survey to learn how many hours the typical student studies each day. She plans to pass out her questionnaire to the members of her health club. You point out that her findings will be flawed because

   a. she has not specified an independent variable.
   b. she has not specified a dependent variable.
   c. the sample will probably not be representative of the population of interest.
   d. of all of these reasons.

3. The concept of control is important in psychological research because

   a. without control over independent and dependent variables, researchers cannot describe, predict, or explain behavior.
   b. experimental control allows researchers to study the influence of one or two independent variables on a dependent variable while holding other potential influences constant.
   c. without experimental control, results cannot be generalized from a sample to a population.
   d. of all of these reasons.

4. Martina believes that high doses of caffeine slow a person's reaction time. To test this belief, she has five friends each drink three 8-ounce cups of coffee and then measures their reaction time on a learning task. What is wrong with Martina's research strategy?

   a. No independent variable is specified.
   b. No dependent variable is specified.
   c. There is no control condition.
   d. There is no provision for replication of the findings.

5. A researcher was interested in determining whether her students' test performance could be predicted from their proximity to the front of the classroom. So she matched her students' scores on a math test with their seating position. This study is an example of
   a. experimentation.
   b. correlational research.
   c. a survey.
   d. naturalistic observation.

6. Your best friend criticizes psychological research for being artificial and having no relevance to behavior in real life. In defense of psychology's use of laboratory experiments you point out that
   a. psychologists make every attempt to avoid artificiality by setting up experiments that closely simulate real-world environments.
   b. psychologists who conduct basic research are not concerned with the applicability of their findings to the real world.
   c. most psychological research is not conducted in a laboratory environment.
   d. psychologists intentionally study behavior in simplified environments in order to gain greater control over variables and to test general principles that help to explain many behaviors.

7. A teacher constructs a questionnaire to determine how students feel about nuclear disarmament. Which of the following techniques should be used to survey a random sample of the student body?
   a. Every student should be sent the questionnaire.
   b. Only students taking psychology should be asked to complete the questionnaire.
   c. Only students living on the east side of town should be asked to complete the questionnaire.
   d. From an alphabetical listing of all students, every tenth (or fifteenth, for example) student should be asked to complete the questionnaire.

8. If eating saturated fat and the likelihood of contracting cancer are positively correlated, which of the following is true?
   a. Saturated fat causes cancer.
   b. People who are prone to develop cancer prefer foods containing saturated fat.
   c. A separate factor links the consumption of saturated fat to cancer.
   d. None of these statements are necessarily true.

9. The scientific attitude in psychology refers to the fact that
   a. psychologists study only observable behaviors.
   b. psychologists study thoughts and actions with an attitude of skepticism and derive their conclusions from direct observations.
   c. psychological research should be free of value judgments.
   d. all of these statements are true.

10. Rashad, who is participating in a psychology experiment on the effects of alcohol on perception, is truthfully told by the experimenter that he has been assigned to the "high-dose condition." What is wrong with this experiment?
    a. There is no control condition.
    b. Rashad's expectations concerning the effects of "high doses" of alcohol on perception may influence his performance.
    c. Rashad was given a placebo, so the results may be tainted.
    d. All of these statements are correct.

11. A friend is critical of psychological research because it often ignores the influence of culture on thoughts and actions. You point out that
    a. there is very little evidence that cultural diversity has a significant effect on specific behaviors and attitudes.
    b. most researchers assign participants to experimental and control conditions in such a way as to fairly represent the cultural diversity of the population under study.
    c. it is impossible for psychologists to control for every possible variable that might influence research participants.
    d. even when specific thoughts and actions vary across cultures, as they often do, the underlying processes are much the same.

12. The scientific attitude of humility is based on the idea that
    a. researchers must evaluate new ideas and theories objectively rather than accept them blindly.
    b. scientific theories must be testable.
    c. simple explanations of behavior make better theories than do complex explanations.
    d. researchers must be prepared to reject their own ideas in the face of conflicting evidence.

13. Which of the following procedures is an example of the use of a placebo?
   a. In a test of the effects of a drug on memory, a participant is led to believe that a harmless pill actually contains an active drug.
   b. A participant in an experiment is led to believe that a pill, which actually contains an active drug, is harmless.
   c. Participants in an experiment are not told which treatment condition is in effect.
   d. Neither the participants nor the experimenter knows which treatment condition is in effect.

14. If height and body weight are positively correlated, which of the following is true?
   a. There is a cause-effect relationship between height and weight.
   b. As height increases, weight decreases.
   c. Knowing a person's height, one can predict his or her weight.
   d. All of these statements are true.

15. The football team's punter wants to determine how consistent his punting distances have been during the past season. He should compute the
   a. mean.   c. mode.
   b. median.   d. standard deviation.

16. Joe believes that his basketball game is always best when he wears his old gray athletic socks. Joe is a victim of the phenomenon called
   a. statistical significance.
   b. overconfidence.
   c. illusory correlation.
   d. hindsight bias.

17. Esteban refuses to be persuaded by an advertiser's claim that people using their brand of gasoline average 50 miles per gallon. His decision probably is based on
   a. the possibility that the average is the mean, which could be artificially inflated by a few extreme scores.
   b. the absence of information about the size of the sample studied.
   c. the absence of information about the variation in sample scores.
   d. all of these statements.

18. Bob scored 43 out of 70 points on his psychology exam. He was worried until he discovered that most of the class earned the same score. Bob's score was equal to the
   a. mean.   c. mode.
   b. median.   d. range.

19. The four families on your block all have annual household incomes of $25,000. If a new family with an annual income of $75,000 moved in, which measure of central tendency would be most affected?
   a. mean   c. mode
   b. median   d. standard deviation

20. Dr. Salazar recently completed an experiment in which she compared reasoning ability in a sample of females and a sample of males. The means of the female and male samples equaled 21 and 19, respectively, on a 25-point scale. A statistical test revealed that her results were not statistically significant. What can Dr. Salazar conclude?
   a. Females have superior reasoning ability.
   b. The difference in the means of the two samples is probably due to chance variation.
   c. The difference in the means of the two samples is reliable.
   d. She cannot reach any of these conclusions.

Essay Question

Elio has a theory that regular exercise for one month can improve thinking. Help him design an experiment evaluating this theory. (Use the space below to list the points you want to make, and organize them. Then write the essay on a separate piece of paper.)

KEY TERMS

Using your own words, on a separate piece of paper write a brief definition or explanation of each of the following.

1. hindsight bias
2. critical thinking
3. theory

4. hypothesis
5. operational definition
6. replication
7. case study
8. survey
9. population
10. random sample
11. naturalistic observation
12. correlation
13. correlation coefficient
14. scatterplot
15. illusory correlation
16. experiment
17. random assignment
18. double-blind procedure
19. placebo effect
20. experimental group
21. control group
22. independent variable
23. confounding variable
24. dependent variable
25. mode
26. mean
27. median
28. range
29. standard deviation
30. normal curve
31. statistical significance
32. culture
33. informed consent
34. debriefing

ANSWERS
Unit Review

The Need for Psychological Science

1. hindsight bias; common; both children and adults
2. overconfidence
3. equally wrong
4. curiosity; skepticism; humility
5. critical thinking

How Do Psychologists Ask and Answer Questions?

1. scientific method; observations; theories; revised; observations
2. theory; hypotheses; research
3. operational definitions; replicate
4. organizes; predictions
5. descriptive; correlational; experimental
6. case study
7. hypotheses; atypical
8. survey; wording
9. vivid
10. random; population; does
11. are
12. naturalistic observation
13. describe
14. social; solitary; varies
15. correlated; predict; correlation coefficient; scatter-plot
16. positively correlated; negatively correlated; inversely
17. strength; weakness; causation; cause-effect

This is an example of a negative correlation. As one factor (time spent studying) increases, the other factor (anxiety level) decreases.

18. predicted
19. event; caused; explanation
20. illusory correlation
21. confirm; superstitious
22. random events
23. more; do not
24. cause; effect; statistically; factors
25. do; experiments; randomly; manipulates; holding constant
26. experimental; effect
27. double-blind
28. placebo; placebo effect
29. experimental; control
30. random assignment
31. independent; confounding; dependent
32. manipulate; independent; dependent; control

Experimentation has the advantage of increasing the investigator's control of both relevant and irrelevant variables that might influence behavior. Experiments also permit the investigator to go beyond observation and description to uncover cause-effect relationships in behavior.

Statistical Reasoning in Everyday Life

1. statistics
2. data; organize; bar graph; scale labels; range
3. mode; median; mean
4. mode
5. sum; number
6. 50th
7. skewed; mean
8. low; high
9. range; standard deviation
10. difference between the lowest and highest scores
11. crude; is
12. more accurate; does
13. mean; normal curve (normal distribution)
14. representative; biased
15. low
16. less
17. significance; chance; reliable; relatively large
18. practical

Frequently Asked Questions About Psychology

1. principles
2. control; general principles
3. ideas; behaviors; attitudes; traditions
4. processes; dyslexia; brain; genders
5. similarities; diseases
6. ethical; well-being
7. safeguards
8. informed consent; debriefed

Ethical guidelines require investigators to (1) obtain informed consent from potential participants, (2) protect them from harm and discomfort, (3) treat information obtained from participants confidentially, and (4) fully explain the research afterward.

9. do
10. can; enlighten

Progress Test 1

Multiple-Choice Questions

1. **a.** is the answer. In a case study, one person is studied in depth. (p. 26)
   b. In survey research, a group of people is interviewed.
   c. Correlations identify whether two factors are related.
   d. In an experiment, an investigator manipulates one variable to observe its effect on another.

2. **c.** is the answer. Exercise is the variable being manipulated in the experiment. (p. 35)
   a. A control condition for this experiment would be a group of people not permitted to exercise.
   b. An intervening variable is a variable other than those being manipulated that may influence behavior.
   d. The dependent variable is the behavior measured by the experimenter—in this case, the effects of exercise.

3. **c.** is the answer. The control condition is that for which the experimental treatment (the new drug) is absent. (p. 35)
   a. A random sample is a subset of a population in which every person has an equal chance of being selected.
   b. The experimental condition is the group for which the experimental treatment (the new drug) is present.
   d. "Test group" is an ambiguous term; both the experimental and control group are tested.

4. **d.** is the answer. (p. 25)
   a. Hypotheses are testable propositions.
   b. Dependent variables are factors that may change in response to manipulated independent variables.
   c. Statistical indexes may be used to test specific hypotheses (and therefore as indirect tests of theories), but they are merely mathematical tools, not general principles, as are theories.

5. **d.** is the answer. In this case, the children are being observed in their normal environment rather than in a laboratory. (p. 28)
   a. Correlational research measures relationships between two factors. The psychologist may later want to determine whether there are correlations between the variables studied under natural conditions.
   b. In a case study, one subject is studied in depth.
   c. This is not an experiment because the psychologist is not directly controlling the variables being studied.

6. **d.** is the answer. (p. 26)

7. **d.** is the answer. (p. 23)

8. **b.** is the answer. Replication is the repetition of an experiment in order to determine whether its findings are reliable. It is not a research method. (p. 26)

9. **c.** is the answer. (p. 46)
   a., b., & d. Psychologists' personal values can influence all of these.

10. **b.** is the answer. (p. 30)
    a. & c. These answers would have been correct had the question stated that there is a *positive* cor-

relation between shoe size and IQ. Actually, there is probably no correlation at all!

11. **d.** is the answer. In an experiment, it would be possible to manipulate alcohol consumption and observe the effects, if any, on memory. (p. 34)
a., b., & c. These answers are incorrect because only by directly controlling the variables of interest can a researcher uncover cause-effect relationships.

12. **d.** is the answer. (p. 28)
a. A sample is a subset of a population.
b. & c. Control and experimental groups are used in experimentation, not in survey research.

13. **c.** is the answer. The mean is the sum of scores divided by the number of scores. $[(2 + 3 + 7 + 6 + 1 + 4 + 9 + 5 + 8 + 2)/10 = 4.7.]$ (p. 38)

14. **d.** is the answer. When the scores are put in order (1, 2, 3, 4, 7, 7, 8), 4 is at the 50th percentile, splitting the distribution in half. (p. 38)

15. **b.** is the answer. The mode is the most frequently occurring score. Because there are more "twos" than any other number in the distribution, 2 is the mode. (p. 37)

16. **d.** is the answer. (pp. 40–41)

17. **c.** is the answer. (p. 40)
a. A statistically significant difference may or may not be of practical importance.
b. This is often the case when a difference is not statistically significant.

18. **c.** is the answer. (p. 38)

19. **d.** is the answer. (pp. 21–22)
a. In an experiment, a placebo effect means that results were achieved by expectation alone.
b. This is the false perception of a relationship between two events.
c. This is the tendency to believe, after learning an outcome, that one could have foreseen it.

20. **a.** is the answer. As an average, calculated by adding all scores and dividing by the number of scores, the mean could easily be affected by the inclusion of a few extreme scores. (p. 38)
b. The range is not a measure of central tendency.
c. & d. The median and mode give equal weight to all scores; each counts only once and its numerical value is unimportant.

Matching Items

1. i (p. 43)
2. f (p. 38)
3. l (p. 35)
4. j (p. 20)
5. e (p. 37)
6. b (p. 39)
7. h (p. 39)
8. g (p. 29)
9. c (p. 38)
10. a (p. 37)
11. d (p. 39)
12. k (p. 24)
13. m (p. 32)

Progress Test 2

Multiple-Choice Questions

1. **d.** is the answer. Only experiments can reveal cause-effect relationships; the other methods can only *describe* relationships. (p. 34)

2. **d.** is the answer. (p. 34)
a. & b. The double-blind procedure is one way to create experimental and control groups.
c. Research participants are randomly assigned to either an experimental or a control group.

3. **d.** is the answer. Animal shelters are forced to kill 50 times as many dogs and cats as are used in research. (p. 44)

4. **d.** is the answer. (p. 35)
a. The control condition is the comparison group, in which the experimental treatment (the treatment of interest) is absent.
b. Memory is a directly observed and measured dependent variable in this experiment.
c. Attention is the independent variable, which is being manipulated.

5. **c.** is the answer. Only about 68 percent of all cases in a normal curve fall within one standard deviation on either side of the mean. (p. 40)

6. **b.** is the answer. (p. 20)
a. The phenomenon is related to hindsight rather than foresight.
c. & d. The phenomenon doesn't involve whether or not the intuitions are correct but rather people's attitude that they had the correct intuition.

7. **b.** is the answer. If enough participants are used in an experiment and they are randomly assigned to the two groups, any differences that emerge between the groups should stem from the experiment itself. (p. 34)
a., c., & d. None of these terms describes precautions taken in setting up groups for experiments.

8. **b.** is the answer. (p. 32)

9. **a.** is the answer. (p. 40)
b. & c. Large, random samples are more likely to be representative of the populations from which they are drawn.

10. **d.** is the answer. Because we are sensitive to dramatic or unusual events, we are especially likely to perceive a relationship between them. (p. 32)
a., b., & c. The relationship between vivid events is no more likely to be significant, positive, or negative than that between less dramatic events.

11. **b.** is the answer. (p. 25)

a. In fact, the artificiality of experiments is part of an intentional attempt to create a controlled environment in which to test theoretical principles that are applicable to all behaviors.
c. Some psychological theories go against what we consider common sense; furthermore, on many issues that psychology addresses, it's far from clear what the "common sense" position is.
d. Psychology has always had ties to other disciplines, and in recent times, these ties have been increasing.

12. **d.** is the answer. Correlations show how well one factor can be predicted from another. (p. 29)
a. Because a case study focuses in great detail on the behavior of an individual, it's probably not useful in showing whether predictions are possible.
b. Naturalistic observation is a method of describing, rather than predicting, behavior.
c. In experimental research the effects of manipulated independent variables on dependent variables are measured. It is not clear how an experiment could help determine whether IQ tests predict academic success.

13. **b.** is the answer. The control condition is the one in which the treatment—in this case, pollution—is absent. (p. 35)
a. Students in the polluted room would be in the experimental condition.
c. Presumably, all students in both conditions were randomly assigned to their groups. Random assignment is a method for establishing groups, rather than a condition.
d. The word *dependent* refers to a kind of variable in experiments; conditions are either experimental or control.

14. **c.** is the answer. The lighting is the factor being manipulated. (p. 35)
a. & d. These answers are incorrect because they involve aspects of the experiment other than the variables.
b. This answer is the dependent, not the independent, variable.

15. **b.** is the answer. (pp. 37–38)

16. **c.** is the answer. The mean is the sum of the scores divided by the number of scores (60/10 = 6). (p. 38)

17. **c.** is the answer. When the scores are put in order (5, 6, 7, 8, 9, 10, 11), 8 is at the 50th percentile, splitting the distribution in half. (p. 38)

18. **d.** is the answer. Since the range is the difference between the highest and lowest scores, it is by definition affected by extreme scores. (p. 39)

a. & c. The mean and mode are measures of central tendency, not of variation.
b. The standard deviation is less affected than the range because, when it is calculated, the deviation of every score from the mean is computed.

19. **b.** is the answer. Averages derived from scores with low variability tend to be more reliable estimates of the populations from which they are drawn. Thus, a. and c. are incorrect. Because the standard deviation is a more accurate estimate of variability than the range, d. is incorrect. (p. 40)

20. **d.** is the answer. A difference that is statistically significant is a true difference, rather than an apparent difference due to factors such as sampling variation, and it is reliable. (p. 41)

Matching Items

1. e (p. 25)	5. j (p. 35)	9. f (p. 26)
2. h (p. 25)	6. d (p. 35)	10. g (p. 34)
3. b (p. 35)	7. a (p. 26)	11. i (p. 34)
4. c (p. 35)	8. k (p. 27)	12. l (p. 34)

Psychology Applied

Multiple-Choice Questions

1. **b.** is the answer. A general belief such as this one is a theory; it helps organize, explain, and generate testable predictions (called hypotheses) such as "boys drink more soft drinks than girls." (p. 25)
c. & d. Independent and dependent variables are experimental treatments and behaviors, respectively. Beliefs and predictions may involve such variables, but are not themselves those variables.

2. **c.** is the answer. The members of one club are likely to share more interests, traits, and attitudes than will the members of a random sample of students. (pp. 27–28)
a. & b. Unlike experiments, surveys do not specify or directly manipulate independent and dependent variables. In a sense, survey questions are independent variables, and the answers, dependent variables.

3. **b.** is the answer. (p. 35)
a. Although the descriptive methods of case studies, surveys, naturalistic observation, and correlational research do not involve control of variables, they nevertheless enable researchers to describe and predict behavior.
c. Whether or not a sample is representative of a population, rather than control over variables, determines whether results can be generalized from a sample to a population.

4. **c.** is the answer. To determine the effects of caffeine on reaction time, Martina needs to measure reaction time in a control, or comparison, group that does not receive caffeine. (p. 35)
   a. Caffeine is the independent variable.
   b. Reaction time is the dependent variable.
   d. Whether or not Martina's experiment can be replicated is determined by the precision with which she reports her procedures, which is not an aspect of research strategy.

5. **b.** is the answer. (p. 29)
   a. This is not an experiment because the researcher is not manipulating the independent variable (seating position); she is merely measuring whether variation in this factor predicts test performance.
   c. If the study were based entirely on students' self-reported responses, this would be a survey.
   d. This study goes beyond naturalistic observation, which merely describes behavior as it occurs, to determine if test scores can be predicted from students' seating position.

6. **d.** is the answer. (p. 42)

7. **d.** is the answer. Selecting every tenth person would probably result in a representative sample of the entire population of students. (pp. 27–28)
   a. It would be difficult, if not impossible, to survey every student.
   b. Psychology students are not representative of the entire student population.
   c. This answer is incorrect for the same reason as b. This would constitute a biased sample.

8. **d.** is the answer. (p. 30)
   a. Correlation does not imply causality.
   b. Again, a positive correlation simply means that two factors tend to increase or decrease together; further relationships are not implied.
   c. A separate factor may or may not be involved. That the two factors are correlated does not imply a separate factor. There may, for example, be a direct causal relationship between the two factors themselves.

9. **b.** is the answer. Psychology is a science because psychologists use the scientific method and approach the study of behavior and mental processes with attitudes of curiosity, skepticism, and humility. (pp. 22–23)
   a. Psychologists study both overt (observable) behaviors and covert thoughts and feelings.
   c. Psychologists' values definitely do influence their research.

10. **b.** is the answer. (p. 34)

a. The low-dose comparison group is the control group.
c. Rashad was not given a placebo.

11. **d.** is the answer. (p. 43)
    a. In fact, just the opposite is true.
    b. Actually, psychological experiments tend to use the most readily available people, often white North American college students.
    c. Although this may be true, psychological experiments remain important because they help explain underlying processes of human behavior everywhere. Therefore, d. is a much better response than c.

12. **d.** is the answer. (p. 23)
    a. This follows from the attitude of skepticism, rather than humility.
    b. & c. Although both of these are true of the scientific method, neither has anything to do with humility.

13. **a.** is the answer. (p. 35)
    b. Use of a placebo tests whether the behavior of a research participant, who mistakenly believes that a treatment (such as a drug) is in effect, is the same as it would be if the treatment were actually present.
    c. & d. These are examples of *blind* and *double-blind* control procedures.

14. **c.** is the answer. If height and weight are positively correlated, increased height is associated with increased weight. Thus, one can predict a person's weight from his or her height. (p. 30)
    a. Correlation does not imply causality.
    b. This situation depicts a negative correlation between height and weight.

15. **d.** is the answer. A small or large standard deviation indicates whether a distribution is homogeneous or variable. (p. 39)
    a., b., & c. These statistics would not give any information regarding the consistency of performance.

16. **c.** is the answer. A correlation that is perceived but doesn't actually exist, as in the example, is known as an illusory correlation. (p. 32)
    a. Statistical significance is a statement of how likely it is that an obtained result occurred by chance.
    b. Overconfidence is the tendency to think we are more right than we actually are.
    d. Hindsight bias is the tendency to believe, after learning an outcome, that one would have foreseen it.

17. **d.** is the answer. (pp. 40–41)

18. c. is the answer. (pp. 37–38)
 a. The mean is computed as the sum of the scores divided by the number of scores.
 b. The median is the midmost score in a distribution.
 d. The range is the difference between the highest and lowest scores in a distribution.

19. a. is the answer. The mean is strongly influenced by extreme scores. In this example, the mean would change from $25,000 to (75,000 + 25,000 + 25,000 + 25,000 + 25,000)/5 = $35,000. (p. 38)
 b. & c. Both the median and the mode would remain $25,000, even with the addition of the fifth family's income.
 d. The standard deviation is a measure of variation, not central tendency.

20. b. is the answer. (p. 40)
 a. If the difference between the sample means is not significant, then the groups probably do not differ in the measured ability.
 c. When a result is not significant it means that the observed difference is unreliable.

Essay Question

Elio's hypothesis is that daily aerobic exercise for one month will improve memory. Exercise is the independent variable. The dependent variable is memory. Exercise could be manipulated by having people in an experimental group jog for 30 minutes each day. Memory could be measured by comparing the number of words they recall from a test list studied before the exercise experiment begins, and again afterward. A control group that does not exercise *is* needed so that any improvement in the experimental group's memory can be attributed to exercise, and not to some other factor, such as the passage of one month's time or familiarity with the memory test. The control group should engage in some nonexercise activity for the same amount of time each day that the experimental group exercises. The participants should be randomly selected from the population at large, and then randomly assigned to the experimental and control groups.

Key Terms

1. **Hindsight bias** refers to the tendency to believe, after learning an outcome, that one would have foreseen it; also called the *I-knew-it-all-along phenomenon.* (p. 20)
2. **Critical thinking** is careful reasoning that examines assumptions, discerns hidden values, evaluates evidence, and assesses conclusions. (p. 24)
3. A **theory** is an explanation using an integrated set of principles that organizes observations and predicts behaviors or events. (p. 25)
4. A **hypothesis** is a testable prediction, often implied by a theory; testing the hypothesis helps scientists to test the theory. (p. 25)
 Example: In order to test his theory of why people conform, Solomon Asch formulated the testable **hypothesis** that an individual would be more likely to go along with the majority opinion of a large group than with that of a smaller group.
5. An **operational definition** is a precise statement of the procedures (operations) used to define research variables. (p. 26)
6. **Replication** is the process of repeating an experiment, often with different participants and in different situations, to see whether the basic finding generalizes to other people and circumstances. (p. 26)
7. The **case study** is an observation technique in which one person is studied in great depth, often with the intention of revealing universal principles. (p. 26)
8. The **survey** is a technique for ascertaining the self-reported attitudes or behaviors of a representative, random sample of people. (p. 27)
9. A **population** consists of all the members of a group being studied. (p. 28)
10. A **random sample** is one that is representative because every member of the population has an equal chance of being included. (p. 28)
11. **Naturalistic observation** involves observing and recording behavior in naturally occurring situations without trying to manipulate and control the situation. (p. 28)
12. **Correlation** is a measure of the extent to which two factors vary together, and thus of how well either factor predicts the other. (p. 29)
13. The **correlation coefficient** is a statistical measure of the relationship; it can be positive or negative (from -1 to $+1$). (p. 29)
 Example: If there is a **positive correlation** between air temperature and ice cream sales, the warmer (higher) it is, the more ice cream is sold. If there is a **negative correlation** between air temperature and sales of cocoa, the cooler (lower) it is, the more cocoa is sold.
14. A **scatterplot** is a depiction of the relationship between two variables by means of a graphed cluster of dots. (p. 29)

15. **Illusory correlation** is the perception of a relationship where none exists. (p. 32)

16. An **experiment** is a research method in which a researcher directly manipulates one or more factors (independent variables) to observe the effect on some behavior or mental process (the dependent variable); experiments therefore make it possible to establish cause-effect relationships. (p. 34)

17. **Random assignment** is the procedure of assigning participants to the experimental and control conditions by chance, thus minimizing preexisting differences between those assigned to the different groups. (p. 34)

18. A **double-blind procedure** is an experimental procedure in which neither the experimenter nor the research participants are aware of which group is receiving the treatment. It is used to prevent experimenters' and participants' expectations from influencing the results of an experiment. (p. 35)

19. The **placebo effect** occurs when the results of an experiment are caused by expectations alone. (p. 35)

20. The **experimental group** in an experiment is one in which participants are exposed to the independent variable being studied. (p. 35)

    Example: In the study of the effects of a new drug on reaction time, participants in the **experimental group** would actually receive the drug being tested.

21. The **control group** in an experiment is one in which the treatment of interest, or independent variable, is withheld so that comparison to the experimental condition can be made. (p. 35)

    Example: The **control group** in an experiment testing the effects of a new drug on reaction time would be a group of participants given a placebo (inactive drug or sugar pill) instead of the drug being tested.

22. The **independent variable** of an experiment is the factor being manipulated and tested by the investigator. (p. 35)

    Example: In the study of the effects of a new drug on reaction time, the drug is the **independent variable**.

23. A **confounding variable** is any factor other than the independent variable that might affect the factor being measured in an experiment. (p. 35)

24. The **dependent variable** of an experiment is the factor being measured by the investigator, that is, the factor that may change in response to manipulations of the independent variable. (p. 35)

Example: In the study of the effects of a new drug on reaction time, the participants' reaction time is the **dependent variable.**

25. The **mode** is the most frequently occurring score in a distribution; it is the simplest measure of central tendency to determine. (pp. 37–38)

26. The **mean** is the arithmetic average, the measure of central tendency computed by adding the scores in a distribution and dividing by the number of scores. (p. 38)

27. The **median**, another measure of central tendency, is the score that falls at the 50th percentile, cutting a distribution in half. (p. 38)

    Example: When the **mean** of a distribution is affected by a few extreme scores, the **median** is the more appropriate measure of central tendency.

28. The **range** is a measure of variation computed as the difference between the highest and lowest scores in a distribution. (p. 39)

29. The **standard deviation** is a computed measure of how much scores in a distribution deviate around the mean. Because it is based on every score in the distribution, it is a more precise measure of variation than the range. (p. 39)

30. The **normal curve** is the symmetrical, bell-shaped distribution describing many types of psychological data, in which most scores fall near the mean, with fewer and fewer at the extremes. (p. 40)

31. **Statistical significance** means that an obtained result, such as the difference between the averages for two samples, very likely reflects a real difference rather than sampling variation or chance factors. Tests of statistical significance help researchers decide when they can justifiably generalize from an observed instance. (p. 41)

32. **Culture** is the enduring behaviors, ideas, attitudes, and traditions shared by a large group of people and transmitted from one generation to the next. (p. 43)

33. **Informed consent** is the ethical principle that research participants should be told enough about an experiment to enable them to decide whether they wish to participate. (p. 45)

34. **Debriefing** occurs when participants are fully informed about an experiment's purpose and procedures once the study has concluded. (p. 45)

Biological Bases of Behavior: 3A: Neural Processing and the Endocrine System

UNIT OVERVIEW

Unit 3A is concerned with neural processing and the endocrine system. Under the direction of the brain, the nervous and endocrine systems coordinate a variety of voluntary and involuntary behaviors and serve as the body's mechanisms for communication with the external environment.

NOTE: Answer guidelines for all Unit 3A questions begin on page 42.

UNIT REVIEW

First, skim each section, noting headings and boldface items. After you have read the section, review each objective by answering the fill-in and essay-type questions that follow it. As you proceed, evaluate your performance by consulting the answers beginning on page 42. Do not continue with the next section until you understand each answer. If you need to, review or reread the section in the textbook before continuing.

Introduction (pp. 51–52)

Objective 1: Explain why psychologists are concerned with human biology, and describe the ill-fated phrenology theory.

1. In the most basic sense, every idea, mood, memory, and behavior that an individual has ever experienced is a _____ phenomenon.

2. The theory that linked our mental abilities to bumps on the skull was _____ .

3. Researchers who study the links between biology and behavior are called _____

   _____ .

4. We are made up of smaller and smaller _____ ; we are also part of larger _____ . Thus, we are _____ systems.

Neural Communication (pp. 52–58)

Objective 2: Describe the parts of a neuron, and explain how its impulses are generated.

1. Our body's neural system is built from billions of nerve cells, or _____ . Information arriving in the brain and spinal cord from the body travels in _____ neurons. Instructions from the brain and spinal cord are sent to the body's tissues via _____ neurons. The neurons that enable internal communication within the brain and spinal cord are called _____ .

2. The extensions of a neuron that receive messages from other neurons are the _____ .

3. The extension of a neuron that transmits information to other neurons is the _____ ; some of these extensions are insulated by a fatty tissue called the _____ _____ , which helps speed the neuron's impulses.

4. Identify the major parts of the neuron diagrammed below.

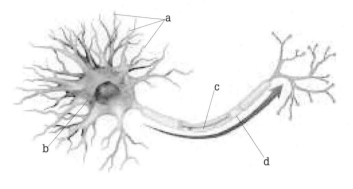

a. _____   c. _____
b. _____   d. _____

5. The neural impulse, or _____ _____ , is a brief electrical charge that travels down a(n) _____ .

6. The fluid interior of a resting axon carries mostly _____ (positively/negatively) charged ions, while the fluid outside has mostly _____ (positively/negatively) charged ions. This polarization, called the _____ _____ , occurs because the cell membrane is _____ _____ .

7. An action potential occurs when the first part of the axon opens its gates and _____ (positively/negatively) charged ions rush in, causing that part of the neuron to become _____ . During the resting pause following an action potential the neuron pumps _____ (positively/negatively) charged ions back outside the cell.

8. To trigger a neural impulse, _____ signals minus _____ signals must exceed a certain intensity, called the _____ . Increasing a stimulus above this level _____ (will/will not) increase the neural impulse's intensity. This phenomenon is called an _____-_____-_____ response.

9. The strength of a stimulus _____ (does/does not) affect the intensity of a neural impulse. A strong stimulus _____ (can/cannot) trigger more neurons to fire.

Objective 3: Describe how nerve cells communicate.

10. The junction between two neurons is called a _____ , and the gap is called the _____ _____ . This discovery was made by _____ .

11. The chemical messengers that convey information across the gaps between neurons are called _____ . These chemicals bind to receptor sites and unlock tiny channels, allowing electrically charged _____ to enter the neuron.

12. Neurotransmitters influence neurons either by _____ or _____ their readiness to fire. Excess neurotransmitters are reabsorbed by the sending neuron in a process called _____ .

Outline the sequence of reactions that occur when a neural impulse is generated and transmitted from one neuron to another.

Objective 4: Describe how neurotransmitters influence behavior, and explain how drugs and other chemicals affect neurotransmission.

13. A neurotransmitter that is important in muscle contraction is _____ ; it is also important in learning and _____ .

14. Naturally occurring opiatelike neurotransmitters that are present in the brain are called _____ . When the brain is flooded with drugs such as _____ or _____ , it may stop producing these neurotransmitters.

15. Drugs that produce their effects by mimicking neurotransmitters are called _____ . Drugs that block the effects of neurotransmitters by occupying their _____ _____ are called _____ . While certain _____ drugs create a temporary "high" by mimicking the endorphins, the poison _____ produces paralysis by blocking the activity of the neurotransmitter ACh.

The Nervous System (pp. 59–62)

Objective 5: Identify the two major divisions of the nervous system, and describe their basic functions.

1. Taken altogether, the neurons of the body form the _____ _____ .

2. The brain and spinal cord form the _____ nervous system. The neurons that link the brain and spinal cord to the body's sense receptors, muscles, and glands form the _____ nervous system.

3. Sensory and motor axons are bundled into electrical cables called _____ .

4. The division of the peripheral nervous system that enables voluntary control of the skeletal muscles is the _____ nervous system.

5. Involuntary, self-regulating responses—those of the glands and muscles of internal organs—are controlled by the _____ nervous system.

6. The body is made ready for action by the _____ division of the autonomic nervous system.

7. The _____ division of the autonomic nervous system produces relaxation.

Describe and explain the sequence of physical reactions that occur in the body as an emergency is confronted and then passes.

8. Neurons cluster into work groups called _____ _____ .

9. Automatic responses to stimuli, called _____ , illustrate the work of the _____ _____ . Simple pathways such as these are involved in the _____-_____ response and in the _____ reflex.

Beginning with the sensory receptors in the skin, trace the course of a spinal reflex as a person reflexively jerks his or her hand away from an unexpectedly hot burner on a stove.

The Endocrine System (pp. 62–63)

Objective 6: Describe the nature and functions of the endocrine system and its interaction with the nervous system.

1. The body's chemical communication network is called the _____ _____ . This system transmits information through chemical messengers called _____ at a much _____ (faster/slower) rate than the nervous system, and its effects last _____ (a longer time/a shorter time).

2. In a moment of danger, the autonomic nervous system orders the _____ glands to release _____ and _____ .

3. The most influential gland is the
_____ , which, under the control of
an adjacent brain area called the
_____ , helps regulate
_____ and the release of hormones
by other endocrine glands.

Write a paragraph describing the feedback system
that links the nervous and endocrine systems.

PROGRESS TEST 1

Multiple-Choice Questions

Circle your answers to the following questions and
check them with the answers beginning on page 43. If
your answer is incorrect, read the explanation for
why it is incorrect and then consult the appropriate
pages of the text (in parentheses following the correct
answer).

1. The axons of certain neurons are covered by a
layer of fatty tissue that helps speed neural transmission. This tissue is
   a. dopamine.
   b. the myelin sheath.
   c. acetylcholine.
   d. an endorphin.

2. Heartbeat, digestion, and other self-regulating
bodily functions are governed by the
   a. voluntary nervous system.
   b. autonomic nervous system.
   c. sympathetic division of the autonomic nervous system.
   d. somatic nervous system.

3. A strong stimulus can increase the
   a. speed of the impulse the neuron fires.
   b. intensity of the impulse the neuron fires.
   c. number of times the neuron fires.
   d. threshold that must be reached before the
neuron fires.

4. The pain of heroin withdrawal may be attributable to the fact that
   a. under the influence of heroin the brain ceases
production of endorphins.
   b. under the influence of heroin the brain ceases
production of all neurotransmitters.
   c. during heroin withdrawal the brain's production of all neurotransmitters is greatly
increased.
   d. heroin destroys endorphin receptors in the
brain.

5. The effect of a drug that is an antagonist is to
   a. cause the brain to stop producing certain
neurotransmitters.
   b. mimic a particular neurotransmitter.
   c. block a particular neurotransmitter.
   d. disrupt a neuron's all-or-none firing pattern.

6. Which is the correct sequence in the transmission
of a simple reflex?
   a. sensory neuron, interneuron, sensory neuron
   b. interneuron, motor neuron, sensory
neuron
   c. sensory neuron, interneuron, motor
neuron
   d. interneuron, sensory neuron, motor
neuron

7. In a resting state, the axon is
   a. depolarized, with mostly negatively charged
ions outside and positively charged ions
inside.
   b. depolarized, with mostly positively charged
ions outside and negatively charged ions
inside.
   c. polarized, with mostly negatively charged
ions outside and positively charged ions
inside.
   d. polarized, with mostly positively charged ions
outside and negatively charged ions inside.

8. Dr. Hernandez is studying neurotransmitter abnormalities in depressed patients. She would
most likely describe herself as a
   a. personality psychologist.
   b. phrenologist.
   c. psychoanalyst.
   d. biological psychologist.

9. Voluntary movements, such as writing with a pencil, are directed by the
   a. sympathetic nervous system.
   b. somatic nervous system.
   c. parasympathetic nervous system.
   d. autonomic nervous system.

10. A neuron will generate action potentials when it
    a. remains below its threshold.
    b. receives an excitatory input.
    c. receives more excitatory than inhibitory inputs.
    d. is stimulated by a neurotransmitter.

11. Which is the correct sequence in the transmission of a neural impulse?
    a. axon, dendrite, cell body, synapse
    b. dendrite, axon, cell body, synapse
    c. synapse, axon, dendrite, cell body
    d. dendrite, cell body, axon, synapse

Matching Items

Match each structure or technique with its corresponding function or description.

Structures

_____ 1. sensory neuron
_____ 2. axon
_____ 3. threshold
_____ 4. motor neuron
_____ 5. dendrite
_____ 6. synapse
_____ 7. reuptake
_____ 8. action potential
_____ 9. myelin sheath
_____ 10. interneuron
_____ 11. neuron

Functions or Descriptions

a. absorption of excess neurotransmitters
b. carries incoming information to the brain and spinal cord
c. insulates the axons of certain neurons
d. neuron extension through which messages pass to other neurons
e. nerve cell
f. level of stimulation required to trigger an action potential
g. carries outgoing information from the brain and spinal cord
h. neuron extension that receives incoming information
i. junction between two neurons
j. neural impulse
k. neurons within the brain and spinal cord

PROGRESS TEST 2

Progress Test 2 should be completed during a final unit review. Answer the following questions after you thoroughly understand the correct answers for the section reviews and Progress Test 1.

Multiple-Choice Questions

1. When Sandy scalded her toe in a tub of hot water, the pain message was carried to her spinal cord by the _____ nervous system.
   a. somatic
   b. sympathetic
   c. parasympathetic
   d. central

2. Which of the following are governed by the simplest neural pathways?
   a. emotions
   b. physiological drives, such as hunger
   c. reflexes
   d. movements, such as walking

3. Melissa has just completed running a marathon. She is so elated that she feels little fatigue or discomfort. Her lack of pain is probably the result of the release of
   a. ACh.
   b. endorphins.
   c. dopamine.
   d. norepinephrine.

4. The myelin sheath that is on some neurons
   a. increases the speed of neural transmission.
   b. slows neural transmission.
   c. regulates the release of neurotransmitters.
   d. prevents positive ions from passing through the membrane.

5. I am a relatively fast-acting chemical messenger that affects mood, hunger, sleep, and arousal. What am I?
   a. acetylcholine
   b. dopamine
   c. norepinephrine
   d. serotonin

6. The neurotransmitter acetylcholine (ACh) is most likely to be found
   a. at the junction between sensory neurons and muscle fibers.
   b. at the junction between motor neurons and muscle fibers.
   c. at junctions between interneurons.
   d. in all of these locations.

7. The gland that regulates body growth is the
   a. adrenal.   c. hypothalamus.
   b. thyroid.   d. pituitary.

8. Epinephrine and norepinephrine are _____ that are released by the _____ gland.
   a. neurotransmitters; pituitary
   b. hormones; pituitary
   c. neurotransmitters; thyroid
   d. hormones; adrenal

9. The effect of a drug that is an agonist is to
   a. cause the brain to stop producing certain neurotransmitters.
   b. mimic a particular neurotransmitter.
   c. block a particular neurotransmitter.
   d. disrupt a neuron's all-or-none firing pattern.

10. Chemical messengers produced by endocrine glands are called
    a. agonists.   c. hormones.
    b. neurotransmitters.   d. enzymes.

11. In the brain, learning occurs as experience strengthens certain connections in cell work groups called
    a. action potentials.   c. endocrine systems.
    b. neural networks.   d. dendrites.

Matching Items
Match each structure or term with its corresponding function or description.

Structures or Terms

_____ 1. biological psychology
_____ 2. endorphins
_____ 3. central nervous system
_____ 4. peripheral nervous system
_____ 5. autonomic nervous system
_____ 6. sympathetic nervous system
_____ 7. nerve
_____ 8. somatic nervous system
_____ 9. endocrine system
_____ 10. parasympathetic nervous system
_____ 11. neurotransmitters

Functions or Descriptions

a. natural, opiatelike neurotransmitters
b. body's system of glands
c. concerned with the links between biology and behavior
d. the brain and spinal cord
e. connects the brain and spinal cord to the rest of the body
f. bundled axons
g. arouses the body
h. calms the body
i. controls the glands and muscles of internal organs
j. enables voluntary control of skeletal muscles
k. chemical messengers released into synapses

PSYCHOLOGY APPLIED

Answer these questions the day before a test as a final check on your understanding of the unit's terms and concepts.

Multiple-Choice Questions

1. A biological psychologist would be *more* likely to study
   a. how you learn to express emotions.
   b. how to help people overcome emotional disorders.
   c. life-span changes in the expression of emotion.
   d. the chemical changes that accompany emotions.

2. You are able to pull your hand quickly away from hot water before pain is felt because
   a. movement of the hand is a reflex that involves intervention of the spinal cord only.
   b. movement of the hand does not require intervention by the central nervous system.
   c. the brain reacts quickly to prevent severe injury.
   d. the autonomic division of the peripheral nervous system intervenes to speed contraction of the muscles of the hand.

3. Several shy neurons send an inhibitory message to neighboring neuron Joni. At the same time, a larger group of party-going neurons sends Joni excitatory messages. What will Joni do?
   a. fire, assuming that her threshold has been reached
   b. not fire, even if her threshold has been reached
   c. enter a resting potential.
   d. become hyperpolarized

4. Following Jayshree's near-fatal car accident, her physician noticed that the pupillary reflex of her eyes was abnormal. This MAY indicate that Jayshree's _____ was damaged in the accident.
   a. myelin sheath
   b. autonomic nervous system
   c. pituitary gland
   d. somatic nervous system

5. I am a relatively fast-acting chemical messenger that influences movement, learning, attention, and emotion. What am I?
   a. dopamine   c. acetylcholine
   b. a hormone   d. glutamate

6. Since Malcolm has been taking a drug prescribed by his doctor, he no longer enjoys the little pleasures of life, such as eating and drinking. His doctor explains that this is because the drug
   a. triggers release of dopamine.
   b. inhibits release of dopamine.
   c. triggers release of ACh.
   d. inhibits release of ACh.

7. Which of the following was a major problem with phrenology?
   a. It was "ahead of its time" and no one believed it could be true.
   b. The brain is not neatly organized into structures that correspond to our categories of behavior.
   c. The brains of humans and animals are much less similar than the theory implied.
   d. All of these were problems with phrenology.

8. I am a relatively slow-acting (but long-lasting) chemical messenger carried throughout the body by the bloodstream. What am I?
   a. a hormone
   b. a neurotransmitter
   c. acetylcholine
   d. dopamine

9. Your brother has been taking prescription medicine and experiencing a number of unpleasant side effects, including unusually rapid heartbeat and excessive perspiration. It is likely that the medicine is exaggerating activity in the
   a. central nervous system.
   b. sympathetic nervous system.
   c. parasympathetic nervous system.
   d. somatic nervous system.

10. A bodybuilder friend suddenly seems to have grown several inches in height. You suspect that your friend's growth spurt has occurred because he has been using drugs that affect the
    a. pituitary gland.
    b. parathyroids.
    c. adrenal glands.
    d. pancreas.

Essay Question

Discuss how the endocrine and nervous systems become involved when a student feels stress—such as that associated with an upcoming final exam. (Use the space below to list the points you want to make, and organize them. Then write the essay on a separate sheet of paper.)

KEY TERMS

Using your own words, on a piece of paper write a brief definition or explanation of each of the following terms.

1. biological psychology
2. neuron
3. sensory neurons
4. motor neurons
5. interneurons
6. dendrite
7. axon
8. myelin sheath
9. action potential
10. threshold
11. synapse
12. neurotransmitters
13. reuptake
14. endorphins
15. nervous system
16. central nervous system (CNS)
17. peripheral nervous system (PNS)
18. nerves
19. somatic nervous system
20. autonomic nervous system
21. sympathetic nervous system
22. parasympathetic nervous system
23. reflex
24. endocrine system
25. hormones
26. adrenal glands
27. pituitary gland

ANSWERS

Unit Review

Introduction

1. biological
2. phrenology
3. biological psychologists
4. subsystems; systems; biopsychosocial

Neural Communication

1. neurons; sensory; motor; interneurons
2. dendrites
3. axon; myelin sheath
4. a. dendrites
   b. cell body
   c. axon
   d. myelin sheath
5. action potential; axon
6. negatively; positively; resting potential; selectively permeable
7. positively; depolarized; positively
8. excitatory; inhibitory; threshold; will not; all-or-none
9. does not; can
10. synapse; synaptic cleft (gap); Sir Charles Sherrington
11. neurotransmitters; atoms
12. exciting; inhibiting; reuptake

A neural impulse is generated by excitatory signals minus inhibitory signals exceeding a certain threshold. The stimuli are received through the dendrites, combined in the cell body, and electrically transmitted in an all-or-none fashion down the length of the axon. When the combined signal reaches the end of the axon, chemical messengers called neurotransmitters are released into the synaptic cleft, or gap, between two neurons. Neurotransmitter molecules bind to receptor sites on the dendrites of neighboring neurons and have either an excitatory or inhibitory influence on that neuron's tendency to generate its own neural impulse.

13. acetylcholine (ACh); memory

14. endorphins; heroin; morphine

15. agonists; receptor sites; antagonists; opiate; curare

The Nervous System

1. nervous system

2. central; peripheral

3. nerves

4. somatic

5. autonomic

6. sympathetic

7. parasympathetic

The sympathetic division of the autonomic nervous system becomes aroused in response to an emergency. The physiological changes that occur include accelerated heartbeat, elevated blood sugar, slowing of digestion, and increased perspiration to cool the body. When the emergency is over, the parasympathetic nervous system produces the opposite physical reactions.

8. neural networks

9. reflexes; spinal cord; knee-jerk; pain

From sensory receptors in the skin the message travels via sensory neurons to an interneuron in the spinal cord, which in turn activates a motor neuron. This motor neuron causes the muscles in the hand to contract, and the person jerks his or her hand away from the heat.

The Endocrine System

1. endocrine system; hormones; slower; a longer time

2. adrenal; epinephrine; norepinephrine

3. pituitary; hypothalamus; growth

The hypothalamus in the brain controls the pituitary. The pituitary regulates other endocrine glands, which release hormones that influence the brain, which directs behavior.

Progress Test 1

Multiple-Choice Questions

1. **b.** is the answer. (p. 53)
   a. Dopamine is a neurotransmitter that influences movement, learning, attention, and emotion.
   c. Acetylcholine is a neurotransmitter that triggers muscle contraction.

d. Endorphins are opiatelike neurotransmitters linked to pain control and to pleasure.

2. **b.** is the answer. The autonomic nervous system controls internal functioning, including heartbeat, digestion, and glandular activity. (p. 59)
   a. The functions mentioned are all automatic, not voluntary, so this answer cannot be correct.
   c. This answer is incorrect because most organs are affected by both divisions of the autonomic nervous system.
   d. The somatic nervous system transmits sensory input to the central nervous system and enables voluntary control of skeletal muscles.

3. **c.** is the answer. Stimulus strength can affect only the number of times a neuron fires or the number of neurons that fire. (p. 55)
   a., b., & d. These answers are incorrect because firing is an all-or-none response, so intensity remains the same regardless of stimulus strength. Nor can stimulus strength change the neuronal threshold or the impulse speed.

4. **a.** is the answer. Endorphins are neurotransmitters that function as natural painkillers. When the body has a supply of artificial painkillers such as heroin, endorphin production stops. (p. 57)
   b. The production of neurotransmitters other than endorphins does not cease.
   c. Neurotransmitter production does not increase during withdrawal.
   d. Heroin makes use of the same receptor sites as endorphins.

5. **c.** is the answer. (p. 58)

6. **c.** is the answer. In a simple reflex, a sensory neuron carries the message that a sensory receptor has been stimulated to an interneuron in the spinal cord. The interneuron responds by activating motor neurons that will enable the appropriate response. (p. 61)

7. **d.** is the answer. (p. 54)

8. **d.** is the answer. Biological psychologists study the links between biology (in this case, neurotransmitters) and psychology (depression, in this example). (p. 52)

9. **b.** is the answer. (p. 59)
   a., c., & d. The autonomic nervous system, which is divided into the sympathetic and parasympathetic divisions, is concerned with regulating basic bodily maintenance functions.

10. **c.** is the answer. (p. 54)
    a. An action potential will occur only when the neuron's threshold is *exceeded*.

b. An excitatory input that does not reach the neuron's threshold will not trigger an action potential.

d. This answer is incorrect because some neurotransmitters inhibit a neuron's readiness to fire.

11. **d.** is the answer. A neuron receives incoming stimuli on its dendrites and cell body. These electrochemical signals are combined in the cell body, generating an impulse that travels down the axon, causing the release of neurotransmitter substances into the synaptic cleft or gap. (pp. 53–55)

Matching Items

1. b (p. 53)	**5.** h (p. 53)	**9.** c (p. 53)
2. d (p. 53)	**6.** i (p. 55)	**10.** k (p. 53)
3. f (p. 54)	**7.** a (p. 55)	**11.** e (p. 53)
4. g (p. 53)	**8.** j (p. 53)	

Progress Test 2

Multiple-Choice Questions

1. **a.** is the answer. Sensory neurons in the somatic nervous system relay such messages. (p. 59)
   b. & c. These divisions of the autonomic nervous system are concerned with the regulation of bodily maintenance functions such as heartbeat, digestion, and glandular activity.
   d. The spinal cord itself is part of the central nervous system, but the message is carried to the spinal cord by the somatic division of the peripheral nervous system.

2. **c.** is the answer. As automatic responses to stimuli, reflexes are the simplest complete units of behavior and require only simple neural pathways. (p. 61)
   a., b., & d. Emotions, drives, and voluntary movements are all behaviors that are much more complex than reflexes and therefore involve much more complicated neural pathways.

3. **b.** is the answer. Endorphins are neurotransmitters that function as natural painkillers and are evidently involved in the "runner's high" and other situations in which discomfort or fatigue is expected but not experienced. (p. 57)
   a. ACh is a neurotransmitter involved in muscular control.
   c. Dopamine is a neurotransmitter involved in, among other things, motor control.
   d. Norepinephrine is an adrenal hormone released to help us respond in moments of danger.

4. **a.** is the answer. (p. 53)

c. & d. Myelin sheaths are not involved in regulating the release of neurotransmitters.

5. **d.** is the answer. (p. 57)

6. **b.** is the answer. ACh is a neurotransmitter that causes the contraction of muscle fibers when stimulated by motor neurons. This function explains its location. (p. 56)
   a. & c. Sensory neurons and interneurons do not directly stimulate muscle fibers.

7. **d.** is the answer. The pituitary regulates body growth, and some of its secretions regulate the release of hormones from other glands. (p. 63)
   a. The adrenal glands are stimulated by the autonomic nervous system to release epinephrine and norepinephrine.
   b. The thyroid gland affects metabolism, among other things.
   c. The hypothalamus regulates the pituitary but does not itself directly regulate growth.

8. **d.** is the answer. Also known as adrenaline and noradrenaline, epinephrine and norepinephrine are hormones released by the adrenal glands. (p. 63)

9. **b.** is the answer. (pp. 57, 58)
   a. Abuse of certain drugs, such as heroin, may have this effect.
   c. This describes the effect of an antagonist.
   d. Drugs do not have this effect on neurons.

10. **c.** is the answer. (p. 62)
    a. Agonists are drugs that excite neural firing by mimicking a particular neurotransmitter.
    b. Neurotransmitters are the chemicals involved in synaptic transmission in the nervous system.
    d. Enzymes are chemicals that facilitate various chemical reactions throughout the body but are not involved in communication within the endocrine system.

11. **b.** is the answer. (p. 61)
    a. Action potentials are neural impulses that occur in all forms of communication in the nervous system.
    c. The endocrine system is the body's glandular system of chemical communication.
    d. Dendrites are the branching extensions of neurons that receive messages from other nerve cells.

Matching Items

1. c (p. 52)	**5.** i (p. 59)	**9.** b (p. 62)
2. a (p. 57)	**6.** g (p. 59)	**10.** h (p. 60)
3. d (p. 59)	**7.** f (p. 59)	**11.** k (p. 55)
4. e (p. 59)	**8.** j (p. 59)	

Psychology Applied

Multiple-Choice Questions

1. **d.** is the answer. Biological psychologists study the links between biology (chemical changes in this example) and behavior (emotions in this example). (p. 52)
   a., b., & c. Experimental, clinical, and developmental psychologists would be more concerned with the learning of emotional expressions, the treatment of emotional disorders, and life-span changes in emotions, respectively.

2. **a.** is the answer. Because this reflex is an automatic response and involves only the spinal cord, the hand is jerked away before the brain has even received the information that causes the sensation of pain. (p. 61)
   b. The spinal cord, which organizes simple reflexes such as this one, is part of the central nervous system.
   c. The brain is not involved in directing spinal reflexes.
   d. The autonomic nervous system controls the glands and the muscles of the internal organs; it does not influence the skeletal muscles controlling the hand.

3. **a.** is the answer. (p. 54)
   b. Because she has reached her threshold, she will probably fire.
   c. Because Joni has received a large number of excitatory messages, she will not be at rest.
   d. *Hyperpolarization* is not a term.

4. **b.** is the answer. Simple reflexes, such as this one, are governed by activity in the autonomic nervous system. (p. 61)
   a. The myelin sheath is the fatty layer of tissue that surrounds some axons.
   c. The pituitary is an endocrine gland that regulates growth and controls other endocrine glands.
   d. The somatic nervous system enables voluntary control of the skeletal muscles.

5. **c.** is the answer. (p. 56)

6. **b.** is the answer. (p. 57)
   a. By triggering release of dopamine, such a drug would probably *enhance* Malcolm's enjoyment of the pleasures of life.
   c. & d. ACh is the neurotransmitter at synapses between motor neurons and muscle fibers.

7. **b.** is the answer. (pp. 51–52)
   a. "Ahead of its time" implies the theory had merit, which later research clearly showed it did not. Moreover, phrenology *was* accepted as an accurate theory of brain organization by many scientists.
   c. Phrenology said nothing about the similarities of human and animal brains.

8. **a.** is the answer. (p. 62)
   b., c., & d. Acetylcholine and dopamine are fast-acting neurotransmitters released at synapses, not in the bloodstream.

9. **b.** is the answer. Sympathetic arousal produces several effects, including accelerated heartbeat and excessive perspiration. (p. 59)
   a. The central nervous system is not involved in heartbeat or other involuntary actions.
   c. Arousal of the parasympathetic nervous system would have effects opposite to those stated.
   d. The somatic nervous system enables voluntary control of the skeletal muscles.

10. **a.** is the answer. Hormones of the pituitary gland regulate body growth. (p. 63)
    b. & d. Because they are not endocrine glands, the thalamus and medulla are not influenced by hormones.
    c. The adrenal glands produce hormones that provide energy during emergencies; they are not involved in regulating body growth.

Essay Question

The body's response to stress is regulated by the nervous system. As the date of the exam approaches, the stressed student's cerebral cortex activates the hypothalamus, triggering the release of hormones that in turn activate the sympathetic branch of the autonomic nervous system and the endocrine system. The autonomic nervous system controls involuntary bodily responses such as breathing, heartbeat, and digestion. The endocrine system contains glands that secrete hormones into the bloodstream that regulate the functions of body organs.

In response to activation by the hypothalamus, the student's pituitary gland would secrete a hormone which in turn triggers the release of epinephrine, norepinephrine, and other stress hormones from the adrenal glands. These hormones would help the student's body manage stress by making nutrients available to meet the increased demands for energy stores the body often faces in coping with stress. These hormones activate the sympathetic division of the autonomic system, causing increased heart rate, breathing, and blood pressure and the suppression of digestion. After the exam date has passed, the student's body would attempt to restore its normal, pre-stress state. The parasympathetic branch of the autonomic system would slow the student's heartbeat and breathing and digestive processes would no longer be suppressed, perhaps causing the student to feel hungry.

Key Terms

1. **Biological psychology** is the study of the links between biology and behavior. (p. 52)

2. The **neuron**, or nerve cell, is the basic building block of the nervous system. (p. 53)

3. **Sensory neurons** carry information from the sensory receptors to the brain and spinal cord for processing. (p. 53)

4. **Motor neurons** carry information and instructions for action from the brain and spinal cord to muscles and glands. (p. 53)

5. **Interneurons** are the neurons of the brain and spinal cord that link the sensory and motor neurons in the transmission of sensory inputs and motor outputs. (p. 53)

6. The **dendrites** of a neuron are the bushy, branching extensions that receive messages from other nerve cells and conduct impulses toward the cell body. (p. 53)

7. The **axon** of a neuron is the extension that sends impulses to other nerve cells or to muscles or glands. (p. 53)

8. The **myelin sheath** is a layer of fatty tissue that segmentally covers many axons and helps speed neural impulses. (p. 53)

9. An **action potential** is a neural impulse generated by the movement of electrically charged atoms down the axon. (p. 53)

10. A neuron's **threshold** is the level of stimulation that must be exceeded for the neuron to fire, or generate an electrical impulse. (p. 54)

11. A **synapse** is the junction between the axon tip of the sending neuron and the dendrite or cell body of the receiving neuron. The tiny gap at this junction is called the synaptic gap or cleft. (p. 55)

12. **Neurotransmitters** are chemicals that are released into synaptic gaps and so transmit neural messages from neuron to neuron. (p. 55)

13. **Reuptake** is the absorption of excess neurotransmitters by a sending neuron. (p. 55)

14. **Endorphins** are natural, opiatelike neurotransmitters linked to pain control and to pleasure. (p. 57)

    Memory aid: Endorphins *end* pain.

15. The **nervous system** is the speedy, electrochemical communication system, consisting of all the nerve cells in the peripheral and central nervous systems. (p. 59)

16. The **central nervous system (CNS)** consists of the brain and spinal cord; it is located at the *center*, or internal core, of the body. (p. 59)

17. The **peripheral nervous system (PNS)** includes the sensory and motor neurons that connect the central nervous system to the body's sense receptors, muscles, and glands; it is at the *periphery* of the body relative to the brain and spinal cord. (p. 59)

18. **Nerves** are bundles of neural axons, which are part of the PNS, that connect the central nervous system with muscles, glands, and sense organs. (p. 59)

19. The **somatic nervous system** is the division of the peripheral nervous system that enables voluntary control of the skeletal muscles; also called the *skeletal nervous system*. (p. 59)

20. The **autonomic nervous system** is the division of the peripheral nervous system that controls the glands and the muscles of internal organs and thereby controls internal functioning; it regulates the *automatic* behaviors necessary for survival. (p. 59)

21. The **sympathetic nervous system** is the division of the autonomic nervous system that arouses the body, mobilizing its energy in stressful situations. (p. 59)

22. The **parasympathetic nervous system** is the division of the autonomic nervous system that calms the body, conserving its energy. (p. 60)

23. A **reflex** is a simple, automatic, inborn response to a sensory stimulus; it is governed by a very simple neural pathway. (p. 61)

24. The **endocrine system**, the body's "slow" chemical communication system, consists of glands that secrete hormones into the bloodstream. (p. 62)

25. **Hormones** are chemical messengers, mostly those manufactured by the endocrine glands, that are produced in one tissue and circulate through the bloodstream to their target tissues, on which they have specific effects. (p. 62)

26. The **adrenal glands** produce epinephrine and norepinephrine, hormones that prepare the body to deal with emergencies or stress. (p. 63)

27. The **pituitary gland**, under the influence of the hypothalamus, regulates growth and controls other endocrine glands; sometimes called the "master gland." (p. 63)

Biological Bases of Behavior:
3B: The Brain

UNIT OVERVIEW

Unit 3B is concerned with the functions of the brain and how our millions of brain cells come together to create our consciousness.

The brain consists of the brainstem, the thalamus, the cerebellum, the limbic system, and the cerebral cortex. Knowledge of the workings of the brain has increased with advances in neuroscientific methods such as the PET scan. Studies of split-brain patients have also given researchers a great deal of information about the specialized functions of the brain's right and left hemispheres.

NOTE: Answer guidelines for all Unit 3B questions begin on page 56.

UNIT REVIEW

First, skim each section, noting headings and boldface items. After you have read the section, review each objective by answering the fill-in and essay-type questions that follow it. As you proceed, evaluate your performance by consulting the answers beginning on page 56. Do not continue with the next section until you understand each answer. If you need to, review or reread the section in the textbook before continuing.

The Tools of Discovery: Having Our Head Examined (pp. 67–68)

Objective 1: Describe several techniques for studying the brain.

1. Researchers sometimes study brain function by producing _____ or by selectively destroying brain cells. The oldest technique for studying the brain involves _____ _____ of patients with brain injuries or diseases.

2. The _____ is an amplified recording of the waves of electrical activity that sweep across the brain's surface.

3. The technique in which X-ray photographs are combined to form a composite representation of a slice through the body is called the

   _____ _____ .

4. The technique depicting the level of activity of brain areas by measuring the brain's consumption of glucose is called the

   _____ _____ .

Briefly explain the purpose of the PET scan.

5. A technique that produces clearer images of the brain (and other body parts) by using magnetic fields and radio waves is known as

   _____ .

6. By comparing scans taken less than a second apart, the _____ _____ detects oxygen-laden bloodflow to the part of the brain thought to control the bodily activity being studied. Using this technique, researchers found that bloodflow to the back of the brain _____ (increases/decreases) when people view a scene because that is where _____ information is processed.

Older Brain Structures (pp. 69–73)

Objective 2: Describe the components of the brainstem, and summarize the functions of the brainstem, thalamus, and cerebellum.

1. The oldest and innermost region of the brain is the _____ .

2. At the base of the brainstem, where the spinal cord enters the skull, lies the _____ , which controls _____ and _____ . Just above this part is the _____ , which helps coordinate movements.

3. Nerves from each side of the brain cross over to connect with the body's opposite side in the _____ .

4. The finger-shaped network of neurons, the _____ _____ , is contained inside the brainstem and plays an important role in controlling _____ . Electrically stimulating this area will produce an _____ animal. Lesioning this area will cause an animal to lapse into a _____ .

5. At the top of the brainstem sits the _____ , which serves as the brain's sensory switchboard, receiving information from all the senses except _____ and routing it to the regions dealing with those senses. These egg-shaped structures also receive replies from the higher regions, which they direct to the _____ and to the _____ .

6. At the rear of the brainstem lies the _____ . It influences one type of _____ _____ and memory. It also coordinates voluntary movement and _____ control.

7. The lower brain functions occur without _____ effort, indicating that our brains process most information _____ (inside/outside) of our awareness.

Objective 3: Describe the structures and functions of the limbic system, and explain how one of these structures controls the pituitary gland.

8. Between the brainstem and cerebral hemispheres is the _____ system. One component of this system that processes memory is the _____ .

9. Aggression or fear will result from stimulation of different regions of the lima bean–sized neural clusters, the _____ .

10. We must remember, however, that the brain _____ (is/is not) neatly organized into structures that correspond to our categories of behavior. For example, aggressive behavior _____ (does/does not) involve neural activity in many brain levels.

11. Below the thalamus is the _____ , which regulates bodily maintenance behaviors such as _____ , _____ , _____ _____ , and _____ behavior. This area also regulates behavior by secreting _____ that enable it to control the _____ gland. Olds and Milner discovered that this region also contains _____ centers, which animals will work hard to have stimulated.

12. Some researchers believe that alcohol dependence, drug abuse, binge eating, and other _____ disorders may stem from a genetically disposed _____ _____ in the natural brain systems for pleasure and well-being.

The Cerebral Cortex (pp. 74–83)

Objective 4: Describe the structure of the cerebral cortex, and explain the various functions of the four lobes.

1. The most complex functions of human behavior are linked to the most developed part of the brain, the _____ _____ . This thin layer of interconnected neural cells is the body's ultimate control and

_____-_____
center.

2. The cells that support, protect, and nourish cortical neurons are called _____ _____ . These cells may also play a role in _____ and _____ .

3. Compared with the cortexes of lower mammals, the human cortex has a _____ (smoother/more wrinkled) surface. This _____ (increases/decreases) the overall surface area of our brains.

4. List the four lobes of the brain.

   a. _____   c. _____

   b. _____   d. _____

Objective 5: Summarize some of the findings on the functions of the motor cortex and the sensory cortex, and discuss the importance of the association areas.

5. Electrical stimulation of one side of the _____ cortex, an arch-shaped region at the back of the _____ lobe, will produce movement on the opposite side of the body. The more precise the control needed, the _____ (smaller/ greater) amount of cortical space occupied. Findings from clinical trials involving _____ _____ , in which, for example, recording electrodes were implanted in this area of a 25-year-old man's brain, raise hopes that people who are _____ may one day be able to control machines directly with their _____ .

6. At the front of the parietal lobes lies the _____ cortex, which, when stimulated, elicits a sensation of _____ .

7. The more sensitive a body region, the greater the area of _____ _____ devoted to it.

8. Visual information is received in the _____ lobes, whereas auditory information is received in the _____ lobes.

9. Areas of the brain that don't receive sensory information or direct movement but, rather, integrate and interpret information received by other regions are known as _____ _____ . Approximately _____ of the human cortex is of this type. Such areas in the _____ lobe are involved in judging, planning, and processing of new memories and in some aspects of personality. In the _____ lobe, these areas enable mathematical and spatial reasoning, and an area of the _____ lobe enables us to recognize faces.

Objective 6: Identify the brain areas involved in language processing, and describe the process that enables us to speak and understand language.

10. Brain injuries may produce an impairment in language use called _____ . Studies of people with such impairments have shown that _____ _____ is involved in producing speech, _____ _____ is involved in understanding speech, and the _____ _____ is involved in recoding printed words into auditory form.

11. Norman Geschwind has explained how we use language. When we read aloud, the words register in the brain's _____ _____ . They are then relayed to the _____ _____ , which transforms them into an auditory code. The code is received and understood in _____ _____ and sent to _____ _____ , which controls the _____ _____ as it creates the pronounced word.

12. Although the mind's subsystems are localized in particular brain regions, the brain acts as a _____ _____ .

Objective 7: Discuss the brain's plasticity following injury or illness.

13. The quality of the brain that makes it possible for undamaged brain areas to take over the functions of damaged regions is known as _____ . This quality is especially apparent in the brains of _____ (young children/adolescents/adults).

14. Although severed neurons usually _____ (will/will not) regenerate, some neural tissue can _____ in response to damage. The form of therapy aimed at helping to reprogram a damaged brain is called _____-_____ therapy. New evidence suggests that adult mice and humans _____ (can/cannot) generate new brain cells through a process called _____ . Research also reveals the existence of master _____ cells in the human embryo that can develop into any type of brain cell.

Our Divided Brain (pp. 83–86)

Objective 8: Describe split-brain research, and explain how it helps us understand the functions of our left and right hemispheres.

1. The brain's two sides serve differing functions, which is referred to as hemispheric specialization, or _____ . Because damage to it will impair language and understanding, the _____ hemisphere came to be known as the _____ hemisphere.

2. In treating several patients with severe epilepsy, Vogel and Bogen separated the two hemispheres of the brain by cutting the _____ _____ . When this structure is severed, the result is referred to as a _____ _____ .

3. In a split-brain patient, only the _____ hemisphere will be aware of an unseen object held in the left hand. In this case, the person would not be able to _____ the object. When different words are shown in the left and right visual fields, if the patient fixates on a point on the center line between the fields, the patient will be able to say only the word shown on the _____ .

Explain why a split-brain patient would be able to read aloud the word *pencil* flashed to his or her right visual field, but would be unable to identify a *pencil* by touch using only the left hand.

4. When the "two minds" of a split brain are at odds, the _____ hemisphere tries to rationalize what it doesn't understand. The _____ hemisphere often acts on autopilot. This phenomenon demonstrates that the _____ mind _____ (can/cannot) control our behavior.

Right-Left Differences in the Intact Brain (pp. 86–89)

Objective 9: Describe the distinct functions of the brain's two hemispheres, and discuss the relationship between brain organization and handedness.

1. Deaf people use the _____ hemisphere to process sign language.

2. Although the _____ hemisphere is better at making literal interpretations of language, the _____ hemisphere excels at quick, intuitive responses and at copying drawings, _____ _____ , perceiving objects, and perceiving _____ .

3. (Close-Up) In all cultures of the world, most of the human population is _____ (right/left)-handed. Genetic factors _____ (play/do not play) a role in handedness.

The Brain and Consciousness (pp. 89–91)

Objective 10: Describe research that leads cognitive neuroscientists to infer how the brain's dual processing affects our perception, memory, and attitudes on conscious and unconscious levels.

1. The study of _____ was central in the early years of psychology and has increased in recent decades.

2. The interdisciplinary study of how brain activity is linked with mental processes is called

   _____ _____ .

3. Much of our everyday thinking, feeling, and acting operates outside of our _____ awareness.

4. Unconscious information processing occurs _____ (sequentially/simultaneously) on _____ (serial/parallel) tracks.

5. Solving new problems _____ (requires/does not require) conscious attention.

6. In comparison with unconscious processing, conscious processing has a(n) _____ (limited/unlimited) capacity, is relatively _____ (fast/slow), and processes pieces of information _____ (simultaneously/serially).

PROGRESS TEST 1

Multiple-Choice Questions

Circle your answers to the following questions and check them with the answers on page 57. If your answer is incorrect, read the explanation for why it is incorrect and then consult the appropriate pages of the text (in parentheses following the correct answer).

1. The brain research technique that involves monitoring the brain's usage of glucose is called (in abbreviated form) the
   a. PET scan.   c. EEG.
   b. fMRI.   d. MRI.

2. Though there is no single "control center" for emotions, their regulation is primarily attributed to the brain region known as the
   a. limbic system.   c. brainstem.
   b. reticular formation. d. cerebellum.

3. Which of the following is typically controlled by the right hemisphere?
   a. language
   b. learned voluntary movements
   c. arithmetic reasoning
   d. perceptual tasks

4. The increasing complexity of animals' behavior is accompanied by an
   a. increase in the size of the brainstem.
   b. increase in the depth of the corpus callosum.
   c. increase in the size of the frontal lobes.
   d. increase in the amount of association area.

5. Following a head injury, a person has ongoing difficulties staying awake. Most likely, the damage occurred to the
   a. thalamus.   c. reticular formation.
   b. corpus callosum.   d. cerebellum.

6. An experimenter flashes the word FLYTRAP onto a screen facing a split-brain patient so that FLY projects to her right hemisphere and TRAP to her left hemisphere. When asked what she saw, the patient will
   a. say she saw FLY.
   b. say she saw TRAP.
   c. point to FLY using her right hand.
   d. point to TRAP using her left hand.

7. Cortical areas that are not primarily concerned with sensory, motor, or language functions are
   a. called projection areas.
   b. called association areas.
   c. located mostly in the parietal lobe.
   d. located mostly in the temporal lobe.

8. Damage to _____ will usually cause a person to lose the ability to comprehend language.
   a. the angular gyrus
   b. Broca's area
   c. Wernicke's area
   d. frontal lobe association areas

9. In a soccer game, Laura suffered damage to her left temporal lobe. As a result, she is unable to speak in meaningful sentences. The damage affected
   a. Wernicke's area.
   b. Broca's area.
   c. the angular gyrus.
   d. the hippoccampus.

10. *Consciousness* is defined in the text as
    a. mental life.
    b. selective attention to ongoing perceptions, thoughts, and feelings.
    c. information processing.
    d. our awareness of ourselves and our environment.

Matching Items

Match each structure or technique with its corresponding function or description.

Structures

_____ 1. hypothalamus
_____ 2. lesion
_____ 3. EEG
_____ 4. fMRI
_____ 5. reticular formation
_____ 6. MRI
_____ 7. thalamus
_____ 8. corpus callosum
_____ 9. cerebellum
_____ 10. amygdala
_____ 11. medulla

Functions or Descriptions

a. amplified recording of brain waves
b. technique that uses radio waves and magnetic fields to image brain anatomy
c. serves as sensory switchboard
d. contains reward centers
e. tissue destruction
f. technique that uses radio waves and magnetic fields to show brain function
g. helps control arousal
h. links the cerebral hemispheres
i. influences rage and fear
j. regulates breathing and heartbeat
k. enables coordinated movement

PROGRESS TEST 2

Progress Test 2 should be completed during a final unit review. Answer the following questions after you thoroughly understand the correct answers for the section reviews and Progress Test 1.

Multiple-Choice Questions

1. The visual cortex is located in the
   a. occipital lobe.   c. frontal lobe.
   b. temporal lobe.   d. parietal lobe.

2. Which of the following is typically controlled by the left hemisphere?
   a. spatial reasoning
   b. word recognition
   c. the left side of the body
   d. perceptual skills

3. In the brain, I outnumber neurons. I also provide nutrients to the neurons and help remove excess neurotransmitters. I am a
   a. hormone.
   b. myelin sheath.
   c. glial cell.
   d. stem cell.

4. The technique that uses magnetic fields and radio waves to produce computer images of structures within the brain is called
   a. the EEG.   c. a PET scan.
   b. a lesion.   d. MRI.

5. Jessica experienced difficulty keeping her balance after receiving a blow to the back of her head. It is likely that she injured her
   a. medulla.   c. hypothalamus.
   b. thalamus.   d. cerebellum.

6. Moruzzi and Magoun caused a cat to lapse into a coma by severing neural connections between the cortex and the
   a. reticular formation.   c. thalamus.
   b. hypothalamus.   d. cerebellum.

7. Research has found that the amount of representation in the motor cortex reflects the
   a. size of the body parts.
   b. degree of precise control required by each of the parts.
   c. sensitivity of the body region.
   d. area of the occipital lobe being stimulated by the environment.

8. The nerve fibers that enable communication between the right and left cerebral hemispheres and that have been severed in split-brain patients form a structure called the
   a. reticular formation.   c. corpus callosum.
   b. association areas.   d. parietal lobes.

9. Beginning at the front of the brain and moving toward the back of the head, then down the skull and back around to the front, which of the following is the correct order of the cortical regions?
   a. occipital lobe; temporal lobe; parietal lobe; frontal lobe
   b. temporal lobe; frontal lobe; parietal lobe; occipital lobe
   c. frontal lobe; occipital lobe; temporal lobe; parietal lobe
   d. frontal lobe; parietal lobe; occipital lobe; temporal lobe

10. Following a nail gun wound to his head, Jack became more uninhibited, irritable, dishonest, and profane. It is likely that his personality change was the result of injury to his
    a. parietal lobe.   c. occipital lobe.
    b. temporal lobe.   d. frontal lobe.

11. Three-year-old Marco suffered damage to the speech area of the brain's left hemisphere when he fell from a swing. Research suggests that
    a. he may never speak again.
    b. his motor abilities may improve so that he can easily use sign language.
    c. his right hemisphere may take over much of the language function.
    d. his earlier experience with speech may enable him to continue speaking.

Matching Items
Match each structure or term with its corresponding function or description.

Structures or Terms

_____ 1. right hemisphere
_____ 2. brainstem
_____ 3. temporal lobes
_____ 4. occipital lobes
_____ 5. plasticity
_____ 6. neurogenesis
_____ 7. Broca's area
_____ 8. limbic system
_____ 9. association areas
_____ 10. left hemisphere
_____ 11. glial cells

Functions or Descriptions

a. the formation of new neurons
b. specializes in rationalizing reactions
c. support cells of the nervous system
d. specializes in spatial relations
e. brain areas containing the auditory cortex
f. brain areas containing the visual cortex
g. oldest part of the brain
h. regulates emotion
i. the brain's capacity for modification
j. controls speech production
k. brain areas involved in higher mental functions

In the diagrams to the right, the numbers refer to brain locations that have been damaged. Match each location with its probable effect on behavior.

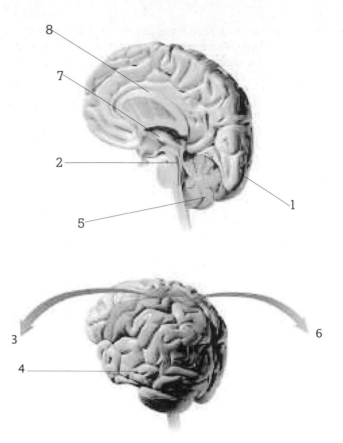

Location		Behavioral Effect
_____	1.	**a.** vision disorder
_____	2.	**b.** insensitivity to touch
_____	3.	**c.** motor paralysis
_____	4.	**d.** hearing problem
_____	5.	**e.** lack of coordination
_____	6.	**f.** abnormal hunger
_____	7.	**g.** split brain
_____	8.	**h.** sleep/arousal disorder

PSYCHOLOGY APPLIED

Answer these questions the day before a test as a final check on your understanding of the unit's terms and concepts.

Multiple-Choice Questions

1. The part of the human brain that is most like that of a fish is the
   a. cortex.
   b. limbic system.
   c. brainstem.
   d. right hemisphere.

2. To pinpoint the location of a tumor, a neurosurgeon electrically stimulated parts of the patient's sensory cortex. If the patient was conscious during the procedure, which of the following was probably experienced?
   a. "hearing" faint sounds
   b. "seeing" random visual patterns
   c. movement of the arms or legs
   d. a sense of having the skin touched

3. If Dr. Rogers wishes to conduct an experiment on the effects of stimulating the reward centers of a rat's brain, he should insert an electrode into the
   a. thalamus.
   b. sensory cortex.
   c. hypothalamus.
   d. corpus callosum.

4. A split-brain patient has a picture of a knife flashed to her left hemisphere and that of a fork to her right hemisphere. She will be able to
   a. identify the fork using her left hand.
   b. identify a knife using her left hand.
   c. identify a knife using either hand.
   d. identify a fork using either hand.

5. Anton is applying for a technician's job with a neurosurgeon. In trying to impress his potential employer with his knowledge of the brain, he says, "After my father's stroke I knew immediately that the blood clot had affected his left cerebral hemisphere because he no longer recognized a picture of his friend." Should Anton be hired?

   a. Yes. Anton obviously understands brain structure and function.

   b. No. The right hemisphere, not the left, specializes in picture recognition.

   c. Yes. Although blood clots never form in the left hemisphere, Anton should be rewarded for recognizing the left hemisphere's role in picture recognition.

   d. No. Blood clots never form in the left hemisphere, and the right hemisphere is more involved than the left in recognizing pictures.

6. Dr. Johnson briefly flashed a picture of a key in the right visual field of a split-brain patient. The patient could probably

   a. verbally report that a key was seen.

   b. write the word *key* using the left hand.

   c. draw a picture of a key using the left hand.

   d. do none of these things.

7. In primitive vertebrate animals, the brain primarily regulates _____ ; in lower mammals, the brain enables _____ .

   a. emotion; memory

   b. memory; emotion

   c. survival functions; emotion

   d. reproduction; emotion

8. A scientist from another planet wishes to study the simplest brain mechanisms underlying emotion and memory. You recommend that the scientist study the

   a. brainstem of a frog.

   b. limbic system of a dog.

   c. cortex of a monkey.

   d. cortex of a human.

9. Dr. Frankenstein made a mistake during neurosurgery on his monster. After the operation, the monster "saw" with his ears and "heard" with his eyes. It is likely that Dr. Frankenstein "rewired" neural connections in the monster's

   a. hypothalamus.

   b. cerebellum.

   c. amygdala.

   d. thalamus.

10. Raccoons have much more precise control of their paws than dogs. You would expect that raccoons have more cortical space dedicated to "paw control" in the _____ of their brains.

    a. frontal lobes   c. temporal lobes
    b. parietal lobes   d. occipital lobes

Essay Question

A patient presents to the hospital complaining of headaches and difficulty speaking. Describe what a physician or cognitive neuroscientist might do to diagnose the patient's problem, and identify the possible results of such an investigation.

KEY TERMS

Using your own words, on a piece of paper write a brief definition or explanation of each of the following terms.

1. lesion

2. electroencephalogram (EEG)

3. CT (computed tomography) scan

4. PET (positron emission tomography) scan

5. MRI (magnetic resonance imaging)

6. fMRI (functional magnetic resonance imaging)

7. brainstem

8. medulla

9. reticular formation

10. thalamus

11. cerebellum

12. limbic system

13. amygdala

14. hypothalamus

15. cerebral cortex

16. glial cells
17. frontal lobes
18. parietal lobes
19. occipital lobes
20. temporal lobes
21. motor cortex
22. sensory cortex
23. association areas
24. aphasia
25. Broca's area
26. Wernicke's area
27. plasticity
28. neurogenesis
29. corpus callosum
30. split brain
31. consciousness
32. cognitive neuroscience
33. dual processing

ANSWERS

Unit Review

The Tools of Discovery: Having Our Head Examined

1. lesions; clinical observation
2. electroencephalogram (EEG)
3. CT scan
4. PET scan

By depicting the brain's consumption of radioactively labeled glucose, the PET scan allows researchers to see which brain areas are most active as a person performs various tasks. This provides additional information on the specialized functions of various regions of the brain.

5. MRI (magnetic resonance imaging)
6. functional MRI; increases; visual

Older Brain Structures

1. brainstem
2. medulla; breathing; heartbeat; pons
3. brainstem
4. reticular formation; arousal; alert (awake); coma
5. thalamus; smell; medulla; cerebellum
6. cerebellum; nonverbal learning; balance
7. conscious; outside

8. limbic; hippocampus
9. amygdala
10. is not; does
11. hypothalamus; hunger; thirst; body temperature; sexual; hormones; pituitary; reward
12. addictive; reward deficiency syndrome

The Cerebral Cortex

1. cerebral cortex; information-processing
2. glial cells; learning; thinking
3. more wrinkled; increases
4. a. frontal lobe
   b. parietal lobe
   c. occipital lobe
   d. temporal lobe
5. motor; frontal; greater; neural prosthetics; paralyzed; thoughts (or brains)
6. sensory; touch
7. sensory cortex
8. occipital; temporal
9. association areas; three-fourths; frontal; parietal; temporal
10. aphasia; Broca's area; Wernicke's area; angular gyrus
11. visual area; angular gyrus; Wernicke's area; Broca's area; motor cortex
12. unified whole
13. plasticity; young children
14. will not; reorganize; constraint-induced; can; neurogenesis; stem

Our Divided Brain

1. lateralization; left; dominant (major)
2. corpus callosum; split brain
3. right; name; right

The word *pencil* when flashed to a split-brain patient's right visual field would project only to the opposite, or left, hemisphere of the patient's brain. Because the left hemisphere contains the language control centers of the brain, the patient would be able to read the word aloud. The left hand is controlled by the right hemisphere of the brain. Because the right hemisphere would not be aware of the word, it would not be able to guide the left hand in identifying a pencil by touch.

4. left; right; unconscious; can

Right-Left Differences in the Intact Brain

1. left

2. left; right; recognizing faces; emotion

3. right; play

The Brain and Consciousness

1. consciousness

2. cognitive neuroscience

3. conscious

4. simultaneously; parallel

5. requires

6. limited; slow; serially

Progress Test 1

1. **a.** is the answer. The PET scan measures glucose consumption in different areas of the brain to determine their levels of activity. (p. 68)
   b. The fMRI compares MRI scans taken less than a second apart to reveal brain structure and function.
   c. The EEG is a measure of electrical activity in the brain.
   d. MRI uses magnetic fields and radio waves to produce computer-generated images of soft tissues of the body.

2. **a.** is the answer. (p. 71)
   b. The reticular formation is linked to arousal.
   c. The brainstem governs the mechanisms of basic survival—heartbeat and breathing, for example—and has many other roles.
   d. The cerebellum coordinates movement output and balance.

3. **d.** is the answer. (p. 87)
   a. In most persons, language is primarily a left hemisphere function.
   b. Learned movements are unrelated to hemispheric specialization.
   c. Arithmetic reasoning is generally a left hemisphere function.

4. **d.** is the answer. As animals increase in complexity, there is an increase in the amount of association areas. (p. 78)
   a. The brainstem controls basic survival functions and is not related to the complexity of an animal's behavior.
   b. The corpus callosum connects the brain's two hemispheres; it's not necessarily related to more complex behaviors.
   c. The frontal lobe is concerned with personality, planning, and other mental functions, but its size

is unrelated to intelligence or the complexity of behavior.

5. **c.** is the answer. The reticular formation plays an important role in arousal. (p. 70)
   a. The thalamus relays sensory input.
   b. The corpus callosum links the two cerebral hemispheres.
   d. The cerebellum is involved in coordination of movement output and balance.

6. **b.** is the answer. (p. 84)

7. **b.** is the answer. Association areas interpret, integrate, and act on information from other areas of the cortex. (p. 78)

8. **c.** is the answer. (p. 80)
   a. The angular gyrus translates the signals into the auditory code.
   b. Broca's area is involved in speech production.
   d. The association areas are involved in higher-order activities such as planning.

9. **a.** is the answer. (p. 80)
   b. Broca's area is involved in speech production.
   c. The angular gyrus converts to auditory code.
   d. The hippocampus has nothing to do with language.

10. **d.** is the answer. (p. 89)

Matching Items

1. d (p. 72)	5. g (p. 70)	9. k (p. 70)
2. e (p. 67)	6. b (p. 68)	10. i (p. 71)
3. a (p. 67)	7. c (p. 70)	11. j (p. 69)
4. f (p. 68)	8. h (p. 84)	

Progress Test 2

Multiple-Choice Questions

1. **a.** is the answer. The visual cortex is located at the very back of the brain. (p. 77)

2. **b.** is the answer. (p. 87)
   a., c., & d. Spatial reasoning, perceptual skills, and the left side of the body are primarily influenced by the right hemisphere.

3. **c.** is the answer. (p. 74)
   a. Hormones are secreted by endocrine glands directly into the bloodstream.
   b. Myelin sheath is the fatty tissue that intermittently surrounds the axons of neurons.
   d. Stem cells in the embryo can develop into any kind of cell.

4. **d.** is the answer. (p. 68)
   a. The EEG is an amplified recording of the brain's electrical activity.

b. A lesion is destruction of tissue.

c. The PET scan is a visual display of brain activity that detects the movement of a radioactive form of glucose as the brain performs a task.

5. **d.** is the answer. The cerebellum is involved in the coordination of voluntary muscular movements. (p. 70)
   a. The medulla regulates breathing and heartbeat.
   b. The thalamus relays sensory inputs to the appropriate higher centers of the brain.
   c. The hypothalamus is concerned with the regulation of basic drives and emotions.

6. **a.** is the answer. The reticular formation controls arousal via its connections to the cortex. Thus, separating the two produces a coma. (p. 70)
   b., c., & d. None of these structures controls arousal. The hypothalamus regulates hunger, thirst, sexual behavior, and other basic drives; the thalamus is a sensory relay station; and the cerebellum is involved in the coordination of voluntary movement.

7. **b.** is the answer. (p. 75)
   c. & d. These refer to the sensory cortex.

8. **c.** is the answer. The corpus callosum is a large band of neural fibers linking the right and left cerebral hemispheres. To sever the corpus callosum is in effect to split the brain. (p. 84)

9. **d.** is the answer. The frontal lobe is in the front of the brain. Just behind is the parietal lobe. The occipital lobe is located at the very back of the head and just below the parietal lobe. Next to the occipital lobe and toward the front of the head is the temporal lobe. (p. 74)

10. **d.** is the answer. As demonstrated in the case of Phineas Gage, injury to the frontal lobe may produce such changes in personality. (p. 79)
    a. Damage to the parietal lobe might disrupt functions involving the sensory cortex.
    b. Damage to the temporal lobe might impair hearing.
    c. Occipital damage might impair vision.

11. **c.** is the answer. (p. 80)

Matching Items

1. d (p. 74)	5. i (p. 82)	9. k (p. 78)
2. g (p. 69)	6. a (p. 83)	10. b (p. 74)
3. e (p. 74)	7. j (p. 80)	11. c (p. 74)
4. f (p. 74)	8. h (p. 71)	

Brain Damage Diagram

1. a	4. d	7. f
2. h	5. e	8. g
3. c	6. b	

Psychology Applied

Multiple-Choice Questions

1. **c.** is the answer. The brainstem is the oldest and most primitive region of the brain. It is found in lower vertebrates, such as fish, as well as in humans and other mammals. The structures mentioned in the other choices are associated with stages of brain evolution beyond that seen in the fish. (p. 69)

2. **d.** is the answer. Stimulation of the sensory cortex elicits a sense of touch, as the experiments of Penfield demonstrated. (p. 77)
   a., b., & c. Hearing, seeing, or movement might be expected if the temporal, occipital, and motor regions of the cortex, respectively, were stimulated.

3. **c.** is the answer. As Olds and Milner discovered, electrical stimulation of the hypothalamus is a highly reinforcing event because it is the location of the animal's reward centers. The other brain regions mentioned are not associated with reward centers. (p. 72)

4. **a.** is the answer. The left hand, controlled by the right hemisphere, would be able to identify the fork, the picture of which is flashed to the right hemisphere. (p. 84)

5. **b.** is the answer. (p. 87)
   a., c., & d. The left hemisphere does not specialize in picture recognition. And blood clots can form anywhere in the brain.

6. **a.** is the answer. The right visual field projects directly to the verbal left hemisphere. (pp. 84–85)
   b. & c. The left hand is controlled by the right hemisphere, which, in this situation, would be unaware of the word since the picture has been flashed to the left hemisphere.

7. **c.** is the answer. (p. 69)
   d. Reproduction is only one of the basic survival functions the brain regulates.

8. **b.** is the answer. The hippocampus of the limbic system is involved in processing memory. The amygdala of the limbic system influences fear and anger. (p. 71)

a. The brainstem controls vital functions such as breathing and heartbeat; it is not directly involved in either emotion or memory.

c. & d. These answers are incorrect because the limbic system is an older brain structure than the cortex. Its involvement in emotions and memory is therefore more basic than that of the cortex.

9. **d.** is the answer. The thalamus relays sensory messages from the eyes, ears, and other receptors to the appropriate projection areas of the cortex. "Rewiring" the thalamus, theoretically, could have the effects stated in this question. (p. 70)

   a., b., & c. These brain structures are not directly involved in brain processes related to sensation or perception.

10. **a.** is the answer. The motor cortex, which determines the precision with which various parts of the body can be moved, is located in the frontal lobes. (pp. 75, 76)

    b. The parietal lobes contain the sensory cortex, which controls sensitivity to touch.

    c. The temporal lobes contain the primary projection areas for hearing and, on the left side, are also involved in language use.

    d. The occipital lobes contain the primary projection areas for vision.

Essay Question

The patient's two key symptoms (headaches and difficulty speaking) implicate the brain, and specifically Broca's area because of its involvement in controlling speech. To pinpoint possible brain damage and its resulting aphasia, a physician or cognitive neuroscientist might order an electroencephalogram (EEG) to determine if electrical activity in the patient's brain is abnormal. To gather more detailed information, a PET scan might be used to measure glucose-related activity in Broca's area. To examine whether structural damage has occurred, an MRI or fMRI might be used.

Key Terms

1. A **lesion** is destruction of tissue; studying the consequences of lesions in different regions of the brain—both surgically produced in animals and naturally occurring—helps researchers to determine the normal functions of these regions. (p. 67)

2. An **electroencephalogram (EEG)** is an amplified recording of the waves of electrical activity of the brain. *Encephalo* comes from a Greek word meaning "related to the brain." (p. 67)

3. A **CT (computed tomography) scan** is a series of X-ray photographs combined by computer into a composite representation of a slice through the body. (p. 68)

4. The **PET (positron emission tomography) scan** measures the levels of activity of different areas of the brain by tracing their consumption of a radioactive form of glucose, the brain's fuel. (p. 68)

5. **MRI (magnetic resonance imaging)** uses magnetic fields and radio waves to produce computer-generated images that show brain structures more clearly. (p. 68)

6. In a **fMRI (functional magnetic resonance imaging),** MRI scans taken less than a second apart are compared to reveal blood flow and, therefore, brain structure and function. (p. 68)

7. The **brainstem**, the oldest and innermost region of the brain, is an extension of the spinal cord and is the central core of the brain; its structures direct automatic survival functions. (p. 69)

8. Located in the brainstem, the **medulla** controls breathing and heartbeat. (p. 69)

9. Also part of the brainstem, the **reticular formation** is a nerve network that plays an important role in controlling arousal. (p. 70)

10. Located atop the brainstem, the **thalamus** routes incoming messages to the sensory receiving areas in the cortex and transmits replies to the medulla and cerebellum. (p. 70)

11. The **cerebellum** processes sensory input and coordinates movement output and balance. (p. 70)

12. The **limbic system** is a neural system associated with emotions such as fear and aggression and basic physiological drives. (p. 71)

    Memory aid: Its name comes from the Latin word *limbus*, meaning "border"; the **limbic system** is at the border of the brainstem and cerebral hemispheres.

13. The **amygdala** is part of the limbic system and influences the emotions of fear and aggression. (p. 71)

14. Also part of the limbic system, the **hypothalamus** regulates hunger, thirst, body temperature, and sexual behavior; helps govern the endocrine system via the pituitary gland; and contains the so-called reward centers of the brain. (p. 72)

15. The **cerebral cortex** is a thin intricate covering of interconnected neural cells atop the cerebral hemispheres. The seat of information processing,

the cortex is responsible for those complex functions that make us distinctively human. (p. 74)

Memory aid: Cortex in Latin means "bark." As bark covers a tree, the **cerebral cortex** is the "bark of the brain."

16. More numerous than cortical neurons, the **glial cells** of the brain guide neural connections, provide nutrients and insulating myelin, and help remove excess ions and neurotransmitters. (p. 74)

17. Located at the front of the brain, just behind the forehead, the **frontal lobes** are involved in speaking and muscle movements and in making plans and judgments. (p. 74)

18. Situated between the frontal and occipital lobes, the **parietal lobes** contain the sensory cortex. (p. 74)

19. Located at the back and base of the brain, the **occipital lobes** contain the visual cortex, which receives information from the eyes. (p. 74)

20. Located on the sides of the brain, the **temporal lobes** contain the auditory cortex, which receives information from the ears. (p. 74)

Memory aid: The **temporal lobes** are located near the *temples.*

21. Located at the back of the frontal lobe, the **motor cortex** controls voluntary movement. (p. 75)

22. The **sensory cortex** is located at the front of the parietal lobes, just behind the motor cortex. It registers and processes body touch and movement sensations. (p. 77)

23. Located throughout the cortex, **association areas** of the brain are involved in higher mental functions, such as learning, remembering, and abstract thinking. (p. 78)

Memory aid: Among their other functions, **association areas** of the cortex are involved in integrating, or *associating,* information from different areas of the brain.

24. **Aphasia** is an impairment of language as a result of damage to any of several cortical areas, including Broca's area and Wernicke's area. (p. 80)

25. **Broca's area,** located in the left frontal lobe, is involved in controlling the motor ability to produce speech. (p. 80)

28. **Wernicke's area,** located in the left temporal lobe, is involved in language comprehension and expression. (p. 80)

27. **Plasticity** is the brain's capacity for modification, as evidenced by brain reorganization following damage (especially in children). (p. 82)

28. **Neurogenesis** is the formation of new neurons. (p. 83)

29. The **corpus callosum** is the large band of neural fibers that links the right and left cerebral hemispheres. Without this band of nerve fibers, the two hemispheres could not interact. (p. 84)

30. **Split brain** is a condition in which the major connections between the two cerebral hemispheres (the corpus callosum) are severed, literally resulting in a split brain. (p. 84)

31. **Consciousness** is awareness of ourselves and the environment. (p. 89)

32. **Cognitive neuroscience** is the interdisciplinary study of brain activity linked with perception, thinking, memory, and language. (p. 89)

33. **Dual processing** is the principle that the brain often processes information simultaneously on separate conscious and unconscious tracks. (p. 90)

Biological Bases of Behavior: 3C: Genetics, Evolutionary Psychology, and Behavior

UNIT OVERVIEW

Unit 3C is concerned with the ways in which our biological heritage, or nature, interacts with our individual experiences, or nurture, to shape who we are. After a brief explanation of basic terminology, the chapter explores the fields of behavior genetics, which studies twins and adopted children to weigh genetic and environmental influences on behaviors. The next section discusses psychology's use of evolutionary principles to answer universal questions about human behavior. This section uses human sexuality to illustrate the evolutionary explanation of human behavior.

The final section of the chapter explores how genes and environment interact to shape us biologically, psychologically, and socially. In the end, the message is clear: Our genes and our experience together form who we are.

NOTE: Answer guidelines for all Unit 3C questions begin on page 68.

UNIT REVIEW

First, skim each section, noting headings and boldface items. After you have read the section, review each objective by answering the fill-in and essay-type questions that follow it. As you proceed, evaluate your performance by consulting the answers on page 68. Do not continue with the next section until you understand each answer. If you need to, review or reread the section in the textbook before continuing.

Introduction (p. 94)

1. Our differences as humans include our

   _____ , _____ , and

_____ and _____

backgrounds.

2. Our similarities as human beings include our

   common _____ _____ ,

   our shared _____ architecture, our

   ability to use _____ , and our

   _____ behaviors.

3. A fundamental question in psychology deals with the extent to which we are shaped by our heredity, called our _____ , and by external influences, called our _____ .

Behavior Genetics: Predicting Individual Differences (pp. 95–103)

Objective 1: Identify the types of questions that interest behavior geneticists, and describe the elements of heredity: *chromosome, DNA, gene,* and *genome.*

1. Researchers who specifically study genetic and environmental influences on behavior are called

   _____ _____ .

2. The term *environment* refers to every

   _____ influence.

3. The master plans for development are stored in the _____ . In number, each person inherits _____ of these structures, _____ from each parent. Each is composed of a coiled chain of the molecule

   _____ .

4. If chromosomes are the "chapters" of heredity, the "words" that make each of us a distinctive human being are called _____ .

Most our our traits are influenced by
_____ (one/many) of these units of
heredity.

5. The complete instructions for making an organism are referred to as the human
_____ .

Objective 2: Describe how twin and adoption studies help us differentiate hereditary and environmental influences on human behavior.

6. To study the power and limits of genetic influences on behavior, researchers use
_____ and _____
studies.

7. Twins who developed from a single egg are genetically _____ . Twins who developed from different fertilized eggs are no more genetically alike than siblings and are called _____ twins.

8. In terms of the personality traits of extraversion and neuroticism, identical twins are
_____ (more/no more) alike than are fraternal twins.

9. Twin pairs reported _____ (being treated alike/being treated differently). However, their similarities _____ (could/could not) be attributed to how they were treated.

10. Through research on identical twins raised apart, psychologists are able to study the influence of the _____ .

11. Studies tend to show that the personalities of adopted children _____ (do/do not) closely resemble those of their adoptive parents. However, adoption studies show that parenting _____ (does/does not) matter. For example, many adopted children score _____ (higher/lower) than their biological parents on intelligence tests.

Objective 3: Explain what is meant by heritability, and give examples of the interaction of genes and environment on specific traits.

12. The extent to which variation among individuals can be attributed to differing genes is called _____ . Heritable individual differ-

ences _____ (imply/do not necessarily imply) heritable group differences.

13. Genes are self-_____ ; rather than acting as _____ that always lead to the same result, they _____ to the environmental context.

14. For _____ phenomena, human differences are nearly always the result of both _____ and _____ influences.

15. Throughout life, we are the product of the _____ of our _____ predispositions and our surrounding _____ .

16. Environments trigger activity in _____ , and our genetically influenced traits evoke _____ in other people. This may explain why _____ twins recall greater variations in their early family life than do _____ twins.

Objective 4: Identify the potential uses of molecular genetics research.

17. The subfield of biology that seeks to identify some of the many genes that influence normal human traits is _____
_____ .

18. To uncover the genes, researchers in this field seek links between certain _____ or _____ segments and specific disorders. They find families with the disorder over several generations, and they compare the _____ of affected and unaffected members, looking for differences.

Evolutionary Psychology: Understanding Human Nature (pp. 103–107)

Objective 5: Describe the area of psychology that interests evolutionary psychologists, and point out some possible effects of natural selection in the development of human characteristics.

1. Researchers who study natural selection and the adaptive nature of human behavior are called
_____ _____ .

2. Researchers in this field focus mostly on what makes people so _____ (much alike/different from one another).

3. According to the principle of _____ _____ , traits that lead to increased reproduction and survival will be most likely to be passed on to succeeding generations.

4. Genetic _____ are random errors in genetic replication that are the source of all genetic _____ .

5. Genetic constraints on human behavior are generally _____ (tighter/looser) than those on animal behavior. The human species' ability to _____ and therefore to _____ in responding to different _____ contributes to our _____ , defined as our ability to _____ and _____ . Because of our genetic legacy, we love the tastes of sweets and _____ , which we tend to _____ , even though famine is unlikely in industrialized societies.

Objective 6: Identify some gender differences in sexuality and mating preferences, and describe evolutionary explanations for those differences.

6. Compared with women, men are _____ (equally/more/less) likely to desire more frequent sex, and they are _____ (equally/more/less) likely to initiate sexual activity. This is an example of a _____ difference.

7. The _____ explanation of gender differences in attitudes toward sex is based on differences in the optimal strategy by which women and men pass on their _____ . According to this view, males and females _____ (are/are not) selected for different patterns of sexuality.

8. Cross-cultural research reveals that men judge women as more attractive if they have a _____ appearance, whereas women judge men who appear _____ ,

_____ , _____ , and _____ as more attractive.

Objective 7: Summarize the criticisms of evolutionary explanations of human behaviors, and describe the evolutionary psychologists' responses to these criticisms.

9. Critics of the evolutionary explanation of the gender sexuality difference argue that it often works _____ (forward/backward) to propose a _____ explanation.

10. Another critique is that gender differences in sexuality vary with _____ expectations. Gender differences in mate preferences are largest in cultures characterized by greater gender _____ (equality/inequality).

11. Evolutionary psychologists counter the criticisms by noting that the sexes, having faced similar adaptive problems, are more _____ (alike/different) than they are _____ (alike/different). They also note that evolutionary principles offer testable _____ .

Reflections on Nature and Nurture
(pp. 108–110)

Objective 8: Discuss some of the ways heredity and environment interact to both "control" who we are and allow us to become who we want to be.

1. As brute strength becomes _____ (more/less) relevant to power and status, gender roles are _____ (converging/diverging).

2. We are the product of both _____ and _____ , but we are also a system that is _____ . We know this because a _____ approach to development shows that no single factor is all-powerful.

3. The principle that we should prefer the simplest of competing explanations for a phenomenon is called _____ _____ .

PROGRESS TEST 1

Multiple-Choice Questions

Circle your answers to the following questions and check them with the answers beginning on page 68. If your answer is incorrect, read the explanation for why it is incorrect and then consult the appropriate pages of the text (in parentheses following the correct answer).

1. Dr. Ross believes that principles of natural selection help explain why infants come to fear strangers about the time they become mobile. Dr. Ross is most likely a(n)
   a. behavior geneticist.
   b. molecular geneticist.
   c. evolutionary psychologist.
   d. molecular biologist.

2. A pair of adopted children or identical twins reared in the same home are most likely to have similar
   a. excitability.
   b. personalities.
   c. religious beliefs.
   d. emotional reactivity.

3. If a fraternal twin develops schizophrenia, the likelihood of the other twin developing serious mental illness is much lower than with identical twins. This suggests that
   a. schizophrenia is caused by genes.
   b. schizophrenia is influenced by genes.
   c. environment is unimportant in the development of schizophrenia.
   d. identical twins are especially vulnerable to mental disorders.

4. Of the following, the best way to separate the effects of genes and environment in research is to study
   a. fraternal twins.
   b. identical twins.
   c. adopted children and their adoptive parents.
   d. identical twins raised in different environments.

5. Through natural selection, the traits that are most likely to be passed on to succeeding generations are those that contribute to
   a. impulsivity.   c. aggression.
   b. survival.   d. social influence.

6. Evolutionary psychologists attribute gender differences in sexuality to the fact that women have
   a. greater reproductive potential than do men.
   b. lower reproductive potential than do men.
   c. weaker sex drives than men.
   d. stronger sex drives than men.

7. According to evolutionary psychology, men are drawn sexually to women who seem _____, while women are attracted to men who seem

   _____ .
   a. nurturing; youthful
   b. youthful and fertile; mature and affluent
   c. slender; muscular
   d. exciting; dominant

8. Unlike _____ twins, who develop from a single fertilized egg, _____ twins develop from separate fertilized eggs.
   a. fraternal; identical
   b. identical; fraternal
   c. placental; nonplacental
   d. nonplacental; placental

9. When evolutionary psychologists use the word *fitness*, they are specifically referring to
   a. an animal's ability to adapt to changing environments.
   b. the diversity of a species' gene pool.
   c. the total number of members of the species currently alive.
   d. our ability to survive and reproduce.

10. A molecular geneticist would be most interested in studying
    a. why most parents are so passionately devoted to their children.
    b. environmental influences on skin color.
    c. why certain diseases are more common among certain age groups.
    d. which genes influence extraversion.

Matching Items

Match each term with its corresponding definition or description.

Terms

_____ 1. natural selection
_____ 2. genome
_____ 3. fraternal
_____ 4. genes
_____ 5. DNA
_____ 6. identical
_____ 7. behavior genetics
_____ 8. chromosomes
_____ 9. molecular genetics
_____ 10. mutation
_____ 11. environment

Functions or Descriptions

a. the biochemical units of heredity
b. twins that develop from a single egg
c. the complete set of instructions for making an organism
d. driving principle behind evolutionary psychology
e. twins that develop from separate eggs
f. threadlike structures composed of DNA
g. nongenetic influences
h. subfield of biology that studies the structure and function of genes
i. study of the relative power of genetic and environmental influences
j. a complex molecule containing the genetic information that makes up the chromosomes
k. random error in gene replication

PROGRESS TEST 2

Progress Test 2 should be completed during a final unit review. Answer the following questions after you thoroughly understand the correct answers for the section reviews and Progress Test 1.

Multiple-Choice Questions

1. Each cell of the human body has a total of
   a. 23 chromosomes.
   b. 23 genes.
   c. 46 chromosomes.
   d. 46 genes.

2. Genes direct our physical development by synthesizing
   a. hormones.
   b. proteins.
   c. DNA.
   d. chromosomes.

3. The *genome* is best defined as
   a. a complex molecule containing genetic information that makes up the chromosomes.
   b. a segment of DNA.
   c. the complete instructions for making an organism.
   d. the code for synthesizing protein.

4. Most human traits are
   a. learned.
   b. determined by a single gene.
   c. influenced by many genes acting together.
   d. unpredictable.

5. Mutations are random errors in _____ replication.
   a. gene
   b. chromosome
   c. DNA
   d. protein

6. Evolutionary explanations of gender differences in sexuality have been criticized because
   a. they offer "after-the-fact" explanations.
   b. standards of attractiveness have not changed over time.
   c. they overestimate cultural influences on sexuality.
   d. they suggest that environment overrides genetic influences.

7. Several studies of long-separated identical twins have found that these twins
   a. have little in common because of the different environments in which they were raised.
   b. have many similarities, in everything from medical histories to personalities.
   c. have similar personalities, but very different likes, dislikes, and life-styles.
   d. are no more similar than are fraternal twins reared apart.

8. Adoption studies show that the personalities of adopted children
   a. closely match those of their adoptive parents.
   b. bear more similarities to their biological parents than to their adoptive parents.
   c. closely match those of the biological children of their adoptive parents.
   d. closely match those of other children reared in the same home, whether or not they are biologically related.

9. Chromosomes are composed of small segments of
   a. DNA called genes.
   b. DNA called neurotransmitters.
   c. genes called DNA.
   d. DNA called enzymes.

10. When the effect of one factor (such as environment) depends on another (such as heredity), we say there is a(n) _____ between the two factors.
    a. norm
    b. positive correlation
    c. negative correlation
    d. interaction

11. An evolutionary psychologist would be most interested in studying
    a. why most parents are so passionately devoted to their children.
    b. hereditary influences on skin color.
    c. why certain diseases are more common among certain age groups.
    d. genetic differences in personality.

True–False Items

Indicate whether each statement is true or false by placing *T* or *F* in the blank next to the item.

_____ 1. Gender differences in mate preferences vary widely from one culture to another.

_____ 2. Most human traits are influenced by many genes acting together.

_____ 3. Research on twins shows a substantial genetic influence on attitudes toward organized religion and many other issues.

_____ 4. Genes act as blueprints that lead to the same result no matter the context.

_____ 5. Compared with identical twins reared in different families, fraternal twins recall their early family life more differently.

_____ 6. Women are more likely than men to take a relational view of sexual activity.

_____ 7. Nature selects behavioral tendencies that increase the likelihood of sending one's genes into the future.

_____ 8. Heritable individual differences in a trait always explain group differences in the same trait.

_____ 9. Women increase their fitness by searching for mates with the potential for long-term investment in their joint offspring.

_____ 10. Environmental events "turn on" genes.

_____ 11. People who grow up together tend to have similar personalities.

PSYCHOLOGY APPLIED

Answer these questions the day before a test as a final check on your understanding of the unit's terms and concepts.

Multiple-Choice Questions

1. If chromosomes are the "chapters" of heredity, the "words" are the
   a. genes.
   b. molecules.
   c. genomes.
   d. DNA.

2. After comparing divorce rates among identical and fraternal twins, Dr. Alexander has concluded that genes do play a role. Dr. Alexander is most likely a(n)
   a. evolutionary psychologist.
   b. behavior geneticist.
   c. molecular geneticist.
   d. divorcee.

3. Despite growing up in the same home environment, Karen and her brother John have personalities as different from each other as two people selected randomly from the population. Why is this so?
   a. Personality is inherited. Because Karen and John are not identical twins, it is not surprising they have very different personalities.
   b. Gender is the most important factor in personality. If Karen had a sister, the two of them would probably be much more alike.
   c. The interaction of their individual genes and nonshared experiences accounts for the common finding that children in the same family are usually very different.
   d. Their case is unusual; children in the same family usually have similar personalities.

4. One of the best ways to distinguish how much genetic and environmental factors affect behavior is to compare children who have
   a. the same genes and environments.
   b. different genes and environments.
   c. similar genes and environments.
   d. the same genes but different environments.

5. My sibling and I developed from a single fertilized egg. Who are we?
   a. opposite-sex identical twins
   b. same-sex identical twins
   c. opposite-sex fraternal twins
   d. same-sex fraternal twins

6. Of the relatively few genetic differences among humans _____ are differences among population groups.
   a. less than 1 percent
   b. less than 10 percent
   c. approximately 25 percent
   d. approximately 40 to 50 percent

7. A person whose twin has Alzheimer's disease has _____ risk of sharing the disease if they are identical twins than if they are fraternal twins.
   a. less
   b. about the same
   c. a much greater
   d. an unpredictable

8. Which of the following is an example of an interaction?
   a. Swimmers swim fastest during competition against other swimmers.
   b. Swimmers with certain personality traits swim fastest during competition, while those with other personality traits swim fastest during solo time trials.
   c. As the average daily temperature increases, sales of ice cream decrease.
   d. As the average daily temperature increases, sales of lemonade increase.

9. Which of the following most accurately summarizes the findings of the 40-year fox-breeding study described in the text?
   a. Wild foxes cannot be domesticated.
   b. "Survival of the fittest" seems to operate only when animals live in their natural habitats.
   c. By mating aggressive and unaggressive foxes, the researchers created a mutant species.
   d. By selecting and mating the tamest males and females, the researchers have produced affectionate, unaggressive offspring.

10. Which of the following is true of women, as compared with men?
    a. They are less likely to be concerned with their partner's maturity.
    b. They are more likely to initiate sexual activity.
    c. They are more likely to perceive warm responses as a sexual come-on.
    d. They are less likely to sacrifice to gain sex.

Essay Question

Lakia's new boyfriend has been pressuring her to become more sexually intimate than she wants to at this early stage in their relationship. Strongly gender typed and "macho" in attitude, Jerome is becoming increasingly frustrated with Lakia's hesitation, while Lakia is starting to wonder if a long-term relationship with this type of man is what she really wants. In light of your understanding of the evolutionary explanation of gender differences in sexuality, explain why the tension between Lakia and Jerome would be considered understandable.

KEY TERMS

Using your own words, on a piece of paper write a brief definition or explanation of each of the following terms.

1. behavior genetics
2. environment
3. chromosomes
4. DNA
5. genes
6. genome
7. identical twins
8. fraternal twins
9. heritability
10. interaction
11. molecular genetics
12. evolutionary psychology
13. natural selection
14. mutation

ANSWERS
Unit Review

Introduction

1. personalities; interests; cultural; family
2. biological heritage; brain; language; social
3. nature; nurture

Behavior Genetics: Predicting Individual Differences

1. behavior geneticists
2. nongenetic
3. chromosomes; 46; 23; DNA
4. genes; many
5. genome
6. twin; adoption
7. identical; fraternal
8. more
9. being treated alike; could not
10. environment
11. do not; does; higher
12. heritability; do not necessarily imply
13. regulating; blueprints; react

14. psychological; genetic; environmental
15. interaction; genetic; environment
16. genes; responses; fraternal; identical
17. molecular genetics
18. genes; chromosome; DNA

Evolutionary Psychology: Understanding Human Nature

1. evolutionary psychologists
2. much alike
3. natural selection
4. mutations; diversity
5. looser; learn; adapt; environments; fitness; survive; reproduce; fats; store
6. more; more; gender
7. evolutionary; genes; are
8. youthful; mature; dominant; bold; affluent
9. backward; hindsight
10. social; inequality
11. alike; different; predictions

Reflections on Nature and Nurture

1. less; converging
2. nature; nurture; open; biopsychosocial
3. Occam's razor

Progress Test 1

Multiple-Choice Questions

1. **c.** is the answer. (p. 103)
   a., b., & d. Whereas evolutionary psychologists attempt to explain universal human tendencies, these researchers investigate genetic differences among individuals.

2. **c.** is the answer. Research has not shown a strong parental influence on personality, temperament, or emotional reactivity. (p. 99)

3. **b.** is the answer. (p. 97)
   a. & c. Although an identical twin is at increased risk, the relationship is far from perfect. Mental disorders, like all psychological traits, are influenced by *both* nature and nurture.
   d. This is not at all implied by the evidence from twin studies.

4. **d.** is the answer. (p. 98)
   a., b., & c. In order to pinpoint the influence of one of the two factors (genes and environment), it is necessary to hold one of the factors constant.

5. **b.** is the answer. (p. 104)

6. **b.** is the answer. Women can incubate only one infant at a time. (p. 106)
   c. & d. The text does not suggest that there is a gender difference in the strength of the sex drive.

7. **b.** is the answer. (p. 106)
   a. According to this perspective, women prefer mates with the potential for long-term nurturing investment in their joint offspring.
   c. While men are drawn to women whose waists are roughly a third narrower than their hips, the text does not suggest that women equate muscularity with fertility.
   d. Excitement was not mentioned as a criterion for mating.

8. **b.** is the answer. (p. 97)
   c. & d. There are no such things as "placental" or "nonplacental" twins. All twins have a placenta during prenatal development.

9. **d.** is the answer. (p. 104)
   a. Survival ability is only one aspect of fitness.
   b. & c. Neither of these is related to fitness.

10. **d.** is the answer. (p. 102)

Matching Items

1. d (p. 103)   5. j (p. 95)   9. h (p. 102)
2. c (p. 96)   6. b (p. 96)   10. k (p. 104)
3. e (p. 97)   7. i (p. 95)   11. g (p. 95)
4. a (p. 95)   8. f (p. 95)

Progress Test 2

Multiple-Choice Questions

1. **c.** is the answer. (p. 95)
   b. & d. Each cell of the human body contains hundreds of genes.

2. **b.** is the answer. (p. 95)
   a. Hormones are chemical messengers produced by the endocrine glands.
   c. & d. Genes are segments of DNA, which are the makeup of chromosomes.

3. **c.** is the answer. (p. 96)
   a. This defines DNA.
   b. This defines a gene.
   d. The genes provide the code for synthesizing proteins.

4. **c.** is the answer. (p. 96)

5. **a.** is the answer. (p. 104)

6. **a.** is the answer. (p. 107)

7. **b.** is the answer. (p. 98)

a., c., & d. Despite being raised in different environments, long-separated identical twins often have much in common, including likes, dislikes, and life-styles. This indicates the significant heritability of many traits.

8. **b.** is the answer. (p. 99)
   a., c., & d. The personalities of adopted children do not much resemble those of their adoptive parents (therefore, not a.) or other children reared in the same home (therefore, not c. or d.).

9. **a.** is the answer. (p. 95)
   b. Neurotransmitters are the chemicals involved in synaptic transmission in the nervous system.
   d. Enzymes are chemicals that facilitate various chemical reactions throughout the body but are not involved in heredity.

10. **d.** is the answer. (p. 101)
    a. A norm is a culturally determined set of expected behaviors for a particular role, such as a gender role.
    b. & c. When two factors are correlated, it means either that increases in one factor are accompanied by increases in the other (positive correlation) or that increases in one factor are accompanied by decreases in the other (negative correlation).

11. **a.** is the answer. This is an example of a trait that contributes to survival of the human species and the perpetuation of one's genes. (p. 104)
    b., c., & d. These traits and issues would likely be of greater interest to a behavior geneticist, since they concern the influence of specific genes on behavior.

True–False Items

1. F (p. 106)   5. T (p. 102)   9. T (p. 106)
2. T (p. 96)   6. T (p. 106)   10. T (p. 101)
3. F (p. 100)   7. T (p. 104)   11. F (p. 99)
4. F (p. 101)   8. F (p. 100)

Psychology Applied

Multiple-Choice Questions

1. **a.** is the answer. (p. 95)
   b. DNA is a molecule.
   c. & d. Genes are segments of DNA, and the genome is the complete instructions for making an organism.

2. **b.** is the answer. (pp. 95, 97)
   a. Evolutionary psychologists study the evolution of behavior using the principles of natural selection.

c. Molecular geneticists search for the specific genes that influence behaviors. In his example, the researcher is merely comparing twins.
d. Who knows?

3. **c.** is the answer. (p. 99)
a. Although heredity does influence certain traits, such as outgoingness and emotional instability, it is the interaction of heredity and experience that ultimately molds personality.
b. There is no single "most important factor" in personality. Moreover, for the same reason two sisters or brothers often have dissimilar personalities, a sister and brother may be very much alike.
d. Karen and John's case is not at all unusual.

4. **d.** is the answer. To separate the influences of heredity and experience on behavior, one of the two must be held constant. (p. 97)
a., b., & c. These situations would not allow one to separate the contributions of heredity and environment.

5. **b.** is the answer. (p. 96)
a. Because they are genetically the same, identical twins are always of the same sex.
c. & d. Fraternal twins develop from two fertilized eggs.

6. **b.** is the answer. Actually, only 5 percent are differences among population groups. (p. 104)

7. **c.** is the answer. (p. 97)

8. **b.** is the answer. (p. 101)
a. An interaction requires at least two variables; in this example there is only one (competition).
c. This is an example of a negative correlation.
d. This is an example of a positive correlation.

9. **d.** is the answer. (pp. 103–104)

10. **d.** is the answer. (p. 105)
a., b., & c. These are typical male attitudes and behaviors.

Essay Question

Evolutionary psychologists would not be surprised by the tension between Lakia and Jerome and would see it as a reflection of women's more relational and men's more recreational approach to sex. Since eggs are expensive, compared with sperm, women prefer mates with the potential for long-term investment in their joint offspring. According to this perspective, this may be why Lakia is not in a hurry to become sexually intimate with Jerome. Men, on the other hand, are selected for "pairing widely" but not necessarily wisely in order to maximize the spreading of their genes. This is especially true of men like Jerome, who have traditional masculine attitudes.

Key Terms

1. **Behavior genetics** is the study of the relative power and limits of genetic and environmental influences on behavior. (p. 95)

2. In behavior genetics, **environment** refers to every nongenetic, or external, influence on our traits and behaviors. (p. 95)

3. **Chromosomes** are threadlike structures made of DNA molecules that contain the genes. In conception, the 23 chromosomes in the egg are paired with the 23 chromosomes in the sperm. (p. 95)

4. **DNA** (*deoxyribonucleic acid*) is a complex molecule containing the genetic information that makes up the chromosomes. (p. 95)

5. **Genes** are the biochemical units of heredity that make up the chromosomes; they are segments of the DNA molecules capable of synthesizing a protein. (p. 95)

6. A **genome** is the complete genetic instructions for making an organism. (p. 96)

7. **Identical twins** develop from a single fertilized egg that splits in two and therefore are genetically identical. (p. 96)

8. **Fraternal twins** develop from two separate eggs fertilized by different sperm and therefore are no more genetically similar than ordinary siblings. (p. 97)

9. **Heritability** refers to the proportion of variation among individuals that can be attributed to genes. (p. 100)

10. An **interaction** occurs when the effects of one factor (such as environment) depend on another factor (such as heredity). (p. 101)

    Example: Because the way people react to us (an environmental factor) depends on our genetically influenced temperament (a genetic factor), there is an **interaction** between environment and heredity.

11. **Molecular genetics** is a subfield of biology that studies the molecular structure and function of specific genes. (p. 102)

12. **Evolutionary psychology** is the study of the evolution of behavior and the mind, using principles of natural selection. (p. 103)

13. **Natural selection** is the evolutionary principle that traits that lead to increased reproduction and survival are the most likely to be passed on to succeeding generations. (p. 103)

14. **Mutations** are random errors in gene replication that are the source of genetic diversity within a species. (p. 104)

Sensation and Perception

UNIT OVERVIEW

Unit 4 explores the processes by which our sense receptors and nervous system represent our external environment (sensation), as well as how we mentally organize and interpret this information (perception). The senses of vision, hearing, taste, touch (including kinesthesis and the vestibular sense), and smell are described, along with the ways in which we organize the stimuli reaching these senses to perceive form; depth; motion; and constant shape, size, and lightness. To enhance your understanding of these processes, the chapter also discusses research findings from studies of subliminal stimulation, sensory restriction, recovery from blindness, adaptation to distorted environments, perceptual set, and extrasensory perception.

In this unit there are many terms to learn and several theories you must understand. Many of the terms are related to the structure of the eye, ear, and other sensory receptors. Doing the chapter review several times, labeling the diagrams, and rehearsing the material frequently will help you to memorize these structures and their functions. The theories discussed include the Young-Helmholtz three-color and opponent-process theories of color vision, the place and frequency theories of hearing, and the Gestalt theory of form perception. As you study these theories, concentrate on understanding the strengths and weaknesses (if any) of each.

NOTE: Answer guidelines for all Unit 4 questions begin on page 89.

UNIT REVIEW

First, skim each section, noting headings and boldface items. After you have read the section, review each objective by answering the fill-in and essay-type questions that follow it. As you proceed, evaluate your performance by consulting the answers beginning on page 89. Do not continue with the next section until you understand each answer. If you need to, review or reread the section in the textbook before continuing.

Introduction and Sensing the World: Some Basic Principles (pp. 115–124)

Objective 1: Contrast sensation and perception, and explain the difference between bottom-up and top-down processing.

1. The perceptual disorder in which a person has lost the ability to recognize familiar faces is

   _____ .

2. The process by which we detect physical energy from the environment and encode it as neural signals is _____ . The process by which sensations are organized and interpreted is

   _____ .

3. Sensory analysis, which starts at the entry level and works up, is called _____ -

   _____ _____ .

   Perceptual analysis, which works from our experience and expectations, is called

   _____ - _____

   _____ .

Objective 2: Discuss how our perceptions are directed and limited by selective attention, noting how we may or may not be affected by unattended stimuli.

4. When we focus our conscious awareness on a particular stimulus, we are using

   _____ _____ .

5. Your ability to attend to only one voice among many is called the _____

_____ _____ .

Failing to see a visible object when our attention is directed elsewhere is called

_____ _____ .

6. When researchers distracted participants with a counting task, the participants displayed

_____ _____ and

failed to notice a gorilla-suited assistant who passed through. Two specific forms of this phenomenon are _____

_____ and_____

_____ . Another result of distraction involves not noticing that different people are speaking, called _____

_____ .

7. Some stimuli are so powerful they demand our attention, causing us to experience

_____-_____ .

Objective 3: Distinguish between absolute and difference thresholds, and discuss whether we can sense and be affected by subliminal or unchanging stimuli.

8. The study of relationships between the physical characteristics of stimuli and our psychological experience of them is _____ .

9. The _____ _____ refers to the minimum stimulation necessary for a stimulus to be detected _____ percent of the time.

10. According to _____

_____ theory, a person's experience, expectations, motivation, and alertness all influence the detection of a stimulus.

11. Some entrepreneurs claim that exposure to "below threshold," or _____ , stimuli can be persuasive, but their claims are probably unwarranted.

12. Some weak stimuli may trigger in our sensory receptors a response that is processed by the brain, even though the response doesn't cross the threshold into _____ awareness.

13. Under certain conditions, an invisible image or word can _____ a person's response to a later question. This illustrates that much of our information processing occurs

_____ .

14. The minimum difference required to distinguish two stimuli 50 percent of the time is called the

_____ _____ .

Another term for this value is the

_____ _____

_____ .

15. The principle that the difference threshold is not a constant amount, but a constant proportion, is known as _____

_____ . The proportion depends on the _____ .

16. After constant exposure to an unchanging stimulus, the receptor cells of our senses begin to fire less vigorously; this phenomenon is called

_____ _____ .

17. This phenomenon illustrates that sensation is designed to focus on _____ changes in the environment.

Vision (pp. 124–133)

Objective 4: Describe the characteristics of visible light, and explain the process by which the eye converts light energy into neural messages.

1. Stimulus energy is _____ (transformed) into _____ messages by our eyes.

2. The visible spectrum of light is a small portion of the larger spectrum of _____ energy.

3. The distance from one light wave peak to the next is called _____ . This value determines the wave's color, or

_____ .

4. The amount of energy in light waves, or _____ , determined by a wave's _____ , or height, influences the _____ of a light.

5. Light enters the eye through the _____ , then passes through a small opening called the _____ ; the size of this opening is controlled by the colored _____ .

6. By changing its curvature, the _____ can focus the image of an object onto the _____ , the light-sensitive inner surface of the eye.

7. The process by which the lens changes shape to focus images is called _____ .

8. The retina's receptor cells are the _____ and _____ .

9. The neural signals produced in the rods and cones activate the neighboring _____ cells, which then activate a network of _____ cells. The axons of ganglion cells converge to form the _____ _____ , which carries the visual information to the _____ .

10. Where this nerve leaves the eye, there are no receptors; thus, the area is called the _____ _____ .

11. Most cones are clustered around the retina's point of central focus, called the _____ , whereas the rods are concentrated in more _____ regions of the retina. Many cones have their own _____ cells to communicate with the visual cortex.

12. It is the _____ (rods/cones) of the eye that permit the perception of color, whereas _____ (rods/cones) enable black-and-white vision.

13. Unlike cones, in dim light the rods are _____ (sensitive/insensitive). Adapting to a darkened room will take the retina approximately _____ minutes.

Objective 5: Discuss the different levels of processing that occur as information travels from the retina to the brain's cortex.

14. Visual information percolates through progressively more _____ levels. In the brain, it is routed by the _____ to the cortex. Hubel and Wiesel discovered that certain neurons in the occipital lobe's _____ respond only to specific features of what is viewed. They called these neurons _____ _____ .

15. Feature detectors pass their information to higher-level cells in the brain, which respond to specific visual scenes. Research has shown that in monkey brains such cells specialize in responding to a specific _____ , _____ _____ , _____ , or _____ . In many cortical areas, teams of cells (_____ _____) respond to complex patterns.

Objective 6: Define *parallel processing*, and discuss its role in visual information processing.

16. The brain achieves its remarkable speed in visual perception by processing several subdivisions of a stimulus _____ (simultaneously/sequentially). This procedure, called _____ _____ , may explain why people who have suffered a stroke may lose just one aspect of vision.

17. Other brain-damaged people may demonstrate _____ by responding to a stimulus that is not consciously perceived.

Objective 7: Explain how the Young-Helmholtz and opponent-process theories help us understand color vision.

18. An object appears to be red in color because it _____ the long wavelengths of red and because of our mental _____ of the color.

19. One out of every 50 people is color deficient; this is usually a male because the defect is genetically _____ - _____ .

20. According to the _____ - _____ _____ theory, the eyes have three types of color receptors: one reacts most strongly to _____ , one to _____ , and one to _____ .

21. After staring at a green square for a while, you will see the color red, its _____ color, as an _____ .

22. Hering's theory of color vision is called the _____ - _____ theory. According to this theory, after visual information leaves the receptors it is analyzed in terms of pairs of opposing colors:

_____ versus _____ ,

_____ versus _____ ,

and _____ versus _____ .

Summarize the two stages of color processing.

Hearing (pp. 133–140)

Objective 8: Describe the auditory process, including the stimulus input and the structure and function of the ear.

1. The stimulus for hearing, or
   _____ , is sound waves, created by
   the compression and expansion of
   _____ _____ .

2. The amplitude of a sound wave determines the
   sound's _____ .

3. The frequency of a sound wave determines the
   _____ we perceive.

4. Sound energy is measured in units called
   _____ . The absolute threshold for
   hearing is arbitrarily defined as
   _____ such units.

5. The ear is divided into three main parts: the
   _____ ear, the
   _____ ear, and the
   _____ ear.

6. The outer ear channels sound waves toward the
   _____ , a tight membrane that then
   vibrates.

7. The middle ear transmits the vibrations through a
   piston made of three small bones: the
   _____ , _____ , and
   _____ .

8. In the inner ear, a coiled, bony, fluid-filled tube
   called the _____ contains the

receptor cells for hearing. The incoming vibrations cause the _____
_____ to vibrate the fluid that fills
the tube, which causes ripples in the

_____ _____ ,

bending the _____
_____ that line its surface. This
movement triggers impulses in the adjacent nerve
fibers that converge to form the auditory nerve,
which carries the neural messages (via the
_____) to the
_____ lobe's auditory cortex.

9. The brain interprets loudness from the
   _____ of hair cells a sound
   activates.

Objective 9: Contrast place and frequency theories, and explain how they help us to understand pitch perception.

10. One theory of pitch perception proposes that different pitches activate different places on the
    cochlea's basilar membrane; this is the
    _____ theory. This theory has difficulty accounting for how we hear
    _____-pitched sounds, which do
    not have such localized effects.

11. A second theory proposes that the frequency of
    neural impulses, sent to the brain at the same frequency as sound waves, allows the perception of
    different pitches. This is the _____
    theory. This theory fails to account for the perception of _____-pitched sounds
    because individual neurons cannot fire faster
    than _____ times per second.

12. For the higher pitches, cells may alternate their
    firing to match the sound's frequency, according
    to the _____ principle.

Objective 10: Describe how we pinpoint sounds, and contrast the two types of hearing loss.

13. We locate a sound by sensing differences in the
    _____ and _____
    with which it reaches our ears.

14. A sound that comes from directly ahead will be
    _____ (easier/harder) to locate
    than a sound that comes from off to one side.

15. Problems in the mechanical conduction of sound waves through the outer or middle ear may cause _____ _____ _____ .

16. Damage to the cochlea's hair cell receptors or their associated auditory nerves can cause _____ hearing loss. It may be caused by disease, but more often it results from the biological changes linked with _____ and prolonged exposure to ear-splitting noise or music.

Objective 11: Describe how cochlear implants function, and explain why Deaf culture advocates object to these devices.

17. An electronic device that restores hearing among nerve-deafened people is a _____ _____ .

18. Advocates of_____ _____ object to the use of these implants on _____ before they have learned to _____ . The basis for their argument is that deafness is not a _____ .

19. Sign language _____ (is/is not) a complete language, _____ (with/without) its own grammar, syntax, and semantics. People who lose one channel of sensation (such as hearing) _____ (seem to/do not seem to) compensate with a slight enhancement in their other sensory abilities.

20. (Close-Up) Deaf children raised in a household where sign language is used express higher _____ and feel more _____ .

Other Senses (pp. 141–150)

Objective 12: Describe the sense of touch, and distinguish between kinesthesis and the vestibular sense.

1. The sense of touch is a mixture of at least four senses: _____ , _____ , _____ , and _____ . Other skin sensations, such

as tickle, itch, hot, and wetness, are _____ of the basic ones.

2. The _____-_____ influence on touch is illustrated by the fact that a self-produced tickle produces less activation in the _____ _____ than someone else's tickle. This influence is also seen in the _____-_____ illusion.

3. The system for sensing the position and movement of body parts is called _____ . The receptors for this sense are located in the _____ , _____ , _____ , and _____ , as well as your skin.

4. The sense that monitors the position and movement of the head (and thus the body) is the _____ _____ . The receptors for this sense are located in the _____ _____ and _____ _____ of the inner ear.

Objective 13: State the purpose of pain, and describe the biopsychosocial approach to pain.

5. People born without the ability to feel pain may be unaware of experiencing severe _____ . More numerous are those who live with _____ pain in the form of persistent headaches and backaches, for example.

6. Pain is a property of our _____ as well as our _____ and _____ , and our surrounding _____ .

7. The pain system _____ (is/is not) triggered by one specific type of physical energy. The body has specialized _____ that detect hurtful stimuli.

8. Melzack and Wall have proposed a theory of pain called the _____-_____ theory, which proposes that there is a neurological _____ in the _____ _____ .

that blocks pain signals or lets them through. It
may be opened by activation of
_____ (small/large) nerve fibers
and closed by activation of _____
(small/large) fibers or by information from the
_____ .

9. Pain-producing brain activity may be triggered
with or without _____
_____ .

10. A sensation of pain in an amputated leg is
referred to as a _____
_____ sensation. Another example
is _____ , experienced by people
who have a ringing-in-the-ears sensation.

List some pain control techniques used in health care
situations.

Objective 14: Describe the senses of taste and smell,
and comment on the nature of sensory interaction.

11. The basic taste sensations are _____ ,
_____ , _____ ,
_____ , and a meaty taste called
_____ .

12. Taste, which is a _____ sense, is
enabled by the 200 or more _____
_____ on the top and sides of the
tongue. Each contains a _____ that
catches food chemicals.

13. Taste receptors reproduce themselves every
_____ . As
we age, the number of taste buds
_____ (increases/decreases/remains
unchanged) and our taste sensitivity
_____ (increases/decreases/remains
unchanged). Taste is also affected by
_____ and by _____ use.

14. When the sense of smell is blocked, as when we
have a cold, foods do not taste the same; this
illustrates the principle of _____
_____ . The _____

effect occurs when we _____ a
speaker saying one syllable while
_____ another.

15. In a few rare individuals, the senses become
joined in a phenomenon called _____ .

16. Like taste, smell, or _____ , is a
_____ sense. There _____
(is/is not) a distinct receptor for each detectable
odor.

17. Odors are able to evoke memories and feelings
because there is a direct link between the brain
area that gets information from the nose and the
ancient _____ centers associated
with memory and emotion.

Perceptual Organization (pp. 151–159)

Objective 15: Describe Gestalt psychology's contribution to our understanding of perception, and identify
principles of perceptual grouping in form perception.

1. According to the _____ school of
psychology, we tend to organize a cluster of sensations into a _____ , or form.

2. When we view a scene, we see the central object,
or _____ , as distinct from sur-
rounding stimuli, or the _____ .

3. Proximity, similarity, closure, continuity, and
connectedness are examples of Gestalt rules of
_____ .

4. The principle that we organize stimuli into
smooth, continuous patterns is called
_____ . The principle that we fill in
gaps to create a complete, whole object is
_____ . The grouping of items that
are close to each other is the principle of
_____ ; the grouping of items that
look alike is the principle of
_____ . The tendency to perceive
uniform or attached items as a single unit is the
principle of _____ .

Objective 16: Explain the binocular and monocular
cues we use to perceive depth.

5. The ability to see objects in three dimensions
despite their two-dimensional representations on

our retinas is called _____

_____ . It enables us to estimate

_____ .

6. Gibson and Walk developed the

_____ _____ to test

depth perception in infants. They found that each

species, by the time it is _____ ,

has the perceptual abilities it needs.

Summarize the results of Gibson and Walk's studies
of depth perception.

For questions 7–15, identify the depth perception cue
that is defined.

7. Any cue that requires both eyes:

_____ .

8. The greater the difference between the images
received by the two eyes, the nearer the object:
_____ _____ . 3-D
movies simulate this cue by photographing each
scene with two cameras.

9. Any cue that requires either eye alone:

_____ .

10. If two objects are presumed to be the same size,
the one that casts a smaller retinal image is perceived as farther away:

_____ _____ .

11. An object partially covered by another is seen as
farther away: _____ .

12. Objects lower in the visual field are seen as
nearer: _____ _____ .

13. As we move, objects at different distances appear
to move at different rates:

_____ _____ .

14. Parallel lines appear to converge in the distance:

_____ _____ .

15. The dimmer of two objects seems farther away:

_____ _____

_____ .

Objective 17: State the basic assumption we make in
our perceptions of motion, and explain how these
perceptions can be deceiving.

16. Our brain normally computes motion based partly on the assumption that shrinking objects are

_____ (approaching/retreating)

and enlarging objects are _____

(approaching/retreating). Sometimes, we are

fooled because larger objects seem to move

_____ (faster/more slowly) than

smaller objects.

17. The brain interprets a rapid series of slightly

varying images as _____ . This

phenomenon is called _____

_____ .

18. The illusion of movement that results when two
adjacent stationary spots of light blink on and off
in quick succession is called the

_____ _____ .

Objective 18: Explain how perceptual constancies
help us to organize our sensations into meaningful
patterns.

19. Our tendency to see objects as unchanging while
the stimuli from them change in size, shape, and

lightness is called _____

_____ .

20. Due to shape and size constancy, familiar objects

_____ (do/do not) appear to

change shape or size despite changes in our

_____ images of them.

21. Several illusions, including the

_____ and_____

illusions, are explained by the interplay between

perceived _____ and perceived

_____ . When distance cues are

removed, these illusions are
_____ (diminished/strengthened).

22. The brain computes an object's brightness
_____ (relative to/independent of)
surrounding objects.

23. The amount of light an object reflects relative to
its surroundings is called

_____ _____ .

24. The experience of color depends on the surrounding _____ in which an object is
seen. In an unvarying context, a familiar object
will be perceived as having consistent color, even
as the light changes. This phenomenon is called

_____ _____ .

25. We see color as a result of our brains' computa-
tions of the light _____ by any
object relative to its _____

_____ .

Perceptual Interpretation (pp. 159–165)

Objective 19: Describe the contributions of restored
vision, sensory deprivation, and perceptual
adaptation research to our understanding of the
nature-nurture interplay in our perceptions.

1. The idea that knowledge comes from inborn
ways of organizing sensory experiences was proposed by the philosopher _____ .

2. On the other side were philosophers who maintained that we learn to perceive the world by
experiencing it. One philosopher of this school
was _____ .

3. Studies of cases in which vision has been restored
to a person who was blind from birth show that,
upon seeing tactilely familiar objects for the first
time, the person _____ (can/can-
not) recognize them.

4. Studies of sensory restriction demonstrate that
visual experiences during _____
are crucial for perceptual development. Such
experiences suggest that there is a

_____ _____ for
normal sensory and perceptual development.

5. Humans given glasses that shift or invert the
visual field _____ (will/will not)
adapt to the distorted perception. This is called

_____ _____ .

6. Animals such as chicks _____
(adapt/do not adapt) to distorting lenses.

Objective 20: Define *perceptual set*, and explain why
the same stimulus can evoke different perceptions in
different contexts.

7. A mental predisposition that influences perception is called a _____

_____ .

8. How a stimulus is perceived depends on the concepts, or _____ , we form and the
_____ in which the stimulus is
experienced.

9. The context of a stimulus creates a
_____ (top-down/bottom-up)
expectation that influences our perception as we
match our _____ (top-down/
bottom-up) signal against it.

10. Our perception is also influenced by
_____ about gender and the
_____ context of our experiences.

11. To best understand perception, we need multiple
levels of analysis because perception is a
_____ phenomenon.

Is There Extrasensory Perception?
(pp. 166–169)

Objective 21: Identify the three most testable forms of
ESP, and explain why most research psychologists
remain skeptical of ESP claims.

1. Perception outside the range of normal sensation
is called _____

_____ .

2. Psychologists who study ESP are called

_____ .

3. The form of ESP in which people claim to be
capable of reading others' minds is called
_____ . A person who "senses"
that a friend is in danger might claim to have the
ESP ability of _____ . An ability to
"see" into the future is called
_____ . A person who claims to be
able to levitate and move objects is claiming the
power of _____ .

4. Analyses of psychic visions and premonitions
reveal _____ (high/chance-level)

accuracy. Nevertheless, some people continue to believe in their accuracy because vague predictions often are later_____ to match events that have already occurred. In addition, people are more likely to recall or _____ dreams that seem to have come true.

5. Critics point out that a major difficulty for parapsychology is that ESP phenomena are not consistently _____ .

6. Researchers who tried to reduce external distractions between a "sender" and a "receiver" in an ESP experiment reported performance levels that _____ (beat/did not beat) chance levels. Follow-up studies _____ (failed to replicate the results/found equally high levels of performance).

PROGRESS TEST 1

Multiple-Choice Questions

Circle your answers to the following questions and check them with the answers beginning on page 91. If your answer is incorrect, read the explanation for why it is correct and then consult the appropriate pages of the text (in parentheses following the correct answer).

1. Which of the following is true?
   a. The absolute threshold for any stimulus is a constant.
   b. The absolute threshold for any stimulus varies somewhat.
   c. The absolute threshold is defined as the minimum amount of stimulation necessary for a stimulus to be detected 75 percent of the time.
   d. The absolute threshold is defined as the minimum amount of stimulation necessary for a stimulus to be detected 60 percent of the time.

2. If you can just notice the difference between 10- and 11-pound weights, which of the following weights could you differentiate from a 100-pound weight?
   a. 101-pound weight
   b. 105-pound weight
   c. 110-pound weight
   d. There is no basis for prediction.

3. A decrease in sensory responsiveness accompanying an unchanging stimulus is called
   a. sensory fatigue.
   b. accommodation.
   c. sensory adaptation.
   d. sensory interaction.

4. The size of the pupil is controlled by the
   a. lens.   c. cornea.
   b. retina.   d. iris.

5. The process by which the lens changes its curvature is
   a. accommodation.   c. feature detection.
   b. sensory adaptation. d. transduction.

6. The receptor of the eye that functions best in dim light is the
   a. fovea.   c. bipolar cell.
   b. cone   d. rod.

7. The Young-Helmholtz theory proposes that
   a. there are three different types of color-sensitive cones.
   b. retinal cells are excited by one color and inhibited by its complementary color.
   c. there are four different types of cones.
   d. rod, not cone, vision accounts for our ability to detect fine visual detail.

8. Frequency is to pitch as _____ is to_____ .
   a. wavelength; loudness
   b. amplitude; loudness
   c. wavelength; intensity
   d. amplitude; intensity

9. Our experience of pain when we are injured depends on
   a. our biological makeup and the type of injury we have sustained.
   b. how well medical personnel deal with our injury.
   c. our physiology, experiences and attention, and surrounding culture.
   d. what our culture allows us to express in terms of feelings of pain.

10. According to the gate-control theory, a way to alleviate chronic pain would be to stimulate the _____ nerve fibers that _____ the spinal gate.
    a. small; open   c. large; open
    b. small; close   d. large; close

11. The transduction of light energy into nerve impulses takes place in the
    a. iris.   c. lens.
    b. retina.   d. optic nerve.

12. The brain breaks vision into separate dimensions such as color, depth, movement, and form and works on each aspect simultaneously. This is called
    a. feature detection.
    b. parallel processing.
    c. accommodation.
    d. opponent processing.

13. Kinesthesis involves
    a. the bones of the middle ear.
    b. information from the bones, ears, tendons, and joints.
    c. membranes within the cochlea.
    d. the body's sense of balance.

14. One light may appear reddish and another greenish if they differ in
    a. wavelength.   c. opponent processes.
    b. amplitude.   d. brightness.

15. Which of the following explains why a rose appears equally red in bright and dim light?
    a. the Young-Helmholtz theory
    b. the opponent-process theory
    c. feature detection
    d. color constancy

16. Which of the following is an example of sensory adaptation?
    a. finding the cold water of a swimming pool warmer after you have been in it for a while
    b. developing an increased sensitivity to salt the more you use it in foods
    c. becoming very irritated at the continuing sound of a dripping faucet
    d. becoming increasingly annoyed by your neighbor's dog's barking.

17. Most color-deficient people will probably
    a. lack functioning red- or green-sensitive cones.
    b. see the world in only black and white.
    c. also suffer from poor vision.
    d. have above-average vision to compensate for the deficit.

18. The historical movement associated with the statement "The whole may exceed the sum of its parts" is
    a. parapsychology.
    b. behavioral psychology.
    c. functional psychology.
    d. Gestalt psychology.

19. Figures tend to be perceived as whole, complete objects, even if spaces or gaps exist in the representation, thus demonstrating the principle of
    a. connectedness.   c. continuity.
    b. similarity.   d. closure.

20. The figure-ground relationship has demonstrated that
    a. perception is largely innate.
    b. perception is simply a point-for-point representation of sensation.
    c. the same stimulus can trigger more than one perception.
    d. different people see different things when viewing a scene.

21. When we stare at an object, each eye receives a slightly different image, providing a depth cue known as
    a. interposition.   c. relative motion.
    b. linear perspective. d. retinal disparity.

22. As we move, viewed objects cast changing shapes on our retinas, although we do not perceive the objects as changing. This is part of the phenomenon of
    a. perceptual constancy.
    b. relative motion.
    c. linear perspective.
    d. continuity.

23. A person claiming to be able to read another's mind is claiming to have the ESP ability of
    a. psychokinesis.   c. clairvoyance.
    b. precognition.   d. telepathy.

24. Which philosopher maintained that knowledge comes from inborn ways of organizing our sensory experiences?
    a. John Locke   c. Eleanor Gibson
    b. Immanuel Kant   d. Richard Walk

25. Kittens and monkeys reared seeing only diffuse, unpatterned light
    a. later had difficulty distinguishing color and brightness.
    b. later had difficulty perceiving color and brightness, but eventually regained normal sensitivity.
    c. later had difficulty perceiving the shape of objects.
    d. showed no impairment in perception, indicating that neural feature detectors develop even in the absence of normal sensory experiences.

26. Adults who are born blind but later have their vision restored
    a. are almost immediately able to recognize familiar objects.
    b. typically fail to recognize familiar objects.
    c. are unable to follow moving objects with their eyes.
    d. have excellent eye-hand coordination.

27. _____ processing refers to how the physical characteristics of stimuli influence their interpretation.
    a. Top-down
    b. Bottom-up
    c. Parapsychological
    d. Psychophysical

28. Which of the following is NOT a monocular depth cue?
    a. light and shadow
    b. relative height
    c. retinal disparity
    d. interposition

29. The Moon illusion occurs in part because distance cues at the horizon make the Moon seem
    a. farther away and therefore larger.
    b. closer and therefore larger.
    c. farther away and therefore smaller.
    d. closer and therefore smaller.

30. Figure is to ground as _____ is to _____ .
    a. night; day
    b. top; bottom
    c. cloud; sky
    d. sensation; perception

31. The study of perception is primarily concerned with how we
    a. detect sights, sounds, and other stimuli.
    b. sense environmental stimuli.
    c. develop sensitivity to illusions.
    d. interpret sensory stimuli.

32. Jack claims that he often has dreams that predict future events. He claims to have the power of
    a. telepathy.
    b. clairvoyance.
    c. precognition.
    d. psychokinesis.

33. Researchers who investigated telepathy found that
    a. when external distractions are reduced, both the "sender" and the "receiver" become much more accurate in demonstrating ESP.
    b. only "senders" become much more accurate.
    c. only "receivers" become much more accurate.
    d. over many studies, neither "senders" nor "receivers" become more accurate.

34. The frequency theory of hearing is better than place theory at explaining our sensation of
    a. the lowest pitches.
    b. pitches of intermediate range.
    c. the highest pitches.
    d. both high and low pitches.

35. The perceptual error in which we fail to see an object when our attention is directed elsewhere is
    a. sensory adaptation.
    b. inattentional blindness.
    c. perceptual adaptation.
    d. transduction.

Matching Items

Match each of the structures with its function or description.

Structures or Conditions

_____ 1. lens
_____ 2. iris
_____ 3. pupil
_____ 4. rods
_____ 5. cones
_____ 6. middle ear
_____ 7. inner ear
_____ 8. large nerve fiber
_____ 9. small nerve fiber
_____ 10. semicircular canals
_____ 11. sensors in joints

Functions or Descriptions

a. amplifies sounds
b. closes pain gate
c. vestibular sense
d. controls pupil
e. accommodation
f. opens pain gate
g. admits light
h. vision in dim light
i. transduction of sound
j. kinesthesis
k. color vision

PROGRESS TEST 2

Progress Test 2 should be completed during a final unit review. Answer the following questions after you thoroughly understand the correct answers for the section reviews and Progress Test 1.

Multiple-Choice Questions

1. Which of the following is NOT one of the basic tastes?
   a. sweet   c. umami
   b. salty   d. bland

2. Of the four distinct skin senses, the only one that has definable receptors is
   a. warmth.   c. pressure.
   b. cold.   d. pain.

3. The process by which sensory information is converted into neural energy is
   a. sensory adaptation.   c. sensory interaction.
   b. feature detection.   d. transduction.

4. The receptors for taste are located in the
   a. taste buds.   c. fovea.
   b. cochlea.   d. cortex.

5. The inner ear contains receptors for
   a. audition and kinesthesis.
   b. kinesthesis and the vestibular sense.
   c. audition and the vestibular sense.
   d. audition, kinesthesis, and the vestibular sense.

6. According to the opponent-process theory
   a. there are three types of color-sensitive cones.
   b. the process of color vision begins in the cortex.
   c. neurons involved in color vision are stimulated by one color's wavelength and inhibited by another's.
   d. people with color-deficient vision lack functioning red-sensitive cones.

7. What enables you to feel yourself wiggling your toes even with your eyes closed?
   a. vestibular sense
   b. kinesthesis
   c. the skin senses
   d. sensory interaction

8. Hubel and Wiesel discovered feature detectors in the visual
   a. fovea.   c. iris.
   b. optic nerve.   d. cortex.

9. Weber's law states that
   a. the absolute threshold for any stimulus is a constant.
   b. the jnd for any stimulus is a constant.
   c. the absolute threshold for any stimulus is a constant proportion.
   d. the jnd for any stimulus is a constant proportion.

10. The principle that one sense may influence another is
    a. transduction.   c. Weber's law.
    b. sensory adaptation. d. sensory interaction.

11. The correct order of the structures through which light passes after entering the eye is
    a. lens, pupil, cornea, retina.
    b. pupil, cornea, lens, retina.
    c. pupil, lens, cornea, retina.
    d. cornea, pupil, lens, retina.

12. In the opponent-process theory, the three pairs of processes are
    a. red-green, blue-yellow, black-white.
    b. red-blue, green-yellow, black-white.
    c. red-yellow, blue-green, black-white.
    d. dependent upon the individual's experience.

13. Wavelength is to _____ as _____ is to brightness.
    a. hue; intensity
    b. intensity; hue
    c. frequency; amplitude
    d. brightness; hue

14. Concerning the evidence for subliminal stimulation, which of the following is the best answer?
    a. The brain processes some information without our awareness.
    b. Stimuli too weak to cross our thresholds for awareness may trigger a response in our sense receptors.
    c. Because the "absolute" threshold is a statistical average, we are able to detect weaker stimuli some of the time.
    d. All of these statements are true.

15. Which of the following is the most accurate description of how we process color?
    a. Throughout the visual system, color processing is divided into separate red, green, and blue systems.
    b. Red-green, blue-yellow, and black-white opponent processes operate throughout the visual system.

c. Color processing occurs in two stages: (1) a three-color system in the retina and (2) opponent-process cells en route to the visual cortex.

d. Color processing occurs in two stages: (1) an opponent-process system in the retina and (2) a three-color system en route to the visual cortex.

16. One reason that your ability to detect fine visual details is greatest when scenes are focused on the fovea of your retina is that

a. there are more feature detectors in the fovea than in the peripheral regions of the retina.

b. cones in the fovea are nearer to the optic nerve than those in peripheral regions of the retina.

c. many rods, which are clustered in the fovea, have individual bipolar cells to relay their information to the cortex.

d. many cones, which are clustered in the fovea, have individual bipolar cells to relay their information to the cortex.

17. Given normal sensory ability, a person standing atop a mountain on a dark, clear night can see a candle flame atop a mountain 30 miles away. This is a description of vision's

a. difference threshold.   c. absolute threshold.
b. jnd.   d. feature detection.

18. The tendency to organize stimuli into smooth, uninterrupted patterns is called

a. closure.   c. similarity.
b. continuity.   d. proximity.

19. Which of the following statements is consistent with the Gestalt theory of perception?

a. Perception develops largely through learning.

b. Perception is the product of heredity.

c. The mind organizes sensations into meaningful perceptions.

d. Perception results directly from sensation.

20. Experiments with distorted visual environments demonstrate that

a. adaptation rarely takes place.

b. animals adapt readily, but humans do not.

c. humans adapt readily, while lower animals typically do not.

d. adaptation is possible during a critical period in infancy but not thereafter.

21. The phenomenon that refers to the ways in which an individual's expectations influence perception is called

a. perceptual set.   c. interposition.
b. retinal disparity.   d. kinesthesis.

22. According to the philosopher _____ , we learn to perceive the world.

a. John Locke   c. Eleanor Gibson
b. Immanuel Kant   d. Richard Walk

23. The phenomenon of size constancy is based on the close connection between an object's perceived _____ and its perceived _____ .

a. size; shape   c. size; brightness
b. size; distance   d. shape; distance

24. Which of the following statements best describes the effects of sensory restriction?

a. It produces functional blindness when experienced for any length of time at any age.

b. It has greater effects on humans than on animals.

c. It has more damaging effects when experienced during infancy.

d. It has greater effects on adults than on children.

25. *Selective attention* is most accurately defined as

a. the focusing of conscious awareness on a particular stimulus.

b. our awareness of ourselves and our environment.

c. failing to see visible objects when our attention is directed elsewhere.

d. separating our conscious awareness to focus on two tasks at the same time.

26. Psychologists who study ESP are called

a. clairvoyants.   c. parapsychologists.
b. telepaths.   d. levitators.

27. The depth cue that occurs when we watch stable objects at different distances as we are moving is

a. linear perspective.   c. relative size.
b. interposition.   d. relative motion.

28. Which of the following statements concerning ESP is true?

a. Most ESP researchers are quacks.

b. There have been a large number of reliable demonstrations of ESP.

c. Most research psychologists are skeptical of the claims of defenders of ESP.

d. There have been reliable laboratory demonstrations of ESP, but the results are no different from those that would occur by chance.

29. Each time you see your car, it projects a different image on the retinas of your eyes, yet you do not perceive it as changing. This is because of
    a. perceptual set.
    b. retinal disparity.
    c. perceptual constancy.
    d. figure-ground.

30. The term *gestalt* means
    a. grouping.   c. perception.
    b. sensation.   d. whole.

31. Studies of the visual cliff have provided evidence that much of depth perception is
    a. innate.
    b. learned.
    c. innate in lower animals, learned in humans.
    d. innate in humans, learned in lower animals.

32. All of the following are laws of perceptual organization EXCEPT
    a. proximity.   c. continuity.
    b. closure.   d. retinal disparity.

● ● ● ● ● ●

33. You probably perceive the diagram above as three separate objects due to the principle of
    a. proximity.   c. closure.
    b. continuity.   d. connectedness.

34. _____ processing refers to how our knowledge and expectations influence perception.
    a. Top-down   c. Parapsychological
    b. Bottom-up   d. Psychophysical

35. The place theory of pitch perception cannot account for how we hear
    a. low-pitched sounds.
    b. middle-pitched sounds.
    c. high-pitched sounds.
    d. chords (three or more pitches simultaneously).

36. Sensorineural hearing loss is caused by
    a. wax buildup in the outer ear.
    b. damage to the eardrum.
    c. blockage in the middle ear because of infection.
    d. damage to the cochlea.

True–False Items

Indicate whether each statement is true or false by placing *T* or *F* in the blank next to the item.

_____ 1. Once we perceive an item as a figure, it is impossible to see it as ground.

_____ 2. Laboratory experiments have laid to rest all criticisms of ESP.

_____ 3. Six-month-old infants will cross a visual cliff if their mother calls.

_____ 4. Unlike other animals, humans have no critical period for visual stimulation.

_____ 5. Immanuel Kant argued that experience determined how we perceive the world.

_____ 6. It is just as easy to touch two pencil tips together with only one eye open as it is with both eyes open.

_____ 7. After a period of time, humans are able to adjust to living in a world made upside down by distorting goggles.

_____ 8. As our distance from an object changes, the object's size seems to change.

_____ 9. Perception is influenced by psychological factors such as set and expectation as well as by physiological events.

_____ 10. John Locke argued that perception is inborn.

PSYCHOLOGY APPLIED

Answer these questions the day before a test as a final check on your understanding of the unit's terms and concepts.

Multiple-Choice Questions

1. In shopping for a new stereo, you discover that you cannot differentiate between the sounds of models X and Y. The difference between X and Y is below your
   a. absolute threshold.   c. receptor threshold.
   b. subliminal threshold.   d. difference threshold.

2. To maximize your sensitivity to fine visual detail you should
   a. stare off to one side of the object you are attempting to see.
   b. close one eye.
   c. decrease the intensity of the light falling upon the object.
   d. stare directly at the object.

3. The phantom limb sensation indicates that
   a. pain is a purely sensory phenomenon.
   b. the central nervous system plays only a minor role in the experience of pain.
   c. pain involves the brain's interpretation of neural activity.
   d. all of these are true.

4. While competing in the Olympic trials, marathoner Kirsten O'Brien suffered a stress fracture in her left leg. That she did not experience significant pain until the race was over is probably attributable to the fact that during the race
   a. the pain gate in her spinal cord was closed by information coming from her brain.
   b. her body's production of endorphins decreased.
   c. an increase in the activity of small pain fibers closed the pain gate.
   d. a decrease in the activity of large pain fibers closed the pain gate.

5. Which of the following is an example of sensory interaction?
   a. finding that despite its delicious aroma, a weird-looking meal tastes awful
   b. finding that food tastes bland when you have a bad cold
   c. finding it difficult to maintain your balance when you have an ear infection
   d. All of these are examples.

6. In comparing the human eye to a camera, the film would be located in the eye's
   a. pupil.   c. cornea.
   b. lens.   d. retina.

7. Sensation is to _____ as perception is to _____ .
   a. recognizing a stimulus; interpreting a stimulus
   b. detecting a stimulus; recognizing a stimulus
   c. interpreting a stimulus; detecting a stimulus
   d. seeing; hearing

8. I am a cell in the thalamus that is excited by red and inhibited by green. I am a(n)
   a. feature detector.   c. bipolar cell.
   b. cone.   d. opponent-process cell.

9. The correct order of structures through which sound travels after entering the ear is
   a. auditory canal, eardrum, middle ear, cochlea.
   b. eardrum, auditory canal, middle ear, cochlea.
   c. eardrum, middle ear, cochlea, auditory canal.
   d. cochlea, eardrum, middle ear, auditory canal.

10. Dr. Frankenstein has forgotten to give his monster an important part; as a result, the monster cannot transduce sound. Dr. Frankenstein omitted the
    a. eardrum.   c. semicircular canals.
    b. middle ear.   d. basilar membrane.

11. Assuming that the visual systems of humans and other mammals function similarly, you would expect that the retina of a nocturnal mammal (one active only at night) would contain
    a. mostly cones.
    b. mostly rods.
    c. an equal number of rods and cones.
    d. more bipolar cells than an animal active only during the day.

12. As the football game continued into the night, LeVar noticed that he was having difficulty distinguishing the colors of the players' uniforms. This is because the _____ , which enable color vision, have a _____ absolute threshold for brightness than the available light intensity.
    a. rods; higher   c. rods; lower
    b. cones; higher   d. cones; lower

13. After staring at a very intense red stimulus for a few minutes, Carrie shifted her gaze to a beige wall and "saw" the color _____ . Carrie's experience provides support for the _____ theory.
    a. green; trichromatic
    b. blue; opponent-process
    c. green; opponent-process
    d. blue; trichromatic

14. Seventy-year-old Mrs. Martinez finds that she must spice her food heavily or she cannot taste it. Unfortunately, her son often finds her cooking inedible because it is so spicy. What is the likely explanation for their taste differences?
    a. Women have higher taste thresholds than men.
    b. Men have higher taste thresholds than women.
    c. Being 70 years old, Mrs. Martinez probably has fewer taste buds than her son.
    d. Her son inherited a taste for bland food.

15. When admiring the texture of a piece of fabric, Calvin usually runs his fingertips over the cloth's surface. He does this because
    a. if the cloth were held motionless, sensory adaptation to its feel would quickly occur.
    b. the sense of touch does not adapt.
    c. a relatively small amount of brain tissue is devoted to processing touch from the fingertips.
    d. he needs to touch the fabric to activate his feature detectors.

16. Superman's eyes used _____ , while his brain used _____ .
    a. perception; sensation
    b. top-down processing; bottom-up processing
    c. bottom-up processing; top-down processing
    d. sensory adaptation; subliminal perception

17. Tamiko hates the bitter taste of her cough syrup. Which of the following would she find most helpful in minimizing the syrup's bad taste?
    a. tasting something very sweet before taking the cough syrup
    b. keeping the syrup in her mouth for several seconds before swallowing it
    c. holding her nose while taking the cough syrup
    d. gulping the cough syrup so that it misses her tongue

18. Although carpenter Smith perceived a briefly viewed object as a screwdriver, police officer Wesson perceived the same object as a knife. This illustrates that perception is guided by
    a. linear perspective.   c. retinal disparity.
    b. shape constancy.   d. perceptual set.

19. The fact that a white object under dim illumination appears lighter than a gray object under bright illumination is called
    a. relative luminance.
    b. perceptual adaptation.
    c. color contrast.
    d. lightness constancy.

20. When two familiar objects of equal size cast unequal retinal images, the object that casts the smaller retinal image will be perceived as being
    a. closer than the other object.
    b. more distant than the other object.
    c. larger than the other object.
    d. smaller than the other object.

21. Concluding her presentation on sensation and perception, Kelly notes that
    a. perception is bottom-up processing.
    b. sensation is top-down processing.
    c. without sensation there is no perception.
    d. sensation and perception blend into one continuous process.

22. As her friend Milo walks toward her, Noriko perceives his size as remaining constant because his perceived distance _____ at the same time that her retinal image of him _____ .
    a. increases; decreases
    b. increases; increases
    c. decreases; decreases
    d. decreases; increases

23. In the absence of perceptual constancy
    a. objects would appear to change size as their distance from us changed.
    b. depth perception would be based exclusively on monocular cues.
    c. depth perception would be based exclusively on binocular cues.
    d. depth perception would be impossible.

24. How do we perceive a pole that partially covers a wall?
    a. as farther away
    b. as nearer
    c. as larger
    d. There is not enough information to determine the object's size or distance.

25. An artist paints a tree orchard so that the parallel rows of trees converge at the top of the canvas. Which cue has the artist used to convey distance?
    a. interposition   c. linear perspective
    b. retinal disparity   d. figure-ground

26. Objects higher in our field of vision are perceived as _____ due to the principle of _____ .
    a. nearer; relative height
    b. nearer; linear perspective
    c. farther away; relative height
    d. farther away; linear perspective

27. Your friend tosses you a frisbee. You know that it is getting closer instead of larger because of
    a. shape constancy.   c. size constancy.
    b. relative motion.   d. all of the above.

28. Regina claims that she can bend spoons, levitate furniture, and perform many other "mind over matter" feats. Regina apparently believes she has the power of

    a. telepathy.
    b. clairvoyance.
    c. precognition.
    d. psychokinesis.

29. Studying the road map before her trip, Colleen had no trouble following the route of the highway she planned to travel. Colleen's ability illustrates the principle of

    a. closure.
    b. similarity.
    c. continuity.
    d. proximity.

Essay Questions

1. A dancer in a chorus line uses many sensory cues when performing. Discuss three senses that dancers rely on, and explain why each is important. (Use the space below to list the points you want to make, and organize them. Then write the essay on a separate sheet of paper.)

2. In many movies from the 1930s, dancers performed seemingly meaningless movements which, when viewed from above, were transformed into intricate patterns and designs. Similarly, the formations of marching bands often create pictures and spell words. Identify and describe at least four Gestalt principles of grouping that explain the audience's perception of the images created by these types of formations. (Use the space below to list the points you want to make, and organize them. Then write the essay on a separate piece of paper.)

Summing Up

Use the diagrams to identify the parts of the eye and ear, then describe how each contributes to vision or hearing. Also, briefly explain the role of each structure.

The Eye

1. _____

    _____

2. _____

    _____

3. _____

    _____

4. _____

    _____

5. _____

    _____

6. _____

    _____

7. _____

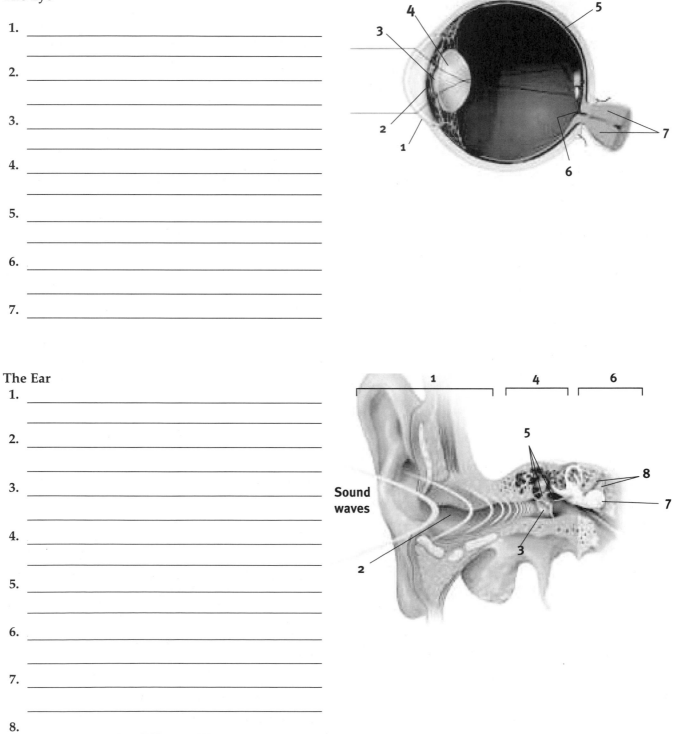

The Ear

1. _____

    _____

2. _____

    _____

3. _____

    _____

4. _____

    _____

5. _____

    _____

6. _____

    _____

7. _____

    _____

8. _____

KEY TERMS

Using your own words, on a piece of paper write a brief definition or explanation of each of the following terms.

1. sensation
2. perception
3. bottom-up processing
4. top-down processing
5. selective attention
6. inattentional blindness
7. change blindness
8. psychophysics
9. absolute threshold
10. signal detection theory
11. subliminal
12. priming
13. difference threshold
14. Weber's law
15. sensory adaptation
16. transduction
17. wavelength and hue
18. intensity
19. pupil
20. iris
21. lens
22. retina
23. accommodation
24. rods and cones
25. optic nerve
26. blind spot
27. fovea
28. feature detectors
29. parallel processing
30. Young-Helmholtz trichromatic (three-color) theory
31. opponent-process theory
32. audition
33. frequency and pitch
34. middle ear
35. cochlea
36. inner ear
37. place theory
38. frequency theory
39. conduction hearing loss
40. sensorineural hearing loss
41. cochlear implant
42. kinesthesis
43. vestibular sense
44. gate-control theory
45. sensory interaction
46. gestalt
47. figure-ground
48. grouping
49. depth perception
50. visual cliff
51. binocular cues
52. retinal disparity
53. monocular cues
54. phi phenomenon
55. perceptual constancy
56. color constancy
57. perceptual adaptation
58. perceptual set
59. extrasensory perception (ESP)
60. parapsychology

ANSWERS
Unit Review

Introduction and *Sensing the World: Some Basic Principles*

1. prosopagnosia
2. sensation; perception
3. bottom-up processing; top-down processing
4. selective attention
5. cocktail party effect; inattentional blindness
6. inattentional blindness; change blindness; choice blindness; change deafness
7. pop-out
8. psychophysics
9. absolute threshold; 50
10. signal detection

11. subliminal

12. conscious

13. prime; automatically

14. difference threshold; just noticeable difference (jnd)

15. Weber's law; stimulus

16. sensory adaptation

17. informative

Vision

1. transduced; neural

2. electromagnetic

3. wavelength; hue

4. intensity; amplitude; brightness

5. cornea; pupil; iris

6. lens; retina

7. accommodation

8. rods; cones

9. bipolar; ganglion; optic nerve; brain

10. blind spot

11. fovea; peripheral; bipolar

12. cones; rods

13. sensitive; 20

14. abstract; thalamus; visual cortex; feature detectors

15. gaze; head angle; posture; body movement; supercell clusters

16. simultaneously; parallel processing

17. blindsight

18. reflects (rejects); construction

19. sex-linked

20. Young-Helmholtz trichromatic; red; green; blue

21. opponent; afterimage

22. opponent-process; red; green; yellow; blue; black; white

In the first stage of color processing, the retina's red, green, and blue cones respond in varying degrees to different color stimuli, as suggested by the three-color theory. The resulting signals are then processed in the thalamus by red-green, blue-yellow, and black-white opponent-process cells, which are turned "on" by one wavelength and turned "off" by its opponent.

Hearing

1. audition; air molecules

2. loudness

3. pitch

4. decibels; zero

5. outer; middle; inner

6. eardrum

7. hammer; anvil; stirrup

8. cochlea; oval window; basilar membrane; hair cells; thalamus; temporal

9. number

10. place; low

11. frequency; high; 1000

12. volley

13. speed (timing); intensity

14. harder

15. conduction hearing loss

16. sensorineural; aging

17. cochlear implant

18. Deaf culture; children; speak; disability

19. is; with; seem to

20. self-esteem; accepted

Other Senses

1. pressure; warmth; cold; pain; variations

2. top-down; somatosensory cortex; rubber-hand

3. kinesthesis; tendons; joints; bones; ears

4. vestibular sense; semicircular canals; vestibular sacs

5. injury; chronic

6. physiology; experiences; attention; culture

7. is not; nociceptors

8. gate-control; gate; spinal cord; small; large; brain

9. sensory input

10. phantom limb; tinnitus

Pain control techniques include drugs, surgery, acupuncture, thought distraction, exercise, hypnosis, relaxation training, electrical stimulation, and massage. Similarly, for burn victims, distraction during painful wound care can be created by immersion in a computer-generated 3-D world.

11. sweet; sour; salty; bitter; umami

12. chemical; taste buds; pore

13. week or two; decreases; decreases; smoking; alcohol

14. sensory interaction; McGurk; see; hearing

15. synaesthesia

16. olfaction; chemical; is not

17. limbic

Perceptual Organization

1. Gestalt; whole
2. figure; ground
3. grouping
4. continuity; closure; proximity; similarity; connectedness
5. depth perception; distance
6. visual cliff; mobile

Research on the visual cliff suggests that in many species the ability to perceive depth is present at, or very shortly after, birth.

7. binocular
8. retinal disparity
9. monocular
10. relative size
11. interposition
12. relative height
13. relative motion
14. linear perspective
15. light and shadow
16. retreating; approaching; more slowly
17. movement; stroboscopic movement
18. phi phenomenon
19. perceptual constancy
20. do not; retinal
21. Moon; Ponzo; size; distance; diminished
22. relative to
23. relative luminance
24. context; color constancy
25. reflected; surrounding objects

Perceptual Interpretation

1. Immanuel Kant
2. John Locke
3. cannot
4. infancy; critical period
5. will; perceptual adaptation
6. do not adapt
7. perceptual set
8. schemas; context
9. top-down; bottom-up
10. stereotypes; emotional
11. biopsychosocial

Is There Extrasensory Perception?

1. extrasensory perception
2. parapsychologists
3. telepathy; clairvoyance; precognition; psychokinesis
4. chance-level; interpreted (retrofitted); reconstruct
5. reproducible
6. beat; failed to replicate the results

Progress Test 1

Multiple-Choice Questions

1. **b.** is the answer. Psychological factors can affect the absolute threshold for a stimulus. (p. 120)
   a. The absolute threshold for detecting a stimulus depends not only on the strength of the stimulus but also on psychological factors such as experience, expectations, motivation, and fatigue. Thus, the threshold cannot be a constant.
   c. & d. The absolute threshold is defined as the minimum stimulus that is detected 50 percent of the time.

2. **c.** is the answer. According to Weber's law, the difference threshold is a constant proportion of the stimulus. There is a 10 percent difference between 10 and 11 pounds; since the difference threshold is a constant proportion, the weight closest to 100 pounds that can nonetheless be differentiated from it is 110 pounds (or 100 pounds plus 10 percent). (pp. 122–123)

3. **c.** is the answer. (p. 123)
   a. "Sensory fatigue" is not a term in psychology.
   b. Accommodation refers to an adaptive change in shape by the lens of the eye.
   d. Sensory interaction is the principle that one sense may influence another.

4. **d.** is the answer. (p. 126)
   a. The lens lies behind the pupil and focuses light on the retina.
   b. The retina is the inner surface of the eyeball and contains the rods and cones.
   c. The cornea lies in front of the pupil and is the first structure that light passes through as it enters the eye.

5. **a.** is the answer. (p. 126)
   b. Sensory adaptation is our diminishing sensitivity to an unchanging stimulus.
   c. Feature detection is the process by which neural cells in the brain respond to specific visual features.

d. Transduction refers to the conversion of an environmental stimulus, such as light, into a neural impulse by a receptor—a rod or a cone.

6. **d.** is the answer. (p. 128)
   a. The fovea is not a receptor; it is a region of the retina that contains only cones.
   b. Cones have a higher threshold for brightness than rods and therefore do not function as well in dim light.
   c. Bipolar cells are not receptors; they are neurons in the retina that link rods and cones with ganglion cells, which make up the optic nerve.

7. **a.** is the answer. The Young-Helmholtz theory proposes that there are red-, green-, and blue-sensitive cones. (p. 132)
   b. This answer describes Hering's opponent-process theory.
   c. The Young-Helmholtz theory proposes that there are three types of cones, not four.
   d. The Young-Helmholtz theory concerns only color vision, not the detection of visual detail.

8. **b.** is the answer. Just as wave frequency determines pitch, so wave amplitude determines loudness. (p. 134)
   a. Amplitude is the physical basis of loudness; wavelength determines frequency and thereby pitch.
   c. & d. Wavelength, amplitude, and intensity are physical aspects of light and sound. Because the question is based on a relationship between a physical property (frequency) of a stimulus and its psychological attribute (pitch), these answers are incorrect.

9. **c.** is the answer. The biopsychosocial approach tells us that our experience of pain depends on biological, psychological, and social-cultural factors. (pp. 143, 145)

10. **d.** is the answer. The small fibers conduct most pain signals; the large fibers conduct most other sensory signals from the skin. The gate either allows pain signals to pass on to the brain or blocks them from passing. When the large fibers are stimulated, the pain gate is closed and other sensations are felt in place of pain. (p. 144)

11. **b.** is the answer. (p. 126)
    a. The iris controls the diameter of the pupil.
    c. The lens accommodates its shape to focus images on the retina.
    d. The optic nerve carries nerve impulses from the retina to the visual cortex.

12. **b.** is the answer. (p. 130)
    a. Feature detection is the process by which nerve cells in the brain respond to specific visual features of a stimulus, such as movement or shape.

c. Accommodation is the process by which the lens changes its curvature to focus images on the retina.
d. The opponent-process theory suggests that color vision depends on the response of brain cells to red-green, yellow-blue, and black-white opposing colors.

13. **b.** is the answer. Kinesthesis, or the sense of the position and movement of body parts, is based on information from the tendons, joints, bones, and ears. (p. 142)
    a. & c. The ear plays no role in kinesthesis.
    d. Equilibrium, or the vestibular sense, is not involved in kinesthesis but is, rather, a companion sense.

14. **a.** is the answer. Wavelength determines hue, or color. (p. 125)
    b. & d. The amplitude of light determines its brightness.
    c. Opponent processes are neural systems involved in color vision, not properties of light.

15. **d.** is the answer. Color constancy is the perception that a familiar object has consistent color, even if changing illumination alters the wavelengths reflected by that object. (p. 158)
    a. & b. These theories explain how the visual system detects color; they do not explain why colors do not seem to change when lighting does.
    c. Feature detection explains how the brain recognizes visual images by analyzing their distinctive features of shape, movement, and angle.

16. **a.** is the answer. Sensory adaptation means a diminishing sensitivity to an unchanging stimulus. Only the adjustment to cold water involves a decrease in sensitivity; the other examples involve an increase. (p. 123)

17. **a.** is the answer. Thus, they have difficulty discriminating these two colors. (p. 132)
    b. Those who are color deficient are usually not "color blind" in a literal sense. Instead, they are unable to distinguish certain hues, such as red from green.
    c. Failure to distinguish red and green is separate from, and does not usually affect, general visual ability.
    d. Color deficiency does not enhance vision. A deficit in one sense often is compensated for by overdevelopment of another sense—for example, hearing in blind people.

18. **d.** is the answer. Gestalt psychology, which developed in Germany early in the twentieth century, was interested in how clusters of sensations are organized into "whole" perceptions. (p. 151)

a. Parapsychology is the study of ESP and other paranormal phenomena.
b. & c. Behavioral and functional psychology developed later in the United States.

19. **d.** is the answer. (p. 152)
    a. Connectedness refers to the tendency to see uniform and linked items as a unit.
    b. Similarity refers to the tendency to group similar items.
    c. Continuity refers to the tendency to group stimuli into smooth, continuous patterns.

20. **c.** is the answer. Although we always differentiate a stimulus into figure and ground, those elements of the stimulus we perceive as figure and those as ground may change. In this way, the same stimulus can trigger more than one perception. (p. 151)
    a. The idea of a figure-ground relationship has no bearing on the issue of whether perception is innate.
    b. Perception cannot be simply a point-for-point representation of sensation, since in figure-ground relationships a single stimulus can trigger more than one perception.
    d. Figure-ground relationships demonstrate the existence of general, rather than individual, principles of perceptual organization. Significantly, even the same person can see different figure-ground relationships when viewing a scene.

21. **d.** is the answer. The greater the retinal disparity, or difference between the images, the less the distance. (p. 153)
    a. Interposition is the monocular distance cue in which an object that partially blocks another object is seen as closer.
    b. Linear perspective is the monocular distance cue in which parallel lines appear to converge in the distance.
    c. Relative motion is the monocular distance cue in which objects at different distances change their relative positions in our visual image, with those closest moving most.

22. **a.** is the answer. Perception of constant shape, like perception of constant size, is part of the phenomenon of perceptual constancy. (p. 156)
    b. Relative motion is a monocular distance cue in which objects at different distances appear to move at different rates.
    c. Linear perspective is a monocular distance cue in which lines we know to be parallel converge in the distance, thus indicating depth.
    d. Continuity is the perceptual tendency to group items into continuous patterns.

23. **d.** is the answer. (p. 166)
    a. Psychokinesis refers to the claimed ability to perform acts of "mind over matter."
    b. Precognition refers to the claimed ability to perceive future events.
    c. Clairvoyance refers to the claimed ability to perceive remote events.

24. **b.** is the answer. (p. 159)
    a. Locke argued that knowledge is not inborn but comes through learning.
    c. & d. Gibson and Walk studied depth perception using the visual cliff; they made no claims about the source of knowledge.

25. **c.** is the answer. (p. 160)
    a. & b. The kittens had difficulty only with lines they had never experienced, and never regained normal sensitivity.
    d. Both perceptual and feature-detector impairment resulted from visual restriction.

26. **b.** is the answer. Because they have not had early visual experiences, these adults typically have difficulty learning to perceive objects. (pp. 159–160)
    a. Such patients typically could not visually recognize objects with which they were familiar by touch, and in some cases this inability persisted.
    c. Being able to perceive figure-ground relationships, patients are able to follow moving objects with their eyes.
    d. This answer is incorrect because eye-hand coordination is an acquired skill and requires much practice.

27. **b.** is the answer. (p. 116)
    a. Top-down processing refers to how our knowledge and expectations influence perception.
    c. Parapsychology is the study of perception outside normal sensory input.
    d. Psychophysics is the study of the relationship between the physical characteristics of objects and our psychological experience of them.

28. **c.** is the answer. Retinal disparity is a *binocular* cue; all the other cues mentioned are monocular. (p. 153)

29. **a.** is the answer. The Moon appears larger at the horizon than overhead in the sky because objects at the horizon provide distance cues that make the Moon seem farther away and therefore larger. In the open sky, of course, there are no such cues. (p. 157)

30. **c.** is the answer. We see a cloud as a figure against the background of sky. (p. 151)

a., b., & d. The figure-ground relationship refers to the organization of the visual field into objects (figures) that stand out from their surroundings (ground).

31. **d.** is the answer. (p. 116)
    a. & b. The study of sensation is concerned with these processes.
    c. Although studying illusions has helped psychologists understand ordinary perceptual mechanisms, it is not the primary focus of the field of perception.

32. **c.** is the answer. (p. 166)
    a. This answer would be correct had Jack claimed to be able to read someone else's mind.
    b. This answer would be correct had Jack claimed to be able to sense remote events, such as a friend in distress.
    d. This answer would be correct had Jack claimed to be able to levitate objects or bend spoons without applying any physical force.

33. **d.** is the answer. (p. 168)

34. **a.** is the answer. Frequency theory best explains the lowest pitches. Place theory best explains the highest pitches, and some combination of the two theories probably accounts for our sensation of intermediate-range pitches. (p. 137)

35. **b.** is the answer. (p. 118)

Matching Items
1. e (p. 126)   6. a (p. 135)   11. j (p. 142)
2. d (p. 126)   7. i (p. 135)
3. g (p. 126)   8. b (p. 144)
4. h (p. 126)   9. f (p. 144)
5. k (p. 126)   10. c (p. 142)

Progress Test 2

Multiple-Choice Questions

1. **d.** is the answer. (pp. 146–147)

2. **c.** is the answer. Researchers have identified receptors for pressure but have been unable to do so for the other skin senses. (p. 141)

3. **d.** is the answer. (p. 124)
   a. Sensory adaptation refers to the diminished sensitivity that occurs with unchanging stimulation.
   b. Feature detection refers to the process by which nerve cells in the brain respond to specific aspects of visual stimuli, such as movement or shape.

c. Sensory interaction is the principle that one sense may influence another.

4. **a.** is the answer. (p. 147)
   b. The cochlea contains receptors for hearing.
   c. The fovea contains receptors for vision (the cones).
   d. The cortex is the outer layer of the brain, where information detected by the receptors is processed.

5. **c.** is the answer. The inner ear contains the receptors for audition (hearing) and the vestibular sense; those for kinesthesis are located in the tendons, joints, bones, and ears. (pp. 135, 142)

6. **c.** is the answer. After leaving the receptor cells, visual information is analyzed in terms of pairs of opponent colors; neurons stimulated by one member of a pair are inhibited by the other. (p. 133)
   a. The idea that there are three types of color-sensitive cones is the basis of the Young-Helmholtz three-color theory.
   b. According to the opponent-process theory, and all other theories of color vision, the process of color vision begins in the retina.

7. **b.** is the answer. Kinesthesis, the sense of movement of body parts, would enable you to feel your toes wiggling. (p. 142)
   a. The vestibular sense is concerned with movement and position, or balance, of the whole body, not of its parts.
   c. The skin, or tactile, senses are pressure, pain, warmth, and cold; they have nothing to do with movement of body parts.
   d. Sensory interaction, the principle that the senses influence each other, does not play a role in this example, which involves only the sense of kinesthesis.

8. **d.** is the answer. Feature detectors are cortical neurons and hence are located in the visual cortex. (p. 129)
   a. The fovea contains cones.
   b. The optic nerve contains neurons that relay nerve impulses from the retina to higher centers in the visual system.
   c. The iris is simply a ring of muscle tissue, which controls the diameter of the pupil.

9. **d.** is the answer. Weber's law concerns difference thresholds (jnd's), not absolute thresholds, and states that these are constant proportions of the stimuli, not that they remain constant. (p. 123)

10. **d.** is the answer. (p. 147)
    a. Transduction is the process by which stimulus energy is converted into nerve impulses.

b. Sensory adaptation is diminished sensitivity to unchanging stimulation.

c. Weber's law states that the jnd is a constant proportion of a stimulus.

11. **d.** is the answer. (p. 126)

12. **a.** is the answer. (p. 133)

13. **a.** is the answer. Wavelength determines hue, and intensity determines brightness. (p. 125)

14. **d.** is the answer. (pp. 121–122)

15. **c.** is the answer. (p. 133)
   a. This answer is incorrect because separate red, green, and blue systems operate only in the retina.
   b. This answer is incorrect because opponent-process systems operate en route to the brain, after visual processing in the receptors is completed.
   d. This answer is incorrect because it reverses the correct order of the two stages of processing.

16. **d.** is the answer. (p. 127)
   a. Feature detectors are nerve cells located in the visual cortex, not in the fovea of the retina.
   b. The proximity of rods and cones to the optic nerve does not influence their ability to resolve fine details.
   c. Rods are concentrated in the peripheral regions of the retina, not in the fovea; moreover, several rods share a single bipolar cell.

17. **c.** is the answer. The absolute threshold is the minimum stimulation needed to detect a stimulus. (p. 120)
   a. & b. The difference threshold, which is also known as the jnd, is the minimum difference between two stimuli that a person can detect. In this example, there is only one stimulus—the sight of the flame.
   d. Feature detection refers to nerve cells in the brain responding to specific features of a stimulus.

18. **b.** is the answer. (p. 152)
   a. Closure refers to the tendency to perceptually fill in gaps in recognizable objects in the visual field.
   c. Similarity refers to the tendency to group items that are similar.
   d. Proximity refers to the tendency to group items that are near one another.

19. **c.** is the answer. (pp. 151)
   a. & b. The Gestalt psychologists did not deal with the origins of perception; they were more concerned with its form.
   d. In fact, they argued just the opposite: Perception is more than mere sensory experience.

20. **c.** is the answer. Humans are able to adjust to upside-down worlds and other visual distortions, figuring out the relationship between the perceived and the actual reality; lower animals, such as chicks, are typically unable to adapt. (p. 160)
   a. Humans are able to adapt quite well to distorted visual environments (and then to readapt).
   b. This answer is incorrect because humans are the most adaptable of creatures.
   d. Humans are able to adapt at any age to distorted visual environments.

21. **a.** is the answer. (p. 161)
   b. Retinal disparity is a binocular depth cue based on the fact that each eye receives a slightly different view of the world.
   c. Interposition is the monocular distance cue in which an object that partially blocks another object is seen as closer.
   d. Kinesthesis is the sense of the position and movement of the parts of the body.

22. **a.** is the answer. (p. 159)
   b. Kant claimed that knowledge is inborn.
   c. & d. Gibson and Walk make no claims about the origins of perception.

23. **b.** is the answer. (p. 156)

24. **c.** is the answer. There appears to be a critical period for perceptual development, in that sensory restriction has severe, even permanent, disruptive effects when it occurs in infancy but not when it occurs later in life. (p. 160)
   a. & d. Sensory restriction does not have the same effects at all ages, and it is more damaging to children than to adults. This is because there is a critical period for perceptual development; whether functional blindness will result depends in part on the nature of the sensory restriction.
   b. Research studies have not indicated that sensory restriction is more damaging to humans than to animals.

25. **a.** is the answer. (p. 117)
   b. This is the definition of consciousness.
   c. This defines inattentional blindness.
   d. In selective attention, awareness is focused on one stimulus.

26. **c.** is the answer. (p. 166)
   a., b., & d. These psychics claim to exhibit the phenomena studied by parapsychologists.

27. **d.** is the answer. When we move, stable objects we see also appear to move, and the distance and speed of the apparent motion cue us to the objects' relative distances. (p. 155)

a., b., & c. These depth cues are unrelated to movement and thus work even when we are stationary.

28. **c.** is the answer. (p. 155)
    a. Many ESP researchers are sincere, reputable researchers.
    b. & d. There have been no reliable demonstrations of ESP.

29. **c.** is the answer. Because of perceptual constancy, we see the car's shape and size as always the same. (p. 156)
    a. Perceptual set is a mental predisposition to perceive one thing and not another.
    b. Retinal disparity means that our right and left eyes each receive slightly different images.
    d. Figure-ground refers to the organization of the visual field into two parts.

30. **d.** is the answer. Gestalt means a "form" or "organized whole." (p. 151)

31. **a.** is the answer. Most infants refused to crawl out over the "cliff" even when coaxed, suggesting that much of depth perception is innate. Studies with the young of "lower" animals show the same thing. (p. 153)

32. **d.** is the answer. (pp. 153, 155)

33. **d.** is the answer. (p. 152)
    a. Proximity is the tendency to group objects near to one another. The diagram is perceived as three distinct units, even though the points are evenly spaced.
    b. Continuity is the tendency to group stimuli into smooth, uninterrupted patterns. There is no such continuity in the diagram.
    c. Closure is the perceptual tendency to fill in gaps in a form. In the diagram, three disconnected units are perceived rather than a single whole.

34. **a.** is the answer. (p. 116)
    b. Bottom-up processing refers to the physical characteristics of stimuli rather than their perceptual interpretation.
    c. Parapsychology is the study of perception outside normal sensory input.
    d. Psychophysics is the study of the relationship between the physical characterstics of objects and our psychological experience of them.

35. **a.** is the answer. (p. 137)
    b. & c. Although the localization of low-pitched sounds along the basilar membrane is poor, that for sounds of middle and, especially, high pitch is good. Therefore, place theory accounts well for high-pitched sounds and, together with frequency theory, can account for middle-pitched sounds.

d. As long as the notes of a chord are within the range of responsiveness of the basilar membrane, place theory can account for chord perception.

36. **d.** is the answer. Sensorineural hearing loss is caused by destruction of neural tissue as a result of problems with the cochlea's receptors or the auditory nerve. (p. 138)
    a. & c. Wax buildup and blockage because of infection are temporary states; sensorineural hearing loss is permanent. Moreover, sensorineural hearing loss involves the inner ear rather than the outer or middle ear.
    b. Damage to the eardrum impairs the mechanical system that conducts sound waves; it could therefore cause conduction hearing loss, not sensorineural hearing loss.

True–False Items

1. F (p. 151)   5. F (p. 159)   9. T (pp. 161–162)
2. F (p. 168)   6. F (p. 153)   10. F (p. 159)
3. F (p. 153)   7. T (p. 160)
4. F (p. 160)   8. F (p. 156)

Psychology Applied

Multiple-Choice Questions

1. **d.** is the answer. (p. 122)
   a. The absolute threshold refers to whether a single stimulus can be detected, not to whether two stimuli can be differentiated.
   b. Subliminal refers to stimuli below the absolute threshold.
   c. A receptor threshold is a minimum amount of energy that will elicit a neural impulse in a receptor cell.

2. **d.** is the answer. Greater sensitivity to fine visual detail is associated with the cones, which have their own bipolar cells to relay information to the cortex. The cones are concentrated in the fovea, the retina's point of central focus. For this reason, staring directly at an object maximizes sensitivity to fine detail. (p. 127)
   a. If you stare off to one side, the image falls onto peripheral regions of the retina, where rods are concentrated and sensitivity to fine visual detail is poor.
   b. Sensitivity to detail is not directly influenced by whether one or both eyes are stimulated.
   c. Decreasing the intensity of light would only impair the functioning of the cones, which are sensitive to visual detail but have a high threshold for light intensity.

3. **c.** is the answer. Since pain is felt in the limb that does not exist, the pain is simply the brain's (mis)interpretation of neural activity. (p. 144)
a. If pain were a purely sensory phenomenon, phantom limb pain would not occur, since the receptors are no longer present.
b. That pain is experienced when a limb is missing indicates that the central nervous system, especially the brain, is where pain is sensed.

4. **a.** is the answer. (p. 144)
b. Since endorphins relieve pain, a decrease in their production would have made Kirsten more likely to experience pain. Moreover, because endorphins are released in response to pain, their production probably would have increased.
c. Neural activity in small fibers tends to open the pain gate.
d. An *increase* in large-fiber activity would tend to *close* the pain gate.

5. **d.** is the answer. Each of these is an example of the interaction of two senses—vision and taste in the case of (a.), taste and smell in the case of (b.), and hearing and the vestibular sense in the case of (c.). (p. 147)

6. **d.** is the answer. Just as light strikes the film of a camera, visual images entering the eye are projected onto the retina. (p. 126)
a. The pupil would be analogous to the aperture of a camera, since both control the amount of light permitted to enter.
b. The lens of the eye performs a focusing function similar to the lens of the camera.
c. The cornea would be analogous to a camera's lens cap in that both protect delicate inner structures.

7. **b.** is the answer. (p. 116)
a. Both recognition and interpretation are examples of perception.
c. This answer would have been correct if the question had read, "Perception is to sensation as _____ is to _____ ."
d. Sensation and perception are important processes in both hearing and seeing.

8. **d.** is the answer. (p. 133)
a. Feature detectors are located in the visual cortex and respond to features such as movement, shape, and angle.
b. & c. Cones and bipolar cells are located in the retina. Moreover, neither are excited by some colors and inhibited by others.

9. **a.** is the answer. (p. 135)

10. **d.** is the answer. The hair cells, which transduce sound energy, are located on the basilar membrane. (p. 135)

a. & b. The eardrum and bones of the middle ear merely conduct sound waves to the inner ear, where they are transduced.
c. The semicircular canals are involved in the vestibular sense, not hearing.

11. **b.** is the answer. Rods and cones enable vision in dim and bright light, respectively. If an animal is active only at night, it is likely to have more rods than cones in its retinas. (p. 128)
d. Bipolar cells link both cones and rods to ganglion cells. There is no reason to expect that a nocturnal mammal would have more bipolar cells than a mammal active both during the day and at night. If anything, because several rods share a single bipolar cell, whereas many cones have their own, a nocturnal animal (with a visual system consisting mostly of rods) might be expected to have fewer bipolar cells than an animal active during the day (with a visual system consisting mostly of cones).

12. **b.** is the answer. (pp. 127–128)
a. & c. It is the cones, rather than the rods, that enable color vision.
d. If the cones' threshold were lower than the available light intensity, they would be able to function and therefore detect the colors of the players' uniforms.

13. **c.** is the answer. (p. 133)
a. The trichromatic theory cannot account for the experience of afterimages.
b. & d. Afterimages are experienced as the complementary color of a stimulus. Green, not blue, is red's complement.

14. **c.** is the answer. As people age they lose taste buds and their taste thresholds increase. For this reason, Mrs. Martinez needs more concentrated tastes than her son to find food palatable. (p. 147)
a. & b. There is no evidence that women and men differ in their absolute thresholds for taste.

15. **a.** is the answer. (p. 123)
b. The sense of touch (pressure) adapts very quickly.
c. On the contrary, the extreme sensitivity of the fingertips is due to the relatively large amount of cortical tissue that processes neural impulses from the fingertips.

16. **c.** is the answer. (p. 116)

17. **c.** is the answer. Because of the powerful sensory interaction between taste and smell, eliminating the odor of the cough syrup should make its taste more pleasant. (p. 147)
a. If anything, the contrasting tastes might make the bitter syrup even less palatable.

b. If Tamiko keeps the syrup in her mouth for several seconds, it will ensure that her taste pores fully "catch" the stimulus, thus intensifying the bitter taste.

d. It's probably impossible to miss the tongue completely.

18. **d.** is the answer. The two people interpreted a briefly perceived object in terms of their perceptual sets, or mental predispositions, in this case conditioned by their work experiences. (p. 161)

a. Both Smith and Wesson had the same sensory experience of the object, so linear perspective cues would not cause their differing perceptions.

b. Shape constancy refers to the perception that objects remain constant in shape even when our retinal images of them change.

c. Retinal disparity is a binocular depth cue; it has nothing to do with individual differences in perception.

19. **d.** is the answer. Although the amount of light reflected from a white object is less in dim light than in bright light—and may be less than the amount of light reflected from a brightly lit gray object—the brightness of the white object is perceived as remaining constant. Because a white object reflects a higher percentage of the light falling on it than does a gray object, and the brightness of objects is perceived as constant despite variations in illumination, white is perceived as brighter than gray even under dim illumination. (p. 158)

a. Relative luminance refers to the relative intensity of light falling on surfaces that are in proximity. Lightness constancy is perceived despite variations in illumination.

b. Perceptual adaptation refers to the ability to adjust to an artificially modified perceptual environment, such as an inverted visual field.

c. Color contrast is not discussed in this text.

20. **b.** is the answer. The phenomenon described is the basis for the monocular cue of relative size. (p. 155)

a. The object casting the *larger* retinal image would be perceived as closer.

c. & d. Because of size constancy, the perceived size of familiar objects remains constant, despite changes in their retinal image size.

21. **d.** is the answer. (p. 116)

22. **d.** is the answer. (p. 156)

23. **a.** is the answer. Because we perceive the size of a familiar object as constant even as its retinal image grows smaller, we perceive the object as being farther away. (p. 156)

b. & c. Perceptual constancy is a cognitive, rather than sensory, phenomenon. Therefore, the absence of perceptual constancy would not alter sensitivity to monocular or binocular cues.

d. Although the absence of perceptual constancy would impair depth perception based on the size-distance relationship, other cues to depth, such as texture gradient, could still be used.

24. **b.** is the answer. This is an example of the principle of interposition in depth perception. (p. 155)

a. The partially obscured object is perceived as farther away.

c. The perceived size of an object is not altered when that object overlaps another.

25. **c.** is the answer. (p. 155)

a. Interposition is a monocular depth cue in which an object that partially covers another is perceived as closer.

b. Retinal disparity refers to the difference between the two images received by our eyes that allows us to perceive depth. It has nothing to do with the way the artist placed the trees.

d. Figure-ground refers to the organization of the field into objects that stand out from their surroundings.

26. **c.** is the answer. (p. 155)

b. & d. Linear perspective is the apparent convergence of parallel lines as a cue to distance.

27. **a.** is the answer. (p. 156)

28. **d.** is the answer. (p. 166)

a. Telepathy is the claimed ability to "read" minds.

b. Clairvoyance refers to the claimed ability to perceive remote events.

c. Precognition refers to the claimed ability to perceive future events.

29. **c.** is the answer. She perceives the line for the road as continuous, even though it is interrupted by lines indicating other roads. (p. 152)

a. Closure refers to the perceptual filling in of gaps in a stimulus to create a complete, whole object.

b. Similarity is the tendency to perceive similar objects as belonging together. On a road map, all the lines representing roads appear similar. Thus, this cue could not be the basis for Colleen's ability to trace the route of a particular road.

d. Proximity is the tendency to group objects near to one another as a single unit.

Essay Question 1

The senses that are most important to dancers are vision, hearing, kinesthesis, and the vestibular sense.

Your answer should refer to any three of these senses and include, at minimum, the following information.

Dancers rely on vision to gauge their body position relative to other dancers as they perform specific choreographed movements. Vision also helps dancers assess the audience's reaction to their performance. Whenever dance is set to music, hearing is necessary so that the dancers can detect musical cues for certain parts of their routines. Hearing also helps the dancers keep their movements in time with the music. Kinesthetic receptors in dancers' tendons, joints, bones, and ears provide their brains with information about the position and movement of body parts to determine if their hands, arms, legs, and heads are in the proper positions. Receptors for the vestibular sense located in the dancers' inner ears send messages to their brains that help them maintain their balance and determine the correctness of the position and movement of their bodies.

Essay Question 2

1. *Proximity.* We tend to perceive items that are near each other as belonging together. Thus, a small section of dancers or members of a marching band may separate themselves from the larger group in order to form part of a particular image.

2. *Similarity.* Because we perceive similar figures as belonging together, choreographers and band directors often create distinct visual groupings within the larger band or dance troupe by having the members of each group wear a distinctive costume or uniform.

3. *Continuity.* Because we perceive smooth, continuous patterns rather than discontinuous ones, dancers or marching musicians moving together (as in a column, for example) are perceived as a separate unit.

4. *Closure.* If a figure has gaps, we complete it, filling in the gaps to create a whole image. Thus, we perceptually fill in the relatively wide spacing between dancers or marching musicians in order to perceive the complete words or forms they are creating.

Summing Up

The Eye

1. Cornea. Light enters the eye through this transparent membrane, which protects the inner structures from the environment.

2. Iris. The colored part of the eye, the iris functions like the aperture of a camera, controlling the size of the pupil to optimize the amount of light that enters the eye.

3. Pupil. The adjustable opening in the iris, the pupil allows light to enter.

4. Lens. This transparent structure behind the pupil changes shape to focus images on the retina.

5. Retina. The light-sensitive inner surface of the eye, the retina contains the rods and cones, which transduce light energy into neural impulses.

6. Blind spot. The region of the retina where the optic nerve leaves the eye, the blind spot contains no rods or cones and so there is no vision here.

7. Optic nerve. This bundle of nerve fibers carries neural impulses from the retina to the brain.

The Ear

1. Outer ear. Hearing begins as sound waves enter the auditory canal of the outer ear.

2. Auditory canal. Sound waves passing through the auditory canal are brought to a point of focus at the eardrum.

3. Eardrum. Lying between the outer and middle ear, this membrane vibrates in response to sound waves.

4. Middle ear. Lying between the outer and inner ear, this air-filled chamber contains the hammer, anvil, and stirrup.

5. Hammer, anvil, and stirrup. These tiny bones of the middle ear concentrate the eardrum's vibrations on the cochlea's oval window.

6. Inner ear. This region of the ear contains the cochlea and the semicircular canals, which play an important role in balance.

7. Cochlea. This fluid-filled multichambered structure contains the hair cell receptors that transduce sound waves into neural impulses.

8. Auditory nerve. This bundle of fibers carries nerve impulses from the inner ear to the brain.

Key Terms

1. **Sensation** is the process by which our sensory receptors and nervous system receive and represent physical energy from the environment. (p. 116)

2. **Perception** is the process by which we organize and interpret sensory information. (p. 116)

3. **Bottom-up processing** is analysis that begins with the sensory receptors and works up to the brain's integration of sensory information. (p. 116)

4. **Top-down processing** is information processing guided by higher-level mental processes. (p. 116)

5. **Selective attention** is the focusing of conscious awareness on a particular stimulus. (p. 117)

6. **Inattentional blindness** is a perceptual error in which we fail to see visible objects when our attention is directed elsewhere. (p. 118)

7. **Change blindness** occurs when we fail to notice changes in the environment. (p. 119)

8. **Psychophysics** is the study of relationships between the physical characteristics of stimuli and our psychological experience of them. (p. 120)

9. The **absolute threshold** is the minimum stimulation needed to detect a stimulus 50 percent of the time. (p. 120)

10. **Signal detection theory** explains precisely how and when we detect the presence of a faint stimulus ("signal") and background stimulation ("noise"). Detection depends partly on experience, expectations, motivation, and alertness. (p. 121)

11. A stimulus that is **subliminal** is one that is below one's absolute threshold for conscious awareness. (p. 121)

    Memory aid: Limen is the Latin word for "threshold." A stimulus that is **subliminal** is one that is *sub-* ("below") the *limen*, or threshold.

12. **Priming** is the activation, often unconsciously, of an association by an imperceptible stimulus, the effect of which is to predispose a perception, memory, or response. (p. 121)

13. The **difference threshold** (also called the *just noticeable difference*, or *jnd*), is the minimum difference between two stimuli required for detection 50 percent of the time. (p. 122)

14. **Weber's law** states that the just noticeable difference between two stimuli is a constant minimum proportion of the stimulus. (p. 123)

    Example: If a difference of 10 percent in weight is noticeable, **Weber's law** predicts that a person could discriminate 10- and 11-pound weights or 50- and 55-pound weights.

15. **Sensory adaptation** refers to the decreased sensitivity that occurs with continued exposure to an unchanging stimulus. (p. 123)

16. In sensation, **transduction** refers to the process by which receptor cells in the eyes, ears, skin, and nose convert stimulus energies into neural impulses our brain can interpret. (p. 124)

17. **Wavelength**, which refers to the distance from the peak of one light wave to the next, gives rise to the perceptual experiences of **hue**, or color, in vision. (p. 125)

18. The **intensity** of light and sound is determined by the amplitude of the waves and is experienced as brightness and loudness, respectively. (p. 125)

    Example: Sounds that exceed 85 decibels in amplitude, or **intensity**, will damage the auditory system.

19. The **pupil** is the adjustable opening in the eye through which light enters. (p. 126)

20. The **iris** is a ring of muscle tissue that forms the colored part of the eye that controls the diameter of the pupil. (p. 126)

21. The **lens** is the transparent structure of the eye behind the pupil that changes shape to focus images on the retina. (p. 126)

22. The **retina** is the light-sensitive, multilayered inner surface of the eye that contains the rods and cones as well as neurons that form the beginning of the optic nerve. (p. 126)

23. **Accommodation** is the process by which the lens of the eye changes shape to focus near objects on the retina. (p. 126)

24. The **rods** and **cones** are visual receptors that convert light energy into neural impulses. The rods are concentrated in the periphery of the retina, the cones in the fovea. The rods have poor sensitivity; detect black, white, and gray; function well in dim light; and are needed for peripheral vision. The cones have excellent sensitivity, enable color vision, and function best in daylight or bright light. (p. 126)

25. Comprised of the axons of retinal ganglion cells, the **optic nerve** carries neural impulses from the eye to the brain. (p. 126)

26. The **blind spot** is the region of the retina where the optic nerve leaves the eye. Because there are no rods or cones in this area, there is no vision here. (pp. 126–127)

27. The **fovea** is the retina's point of central focus. It contains only cones; therefore, images focused on the fovea are the clearest. (p. 127)

28. **Feature detectors**, located in the visual cortex of the brain, are nerve cells that selectively respond to specific visual features, such as movement, shape, or angle. Feature detectors are evidently the basis of visual information processing. (p. 129)

29. **Parallel processing** is information processing in which several aspects of a stimulus, such as light or sound, are processed simultaneously. (p. 130)

30. The **Young-Helmholtz trichromatic (three-color) theory** maintains that the retina contains red-, green-, and blue-sensitive color receptors that in combination can produce the perception of any

color. This theory explains the first stage of color processing. (p. 132)

31. The **opponent-process theory** maintains that color vision depends on pairs of opposing retinal processes (red-green, yellow-blue, and white-black). This theory explains the second stage of color processing. (p. 133)

32. **Audition** refers to the sense of hearing. (p. 134)

33. **Frequency** is directly related to wavelength: Longer waves produce lower pitch; shorter waves produce higher pitch. The **pitch** of a sound is determined by its frequency, that is, the number of complete wavelengths that can pass a point in a given time. (p. 134)

34. The **middle ear** is the chamber between the eardrum and cochlea containing the three bones (hammer, anvil, and stirrup) that concentrate the eardrum's vibrations on the cochlea's oval window. (p. 135)

35. The **cochlea** is the coiled, bony, fluid-filled tube of the inner ear through which sound waves trigger neural impulses. (p. 135)

36. The **inner ear** contains the semicircular canals and the cochlea, which includes the receptors that transform sound energy into neural impulses. Because it also contains the vestibular sac, the inner ear plays an important role in balance, as well as in audition. (p. 135)

37. The **place theory** of hearing states that we hear different pitches because sound waves of various frequencies trigger activity at different places on the cochlea's basilar membrane. (p. 137)

   Memory aid: **Place theory** maintains that the *place* of maximum vibration along the cochlea's membrane is the basis of pitch discrimination.

38. The **frequency theory** of hearing presumes that the rate, or frequency, of nerve impulses in the auditory nerve matches the frequency of a tone, thus enabling us to sense its pitch. (p. 137)

39. **Conduction hearing loss** refers to the hearing loss that results from damage in the mechanics of the outer or middle ear, which impairs the conduction of sound waves to the cochlea. (p. 138)

40. **Sensorineural hearing loss** (nerve deafness) is hearing loss caused by damage to the auditory receptors of the cochlea or to the auditory nerve due to disease, aging, or prolonged exposure to ear-splitting noise. (p. 138)

41. A **cochlear implant** is an electronic device that converts sounds into electrical signals that stimulate the auditory nerve. (p. 138)

42. **Kinesthesis** is the sense of the position and movement of the individual parts of the body. (p. 142)

43. The sense of body movement and position, including the sense of balance, is called the **vestibular sense**. (p. 142)

44. Melzack and Wall's **gate-control theory** maintains that a "gate" in the spinal cord determines whether pain signals are permitted to reach the brain. Neural activity in small nerve fibers opens the gates; activity in large fibers or information from the brain closes the gate. (pp. 143–144)

   Example: The **gate-control theory** gained support with the discovery of endorphins. Production of these opiatelike chemicals may be the brain's mechanism for closing the spinal gate.

45. **Sensory interaction** is the principle that one sense may influence another. (p. 147)

46. **Gestalt** means "organized whole." The Gestalt psychologists emphasized our tendency to integrate pieces of information into meaningful wholes. (p. 151)

47. **Figure-ground** refers to the organization of the visual field into two parts: the figure, which stands out from its surroundings, and the surroundings, or background. (p. 151)

48. **Grouping** is the perceptual tendency to organize stimuli into coherent groups. Gestalt psychologists identified various principles of grouping. (p. 152)

49. **Depth perception** is the ability to see objects in three dimensions although the images that strike the retina are two-dimensional; it allows us to judge distance. (p. 153)

50. The **visual cliff** is a laboratory device for testing depth perception, especially in infants and young animals. In their experiments with the visual cliff, Gibson and Walk found strong evidence that depth perception is at least in part innate. (p. 153)

51. **Binocular cues** are depth cues that depend on information from both eyes. (p. 153)

   Memory aid: *Bi-* indicates "two"; *ocular* means something pertaining to the eye. **Binocular cues** are cues for the "two eyes."

52. **Retinal disparity** refers to the differences between the images received by the left eye and the right eye as a result of viewing the world from slightly different angles. It is a binocular depth cue because the greater the difference between the two images, the nearer the object. (p. 153)

53. **Monocular cues** are depth cues that depend on information from either eye alone. (p. 154)

    Memory aid: *Mono-* means one; a monocle is an eyeglass for one eye. A **monocular cue** is one that is available to either the left or the right eye.

54. The **phi phenomenon** is an illusion of movement created when two or more adjacent lights blink on and off in succession. (p. 156)

55. **Perceptual constancy** is the perception that objects have consistent lightness, color, shape, and size, even as illumination and retinal images change. (p. 156)

56. **Color constancy** is the perception that familiar objects have consistent color despite changes in illumination that shift the wavelengths they reflect. (p. 158)

57. **Perceptual adaptation** refers to our ability to adjust to an artificially displaced or even inverted visual field. Given distorting lenses, we perceive things accordingly but soon adjust by learning the relationship between our distorted perceptions and the reality. (p. 160)

58. **Perceptual set** is a mental predisposition to perceive one thing and not another. (p. 161)

59. **Extrasensory perception (ESP)** refers to the controversial claim that perception can occur without sensory input. Supposed ESP powers include telepathy, clairvoyance, and precognition. (p. 166)

    Memory aid: *Extra-* means "beyond" or "in addition to"; **extrasensory perception** is perception outside or beyond the normal senses.

60. **Parapsychology** is the study of ESP, psychokinesis, and other paranormal forms of interaction between the individual and the environment. (p. 166)

    Memory aid: *Para-*, like *extra-*, indicates "beyond"; thus, paranormal is beyond the normal and **parapsychology** is the study of phenomena beyond the realm of psychology and known natural laws.

States of Consciousness

UNIT OVERVIEW

Consciousness—our awareness of ourselves and our environment—can be experienced in various states. Unit 5 examines not only normal consciousness but also sleep and dreaming, hypnotic states, drug-altered states, and near-death experiences.

Most of the terminology in this unit is introduced in the sections on Sleep and Dreams and on Drugs and Consciousness. Among the issues discussed are why we sleep and dream, whether hypnosis is a unique state of consciousness, and possible psychological and social-cultural roots of drug use.

NOTE: Answer guidelines for all Unit 5 questions begin on page 116.

UNIT REVIEW

First, skim each section, noting headings and boldface items. After you have read the section, review each objective by answering the fill-in and essay-type questions that follow it. As you proceed, evaluate your performance by consulting the answers beginning on page 116. Do not continue with the next section until you understand each answer. If you need to, review or reread the section in the textbook before continuing.

Introduction (pp. 175–176)

Objective 1: Discuss the significance of consciousness in the history of psychology.

1. The study of _____ was central in the early years of psychology and in recent decades, but for quite some time it was displaced by the study of observable _____ .

2. Advances in neuroscience made it possible to relate _____ _____

to various mental states; as a result, psychologists once again affirmed the importance of

_____ .

Define consciousness in a sentence.

Sleep and Dreams (pp. 176–192)

Objective 2: Describe the cycle of our circadian rhythm, and identify some events that can disrupt this biological clock.

1. Our bodies' internal "clocks" control several

_____ _____ .

2. The sleep-waking cycle follows a 24-hour clock called the _____

_____ .

3. Body temperature _____ (rises/falls) as morning approaches and begins to _____ (rise/fall) again before we go to sleep.

4. When people are at their daily peak in circadian arousal, _____ is sharpest and _____ is most accurate.

5. Our biological clock is reset each day by exposure to _____ _____ , which triggers proteins in the _____ of the eyes to signal the brain's _____ _____ , which causes the _____ gland to increase or decrease its production of _____ .

6. Under unnatural conditions, most animals _____ (will/will not) exceed a 24-hour day.

Objective 3: List the stages of the sleep cycle, and explain how they differ.

7. The sleep cycle consists of _____ distinct stages.

8. The rhythm of sleep cycles was discovered when Aserinsky noticed that, at periodic intervals during the night, the _____ of a sleeping child moved rapidly. This stage of sleep, during which _____ occur, is called _____ _____ .

9. The relatively slow brain waves of the awake but relaxed state are known as _____ waves.

10. During Stage 1 sleep, people often experience _____ sensations similar to _____ . These sensations may later be incorporated into _____ .

11. The bursts of brain-wave activity that occur during Stage 2 sleep are called _____ _____ .

12. Large, slow brain waves are called _____ waves. They occur first in Stage _____ , and increasingly during Stage _____ sleep, which are therefore called _____-_____ sleep. A person in the latter stage of sleep generally will be _____ (easy/difficult) to awaken. It is during this stage that children may wet the bed or begin _____ .

Describe the bodily changes that accompany REM sleep.

13. During REM sleep, the motor cortex is _____ (active/relaxed), while the muscles are _____ (active/relaxed). For this reason, REM is often referred to as _____ sleep.

14. The rapid eye movements generally signal the beginning of a _____ , which during REM sleep is often storylike, _____ , and more richly hallucinatory.

15. The sleep cycle repeats itself about every _____ minutes. As the night progresses, Stage 4 sleep becomes _____ (longer/briefer) and REM periods become _____ (longer/briefer). Approximately _____ percent of a night's sleep is spent in REM sleep.

Objective 4: Describe individual differences in sleep duration and the effects of sleep loss, noting five reasons that we need sleep.

16. Newborns spend nearly _____ (how much?) of their day asleep, while adults spend no more than _____ .

17. Sleep patterns are influenced by _____ , as indicated by the fact that sleep patterns among _____ (identical/fraternal) twins are very similar. Sleep is also influenced by _____ , as indicated by the fact that people now sleep _____ (more/less) than they did a century ago.

18. Allowed to sleep unhindered, most people will sleep _____ (how many?) hours a night.

19. Teenagers typically need _____ hours of sleep but now average nearly _____ hours less sleep than teenagers of 80 years ago. To psychologist William _____ , this indicates that the vast majority of students are dangerously sleep-deprived. One effect of this state is to promote weight gain by increasing the hormone

_____ , decreasing the hormone _____ , and increasing the stress hormone _____ . Another is that sleep deprivation may suppress the functioning of the body's _____ system and alter metabolic and hormonal functioning in ways that mimic _____ and are conducive to _____ and _____ _____ . Another indication of the hazards of this state is that the rate of _____ tends to increase immediately after the spring time change in Canada and the United States.

Describe the behavioral effects of sleep loss.

20. Two possible reasons for sleep are to _____ us and to help restore body tissues, especially those of the _____ . Animals with high waking _____ produce an abundance of chemical _____ _____ that are toxic to _____ . Sleep also facilitates our _____ of the day's experiences and stimulates _____ thinking.

21. During sleep a growth hormone is released by the _____ gland. Adults spend _____ (more/less) time in deep sleep than children and so release _____ (more/less) growth hormone.

Objective 5: Identify the major sleep disorders.

22. A persistent difficulty in falling or staying asleep is characteristic of _____ . Sleeping pills and alcohol may make the problem worse because they tend to _____ (increase/reduce) REM sleep.

State several tips for those suffering from insomnia.

23. The sleep disorder in which a person experiences uncontrollable sleep attacks is _____ . People with severe cases of this disorder may collapse directly into _____ sleep and experience a loss of _____ _____ . This disorder may be linked to low levels of the neurotransmitter _____ , which is linked to alertness.

24. Individuals suffering from _____ _____ stop breathing while sleeping. This disorder is especially prevalent among _____ _____ .

25. The sleep disorder characterized by extreme fright and rapid heartbeat and breathing is called _____ _____ . Unlike nightmares, these episodes usually happen early in the night, during Stage _____ sleep. The same is true of episodes of _____ and _____ , problems that _____ (run/do not run) in families. These sleep episodes are most likely to be experienced by _____ (young children/adolescents/older adults), in whom this stage tends to be the _____ and _____ .

Objective 6: Describe the most common content of dreams, and compare the five major perspectives on why we dream.

26. Dreams experienced during _____ sleep are vivid, emotional, and bizarre.

27. For both men and women, 8 in 10 dreams are marked by _____ (positive/negative) emotions, such as fears of being _____ .

28. Freud referred to the actual content of a dream as its _____ content. Freud believed

that this is a censored, symbolic version of the true meaning, or _____ _____ , of the dream.

29. According to Freud, most of the dreams of adults reflect _____ wishes and are the key to understanding inner _____ . To Freud, dreams serve as a psychic _____ _____ that discharges otherwise unacceptable feelings.

30. Researchers who believe that dreams serve an _____-processing function receive support from the fact that REM sleep facilitates _____ .

31. Brain scans confirm the link between _____ sleep and _____ .

32. Other theories propose that dreaming serves some _____ function, for example, that REM sleep provides the brain with needed _____ . Such an explanation is supported by the fact that _____ (infants/adults) spend the most time in REM sleep.

33. Still other theories propose that dreams are elicited by random bursts of _____ activity originating in lower regions of the brain, such as the _____ . According to the _____-_____ theory, dreams are the brain's attempt to make sense of this activity. The bursts are believed to be given their emotional tone by the brain's _____ system. PET scans of sleeping people reveal increased activity in the brain's _____ system, especially the _____ . Other theorists see dreams as a natural part of brain _____ and _____ development.

34. Researchers agree that we _____ (need/do not need) REM sleep. After being deprived of REM sleep, a person spends more time in REM sleep; this is the _____ _____ effect.

35. REM sleep _____ (does/does not) occur in other mammals. Animals such as fish, whose behavior is less influenced by learning,

_____ (do/do not) dream. This finding supports the _____-_____ theory of dreaming.

Hypnosis (pp. 192–196)

Objective 7: Discuss the characteristics of people who are susceptible to hypnosis, and evaluate claims that hypnosis can influence people's memory, will, health, and perception of pain.

1. Hypnosis is a _____ _____ in which a hypnotist suggests that a subject will experience certain feelings or thoughts, for example.

2. Most people are _____ (somewhat/not at all) hypnotically suggestible.

Describe people who are the most susceptible to hypnosis.

3. The idea that we can relive childhood experiences through hypnosis—referred to as _____ _____—has not been supported by research.

4. Research studies show that "hypnotically refreshed" memories combine _____ with _____ .

5. An _____ person in a legitimate _____ can induce people— hypnotized or not—to perform some unlikely acts.

6. Hypnotherapists have helped some people alleviate headaches, asthma, and stress-related skin disorders through the use of _____ suggestions.

7. Hypnosis _____ (is/is not) especially helpful for the treatment of obesity. It _____ (is/is not) useful in treating smoking, drug, and alcohol addictions.

8. Hypnosis _____ (can/cannot) relieve pain.

9. In surgical experiments, hypnotized patients have required less _____ , have recovered _____ , and have left the hospital _____ than unhypnotized controls.

Objective 8: Give arguments for and against hypnosis as an altered state of consciousness.

10. Skeptics believe that hypnosis may reflect the workings of _____ _____ . These findings provide support for the _____ _____ theory of hypnosis.

Summarize the argument that hypnosis is not an altered state of consciousness.

11. Hilgard has advanced the idea that during hypnosis there is a _____ , or split, between different levels of consciousness. For example, he believes that there is a split between the _____ and _____ aspects of pain. Hypnotic pain relief may also be due to selective _____ , that is, to the person's focusing on stimuli other than pain.

Discuss the current view of hypnosis as a blend of the two views.

Drugs and Consciousness (pp. 197–210)

Objective 9: Discuss the nature of drug dependence and addiction, and identify three common misconceptions about addiction.

1. Drugs that alter moods and perceptions are called _____ drugs.

2. Drug users who require increasing doses to experience a drug's effects have developed _____ for the drug. The user's brain counteracts the disruption to its normal functioning; thus, the user experiences _____ .

3. After ceasing to use a drug, a person who experiences _____ symptoms has developed a physical _____ . Regular use of a drug to relieve stress is an example of a _____ dependence. A person who has a compulsive craving for a substance despite adverse consequences is _____ to that substance.

Briefly state three common misconceptions about addiction.

4. The three broad categories of drugs discussed in the text include _____ , which tend to slow body functions; _____ , which speed body functions; and _____ , which alter perception. These drugs all work by mimicking, stimulating, or inhibiting the activity of the brain's _____ . Psychologically, our culturally influenced _____ also play a role.

Objective 10: Explain how depressants affect nervous system activity and behavior, and summarize the findings on alcohol use and abuse.

5. Depressants _____ nervous system activity and _____ body function. Low doses of alcohol, which is classified as a _____ , slow the activity of the _____ nervous system.

6. Alcohol may make a person more
_____ , more _____ , or
more _____ daring. Alcohol affects
memory by interfering with the process of transferring experiences into _____-
_____ memory. Also, blackouts
after drinking result from alcohol's suppression
of _____ _____ .

7. Excessive use of alcohol can also affect cognition
by _____ the brain, especially in
_____ (men/women). Alcohol also
reduces _____ and focuses one's
attention on the _____ situation
and away from _____ consequences,
thus lessening _____ _____ .

Describe how a person's expectations can influence
the behavioral effects of alcohol.

8. Tranquilizers, which are also known as
_____ , have effects similar to those
of alcohol.

9. Opium, morphine, and heroin all
_____ (excite/depress) neural
functioning. Together, these drugs are called the
_____ . When they are present, the
brain eventually stops producing
_____ .

Objective 11: Identify the major stimulants, and
explain how they affect neural activity and behavior.

10. The most widely used stimulants are
_____ , _____ ,
the _____ , _____ ,
_____ , and _____ .

Stimulants _____ (are/are not)
addictive.

11. Methamphetamine triggers the release of the
neurotransmitter _____ , which
stimulates brain cells that enhance
_____ and _____ .

12. Eliminating _____ would increase
life expectancy more than any other preventive
measure. Smoking usually begins during
_____ _____ . Smokers
_____ (do/do not) become dependent on _____ , and they
_____ (do/do not) develop tolerance to the drug. Quitting causes
_____-_____ symp-
toms that include _____
_____ .

13. Nicotine quickly triggers the release of
_____ and _____ , two
neurotransmitters that diminish _____
and boost _____ and
_____ _____ . Nicotine
also stimulates the _____
_____ system to release
_____ and _____ , neu-
rotransmitters that calm _____ and
reduce sensitivity to _____ .

14. Cocaine and crack deplete the brain's supply of
the neurotransmitters _____ ,
_____ , and _____
and result in depression as the drugs' effects
wear off. They do this by blocking the
_____ of the neurotransmitters,
which remain in the nerve cells' _____ .

15. Cocaine's psychological effects depend not only
on dosage and form but also on
_____ , _____ , and the
_____ .

16. The drug _____ , or MDMA,
is both a _____
and a _____ _____ .
This drug triggers the release of the

neurotransmitters _____ and _____ and blocks the reabsorption of _____ . Among the adverse effects of this drug are disruption of the body's _____ clock, suppression of the _____ _____ , and impaired _____ and other _____ functions.

Objective 12: Describe the physiological and psychological effects of hallucinogens, and summarize the effects of LSD and marijuana.

17. Hallucinogens are also referred to as _____ . Two common synthetic hallucinogens are _____ and LSD, which is chemically similar to a subtype of the neurotransmitter _____ . LSD works by _____ the actions of this neurotransmitter.

18. The reports of people who have had near-death experiences are very similar to the _____ reported by drug users. These experiences may be the result of a deficient supply of _____ or other insults to the brain.

19. The active ingredient in marijuana is abbreviated _____ .

Describe some of the physical and psychological effects of marijuana.

20. All psychoactive drugs trigger _____ _____ , which helps explain both _____ and _____ .

Objective 13: Discuss the biological, psychological, and social-cultural factors that contribute to drug use.

21. Drug use by North American youth _____ (increased/declined) during the 1970s, then declined until the early 1990s due to increased _____ _____ and efforts by the media to deglamorize drug use.

22. Adopted individuals are more susceptible to alcohol dependence if they had a(n) _____ (adoptive/biological) parent with a history of alcohol dependence. Also having an _____ _____ with alcohol dependence increases the risk of dependence. Boys who at age 6 are _____ (more/less) excitable are more likely as teens to smoke, drink, and use other drugs. Genes that are more common among people predisposed to alcohol dependence may cause deficiencies in the brain's _____ _____ system.

Identify some of the psychological and social-cultural roots of drug use.

23. Among teenagers, drug use _____ (varies/is about the same) across _____ and _____ groups.

24. African-American high school seniors report the _____ (highest/lowest) rates of drug use. A major social influence on drug use is the _____ culture.

25. State three possible channels of influence for drug prevention and treatment programs.

   a. _____

   b. _____

   c. _____

PROGRESS TEST 1

Multiple-Choice Questions

Circle your answers to the following questions and check them with the answers beginning on page 118. If your answer is incorrect, read the explanation for why it is incorrect and then consult the appropriate pages of the text (in parentheses following the correct answer).

1. As defined by the text, *consciousness* includes which of the following?
   a. focused attention
   b. sleeping
   c. hypnosis
   d. all of these conditions

2. The cluster of brain cells that control the circadian rhythm is the
   a. amygdala.
   b. suprachiasmatic nucleus.
   c. NPY.
   d. pineal.

3. Compared with their counterparts of 80 years ago, teenagers today average _____ sleep each night.
   a. 2 hours less
   b. 4 hours less
   c. 1 hour more
   d. about the same amount of

4. Sleep spindles predominate during which stage of sleep?
   a. Stage 2   c. Stage 4
   b. Stage 3   d. REM sleep

5. During which stage of sleep does the body experience increased heart rate, rapid breathing, and genital arousal?
   a. Stage 2   c. Stage 4
   b. Stage 3   d. REM sleep

6. The sleep cycle is approximately _____ minutes.
   a. 30   c. 75
   b. 50   d. 90

7. The effects of chronic sleep deprivation include
   a. suppression of the immune system.
   b. altered metabolic and hormonal functioning.
   c. impaired creativity.
   d. all of these effects.

8. One effect of sleeping pills is to
   a. decrease REM sleep.
   b. increase REM sleep.
   c. decrease Stage 2 sleep.
   d. increase Stage 2 sleep.

9. Cocaine and crack produce a euphoric rush by
   a. blocking the actions of serotonin.
   b. depressing neural activity in the brain.
   c. blocking the reuptake of dopamine in brain cells.
   d. stimulating the brain's production of endorphins.

10. Which of the following is classified as a depressant?
    a. methamphetamine   c. marijuana
    b. LSD   d. alcohol

11. Which of the following preventive measures would have the greatest impact on average life expectancy?
    a. eliminating obesity
    b. eliminating smoking
    c. eliminating sleep deprivation
    d. eliminating binge drinking

12. Which of the following statements concerning hypnosis is true?
    a. People will do anything under hypnosis.
    b. Hypnosis is the same as sleeping.
    c. Hypnosis is in part an extension of the division between conscious awareness and automatic behavior.
    d. Hypnosis improves memory recall.

13. People who heard unusual phrases prior to sleep were awakened each time they began REM sleep. The fact that they remembered less the next morning provides support for the _____ theory of dreaming.
    a. manifest content
    b. physiological
    c. information-processing
    d. activation-synthesis

14. According to Freud, dreams are
    a. a symbolic fulfillment of erotic wishes.
    b. the result of random neural activity in the brainstem.
    c. the brain's mechanism for self-stimulation.
    d. the disguised expressions of inner conflicts.

15. Psychoactive drugs affect behavior and perception through
    a. the power of suggestion.
    b. the placebo effect.
    c. alteration of neural activity in the brain.
    d. psychological, not physiological, influences.

16. All of the following are common misconceptions about addiction, EXCEPT the statement that
    a. to overcome an addiction a person almost always needs professional therapy.
    b. psychoactive and medicinal drugs very quickly lead to addiction.
    c. biological factors place some individuals at increased risk for addiction.
    d. many other repetitive, pleasure-seeking behaviors fit the drug-addiction-as-disease-needing-treatment model.

17. At its beginning, psychology focused on the study of
    a. observable behavior.
    b. consciousness.
    c. abnormal behavior.
    d. all of these factors.

18. Which of the following is NOT a theory of dreaming mentioned in the text?
    a. Dreams facilitate information processing.
    b. Dreaming stimulates the developing brain.
    c. Dreams result from random neural activity originating in the brainstem.
    d. Dreaming is an attempt to escape from social stimulation.

19. The sleep-waking cycles of young people who stay up too late typically are _____ hours in duration.
    a. 23
    b. 24
    c. 25
    d. 26

Matching Items

Match each term with its appropriate definition or description.

Definitions or Descriptions

_____ 1. surface meaning of dreams
_____ 2. deeper meaning of dreams
_____ 3. stage(s) of sleep associated with delta waves
_____ 4. stage(s) of sleep associated with muscular relaxation
_____ 5. sleep disorder in which breathing stops
_____ 6. sleep disorder occurring in Stage 4 sleep
_____ 7. depressant
_____ 8. hallucinogen
_____ 9. stimulant
_____ 10. disorder in which sleep attacks occur
_____ 11. twilight stage of sleep associated with imagery resembling hallucinations

Terms

a. marijuana
b. alcohol
c. Stage 1 sleep
d. manifest content
e. cocaine
f. narcolepsy
g. sleep apnea
h. Stages 3 and 4 sleep
i. REM sleep
j. latent content
k. night terrors

PROGRESS TEST 2

Progress Test 2 should be completed during a final unit review. Answer the following questions after you thoroughly understand the correct answers for the section reviews and Progress Test 1.

Multiple-Choice Questions

1. Which of the following statements regarding REM sleep is true?
   a. Adults spend more time than infants in REM sleep.
   b. REM sleep deprivation results in a REM rebound.
   c. People deprived of REM sleep adapt easily.
   d. Sleeping medications tend to increase REM sleep.

2. Alcohol has the most profound effect on
   a. the transfer of experiences to long-term memory.
   b. immediate memory.
   c. previously established long-term memories.
   d. all of these factors.

3. A person whose EEG shows a high proportion of alpha waves is most likely
   a. dreaming.   c. in Stage 3 or 4 sleep.
   b. in Stage 2 sleep.   d. awake and relaxed.

4. Circadian rhythms are the
   a. brain waves that occur during Stage 4 sleep.
   b. muscular tremors that occur during opiate withdrawal.
   c. regular body cycles that occur on a 24-hour schedule.
   d. brain waves that are indicative of Stage 2 sleep.

5. A person who requires increasing amounts of a drug to feel its effect is said to have developed
   a. tolerance.
   b. physical dependency.
   c. psychological dependency.
   d. resistance.

6. Which of the following is NOT an example of a biological rhythm?
   a. the circadian rhythm
   b. the 90-minute sleep cycle
   c. the five sleep stages
   d. sudden sleep attacks during the day

7. Which of the following is characteristic of REM sleep?
   a. genital arousal
   b. increased muscular tension
   c. night terrors
   d. alpha waves

8. Which of the following is NOT a stimulant?
   a. amphetamines   c. nicotine
   b. caffeine   d. alcohol

9. Hypnotic responsiveness is
   a. the same in all people.
   b. generally greater in women than men.
   c. generally greater in men than women.
   d. greater when people are led to expect it.

10. According to Hilgard, hypnosis is
    a. no different from a state of heightened motivation.
    b. the same as dreaming.
    c. a dissociation between different levels of consciousness.
    d. a form of Stage 4 sleep.

11. Which of the following was NOT cited in the text as evidence that heredity influences alcohol use?
    a. Children whose parents abuse alcohol have a lower tolerance for multiple alcoholic drinks taken over a short period of time.
    b. Boys who are impulsive and fearless at age 6 are more likely to drink as teenagers.
    c. Laboratory mice have been selectively bred to prefer alcohol to water.
    d. Adopted children are more susceptible if one or both of their biological parents have a history of alcohol dependence.

12. As a form of therapy for relieving problems such as warts, hypnosis is
    a. ineffective.
    b. no more effective than positive suggestions given without hypnosis.
    c. highly effective.
    d. more effective with adults than children.

13. Which of the following is usually the most powerful determinant of whether teenagers begin using drugs?
    a. family strength   c. school adjustment
    b. religiosity   d. peer influence

14. THC is the major active ingredient in
    a. nicotine.   c. marijuana.
    b. MDMA.   d. cocaine.

15. Those who believe that hypnosis is a social phenomenon argue that "hypnotized" individuals are
   a. consciously faking their behavior.
   b. merely acting out a role.
   c. underachievers striving to please the hypnotist.
   d. doing all of these things.

16. *Consciousness* is defined in the text as
   a. mental life.
   b. selective attention to ongoing perceptions, thoughts, and feelings.
   c. information processing.
   d. our awareness of ourselves and our environment.

17. I am a synthetic stimulant and mild hallucinogen that produces euphoria and social intimacy by triggering the release of dopamine and serotonin. What am I?
   a. LSD   c. THC
   b. MDMA   d. cocaine

18. According to the activation-synthesis theory, dreaming represents
   a. the brain's efforts to integrate unrelated bursts of activity in visual brain areas with the emotional tone provided by limbic system activity.
   b. a mechanism for coping with the stresses of daily life.
   c. a symbolic depiction of a person's unfulfilled wishes.
   d. an information-processing mechanism for converting the day's experiences into long-term memory.

19. How a particular psychoactive drug affects a person depends on
   a. the dosage and form in which the drug is taken.
   b. the user's expectations and personality.
   c. the situation in which the drug is taken.
   d. all of these conditions.

Matching Items

Match each term with its appropriate definition or description.

Terms

   a. Freud's theory
   b. serotonin
   c. Ecstasy
   d. alpha
   e. dissociation
   f. amphetamines
   g. consciousness
   h. sleep spindle
   i. endorphins
   j. REM
   k. barbiturates

Definitions or Descriptions

_____ 1. drug that is both a stimulant and mild hallucinogen

_____ 2. drugs that increase energy and stimulate neural activity

_____ 3. brain wave of awake, relaxed person

_____ 4. brain-wave activity during Stage 2 sleep

_____ 5. sleep stage associated with dreaming

_____ 6. drugs that reduce anxiety and depress central nervous system activity

_____ 7. natural painkillers produced by the brain

_____ 8. our awareness of ourselves and our environment

_____ 9. theory that dreaming reflects our erotic drives

_____ 10. a split between different levels of consciousness

_____ 11. neurotransmitter that LSD resembles

PSYCHOLOGY APPLIED

Answer these questions the day before a test as a final check on your understanding of the unit's terms and concepts.

Multiple-Choice Questions

1. A person who falls asleep in the midst of a heated argument probably suffers from
    a. sleep apnea.
    b. narcolepsy.
    c. night terrors.
    d. insomnia.

2. Which of the following was NOT suggested by the text as an important aspect of drug prevention and treatment programs?
    a. education about the long-term costs of a drug's temporary pleasures
    b. efforts to boost people's self-esteem and purpose in life
    c. attempts to modify peer associations
    d. "scare tactics" that frighten prepubescent children into avoiding drug experimentation

3. REM sleep is referred to as *paradoxical sleep* because
    a. studies of people deprived of REM sleep indicate that REM sleep is unnecessary.
    b. the body's muscles remain relaxed while the brain and eyes are active.
    c. it is very easy to awaken a person from REM sleep.
    d. the body's muscles are very tense while the brain is in a nearly meditative state.

4. An attorney wants to know if the details and accuracy of an eyewitness's memory for a crime would be improved under hypnosis. Given the results of relevant research, what should you tell the attorney?
    a. Most hypnotically retrieved memories are either false or contaminated.
    b. Hypnotically retrieved memories are usually more accurate than conscious memories.
    c. Hypnotically retrieved memories are purely the product of the subject's imagination.
    d. Hypnosis only improves memory of anxiety-provoking childhood events.

5. Dan has recently begun using an addictive, euphoria-producing drug. Which of the following will probably occur if he repeatedly uses this drug?
    a. As tolerance to the drug develops, Dan will experience increasingly pleasurable "highs."
    b. The dosage needed to produce the desired effect will increase.
    c. After each use, he will become more and more elated.
    d. Dependence will become less of a problem.

6. Although her eyes are closed, Adele's brain is generating bursts of electrical activity. It is likely that Adele is
    a. under the influence of a depressant.
    b. under the influence of an opiate.
    c. in REM sleep.
    d. having a near-death experience.

7. The lowest rates of drug use among high school seniors is reported by
    a. Asian-Americans.
    b. Hispanic-Americans.
    c. African-Americans.
    d. Native Americans.

8. Roberto is moderately intoxicated by alcohol. Which of the following changes in his behavior is likely to occur?
    a. If angered, he is more likely to become aggressive than when he is sober.
    b. He will be less self-conscious about his behavior.
    c. If sexually aroused, he will be less inhibited about engaging in sexual activity.
    d. All of these changes are likely.

9. Jill dreams that she trips and falls as she walks up the steps to the stage to receive her diploma. Her psychoanalyst suggests that the dream might symbolize her fear of moving on to the next stage of her life—a career. The analyst is evidently attempting to interpret the _____ content of Jill's dream.
    a. manifest
    b. latent
    c. dissociated
    d. overt

10. Barry has participated in a sleep study for the last four nights. He was awakened each time he entered REM sleep. Now that the experiment is over, which of the following can be expected to occur?
    a. Barry will be too tired to sleep, so he'll continue to stay awake.
    b. Barry will sleep so deeply for several nights that dreaming will be minimal.
    c. There will be an increase in sleep Stages 1–4.
    d. There will be an increase in Barry's REM sleep.

11. Of the following individuals, who is likely to be the most hypnotically suggestible?
    a. Bill, a reality-oriented stockbroker
    b. Janice, an actress with a rich imagination
    c. Megan, a sixth-grader who has trouble focusing her attention on a task
    d. Darren, who has never been able to really "get involved" in movies or novels

12. Which of the following statements concerning alcohol dependence is NOT true?
    a. Adopted individuals are more susceptible to alcohol dependence if they had an adoptive parent with alcohol dependence.
    b. Having an identical twin with alcohol dependence puts a person at increased risk for alcohol problems.
    c. Geneticists have identified genes that are more common among people predisposed to alcohol dependence.
    d. Researchers have bred rats that prefer alcohol to water.

13. Research studies of the effectiveness of hypnosis as a form of therapy have demonstrated that
    a. for problems of addiction, such as smoking, hypnosis has not been especially effective.
    b. posthypnotic suggestions have helped alleviate headaches, asthma, and stress-related skin disorders.
    c. as a form of therapy, hypnosis is no more effective than positive suggestions given without hypnosis.
    d. all of these statements are true.

14. A PET scan of a sleeping person's brain reveals increased activity in the amygdala of the limbic system. This most likely indicates that the sleeper
    a. has a neurological disorder.
    b. is not truly asleep.
    c. is in REM sleep.
    d. suffers from narcolepsy.

15. Which of the following statements concerning marijuana is true?
    a. The by-products of marijuana are cleared from the body more slowly than are the by-products of alcohol.
    b. Regular users may need a larger dose of the drug to achieve a high than occasional users would need to get the same effect.
    c. Marijuana is as addictive as nicotine or cocaine.
    d. Even small doses of marijuana hasten the loss of brain cells.

16. Which of the following statements concerning near-death experiences is true?
    a. They do not produce hallucinations such as those produced by LSD.
    b. They typically consist of fantastic, mystical imagery.
    c. They are more commonly experienced by females than by males.
    d. They are more commonly experienced by males than by females.

17. Those who consider hypnosis a social phenomenon contend that
    a. hypnosis is an altered state of consciousness.
    b. hypnotic phenomena are unique to hypnosis.
    c. hypnotized subjects become unresponsive when they are no longer motivated to act as instructed.
    d. hypnosis involves different brain states.

18. Which of the following statements concerning the roots of drug use is true?
    a. Heavy users of alcohol, marijuana, and cocaine often are always on a high.
    b. If an adolescent's friends use drugs, odds are that he or she will, too.
    c. Teenagers who are academically average students seldom use drugs.
    d. It is nearly impossible to predict whether a particular adolescent will experiment with drugs.

19. Concluding her presentation on contemporary theories of why sleep is necessary, Marilynn makes all of the following points EXCEPT
    a. Sleep may have evolved because it kept our ancestors safe during potentially dangerous periods.
    b. Sleep gives the brain time to heal, as it restores and repairs damaged neurons.
    c. Sleep encourages growth through a hormone secreted during Stage 4.
    d. Slow-wave sleep provides a "psychic safety valve" for stressful waking experiences.

Essay Question

You have just been assigned the task of writing an article tentatively titled "Alcohol and Alcohol Dependence: Roots, Effects, and Prevention." What information should you include in your article? (Use the space below to list the points you want to make, and organize them. Then write the essay on a separate piece of paper.)

KEY TERMS

Using your own words, on a separate piece of paper write a brief definition or explanation of each of the following terms.

1. consciousness
2. circadian rhythm
3. REM sleep
4. alpha waves
5. sleep
6. hallucinations
7. delta waves
8. NREM sleep
9. insomnia
10. narcolepsy
11. sleep apnea
12. night terrors
13. dream
14. manifest content
15. latent content
16. REM rebound
17. hypnosis

18. posthypnotic suggestion
19. dissociation
20. psychoactive drugs
21. tolerance
22. withdrawal
23. physical dependence
24. psychological dependence
25. addiction
26. depressants
27. barbiturates
28. opiates
29. stimulants
30. amphetamines
31. methamphetamines
32. Ecstasy (MDMA)
33. hallucinogens
34. LSD
35. near-death experience
36. THC

ANSWERS

Unit Review

Introduction

1. consciousness; behavior
2. brain activity; cognition

Consciousness is our awareness of ourselves and our environment.

Sleep and Dreams

1. biological rhythms
2. circadian rhythm
3. rises; fall
4. thinking; memory
5. bright light; retinas; suprachiasmatic nucleus; pineal; melatonin
6. will
7. five
8. eyes; dreams; REM sleep
9. alpha
10. hypnagogic; hallucinations; memories
11. sleep spindles
12. delta; 3; 4; slow-wave; difficult; sleepwalking

During REM sleep, brain waves become as rapid as those of Stage 1 sleep, heart rate rises and breathing becomes more rapid and irregular, and genital arousal and rapid eye movements occur.

13. active; relaxed; paradoxical
14. dream; emotional
15. 90; briefer; longer; 20 to 25
16. two-thirds; one-third
17. genes; identical; culture; less
18. 9
19. 8 or 9; 2; Dement; ghrelin; leptin; cortisol; immune; aging; hypertension; memory impairment; accidents

The major effect of sleep deprivation is sleepiness. Other effects include impaired creativity, concentration, and communication; slowed performance; and irritability.

20. protect; brain; metabolism; free radicals; neurons; memory; creative
21. pituitary; less; less
22. insomnia; reduce

Tips for promoting healthy sleep include exercising during the day, avoiding caffeine after early afternoon and rich foods before bedtime, sleeping on a regular schedule, and relaxing before bedtime.

23. narcolepsy; REM; muscular tension; orexin
24. sleep apnea; overweight men
25. night terrors; 4; sleepwalking; sleeptalking; run; young children; lengthiest; deepest
26. REM
27. negative; attacked, pursued, or rejected, or of experiencing misfortune
28. manifest; latent content
29. erotic; conflicts; safety valve
30. information; memory
31. REM; memory
32. physiological; stimulation; infants
33. neural; brainstem; activation-synthesis; limbic; limbic; amygdala; maturation; cognitive
34. need; REM rebound
35. does; do not; information-processing

Hypnosis

1. social interaction
2. somewhat

Those who are most susceptible frequently become deeply absorbed in imaginative activities. They also tend to have rich fantasy lives.

3. age regression
4. fact; fiction
5. authoritative; context
6. posthypnotic
7. is; is not
8. can
9. medication; sooner; earlier
10. normal consciousness; social influence

The behavior of hypnotized subjects is not fundamentally different from that of other people. Therefore, hypnosis may be mainly a social phenomenon, with hypnotized subjects acting out the role of a "good hypnotic subject."

11. dissociation; sensory; emotional; attention

The social influence and divided consciousness views work together to explain hypnosis as an extension both of normal principles of social influence and of everyday dissociations between our conscious awareness and our automatic behaviors.

Drugs and Consciousness

1. psychoactive
2. tolerance; neuroadaptation
3. withdrawal; dependence; psychological; addicted

The following myths about addiction are false:
a. Taking a psychoactive drug automatically leads to addiction.
b. A person cannot overcome an addiction without professional help.
c. The addiction-as-disease-needing-treatment model is applicable to a broad spectrum of pleasure-seeking behaviors.

4. depressants; stimulants; hallucinogens; neurotransmitters; expectations
5. calm; slow; depressant; sympathetic
6. aggressive; helpful; sexually; long-term; REM sleep
7. shrinking; women; self-awareness; immediate; future; impulse control

Studies have found that if people believe that alcohol affects social behavior in certain ways, then, when they drink alcohol (or even mistakenly think that they have been drinking alcohol), they will behave according to their expectations, which vary by culture. For example, if people believe alcohol promotes sexual feeling, on drinking they are likely to behave in a sexually aroused way.

8. barbiturates
9. depress; opiates; endorphins

10. caffeine; nicotine; amphetamines; cocaine; Ecstasy; methamphetamine; are

11. dopamine; energy; mood

12. smoking; early adolescence; do; nicotine; do; nicotine-withdrawal; craving, insomnia, anxiety, and irritability

13. epinephrine; norepinephrine; appetite; alertness; mental efficiency; central nervous; dopamine; opioids; anxiety; pain

14. dopamine; serotonin; norepinephrine; reuptake (reabsorption); synapses

15. expectations; personality; situation

16. Ecstasy; stimulant; mild hallucinogen; dopamine; serotonin; serotonin; circadian; immune system; memory; cognitive

17. psychedelics; MDMA; serotonin; blocking

18. hallucinations; oxygen

19. THC

Like alcohol, marijuana relaxes, disinhibits, and may produce a euphoric feeling. Also like alcohol, marijuana impairs perceptual and motor skills. Unlike alcohol, marijuana is a mild hallucinogen; it can amplify sensitivity to colors, sounds, tastes, and smells. Marijuana also interrupts memory formation. Its by-products remain in the body for a month or more.

20. negative aftereffects; tolerance; withdrawal

21. increased; drug education

22. biological; identical twin; more; dopamine reward

A psychological factor in drug use is the feeling that one's life is meaningless and lacks direction. Regular users of psychoactive drugs often have experienced stress or failure and are somewhat depressed. Drug use often begins as a temporary way to relieve depression, anger, anxiety, or insomnia. A powerful social factor in drug use, especially among adolescents, is peer influence. Peers shape attitudes about drugs, provide drugs, and establish the social context for their use.

23. varies; cultural; ethnic

24. lowest; peer

25. a. education about the long-term costs of a drug's temporary pleasures

    b. efforts to boost people's self-esteem and purpose in life

    c. attempts to "inoculate" youths against peer pressures

Progress Test 1

Multiple-Choice Questions

1. **d.** is the answer. (p. 176)

2. **b.** is the answer. (p. 177)
   a. The amygdala is an emotion center in the limbic system.
   c. NPY is a brain chemical that has been found to be reduced in rats who prefer alcohol to water.
   d. The pineal is a gland that produces the sleep-inducing hormone melatonin.

3. **a.** is the answer. (p. 183)

4. **a.** is the answer. (p. 179)
   b. & c. Delta waves predominate during Stages 3 and 4. Stage 3 is the transition between Stages 2 and 4 and is associated with a pattern that has elements of both stages.
   d. Faster, nearly waking brain waves occur during REM sleep.

5. **d.** is the answer. (pp. 180–181)
   a., b., & c. During non-REM Stages 1–4 heart rate and breathing are slow and regular and the genitals are not aroused.

6. **d.** is the answer. (p. 181)

7. **d.** is the answer. (pp. 183–184)

8. **a.** is the answer. Like alcohol, sleeping pills carry the undesirable consequence of reducing REM sleep and may make insomnia worse in the long run. (p. 186)
   b., c., & d. Sleeping pills do not produce these effects.

9. **c.** is the answer. They also block the reuptake of serotonin and norepinephrine. (p. 204)
   a. This answer describes the effect of LSD.
   b. Depressants such as alcohol have this effect. Cocaine and crack are classified as stimulants.
   d. None of the psychoactive drugs has this effect. Opiates, however, *suppress* the brain's production of endorphins.

10. **d.** is the answer. Alcohol, which slows body functions and neural activity, is a depressant. (p. 199)
    a. Methamphetamine is a stimulant.
    b. & c. LSD and marijuana are hallucinogens.

11. **b.** is the answer. (p. 202)

12. **c.** is the answer. (p. 196)
    a. Hypnotized subjects usually perform only acts they might perform normally.
    b. The text does not suggest that sleeping and hypnosis are the same states. In fact, the brain waves of hypnotized subjects are not like those associated with sleeping.

d. Hypnosis typically *disrupts*, or contaminates, memory.

13. **c.** is the answer. They remembered less than if they were awakened during other stages. (pp. 189–190)

14. **a.** is the answer. Freud saw dreams as psychic safety valves that discharge unacceptable feelings that are often related to erotic wishes. (p. 189)
b. & c. These physiological theories of dreaming are not associated with Freud.
d. According to Freud, dreams represent the individual's conflicts and wishes but in disguised, rather than transparent, form.

15. **c.** is the answer. Such drugs work primarily at synapses, altering neural transmission. (p. 197)
a. What people believe will happen after taking a drug will likely have some effect on their individual reactions, but psychoactive drugs actually work by altering neural transmission.
b. Because a placebo is a substance without active properties, this answer is incorrect.
d. This answer is incorrect because the effects of psychoactive drugs on behavior, perception, and so forth have a physiological basis.

16. **c.** is the answer. This is true. Heredity, for example, influences tendencies toward alcohol dependence. (pp. 198, 208)

17. **b.** is the answer. (p. 175)
a. The behaviorists' emphasis on observable behavior occurred much later in the history of psychology.
c. Psychology has never been primarily concerned with abnormal behavior.

18. **d.** is the answer. (pp. 189–191)
a., b., & c. Each of these describes a valid theory of dreaming that was mentioned in the text.

19. **c.** is the answer. We can reset our biological clocks by adjusting our sleep schedules. Thus, young adults adopt something closer to a 25-hour day by staying up too late to get 8 hours of sleep. (p. 178)

Matching Items

1. d (p. 188)
2. j (p. 189)
3. h (p. 180)
4. i (p. 178)
5. g (p. 187)
6. k (p. 187)
7. b (p. 199)
8. a (p. 206)
9. e (p. 204)
10. f (p. 186)
11. c (p. 179)

Progress Test 2

Multiple-Choice Questions

1. **b.** is the answer. Following REM deprivation, people temporarily increase their amount of REM sleep, in a phenomenon known as REM rebound. (p. 191)
a. Just the opposite is true: The amount of REM sleep is greatest in infancy.
c. Deprived of REM sleep by repeated awakenings, people return more and more quickly to the REM stages after falling back to sleep. They by no means adapt easily to the deprivations.
d. Just the opposite occurs: They tend to suppress REM sleep.

2. **a.** is the answer. Alcohol disrupts the processing of experiences into long-term memory but has little effect on either immediate or previously established memories. (p. 199)

3. **d.** is the answer. (p. 178)
a. The brain waves of REM sleep (dream sleep) are more like those of Stage 1 sleepers.
b. Stage 2 is characterized by sleep spindles.
c. Stages 3 and 4 are characterized by slow delta waves.

4. **c.** is the answer. (p. 177)

5. **a.** is the answer. (p. 197)
b. Physical dependence may occur in the absence of tolerance. The hallmark of physical dependence is the presence of withdrawal symptoms when the person is off the drug.
c. Psychological dependence refers to a felt, or psychological, need to use a drug, for example, a drug that relieves stress.
d. There is no such thing as drug "resistance."

6. **d.** is the answer. (p. 186)

7. **a.** is the answer. (p. 180)
b. During REM sleep, muscular tension is low.
c. Night terrors are associated with Stage 4 sleep.
d. Alpha waves are characteristic of the relaxed, awake state.

8. **d.** is the answer. Alcohol is a depressant. (p. 199)

9. **d.** is the answer. (p. 193)
a. Hypnotic responsiveness varies greatly from person to person.
b. & c. There is no evidence of a gender difference in hypnotic responsiveness.

10. **c.** is the answer. Hilgard believes that hypnosis reflects a dissociation, or split, in consciousness, as occurs normally, only to a much greater extent. (p. 195)

11. **a.** is the answer. Although this is not discussed, the fact that alcohol dependence has a genetic component suggests that compared with other children, children whose parents abuse alcohol have a *higher* tolerance for multiple drinks, making it more likely that they will, in fact, consume more alcohol. (pp. 208–209)

12. **b.** is the answer. (p. 194)
a. & c. Hypnosis *can* be helpful in treating these problems, but it is no more effective than other forms of therapy.
d. Adults are not more responsive than children to hypnosis.

13. **d.** is the answer. If adolescents' friends use drugs, the odds are that they will, too. (p. 209)
a., b., & c. These are also predictors of drug use but seem to operate mainly through their effects on peer association.

14. **c.** is the answer. (p. 206)

15. **b.** is the answer. (p. 195)
a. & c. There is no evidence that hypnotically responsive individuals fake their behaviors or that they are underachievers.

16. **d.** is the answer. (p. 176)

17. **b.** is the answer. (p. 205)
a. & c. Unlike stimulants, LSD and THC do not speed up body functions.
d. Unlike hallucinogens, cocaine is a stimulant and does not generally distort perceptions.

18. **a.** is the answer. (p. 190)
b. & c. These essentially Freudian explanations of the purpose of dreaming are based on the idea that a dream is a psychic safety valve that harmlessly discharges otherwise inexpressible feelings.
d. This explanation of the function of dreaming is associated with the information-processing viewpoint.

19. **d.** is the answer. (p. 205)

Matching Items

1. c (p. 205)   5. j (p. 178)   9. a (p. 189)
2. f (p. 201)   6. k (p. 200)   10. e (p. 195)
3. d (p. 178)   7. i (p. 201)   11. b (p. 204)
4. h (pp. 179–180) 8. g (p. 176)

Psychology Applied

Multiple-Choice Questions

1. **b.** is the answer. Narcolepsy is characterized by uncontrollable sleep attacks. (p. 186)
a. Sleep apnea is characterized by the temporary cessation of breathing while asleep.
c. Night terrors are characterized by high arousal and terrified behavior, occurring during Stage 4 sleep.
d. Insomnia refers to chronic difficulty in falling or staying asleep.

2. **d.** is the answer. (p. 210)

3. **b.** is the answer. Although the body is aroused internally, the messages of the activated motor cortex do not reach the muscles. (pp. 180–181)
a. Studies of REM-deprived people indicate just the opposite.
c. It is difficult to awaken a person from REM sleep.
d. Just the opposite occurs in REM sleep: The muscles are relaxed, yet the brain is aroused.

4. **a.** is the answer. Although people recall more under hypnosis, they "recall" a lot of fiction along with fact and appear unable to distinguish between the two. (p. 193)
b. Hypnotically refreshed memories are usually no more accurate than conscious memories.
c. Although the hypnotized subject's imagination may influence the memories retrieved, some actual memory retrieval also occurs.
d. Hypnotically retrieved memories don't normally focus on anxiety-provoking events.

5. **b.** is the answer. Continued use of a drug produces a tolerance; to experience the same "high," Dan will have to use larger and larger doses. (p. 197)

6. **c.** is the answer. The rapid eye movements of REM sleep coincide with bursts of activity in brain areas that process visual images. (p. 180)

7. **c.** is the answer. (p. 209)

8. **d.** is the answer. Alcohol loosens inhibitions and reduces self-consciousness, making people more likely to act on their feelings of anger or sexual arousal. It also disrupts the processing of experience into long-term memory. (pp. 199–200)

9. **b.** is the answer. The analyst is evidently trying to go beyond the events in the dream and understand the dream's hidden meaning, or the dream's latent content. (p. 189)
a. The manifest content of a dream is its actual story line.

c. Dissociation refers to a split in levels of consciousness.

d. There is no such term. In any case, "overt" would be the same as "manifest" content.

10. **d.** is the answer. Because of the phenomenon known as REM rebound, Barry, having been deprived of REM sleep, will now increase his REM sleep. (p. 191)

a. Increased irritability is an effect of sleep deprivation in general, not of REM deprivation specifically.

b. REM rebound will cause Barry to dream more than normal.

c. The increase in REM sleep is necessarily accompanied by decreases in Stages 1–4 sleep.

11. **b.** is the answer. People with rich fantasy lives and the ability to become imaginatively absorbed have essentially the characteristics associated with hypnotic suggestibility. The fact that Janice is an actress also suggests she possesses such traits. (p. 193)

a. Bill's reality orientation makes him an unlikely candidate for hypnosis.

c. The hypnotically suggestible are generally able to focus on tasks or on imaginative activities.

d. People who are hypnotically suggestible tend to become deeply engrossed in novels and movies.

12. **a.** is the answer. Adopted individuals are more susceptible to alcohol dependence if they had a *biological* parent with alcohol dependence. (p. 208)

b., c., & d. Each of these is true, which indicates that susceptibility to alcohol dependence is at least partially determined by heredity.

13. **d.** is the answer. (p. 194)

14. **c.** is the answer. (pp. 190–191)

a. & d. Increased activity in the visual and auditory areas of the sleeping brain is perfectly normal during REM sleep.

b. In fact, people cannot easily be awakened from REM sleep.

15. **a.** is the answer. THC, the active ingredient in marijuana, and its by-products linger in the body for a month or more. (p. 206)

16. **b.** is the answer. (p. 206)

a. The hallucinations of a near-death experience are very similar to those of an LSD trip.

c. & d. The text does not mention a gender difference in the prevalence of near-death experiences.

17. **c.** is the answer. (p. 195)

18. **b.** is the answer. (p. 209)

19. **d.** is the answer. Freud's theory proposed that dreams, which occur during fast-wave, REM sleep, serve as a psychic safety valve. (p. 189)

Essay Question

As a depressant, alcohol slows neural activity and body functions. Although low doses of alcohol may produce relaxation, with larger doses reactions slow, speech slurs, skilled performance deteriorates, and the processing of recent experiences into long-term memories is disrupted. Alcohol also reduces self-awareness and may facilitate sexual and aggressive urges the individual might otherwise resist.

Some people may be biologically vulnerable to alcohol dependence. This is indicated by the fact that individuals who have a biological parent with alcohol dependence, or people who have an identical twin with alcohol dependence, are more susceptible to alcohol dependence.

Stress, depression, and the feeling that life is meaningless and without direction are common feelings among heavy users of alcohol and may create a psychological vulnerability to alcohol dependence.

Especially for teenagers, peer group influence is strong. If an adolescent's friends use alcohol, odds are that he or she will too.

Research suggests three important channels of influence for drug prevention and treatment programs: (1) education about the long-term consequences of alcohol use; (2) efforts to boost people's self-esteem and purpose in life; and (3) attempts to counteract peer pressure that leads to experimentation with drugs.

Key Terms

1. For most psychologists, **consciousness** is our awareness of ourselves and our environment. (p. 176)

2. A **circadian rhythm** is any regular bodily rhythm, such as body temperature and sleep-wakefulness, that follows a 24-hour cycle. (p. 177)

   Memory aid: In Latin, *circa* means "about" and *dies* means "day." A **circadian rhythm** is one that is about a day, or 24 hours, in duration.

3. **REM sleep** (rapid eye movement sleep) is the sleep stage in which the brain and eyes are active, the muscles are relaxed, and vivid dreaming occurs; also known as *paradoxical sleep*. (p. 178)

Memory aid: **REM** is an acronym for rapid eye movement, the distinguishing feature of this sleep stage that led to its discovery.

4. **Alpha waves** are the relatively slow brain waves characteristic of an awake, relaxed state. (p. 178)

5. **Sleep** is the natural, periodic loss of consciousness, on which the body and mind depend for healthy functioning. (p. 178)

6. **Hallucinations** are false sensory experiences that occur without any sensory stimulus. (p. 179)

7. **Delta waves** are the large, slow brain waves associated with deep sleep. (p. 180)

8. **NREM sleep** (non–rapid eye movement sleep) is the stage of sleep associated with muscular relaxation. It encompasses all sleep stages except REM sleep. (p. 180)

9. **Insomnia** is a sleep disorder in which the person regularly has difficulty in falling or staying asleep. (p. 185)

10. **Narcolepsy** is a sleep disorder in which the victim suffers sudden, uncontrollable sleep attacks, often characterized by entry directly into REM. (p. 186)

11. **Sleep apnea** is a sleep disorder in which the person ceases breathing while asleep, briefly arouses to gasp for air, falls back asleep, and repeats this cycle throughout the night. (p. 187)

    Example: One theory of the sudden infant death syndrome is that it is caused by **sleep apnea**.

12. A person suffering from **night terrors** experiences episodes of high arousal with apparent terror. Night terrors usually occur during Stage 4 sleep. (p. 187)

13. **Dreams** are sequences of images, emotions, and thoughts, the most vivid of which occur during REM sleep. (p. 188)

14. In Freud's theory of dreaming, the **manifest content** is the remembered story line. (p. 188)

15. In Freud's theory of dreaming, the **latent content** is the underlying but censored meaning of a dream. (p. 189)

    Memory aids for 14 and 15: *Manifest* means "clearly apparent, obvious"; *latent* means "hidden, concealed." A dream's **manifest content** is that which is obvious; its **latent content** remains hidden until its symbolism is interpreted.

16. **REM rebound** is the tendency for REM sleep to increase following REM sleep deprivation. (p. 191)

17. **Hypnosis** is a social interaction in which one person (the hypnotist) suggests to another (the sub-ject) that certain perceptions, feelings, thoughts, or behaviors will spontaneously occur. (p. 192)

18. A **posthypnotic suggestion** is a suggestion made during a hypnosis session that is to be carried out when the subject is no longer hypnotized. (p. 194)

19. **Dissociation** is a split between different levels of consciousness, allowing a person to divide attention between two or more thoughts or behaviors. (p. 195)

20. **Psychoactive drugs**—which include stimulants, depressants, and hallucinogens—are chemical substances that alter moods and perceptions. They work by affecting or mimicking the activity of neurotransmitters. (p. 197)

21. **Tolerance** is the diminishing of a psychoactive drug's effect that occurs with repeated use, requiring progressively larger doses to produce the same effect. (p. 197)

22. **Withdrawal** refers to the discomfort and distress that follow the discontinued use of addictive drugs. (p. 197)

23. **Physical dependence** is a physiological need for a drug that is indicated by the presence of unpleasant withdrawal symptoms when the drug is not taken. (p. 197)

24. The psychological need to use a drug is referred to as **psychological dependence**. (p. 197)

25. An **addiction** is a compulsive craving for a drug despite adverse consequences and withdrawal symptoms. (p. 197)

26. **Depressants** are psychoactive drugs, such as alcohol, opiates, and barbiturates, that reduce neural activity and slow body functions. (p. 199)

27. **Barbiturates** are depressants, sometimes used to induce sleep or reduce anxiety. (p. 200)

28. **Opiates** are depressants derived from the opium poppy, such as opium, morphine, and heroin; they reduce neural activity and temporarily lessen pain and anxiety. (p. 201)

29. **Stimulants** are psychoactive drugs, such as caffeine, nicotine, amphetamines, and cocaine, that excite neural activity and speed up body functions. (p. 201)

30. **Amphetamines** are a type of stimulant and, as such, speed up body functions and neural activity. (p. 201)

31. **Methamphetamine** is a powerfully addictive stimulant that speeds up body functions and is associated with energy and mood changes. (p. 201)

32. Classified as both a synthetic stimulant and a mild hallucinogen, **Ecstasy (MDMA)** produces short-term euphoria by increasing serotonin levels in the brain. Repeated use may permanently damage serotonin neurons, suppress immunity, and impair memory and other cognitive functions. (p. 205)

33. **Hallucinogens** are psychedelic drugs, such as LSD and marijuana, that distort perceptions and evoke sensory images in the absence of sensory input. (p. 205)

34. **LSD** (lysergic acid diethylamide) is a powerful hallucinogen capable of producing vivid false perceptions and disorganization of thought processes. LSD produces its unpredictable effects partially because it blocks the action of a subtype of the neurotransmitter serotonin. (p. 205)

35. The **near-death experience** is an altered state of consciousness that has been reported by some people who have had a close brush with death. (p. 206)

36. The major active ingredient in marijuana, **THC** is classified as a mild hallucinogen. (p. 206)

Learning

UNIT OVERVIEW

"No topic is closer to the heart of psychology than learning, a relatively permanent change in an organism's behavior due to experience." Unit 6 covers the basic principles of three forms of learning: classical, or respondent, conditioning, in which we learn associations between events; operant conditioning, in which we learn to engage in behaviors that are rewarded and to avoid behaviors that are punished; and observational learning, in which we learn by observing and imitating others.

The chapter also covers several important issues, including the generality of principles of learning, the role of cognitive processes in learning, and the ways in which learning is constrained by the biological predispositions of different species.

NOTE: Answer guidelines for all Unit 6 questions begin on page 138.

UNIT REVIEW

First, skim each section, noting headings and boldface items. After you have read the section, review each objective by answering the fill-in and essay-type questions that follow it. As you proceed, evaluate your performance by consulting the answers beginning on page 138. Do not continue with the next section until you understand each answer. If you need to, review or reread the section in the textbook before continuing.

Introduction and How Do We Learn?
(pp. 215–217)

Objective 1: Define *learning*, and identify two forms of learning.

1. A relatively permanent change in an organism's behavior due to experience is called

   _____ .

2. More than 200 years ago, philosophers such as John Locke and David Hume argued that an important factor in learning is our tendency to _____ events that occur in sequence. Even simple animals, such as the sea slug *Aplysia*, can learn simple _____ between stimuli. This type of learning is called

   _____ _____ .

   When the stimulus occurs repeatedly, the response diminishes. We say the organism

   _____ .

3. The type of learning in which the organism learns to associate two stimuli is _____ conditioning.

4. The tendency of organisms to associate a response and its consequence forms the basis of _____ conditioning.

5. Complex animals often learn behaviors merely by _____ others perform them.

Classical Conditioning (pp. 218–228)

Objective 2: Define *classical conditioning* and *behaviorism*, and describe the basic components of classical conditioning.

1. Classical conditioning was first explored by the Russian physiologist _____ . Early in the twentieth century, psychologist _____ urged psychologists to discard references to mental concepts in favor of studying observable behavior. This view, called _____ , influenced American psychology during the first half of that century.

2. In Pavlov's classic experiment, a tone, or

   _____ _____ ,

   is sounded just before food, the

   _____ _____ ,

   is placed in the animal's mouth.

3. An animal will salivate when food is placed in its mouth. This salivation is called the

   _____ _____ .

4. Eventually, the dogs in Pavlov's experiment would salivate on hearing the tone. This salivation is called the _____

   _____ .

Objective 3: Summarize the processes and adaptive value of acquisition, higher-order conditioning, extinction, spontaneous recovery, generalization, and discrimination.

5. The initial learning of a conditioned response is called _____ . For many conditioning situations, the optimal interval between a neutral stimulus and the US is

   _____ _____ .

6. When the US is presented prior to a neutral stimulus, conditioning _____ (does/does not) occur.

Explain why learning theorists consider classically conditioned behaviors to be biologically adaptive.

7. Michael Domjan's sexual conditioning studies with quail demonstrate that classical conditioning is highly adaptive because it helps animals _____ and _____ .

8. The procedure in which an established conditioned stimulus is paired with a different _____ stimulus, thereby establishing the latter as a _____ stimulus, is called _____-_____

   _____ . Associations that are not

consciously noticed _____ (can/cannot) influence attitudes.

9. If a CS is repeatedly presented without the US, _____ soon occurs; that is, the CR diminishes.

10. Following a rest, however, the CR reappears in response to the CS; this phenomenon is called

    _____ _____ .

11. Subjects often respond to a similar stimulus as they would to the original CS. This phenomenon is called _____ .

12. Humans and other animals can also be trained not to respond to _____ stimuli. This learned ability is called

    _____ . Being able to recognize differences among stimuli has _____ value because it lets us limit our learned responses to appropriate stimuli.

Objective 4: Discuss the importance of cognitive processes and biological predispositions in classical conditioning.

13. The early behaviorists believed that to understand behavior in various organisms, any presumption of _____ was unnecessary.

14. Experiments by Robert Rescorla and Allan Wagner demonstrate that a CS must reliably _____ the US for an association to develop and, more generally, that _____ processes play a role in conditioning. It is as if the animal learns to _____ that the US will occur.

15. Researcher Martin Seligman found that dogs strapped in a harness and given repeated shocks, with no opportunity to avoid them, learned a sense of _____ . When they could escape the shocks, they _____ (did/did not). This passive resignation is called

    _____ _____ .

16. The importance of cognitive processes in human conditioning is demonstrated by the failure of classical conditioning as a treatment for

   _____ _____ .

17. Some psychologists once believed that any natural _____ could be conditioned to any neutral _____ .

18. John Garcia discovered that rats would associate _____ with taste but not with other stimuli. Garcia found that taste-aversion conditioning _____ (would/would not) occur when the delay between the CS and the US was more than an hour. Conditioning is speedier, stronger, and more durable when the CS is _____ relevant.

19. Results such as these demonstrate that the principles of learning are constrained by the _____ predispositions of each animal species and that they help each species _____ to its environment. They also demonstrate the importance of different

   _____ _____

   _____ in understanding complex phenomena.

Objective 5: Summarize Pavlov's contribution to our understanding of learning and to improvements in human health and well-being.

20. Classical conditioning is one way that virtually all organisms learn to _____ to their environment.

21. Another aspect of Pavlov's legacy is that he showed how a process such as learning could be studied _____ .

Explain why the study of classical conditioning is important.

22. Through classical conditioning, drug users often feel a _____ when they are in the _____ associated with previous highs.

23. Research studies demonstrate that the body's immune system _____ (can/cannot) be classically conditioned.

Describe the experiment by John Watson and Rosalie Rayner.

Operant Conditioning (pp. 218–242)

Objective 6: Identify the two major characteristics that distinguish classical conditioning from operant conditioning.

1. Classical conditioning associates _____ stimuli with stimuli that trigger responses that are _____ . Thus, in this form of conditioning, the organism _____ (does/does not) control the responses.

2. The reflexive responses of classical conditioning involve _____ behavior.

3. In contrast, behavior that is more spontaneous and that is influenced by its consequences is called _____ behavior.

Objective 7: Describe the process of operant conditioning, including the shaping procedure.

4. B. F. Skinner used Thorndike's _____

   _____ _____

   as a starting point in developing a *behavioral technology*. This principle states that _____ behavior is likely to

   _____ .

5. Skinner designed an apparatus, called the

   _____ _____ , to

   investigate learning in animals.

6. The procedure in which a person teaches an animal to perform an intricate behavior by building up to it in small steps is called _____ . This method involves reinforcing successive _____ of the desired behavior.

7. In experiments to determine what an animal can perceive, researchers have found that animals are capable of forming _____ and _____ between stimuli. Similar experiments have been conducted with babies, who also can't verbalize their responses.

8. A situation, event, or signal that a certain response will be reinforced is a _____ _____ .

Objective 8: Identify the different types of reinforcers, and describe the major schedules of reinforcement.

9. An event that increases the frequency of a preceding response is a _____ .

10. A stimulus that strengthens a response by presenting a typically pleasurable stimulus after a response is a _____ _____ .

11. A stimulus that strengthens a response by reducing or removing an aversive (unpleasant) stimulus is a _____ _____ .

12. Reinforcers, such as food and shock, that are related to basic needs and therefore do not rely on learning are called _____ _____ . Reinforcers that must be conditioned and therefore derive their power through association are called _____ _____ .

13. Children who are able to delay gratification tend to become _____ (more/less) socially competent and high achieving as they mature.

14. Immediate reinforcement _____ (is/is not) more effective than its alternative, _____ reinforcement. This explains in part the difficulty that gamblers have in quitting playing the slot machines.

15. The procedure involving reinforcement of each and every response is called _____ _____ . Under these conditions, learning is _____ (rapid/slow). When this type of reinforcement is discontinued, extinction is _____ (rapid/slow).

16. The procedure in which responses are reinforced only part of the time is called _____ reinforcement. Under these conditions, learning is generally _____ (faster/slower) than it is with continuous reinforcement. Behavior reinforced in this manner is _____ (very/not very) resistant to extinction.

17. When behavior is reinforced after a set number of responses, a _____-_____ schedule is in effect.

18. Three-year-old Yusef knows that if he cries when he wants a treat, his mother will sometimes give in. When, as in this case, reinforcement occurs after an unpredictable number of responses, a _____-_____ schedule is being used.

19. Reinforcement of the first response after a set interval of time defines the _____-_____ schedule. An example of this schedule is _____ .

20. When the first response after varying amounts of time is reinforced, a _____-_____ schedule is in effect.

Describe the typical patterns of response under fixed-interval, fixed-ratio, variable-interval, and variable-ratio schedules of reinforcement.

Objective 9: Discuss how punishment and negative reinforcement differ, and list some drawbacks of punishment as a behavior-control technique.

21. An aversive consequence that decreases the likelihood of the behavior that preceded it is called _____ . If an aversive stimulus is administered, it is called _____ _____ . If a desirable stimulus is withdrawn, it is called _____ _____ .

22. Because punished behavior is merely _____ , it may reappear. Also, punishment teaches _____ , that behavior that is unacceptable in one context may be acceptable in another.

23. Punishment can also lead to _____ and a sense of helplessness, as well as to the association of the aversive event with _____ .

24. Punishment also often increases _____ and does not guide the individual toward more desirable behavior.

Objective 10: Explain the importance of cognitive processes and biological predispositions in operant conditioning.

25. Skinner and other behaviorists resisted the growing belief that expectations, perceptions, and other _____ processes have a valid place in the science of psychology.

26. When a well-learned route in a maze is blocked, rats sometimes choose an alternative route, acting as if they were consulting a _____ _____ .

    During their explorations, the rats may have experienced _____ _____ , learning that becomes apparent only when there is some incentive to demonstrate it.

27. Some learning occurs after little or no interaction with our environment. Our sudden solution to a problem may reflect a flash of _____ .

28. Excessive rewards may undermine _____ _____ , which is the desire to perform a behavior for its own sake. The motivation to seek external rewards and avoid punishment is called _____ _____ .

29. Operant conditioning _____ (is/is not) constrained by an animal's biological predispositions.

30. For instance, with animals it is difficult to use food as a _____ to _____ behaviors that are not naturally associated with _____ .

31. Biological constraints predispose organisms to learn associations that are naturally _____ . When animals revert to their biologically predisposed patterns, they are exhibiting what is called _____ .

Objective 11: Describe the controversy over Skinner's views of human behavior, and identify some ways to apply operant conditioning principles at school, in sports, at work, and at home.

32. Skinner's views were controversial because he insisted that _____ influences, rather than _____ _____ and _____ , shape behavior.

33. Skinner also advocated the use of _____ principles to influence people in ways that promote more desirable _____ .

34. Skinner's critics argued that he _____ people by neglecting their personal _____ and by seeking to _____ their actions.

35. The use of teaching machines and programmed textbooks was an early application of the operant conditioning procedure of _____ to education. Online _____ systems, software that is _____ , and _____-based learning are newer examples of this application of operant

principles. Reinforcement principles can also be used to enhance _____ abilities by shaping successive approximations of new skills.

36. In boosting productivity in the workplace, positive reinforcement is _____ (more/less) effective when applied to specific behaviors than when given to reward general merit and when the desired performance is well defined and _____ . For such behaviors, immediate reinforcement is _____ (more/no more) effective than delayed reinforcement.

37. In using operant conditioning to change your own behavior, you would follow these four steps

    a. _____

    b. _____

    c. _____

    d. _____

38. A system for recording a physiological response and providing information concerning it is called _____ . The instrument used in this system was supposed to provide the individual with a means of _____ a particular physiological response, but it seems to work best on _____

    _____ .

Objective 12: Identify the major similarities and differences between classical and operant conditioning.

39. Classical conditioning and operant conditioning are both forms of _____

    _____ .

40. Both types of conditioning involve similar processes of _____ ,

    _____ , _____

    _____ , _____ ,

    and _____ .

41. Classical and operant conditioning are both subject to the influences of _____ processes and _____ predispositions.

42. Through classical conditioning, an organism associates different _____ that it does not _____ and responds

    _____ .

43. Through operant conditioning, an organism associates its _____ _____ with their _____ .

Learning by Observation (pp. 242–249)

Objective 13: Describe the process of observational learning, and Bandura's findings on what determines whether we will imitate a model.

1. Learning by observing and imitating others is called _____ , or _____ . This form of learning _____ (occurs/does not occur) in species other than our own.

2. Neuroscientists have found _____ neurons in the brain's _____ lobe that provide a neural basis for _____ learning. These neurons have been observed to fire when monkeys perform a simple task and when they _____ . This type of neuron _____ (has/has not) been found in human brains.

3. By age _____ , infants will imitate novel gestures. By age _____ , they will imitate acts modeled on TV. Mirror neurons help give rise to children's _____ and their _____ _____ .

4. The psychologist best known for research on observational learning is _____ .

5. In one experiment, the child who viewed an adult punch an inflatable doll played _____ (more/less) aggressively than the child who had not observed the adult.

6. Bandura believes people imitate a model because of _____ and _____ , those received by the model as well as by imitators.

7. We are especially likely to imitate people we perceive as _____ to ourselves, as _____ , or as _____ .

Objective 14: Discuss the impact of prosocial modeling and the relationship between watching violent TV and antisocial behavior.

8. Children will also model positive, or
   _____ , behaviors. Models are also most effective when their words and actions are
   _____ .

9. Modeling may also have _____ effects. This fact may help explain why
   _____ parents might have
   _____ children. However,
   _____ factors may also be involved.

10. Children in developed countries spend more time
    _____ _____ than they spend in school.

11. Compared with the real world, television depicts a much higher percentage of crimes as being
    _____ in nature.

12. Correlational studies _____
    (link/do not link) watching television violence with violent behavior.

13. Correlation does not prove _____ .
    Most researchers believe that watching violence on television _____ (does/does not) lead to aggressive behavior.

14. The violence-viewing effect stems from several factors, including _____ of observed aggression and the tendency of prolonged exposure to violence to _____ viewers.

PROGRESS TEST 1

Multiple-Choice Questions

Circle your answers to the following questions and check them with the answers beginning on page 139. If your answer is incorrect, read the explanation for why it is incorrect and then consult the appropriate pages of the text (in parentheses following the correct answer).

1. *Learning* is best defined as
   a. any behavior produced by an organism without being provoked.
   b. a change in the behavior of an organism.
   c. a relatively permanent change in the behavior of an organism due to experience.
   d. behavior based on operant rather than respondent conditioning.

2. The type of learning associated with Skinner is
   a. classical conditioning.
   b. operant conditioning.
   c. respondent conditioning.
   d. observational learning.

3. In Pavlov's original experiment with dogs, the meat served as a
   a. CS.   c. US.
   b. CR.   d. UR.

4. In Pavlov's original experiment with dogs, the tone was initially a(n) _____ stimulus; after it was paired with meat, it became a(n) _____ stimulus.
   a. conditioned; neutral
   b. neutral; conditioned
   c. conditioned; unconditioned
   d. unconditioned; conditioned

5. To obtain a reward, a monkey learns to press a lever when a 1000-Hz tone is on but not when a 1200-Hz tone is on. What kind of training is this?
   a. extinction
   b. generalization
   c. classical conditioning
   d. discrimination

6. Which of the following statements concerning reinforcement is correct?
   a. Learning is most rapid with intermittent reinforcement, but continuous reinforcement produces the greatest resistance to extinction.
   b. Learning is most rapid with continuous reinforcement, but intermittent reinforcement produces the greatest resistance to extinction.
   c. Learning is fastest and resistance to extinction is greatest after continuous reinforcement.
   d. Learning is fastest and resistance to extinction is greatest following intermittent reinforcement.

7. Martin Seligman has found that humans and animals who are exposed to aversive events they cannot escape may develop
   a. mirror neurons.
   b. a cognitive map.
   c. learned helplessness.
   d. an unconditioned response.

8. The highest and most consistent rate of response is produced by a _____ schedule.
   a. fixed-ratio
   b. variable-ratio
   c. fixed-interval
   d. variable-interval

9. A response that leads to the removal of an unpleasant stimulus is one being
   a. positively reinforced.
   b. negatively reinforced.
   c. punished.
   d. extinguished.

10. When a conditioned stimulus is presented without an accompanying unconditioned stimulus, _____ will soon take place.
    a. generalization
    b. discrimination
    c. extinction
    d. aversion

11. One difference between classical and operant conditioning is that
    a. in classical conditioning, the responses operate on the environment to produce rewarding or punishing stimuli.
    b. in operant conditioning, the responses are triggered by preceding stimuli.
    c. in classical conditioning, the responses are automatically triggered by stimuli.
    d. in operant conditioning, the responses are reflexive.

12. In Garcia and Koelling's studies of taste-aversion learning, rats learned to associate
    a. taste with electric shock.
    b. sights and sounds with sickness.
    c. taste with sickness.
    d. taste and sounds with electric shock.

13. In Pavlov's original experiment with dogs, salivation to meat was the
    a. CS.
    b. CR.
    c. US.
    d. UR.

14. Learning by imitating others' behaviors is called _____ learning. The researcher best known for studying this type of learning is _____ .
    a. secondary; Skinner
    b. observational; Bandura
    c. secondary; Pavlov
    d. observational; Watson

15. Punishment is a controversial way of controlling behavior because
    a. the behavior is forgotten.
    b. punishing stimuli often create fear.
    c. punishment often decreases aggressiveness.
    d. punishment prevents the child from learning discrimination.

16. Classical conditioning experiments by Robert Rescorla and Allan Wagner demonstrate that an important factor in conditioning is
    a. the research participant's age.
    b. the strength of the stimuli.
    c. the predictability of an association.
    d. the similarity of stimuli.

17. Which of the following is an example of reinforcement?
    a. presenting a positive stimulus after a response
    b. removing an unpleasant stimulus after a response
    c. being told that you have done a good job
    d. All of these are examples.

18. When a sea slug is disturbed by a squirt of water, it protectively withdraws its gill. If the squirts continue, the withdrawal response diminishes. This illustrates
    a. discrimination.
    b. spontaneous recovery.
    c. habituation.
    d. shaping.

19. For the most rapid conditioning, a CS should be presented
    a. about 1 second after the US.
    b. about one-half second before the US.
    c. about 15 seconds before the US.
    d. at the same time as the US.

20. Mirror neurons are found in the brain's _____ and are believed to be the neural basis for _____ .
    a. frontal lobe; observational learning
    b. frontal lobe; classical conditioning
    c. temporal lobe; operant conditioning
    d. temporal lobe; observational learning

Matching Items

Match each definition or description with the appropriate term.

Definitions or Descriptions

_____ 1. presentation of a desired stimulus
_____ 2. tendency for similar stimuli to evoke a CR
_____ 3. removal of an aversive stimulus
_____ 4. an innately reinforcing stimulus
_____ 5. an acquired reinforcer
_____ 6. responses are reinforced after an unpredictable amount of time
_____ 7. the motivation to perform a behavior for its own sake
_____ 8. reinforcing closer and closer approximations of a behavior
_____ 9. the reappearance of a weakened CR
_____ 10. a sudden and often novel realization of the solution to a problem
_____ 11. presentation of an aversive stimulus
_____ 12. learning that becomes apparent only after reinforcement is provided
_____ 13. each and every response is reinforced
_____ 14. a desire to perform a behavior due to promised rewards

Terms

a. shaping
b. punishment
c. spontaneous recovery
d. latent learning
e. positive reinforcement
f. negative reinforcement
g. primary reinforcer
h. generalization
i. conditioned reinforcer
j. continuous reinforcement
k. variable-interval schedule
l. extrinsic motivation
m. intrinsic motivation
n. insight

PROGRESS TEST 2

Progress Test 2 should be completed during a final unit review. Answer the following questions after you thoroughly understand the correct answers for the section reviews and Progress Test 1.

Multiple-Choice Questions

1. During extinction, the _____ is omitted; as a result, the _____ seems to disappear.
   a. US; UR
   b. CS; CR
   c. US; CR
   d. CS; UR

2. In the experiment by John Watson and Rosalie Rayner, the loud noise was the _____ and the white rat was the

   _____ .

   a. CS; CR
   b. US; CS
   c. CS; US
   d. US; CR

3. In which of the following may classical conditioning play a role?
   a. emotional problems
   b. the body's immune response
   c. helping drug addicts
   d. in all of these cases

4. Shaping is a(n) _____ technique for _____ a behavior.
   a. operant; establishing
   b. operant; suppressing
   c. respondent; establishing
   d. respondent; suppressing

5. In Pavlov's studies of classical conditioning of a dog's salivary responses, spontaneous recovery occurred
   a. during acquisition, when the CS was first paired with the US.
   b. during extinction, when the CS was first presented by itself.
   c. when the CS was reintroduced following extinction of the CR and a rest period.
   d. during discrimination training, when several conditioned stimuli were introduced.

6. For operant conditioning to be most effective, when should the reinforcers be presented in relation to the desired response?
   a. immediately before
   b. immediately after
   c. at the same time as
   d. at least a half hour before

7. In distinguishing between negative reinforcers and punishment, we note that

    a. punishment, but not negative reinforcement, involves use of an aversive stimulus.

    b. in contrast to punishment, negative reinforcement decreases the likelihood of a response by the presentation of an aversive stimulus.

    c. in contrast to punishment, negative reinforcement increases the likelihood of a response by the presentation of an aversive stimulus.

    d. in contrast to punishment, negative reinforcement increases the likelihood of a response by the termination of an aversive stimulus.

8. The "piecework," or commission, method of payment is an example of which reinforcement schedule?

    a. fixed-interval   c. fixed-ratio

    b. variable-interval   d. variable-ratio

9. Putting on your coat when it is cold outside is a behavior that is maintained by

    a. discrimination learning.

    b. punishment.

    c. negative reinforcement.

    d. classical conditioning.

10. On an intermittent reinforcement schedule, reinforcement is given

    a. in very small amounts.

    b. randomly.

    c. for successive approximations of a desired behavior.

    d. only some of the time.

11. You teach your dog to fetch the paper by giving him a cookie each time he does so. This is an example of

    a. operant conditioning.

    b. classical conditioning.

    c. conditioned reinforcement.

    d. partial reinforcement.

12. In promoting observational learning, the most effective models are those that we perceive as

    a. similar to ourselves.

    b. older than us.

    c. authoritative.

    d. attractive.

13. A cognitive map is a

    a. mental representation of one's environment.

    b. sequence of thought processes leading from one idea to another.

    c. set of instructions detailing the most effective means of teaching a particular concept.

    d. biological predisposition to learn a particular skill.

14. After exploring a complicated maze for several days, a rat subsequently ran the maze with very few errors when food was placed in the goal box for the first time. This performance illustrates

    a. classical conditioning.

    b. discrimination learning.

    c. observational learning.

    d. latent learning.

15. Leon's psychology teacher has scheduled a test every third week of the term. Leon will probably study the most just before a test and the least just after a test. This is because the schedule of tests is reinforcing studying according to which schedule?

    a. fixed-ratio   c. fixed-interval

    b. variable-ratio   d. variable-interval

16. Operant conditioning is to _____ as classical conditioning is to _____ .

    a. Ivan Pavlov; John Watson

    b. B. F. Skinner; Albert Bandura

    c. Ivan Pavlov; B. F. Skinner

    d. B. F. Skinner; Ivan Pavlov

17. Online testing systems and interactive software are applications of the operant conditioning principles of

    a. shaping and immediate reinforcement.

    b. immediate reinforcement and punishment.

    c. shaping and primary reinforcement.

    d. continuous reinforcement and punishment.

18. Which of the following is the best example of a conditioned reinforcer?

    a. putting on a coat on a cold day

    b. relief from pain after the dentist stops drilling your teeth

    c. receiving a cool drink after washing your mother's car on a hot day

    d. receiving an approving nod from the boss for a job well done

19. Experiments on taste-aversion learning demonstrate that

    a. for the conditioning of certain stimuli, the US need not immediately follow the CS.

    b. any perceivable stimulus can become a CS.

    c. all animals are biologically primed to associate illness with the taste of a tainted food.

    d. for learning to occur, the US must precede the CS.

20. Regarding the impact of watching television violence on children, most researchers believe that
    a. aggressive children simply prefer violent programs.
    b. television simply reflects, rather than contributes to, violent social trends.
    c. watching violence on television leads to aggressive behavior.
    d. there is only a weak correlation between exposure to violence and aggressive behavior.

True–False Items

Indicate whether each statement is true or false by placing *T* or *F* in the blank next to the item.

_____ 1. Operant conditioning involves behavior that is primarily reflexive.
_____ 2. The optimal interval between CS and US is about 15 seconds.
_____ 3. Negative reinforcement decreases the likelihood that a response will recur.
_____ 4. The learning of a new behavior proceeds most rapidly with continuous reinforcement.
_____ 5. As a rule, variable schedules of reinforcement produce more consistent rates of responding than fixed schedules.
_____ 6. Cognitive processes are of relatively little importance in learning.
_____ 7. Although punishment may be effective in suppressing behavior, it can have several undesirable side effects.
_____ 8. All animals, including rats and birds, are biologically predisposed to associate taste cues with sickness.
_____ 9. Whether the CS or US is presented first seems not to matter in terms of the ease of classical conditioning.
_____ 10. Spontaneous recovery refers to the tendency of extinguished behaviors to reappear suddenly.
_____ 11. Researchers have discovered brain neurons that fire when a person performs a task *or* when another person is observed performing the same task.
_____ 12. An organism's response to a stimulus increases the more often the organism is exposed to that stimulus.
_____ 13. A discriminative stimulus signals that a response will be reinforced.

PSYCHOLOGY APPLIED

Answer these questions the day before a test as a final check on your understanding of the unit's terms and concepts.

Multiple-Choice Questions

1. You always rattle the box of dog biscuits before giving your dog a treat. As you do so, your dog salivates. Rattling the box is a _____ ; your dog's salivation is a _____ .
   a. CS; CR   c. US; CR
   b. CS; UR   d. US; UR

2. You are expecting an important letter in the mail. As the regular delivery time approaches you glance more and more frequently out the window, searching for the letter carrier. Your behavior in this situation typifies that associated with which schedule of reinforcement?
   a. fixed-ratio   c. fixed-interval
   b. variable-ratio   d. variable-interval

3. Jack finally takes out the garbage in order to get his father to stop pestering him. Jack's behavior is being influenced by
   a. positive reinforcement.
   b. negative reinforcement.
   c. a primary reinforcer.
   d. punishment.

4. Mrs. Ramirez often tells her children that it is important to buckle their seat belts while riding in the car, but she rarely does so herself. Her children will probably learn to
   a. use their seat belts and tell others it is important to do so.
   b. use their seat belts but not tell others it is important to do so.
   c. tell others it is important to use seat belts but rarely use them themselves.
   d. neither tell others that seat belts are important nor use them.

5. A pigeon can easily be taught to flap its wings to avoid shock but not for food reinforcement. This is most likely so because
   a. pigeons are biologically predisposed to flap their wings to escape aversive events and to use their beaks to obtain food.
   b. shock is a more motivating stimulus for birds than food is.
   c. hungry animals have difficulty delaying their eating long enough to learn *any* new skill.
   d. an extinguished response will usually recover after a couple of days.

6. From a casino owner's viewpoint, which of the following jackpot-payout schedules would be the most desirable for reinforcing customer use of a slot machine?
   a. variable-ratio   c. variable-interval
   b. fixed-ratio   d. fixed-interval

7. After discovering that her usual route home was closed due to road repairs, Sharetta used her knowledge of the city and sense of direction to find an alternate route. This is an example of
   a. latent learning.
   b. observational learning.
   c. shaping.
   d. using a cognitive map.

For questions 8–11, use the following information. As a child, you were playing in the yard one day when a neighbor's cat wandered over. Your mother (who has a terrible fear of animals) screamed and snatched you into her arms. Her behavior caused you to cry. You now have a fear of cats.

8. Identify the CS.
   a. your mother's behavior   c. the cat
   b. your crying   d. your fear today

9. Identify the US.
   a. your mother's behavior   c. the cat
   b. your crying   d. your fear today

10. Identify the CR.
   a. your mother's behavior   c. the cat
   b. your crying   d. your fear today

11. Identify the UR.
   a. your mother's behavior   c. the cat
   b. your crying   d. your fear today

12. The manager of a manufacturing plant wishes to use positive reinforcement to increase the productivity of workers. Which of the following procedures would probably be the most effective?
   a. Deserving employees are given a general merit bonus at the end of each fiscal year.
   b. A productivity goal that seems attainable, yet is unrealistic, is set for each employee.
   c. Employees are given immediate bonuses for specific behaviors related to productivity.
   d. Employees who fail to meet standards of productivity receive pay cuts.

13. Bill once had a blue car that was in the shop more than it was out. Since then he will not even consider owning blue- or green-colored cars. Bill's aversion to green cars is an example of
   a. discrimination.
   b. generalization.
   c. latent learning.
   d. extinction.

14. After watching coverage of the Olympics on television recently, Lynn and Susan have been staging their own "summer games." Which of the following best accounts for their behavior?
   a. classical conditioning   c. latent learning
   b. observational learning   d. shaping

15. Two groups of rats receive classical conditioning trials in which a tone and electric shock are presented. For Group 1 the electric shock always follows the tone. For Group 2 the tone and shock occur randomly. Which of the following is likely to result?
   a. The tone will become a CS for Group 1 but not for Group 2.
   b. The tone will become a CS for Group 2 but not for Group 1.
   c. The tone will become a CS for both groups.
   d. The tone will not become a CS for either group.

16. Last evening May-ling ate her first cheeseburger and french fries at an American fast-food restaurant. A few hours later she became ill. It can be expected that
   a. May-ling will develop an aversion to the sight of a cheeseburger and french fries.
   b. May-ling will develop an aversion to the taste of a cheeseburger and french fries.
   c. May-ling will not associate her illness with the food she ate.
   d. May-ling will associate her sickness with something she experienced immediately before she became ill.

17. Reggie's mother tells him that he can watch TV after he cleans his room. Evidently, Reggie's mother is attempting to use _____ to increase room cleaning.
   a. operant conditioning
   b. secondary reinforcement
   c. positive reinforcement
   d. all of these procedures

18. Which of the following is an example of shaping?
    a. A dog learns to salivate at the sight of a box of dog biscuits.
    b. A new driver learns to stop at an intersection when the light changes to red.
    c. A parrot is rewarded first for making any sound, then for making a sound similar to "Laura," and then for "speaking" its owner's name.
    d. A psychology student reinforces a laboratory rat only occasionally, to make its behavior more resistant to extinction.

19. Lars, a shoe salesman, is paid every two weeks, whereas Tom receives a commission for each pair of shoes he sells. Evidently, Lars is paid on a _____ schedule of reinforcement, and Tom on a _____ schedule of reinforcement.
    a. fixed-ratio; fixed-interval
    b. continuous; intermittent
    c. fixed-interval; fixed-ratio
    d. variable-interval; variable-ratio

20. Nancy decided to take introductory psychology because she has always been interested in human behavior. Jack enrolled in the same course because he thought it would be easy. Nancy's behavior was motivated by _____ , Jack's by _____ .
    a. extrinsic motivation; intrinsic motivation
    b. intrinsic motivation; extrinsic motivation
    c. drives; incentives
    d. incentives; drives

Essay Question

Describe the best way for a pet owner to condition her dog to roll over. (Use the space below to list the points you want to make, and organize them. Then write the essay on a separate piece of paper.)

KEY TERMS

Using your own words, on a piece of paper write a brief definition or explanation of each of the following terms.

1. learning
2. habituation
3. associative learning
4. classical conditioning
5. behaviorism
6. unconditioned response (UR)
7. unconditioned stimulus (US)
8. conditioned response (CR)
9. conditioned stimulus (CS)
10. acquisition
11. higher-order conditioning
12. extinction
13. spontaneous recovery
14. generalization
15. discrimination
16. learned helplessness
17. respondent behavior
18. operant conditioning
19. operant behavior
20. law of effect
21. operant chamber (Skinner box)
22. shaping
23. discriminative stimulus
24. reinforcer
25. positive reinforcement
26. negative reinforcement
27. primary reinforcers
28. conditioned reinforcers
29. continuous reinforcement
30. partial (intermittent) reinforcement
31. fixed-ratio schedule
32. variable-ratio schedule
33. fixed-interval schedule
34. variable-interval schedule
35. punishment
36. cognitive map

37. latent learning
38. insight
39. intrinsic motivation
40. extrinsic motivation
41. biofeedback
42. observational learning
43. modeling
44. mirror neurons
45. prosocial behavior

ANSWERS

Unit Review

Introduction and *How Do We Learn?*

1. learning
2. associate; associations; associative learning; habituates
3. classical
4. operant
5. observing

Classical Conditioning

1. Ivan Pavlov; John Watson; behaviorism
2. conditioned stimulus; unconditioned stimulus
3. unconditioned response
4. conditioned response
5. acquisition; one-half second
6. does not

Learning theorists consider classical conditioning to be adaptive because conditioned responses help organisms to *prepare* for good or bad events (unconditioned stimuli).

7. survive; reproduce
8. neutral; conditioned; higher-order conditioning; can
9. extinction
10. spontaneous recovery
11. generalization
12. similar; discrimination; adaptive
13. cognition
14. predict; cognitive; expect
15. helplessness; did not; learned helplessness
16. alcohol dependency
17. response; stimulus
18. sickness; would; ecologically
19. biological; adapt; levels of analysis
20. adapt
21. objectively

Classical conditioning led to the discovery of general principles of learning that are the same for all species tested, including humans. Classical conditioning also provided an example to the young field of psychology of how complex, internal processes could be studied objectively. In addition, classical conditioning has proven to have many helpful applications to human health and well-being.

22. craving; context
23. can

In Watson and Rayner's experiment, classical conditioning was used to condition fear of a rat in Albert, an 11-month-old infant. When Albert touched the white rat (neutral stimulus), a loud noise (unconditioned stimulus) was sounded. After several pairings of the rat with the noise, Albert began crying at the mere sight of the rat. The rat had become a conditioned stimulus, triggering a conditioned response of fear.

Operant Conditioning

1. neutral; automatic; does not
2. respondent
3. operant
4. law of effect; rewarded; recur
5. Skinner box (operant chamber)
6. shaping; approximations
7. concepts; discriminating
8. discriminative stimulus
9. reinforcer
10. positive reinforcer
11. negative reinforcer
12. primary reinforcers; conditioned (secondary) reinforcers
13. more
14. is; delayed
15. continuous reinforcement; rapid; rapid
16. partial (intermittent); slower; very
17. fixed-ratio
18. variable-ratio
19. fixed-interval; checking the mail as delivery time approaches
20. variable-interval

Following reinforcement on a fixed-interval schedule, there is a pause in responding and then an increasing rate of response as time for the next reinforcement draws near. On a fixed-ratio schedule there also is a post-reinforcement pause, followed, however, by a return to a consistent, high rate of response. Both kinds of variable schedules produce steadier rates of response, without the pauses associated with fixed schedules. In general, schedules linked to responses produce higher response rates and variable schedules produce more consistent responding than the related fixed schedules.

21. punishment; positive punishment; negative punishment
22. suppressed; discrimination
23. fear; the person who administered it
24. aggressiveness
25. cognitive
26. cognitive map; latent learning
27. insight
28. intrinsic motivation; extrinsic motivation
29. is
30. reinforcer; shape; food
31. adaptive; instinctive drift
32. external; internal thoughts; feelings
33. operant; behavior
34. dehumanized; freedom; control
35. shaping; testing; interactive; Web; athletic
36. more; achievable; more
37. a. State your goal.

    b. Monitor the behavior (when and where it occurs).

    c. Reinforce the desired behavior.

    d. Reduce the rewards gradually.
38. biofeedback; controlling; tension headaches
39. associative learning
40. acquisition; extinction; spontaneous recovery; generalization; discrimination
41. cognitive; biological
42. stimuli; control; automatically
43. operant behaviors; consequences

Learning by Observation

1. modeling; observational learning; occurs
2. mirror; frontal; observational; observe other monkeys performing the same task; has
3. 8 to 16 months; 14 months; empathy; theory of mind
4. Albert Bandura
5. more

6. rewards; punishments
7. similar; successful; admirable
8. prosocial; consistent
9. antisocial; abusive; aggressive; genetic
10. watching television
11. violent
12. link
13. causation; does
14. imitation; desensitize

Progress Test 1

Multiple-Choice Questions

1. **c.** is the answer. (p. 215)
   a. This answer is incorrect because it simply describes any behavior that is automatic rather than being triggered by a specific stimulus.

   b. This answer is too general, since behaviors can change for reasons other than learning.

   d. Respondently conditioned behavior also satisfies the criteria of our definition of learning.

2. **b.** is the answer. (p. 229)
   a. & c. Classical conditioning is associated with Pavlov; respondent conditioning is another name for classical conditioning.

   d. Observational learning is most closely associated with Bandura.

3. **c.** is the answer. Meat automatically triggers the response of salivation and is therefore an unconditioned stimulus. (p. 219)
   a. A conditioned stimulus acquires its response-triggering powers through learning. A dog does not learn to salivate to meat.

   b. & d. Responses are behaviors triggered in the organism, in this case the dog's salivation. The meat is a stimulus.

4. **b.** is the answer. Prior to its pairing with meat (the US), the tone did not trigger salivation and was therefore a neutral stimulus. Afterward, the tone triggered salivation (the CR) and was therefore a conditioned stimulus (CS). (p. 219)
   c. & d. Unconditioned stimuli, such as meat, innately trigger responding. Pavlov's dogs had to learn to associate the tone with the food.

5. **d.** is the answer. In learning to distinguish between the conditioned stimulus and another, similar stimulus, the monkey has received training in discrimination. (p. 222)
   a. In extinction training, a stimulus and/or response is allowed to go unreinforced.

   b. Generalization training involves responding to stimuli similar to the conditioned stimulus; here the monkey is being trained not to respond to a similar stimulus.

c. This cannot be classical conditioning since the monkey is acting in order to obtain a reward. Thus, this is an example of operant conditioning.

6. **b.** is the answer. A continuous association will naturally be easier to learn than one that occurs on only some occasions, so learning is most rapid with continuous reinforcement. Yet, once the continuous association is no longer there, as in extinction training, extinction will occur more rapidly than it would have had the organism not always experienced reinforcement. (p. 232)

7. **c.** is the answer. (p. 223)

8. **b.** is the answer. (p. 233)
   a. With fixed-ratio schedules, there is a pause following each reinforcement.
   c. & d. Because reinforcement is not contingent on the rate of response, interval schedules, especially fixed-interval schedules, produce lower response rates than ratio schedules.

9. **b.** is the answer. (p. 231)
   a. Positive reinforcement involves presenting a favorable stimulus following a response.
   c. Punishment involves presenting an unpleasant stimulus following a response.
   d. In extinction, a previously reinforced response is no longer followed by reinforcement. In this situation, a response causes a stimulus to be terminated or removed.

10. **c.** is the answer. In this situation, the CR will decline, a phenomenon known as extinction. (p. 221)
    a. Generalization occurs when the subject makes a CR to stimuli similar to the original CS.
    b. Discrimination is when the subject does not make a CR to stimuli other than the original CS.
    d. An aversion is a CR to a CS that has been associated with an unpleasant US, such as shock or a nausea-producing drug.

11. **c.** is the answer. (p. 228)
    a. In *operant* conditioning, the responses operate on the environment.
    b. In *classical* conditioning, responses are triggered by preceding stimuli.
    d. In *classical* conditioning, responses are reflexive.

12. **c.** is the answer. (p. 224)
    a. & d. These studies also indicated that rats are biologically predisposed to associate visual and auditory stimuli, but not taste, with shock.
    b. Rats are biologically predisposed to associate taste with sickness.

13. **d.** is the answer. A dog does not have to learn to salivate to food; therefore, this response is unconditioned. (p. 219)
    a. & c. Salivation is a response, not a stimulus.

14. **b.** is the answer. (pp. 242, 244–245)
    a. Skinner is best known for studies of *operant* learning. Moreover, there is no such thing as secondary learning.
    c. Pavlov is best known for classical conditioning.
    d. Watson is best known as an early proponent of behaviorism.

15. **b.** is the answer. (p. 234)

16. **c.** is the answer. (p. 223)
    a., b., & d. Rescorla and Wagner's research did not address the importance of these factors in classical conditioning.

17. **d.** is the answer. a. is an example of positive reinforcement, b. is an example of negative reinforcement, and c. is an example of conditioned reinforcement. (p. 231)

18. **c.** is the answer. (p. 216)
    a. Discrimination is the ability to distinguish between a conditioned stimulus and other irrelevant stimuli.
    b. Spontaneous recovery is the return of an extinguished response that may occur after a period.
    d. Shaping is an operant conditioning technique involving rewarding behavior as it more closely approximates the desired behavior.

19. **b.** is the answer. (p. 220)
    a. Backward conditioning, in which the US precedes the CS, is ineffective.
    c. This interval is longer than is optimum for the most rapid acquisition of a CS-US association.
    d. Simultaneous presentation of CS and US is ineffective because it does not permit the subject to anticipate the US.

20. **a.** is the answer. (p. 243)

Matching Items

1. e (p. 231)	6. k (p. 233)	11. b (p. 234)
2. h (p. 222)	7. m (p. 237)	12. d (p. 236)
3. f (p. 231)	8. a (p. 229)	13. j (p. 232)
4. g (p. 231)	9. c (p. 221)	14. l (p. 237)
5. i (p. 231)	10. n (p. 236)	

Progress Test 2

Multiple-Choice Questions

1. **c.** is the answer. (p. 221)

2. **b.** is the answer. The loud noise automatically triggered Albert's fear and therefore functioned

as a US. After being associated with the US, the white rat acquired the power to trigger fear and thus became a CS. (p. 227)

3. **d.** is the answer. (pp. 226–227)

4. **a.** is the answer. Shaping works on operant behaviors by reinforcing successive approximations to a desired goal. (p. 229)

5. **c.** is the answer. (p. 221)
a., b., & d. Spontaneous recovery occurs after a CR has been extinguished, and in the absence of the US. The situations described here all involve the continued presentation of the US and, therefore, the further strengthening of the CR.

6. **b.** is the answer. (p. 231)
a., c., & d. Reinforcement that is delayed, presented before a response, or at the same time as a response does not always increase the response's frequency of occurrence.

7. **d.** is the answer. (p. 234)
a. Both involve an aversive stimulus.
b. All reinforcers, including negative reinforcers, increase the likelihood of a response.
c. In negative reinforcement, an aversive stimulus is withdrawn following a desirable response.

8. **c.** is the answer. Payment is given after a fixed number of pieces have been completed. (p. 232)
a. & b. Interval schedules reinforce according to the passage of time, not the amount of work accomplished.
d. Fortunately for those working on commission, the work ratio is fixed and therefore predictable.

9. **c.** is the answer. By learning to put on your coat before going outside, you have learned to reduce the aversive stimulus of the cold. (p. 231)
a. Discrimination learning involves learning to make a response in the presence of the appropriate stimulus and not other stimuli.
b. Punishment is the suppression of an undesirable response by the presentation of an aversive stimulus.
d. Putting on a coat is a response that operates on the environment. Therefore, this is an example of operant, not classical, conditioning.

10. **d.** is the answer. (p. 232)
a. Intermittent reinforcement refers to the ratio of responses to reinforcers, not the overall quantity of reinforcement delivered.
b. Unlike intermittent reinforcement, in which the delivery of reinforcement is contingent on responding, random reinforcement is delivered independently of the subject's behavior.
c. This defines the technique of shaping, not intermittent reinforcement.

11. **a.** is the answer. You are teaching your dog by rewarding him when he produces the desired behavior. (p. 229)
b. This is not classical conditioning because the cookie is a primary reinforcer presented after the operant behavior of the dog fetching the paper.
c. Food is a primary reinforcer; it satisfies an innate need.
d. Rewarding your dog each time he fetches the paper is continuous reinforcement.

12. **a.** is the answer. (p. 245)

13. **a.** is the answer. (p. 236)

14. **d.** is the answer. The rat had learned the maze but did not display this learning until reinforcement became available. (p. 236)
a. Negotiating a maze is clearly operant behavior.
b. This example does not involve learning to distinguish between stimuli.
c. This is not observational learning because the rat has no one to observe!

15. **c.** is the answer. Because reinforcement (earning a good grade on the test) is available according to the passage of time, studying is reinforced on an interval schedule. Because the interval between tests is constant, this is an example of a fixed-interval schedule. (p. 233)

16. **d.** is the answer. (pp. 218, 229)
a. Pavlov and Watson are both associated with classical conditioning.
b. Skinner is associated with operant conditioning, and Bandura is associated with observational learning.

17. **a.** is the answer. Online testing systems apply operant principles such as reinforcement, immediate feedback, and shaping to the teaching of new skills. (p. 238)
b. & d. Online testing systems provide immediate, and continuous, reinforcement for correct responses, but do not use aversive control procedures such as punishment.
c. Online testing systems are based on feedback for correct responses; this feedback constitutes conditioned, rather than primary, reinforcement.

18. **d.** is the answer. An approving nod from the boss is a conditioned reinforcer in that it doesn't satisfy an innate need but has become linked with desirable consequences. Cessation of cold, cessation of pain, and a drink are all primary reinforcers, which meet innate needs. (p. 231)

19. **a.** is the answer. Taste-aversion experiments demonstrate conditioning even with CS-US intervals as long as several hours. (p. 224)

b. Despite being perceivable, a visual or auditory stimulus cannot become a CS for illness in some animals, such as rats.

c. Some animals, such as birds, are biologically primed to associate the *appearance* of food with illness.

d. The US should always follows the CS.

20. **c.** is the answer. (p. 248)

True–False Items

1. F (p. 228)	6. F (pp. 223, 235)	10. T (p. 221)
2. F (p. 220)	7. T (p. 234)	11. T (p. 243)
3. F (p. 231)	8. F (p. 224)	12. F (p. 216)
4. T (p. 232)	9. F (p. 220)	13. T (p. 230)
5. T (p. 233)		

Psychology Applied

Multiple-Choice Questions

1. **a.** is the answer. Your dog had to learn to associate the rattling sound with the food. Rattling is therefore a conditioned, or learned, stimulus, and salivation in response to this rattling is a learned, or conditioned, response. (p. 219)

2. **c.** is the answer. Reinforcement (the letter) comes after a fixed interval, and as the likely end of the interval approaches, your behavior (glancing out the window) becomes more frequent. (p. 233)
   a. & b. These answers are incorrect because with ratio schedules, reinforcement is contingent upon the number of responses rather than on the passage of time.
   d. Assuming that the mail is delivered at about the same time each day, the interval is fixed rather than variable. Your behavior reflects this, since you glance out the window more often as the delivery time approaches.

3. **b.** is the answer. By taking out the garbage, Jack terminates an aversive stimulus—his father's nagging. (p. 231)
   a. Positive reinforcement would involve a desirable stimulus that increases the likelihood of the response that preceded it.
   c. This answer would have been correct if Jack's father had rewarded Jack for taking out the garbage by providing his favorite food.
   d. Punishment suppresses behavior; Jack is behaving in order to obtain reinforcement.

4. **c.** is the answer. Studies indicate that when a model says one thing but does another, subjects do the same and learn not to practice what they preach. (p. 246)

5. **a.** is the answer. As in this example, conditioning must be consistent with the particular organism's biological predispositions. (p. 224)
   b. Some behaviors, but certainly not all, are acquired more rapidly than others when shock is used as negative reinforcement.
   c. Pigeons are able to acquire many new behaviors when food is used as reinforcement.

6. **a.** is the answer. Ratio schedules maintain higher rates of responding—gambling in this example—than do interval schedules. Furthermore, variable schedules are not associated with the pause in responding following reinforcement that is typical of fixed schedules. The slot machine would therefore be used more often, and more consistently, if jackpots were scheduled according to a variable-ratio schedule. (p. 233)

7. **d.** is the answer. Sharetta is guided by her mental representation of the city, or cognitive map. (p. 236)
   a. Latent learning, or learning in the absence of reinforcement that is demonstrated when reinforcement becomes available, has no direct relevance to the example.
   b. Observational learning refers to learning from watching others.
   c. Shaping is the technique of reinforcing successive approximations of a desired behavior.

8. **c.** is the answer. Because the cat was associated with your mother's scream, it triggered a fear response, and is thus the CS. (p. 219)

9. **a.** is the answer. Your mother's scream and evident fear, which naturally caused you to cry, was the US. (p. 219)

10. **d.** is the answer. Your fear of cats is the CR. An acquired fear is always a conditioned response. (p. 219)

11. **b.** is the answer. Your crying, automatically triggered by your mother's scream and fear, was the UR. (p. 219)

12. **c.** is the answer. (p. 239)
    a. Positive reinforcement is most effective in boosting productivity in the workplace when specific behavior, rather than vaguely defined general merit, is rewarded. Also, immediate reinforcement is much more effective than the delayed reinforcement described in a.
    b. Positive reinforcement is most effective in boosting productivity when performance goals are achievable, rather than unrealistic.
    d. The text does not specifically discuss the use of punishment in the workplace. However, it makes the general point that although punishment may temporarily suppress unwanted behavior, it does

not guide one toward more desirable behavior. Therefore, workers who receive pay cuts for poor performance may learn nothing about how to improve their productivity.

13. **b.** is the answer. Not only is Bill extending a learned aversion to a specific blue car to all blue cars but also to cars that are green. (p. 222)
a. Whereas discrimination involves responding only to a particular stimulus, Bill is extending his aversive response to other stimuli (green cars) as well.
c. Latent learning is learning that becomes apparent only after reinforcement becomes available.
d. Extinction is the weakening of the CR when the CS is no longer followed by the US.

14. **b.** is the answer. The girls are imitating behavior they have observed and admired. (p. 242)
a. Because these behaviors are clearly willful rather than involuntary, classical conditioning plays no role.
c. Latent learning plays no role in this example.
d. Shaping is a procedure for teaching the acquisition of a new response by reinforcing successive approximations of the behavior.

15. **a.** is the answer. Classical conditioning proceeds most effectively when the CS and US are reliably paired and therefore appear predictably associated. Only for Group 1 is this likely to be true. (p. 220)

16. **b.** is the answer. (p. 223)
a., c., & d. Taste-aversion research demonstrates that humans and some other animals, such as rats, are biologically primed to associate illness with the taste of tainted food, rather than with other cues, such as the food's appearance. Moreover, taste aversions can be acquired even when the interval between the CS and the illness is several hours.

17. **d.** is the answer. By making a more preferred activity (watching TV) contingent on a less preferred activity (room cleaning), Reggie's mother is employing the operant conditioning technique of positive reinforcement. (pp. 229, 231)

18. **c.** is the answer. The parrot is reinforced for making successive approximations of a goal behavior. This defines shaping. (p. 229)
a. Shaping is an operant conditioning procedure; salivation at the sight of dog biscuits is a classically conditioned response.
b. Shaping involves the systematic reinforcement of successive approximations of a more complex behavior. In this example there is no indication that the response of stopping at the intersection involved the gradual acquisition of simpler behaviors.
d. This is an example of the partial reinforcement of an established response, rather than the shaping of a new response.

19. **c.** is the answer. Whereas Lars is paid (reinforced) after a fixed period of time (fixed-interval), Tom is reinforced for each sale (fixed-ratio) he makes. (pp. 232, 233)

20. **b.** is the answer. Wanting to do something for its own sake is intrinsic motivation; wanting to do something for a reward (in this case, presumably, a high grade) is extrinsic motivation. (p. 237)
a. The opposite is true. Nancy was motivated to take the course for its own sake, whereas Jack was evidently motivated by the likelihood of a reward in the form of a good grade.
c. & d. A good grade, such as the one Jack is expecting, is an incentive. Drives, however, are aroused states that result from physical deprivation; they are not involved in this example.

Essay Question

The first step in shaping an operant response, such as rolling over, is to find an effective reinforcer. Some sort of biscuit or dog treat is favored by animal trainers. This primary reinforcement should be accompanied by effusive praise (secondary reinforcement) whenever the dog makes a successful response.

Rolling over (the goal response) should be divided into a series of simple approximations, the first of which is a response, such as lying down on command, that is already in the dog's repertoire. This response should be reinforced several times. The next step is to issue a command, such as "Roll over," and withhold reinforcement until the dog (usually out of frustration) makes a closer approximation (such as rotating slightly in one direction). Following this example, the trainer should gradually require closer and closer approximations until the goal response is attained. When the new response has been established, the trainer should switch from continuous to partial reinforcement, in order to strengthen the skill.

Key Terms

1. **Learning** is any relatively permanent change in an organism's behavior due to experience. (p. 215)

2. **Habituation** is an organism's decreasing response to a stimulus with repeated exposure to it. (p. 216)

3. In **associative learning**, organisms learn that certain events occur together. Two variations of associative learning are classical conditioning and operant conditioning. (p. 216)

4. Also known as Pavlovian conditioning, **classical conditioning** is a type of learning in which a neutral stimulus becomes capable of triggering a conditioned response after having become associated with an unconditioned stimulus. (p. 218)

5. **Behaviorism** is the view that psychology should be an objective science that studies only observable behaviors without reference to mental processes. (p. 218)

   Example: Because he was an early advocate of the study of observable behavior, John Watson is often called the father of behaviorism.

6. In classical conditioning, the **unconditioned response (UR)** is the unlearned, involuntary response to the unconditioned stimulus. (p. 219)

7. In classical conditioning, the **unconditioned stimulus (US)** is the stimulus that naturally and automatically triggers the reflexive unconditioned response. (p. 219)

8. In classical conditioning, the **conditioned response (CR)** is the learned response to a previously neutral conditioned stimulus, which results from the acquired association between the CS and US. (p. 219)

9. In classical conditioning, the **conditioned stimulus (CS)** is an originally neutral stimulus that comes to trigger a CR after association with an unconditioned stimulus. (p. 219)

10. In a learning experiment, **acquisition** refers to the initial stage of conditioning in which the new response is established and gradually strengthened. In operant conditioning, it is the strengthening of a reinforced response. (p. 220)

11. In **higher-order conditioning,** pairing an established conditioned stimulus (CS) with a neutral stimulus may cause the latter to become a weak CS itself. (p. 220)

12. **Extinction** refers to the weakening of a CR when the CS is no longer followed by the US; in operant conditioning extinction occurs when a response is no longer reinforced. (p. 221)

13. **Spontaneous recovery** is the reappearance of an extinguished CR after a rest period. (p. 221)

14. **Generalization** refers to the tendency, once a response has been conditioned, for stimuli similar to the original CS to evoke a CR. (p. 222)

15. **Discrimination** in classical conditioning refers to the ability to distinguish the CS from similar stimuli that do not signal a US. In operant conditioning, it refers to responding differently to stimuli that signal a behavior will be reinforced or will not be reinforced. (p. 222)

16. **Learned helplessness** is the passive resignation an animal or human learns when unable to avoid repeated aversive events. (p. 223)

17. **Respondent behavior** is that which occurs as an automatic response to some stimulus. (p. 228)

    Example: In classical conditioning, conditioned and unconditioned responses are examples of **respondent behavior** in that they are automatic responses triggered by specific stimuli.

18. **Operant conditioning** is a type of learning in which behavior is strengthened if followed by a reinforcer or diminished if followed by a punisher. (p. 228)

    Example: Unlike classical conditioning, which works on automatic behaviors, **operant conditioning** works on behaviors that operate on the environment.

19. **Operant behavior** is behavior that operates on the environment, producing consequences. (p. 228)

20. E. L. Thorndike proposed the **law of effect**, which states that behaviors followed by favorable consequences are likely to recur, and that behaviors followed by unfavorable consequences become less likely. (p. 229)

21. An **operant chamber** (*Skinner box*) is an experimental chamber for the operant conditioning of an animal such as a pigeon or rat. The controlled environment enables the investigator to present visual or auditory stimuli, deliver reinforcement or punishment, and precisely measure simple responses such as bar presses or key pecking. (p. 229)

22. **Shaping** is the operant conditioning procedure for establishing a new response by reinforcing successive approximations of the desired behavior. (p. 229)

23. In operant conditioning, a **discriminative stimulus** is a stimulus that elicits a response after association with reinforcement. (p. 230)

24. In operant conditioning, a **reinforcer** is any event that strengthens the behavior it follows. (p. 230)

25. In operant conditioning, **positive reinforcement** strengthens a response by *presenting* a typically pleasurable stimulus after that response. (p. 231)

26. In operant conditioning, **negative reinforcement** strengthens a response by *removing* an aversive stimulus after that response. (p. 231)

27. The powers of **primary reinforcers** are inborn and do not depend on learning. (p. 231)

28. **Conditioned reinforcers** are stimuli that acquire their reinforcing power through their association with primary reinforcers; also called *secondary reinforcers*. (p. 231)

29. **Continuous reinforcement** is the operant procedure of reinforcing the desired response every time it occurs. In promoting the acquisition of a new response it is best to use continuous reinforcement. (p. 232)

30. **Partial (intermittent) reinforcement** is the operant procedure of reinforcing a response intermittently. A response that has been partially reinforced is much more resistant to extinction than one that has been continuously reinforced. (p. 232)

31. In operant conditioning, a **fixed-ratio schedule** is one in which reinforcement is presented after a set number of responses. (p. 232)

    Example: Continuous reinforcement is a special kind of **fixed-ratio schedule**: Reinforcement is presented after *each* response, so the ratio of reinforcements to responses is one to one.

32. In operant conditioning, a **variable-ratio schedule** is one in which reinforcement is presented after a varying number of responses. (p. 233)

33. In operant conditioning, a **fixed-interval schedule** is one in which a response is reinforced after a specified time has elapsed. (p. 233)

34. In operant conditioning, a **variable-interval schedule** is one in which responses are reinforced after varying intervals of time. (p. 233)

35. In operant conditioning, **punishment** is the presentation of an aversive stimulus, such as shock, which decreases the behavior it follows. (p. 234)

    Memory aid: People often confuse negative reinforcement and **punishment**. The former strengthens behavior, while the latter weakens it.

36. A **cognitive map** is a mental picture of one's environment. (p. 236)

37. **Latent learning** is learning that occurs in the absence of reinforcement but only becomes apparent when there is an incentive to demonstrate it. (p. 236)

38. **Insight** is a sudden and often novel realization of the solution to a problem. (p. 236)

39. **Intrinsic motivation** is the desire to perform a behavior for its own sake, rather than for some external reason, and to be effective. (p. 237)

    Memory aid: Intrinsic means "internal": A person who is **intrinsically motivated** is motivated from within.

40. **Extrinsic motivation** is the desire to perform a behavior in order to obtain a reward or avoid a punishment. (p. 237)

    Memory aid: Extrinsic means "external": A person who is extrinsically motivated is motivated by some outside factor.

41. **Biofeedback** is a system for recording, amplifying, and feeding back information regarding a subtle physiological state. (p. 241)

42. **Observational learning** is learning by watching and imitating the behavior of others. (p. 242)

43. **Modeling** is the process of watching and then imitating a specific behavior and is thus an important means through which observational learning occurs. (p. 242)

44. Found in the brain's frontal lobe, **mirror neurons** may be the neural basis for observational learning. These neurons generate impulses when certain actions are performed or when another individual who performs those actions is observed. (p. 243)

45. The opposite of antisocial behavior, **prosocial behavior** is positive, helpful, and constructive and is subject to the same principles of observational learning as is undesirable behavior, such as aggression. (p. 246)

Cognition:
7A: Memory

UNIT OVERVIEW

Unit 7A explores human memory as a system that processes information in three steps. Encoding refers to the process of putting information into the memory system. Storage is the purely passive mechanism by which information is maintained in memory. Retrieval is the process by which information is accessed from memory through recall or recognition.

Unit 7A also discusses the important role of meaning, imagery, and organization in encoding new memories, how memory is represented physically in the brain, and how forgetting may result from failure to encode or store information or to find appropriate retrieval cues. The final section of the unit discusses the issue of memory construction. How "true" are our memories of events? A particularly controversial issue in this area involves suspicious claims of long-repressed memories of sexual abuse and other traumas that are "recovered" with the aid of hypnosis and other techniques. As you study this unit, try applying some of the memory and studying tips discussed in the text.

NOTE: Answer guidelines for all Unit 7A questions begin on page 160.

UNIT REVIEW

First, skim this section, noting headings and boldface items. After you have read the section, review each objective by completing the sentences and answering the questions that follow it. As you proceed, evaluate your performance by consulting the answers beginning on page 160. Do not continue with the next section until you understand each answer. If you need to, review or reread the section in the textbook before continuing.

The Phenomenon of Memory and Information Processing (pp. 255–278)

1. Learning that persists over time indicates the existence of _____ for that learning.

Objective 1: Describe Atkinson-Shiffrin's classic three-stage processing model of memory, and explain how the concept of working memory clarifies the processing that occurs in short-term memory.

2. Both human memory and computer memory can be viewed as _____-_____ systems that perform three tasks: _____ , _____ , and _____ . The model called _____ views memory as emerging from interconnected _____ _____ .

3. The classic model of memory has been Atkinson and Shiffrin's _____-_____ _____ model. According to this model, we first record information as a fleeting _____ . _____ , from which it is processed into _____-_____ memory, where the information is _____ through rehearsal into _____ -_____ memory for later retrieval.

4. A modified form of this model accommodates two important new concepts. First, some information is processed _____ and _____ into long-term memory, without our _____ awareness.

5. Second, the phenomenon of short-term memory has been clarified by the concept of _____ memory, which focuses more on the _____ processing of briefly stored information. This form of memory processes incoming _____ as well as information retrieved from _____-_____ memory.

Objective 2: Describe the types of information we encode automatically, and contrast effortful processing with automatic processing, giving examples of each.

6. Most computers engage in _____ processing of information. The human brain is capable of _____ processing. Encoding that does not require conscious attention or effort is called _____ _____ . Some processing requires effort at first but with _____ it becomes effortless.

Give examples of material that is typically encoded with little or no effort.

7. Encoding that requires attention and conscious effort is called _____ _____ .

8. With novel information, conscious repetition, or _____ , boosts memory.

9. A pioneering researcher in verbal memory was _____ . In one experiment, he found that the longer he studied a list of nonsense syllables, the _____ (fewer/greater) the number of repetitions he required to relearn it later. Additional rehearsal (or _____) increases retention.

10. Memory studies also reveal that distributed rehearsal is more effective for retention; this is called the _____ _____ .

11. The tendency to remember the first and last items in a list best is called the _____ _____ _____ .

12. People briefly recall the last items in a list quickly and well, called the _____ effect. Following a delay, first items are remembered _____ (better/less well) than last items, called the _____ effect.

Objective 3: Compare the benefits of visual, acoustic, and semantic encoding in remembering verbal information, and describe some memory-enhancing encoding strategies.

13. Encoding the meaning of words is referred to as _____ encoding; encoding by sound is called _____ encoding; encoding picture images of words is _____ encoding.

14. Comparing visual, acoustic, and semantic encoding has shown that memory is best with _____ encoding. We have especially good recall for information we can meaningfully relate to ourselves, called the _____-_____ effect.

15. Memory that consists of mental pictures is based on the use of _____ .

16. Concrete, high-imagery words tend to be remembered _____ (better/less well) than abstract, low-imagery words.

17. Memory for concrete nouns is facilitated when we encode them both _____ and _____ .

18. Our tendency to recall the high points of events such as family vacations illustrates the phenomenon of _____ _____ .

19. Memory aids are known as _____ devices.

20. Using a jingle, such as the one that begins "one is a bun," is an example of the _____-_____ system.

21. Memory may be aided by grouping information into meaningful units called _____ . An example of this technique involves forming words from the first letters of to-be-remembered words; the resulting word is called an _____ .

22. In addition, material may be processed into _____ , which are composed of a few broad concepts divided into lesser concepts, categories, and facts.

Objective 4: Contrast two types of sensory memory, and describe the duration and capacity of working/short-term memory.

23. Stimuli from the environment are first recorded in _____ memory.

24. George Sperling found that when people were briefly shown three rows of letters, they could recall _____ (virtually all/about half) of them. When Sperling sounded a tone immediately after a row of letters was flashed to indicate which letters were to be recalled, the subjects were much _____ (more/less) accurate. This suggests that people have a brief photographic, or _____ , memory lasting about a few tenths of a second.

25. Sensory memory for sounds is called _____ memory. This memory fades _____ (more/less) rapidly than photographic memory, lasting for as long as _____ .

26. Peterson and Peterson found that when _____ was prevented by asking people to count backward, memory for letters was gone after 12 seconds. Without _____ processing, short-term memories have a limited life.

27. Our short-term memory capacity is about _____ chunks of information. This capacity was discovered by _____ .

28. Short-term memory for random _____ (digits/letters) is slightly better than for random _____ (digits/letters), and memory for information we hear is somewhat _____ (better/worse) than that for information we see.

29. Both children and adults have short-term recall for roughly as many words as they can speak in _____ (how many?) seconds.

Objective 5: Describe the capacity and duration of long-term memory, and discuss the biological changes that may underlie memory formation and storage.

30. In contrast to short-term memory—and contrary to popular belief—the capacity of permanent memory is essentially _____ .

31. Psychologist _____ attempted to locate memory by cutting out pieces of rats' _____ after they had learned a maze. He found that no matter where he cut, the rats _____ (remembered/forgot) the maze.

32. Researchers believe that the physical basis of memory, or the _____ _____ , involves a strengthening of certain neural connections, which occurs at the _____ between neurons.

33. Kandel and Schwartz have found that when learning occurs in the sea slug *Aplysia*, the neurotransmitter _____ is released in greater amounts, making synapses more efficient.

34. After learning has occurred, a sending neuron needs _____ (more/less) prompting to fire, and the number of _____ _____ it stimulates may increase. This phenomenon, called _____-_____ _____ , may be the neural basis for learning and memory. Blocking this process with a specific _____ , or by genetic engineering that causes the absence of an _____ , interferes with learning. Rats given a drug that enhances _____ will learn a maze _____ (faster/more slowly).

35. After LTP has occurred, an electric current passed through the brain _____ (will/will not) disrupt old memories and _____ (will/will not) wipe out recent experiences.

36. Hormones released when we are excited or under stress often _____ (facilitate/impair) learning and memory.

37. Two emotion-processing clusters, the _____ , in the brain's _____ system increase activity in the brain's memory-forming areas.

38. Drugs that block the effects of stress hormones _____ (facilitate/disrupt) memories of emotional events.

39. Memories for surprising, significant moments that are especially clear are called _____ memories. Like other memories, these memories _____ (can/cannot) err.

Objective 6: Distinguish between implicit and explicit memory, and identify the main brain structure associated with each.

40. The loss of memory is called _____ . Studies of people who have lost their memory suggest that there _____ (is/is not) a single unified system of memory.

41. Although amnesia victims typically _____ (have/have not) lost their capacity for learning, which is called _____ memory, they _____ (are/are not) able to declare their memory, suggesting a deficit in their _____ memory systems.

42. Amnesia patients typically have suffered damage to the _____ of their limbic system. This brain structure is important in the processing and storage of _____ memories. Damage on the left side of this structure impairs _____ memory; damage on the right side impairs memory for _____ designs and locations. The rear part of this structure processes _____ memory.

43. The hippocampus seems to function as a zone where the brain _____ (temporarily/permanently) stores the elements of a memory. However, memories _____ (do/do not) migrate for storage elsewhere. The hippocampus is active during _____-_____ sleep, as memories are processed for later retrieval. Recalling past experiences activates various parts of the _____ and _____ lobes.

44. The cerebellum is important in the processing of _____ memories. Humans and laboratory animals with a damaged cerebellum are incapable of simple _____ conditioning.

45. The dual explicit-implicit memory system helps explain _____ amnesia. We do not have explicit memories of our first three years because the _____ is one of the last brain structures to mature.

Objective 7: Contrast the recall, recognition, and relearning measures of memory, and explain how retrieval cues can help us access stored memories.

46. The ability to retrieve information not in conscious awareness is called _____ .

47. Bahrick found that 25 years after graduation, people were not able to _____ (recall/recognize) the names of their classmates but were able to _____ (recall/recognize) 90 percent of their names and their yearbook pictures.

48. If you have learned something and then forgotten it, you will probably be able to _____ it _____ (more/less) quickly than you did originally.

49. The best retrieval cues come from the associations formed at the time we _____ a memory.

50. The process by which associations can lead to retrieval is called _____ .

Objective 8: Describe the impact of environmental contexts and internal emotional states on retrieval.

51. Studies have shown that retention is best when learning and testing are done in _____ (the same/different) contexts.

Summarize the text explanation of the déjà vu experience.

52. The type of memory in which emotions serve as retrieval cues is referred to as _____-_____ memory.

53. Our tendency to recall experiences that are consistent with our current emotional state is called _____-_____ memory.

Describe the effects of mood on memory.

54. People who are currently depressed may recall their parents as _____ _____ . People who have recovered from depression typically recall their parents about the same as do people who _____ _____ .

Forgetting (pp. 278–285)

Objective 9: Explain why we should value our ability to forget, and discuss the roles of encoding failure and storage decay in the process of forgetting.

1. Without the ability to _____ , we would constantly be overwhelmed by information.

2. Memory researcher Daniel Schacter has identified the seven sins of memory, divided into three categories that identify the ways in which our memory can fail: the three sins of _____ , the three sins of _____ , and the one sin of _____ .

3. The first type of forgetting is caused by _____ failure.

4. This type of forgetting occurs because some of the information that we sense never actually _____ .

5. One reason for age-related memory decline is that the brain areas responsible for _____ new information are _____ (more/less) responsive in older adults.

6. Studies by Ebbinghaus and by Bahrick indicate that most forgetting occurs _____ (soon/a long time) after the material is learned.

7. This type of forgetting is known as _____ _____ , which may be caused by a gradual fading of the physical _____ _____ .

8. When information that is stored in memory temporarily cannot be found, _____ failure has occurred.

Objective 10: Explain what is meant by retrieval failure, and discuss the effects of interference and motivated forgetting on retrieval.

9. Research suggests that memories are also lost as a result of _____ , which is especially possible if we simultaneously learn similar, new material.

10. The disruptive effect of previous learning on current learning is called _____ _____ . The disruptive effect of

learning new material on efforts to recall material previously learned is called _____ _____ .

11. Jenkins and Dallenbach found that if people went to sleep after learning, their memory for a list of nonsense syllables was _____ (better/worse) than it was if they stayed awake.

12. In some cases, old information facilitates our learning of new information. This is called

_____ _____ .

13. Freud proposed that motivated forgetting, or _____ , may protect a person from painful memories.

14. Increasing numbers of memory researchers think that motivated forgetting is _____ (less/more) common than Freud believed.

Memory Construction (pp. 285–293)

Objective 11: Explain how misinformation, imagination, and source amnesia can distort our memory of an event, and discuss why it is difficult to distinguish between true and false memories.

1. Research has shown that recall of an event is often influenced by our experiences and assumptions. The workings of these influences illustrate the process of memory _____ .

2. When witnesses to an event receive misleading information about it, they may experience a _____ _____ and misremember the event. A number of experiments have demonstrated that false memories _____ (can/cannot) be created when people are induced to imagine nonexistent events; that is, these people later experience _____ _____ . People who believe they have recovered memories of alien abduction and child sex abuse tend to have _____ _____ .

Describe what Loftus' studies have shown about the effects of misleading postevent information on eyewitness reports.

3. At the heart of many false memories is _____ _____ , which occurs when we _____ an event to the wrong source.

4. Because memory is reconstruction as well as reproduction, we _____ (can/cannot) be sure whether a memory is real by how real it feels.

5. The persistence of a memory _____ (does/does not) reveal whether it derives from an actual experience. Whereas real memories have more _____ , gist memories are more _____ .

6. Eyewitnesses' confidence in their memories _____ (is/is not) related to the accuracy of those memories.

7. Memory construction explains why memories "refreshed" under _____ are often inaccurate.

Objective 12: Discuss whether young children's eyewitness reports are reliable and the controversy over reports of repressed and recovered memories.

8. Research studies of children's eyewitness recall reveal that preschoolers _____ (are/are not) more suggestible than older children or adults. For this reason, whether a child produces an accurate eyewitness memory depends heavily on how he or she is _____ .

9. Children are most accurate when it is a first interview with a _____ person who asks _____ questions.

10. Researchers increasingly agree that memories obtained under the influence of hypnosis or using other "memory work" techniques _____ (are/are not) reliable.

11. Memories of events that happened before age _____ are unreliable. This phenomenon is called _____ _____ .

Improving Memory (pp. 293–294)

Objective 13: Explain how an understanding of memory can contribute to effective study techniques.

1. The SQ3R study technique identifies five strategies for boosting memory: _____ , _____ , _____ , _____ , and _____ .

Discuss several specific strategies for improving memory.

PROGRESS TEST 1

Multiple-Choice Questions

Circle your answers to the following questions and check them with the answers beginning on page 162. If your answer is incorrect, read the explanation for why it is incorrect and then consult the appropriate pages of the text (in parentheses following the correct answer).

1. The three steps in memory information processing are
   a. input, processing, output.
   b. input, storage, output.
   c. input, storage, retrieval.
   d. encoding, storage, retrieval.

2. Visual sensory memory is referred to as
   a. iconic memory.   c. photomemory.
   b. echoic memory.   d. semantic memory.

3. Echoic memories fade after approximately
   a. 1 hour.   c. 1 second.
   b. 1 minute.   d. 3 to 4 seconds.

4. Which of the following is NOT a measure of retention?
   a. recall   c. relearning
   b. recognition   d. retrieval

5. Our short-term memory span is approximately _____ items.
   a. 2   c. 7
   b. 5   d. 10

6. Memory techniques such as acronyms and the peg-word system are called
   a. consolidation devices.
   b. imagery techniques.
   c. encoding strategies.
   d. mnemonic devices.

7. One way to increase the amount of information in memory is to group it into larger, familiar units. This process is referred to as
   a. consolidating.   c. encoding.
   b. organization.   d. chunking.

8. Kandel and Schwartz have found that when learning occurs, more of the neurotransmitter _____ is released into synapses.
   a. ACh   c. serotonin
   b. dopamine   d. noradrenaline

9. Research on memory construction reveals that memories
   a. are stored as exact copies of experience.
   b. reflect a person's biases and assumptions.
   c. may be chemically transferred from one organism to another.
   d. even if long term, usually decay within about five years.

10. In a study on context cues, people learned words while on land or when they were underwater. In a later test of recall, those with the best retention had
    a. learned the words on land, that is, in the more familiar context.
    b. learned the words underwater, that is, in the more exotic context.
    c. learned the words and been tested on them in different contexts.
    d. learned the words and been tested on them in the same context.

11. The spacing effect means that
    a. distributed study yields better retention than cramming.
    b. retention is improved when encoding and retrieval are separated by no more than 1 hour.
    c. learning causes a reduction in the size of the synaptic gap between certain neurons.
    d. delaying retrieval until memory has consolidated improves recall.

12. Studies demonstrate that learning causes permanent neural changes in the _____ of animals' neurons.
    a. myelin   c. synapses
    b. cell bodies   d. dendrites

13. In Sperling's memory experiment, research participants were shown three rows of three letters, followed immediately by a low, medium, or high tone. The participants were able to report
    a. all three rows with perfect accuracy.
    b. only the top row of letters.
    c. only the middle row of letters.
    d. any one of the three rows of letters.

14. Studies of amnesia victims suggest that
    a. memory is a single, unified system.
    b. there are two distinct types of memory.
    c. there are three distinct types of memory.
    d. memory losses following brain trauma are unpredictable.

15. Memory for skills is called
    a. explicit memory.   c. prime memory.
    b. declarative memory.   d. implicit memory.

16. The eerie feeling of having been somewhere before is an example of
    a. state dependency.   c. priming.
    b. encoding failure.   d. déjà vu.

17. When Gordon Bower presented words grouped by category or in random order, recall was
    a. the same for all words.
    b. better for the categorized words.
    c. better for the random words.
    d. improved when participants developed their own mnemonic devices.

18. The three-stage processing model of memory was proposed by
    a. Richard Atkinson and Richard Shiffrin.
    b. Herman Ebbinghaus.
    c. Elizabeth Loftus and John Palmer.
    d. George Sperling.

19. Hypnotically "refreshed" memories may prove inaccurate—especially if the hypnotist asks leading questions—because of
    a. encoding failure.
    b. state-dependent memory.
    c. proactive interference.
    d. memory construction.

20. Which area of the brain is most important in the processing of implicit memories?
    a. hippocampus   c. hypothalamus
    b. cerebellum   d. amygdala

21. Which of the following terms does NOT belong with the others?
    a. misattribution   c. suggestibility
    b. blocking   d. bias

Matching Items

Match each definition or description with the appropriate term.

Definitions or Descriptions

_____ 1. sensory memory that decays more slowly than visual sensory memory

_____ 2. the process by which information gets into the memory system

_____ 3. mental pictures that aid memory

_____ 4. the blocking of painful memories

_____ 5. the phenomenon in which one's mood can influence retrieval

_____ 6. memory for a list of words is affected by word order

_____ 7. "one is a bun, two is a shoe" mnemonic device

_____ 8. word that chunks to-be-remembered information into a more familiar form

_____ 9. new learning interferes with previous knowledge

_____ 10. a measure of memory

_____ 11. old knowledge interferes with new learning

_____ 12. misattributing the origin of an event

_____ 13. the fading of unused information over time

_____ 14. the lingering effects of misinformation

_____ 15. a memory sin of intrusion

Terms

a. repression
b. relearning
c. serial position effect
d. persistence
e. peg-word system
f. acronym
g. proactive interference
h. transience
i. retroactive interference
j. source amnesia
k. suggestibility
l. imagery
m. mood-congruent memory
n. echoic memory
o. encoding

PROGRESS TEST 2

Progress Test 2 should be completed during a final unit review. Answer the following questions after you thoroughly understand the correct answers for the section reviews and Progress Test 1.

Multiple-Choice Questions

1. Which of the following best describes the typical forgetting curve?
   a. a steady, slow decline in retention over time
   b. a steady, rapid decline in retention over time
   c. a rapid initial decline in retention becoming stable thereafter
   d. a slow initial decline in retention becoming rapid thereafter

2. Jenkins and Dallenbach found that memory was better in people who were
   a. awake during the retention interval, presumably because decay was reduced.
   b. asleep during the retention interval, presumably because decay was reduced.
   c. awake during the retention interval, presumably because interference was reduced.
   d. asleep during the retention interval, presumably because interference was reduced.

3. Which of the following measures of retention is the least sensitive in triggering retrieval?
   a. recall   c. relearning
   b. recognition   d. They are equally sensitive.

4. Amnesia victims typically have experienced damage to the _____ of the brain.
   a. frontal lobes   c. thalamus
   b. cerebellum   d. hippocampus

5. According to the serial position effect, when recalling a list of words you should have the greatest difficulty with those
   a. at the beginning of the list.
   b. at the end of the list.
   c. at the end and in the middle of the list.
   d. in the middle of the list.

6. Experimenters gave people a list of words to be recalled. When the participants were tested after a delay, the items that were best recalled were those
   a. at the beginning of the list.
   b. in the middle of the list.
   c. at the end of the list.
   d. at the beginning and the end of the list.

7. Which type of word processing—visual, acoustic, or semantic—results in the greatest retention?
   a. visual
   b. acoustic
   c. semantic
   d. Acoustic and semantic processing are equally beneficial.

8. Lashley's studies, in which rats learned a maze and then had various parts of their brains surgically removed, showed that the memory
   a. was lost when surgery took place within 1 hour of learning.
   b. was lost when surgery took place within 24 hours of learning.
   c. was lost when any region of the brain was removed.
   d. remained no matter which area of the brain was tampered with.

9. The disruption of memory that occurs when football players have been knocked out provides evidence for the importance of
   a. consolidation in the formation of new memories.
   b. consolidation in the retrieval of long-term memories.
   c. nutrition in normal neural functioning.
   d. semantic encoding of recent information.

10. *Long-term potentiation* refers to
   a. the disruptive influence of old memories on the formation of new memories.
   b. the disruptive influence of recent memories on the retrieval of old memories.
   c. our tendency to recall experiences that are consistent with our current mood.

   d. the increased efficiency of synaptic transmission between certain neurons following learning.

11. Repression is an example of
   a. encoding failure.　　c. motivated forgetting.
   b. memory decay.　　d. a memory trace.

12. Studies by Loftus and Palmer, in which people were quizzed about a film of an accident, indicate that
   a. when quizzed immediately, people can recall very little, due to the stress of witnessing an accident.
   b. when questioned as little as one day later, their memory was very inaccurate.
   c. most people had very accurate memories as much as 6 months later.
   d. people's recall may easily be affected by misleading information.

13. Which of the following was NOT recommended as a strategy for improving memory?
   a. active rehearsal
   b. distributed study
   c. speed reading
   d. encoding meaningful associations

14. The process of getting information out of memory storage is called
   a. encoding.　　c. rehearsal.
   b. retrieval.　　d. storage.

15. Amnesia patients typically experience disruption of
   a. implicit memories.　　c. iconic memories.
   b. explicit memories.　　d. echoic memories.

16. Information is maintained in short-term memory only briefly unless it is
   a. encoded.　　c. iconic or echoic.
   b. rehearsed.　　d. retrieved.

17. Textbook chapters are often organized into _____ to facilitate information processing.
   a. mnemonic devices　　c. hierarchies
   b. chunks　　d. recognizable units

18. Memory researchers are suspicious of long-repressed memories of traumatic events that are "recovered" with the aid of drugs or hypnosis because
   a. such experiences usually are vividly remembered.

b. such memories are unreliable and easily influenced by misinformation.

c. memories of events happening before about age 3 are especially unreliable.

d. of all of these reasons.

19. It is easier to recall information that has just been presented when the information

   a. consists of random letters rather than words.
   b. is seen rather than heard.
   c. is heard rather than seen.
   d. is experienced in an unusual context.

20. The misinformation effect provides evidence that memory

   a. is constructed during encoding.
   b. is unchanging once established.
   c. may be reconstructed during recall according to how questions are framed.
   d. is highly resistant to misleading information.

21. According to memory researcher Daniel Schacter, blocking occurs when

   a. our inattention to details produces encoding failure.
   b. we confuse the source of information.
   c. our beliefs influence our recollections.
   d. information is on the tip of our tongue, but we can't get it out.

True–False Items

Indicate whether each statement is true or false by placing *T* or *F* in the blank next to the item.

_____ 1. Studying that is distributed over time produces better retention than cramming.

_____ 2. Generally speaking, memory for random digits is better than memory for random letters.

_____ 3. Preschool children can be induced to report false events through the use of suggestive interview techniques.

_____ 4. Most people do not have memories of events that occurred before the age of 3.

_____ 5. Studies by Ebbinghaus show that most forgetting takes place soon after learning.

_____ 6. The persistence of a memory is a good clue as to whether or not it derives from an actual experience.

_____ 7. Recall of newly acquired knowledge is no better after sleeping than after being awake for the same period of time.

_____ 8. Time spent in developing imagery, chunking, and associating material with what you already know is more effective than time spent repeating information again and again.

_____ 9. Although repression has not been confirmed experimentally, most psychologists believe it happens.

_____ 10. Overlearning material by continuing to restudy it beyond mastery often disrupts recall.

PSYCHOLOGY APPLIED

Answer these questions the day before a test as a final check on your understanding of the unit's terms and concepts.

Multiple-Choice Questions

1. Complete this analogy: Fill-in-the-blank test questions are to multiple-choice questions as

   a. encoding is to storage.
   b. storage is to encoding.
   c. recognition is to recall.
   d. recall is to recognition.

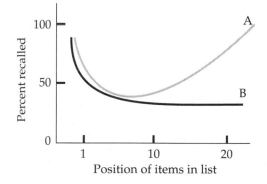

2. The above figure depicts the recall of a list of words under two conditions. Which of the following best describes the difference between the conditions?

   a. In *A*, the words were studied and retrieved in the same context; in *B*, the contexts were different.
   b. In *B*, the words were studied and retrieved in the same context; in *A*, the contexts were different.
   c. The delay between presentation of the last word and the test of recall was longer for *A* than for *B*.
   d. The delay between presentation of the last word and the test of recall was longer for *B* than for *A*.

3. Darren was asked to memorize a list of letters that included *v, q, y,* and *j.* He later recalled these letters as *e, u, i,* and *k,* suggesting that the original letters had been encoded
   a. automatically.   c. semantically.
   b. visually.   d. acoustically.

4. After finding her old combination lock, Janice can't remember its combination because she keeps confusing it with the combination of her new lock. She is experiencing
   a. proactive interference.
   b. retroactive interference.
   c. encoding failure.
   d. storage failure.

5. Which of the following sequences would be best to follow if you wanted to minimize interference-induced forgetting in order to improve your recall on the AP psychology exam?
   a. study, eat, test
   b. study, sleep, test
   c. study, listen to music, test
   d. study, exercise, test

6. Being in a bad mood after a hard day of work, Susan could think of nothing positive in her life. This is best explained as an example of
   a. priming.
   b. memory construction.
   c. mood-congruent memory.
   d. retrieval failure.

7. In an effort to remember the name of the class-mate who sat behind her in fifth grade, Martina mentally recited the names of other classmates who sat near her. Martina's effort to refresh her memory by activating related associations is an example of
   a. priming.   c. encoding.
   b. déjà vu.   d. relearning.

8. Walking through the halls of his high school 10 years after graduation, Tom experienced a flood of old memories. Tom's experience showed the role of
   a. state-dependent memory.
   b. context effects.
   c. retroactive interference.
   d. echoic memory.

9. The first thing Karen did when she discovered that she had misplaced her keys was to re-create in her mind the day's events. That she had little difficulty in doing so illustrates
   a. automatic processing.
   b. effortful processing.
   c. state-dependent memory.
   d. priming.

10. Which of the following is the best example of a flashbulb memory?
    a. suddenly remembering to buy bread while standing in the checkout line at the grocery store
    b. recalling the name of someone from high school while looking at his or her yearbook snapshot
    c. remembering to make an important phone call
    d. remembering what you were doing on September 11, 2001, when terrorists crashed planes into the World Trade Center towers.

11. When Carlos was promoted, he moved into a new office with a new phone extension. Every time he is asked for his phone number, Carlos first thinks of his old extension, illustrating the effects of
    a. proactive interference.
    b. retroactive interference.
    c. encoding failure.
    d. storage failure.

12. Elderly Mr. Flanagan, a retired electrician, can easily remember how to wire a light switch, but he cannot remember the name of the president of the United States. Evidently, Mr. Flanagan's _____ memory is better than his _____ memory.
    a. implicit; explicit
    b. explicit; implicit
    c. declarative; nondeclarative
    d. explicit; declarative

13. Although you can't recall the answer to a question on your psychology test, you have a clear mental image of the textbook page on which it appears. Evidently, your _____ encoding of the answer was _____ .
    a. semantic; automatic
    b. visual; automatic
    c. semantic; effortful
    d. visual; effortful

14. You're visiting your elementary school for the first since you graduated. You cannot remember the last name of your fourth-grade teacher. Your failure to remember is most likely the result of
    a. encoding failure.
    b. storage failure.
    c. retrieval failure.
    d. state-dependent memory.

15. Brenda has trouble remembering her new five-digit ZIP plus four-digit address code. What is the most likely explanation for the difficulty Brenda is having?
    a. Nine digits are at or above the upper limit of most people's short-term memory capacity.
    b. Nine digits are at or above the upper limit of most people's iconic memory capacity.
    c. The extra four digits cannot be organized into easily remembered chunks.
    d. Brenda evidently has an impaired implicit memory.

16. Lewis cannot remember the details of the torture he experienced as a prisoner of war. According to Freud, Lewis' failure to remember these painful memories is an example of
    a. repression.
    b. retrieval failure.
    c. state-dependent memory.
    d. flashbulb memory.

17. Which of the following illustrates the constructive nature of memory?
    a. Janice keeps calling her new boyfriend by her old boyfriend's name.
    b. After studying all afternoon and then getting drunk in the evening, Don can't remember the material he studied.
    c. After getting some good news, elated Kareem has a flood of good memories from his younger years.
    d. Although Mrs. Harvey, who has Alzheimer's disease, has many gaps in her memory, she invents sensible accounts of her activities so that her family will not worry.

18. Brad, who suffered accidental damage to the left side of his hippocampus, has trouble remembering
    a. visual designs.
    b. locations.
    c. all nonverbal information.
    d. verbal information.

19. During basketball practice Jan's head was painfully elbowed. If the trauma to her brain disrupts her memory, we would expect that Jan would be most likely to forget
    a. the name of her teammates.
    b. her telephone number.
    c. the name of the play during which she was elbowed.
    d. the details of events that happened shortly after the incident.

20. After suffering damage to the hippocampus, a person would probably
    a. lose memory for skills such as bicycle riding.
    b. be incapable of being classically conditioned.
    c. lose the ability to store new facts.
    d. experience all of these changes.

21. When he was 8 years old, Frank was questioned by the police about a summer camp counselor suspected of molesting children. Even though he was not, in fact, molested by the counselor, today 19-year-old Frank "remembers" the counselor touching him inappropriately. Frank's false memory is an example of which "sin" of memory?
    a. blocking
    b. transience
    c. misattribution
    d. suggestibility

Essay Question

Discuss the points of agreement among experts regarding the validity of recovered memories of child abuse. (Use the space below to list the points you want to make, and organize them. Then write the essay on a separate piece of paper.)

KEY TERMS

Using your own words, on a separate piece of paper write a brief definition or explanation of each of the following terms.

1. memory
2. encoding
3. storage
4. retrieval
5. sensory memory
6. short-term memory
7. long-term memory
8. working memory
9. parallel processing
10. automatic processing
11. effortful processing
12. rehearsal
13. spacing effect
14. serial position effect
15. visual encoding
16. acoustic encoding
17. semantic encoding
18. imagery
19. mnemonics
20. chunking
21. iconic memory
22. echoic memory
23. long-term potentiation (LTP)
24. flashbulb memory
25. amnesia
26. implicit memory
27. explicit memory
28. hippocampus
29. recall
30. recognition
31. relearning
32. priming
33. déjà vu
34. mood-congruent memory
35. proactive interference
36. retroactive interference
37. repression
38. misinformation effect
39. source amnesia

ANSWERS

Unit Review

The Phenomenon of Memory and *Information Processing*

1. memory
2. information-processing; encoding; storage; retrieval; connectionism; neural networks
3. three-stage processing; sensory memory; short-term; encoded; long-term
4. directly; automatically; conscious
5. working; active; stimuli; long-term
6. serial; parallel; automatic processing; practice

Automatic processing includes the encoding of information about space, time, and frequency. It also includes well-learned information, such as words in your native language.

7. effortful processing
8. rehearsal
9. Hermann Ebbinghaus; fewer; overlearning
10. spacing effect
11. serial position effect
12. recency; better; primacy
13. semantic; acoustic; visual
14. semantic; self-reference
15. imagery
16. better
17. semantically; visually
18. rosy retrospection
19. mnemonic
20. peg-word
21. chunks; acronym
22. hierarchies
23. sensory

24. about half; more; iconic

25. echoic; less; 3 or 4 seconds

26. rehearsal; active

27. 7; George Miller

28. digits; letters; better

29. 2

30. unlimited (limitless)

31. Karl Lashley; cortexes; remembered

32. memory trace; synapses

33. serotonin

34. less; receptor sites; long-term potentiation; drug; enzyme; LTP; faster

35. will not; will

36. facilitate

37. amygdala; limbic

38. disrupt

39. flashbulb; can

40. amnesia; is not

41. have not; implicit; are not; explicit

42. hippocampus; explicit; verbal; visual; spatial

43. temporarily; do; slow-wave; frontal; temporal

44. implicit; eyeblink

45. infantile; hippocampus

46. recall

47. recall; recognize

48. relearn; more

49. encode

50. priming

51. the same

The déjà vu experience is most likely the result of being in a context similar to one that we have actually been in before. If we have previously been in a similar situation, though we cannot recall what it was, the current situation may present cues that subconsciously help us to retrieve the earlier experience.

52. state-dependent

53. mood-congruent

When happy, for example, we perceive things in a positive light and recall happy events; these perceptions and memories, in turn, prolong our good mood.

54. rejecting, punitive, and guilt-promoting; have never suffered depression

Forgetting

1. forget

2. forgetting; distortion; intrusion

3. encoding

4. enters the memory system

5. encoding; less

6. soon

7. storage decay; memory trace

8. retrieval

9. interference

10. proactive interference; retroactive interference

11. better

12. positive transfer

13. repression

14. less

Memory Construction

1. construction

2. misinformation effect; can; imagination inflation; vivid imaginations

When people viewed a film of a traffic accident and were quizzed a week later, phrasing of questions affected answers; the word "smashed," for instance, made viewers mistakenly think they had seen broken glass.

3. source amnesia; misattribute

4. cannot

5. does not; details; durable

6. is not

7. hypnosis

8. are; questioned

9. neutral; nonleading

10. are not

11. 3; infantile amnesia

Improving Memory

1. Survey; Question; Read; Rehearse; Review

Suggestions for improving memory include rehearsing material over many separate and distributed study sessions with the objective of overlearning material. Studying should also involve making the material meaningful rather than mindlessly repeating information. Using mnemonic devices that incorporate vivid imagery is helpful, too. Frequent activation of retrieval cues, such as the context and mood in which the original learning occurred, can also help strengthen memory. Studying should also be arranged to minimize potential sources of interference. And, of course, sleep more, so the brain has a chance to organize and consolidate information. Finally, self-tests in the same format (recall or recognition) that will later be used on the actual test are useful.

Progress Test 1

Multiple-Choice Questions

1. **d.** is the answer. Information must be encoded, or put into appropriate form; stored, or retained over time; and retrieved, or located and gotten out when needed. (p. 257)

2. **a.** is the answer. Iconic memory is our fleeting memory of visual stimuli. (p. 266)
   b. Echoic memory is auditory sensory memory.
   c. There is no such thing as photomemory.
   d. Semantic memory is memory for meaning, not a form of sensory memory.

3. **d.** is the answer. Echoic memories last 3 to 4 seconds. (p. 266)

4. **d.** is the answer. Retrieval refers to the *process* of remembering. (p. 274)

5. **c.** is the answer. (p. 266)

6. **d.** is the answer. (p. 263)
   a. There is no such term as "consolidation techniques."
   b. & c. Imagery and encoding strategies are important in storing new memories, but mnemonic device is the general designation of techniques that facilitate memory, such as acronyms and the peg-word system.

7. **d.** is the answer. (p. 264)
   a. There is no such process of "consolidating."
   b. Organization *does* enhance memory, but it does so through hierarchies, not grouping.
   c. Encoding refers to the processing of information into the memory system.

8. **c.** is the answer. Kandel and Schwartz found that when learning occurred in the sea slug *Aplysia*, serotonin was released at certain synapses, which then became more efficient at signal transmission. (pp. 268–269)

9. **b.** is the answer. In essence, we construct our memories, bringing them into line with our biases and assumptions, as well as with our subsequent experiences. (p. 285)
   a. If this were true, it would mean that memory construction does not occur. Through memory construction, memories may deviate significantly from the original experiences.
   c. There is no evidence that such chemical transfers occur.
   d. Many long-term memories are apparently unlimited in duration.

10. **d.** is the answer. In general, being in a context similar to that in which you experienced something will tend to help you recall the experience. (pp. 276, 277)
    a. & b. The learning environment per se—and its familiarity or exoticness—did not affect retention.

11. **a.** is the answer. (p. 260)
    b. & d. The text does not suggest that there is an optimal interval between encoding and retrieval.
    c. Learning increases the efficiency of synaptic transmission in certain neurons, but not by altering the size of the synapse.

12. **c.** is the answer. (p. 268)

13. **d.** is the answer. When asked to recall all the letters, participants could recall only about half; however, if immediately after the presentation they were signaled to recall a particular row, their recall was near perfect. This showed that they had a brief photographic memory—so brief that it faded in less time than it would have taken to say all nine letters. (p. 266)

14. **b.** is the answer. Because amnesia victims lose their fact (explicit) memories but not their skill (implicit) memories or their capacity to learn, it appears that human memory can be divided into two distinct types. (pp. 271–272)
    d. As studies of amnesia victims show, memory losses following damage to the hippocampus are quite predictable.

15. **d.** is the answer. (p. 272)
    a. & b. Explicit memory (also called declarative memory) is memory of facts and experiences that one can consciously know and declare.
    c. There is no such thing as prime memory.

16. **d.** is the answer. (p. 276)
    a. State-dependent memory is the phenomenon in which information is best retrieved when the person is in the same emotional or physiological state he or she was in when the material was learned.

b. Encoding failure occurs when a person has not processed information sufficiently for it to enter the memory system.

c. Priming is the process by which a memory is activated through retrieval of an associated memory.

17. **b.** is the answer. When the words were organized into categories, recall was two to three times better, indicating the benefits of hierarchical organization in memory. (p. 265)

d. This study did not examine the use of mnemonic devices.

18. **a.** is the answer. (p. 257)

b. Herman Ebbinghaus conducted pioneering studies of verbal learning and memory.

c. Loftus and Palmer conducted influential research studies of eyewitness memory.

d. George Sperling is known for his research studies of iconic memory.

19. **d.** is the answer. It is in both encoding and retrieval that we construct our memories, and as Loftus' studies showed, leading questions affect people's memory construction. (p. 288)

a. The memory encoding occurred at the time of the event in question, not during questioning by the hypnotist.

b. State-dependent memory refers to the influence of one's own emotional or physiological state on encoding and retrieval, and would not apply here.

c. Proactive interference is the interfering effect of prior learning on the recall of new information.

20. **b.** is the answer. (p. 273)

a. The hippocampus is a temporary processing site for *explicit memories.*

c. & d. These areas of the brain are not directly involved in the memory system.

21. **b.** is the answer. Blocking is an example of retrieval failure. Each of the others is an example of a "sin of distortion," in which memories, although inaccurate, are retrieved. (p. 279)

Matching Items

1. n (p. 266)	**6.** c (p. 260)	**11.** g (p. 282)
2. o (p. 257)	**7.** e (p. 263)	**12.** j (p. 287)
3. l (p. 263)	**8.** f (p. 264)	**13.** h (p. 279)
4. a (p. 284)	**9.** i (p. 282)	**14.** k (p. 279)
5. m (p. 278)	**10.** b (p. 274)	**15.** d (p. 279)

Progress Test 2

Multiple-Choice Questions

1. **c.** is the answer. As Ebbinghaus and Bahrick both showed, most of the forgetting that is going to occur happens soon after learning. (pp. 280–281)

2. **d.** is the answer. (p. 282)

a. & b. This study did not find evidence that memories fade (decay) with time.

c. When one is awake, there are many *more* potential sources of memory interference than when one is asleep.

3. **a.** is the answer. A test of recall presents the fewest retrieval cues and usually produces the most limited retrieval. (p. 274)

4. **d.** is the answer. (pp. 271–272)

5. **d.** is the answer. According to the serial position effect, items at the beginning and end of a list tend to be remembered best. (p. 260)

6. **a.** is the answer. (p. 260)

b. In the serial position effect, the items in the middle of the list always show the *poorest* retention.

c. & d. Delayed recall erases the memory facilitation for items at the end of the list.

7. **c.** is the answer. Processing a word in terms of its meaning (semantic encoding) produces much better retention than does visual or acoustic encoding. (p. 262)

8. **d.** is the answer. Surprisingly, Lashley found that no matter where he cut, the rats had at least a partial memory of how to solve the maze. (p. 268)

a. & b. Lashley's studies did not investigate the significance of the interval between learning and cortical lesioning.

9. **a.** is the answer. A blow to the head wipes out recent experiences because information in STM did not have time to consolidate into LTM. (p. 270)

b. Such injuries disrupt the formation, rather than the retrieval, of memories.

c. Although nutrition plays an important role in neural functioning, the effects of such injuries are independent of nutrition.

10. **d.** is the answer. (p. 269)

11. **c.** is the answer. According to Freud, we repress painful memories to preserve our self-concepts. (p. 284)

a. & b. The fact that repressed memories can sometimes be retrieved suggests that they were encoded and have not decayed with time.

12. **d.** is the answer. When misled by the phrasings of questions, subjects incorrectly recalled details of the film and even "remembered" objects that weren't there. (pp. 285–286)

13. **c.** is the answer. Speed reading, which entails little active rehearsal, yields poor retention. (pp. 293–294)

14. **b.** is the answer. (p. 257)
   a. Encoding is the process of getting information *into* memory.
   c. Rehearsal is the conscious repetition of information in order to maintain it in memory.
   d. Storage is the maintenance of encoded material over time.

15. **b.** is the answer. Amnesia patients typically have suffered damage to the hippocampus, a brain structure involved in processing explicit memories for facts. (p. 272)
   a. Amnesia patients do retain implicit memories for how to do things; these are processed in the cerebellum.
   c. & d. Amnesia patients generally do not experience impairment in their iconic and echoic sensory memories.

16. **b.** is the answer. (p. 266)
   a. Information in short-term memory has *already* been encoded.
   c. Iconic and echoic are types of *sensory* memory.
   d. Retrieval is the process of getting material out of storage and into conscious, short-term memory. Thus, all material in short-term memory has either already been retrieved or is about to be placed in storage.

17. **c.** is the answer. By breaking concepts down into subconcepts and yet smaller divisions and showing the relationships among these, hierarchies facilitate information processing. Use of main heads and subheads is an example of the organization of textbook chapters into hierarchies. (p. 265)
   a. Mnemonic devices are the method of loci, acronyms, and other memory *techniques* that facilitate retention.
   b. Chunks are organizations of knowledge into familiar, manageable units.
   d. Recognition is a measure of retention.

18. **d.** is the answer. (p. 288)

19. **c.** is the answer. Short-term recall is slightly better for information we hear rather than see, because echoic memory momentarily outlasts iconic memory. (p. 267)
   a. Meaningful stimuli, such as words, are usually remembered more easily than meaningless stimuli, such as random letters.

   b. Iconic memory does not last as long as echoic memory in short-term recall.
   d. Although context is a powerful retrieval cue, there is no general facilitation of memory in an unusual context.

20. **c.** is the answer. Loftus and Palmer found that eyewitness testimony could easily be altered when questions were phrased to imply misleading information. (p. 286)
   a. Although memories *are* constructed during encoding, the misinformation effect is a retrieval, rather than an encoding, phenomenon.
   b. & d. In fact, just the opposite is true.

21. **d.** is the answer. (p. 279)
   a. This defines absent-mindedness.
   b. This is misattribution.
   c. This is bias.

True–False Items

1. T (p. 293)	**6.** F (p. 288)
2. T (p. 267)	**7.** F (pp. 282–283)
3. T (pp. 289–290)	**8.** T (p. 294)
4. T (p. 291)	**9.** F (p. 284)
5. T (pp. 280–281)	**10.** F (p. 293)

Psychology Applied

Multiple-Choice Questions

1. **d.** is the answer. (p. 274)
   a. & b. In order to correctly answer either type of question, the knowledge must have been encoded and stored.
   c. With fill-in-the-blank questions, the answer must be recalled with no retrieval cues other than the question. With multiple-choice questions, the correct answer merely has to be recognized from among several alternatives.

2. **d.** is the answer. (p. 276)
   a. & b. A serial position effect would presumably occur whether the study and retrieval contexts were the same or different.
   c. As researchers found, when recall is delayed, only the first items in a list are recalled more accurately than the others. With immediate recall, both the first and last items are recalled more accurately.

3. **d.** is the answer. That all four mistakes are based on a sound confusion suggests that the letters were encoded acoustically. (p. 261)
   a. Memorizing a list of letters would involve effortful, rather than automatic, processing.
   b. The mistakes do not involve letters that are similar in appearance.

c. Semantic encoding would have been suggested by errors based on similarities in meaning.

4. **b.** is the answer. Retroactive interference is the disruption of something you once learned by new information. (p. 282)

a. Proactive interference occurs when old information makes it difficult to correctly remember new information.

c. & d. Interference produces forgetting even when the forgotten material was effectively encoded and stored. Janice's problem is at the level of retrieval.

5. **b.** is the answer. (pp. 282–283)

a., c., & d. Involvement in other activities, even just eating or listening to music, is more disruptive than sleeping.

6. **c.** is the answer. Susan's memories are affected by her bad mood. (p. 278)

a. Priming refers to the conscious or unconscious activation of particular associations in memory.

b. Memory construction refers to changes in memory as new experiences occur.

d. Although Susan's difficulty in recalling the good could be considered retrieval failure, it is caused by the mood-congruent effect, which is therefore the best explanation.

7. **a.** is the answer. Priming is the conscious or unconscious activation of particular associations in memory. (p. 275)

b. Déjà vu is the false impression of having previously experienced a current situation.

c. That Martina is able to retrieve her former classmates' names implies that they already have been encoded.

d. Relearning is a measure of retention based on how long it takes to relearn something already mastered. Martina is recalling her former classmates' names, not relearning them.

8. **b.** is the answer. Being back in the context in which the original experiences occurred triggered memories of these experiences. (p. 276)

a. The memories were triggered by similarity of place, not mood.

c. Retroactive interference would involve difficulties in retrieving old memories.

d. Echoic memory refers to momentary memory of auditory stimuli.

9. **a.** is the answer. Time and space—and therefore sequences of events—are often automatically processed. (p. 259)

b. That she had *little difficulty* indicates that the processing was automatic, rather than effortful.

c. & d. State-dependent memory and priming have nothing to do with the automatic processing of space and time.

10. **d.** is the answer. Flashbulb memories are unusually clear memories of emotionally significant moments in life. (p. 270)

11. **a.** is the answer. Proactive interference occurs when old information makes it difficult to recall new information. (p. 282)

b. If Carlos were having trouble remembering the old extension, this answer would be correct.

c. & d. Carlos has successfully encoded and stored the extension; he's just having problems retrieving it.

12. **a.** is the answer. (p. 272)

b., c., & d. Explicit memory, also called declarative memory, is the memory of facts that one can consciously "declare." Nondeclarative memory is what Mr. Flanagan has retained.

13. **b.** is the answer. (p. 259)

a. & c. Your failure to recall the answer indicates that it was never encoded semantically.

d. Spatial information, such as the location of an answer (but not the actual answer) on a textbook page, is often encoded automatically.

14. **c.** is the answer. (p. 282)

a. & b. The name of your homeroom teacher, which you probably heard at least once each day of school, was surely processed into memory (encoded) and maintained there for some time (stored).

d. State-dependent memory is the tendency to recall information best in the same emotional or physiological state as when it was learned. It is unlikely that a single state was associated with learning your homeroom teacher's name.

15. **a.** is the answer. Short-term memory capacity is approximately seven digits. (p. 266)

b. Because iconic memory lasts no more than a tenth of a second, regardless of how much material is experienced, this cannot be the explanation for Brenda's difficulty.

c. The final four digits should be no more difficult to organize into chunks than the first five digits of the address code.

d. Memory for digits is an example of explicit, rather than implicit, memory.

16. **a.** is the answer. (p. 284)

b. Although Lewis' difficulty in recalling these memories could be considered retrieval failure, it is caused by repression, which is therefore the *best* explanation.

c. This answer is incorrect because it is clear that Lewis fails to remember these experiences because they are painful memories and not because he is in a different emotional or physiological state.

d. Flashbulb memories are especially *vivid* memories for emotionally significant events. Lewis has no memory at all.

17. **d.** is the answer. (p. 286)
    a. This is an example of proactive interference.
    b. This is an example of the disruptive effects of depressant drugs, such as alcohol, on the formation of new memories.
    c. This is mood-congruent memory.

18. **d.** is the answer. (p. 272)
    a., b., & c. Damage to the right side, not the left side, of the hippocampus would cause these types of memory deficits.

19. **c.** is the answer. Blows to the head usually disrupt the most recent experiences, such as this one, rather than long-term memories like those in choices a. and b., or new learning such as that in choice d. (p. 270)

20. **c.** is the answer. The hippocampus is involved in processing new facts for storage. (p. 272)
    a., b., & d. Studies of amnesia victims with hippocampal damage show that neither classical conditioning nor skill memory are impaired, indicating that these aspects of memory are controlled by other regions of the brain.

21. **d.** is the answer. In this example, the questions Frank was asked to answer created misinformation that later became part of his memory. (p. 279)
    a. This answer would have been correct if Frank had been molested by the counselor but had failed to encode it in his memory.
    b. This answer would have been correct if Frank had been molested but the memory trace had faded with time.
    c. Misattribution might have occurred if Frank had witnessed another camper being molested and later recalled himself as the actual victim.

Essay Question

Experts agree that child abuse is a real problem that can have long-term adverse effects on individuals. They also acknowledge that forgetting of isolated events, both good and bad, is an ordinary part of life. Although experts all accept the fact that recovered memories are commonplace, they warn that memories "recovered" under hypnosis or with the use of drugs are unreliable, as are memories of events before age 3. Finally, they agree that memories can be traumatic, whether real or false.

Key Terms

1. **Memory** is the persistence of learning over time through the storage and retrieval of information. (p. 255)

2. **Encoding** is the first step in memory; information is translated into some form that enables it to enter our memory system. (p. 257)

3. **Storage** is the process by which encoded information is maintained over time. (p. 257)

4. **Retrieval** is the process of getting information out of memory storage. (p. 257)

5. **Sensory memory** is the immediate, very brief recording of sensory information in the memory system. (p. 257)

6. **Short-term memory** is activated memory, which can hold about seven items for a short time. (p. 257)

7. **Long-term memory** is the relatively permanent and unlimited capacity memory system into which information from short-term memory may pass. It includes knowledge, skills, and experiences. (p. 257)

8. **Working memory** is the newer way of conceptualizing short-term memory as a work site for the active processing of incoming auditory and visual-spatial information, and of information retrieved from long-term memory. (p. 258)

9. **Parallel processing** refers to the human brain's ability to process several aspects of a problem at the same time. (p. 258)

10. **Automatic processing** refers to our unconscious encoding of incidental information such as space, time, and frequency and of well-learned information. (p. 258)

11. **Effortful processing** is encoding that requires attention and conscious effort. (p. 259)

12. **Rehearsal** is the conscious, effortful repetition of information that you are trying either to maintain in consciousness or to encode for storage. (p. 259)

13. The **spacing effect** is the tendency for distributed study or practice to yield better long-term retention than massed study or practice. (p. 260)

14. The **serial position effect** is the tendency for items at the beginning and end of a list to be more easily retained than those in the middle. (p. 260)

15. **Visual encoding** is the use of picture images to process information into memory. (p. 261)

16. **Acoustic encoding** is the processing of information into memory according to its sound. (p. 261)

17. **Semantic encoding** is the processing of information into memory according to its meaning. (p. 261)

18. **Imagery** refers to mental pictures and can be an important aid to effortful processing. (p. 263)

19. **Mnemonics** are memory aids (acronyms, pegwords, etc.), which often use vivid imagery and organizational devices. (p. 263)

20. **Chunking** is the memory technique of organizing material into familiar, meaningful units. (p. 264)

21. **Iconic memory** is the visual sensory memory consisting of a perfect photographic memory, which lasts no more than a few tenths of a second. (p. 266)

    Memory aid: *Icon* means "image" or "representation." **Iconic memory** consists of brief visual images.

22. **Echoic memory** is the momentary sensory memory of auditory stimuli, lasting about 3 or 4 seconds. (p. 266)

23. **Long-term potentiation (LTP)** is an increase in a synapse's firing potential following brief, rapid stimulation. LTP is believed to be the neural basis for learning and memory. (p. 269)

24. A **flashbulb memory** is an unusually vivid memory of an emotionally important moment or event. (p. 270)

25. **Amnesia** is the loss of memory. (p. 271)

26. **Implicit memories** are memories of skills, preferences, and dispositions. These memories are evidently processed, not by the hippocampus, but by a more primitive part of the brain, the cerebellum. They are also called *nondeclarative memories*. (p. 272)

27. **Explicit memories** are memories of facts, including names, images, and events. They are also called *declarative memories*. (p. 272)

28. The **hippocampus** is a temporal lobe neural center located in the limbic system that is important in the processing of explicit memories for storage. (p. 272)

29. **Recall** is a measure of memory in which the person must retrieve information, with few retrieval cues, information learned earlier. (p. 274)

30. **Recognition** is a measure of memory in which one need only identify, rather than recall, previously learned information. (p. 274)

31. **Relearning** is also a measure of memory in that the less time it takes to relearn information, the more that information has been retained. (p. 274)

32. **Priming** is the activation, often unconsciously, of a web of associations in memory in order to retrieve a specific memory. (p. 275)

33. **Déjà vu** is the false sense that you have already experienced a current situation. (p. 276)

34. **Mood-congruent memory** is the tendency to recall experiences that are consistent with our current mood. (p. 278)

35. **Proactive interference** is the disruptive effect of something you already have learned on your efforts to learn or recall new information. (p. 282)

36. **Retroactive interference** is the disruptive effect of new learning on the recall of old knowledge. (p. 282)

    Memory aid: *Retro* means "backward." **Retroactive interference** is "backward-acting" interference.

37. **Repression** is an example of motivated forgetting in that painful and unacceptable memories are prevented from entering consciousness. In psychoanalytic theory, it is the basic defense mechanism. (p. 284)

38. The **misinformation effect** is the tendency of eyewitnesses to an event to incorporate misleading information about the event into their memories. (p. 286)

39. At the heart of many false memories, **source amnesia** refers to attributing an event to the wrong source. (p. 287)

Cognition:
7B: Thinking, Problem Solving, Creativity, and Language

UNIT OVERVIEW

The first part of Unit 7B deals with thinking, with emphasis on how people logically—or at times illogically—use tools such as algorithms and heuristics when making decisions and solving problems. Also discussed is the type of thinking that leads to creativity, as well as several common obstacles to problem solving. These include fixations that prevent us from taking a fresh perspective on a problem and our bias to search for information that confirms rather than challenges existing hypotheses. The section concludes with discussions of the power and perils of intuition and the effects of framing on decision making.

The rest of the unit is concerned with language, including its structure, development in children, and relationship to thinking. Two theories of language acquisition are evaluated: Skinner's theory that language acquisition is based entirely on learning and Chomsky's theory that humans have a biological predisposition to acquire language.

NOTE: Answer guidelines for all Unit 7B questions begin on page 179.

UNIT REVIEW

First, skim each section, noting headings and boldface items. After you have read the section, review each objective by answering the fill-in and essay-type questions that follow it. As you proceed, evaluate your performance by consulting the answers beginning on page 179. Do not continue with the next section until you understand each answer. If you need to, review or reread the section in the textbook before continuing.

Thinking (pp. 298–312)

Objective 1: Define *cognition*, and describe the roles of categories, hierarchies, and prototypes in concept formation.

1. Cognition, or _____ , can be defined as _____ _____ .

2. Scientists who study these mental activities are called _____ _____ .

3. People tend to organize specific items into mental groupings called_____ , and many such groupings often are further organized into

   _____ .

4. Concepts are typically formed through the development of a best example, or _____ , of a category. People more easily detect _____ (male/female) prejudice against _____ (males/females) than vice versa.

Objective 2: Compare algorithms, heuristics, and insight as problem-solving strategies, and identify the factors associated with creativity.

5. Humans are especially capable of using their reasoning powers for coping with new situations, and thus for _____

   _____ .

6. When we try each possible solution to a problem, we are using _____

   _____ _____ .

7. Logical, methodical, step-by-step procedures for solving problems are called

_____ .

8. Simple thinking strategies that provide us with problem-solving shortcuts are referred to as

_____ .

9. When you suddenly realize a problem's solution, _____ has occurred. Research studies show that such moments are preceded by _____ _____ activity involved in focusing attention and accompanied by a burst of activity in the _____

_____ _____ .

10. The ability to produce ideas that are both novel and valuable is called _____ . Studies suggest that a certain level of _____ is necessary but _____ (is/is not) sufficient for this ability.

11. Standard intelligence tests, which demand single correct answers to questions, measure _____ thinking. Tests that allow multiple possible answers to problems measure _____ thinking.

Describe five components of creativity.

Objective 3: Explain how confirmation bias and fixation can interfere with problem solving.

12. The tendency of people to look for information that supports their preconceptions is called

_____ _____ .

13. It is human nature to seek evidence that _____ our ideas more eagerly than to seek evidence that might _____ them.

14. Not being able to take a new perspective when attempting to solve a problem is referred to as _____ . One example of this obstacle to problem solving is the tendency to repeat solutions that have worked previously; this phenomenon is known as the development of a

_____ _____ .

15. When a person is unable to envision using an object in an atypical way, _____ _____ is operating.

Objective 4: Explain how the representativeness and availability heuristics can cause us to underestimate or ignore important information, and describe the drawbacks and advantages of overconfidence in decision making.

16. People judge how well something matches a particular prototype; this is the _____

_____ .

17. When we judge the likelihood of something occurring in terms of how readily it comes to mind, we are using the _____

_____ .

Explain how these two heuristics may lead us to make judgmental errors.

18. (Thinking Critically) Many people fear _____ more than driving and _____ more than accidents, despite the fact that these fears are not supported by death and injury statistics. This type of faulty thinking occurs because we fear

a. _____

b. _____

c. _____

d. _____

19. The tendency of people to overestimate the accuracy of their knowledge results in

_____ .

20. Overconfidence has _____ value because self-confident people tend to live _____ (more/less) happily, find it _____ (easier/harder) to make tough decisions, and seem _____ (more/less) credible.

21. When research participants are given feedback on the accuracy of their judgments, such feedback generally _____ (does/does not) help them become more realistic about how much they know.

Objective 5: Describe the effects that belief perseverance, intuition, and framing can have on our judgments and decision making.

22. Research has shown that once we form a belief or a concept, it may take more convincing evidence for us to change the concept than it did to create it; this is because of _____

_____ .

23. A cure for this is to _____

_____ .

24. Intuitive reactions allow us to react _____ and in ways that are usually _____ . They do so thanks, first, to our fast and frugal _____ and, second, thanks to our _____

_____ .

25. The way an issue is posed is called _____ . This effect influences political and business decisions, suggesting that our judgments _____ (may/may not) always be well reasoned.

Language (pp. 313–319)

Objective 6: Describe the basic structural units of a language, including the rules that enable us to commununicate meaning.

1. The basic sound units of language are its _____ . English has approximately

_____ of these units. The basic units of sign language are defined by _____ _____ and

_____ .

2. Phonemes are grouped into units of meaning called _____ .

3. The system of rules that enables us to use our language to speak to and understand others is called _____ .

4. The system by which meaning is derived from morphemes, words, and sentences is the _____ of a language.

5. The system of rules we use to combine words into grammatically sensible sentences is called _____ .

Objective 7: Trace the course of language acquisition from the babbling stage through the two-word stage.

6. By _____ months of age, babies can read lips and discriminate speech sounds. This marks the beginning of their _____ _____ , their ability to comprehend speech. This ability begins to mature before their _____ _____ , or ability to produce words.

7. The first stage of language development, in which children spontaneously utter different sounds, is the _____ stage. This stage typically begins at about _____ months of age. The sounds children make during this stage _____ (do/do not) include only the sounds of the language they hear.

8. Deaf infants _____ (do/do not) babble. Many natural babbling sounds are _____-_____ pairs formed by _____

_____ .

9. By about _____ months of age, infant babbling begins to resemble the household language. At about the same time, the ability to perceive speech sounds outside their native language is _____ (lost/acquired).

10. During the second stage, called the _____-_____ stage, children convey complete thoughts using single words. This stage begins at about _____ year(s) of age.

11. During the _____-_____ stage, children speak in sentences containing mostly nouns and verbs. This type of speech is called _____ speech. It _____ (does/does not) follow the rules of syntax.

Objective 8: Discuss Skinner's and Chomsky's contributions to the nature-nurture debate over how children acquire language, and explain why statistical learning and critical periods are important concepts in children's language learning.

12. B. F. Skinner believed that language development follows the general principles of learning, including _____ , _____ , and _____ .

13. Other theorists believe that humans are biologically predisposed to learn language. One such theorist is _____ , who believes that we all are born with a _____ _____ _____ in which _____ switches are thrown as children experience their language. This theorist contends that all human languages have the same grammatical building blocks, which suggests that there is a _____ _____ .

14. Research by Jenny Saffran has demonstrated that even before _____ year(s) of age, infants are able to discern _____ _____ and _____ analyze which syllables most often go together.

15. Research studies of infants' knack for soaking up language suggest that babies come with a built-in readiness to learn _____ _____ .

16. Childhood seems to represent a _____ _____ for mastering certain aspects of language. Those who learn a second language as adults usually speak it with the _____ of their first language. Moreover, they typically show _____ (poorer/better) mastery of the _____ of the second language.

17. The window for learning language gradually begins to close after age _____ . When a young brain doesn't learn any language, its language-learning capacity _____ (never/may still) fully develop(s).

18. Considering the two theories together, we can say that although we are born with a readiness to learn language, _____ is also important, as shown in linguistically stunted children who have been isolated from language during the _____ _____ for its acquisition.

Thinking and Language (pp. 319–322)

Objective 9: Discuss Whorf's linguistic determinism hypothesis in relation to current views regarding thinking and language, and describe the value of thinking in images.

1. According to the _____ _____ hypothesis, language shapes our thinking. The linguist who proposed this hypothesis is _____ .

2. Many people who are bilingual report feeling a different sense of _____ , depending on which language they are using.

3. In several studies, researchers have found that using the pronoun *he* (instead of *he or she*) _____ (does/does not) influence people's thoughts concerning gender.

4. Bilingual children, who learn to inhibit one language while using their other language, are better able to inhibit their _____ to irrelevant information. This has been called the _____ _____ .

5. One study of Canadian children found that English-speaking children who were _____ in French had higher _____ scores and math scores than control children.

6. It appears that thinking _____ (can/cannot) occur without the use of language. Athletes often supplement physical with _____ practice.

7. In one study of psychology students preparing for a midterm exam, the greatest benefits were achieved by those who visualized themselves _____ (receiving a high grade/studying effectively).

Summarize the probable relationship between thinking and language.

PROGRESS TEST 1

Multiple-Choice Questions

Circle your answers to the following questions and check them with the answers beginning on page 180. If your answer is incorrect, read the explanation for why it is incorrect and then consult the appropriate pages of the text (in parentheses following the correct answer).

1. The text defines *cognition* as
   a. silent speech.
   b. all mental activity.
   c. the mental activities associated with thinking, knowing, remembering, and communicating information.
   d. logical reasoning.

2. A mental grouping of similar things, events, or people is called a(n)
   a. prototype.   c. algorithm.
   b. concept.   d. heuristic.

3. When forming a concept, people often develop a best example, or _____ , of a category.
   a. denoter   c. prototype
   b. heuristic   d. algorithm

4. Confirmation bias refers to the tendency to
   a. allow preexisting beliefs to distort logical reasoning.
   b. cling to one's initial conceptions after the basis on which they were formed has been discredited.
   c. search randomly through alternative solutions when problem solving.
   d. look for information that is consistent with one's beliefs.

5. The English language has approximately _____ phonemes.
   a. 25   c. 40
   b. 30   d. 45

6. Which of the following is NOT true of babbling?
   a. It is imitation of adult speech.
   b. It is the same in all cultures.
   c. It typically occurs from about age 4 months to 1 year.
   d. Babbling increasingly comes to resemble a particular language.

7. Mental set and functional fixedness are two types of
   a. algorithms.   c. fixation.
   b. heuristics.   d. insight.

8. Which of the following best describes the relationship between creativity and aptitude, as reflected in intelligence test scores?
   a. Creativity appears to depend on the ability to think imaginatively and has little if any relationship to aptitude.
   b. Creativity is best understood as a certain kind of intelligence.
   c. The better a person's intelligence scores are, the greater his or her creativity.
   d. A certain level of aptitude is necessary but not sufficient for creativity.

9. Whorf's linguistic determinism hypothesis states that
   a. language is primarily a learned ability.
   b. language is partially an innate ability.
   c. the size of a person's vocabulary reflects his or her intelligence.
   d. our language shapes our thinking.

10. Which of the following BEST describes Chomsky's view of language development?
    a. Language is an entirely learned ability.
    b. Language is an innate ability.
    c. Humans have a biological predisposition to acquire language.
    d. There are no cultural influences on the development of language.

11. Failing to solve a problem that requires using an object in an unusual way illustrates the phenomenon of
    a. mental set.
    b. functional fixedness.
    c. framing.
    d. belief perseverance.

12. Which of the following is an example of the use of heuristics?
    a. trying every possible letter ordering when unscrambling a word
    b. considering each possible move when playing chess
    c. using the formula "area = length × width" to find the area of a rectangle
    d. playing chess using a defensive strategy that has often been successful for you

13. The chimpanzee Sultan used a short stick to pull a longer stick that was out of reach into his cage. He then used the longer stick to reach a piece of fruit. Researchers hypothesized that Sultan's discovery of the solution to his problem was the result of:
    a. trial and error.
    b. heuristics.
    c. functional fixedness.
    d. insight.

14. You hear that one of the Smith children is an outstanding Little League player and immediately conclude it's their one son rather than any of their four daughters. You reached your quite possibly erroneous conclusion as the result of
    a. the confirmation bias.
    b. the availability heuristic.
    c. the representativeness heuristic.
    d. belief perseverance.

15. Deaf children who are not exposed to sign language until they are teenagers
    a. are unable to master the basic words of sign language.
    b. learn the basic words but not how to order them.
    c. are unable to master either the basic words or syntax of sign language.
    d. never become as fluent as those who learned to sign at a younger age.

16. According to the text, language acquisition is best described as
    a. the result of conditioning and reinforcement.
    b. a biological process of maturation.
    c. an interaction between biology and experience.
    d. a mystery of which researchers have no real understanding.

17. Infants as young as 6 months old display a remarkable ability to learn statistical aspects of speech. Specifically, research studies have shown that they
    a. are quickly able to recognize syllable sequences that appear repeatedly.
    b. respond to changes in the pitch of a speaker's voice.
    c. pay less attention to a same-gender voice.
    d. do all of these things.

18. The linguistic determinism hypothesis is challenged by the finding that
    a. many of the language errors children make result from overgeneralizing grammatical rules.
    b. people with no word for a certain color can still perceive that color accurately.
    c. the Eskimo language contains a number of words for snow, whereas English has only one.
    d. infants' babbling contains many phonemes that do not occur in their own language and that they therefore cannot have heard.

19. Several studies have indicated that the generic pronoun *he*
    a. tends for children and adults alike to trigger images of both males and females.
    b. tends for adults to trigger images of both males and females, but for children to trigger images of males.
    c. tends for both children and adults to trigger images of males but not females.
    d. for both children and adults triggers images of females about one-fourth of the time it is used.

Matching Items

Match each definition or description with the appropriate term.

Definitions or Descriptions

_____ 1. the basic units of sound in a language
_____ 2. the way an issue or question is posed
_____ 3. rules for combining words into sentences
_____ 4. the rules by which meaning is derived from sentences
_____ 5. presuming that something is likely if it comes readily to mind
_____ 6. the tendency to overestimate the accuracy of one's judgments
_____ 7. being unable to see a problem from a different angle
_____ 8. haphazard problem solving by trying one solution after another
_____ 9. the sudden realization of the solution to a problem
_____ 10. the tendency to repeat problem-solving techniques that worked in the past even though a fresh approach may be more appropriate
_____ 11. the basic units of meaning in a language
_____ 12. the ability to produce valuable and novel ideas

Terms

a. syntax
b. morphemes
c. mental set
d. trial and error
e. availability heuristic
f. phonemes
g. semantics
h. insight
i. framing
j. overconfidence
k. fixation
l. creativity

PROGRESS TEST 2

Progress Test 2 should be completed during a final unit review. Answer the following questions after you thoroughly understand the correct answers for the section reviews and Progress Test 1.

Multiple-Choice Questions

1. A common problem in everyday reasoning is our tendency to
   a. accept as logical those conclusions that agree with our own opinions.
   b. accept as logical those conclusions that disagree with our own opinions.
   c. underestimate the accuracy of our knowledge.
   d. accept as logical conclusions that involve unfamiliar concepts.

2. Phonemes are the basic units of ___ in language.
   a. sound
   b. meaning
   c. grammar
   d. semantics

3. Syntax refers to the
   a. sounds in a word.
   b. rules for grouping words into sentences.
   c. rules by which meaning is derived from sentences.
   d. overall rules of a language.

4. Skinner and other behaviorists have argued that language development is the result of
   a. imitation.
   b. reinforcement.
   c. association.
   d. all of these.

5. Representativeness and availability are examples of
   a. mental sets.
   b. belief bias.
   c. algorithms.
   d. heuristics.

6. The basic units of cognition are
   a. phonemes.
   b. concepts.
   c. prototypes.
   d. morphemes.

7. Assume that Congress is considering revising its approach to welfare and to this end is hearing a range of testimony. A member of Congress who uses the availability heuristic would be most likely to

    a. want to experiment with numerous possible approaches to see which of these seems to work best.

    b. want to cling to approaches to welfare that seem to have had some success in the past.

    c. refuse to be budged from his or her beliefs despite persuasive testimony to the contrary.

    d. base his or her ideas on the most vivid, memorable testimony given, even though many of the statistics presented run counter to this testimony.

8. If you want to be absolutely certain that you will find the solution to a problem you know *is* solvable, you should use

    a. a heuristic.   c. insight.

    b. an algorithm.   d. trial and error.

9. Complete the following: *-ed* is to *sh* as _____ is to _____ .

    a. phoneme; morpheme   c. grammar; syntax

    b. morpheme; phoneme   d. syntax; grammar

10. Which of the following is NOT cited by Chomsky as evidence that language acquisition cannot be explained by learning alone?

    a. Children master the complicated rules of grammar with ease.

    b. Children create sentences they have never heard.

    c. Children make the kinds of mistakes that suggest they are attempting to apply rules of grammar.

    d. Children raised in isolation from language spontaneously begin speaking words.

11. Telegraphic speech is typical of the _____ stage.

    a. babbling   c. two-word

    b. one-word   d. three-word

12. Children first demonstrate a rudimentary understanding of syntax during the _____ stage.

    a. babbling   c. two-word

    b. one-word   d. three-word

13. The study in which people who immigrated to the United States at various ages were compared in terms of their ability to understand English grammar found that

    a. age of arrival had no effect on mastery of grammar.

    b. those who immigrated as children understood grammar as well as native speakers.

    c. those who immigrated as adults understood grammar as well as native speakers.

    d. whether or not English was spoken in the home was the most important factor in mastering the rules of grammar.

14. Regarding the relationship between thinking and language, which of the following most accurately reflects the position taken in the text?

    a. Language determines everything about our thinking.

    b. Language determines the way we think.

    c. Thinking without language is not possible.

    d. Thinking affects our language, which then affects our thought.

15. The rules most directly involved in permitting a person to derive meaning from words and sentences are rules of

    a. syntax.   c. phonemic structure.

    b. grammar.   d. semantics.

16. Which of the following is true regarding the relationship between thinking and language?

    a. "Real" thinking requires the use of language.

    b. People sometimes think in images rather than in words.

    c. A thought that cannot be expressed in a particular language cannot occur to speakers of that language.

    d. Even when we use the generic *he*, people understand that we are referring to males and females.

17. One reason an English-speaking adult may have difficulty pronouncing Russian words is that

    a. the vocal tracts of English- and Russian-speaking people develop differently in response to the demands of the two languages.

    b. although English and Russian have very similar morphemes, their phonemic inventories are very different.

    c. although English and Russian have very similar phonemes, their morphemic inventories are very different.

    d. after the babbling stage, a child who hears only English stops uttering other phonemes.

True–False Items

Indicate whether each statement is true or false by placing *T* or *F* in the blank next to the item.

_____ 1. The order in which children acquire an understanding of various morphemes is unpredictable.

_____ 2. According to the confirmation bias, people often interpret ambiguous evidence as support for their beliefs.

_____ 3. Most human problem solving involves the use of heuristics rather than reasoning that systematically considers every possible solution.

_____ 4. When asked, most people underestimate the accuracy of their judgments.

_____ 5. Studies have shown that even animals may sometimes have insight reactions.

_____ 6. Mental set is the tendency to repeat problem-solving solutions that have worked in the past.

_____ 7. Although the morphemes differ from language to language, the phonemes for all languages are the same.

_____ 8. Children of all cultures babble using the same phonemes.

_____ 9. Thinking without using language is not possible.

_____ 10. Most researchers believe that we can perform statistical analyses of language throughout our lives.

PSYCHOLOGY APPLIED

Answer these questions the day before a test as a final check on your understanding of the unit's terms and concepts.

Multiple-Choice Questions

1. The word "predates" contains _____ phonemes and _____ morphemes.
   a. 7; 3
   b. 3; 7
   c. 7; 2
   d. 3; 2

2. Vanessa is a very creative sculptress. We would expect that Vanessa also
   a. has an exceptionally high intelligence test score.
   b. is quite introverted.
   c. has a venturesome personality and is intrinsically motivated.
   d. lacks expertise in most other skills.

3. A listener hearing a recording of Japanese, Spanish, and North American children babbling would
   a. not be able to tell them apart.
   b. be able to tell them apart if they were older than 6 months.
   c. be able to tell them apart if they were older than 8 to 10 months.
   d. be able to tell them apart at any age.

4. Which of the following illustrates belief perseverance?
   a. Your belief remains intact even in the face of evidence to the contrary.
   b. You refuse to listen to arguments counter to your beliefs.
   c. You tend to become flustered and angered when your beliefs are refuted.
   d. You tend to search for information that supports your beliefs.

5. Complete the following analogy: Rose is to flower as
   a. concept is to prototype.
   b. prototype is to concept.
   c. concept is to hierarchy.
   d. hierarchy is to concept.

6. Your stand on an issue such as the use of nuclear power for electricity involves personal judgment. In such a case, one memorable occurrence can weigh more heavily than a bookful of data, thus illustrating
   a. belief perseverance.
   b. confirmation bias.
   c. the representativeness heuristic.
   d. the availability heuristic.

7. A dessert recipe that gives you the ingredients, their amounts, and the steps to follow is an example of a(n)
   a. prototype.
   b. algorithm.
   c. heuristic.
   d. mental set.

8. Marilyn was asked to solve a series of five math problems. The first four problems could only be solved by a particular sequence of operations. The fifth problem could also be solved following this sequence; however, a much simpler solution was possible. Marilyn did not realize this simpler solution and solved the problem in the way she had solved the first four. Her problem-solving strategy was hampered by
   a. functional fixedness.
   b. the overconfidence phenomenon.
   c. mental set.
   d. her lack of a prototype for the solution.

9. Dr. Mendoza is studying the mental strategies people use when solving problems. Dr. Mendoza is clearly a(n)
   a. cognitive psychologist.
   b. experimental psychologist.
   c. organizational psychologist.
   d. developmental psychologist.

10. Boris the chess master selects his next move by considering moves that would threaten his opponent's queen. His opponent, a chess-playing computer, selects its next move by considering *all* possible moves. Boris is using a(n) _____ and the computer is using a(n) _____ .
    a. algorithm; heuristic
    b. prototype; mental set
    c. mental set; prototype
    d. heuristic; algorithm

11. During a televised political debate, the Republican and Democratic candidates each argued that the results of a recent public opinion poll supported their party's platform regarding job creation. Because both candidates saw the information as supporting their belief, it is clear that both were victims of
    a. functional fixedness.   c. belief perseverance.
    b. mental set.   d. confirmation bias.

12. The child who says "Milk gone" is engaging in _____ . This type of utterance demonstrates that children are actively experimenting with the rules of _____ .
    a. babbling; syntax
    b. telegraphic speech; syntax
    c. babbling; semantics
    d. telegraphic speech; semantics

13. Experts in a field prefer heuristics to algorithms because heuristics
    a. guarantee solutions to problems.
    b. prevent mental sets.
    c. often save time.
    d. prevent fixation.

14. Rudy is 6 feet 6 inches tall, weighs 210 pounds, and is very muscular. If you think that Rudy is more likely to be a basketball player than a computer programmer, you are a victim of
    a. belief perseverance.
    b. mental set.
    c. functional fixedness.
    d. the representativeness heuristic.

15. Failing to see that an article of clothing can be inflated as a life preserver is an example of
    a. belief perseverance.
    b. the availability heuristic.
    c. the representativeness heuristic.
    d. functional fixedness.

16. Airline reservations typically decline after a highly publicized airplane crash because people overestimate the incidence of such disasters. In such instances, their decisions are being influenced by
    a. belief perseverance.
    b. the availability heuristic.
    c. the representativeness heuristic.
    d. functional fixedness.

17. Most people tend to
    a. accurately estimate the accuracy of their knowledge and judgments.
    b. underestimate the accuracy of their knowledge and judgments.
    c. overestimate the accuracy of their knowledge and judgments.
    d. lack confidence in their decision-making strategies.

18. In relation to ground beef, consumers respond more positively to an ad describing it as "75 percent lean" than to one referring to its "25 percent fat" content. This is an example of
    a. the framing effect.   c. mental set.
    b. confirmation bias.   d. overconfidence.

19. The sentence "Blue jeans wear false smiles" has correct _____ but incorrect _____ .
    a. morphemes; phonemes
    b. phonemes; morphemes
    c. semantics; syntax
    d. syntax; semantics

20. In preparing her class presentation, "Updating Chomsky's Understanding of Language Development," Britney's outline includes all of the following evidence EXCEPT that
   a. computers programmed to learn to form the past tense of irregular verbs can learn to do so, even without "inborn" linguistic rules.
   b. infants rapidly learn to detect subtle differences between simple sequences of syllables.
   c. infants can recognize color differences even before they can name different colors.
   d. children isolated from language during the first seven years of life never fully develop language.

Essay Question

The lectures of your linguistics professor, who happens to be a staunch behaviorist, clearly imply that she believes language development can be explained according to principles of conditioning. What evidence should you present to convince her that she is wrong? (Use the space below to list the points you want to make, and organize them. Then write the essay on a separate piece of paper.)

KEY TERMS

Using your own words, on a piece of paper write a brief definition or explanation of each of the following terms.

1. cognition
2. concept
3. prototype
4. algorithm
5. heuristic
6. insight
7. creativity

8. confirmation bias
9. fixation
10. mental set
11. functional fixedness
12. representativeness heuristic
13. availability heuristic
14. overconfidence
15. belief perseverance
16. intuition
17. framing
18. language
19. phoneme
20. morpheme
21. grammar
22. semantics
23. syntax
24. babbling stage
25. one-word stage
26. two-word stage
27. telegraphic speech
28. linguistic determinism

ANSWERS

Unit Review

Thinking

1. thinking; the mental activities associated with thinking, knowing, remembering, and communicating
2. cognitive psychologists
3. concepts; hierarchies
4. prototype; male; females
5. problem solving
6. trial and error
7. algorithms
8. heuristics
9. insight; frontal lobe; right temporal lobe
10. creativity; aptitude; is not
11. convergent; divergent

Creative people tend to have expertise, or a solid base of knowledge; imaginative thinking skills, which allow them to see things in new ways, to recognize patterns, and to make connections; intrinsic motivation, or the tendency to focus on the pleasure and challenge of their work; and a venturesome personality that tolerates ambiguity and risk and seeks new experiences. Creative people also have generally benefited from living in creative environments.

12. confirmation bias
13. verifies; refute
14. fixation; mental set
15. functional fixedness
16. representativeness heuristic
17. availability heuristic

Using these heuristics often prevents us from processing other relevant information; because we overlook this information, we make judgmental errors. Thus, in the text example, the representativeness heuristic leads people to overlook the fact that there are many more truck drivers than Ivy League classics professors and, as a result, to wrongly conclude that the poetry reader is more likely to be an Ivy League classics professor.

18. flying; terrorism
    a. what our ancestral history has prepared us to fear.
    b. what we cannot control.
    c. what is immediate.
    b. what is most readily available in memory.
19. overconfidence
20. adaptive; more; easier; more
21. does
22. belief perseverance
23. consider the opposite
24. quickly; adaptive; heuristics; learned associations
25. framing; may not

Language

1. phonemes; 40; hand shapes; movements
2. morphemes
3. grammar
4. semantics
5. syntax
6. 4; receptive language; productive language
7. babbling; 4; do not
8. do; consonant-vowel; bunching the tongue in the front of the mouth
9. 10; lost
10. one-word; 1

11. two-word; telegraphic; does
12. association; imitation; reinforcement
13. Noam Chomsky; language acquisition device; grammar; universal grammar
14. 1; word breaks; statistically
15. grammatical rules
16. critical period; accent; poorer; grammar
17. 7; never
18. experience; critical period

Thinking and Language

1. linguistic determinism; Benjamin Whorf
2. self
3. does
4. attention; bilingual advantage
5. immersed; aptitude
6. can; mental
7. studying effectively

The relationship is probably a two-way one: the linguistic determinism hypothesis suggests that language helps shape thought; that words come into the language to express new ideas indicates that thought also shapes language.

Progress Test 1

Multiple-Choice Questions

1. **c.** is the answer. (p. 298)
2. **b.** is the answer. (p. 299)
   a. A prototype is the best example of a particular category, or concept.
   c. & d. Algorithms and heuristics are problem-solving strategies.
3. **c.** is the answer. (p. 299)
   a. There is no such thing as a "denoter."
   b. & d. Heuristics and algorithms are problem-solving strategies.
4. **d.** is the answer. It is a major obstacle to problem solving. (pp. 302–303)
   a. & b. These refer to belief bias and belief perseverance, respectively.
   c. This is trial-and-error problem solving.
5. **c.** is the answer. (p. 313)
6. **a.** is the answer. Babbling is not the imitation of adult speech since babbling infants produce phonemes from languages they have not heard and could not be imitating. (p. 315)
7. **c.** is the answer. Both involve failing to see a problem from a new perspective. (p. 303)

a. & b. Algorithms and heuristics are problem-solving strategies.

d. Insight is the sudden realization of a problem's solution.

8. **d.** is the answer. (p. 301)

   a. The ability to think imaginatively and intelligence are both components of creativity.

   b. & c. Creativity, the capacity to produce ideas that are novel and valuable, requires a certain level of aptitude, but creative people do not necessarily score higher on intelligence tests than their less creative peers.

9. **d.** is the answer. (p. 319)

   a. This is Skinner's position regarding language development.

   b. This is Chomsky's position regarding language development.

   c. The linguistic determinism hypothesis is concerned with the content of thought, not intelligence.

10. **c.** is the answer. (p. 317)

    a. This is Skinner's position.

    b. According to Chomsky, although the *ability* to acquire language is innate, the child can only acquire language in association with others.

    d. Cultural influences are an important example of the influence of learning on language development, an influence Chomsky fully accepts.

11. **b.** is the answer. Functional fixedness is the tendency to think of things only in terms of their usual functions. (p. 303)

    a. Mental set is the tendency to approach a problem in a particular way that worked previously.

    c. Framing refers to the way an issue is posed; this often influences our judgment.

    d. Belief perseverance is the tendency to cling to one's beliefs even after they have been refuted.

12. **d.** is the answer. Heuristics are simple thinking strategies—such as playing chess defensively—that are based on past successes in similar situations. (p. 300)

    a., b., & c. These are all algorithms.

13. **d.** is the answer. Sultan suddenly arrived at a novel solution to his problem, thus displaying apparent insight. (p. 300)

    a. Sultan did not randomly try various strategies of reaching the fruit; he demonstrated the "light bulb" reaction that is the hallmark of insight.

    b. Heuristics are simple thinking strategies.

    c. Functional fixedness is an impediment to problem solving. Sultan obviously solved his problem.

14. **c.** is the answer. Your conclusion is based on sex stereotypes, that is, athletic ability and participa-

tion are for you more *representative* of boys. Your conclusion is by no means necessarily right, however, especially because the Smiths have four daughters and only one son! (p. 304)

   a. The confirmation bias is the tendency to look for information that confirms one's preconceptions.

   b. The availability heuristic involves judging the probability of an event in terms of how readily it comes to mind.

   d. Belief perseverance is the tendency to cling to beliefs, even when the evidence has shown that they are wrong.

15. **d.** is the answer. Compared with deaf children exposed to sign language from birth, those who learn to sign as teens have the same grammatical difficulties as do hearing adults trying to learn a second spoken language. (p. 318)

16. **c.** is the answer. Children are biologically prepared to learn language as they and their caregivers interact. (p. 318)

    a. This is Skinner's position.

    b. No psychologist, including Chomsky, believes that language is entirely a product of biological maturation.

    d. Although language acquisition is not completely understood, research has shed sufficient light on it to render it less than a complete mystery.

17. **a.** is the answer. (p. 317)

    b. & c. This research is unrelated to infants' ability to detect different pitches of voices or distinguish between male and female voices.

18. **b.** is the answer. The evidence that absence of a term for a color does not affect ability to perceive the color challenges the idea that language always shapes thought. (p. 320)

    a. & d. These findings are not relevant to the linguistic determinism hypothesis, which addresses the relationship between language and thought.

    c. This finding is in keeping with the linguistic determinism hypothesis.

19. **c.** is the answer. The generic pronoun *he* evidently tends, for both adults and children, to conjure up images of males. (p. 320)

Matching Items

1. f (p. 313)	**6.** j (p. 306)	**11.** b (p. 314)
2. i (p. 311)	**7.** k (p. 303)	**12.** l (p. 301)
3. a (p. 314)	**8.** d (p. 300)	
4. g (p. 314)	**9.** h (p. 300)	
5. e (p. 305)	**10.** c (p. 303)	

Progress Test 2

Multiple-Choice Questions

1. **a.** is the answer. Reasoning in daily life is often distorted by our beliefs, which may lead us, for example, to accept conclusions that haven't been arrived at logically. (pp. 302–303)
   b., c., & d. These are just the opposite of what we tend to do.

2. **a.** is the answer. (p. 313)
   b. Morphemes are the basic units of meaning.
   c. & d. The text does not refer to basic units of grammar or semantics.

3. **b.** is the answer. (p. 314)
   a. Phonemes are the sounds in a word.
   c. Such rules are known as semantics.
   d. Such rules are the language's grammar, which would include its syntax as well as its semantics.

4. **d.** is the answer. These are all basic principles of learning and, according to Skinner, explain language development. (p. 316)

5. **d.** is the answer. Both are simple thinking strategies that allow us to make quick judgments. (pp. 304, 305)
   a. Mental sets are obstacles to problem solving, in which the person tends to repeat solutions that have worked in the past and is unable to conceive of other possible solutions.
   b. Belief bias is the tendency for preexisting beliefs to distort logical reasoning.
   c. Algorithms are methodical strategies that guarantee a solution to a particular problem.

6. **b.** is the answer. (p. 299)
   a. & d. Phonemes and morphemes are units of sound and meaning in language, respectively.
   c. Prototypes are the best examples of specific categories.

7. **d.** is the answer. If we use the availability heuristic, we base judgments on the availability of information in our memories, and more vivid information is often the most readily available. (p. 305)
   a. This would exemplify use of the trial-and-error approach to problem solving.
   b. This would exemplify a mental set.
   c. This would exemplify belief perseverance.

8. **b.** is the answer. Because they involve the systematic examination of all possible solutions to a problem, algorithms guarantee that a solution will be found. (p. 299)
   a., c., & d. None of these methods guarantees that a problem's solution will be found.

9. **b.** is the answer. The morpheme *-ed* changes the *meaning* of a regular verb to form its past tense;

the phoneme *sh* is a unique *sound* in the English language. (pp. 313, 314)
   c. & d. Syntax, which specifies rules for combining words into grammatical sentences, is one aspect of the grammar of a language.

10. **d.** is the answer. Chomsky believes that the inborn capacity for language acquisition must be activated by exposure to language. And, in fact, children raised in isolation will *not* begin to speak spontaneously. (p. 317)

11. **c.** is the answer. (p. 316)

12. **c.** is the answer. Although the child's utterances are only two words long, the words are placed in a sensible order. In English, for example, adjectives are placed before nouns. (p. 316)
    a. & b. Syntax specifies rules for *combining* two or more units in speech.
    d. There is no three-word stage.

13. **b.** is the answer. (pp. 318, 319)

14. **d.** is the answer. (p. 322)

15. **d.** is the answer. Semantic rules are directly concerned with the derivation of meaning from morphemes, words, and sentences. (p. 314)
    a. Syntax is the set of rules for a language that permits the combination of words into sentences.
    b. Grammar is the overall system of rules for using a language and, as such, includes syntax as well as semantics.
    c. Phonemic structure concerns the basic sounds, or phonemes, of a language.

16. **b.** is the answer. (p. 321)
    a. Researchers do not make a distinction between "real" and other thinking, nor do they consider nonlinguistic thinking less valid than linguistic thinking.
    c. As indicated by several studies cited in the text, this is not true.
    d. Research shows that the wordds we use do make a difference.

17. **d.** is the answer. Following the babbling stage, the child's ability to produce all phonemes becomes in a sense shaped and limited to the ability to produce those phonemes he or she hears. (p. 315)
    a. The vocal tract of *Homo sapiens* does not develop in specialized ways for different languages.
    b. & c. English and Russian differ significantly in both their phonemes and their morphemes. Nor is there any reason why differences in morphemes would in and of themselves cause pronunciation difficulties.

True–False Items

1.	F (pp. 315–316)	**6.**	T (p. 303)
2.	T (pp. 302–303)	**7.**	F (p. 313)
3.	T (p. 300)	**8.**	T (p. 313)
4.	F (p. 306)	**9.**	F (p. 321)
5.	T (p. 300)	**10.**	F (p. 318)

Psychology Applied

Multiple-Choice Questions

1. **a.** is the answer. Each sound of the word is a phoneme (note that the second letter "e" does not itself represent a sound); the morphemes are "pre," which means before; "date"; and "s," which indicates the plural. (pp. 313, 314)

2. **c.** is the answer. (pp. 301–302)
   a. Beyond a certain level of aptitude, creativity and intelligence scores are not correlated.
   b. & d. There is no evidence that creative people are more likely to be introverted or that they lack expertise in other areas.

3. **a.** is the answer. (p. 315)

4. **a.** is the answer. (p. 307)
   b. & c. These may very well occur, but they do not define belief perseverance.
   d. This is the confirmation bias.

5. **b.** is the answer. A rose is a prototypical example of the concept *flower.* (p. 299)
   c. & d. Hierarchies are organized clusters of concepts. In this example, there is only the single concept *flower.*

6. **d.** is the answer. The availability heuristic is the judgmental strategy that estimates the likelihood of events in terms of how readily they come to mind, and the most vivid information is often the most readily available. (p. 305)

7. **b.** is the answer. Follow the directions precisely and you can't miss! (p. 299)
   a. A prototype is the best example of a concept.
   c. Heuristics are simple thinking strategies that help solve problems but, in contrast to a recipe that is followed precisely, do not guarantee success.
   d. A mental set is a tendency to approach a problem in a way that has been successful in the past.

8. **c.** is the answer. By simply following a strategy that has worked well in the past, Marilyn is hampered by the type of fixation called mental set. (p. 303)
   a. Functional fixedness is being unable to conceive of an unusual function for an object.

b. Overconfidence is exhibited by the person who overestimates the accuracy of his or her judgments.
d. Prototypes are best examples of categories, not strategies for solving problems.

9. **a.** is the answer. Cognitive psychologists study how we process, understand, and communicate knowledge. Problem solving involves processing information and is therefore a topic explored by cognitive psychologists. (p. 298)
   b. Cognitive psychologists often use experimentation to study phenomena but, because not all experimental psychologists study cognition, a. is the best answer.
   c. Organizational psychologists study behavior in the workplace.
   d. Developmental psychologists study the ways in which behavior changes over the life span.

10. **d.** is the answer. (p. 299)
    b. & c. If Boris always attacks his opponent's queen when playing chess, he is a victim of mental set; prototypes, however, have nothing to do with chess playing.

11. **d.** is the answer. Confirmation bias is the tendency to search for information that confirms one's preconceptions. In this example, the politicians' preconceptions are biasing their interpretation of the survey results. (pp. 302–303)
    a. Functional fixedness is the inability to perceive an unusual use for a familiar object.
    b. Mental set is the tendency to approach a problem in a particular way. There is no problem per se in this example.
    c. Belief perseverance is the tendency to cling to one's beliefs despite evidence to the contrary.

12. **b.** is the answer. Such utterances, characteristic of a child of about 2 years, are like telegrams, in that they consist mainly of nouns and verbs and show use of syntax. (p. 316)
    a. & c. Babbling consists of phonemes, not words.
    d. Semantics refers to the rules by which meaning is derived from sentences; this speech example indicates nothing in particular about the child's understanding of semantics.

13. **c.** is the answer. (p. 299)
    a., b., & d. Heuristics do not guarantee solutions or prevent mental sets.

14. **d.** is the answer. Your conclusion is based on the stereotype that muscular build is more *representative* of athletes than computer programmers. (p. 304)
    a. Belief perseverance is the tendency to cling to one's beliefs despite evidence to the contrary.

b. Mental set is the tendency to repeat solutions that have worked in the past.
c. Functional fixedness is the tendency to think of things only in terms of their usual functions.

15. **d.** is the answer. (p. 303)

16. **b.** is the answer. The publicity surrounding disasters makes such events vivid and seemingly more probable than they actually are. (p. 305)
a. Belief perseverance is the tendency to cling to one's beliefs despite evidence to the contrary.
c. The representativeness heuristic operates when we judge the likelihood of things in terms of how well they represent particular prototypes. This example does not involve such a situation.
d. Functional fixedness operates in situations in which effective problem solving requires using an object in an unfamiliar manner.

17. **c.** is the answer. This is referred to as overconfidence. (p. 306)

18. **a.** is the answer. In this example, the way the issue is posed, or framed, has evidently influenced consumers' judgments. (p. 311)
b. Confirmation bias is the tendency to search for information that confirms one's preconceptions.
c. Mental set is the tendency to approach a problem in a particular way.
d. Overconfidence is the tendency to be more confident than correct.

19. **d.** is the answer. This sentence, although semantically meaningless, nevertheless follows the grammatical rules of English syntax for combining words into sentences. (p. 314)
a. & b. The phonemes (smallest units of sound) and morphemes (smallest units of meaning) of this sentence are equally correct.

20. **c.** is the answer. This fact challenges the linguistic determinism hypothesis; it neither supports nor refutes Chomsky's concept of an inborn universal grammar. (p. 320)

Essay Question

You should point out that the rate at which children acquire words and grammar is too extraordinary to be explained solely according to principles of learning. Children also utter all sorts of word forms they have never heard and could not, therefore, be imitating. Furthermore, children begin using morphemes in a predictable order, which learning theorists would not expect since each child experiences a unique linguistic environment. It therefore seems clear that children are biologically prepared to acquire language and that the behaviorist position is incorrect.

Key Terms

1. **Cognition** refers to all the mental activities associated with thinking, knowing, remembering, and communicating information. (p. 298)

2. A **concept** is a mental grouping of similar objects, events, and people. (p. 299)

3. A **prototype** is the best example of a particular category. (p. 299)

4. An **algorithm** is a methodical, logical procedure that, while sometimes slow, guarantees success. (p. 300)

5. A **heuristic** is a simple thinking strategy that often allows us to make judgments and solve problems efficiently. Although heuristics are more efficient than algorithms, they do not guarantee success and sometimes even impede problem solving. (p. 300)

6. **Insight** is a sudden and often novel realization of the solution to a problem. Insight contrasts with trial and error and, indeed, may often follow an unsuccessful episode of trial and error. (p. 300)

7. Most experts agree that **creativity** refers to an ability to produce novel and valuable ideas. A certain level of aptitude is necessary but not sufficient for creativity. (p. 301)

8. **Confirmation bias** is an obstacle to problem solving in which people tend to search for information that supports their preconceptions. (pp. 302–303)

9. **Fixation** is an inability to approach a problem in a new way. (p. 303)

10. **Mental set** refers to the tendency to continue applying a particular problem-solving strategy even when it is no longer helpful. (p. 303)

11. **Functional fixedness** is a type of fixation in which a person can think of things only in terms of their usual functions. (p. 303)

12. The **representativeness heuristic** is the tendency to judge the likelihood of things in terms of how well they match particular prototypes. (p. 304)

13. The **availability heuristic** is based on estimating the probability of certain events in terms of how readily they come to mind. (p. 305)

14. Another obstacle to problem solving, **overconfidence** refers to the tendency to overestimate the accuracy of our beliefs and judgments. (p. 306)

15. **Belief perseverance** is the tendency for people to cling to a particular belief even after the information that led to the formation of the belief is discredited. (p. 307)

16. **Intuition** is an immediate, automatic, and effortless feeling or thought. (p. 308)

17. **Framing** refers to the way an issue or question is posed. It can affect people's perception of the issue or answer to the question. (p. 311)

18. **Language** refers to spoken, written, or signed words and how we combine them to communicate meaning. (p. 313)

19. **Phonemes** are the smallest units of sound in a language that are distinctive for speakers of the language. (p. 313)

20. **Morphemes** are the smallest units of language that carry meaning. (p. 314)

    Example: The word "dogs," which contains four phonemes, contains only two **morphemes**—"dog" and "-s." Although most morphemes are combinations of two or more phonemes, the plural "-s" conveys a distinctive meaning of "more than one."

21. **Grammar** is a system of rules that enables us to communicate with and understand others. (p. 314)

22. **Semantics** is the set of rules used to derive meaning from morphemes, words, and sentences in a given language. (p. 314)

    Example: One **semantic** rule of English is that adding *-ed* to a verb gives the verb a past-tense meaning.

23. **Syntax** is the rules for combining words into grammatically sensible sentences in a given language. (p. 314)

    Example: One **syntactic** rule of English is that adjectives are positioned before nouns.

24. The **babbling stage** of speech development, which begins around 4 months, is characterized by the spontaneous utterance of speech sounds. During the babbling stage, children the world over sound alike. (p. 315)

25. Between 1 and 2 years of age, children speak mostly in single words; they are therefore in the **one-word stage** of linguistic development. (p. 316)

26. Beginning about age 2, children are in the **two-word stage** and speak mostly in two-word sentences. (p. 316)

27. **Telegraphic speech** is the economical, telegram-like speech of children in the two-word stage. Utterances consist mostly of nouns and verbs; however, words occur in the correct order, showing that the child has learned some of the language's syntactic rules. (p. 316)

28. **Linguistic determinism** is Benjamin Whorf's hypothesis that language determines the way we think. (p. 319)

Motivation and Emotion:
8A: Motivation

UNIT OVERVIEW

Motivation is the study of forces that energize and direct our behavior. Unit 8A discusses various motivational concepts and looks closely at three motives: hunger, sex, and the need to belong. Research on hunger points to the fact that our biological drive to eat is strongly influenced by psychological and social-cultural factors. Sexual motivation in men and women is triggered less by physiological factors and more by external incentives. Even so, research studies demonstrate that sexual orientation is neither willfully chosen nor easily changed.

The last part of the unit discusses the need to belong. Our need to feel connected with others had survival value for our ancestors, and may explain why humans everywhere live in groups.

NOTE: Answer guidelines for all Unit 8A questions begin on page 200.

UNIT REVIEW

First, skim each section, noting headings and boldface items. After you have read the section, review each objective by answering the fill-in and essay-type questions that follow it. As you proceed, evaluate your performance by consulting the answers beginning on page 200. Do not continue with the next section until you understand each answer. If you need to, review or reread the section in the textbook before continuing.

Introduction and **Motivational Concepts**
(pp. 328–331)

Objective 1: Define *motivation* as psychologists use the term today, and identify four perspectives useful for studying motivated behavior.

1. Motivation is defined as _____ _____ _____ .

2. Four perspectives on motivation are _____ theory (which has been replaced by the _____ perspective), _____ - _____ theory, _____ theory, and the _____ of needs proposed by _____ .

3. As a result of Darwin's influence, many complex behaviors were classified as rigid, unlearned behavior patterns that are characteristic of a species, called _____ . Although early instinct theory_____ (did/did not) explain human motives, the underlying assumption that _____ predispose species-typical behavior remains strong.

4. According to another view of motivation, organisms may experience a physiological _____ , which creates a state of arousal that _____ the organism to reduce the need.

5. The aim of drive reduction is to maintain a constant internal state, called _____ .

6. Behavior is often not so much pushed by our drives as it is pulled by _____ in the environment.

7. Rather than reduce a physiological need, some motivated behaviors actually _____ arousal. This demonstrates that human motives _____ (do/do not) always satisfy some biological need.

8. Human motivation aims not to eliminate _____ but to seek

_____ _____

of arousal.

Objective 2: Describe Maslow's hierarchy of needs.

9. Starting from the idea that _____- _____ needs such as the need for water take precedence over others, Maslow constructed a hierarchy of needs.

10. According to Maslow, the _____ needs are the most pressing, whereas the highest-order needs relate to _____ and _____ .

11. A criticism of Maslow's theory is that the sequence is _____ and not _____ experienced.

12. Surveys of life satisfaction reveal that _____ satisfaction is strongly predictive of well-being in poorer nations, whereas _____-_____ satisfaction matters more in wealthy nations and _____ in individualist nations.

Hunger (pp. 331–348)

Objective 3: Describe the physiological determinants of hunger.

1. Ancel Keys observed that men became preoccupied with thoughts of food when they underwent

_____ .

2. Cannon and Washburn's experiment using a balloon indicated that there is an association between hunger and _____

_____ .

3. When rats had their stomachs removed, hunger _____ (did/did not) continue.

4. Increases in the hormone _____ diminish blood _____ , partly by converting it to stored fat, which causes hunger to _____ .

5. The brain area that plays a role in hunger and other bodily maintenance functions is the _____ . Animals will begin eating when the _____ _____ is electrically stimulated. When this region is destroyed, hunger _____ (increases/ decreases). Animals will stop eating when the

_____ _____

is stimulated. When this area is destroyed, animals _____ (overeat/ undereat).

6. The hypothalamus also secretes the hunger-triggering hormone _____ .

7. The hunger-arousing hormone secreted by an empty stomach is _____ .

8. When a portion of an obese person's stomach is surgically sealed off, the remaining stomach produces _____ (more/less) of this hormone.

For questions 9–11, identify the appetite hormone that is described.

9. Chemical secreted by bloated fat cells:

_____ .

10. Digestive tract hormone that signals fullness:

_____ .

11. Hormone secreted by the stomach that signals fullness: _____

12. The weight level at which an individual's body is programmed to stay is referred to as the body's

_____ _____ .

A person whose weight goes beyond this level will tend to feel _____ (more/less) hungry than usual and expend _____ (more/less) energy.

13. The rate of energy expenditure in maintaining basic functions when the body is at rest is the

_____ _____ rate. When food intake is reduced, the body compensates by _____ (raising/lowering) this rate.

14. The concept of a precise body set point that drives hunger _____ (is accepted/is not accepted) by all researchers. Some researchers believe that set point can be altered by _____

_____ .

In support of this idea is evidence that when people and other animals are given unlimited access to tasty foods, they tend to_____ and _____ _____ .
For these reasons, some researchers prefer to use the term _____ _____ as an alternative to the idea that there is a fixed set point.

Objective 4: Discuss psychological, cultural, and situational influences on hunger.

15. Research with amnesia patients indicates that part of knowing when to eat is our _____ of our last meal.

16. Carbohydrates boost levels of the neurotransmitter _____ , which _____ (calms/arouses) the body.

17. Taste preferences for sweet and salty are _____ (genetic/learned). Other influences on taste include _____ and _____ .

18. We have a natural dislike of many foods that are _____ ; this _____ was probably adaptive for our ancestors, and protected them from toxic substances.

19. Because of _____ facilitation, people tend to eat _____ (less/more) when they are with other people. The phenomenon of _____ _____ is the tendency to mindlessly eat more when portions are larger.

Objective 5: Explain how the eating disorders demonstrate the influence of psychological forces on physiologically motivated behavior.

20. The disorder in which a person becomes significantly underweight and yet feels fat is known as _____ _____ .

21. A more common disorder is

_____ _____ , which is characterized by repeated

_____-_____ episodes and by feelings of depression or anxiety. When bouts of excessive eating followed by remorse are not accompanied by excessive exercise or fasting, the _____-_____ disorder may be diagnosed.

22. The families of bulimia patients have a high incidence of childhood _____ and _____ self-evaluation. The families of anorexia patients tend to be

_____ , _____-_____ , and _____ .

23. Genetic factors _____ (may/do not) influence susceptibility to eating disorders.

24. Vulnerability to eating disorders _____ (increases/does not increase) with greater body dissatisfaction.

25. Women students in _____ rate their actual shape as closer to the cultural ideal. In _____ cultures, however, the rise in eating disorders has coincided with an increasing number of women having a poor _____ _____ .

26. Stice and Shaw found that when young women were shown pictures of unnaturally thin models, they felt more _____ ,

_____ , and _____ with their own bodies.

Objective 6: Describe research findings on obesity and weight control.

27. Being slightly overweight _____ (poses/does not pose) serious health risks. In the United States, over _____ (how many?) percent of adults are obese. Significant obesity increases the risk of _____ _____ _____ .

28. In developing societies where people face _____ , obesity is considered a sign of _____ and _____ _____ .

29. The risks of obesity are greater for people who carry their weight at their _____ . It also has been linked in women to their risk of late-life _____ disease and brain tissue loss.

30. Obese people are often stereotyped as _____ , _____ , and _____ .

31. One study found that obese women earned _____ than a control group of nonobese women and were less likely to be _____ .

32. In one experiment, job applicants were rated as less worthy of hiring when they were made to appear _____ .

33. The energy equivalent of a pound of fat is approximately _____ calories.

34. The immediate determinant of body fat is the size and number of _____ _____ one has. This number is, in turn, determined by several factors, including _____ _____ .

35. The size of fat cells _____ (can/cannot) be decreased by dieting; the number of fat cells _____ (can/cannot) be decreased by dieting.

36. Fat tissue has a _____ (higher/lower) metabolic rate than lean tissue.

The result is that fat tissue requires _____ (more/less) food energy to be maintained.

37. The body weight "thermostat" of obese people _____ (is/is not) set to maintain a higher-than-average weight. When weight drops below this setting, _____ increases and _____ decreases.

Explain why, metabolically, many obese people find it so difficult to become and stay thin.

38. Studies of adoptees and twins _____ (do/do not) provide evidence of a genetic influence on obesity. A particular variant of the gene called _____ has been shown to nearly double a person's risk of becoming obese.

39. People are _____ (less/more) likely to become obese when a friend becomes obese, thus demonstrating _____ influence as a factor in obesity. Obesity is _____ (more/less) common among those who watch more daily TV and _____ (more/less) common among people living in communities where walking is common.

40. Most obese persons who lose weight _____ (gain/do not gain) it back.

(Close-Up) State several pieces of advice for those who want to lose weight.

Sexual Motivation (pp. 348–359)

Objective 7: Describe the human sexual response cycle.

1. The two researchers who identified a four-stage sexual response cycle are _____ and _____ . In order, the stages of the cycle are the _____ phase, the _____ phase, _____ , and the _____ phase.

2. During resolution, males experience a _____ _____ , during which they are incapable of another orgasm.

Objective 8: Discuss the impact of hormones, external stimuli, and fantasies on sexual motivation and behavior.

3. In most mammals, females are sexually receptive only during ovulation, when the hormones, the _____ (such as _____), have peaked.

4. The importance of the hormone _____ to male sexual arousal is confirmed by the fact that sexual interest declines in animals if their _____ are removed. In women, low levels of the hormone _____ may cause a waning of sexual interest.

5. Normal hormonal fluctuations in humans have _____ (little/significant) effect on sexual motivation. In later life, frequency of intercourse _____ (increases/ decreases) as sex hormone levels _____ (increase/decline).

6. Research has shown that erotic stimuli _____ (are/are not) nearly as arousing for women as for men.

7. Brain scans reveal more activity in the _____ among _____ (women/men) who are viewing erotica.

Explain some of the possible harmful consequences of sexually explicit material.

8. Most women and men _____ (have/ do not have) sexual fantasies. Compared with women's fantasies, men's sexual fantasies are more _____ _____ . Sexual fantasies _____ (do/do not) indicate sexual problems or dissatisfaction.

Objective 9: Discuss some of the factors that influence adolescent sexual behavior, and describe trends in the spread of sexually transmitted infections.

9. Sexual expression varies widely from one _____ to another and with the passage of _____ .

10. Rates of teen intercourse are roughly similar in _____ _____ and _____ _____ but much lower in _____ and _____ countries and among North Americans of _____ descent.

11. Because teenage sex is often _____ , there is increased risk of pregnancy and _____ _____ . Compared with European teens, American teens have _____ (higher/lower) rates of intercourse, _____ (higher/lower) rates of contraceptive use, and thus _____ (higher/lower) rates of teen pregnancy and abortion.

State five factors that contribute to the high rate of unprotected sex among teenagers.

12. Unprotected sex has led to an increase in adolescent rates of _____

_____ _____ .

Teenage girls, because of their not yet fully mature biological development and lower levels of protective _____ , may be especially vulnerable to STIs.

State several predictors of sexual restraint (reduced teen sexuality and pregnancy).

Objective 10: Summarize current views on the number of people whose sexual orientation is homosexual, and discuss the research on environmental and biological influences on sexual orientation.

13. A person's sexual attraction toward members of a particular gender is referred to as

_____ _____ .

14. Historically, _____ (all/a slight majority) of the world's cultures have been predominantly heterosexual. Most homosexuals begin thinking of themselves as gay or lesbian around _____ .

15. Studies in Europe and the United States indicate that approximately _____ percent of men and _____ percent of women are exclusively homosexual. This finding suggests that popular estimates of the rate of homosexuality are _____ (high/low/accurate).

16. Some homosexuals struggle with their sexual orientation and are at increased risk of _____ attempts.

17. A person's sexual orientation _____ (does/does not) appear to be voluntarily chosen. Several research studies reveal that sexual orientation among _____ (women/men) tends to be less strongly felt and potentially more changeable than among the other gender. This phenomenon has been called the gender difference in _____

_____ .

18. Childhood events and family relationships _____ (are/are not) important factors in determining a person's sexual orientation. Also, homosexuality _____ (does/does not) involve a fear of the other gender that leads people to direct their sexual desires toward members of their own gender.

19. Sex hormone levels _____ (do/do not) predict sexual orientation.

20. As children, most homosexuals _____ (were/were not) sexually victimized.

21. Homosexual and bisexual people appear more often in certain populations, including

_____ ,

_____ _____ ,

_____ , and _____ .

22. Men who have older brothers are somewhat _____ (more/less) likely to be gay. This phenomenon, which has been called the

_____ _____ -

_____ _____ ,

may represent a defensive maternal

_____ response to substances produced by _____ (male/ female) fetuses.

23. Same-sex attraction _____ (does/does not) occur among animals.

24. Researcher Simon LeVay discovered a cluster of cells in the _____ that is larger in _____ men than in all others. Gays and lesbians differ from their straight counterparts in their preference for sex-related _____ . Other studies have

found that the brain's _____ _____ is larger in lesbian women and heterosexual men.

25. Studies of twins suggest that genes probably _____ (do/do not) play a role in homosexuality. Research has confirmed that homosexual men have more homosexual relatives on their _____ (mother's/father's) side than on their _____ (mother's/father's) side.

26. In animals and some rare human cases, sexual orientation has been altered by abnormal _____ conditions during prenatal development. In humans, prenatal exposure to hormone levels typical of _____ , particularly between _____ and _____ months after conception, may predispose an attraction to males.

27. Gays and lesbians may have certain physical traits that fall midway between straight males and females, including _____ ridges, greater odds of being _____ (right/left)-handed, and anatomical traits of the _____ within the hearing system.

28. A number of scientists today believe that biological factors may predispose a _____ that influences sexuality, and thus explains why sexual orientation is _____ (difficult/relatively easy) to change. Most psychiatrists now believe that _____ plays the larger role in predisposing sexual orientation. Those who believe that sexual orientation is determined by _____ express more accepting attitudes toward homosexual persons.

The Need to Belong (pp. 359–362)

Objective 11: Describe the adaptive value of social attachments, and discuss both healthy and unhealthy consequences of our need to belong.

1. The philosopher _____ referred to humans as the _____ animal.

From an evolutionary standpoint, social bonds in humans boosted our ancestors' _____ rates. As adults, those who formed _____ were more likely to _____ and co-nurture their offspring to maturity.

2. When asked what makes life meaningful, most people mention _____ _____ .

3. Feeling accepted and loved by others boosts our _____ .

4. Much of our _____ behavior aims to increase our belonging. For most people, familiarity leads to _____ (liking/disliking).

5. After years of placing individual refugee and immigrant families in _____ communities, U.S. policies today encourage _____ _____ .

6. _____ (Throughout the world/Only in certain cultures do) people use social exclusion, or _____ , to control social behavior.

7. Researchers have found that people who are rejected are more likely to engage in _____ behaviors, to underperform on _____ _____ , and to act in disparaging or _____ ways.

PROGRESS TEST 1

Multiple-Choice Questions

Circle your answers to the following questions and check them with the answers beginning on page 201. If your answer is incorrect, read the explanation for why it is incorrect and then consult the appropriate pages of the text (in parentheses following the correct answer).

1. Motivation is best understood as a state that
   a. reduces a drive.
   b. aims at satisfying a biological need.
   c. energizes an organism to act.
   d. energizes and directs behavior.

2. Which of the following is a difference between a drive and a need?
   a. Needs are learned; drives are inherited.
   b. Needs are physiological states; drives are psychological states.
   c. Drives are generally stronger than needs.
   d. Needs are generally stronger than drives.

3. One problem with the idea of motivation as drive reduction is that
   a. because some motivated behaviors do not seem to be based on physiological needs, they cannot be explained in terms of drive reduction.
   b. it fails to explain any human motivation.
   c. it cannot account for homeostasis.
   d. it does not explain the hunger drive.

4. Some scientific evidence makes a preliminary link between homosexuality and
   a. late sexual maturation.
   b. the age of an individual's first erotic experience.
   c. atypical prenatal hormones.
   d. early problems in relationships with parents.

5. Increases in insulin will
   a. lower blood sugar and trigger hunger.
   b. raise blood sugar and trigger hunger.
   c. lower blood sugar and trigger satiety.
   d. raise blood sugar and trigger satiety.

6. Electrical stimulation of the lateral hypothalamus will cause an animal to
   a. begin eating.
   b. stop eating.
   c. become obese.
   d. begin copulating.

7. The text suggests that a *neophobia* for unfamiliar tastes
   a. is more common in children than in adults.
   b. protected our ancestors from potentially toxic substances.
   c. may be an early warning sign of an eating disorder.
   d. only grows stronger with repeated exposure to those tastes.

8. I am a protein produced by fat cells and monitored by the hypothalamus. When in abundance, I cause the brain to increase metabolism. What am I?
   a. PYY
   b. ghrelin
   c. orexin
   d. leptin

9. Instinct theory and drive-reduction theory both emphasize _____ factors in motivation.
   a. environmental
   b. cognitive
   c. psychological
   d. biological

10. The correct order of the stages of Masters and Johnson's sexual response cycle is
    a. plateau; excitement; orgasm; resolution.
    b. excitement; plateau; orgasm; resolution.
    c. excitement; orgasm; resolution; refractory.
    d. plateau; excitement; orgasm; refractory.

11. Few human behaviors are rigidly patterned enough to qualify as
    a. needs.
    b. drives.
    c. instincts.
    d. incentives.

12. Which of the following is NOT true regarding sexual orientation?
    a. Sexual orientation is neither willfully chosen nor willfully changed.
    b. Some homosexuals struggle with their sexual orientation.
    c. Men's sexual orientation is potentially more fluid and changeable than women's.
    d. Women, regardless of sexual orientation, respond to both female and male erotic stimuli.

13. In his study of men on a semistarvation diet, Keys found that
    a. the metabolic rate of the men increased.
    b. the men eventually lost interest in food.
    c. the men became obsessed with food.
    d. the men's behavior directly contradicted predictions made by Maslow's hierarchy of needs.

14. When asked what makes life meaningful, most people first mention
    a. good health.
    b. challenging work.
    c. satisfying relationships.
    d. serving others.

15. Which of the following is true of bulimia nervosa?
    a. It involves bingeing and purging.
    b. Sufferers are usually females from competitive families.
    c. It results in dramatic weight loss.
    d. Victims set perfectionist standards for themselves.

16. Castration of male rats results in
    a. reduced testosterone and sexual interest.
    b. reduced testosterone, but no change in sexual interest.
    c. reduced estradiol and sexual interest.
    d. reduced estradiol, but no change in sexual interest.

17. Research on genetic influences on obesity reveals that
    a. the body weights of adoptees correlate with that of their biological parents.
    b. the body weights of adoptees correlate with that of their adoptive parents.
    c. identical twins usually have very different body weights.
    d. the body weights of identical twin women are more similar than those of identical twin men.

18. Research on obesity indicates that
    a. pound for pound, fat tissue requires more calories to maintain than lean tissue.
    b. once fat cells are acquired they are never lost, no matter how rigorously one diets.
    c. one pound of weight is lost for every 3500-calorie reduction in diet.
    d. when weight drops below the set point, hunger and metabolism also decrease.

19. The number of fat cells a person has is influenced by
    a. genetic predisposition.
    b. childhood eating patterns.
    c. adulthood eating patterns.
    d. all of these factors.

Matching Items

Match each term with its definition or description.

Terms

_____ 1. anorexia nervosa
_____ 2. set point
_____ 3. incentive
_____ 4. testosterone
_____ 5. binge-eating disorder
_____ 6. refractory period
_____ 7. estrogen
_____ 8. homeostasis
_____ 9. basal metabolic rate
_____ 10. glucose
_____ 11. sexual orientation
_____ 12. bulimia nervosa

Definitions or Descriptions

a. hormone secreted more by females than by males
b. the body's tendency to maintain a balanced internal state
c. hormone secreted more by males than by females
d. resting period after orgasm
e. environmental stimulus that motivates behavior
f. a person's attraction to members of a particular sex
g. an eating disorder characterized by significantly below normal weight
h. the major source of energy for body tissues
i. resting rate of energy expenditure
j. an eating disorder characterized by repeated episodes of overeating followed by vomiting, fasting, or laxative use
k. the body's weight-maintenance setting
l. characterized by bouts of overeating and remorse, but without excessive exercise or fasting

PROGRESS TEST 2

Progress Test 2 should be completed during a final unit review. Answer the following questions after you thoroughly understand the correct answers for the section reviews and Progress Test 1.

Multiple-Choice Questions

1. Which of the following influences on hunger motivation does NOT belong with the others?
   a. set/settling point
   b. attraction to sweet and salty tastes
   c. reduced production of ghrelin after stomach bypass surgery
   d. memory of time elapsed since your last meal

2. Homeostasis refers to
   a. the tendency to maintain a steady internal state.
   b. the tendency to seek external incentives for behavior.
   c. the setting of the body's "weight thermostat."
   d. a theory of the development of sexual orientation.

3. The tendency to overeat when food is plentiful
   a. is a recent phenomenon that is associated with the luxury of having ample food.
   b. emerged in our prehistoric ancestors as an adaptive response to alternating periods of feast and famine.
   c. is greater in developed, than in developing, societies.
   d. is stronger in women than in men.

4. Although the cause of eating disorders is still unknown, proposed explanations focus on all the following EXCEPT
   a. metabolic factors.
   b. genetic factors.
   c. family background factors.
   d. cultural factors.

5. The brain area that when stimulated suppresses eating is the
   a. lateral hypothalamus.
   b. ventromedial hypothalamus.
   c. lateral thalamus.
   d. ventromedial thalamus.

6. Exposure of a fetus to the hormones typical of females between _____ and _____ months after conception may predispose the developing human to become attracted to males.
   a. 1; 3   c. 4; 7
   b. 2; 5   d. 6; 9

7. Which of the following statements concerning homosexuality is true?
   a. Homosexuals have abnormal hormone levels.
   b. As children, most homosexuals were molested by an adult homosexual.
   c. Homosexuals had a domineering opposite-sex parent.
   d. Research indicates that sexual orientation may be at least partly physiological.

8. Women in _____ rate their body ideals closest to their actual shape.
   a. Western cultures
   b. countries such as Africa, where thinness can signal poverty,
   c. countries such as India, where thinness is not idealized,
   d. Australia, New Zealand, and England

9. According to Maslow's theory
   a. the most basic motives are based on safety needs.
   b. needs are satisfied in a specified order.
   c. the highest motives relate to self-actualization.
   d. the order of these is not universally fixed.

10. Which of the following is INCONSISTENT with the drive-reduction theory of motivation?
    a. When body temperature drops below 98.6° Fahrenheit, blood vessels constrict to conserve warmth.
    b. A person is driven to seek a drink when his or her cellular water level drops below its optimum point.
    c. Monkeys will work puzzles even if not given a food reward.
    d. A person becomes hungry when body weight falls below its biological set point.

11. Which of the following is true concerning eating disorders?

    a. Genetic factors may influence susceptibility.
    b. Cultural pressures for thinness strongly influence teenage girls.
    c. Family background is a significant factor.
    d. All of these statements are true.

12. Sexual orientation refers to

    a. a person's tendency to display behaviors typical of males or females.
    b. a person's sense of identity as a male or female.
    c. a person's enduring sexual attraction toward members of a particular gender.
    d. a person's level of arousal during the response cycle.

13. Hunger and sexual motivation are alike in that both are influenced by

    a. internal physiological factors.
    b. external and imagined stimuli.
    c. cultural expectations.
    d. all of these factors.

14. According to Masters and Johnson, the sexual response of males is most likely to differ from that of females during

    a. the excitement phase.
    b. the plateau phase.
    c. orgasm.
    d. the resolution phase.

15. In animals, destruction of the lateral hypothalamus results in _____ , whereas destruction of the ventromedial hypothalamus results in _____ .

    a. overeating; loss of hunger
    b. loss of hunger; overeating
    c. an elevated set point; a lowered set point
    d. increased thirst; loss of thirst

16. Which of the following is NOT necessarily a reason that obese people have trouble losing weight?

    a. Fat tissue has a lower metabolic rate than lean tissue.
    b. Once a person has lost weight, it takes fewer calories to maintain his or her current weight.
    c. The tendency toward obesity may be genetically based.
    d. Obese people tend to lack willpower.

17. Beginning with the most basic needs, which of the following represents the correct sequence of needs in the hierarchy described by Maslow?

    a. safety; physiological; esteem; belongingness and love; self-fulfillment; self-transcendence
    b. safety; physiological; belongingness and love; esteem; self-fulfillment; self-transcendence
    c. physiological; safety; esteem; belongingness and love; self-fulfillment; self-transcendence
    d. physiological; safety; belongingness and love; esteem; self-fulfillment; self-transcendence

18. While viewing erotica, men and women differ in the activity levels of which brain area?

    a. anterior cingulate cortex
    b. amygdala
    c. occipital lobe
    d. temporal lobe

True–False Items

Indicate whether each statement is true or false by placing *T* or *F* in the blank next to the item.

_____ 1. When body weight rises above set point, hunger increases.

_____ 2. According to Masters and Johnson, only males experience a plateau period in the cycle of sexual arousal.

_____ 3. Testosterone affects the sexual arousal of the male only.

_____ 4. Unlike men, women tend not to be aroused by sexually explicit material.

_____ 5. All taste preferences are conditioned.

_____ 6. Separated or divorced people are half as likely as married people to say they are happy.

_____ 7. An increase in insulin increases blood glucose levels and triggers hunger.

_____ 8. Most obese people who lose weight eventually gain it back.

_____ 9. One's sexual orientation is not voluntarily chosen.

_____ 10. Obesity is often a sign of social status and affluence in developing countries.

PSYCHOLOGY APPLIED

Answer these questions the day before a test as a final check on your understanding of the unit's terms and concepts.

Multiple-Choice Questions

1. After an initial rapid weight loss, a person on a diet loses weight much more slowly. This slow-down occurs because
   a. most of the initial weight loss is simply water.
   b. when a person diets, metabolism decreases.
   c. people begin to "cheat" on their diets.
   d. insulin levels tend to increase with reduced food intake.

2. (Close-Up) Which of the following would be the worst piece of advice to offer to someone trying to lose weight?
   a. "To treat yourself to one 'normal' meal each day, eat very little until the evening meal."
   b. "Reduce your consumption of saturated fats."
   c. "Boost your metabolism by exercising regularly."
   d. "Without increasing total caloric intake, increase the relative proportion of carbohydrates in your diet."

3. Mary loves hang-gliding. It would be most difficult to explain Mary's behavior according to
   a. incentives.
   b. arousal theory.
   c. drive-reduction theory.
   d. Maslow's hierarchy of needs.

4. For two weeks, Orlando has been on a hunger strike in protest of his country's involvement in what he perceives as an immoral war. Orlando's willingness to starve himself to make a political statement conflicts with the theory of motivation advanced by
   a. Masters.   c. Keys.
   b. Murray.   d. Maslow.

5. Kathy has been undergoing treatment for bulimia. There is an above-average probability that one or more members of Kathy's family have a problem with
   a. high achievement.
   b. overprotection.
   c. obesity.
   d. their appearance.

6. Which of the following was NOT identified as a contributing factor in the low rate of contraceptive use among adolescents?
   a. alcohol use
   b. thrill-seeking
   c. mass media sexual norms
   d. ignorance

7. One shortcoming of the instinct theory of motivation is that it
   a. places too much emphasis on environmental factors.
   b. focuses on cognitive aspects of motivation.
   c. applies only to animal behavior.
   d. does not explain human behaviors; it simply names them.

8. Which of the following is NOT typical of both anorexia and bulimia?
   a. far more frequent occurrence in women than in men
   b. preoccupation with food and fear of being overweight
   c. weight significantly and noticeably outside normal ranges
   d. low self-esteem and feelings of depression

9. Which of the following is NOT an example of homeostasis?
   a. perspiring to restore normal body temperature
   b. feeling hungry and eating to restore the level of blood glucose to normal
   c. feeling hungry at the sight of an appetizing food
   d. drinking water to prevent dehydration.

10. Two rats have escaped from their cages in the neurophysiology lab. The technician needs your help in returning them to their proper cages. One rat is grossly overweight; the other is severely underweight. You confidently state that the overweight rat goes in the "_____-destruction" cage, while the underweight rat goes in the "_____-destruction" cage.
    a. hippocampus; amygdala
    b. amygdala; hippocampus
    c. lateral hypothalamus; ventromedial hypothalamus
    d. ventromedial hypothalamus; lateral hypothalamus

11. Kenny and his brother have nearly identical eating and exercise habits, yet Kenny is obese and his brother is very thin. The MOST LIKELY explanation for the difference in their body weights is that they differ in
    a. their bone structure.
    b. amygdala activity.
    c. their set points and their metabolic rates.
    d. their differing exposure to carbohydrate-laden foods.

12. Ali's parents have tried hard to minimize their son's exposure to sweet, fattening foods. If Ali has the occasion to taste sweet foods in the future, which of the following is likely?
    a. He will have a strong aversion to such foods.
    b. He will have a neutral reaction to sweet foods.
    c. He will display a preference for sweet tastes.
    d. It is impossible to predict Ali's reaction.

13. Summarizing his presentation on the origins of homosexuality, Dennis explains that the fraternal birth-order effect refers to the fact that
    a. men who have younger brothers are somewhat more likely to be gay.
    b. men who have older brothers are somewhat more likely to be gay.
    c. women with older sisters are somewhat more likely to be gay.
    d. women with younger sisters are somewhat more likely to be gay.

14. Summarizing her report on the need to belong, Rolanda states that
    a. "Cooperation amongst our ancestors was uncommon."
    b. "Social bonding is not in our nature; it is a learned human trait."
    c. "Because bonding with others increased our ancestors' success at reproduction and survival, it became part of our biological nature."
    d. "Our male ancestors were more likely to bond than were females."

15. Of the following individuals, who might be most prone to developing an eating disorder?
    a. Jason, an adolescent boy who is somewhat overweight and is unpopular with his peers
    b. Jennifer, a teenage girl who has a poor self-image and a fear of not being able to live up to her parents' high standards
    c. Susan, a 35-year-old woman who is a "workaholic" and devotes most of her energies to her high-pressured career

    d. Bill, a 40-year-old man who has had problems with alcoholism and is seriously depressed after losing his job of 20 years

16. Lucille has been sticking to a strict diet but can't seem to lose weight. What is the most likely explanation for her difficulty?
    a. Her body has a very low set point.
    b. Her prediet weight was near her body's set point.
    c. Her weight problem is actually caused by an underlying eating disorder.
    d. Lucille is influenced primarily by external factors.

17. Randy, who has been under a lot of stress lately, has intense cravings for sugary junk foods, which tend to make him feel more relaxed. Which of the following is the most likely explanation for his craving?
    a. Randy feels that he deserves to pamper himself with sweets because of the stress he is under.
    b. The extra sugar gives Randy the energy he needs to cope with the demands of daily life.
    c. Carbohydrates boost levels of serotonin, which has a calming effect.
    d. The extra sugar tends to lower blood insulin level, which promotes relaxation.

18. Which of the following teens is most likely to delay the initiation of sex?
    a. Jack, who has below-average intelligence
    b. Jason, who is not religiously active
    c. Ron, who regularly volunteers his time in community service
    d. It is impossible to predict.

Essay Question

Differentiate the three major theories of motivation, discuss their origins, and explain why they cannot fully account for human behavior. (Use the space below to list the points you want to make, and organize them. Then write the essay on a separate sheet of paper.)

KEY TERMS

Using your own words, write on a separate piece of paper a brief definition or explanation of each of the following terms.

1. motivation
2. instinct
3. drive-reduction theory
4. homeostasis
5. incentives
6. hierarchy of needs
7. glucose
8. set point
9. basal metabolic rate
10. anorexia nervosa
11. bulimia nervosa
12. binge-eating disorder
13. sexual response cycle
14. refractory period
15. estrogen
16. testosterone
17. sexual orientation

ANSWERS
Unit Review

Introduction and *Motivational Concepts*

1. a need or desire that energizes behavior and directs it toward a goal
2. instinct; evolutionary; drive-reduction; arousal; hierarchy; Abraham Maslow
3. instincts; did not; genes
4. need; drives
5. homeostasis
6. incentives
7. increase; do not
8. arousal; optimum levels
9. lower-level
10. physiological; self-actualization; self-transcendence
11. arbitrary; universally
12. financial; home-life; self-esteem

Hunger

1. semistarvation
2. stomach contractions
3. did
4. insulin; glucose; increase
5. hypothalamus; lateral hypothalamus; decreases; ventromedial hypothalamus; overeat
6. orexin
7. ghrelin
8. less
9. leptin
10. PYY
11. obestatin
12. set point; less; more
13. basal metabolic; lowering
14. is not accepted; slow, sustained changes in body weight; overeat; gain weight; settling point
15. memory
16. serotonin; calms
17. genetic; conditioning; culture
18. unfamiliar; neophobia
19. social; more; unit bias
20. anorexia nervosa
21. bulimia nervosa; binge-purge; binge-eating
22. obesity; negative; competitive; high-achieving; protective
23. may
24. increases
25. India; Western; body image
26. ashamed; depressed; dissatisfied
27. does not pose; 34; diabetes, high blood pressure, heart disease, gallstones, arthritis, and certain types of cancer
28. famine; affluence; social status
29. abdomens (stomachs); Alzheimer's
30. slow; lazy; sloppy
31. less; married
32. overweight
33. 3500
34. fat cells; genetic predisposition, early childhood eating patterns, adult overeating
35. can; cannot
36. lower; less
37. is; hunger; metabolism

Obese persons have higher set-point weights than nonobese persons. During a diet, metabolic rate drops to defend the set-point weight. The dieter therefore finds it hard to progress beyond an initial weight loss. When the diet is concluded, the lowered metabolic rate continues, so that relatively small amounts of food may prove fattening. Also, some people have lower metabolic rates than others.

38. do; FTO

39. more; social; more; less

40. gain

Begin only if you are motivated and self-disciplined. Minimize exposure to tempting food cues. Eat healthy foods. Don't starve all day and eat one big meal at night. Beware of binge eating. Be realistic and moderate. Boost your metabolism through exercise.

Sexual Motivation

1. Masters; Johnson; excitement; plateau; orgasm; resolution

2. refractory period

3. estrogens; estradiol

4. testosterone; testes; testosterone

5. little; decreases; decline

6. are

7. amygdala; men

Erotic material may increase the viewer's acceptance of the false idea that women enjoy rape, may increase men's willingness to hurt women, may lead people to devalue their partners and relationships, and may diminish people's satisfaction with their own sexual partners.

8. have; frequent, physical, and less romantic; do not

9. culture; time

10. Western Europe; Latin America; Asian; Arab; Asian

11. unprotected; sexually transmitted infections (STIs); lower; lower; higher

Among the factors that contribute to unprotected sex among adolescents are (1) ignorance about the safe and risky times of the menstrual cycle, (2) guilt related to sexual activity, (3) minimal communication about birth control, (4) alcohol use that influences judgment, and (5) mass media norms of unprotected promiscuity.

12. sexually transmitted infection (STI); antibodies

Teens with high intelligence test scores, those who are actively religious, those whose father is present, and those who participate in service learning programs more often delay sex. Trends toward commitment show declining teen birth rates and sexual activity.

13. sexual orientation

14. all; the late teens or early twenties

15. 3 or 4; 1 or 2; high

16. suicide

17. does not; women; erotic plasticity

18. are not; does not

19. do not

20. were not

21. poets; fiction writers; artists; musicians

22. more; fraternal birth-order effect; immune; male

23. does

24. hypothalamus; heterosexual; odors; right hemisphere

25. do; mother's; father's

26. hormone; females; two; five

27. fingerprint; left; cochlea

28. temperament; difficult; biology; biology

The Need to Belong

1. Aristotle; social; survival; attachments; reproduce

2. close, satisfying relationships with family, friends, or romantic partners

3. self-esteem

4. social; liking

5. isolated; chain migration

6. Throughout the world; ostracism

7. self-defeating; aptitude tests; aggressive

Progress Test 1

Multiple-Choice Questions

1. **d.** is the answer. (p. 328)
   a. & b. Although motivation is often aimed at reducing drives and satisfying biological needs, this is by no means always the case, as achievement motivation illustrates.
   c. Motivated behavior not only is energized but also is directed at a goal.

2. **b.** is the answer. A drive is the psychological consequence of a physiological need. (p. 329)
   a. Needs are unlearned states of deprivation.
   c. & d. Since needs are physical and drives psychological, their strengths cannot be compared directly.

3. **a.** is the answer. The curiosity of a child or a scientist is an example of behavior apparently

motivated by something other than a physiological need. (p. 329)

b. & d. Some behaviors, such as thirst and hunger, are partially explained by drive reduction.

c. Drive reduction is directly based on the principle of homeostasis.

4. **c.** is the answer. (p. 358)

a., b., & d. None of these is linked to homosexuality.

5. **a.** is the answer. Increases in insulin increase hunger indirectly by lowering blood sugar, or glucose. (p. 333)

6. **a.** is the answer. This area of the hypothalamus seems to elevate hunger. (p. 333)

b. Stimulating the ventromedial hypothalamus has this effect.

c. Destroying the ventromedial hypothalamus has this effect.

d. The hypothalamus is involved in sexual motivation, but not in this way.

7. **b.** is the answer. (p. 336)

a. Neophobia for taste is typical of all age groups.

c. Neophobia for taste is *not* an indicator of an eating disorder.

d. With repeated exposure, our appreciation for a new taste typically *increases*.

8. **d.** is the answer. (p. 334)

a. PYY signals fullness, which is associated with decreased metabolism.

b. Ghrelin is a hormone secreted by the empty stomach that sends hunger signals.

c. Orexin is a hormone secreted by the hypothalamus.

9. **d.** is the answer. (pp. 328–329)

10. **b.** is the answer. (p. 349)

11. **c.** is the answer. (p. 328)

a. & b. Needs and drives are biologically based states that stimulate behaviors but are not themselves behaviors.

d. Incentives are the external stimuli that motivate behavior.

12. **c.** is the answer. Research studies suggest that women's sexual orientation is potentially more fluid and changeable than men's. (p. 355)

13. **c.** is the answer. The deprived men focused on food almost to the exclusion of anything else. (p. 332)

a. In order to conserve energy, the men's metabolic rate actually *decreased*.

b. & d. Far from losing interest in food, the men came to care only about food—a finding consistent with Maslow's hierarchy, in which physiological needs are at the base.

14. **c.** is the answer. (p. 360)

15. **a.** is the answer. (p. 337)

b., c., & d. All of these are characteristic of anorexia nervosa.

16. **a.** is the answer. (p. 350)

c. & d. Castration of the testes, which produce testosterone, does not alter estrogen levels.

17. **a.** is the answer. (p. 344)

18. **b.** is the answer. (pp. 342–343)

19. **d.** is the answer. (pp. 342–343)

Matching Items

1. g (p. 337)
2. k (p. 335)
3. e (p. 329)
4. c (p. 350)
5. l (p. 337)
6. d (p. 349)
7. a (p. 350)
8. b (p. 329)
9. i (p. 335)
10. h (p. 333)
11. f (p. 354)
12. j (p. 337)

Progress Test 2

Multiple-Choice Questions

1. **d.** is the answer. Memory of the time of the last meal is an example of a psychological influence on hunger motivation. (p. 335)

a., b., & c. Each of these is a biological influence on hunger motivation.

2. **a.** is the answer. (p. 329)

b. This describes extrinsic motivation.

c. This describes set point.

d. Homeostasis has nothing to do with sexual orientation.

3. **b.** is the answer. (p. 340)

c. If anything, just the opposite is true.

d. Men and women do not differ in the tendency to overeat.

4. **a.** is the answer. The text does not indicate whether their metabolism is higher or lower than most. (pp. 338–339)

b., c., & d. Genes, family background, and cultural influence have all been proposed as factors in eating disorders.

5. **b.** is the answer. (p. 333)

a. Stimulation of the lateral hypothalamus triggers eating.

c. & d. The thalamus is a sensory relay station; stimulation of it has no effect on eating.

6. **b.** is the answer. The time between the middle of the second and fifth months after conception may be a critical period for the brain's neuro-hormonal control system. Exposure to abnormal hormonal conditions at other times has no effect on sexual orientation. (p. 358)

7. **d.** is the answer. Researchers have not been able to find any clear differences, psychological or otherwise, between homosexuals and heterosexuals. Thus, the basis for sexual orientation remains unknown, although recent evidence points more to a physiological basis. (pp. 357–358)

8. **c.** is the answer. (p. 338)

9. **b.** is the answer. (p. 330)

10. **c.** is the answer. Such behavior, presumably motivated by curiosity rather than any biological need, is inconsistent with a drive-reduction theory of motivation. (p. 329)
a., b., & d. Each of these examples is consistent with a drive-reduction theory of motivation.

11. **d.** is the answer. (pp. 337–338)

12. **c.** is the answer. (p. 354)

13. **d.** is the answer. (p. 339, 351)

14. **d.** is the answer. During the resolution phase males experience a refractory period. (p. 349)
a., b., & c. The male and female responses are very similar in each of these phases.

15. **b.** is the answer. (p. 333)
a. These effects are the reverse of what takes place.
c. If anything, set point is lowered by destruction of the lateral hypothalamus and elevated by destruction of the ventromedial hypothalamus.
d. These effects do not occur.

16. **d.** is the answer. Most researchers today discount the idea that people are obese because they lack willpower. (p. 342)

17. **d.** is the answer. (p. 330)

18. **b.** is the answer. (p. 351)
a. The anterior cingulate cortex has been found to be implicated in feelings of ostracism.
c. & d. The occipital and temporal lobes do not play a major role in motivation.

True–False Items

1. F (p. 335)
2. F (p. 349)
3. F (p. 350)
4. F (p. 351)
5. F (p. 335)
6. T (p. 361)
7. F (p. 333)
8. T (p. 346)
9. T (p. 355)
10. T (p. 340)

Psychology Applied

Multiple-Choice Questions

1. **b.** is the answer. Following the initial weight loss, metabolism drops as the body attempts to defend its set-point weight. This drop in metabolism means that eating an amount that once produced a loss in weight may now actually result in weight gain. (p. 343)

2. **a.** is the answer. Dieting, including fasting, lowers the body's metabolic rate and reduces the amount of food energy needed to maintain body weight. (p. 347)
b., c., & d. Each of these strategies would be a good piece of advice to a dieter.

3. **c.** is the answer. Drive-reduction theory maintains that behavior is motivated when a biological need creates an aroused state, driving the individual to satisfy the need. It is difficult to believe that Mary's hang-gliding is satisfying a biological need. (p. 329)
a., b., & d. Mary may enjoy hang-gliding because it is a challenge that "is there" (incentive), because it satisfies a need to do something challenging (arousal), or because it increases her self-esteem and sense of fulfillment in life (Maslow's hierarchy of needs).

4. **d.** is the answer. According to Maslow's theory, physiological needs, such as the need to satisfy hunger, must be satisfied before a person pursues loftier needs, such as making political statements. (p. 330)
a. Masters was concerned with sexual behavior.
b. Murray was concerned with achievement motivation.
c. Keys was concerned with hunger.

5. **c.** is the answer. (p. 337)
a. & b. These are more typical of the families of anorexia patients.

6. **b.** is the answer. (pp. 352–353)

7. **d.** is the answer. (pp. 328–329)
a. & b. Instinct theory emphasizes biological factors rather than environmental or cognitive factors.
c. Instinct theory applies to both humans and other animals.

8. **c.** is the answer. Although people with anorexia are significantly underweight, those with bulimia often are not unusually thin or overweight. (p. 337)
a., b., & d. Both anorexia and bulimia victims are more likely to be women than men, preoccupied

with food, fearful of becoming overweight, and suffer from depression or low self-esteem.

9. **c.** is the answer. This is an example of salivating in response to an incentive rather than to maintain a balanced internal state. (p. 329)
   a. & b. Both examples are behaviors that maintain a balanced internal state (homeostasis).

10. **d.** is the answer. Destruction of the ventromedial hypothalamus produces overeating and rapid weight gains. Destruction of the lateral hypothalamus suppresses hunger and produces weight loss. (p. 333)
    a. & b. The hippocampus and amygdala are not involved in regulating eating behavior.

11. **c.** is the answer. Individual differences in metabolism and set point explain why it is possible for two people to have very different weights despite similar patterns of eating and exercise. (p. 335)

12. **c.** is the answer. Our preferences for sweet and salty tastes are genetic and universal. (p. 335)

13. **b.** is the answer. (p. 356)

14. **c.** is the answer. (p. 360)

15. **b.** is the answer. Adolescent females with low self-esteem and high-achieving families seem especially prone to eating disorders such as anorexia nervosa. (pp. 337–338)
    a. & d. Eating disorders occur much more frequently in women than in men.
    c. Eating disorders usually develop during adolescence, rather than during adulthood.

16. **b.** is the answer. The body acts to defend its set point, or the weight to which it is predisposed. If Lucille was already near her set point, weight loss would prove difficult. (p. 343)
    a. If the weight level to which her body is predisposed is low, weight loss upon dieting should not be difficult.
    c. The eating disorders relate to eating behaviors and psychological factors and would not explain a difficulty with weight loss.
    d. People influenced by external factors might have greater problems losing weight because they tend to respond to food stimuli, but this can't be the explanation in Lucille's case because she has been sticking to her diet.

17. **c.** is the answer. Serotonin is a neurotransmitter that is elevated by the consumption of carbohydrates and has a calming effect. (p. 335)
    a. & b. These answers do not explain the feelings of relaxation that Randy associates with eating junk food.

d. The consumption of sugar tends to elevate insulin level rather than lower it.

18. **c.** is the answer. (p. 354)
    a., b., & d. Teens with high rather than average intelligence (therefore, not a.), and those who are religiously active (therefore, not b.) are most likely to delay sex.

Essay Question
Under the influence of Darwin's evolutionary theory, it became fashionable to classify all sorts of behaviors as instincts. Instinct theory fell into disfavor for several reasons. First, instincts do not explain behaviors, they merely name them. Second, to qualify as an instinct, a behavior must have a fixed and automatic pattern and occur in all people, regardless of differing cultures and experiences. Apart from a few simple reflexes, however, human behavior is not sufficiently automatic and universal to meet these criteria. Although instinct theory failed to explain human motives, the underlying assumption that genes predispose many behaviors is as strongly believed as ever.

Instinct theory was replaced by drive-reduction theory and the idea that biological needs create aroused drive states that motivate the individual to satisfy these needs and preserve homeostasis. Drive-reduction theory failed as a complete account of human motivation because many human motives do not satisfy any obvious biological need. Instead, such behaviors are motivated by environmental incentives.

Arousal theory emerged in response to evidence that some motivated behaviors *increase*, rather than decrease, arousal.

Key Terms

1. **Motivation** is a need or desire that energizes and directs behavior. (p. 328)

2. An **instinct** is a complex behavior that is rigidly patterned throughout a species and is unlearned. (p. 328)

3. **Drive-reduction theory** attempts to explain behavior as arising from a physiological need that creates an aroused tension state (drive) that motivates an organism to satisfy the need. (p. 329)

4. **Homeostasis** refers to the body's tendency to maintain a balanced or constant internal state. (p. 329)

5. **Incentives** are positive or negative environmental stimuli that motivate behavior. (p. 329)

6. Maslow's **hierarchy of needs** proposes that human motives may be ranked from the basic, physiological level through higher-level needs for safety, love, esteem, self-actualization, and self-transcendence; until they are satisfied, the more basic needs are more compelling than the higher-level ones. (p. 330)

7. **Glucose**, or blood sugar, is the major source of energy for the body's tissues. Elevating the level of glucose in the body will reduce hunger. (p. 333)

8. **Set point** is an individual's regulated weight level, which is maintained by adjusting food intake and energy output. (p. 335)

9. **Basal metabolic rate** is the body's base rate of energy expenditure when resting. (p. 335)

10. **Anorexia nervosa** is an eating disorder, most common in adolescent females, in which a person restricts food intake to become significantly underweight and yet, still feeling fat, continues to starve. (p. 337)

11. **Bulimia nervosa** is an eating disorder characterized by episodes of overeating, usually of high-calorie foods, followed by vomiting, laxative use, fasting, or excessive exercise. (p. 337)

12. **Binge-eating disorder** is characterized by episodes of overeating, followed by remorse, but not by purging, fasting, or excessive exercise. (p. 337)

13. The **sexual response cycle** described by Masters and Johnson consists of four stages of bodily reaction: excitement, plateau, orgasm, and resolution. (p. 349)

14. The **refractory period** is a resting period after orgasm, during which a male cannot be aroused to another orgasm. (p. 349)

15. **Estrogens** are sex hormones, such as estradiol, secreted in greater amounts by females than by males. In mammals other than humans, estrogen levels peak during ovulation and trigger sexual receptivity. (p. 350)

16. **Testosterone** is a sex hormone secreted in greater amounts by males than by females. In males, higher testosterone levels stimulate the prenatal growth of the male sex organs and the development of the male sex characteristics during puberty. (p. 350)

17. **Sexual orientation** refers to a person's enduring attraction to members of either the same or the opposite gender. (p. 354)

Motivation and Emotion:
8B: Emotions, Stress, and Health

UNIT OVERVIEW

Emotions are responses of the whole individual, involving physiological arousal, expressive behaviors, and conscious experience. Unit 8B first discusses several theoretical controversies concerning the relationship and sequence of the components of emotion, primarily regarding whether the body's response to a stimulus causes the emotion that is felt and whether thinking is necessary to and must precede the experience of emotion. After describing the physiology of emotion and emotional expressiveness, it examines the components of emotion in detail, particularly as they relate to the emotions of fear, anger, and happiness.

Behavioral factors play a major role in maintaining health and causing illness. The effort to understand this role more fully has led to the emergence of the interdisciplinary field of behavioral medicine. The subfield of health psychology focuses on questions such as: How do our perceptions of a situation determine the stress we feel? How do our emotions and personality influence our risk of disease? How can psychology contribute to the prevention of illness?

Unit 8B addresses a key topic in health psychology: stress—its nature, its effects on the body, psychological factors that determine how it affects us, and how stress contributes to heart disease, infectious diseases, and cancer.

NOTE: Answer guidelines for all Unit 8B questions begin on page 223.

UNIT REVIEW

First, skim each section, noting headings and boldface items. After you have read the section, review each objective by answering the fill-in and essay-type questions that follow it. As you proceed, evaluate your performance by consulting the answers beginning on page 223. Do not continue with the next section until you understand each answer. If you need to, review or reread the section in the textbook before continuing.

Theories of Emotion (pp. 366–368)

Objective 1: Identify the three components of emotion, and contrast the James-Lange, Cannon-Bard, and two-factor theories of emotion.

1. Emotions have three components: _____

   _____ , _____

   _____ , and _____

   _____ .

2. According to the James-Lange theory, emotional states _____ (precede/follow) physiological responses.

Describe two problems that Walter Cannon identified with the James-Lange theory.

3. Cannon proposed that emotional stimuli in the environment are routed simultaneously to the _____ , which results in awareness of the emotion, and to the _____ nervous system, which causes the body's reaction. Because another scientist concurrently proposed similar ideas, this theory has come to be known as the _____-_____ theory.

4. The two-factor theory of emotion proposes that emotion has two components: _____ arousal and a _____ label. This theory was proposed by _____ and _____ .

Embodied Emotion (pp. 369–377)

Objective 2: Describe the physiological changes that occur during emotional arousal, and discuss the relationship between arousal and performance.

1. Describe the major physiological changes that each of the following undergoes during emotional arousal
   a. heart: _____
   b. muscles _____
   c. liver: _____
   d. breathing: _____
   e. digestion: _____
   f. pupils: _____
   g. blood: _____
   h. skin: _____

2. The responses of arousal are activated by the _____ nervous system. In response to its signal, the _____ glands release the stress hormones _____ and _____ , which increase heart rate, respiration, blood pressure, and blood sugar.

3. When the need for arousal has passed, the body is calmed through activation of the _____ nervous system.

Objective 3: Describe the relationship between physiological states and specific emotions, and discuss the effectiveness of the polygraph in detecting lies.

4. The various emotions are associated with _____ (similar/different) forms of physiological arousal. In particular, the emotions of _____ , _____ , and _____ are difficult to distinguish physiologically.

5. The emotions _____ and _____ are sometimes accompanied by differing _____ temperatures and _____ secretions.

6. The emotions _____ and _____ stimulate different facial muscles.

7. The brain circuits underlying different emotions _____ (are/are not) different. For example, seeing a fearful face elicits greater activity in the _____ than seeing a(n) _____ face. People who have generally negative personalities, and those who are prone to _____ , show more _____ _____ lobe activity.

8. When people experience positive moods, brain scans reveal more activity in the _____ _____ _____ .

9. Individuals with more active _____ (right/left) _____ lobes tend to be more cheerful than those in whom this pattern of brain activity is reversed. A cluster of neurons called the _____ _____ becomes activated when people experience natural or drug-induced pleasure.

10. (Thinking Critically) The technical name for the "lie detector" is the _____ .

(Thinking Critically) Explain how lie detectors supposedly indicate whether a person is lying.

11. (Thinking Critically) How well the lie detector works depends on whether a person exhibits _____ while lying.

12. (Thinking Critically) Those who criticize lie detectors feel that the tests are particularly likely

to err in the case of the _____ (innocent/guilty) because different _____ all register as _____ .

13. (Thinking Critically) By and large, experts _____ (agree/do not agree) that lie detector tests are highly accurate.

14. (Thinking Critically) A test that assesses a suspect's knowledge of details of a crime that only the guilty person should know is the

_____ _____

_____ .

Objective 4: Explain the role of cognition in emotion, and discuss how neurological processes may enable us to experience some emotions prior to conscious thought.

15. The *spillover effect* refers to occasions when our _____ response to one event carries over into our response to another event.

16. Schachter and Singer found that physically aroused college men told that an injection would cause arousal _____ (did/did not) become emotional in response to an accomplice's aroused behavior. Physically aroused volunteers not expecting arousal _____ (did/did not) become emotional in response to an accomplice's behavior.

17. Arousal _____ emotion; cognition _____ emotion.

18. Robert Zajonc believes that the feeling of emotion _____ (can/cannot) precede our cognitive labeling of that emotion.

Cite two pieces of evidence that support Zajonc's position.

19. A pathway from the _____ via the _____ to the _____ enables us to experience emotion before _____ . For more complex emotions, sensory input is routed through the _____ for interpretation.

20. The researcher who disagrees with Zajonc and argues that most emotions require cognitive processing is _____ . According to this view, emotions arise when we _____ an event as beneficial or harmful to our well-being.

21. Complex emotions are affected by our

_____ , _____ ,

and _____ .

Express some general conclusions that can be drawn about cognition and emotion.

Expressed Emotion (pp. 377–384)

Objective 5: Describe our ability to perceive and communicate emotions nonverbally, and discuss gender differences in this capacity.

1. Most people are especially good at interpreting nonverbal _____ . We read fear and _____ mostly from the _____ , and happiness from the _____ . Although we are good at detecting emotions, we find it difficult to detect _____ expressions.

2. Introverts are _____ (better/ worse) at reading others' emotions, whereas extraverts are themselves _____ (easier/harder) to read.

3. The absence of nonverbal cues to emotion is one reason that communications sent as _____ are easy to misread.

4. Women are generally _____ (better/worse) than men at detecting nonverbal signs of emotion and in spotting _____ . Women possess greater emotional _____ than men, as revealed by the tendency of men to describe their emotions in _____ terms. This gender difference may contribute to women's greater emotional _____ .

5. Although women are _____ (more/less) likely than men to describe themselves as empathic, physiological measures reveal a much _____ (smaller/larger) gender difference. Women are _____ (more/less) likely than men to express empathy.

Objective 6: Discuss the culture-specific and culturally universal aspects of emotional expression, and describe the effects of facial expressions on emotional experience.

6. Gestures have _____ (the same/different) meanings in different cultures.

7. Studies of adults indicate that in different cultures facial expressions have _____ (the same/different) meanings. Even our emotional _____ _____ cross world cultures. Studies of children indicate that the meaning of their facial expressions _____ (varies/does not vary) across cultures. The emotional facial expressions of blind children _____ (are/are not) the same as those of sighted children.

8. According to _____ , human emotional expressions evolved because they helped our ancestors communicate before language developed. It has also been adaptive for us to _____ faces in particular _____ .

9. In cultures that encourage _____ , emotional expressions are often intense and prolonged. Cultures such as that of Japan _____ (also show intense emotion/hide their emotions). This points to the importance of realizing that emotions are not only biological and psychological but also _____-_____ .

10. Darwin believed that when an emotion is accompanied by an outward facial expression, the emotion is _____ (intensified/diminished).

11. In one study, students who were induced to smile _____ (found/did not find) cartoons more amusing.

12. The _____ _____ effect occurs when expressions amplify our emotions by activating muscles associated with specific states.

13. Studies have found that imitating another person's facial expressions _____ (leads/does not lead) to greater empathy with that person's feelings.

14. Similarly, moving our body as we would when experiencing a particular emotion causes us to feel that emotion. This is the _____ _____ effect.

Experienced Emotion (pp. 384–396)

Objective 7: Name several basic emotions, and describe two dimensions psychologists use to differentiate emotions.

1. Izard believes that there are _____ basic emotions, most of which _____ (are/are not) present in infancy. Although others claim that emotions such as pride and love should be added to the list, Izard contends that they are _____ of the basic emotions.

2. Throughout the world, people place emotions along two dimensions: _____ , which refers to whether a feeling is _____ or _____ , and high versus low _____ .

Objective 8: State two ways we learn our fears, and discuss some of the biological components of fear.

3. Fear can by and large be seen as a(n) _____ (adaptive/maladaptive) response.

4. Most human fears are acquired through _____ .

5. In addition, some fears are acquired by
   _____ parents and friends.

Explain why researchers think that some fears are
biologically predisposed.

6. A key to fear learning lies in the
   _____ , a neural center in the
   _____ system. Following damage
   to this area, humans who have been conditioned
   to fear a loud noise will _____
   the conditioning but show no _____
   effect of it.

7. People who have suffered damage to the
   _____ will show the
   _____ _____ but
   _____ (will/will not) be able to
   remember why.

8. Patients who have lost use of the
   _____ are unusually trusting of
   scary-looking people.

9. Fears that fall outside the average range are
   called _____ . Fearfulness is
   shaped by both our _____ and
   our _____ .

Objective 9: Identify some common causes and
consequences of anger, and assess the catharsis
hypothesis.

10. Most people become angry when another per-
    son's act seems _____ ,
    _____ , and _____ .

11. The belief that expressing pent-up emotion is
    adaptive is most commonly found in cultures that
    emphasize _____ . This is the
    _____ hypothesis. In cultures that
    emphasize _____ , such as those
    of _____ or _____ ,
    expressions of anger are less common.

12. Psychologists have found that when anger has
    been provoked, retaliation may have a calming

effect under certain circumstances. List the circumstances.
   a. _____
   b. _____
   c. _____

Identify some potential problems with expressing
anger.

13. List two suggestions offered by experts for
    handling anger.
    a. _____
    b. _____

14. Researchers have found that students who
    mentally rehearsed the times they
    _____ someone who had hurt
    them had lower bodily arousal than when they
    thought of times when they did not.

Objective 10: Identify some potential causes and consequences of happiness, and describe two psychological phenomena that help explain the relatively short
duration of emotions

15. Happy people tend to perceive the world as
    _____ and live
    _____ and more energized and
    satisfied lives.

16. Happy people are also _____
    (more/less) willing to help others. This is called
    the _____-_____ ,
    _____-_____
    phenomenon.

17. An individual's self-perceived happiness or satis-
    faction with life is called his or her
    _____ .

18. Positive emotions _____
    (rise/fall) in the early to middle part of most
    days. The gloom of stressful events usually
    _____ (is gone by/continues into)
    the next day.

19. After experiencing tragedy or dramatically positive events, people generally _____
(regain/do not regain) their previous degree of
happiness.

20. Most people tend to _____
(underestimate/overestimate) the duration of
emotions and _____ (underesti-
mate/overestimate) their capacity to adapt.

21. Researchers have found that levels of happiness
_____ (do/do not) mirror differ-
ences in standards of living.

22. During the last four decades, buying power in the
United States has almost tripled; personal happiness has _____ (increased/
decreased/remained almost unchanged).

23. Research has demonstrated that people generally
experience a higher quality of life and greater
well-being when they strive for _____
_____
_____ than
when they strive for _____ .

24. The idea that happiness is relative to one's recent
experience is stated by the _____-
_____ phenomenon.

Explain how this principle accounts for the fact that,
for some people, material desires can never be
satisfied.

(Close-Up) State several research-based suggestions
for increasing your satisfaction with life.

25. The principle that one feels worse off than others
is known as _____
_____ . This helps to explain why
the middle- and upper-income people who compare themselves with the relatively poor are
_____ (slightly more/slightly
less/equally) satisfied with life.

26. List six factors that have been shown to be positively correlated with feelings of happiness.

_____
_____
_____
_____
_____
_____

27. List four factors that are evidently unrelated to
happiness.

_____
_____
_____
_____

28. Research studies of identical and fraternal twins
have led to the estimate that _____
percent of the variation in people's happiness ratings is heritable.

Stress and Health (pp. 397–406)

Objective 11: Identify the role of health psychologists
in studying the effects of stress on health and illness,
and discuss the concept of stress as a process that
involves cognitive appraisal.

1. The field that integrates behavioral and medical
knowledge relevant to health and disease is
_____ _____ . The
subfield of psychology that contributes to behavioral medicine is called _____
psychology.

2. Stress is not merely a _____ or a
_____ . Rather, it is the
_____ by which we perceive and
respond to environmental threats and challenges.

3. This definition highlights the fact that stress arises less from the events than from how we _____ them and that stressors can have _____ (only negative/both positive and negative) effects, depending on how they are perceived.

Objective 12: Describe the biology of the "fight-or-flight" response as well as the physical characteristics and phases of the general adaptation syndrome.

4. In the 1920s, physiologist Walter _____ began studying the effect of stress on the body. He discovered that the hormones _____ and _____ are released into the bloodstream in response to stress. This and other bodily changes due to stress are mediated by the _____ nervous system, thus preparing the body for _____ _____.

5. Physiologists have discovered that in response to stress the cerebral cortex, via the _____ and the _____ gland, triggers the outer part of the _____ _____ to release _____ stress hormones such as _____ .

6. Another common response to stress among women has been called "_____ _____ _____," which refers to the increased tendency to _____ .

7. In studying animals' reactions to stressors, Hans Selye referred to the bodily response to stress as the _____ _____ _____ .

8. During the first phase of the GAS—the _____ reaction—the person is in a state of shock due to the sudden arousal of the _____ nervous system.

9. This is followed by the stage of _____ , in which the body's resources are mobilized to cope with the stressor.

10. If stress continues, the person enters the stage of _____ . During this stage, a person is _____ (more/less) vulnerable to disease.

11. One study found that women who suffered enduring caregiver stress had especially short _____ , which are pieces of _____ at the ends of _____ that are important in allowing cells to _____ .

Objective 13: Discuss the health consequences of catastrophes, significant life changes, and daily hassles.

12. In the wake of catastrophic events, such as floods, hurricanes, and fires, there often is an increase in the rates of _____ _____ .

13. Research studies have found that people who have recently been widowed, fired, or divorced are _____ (more/no more) vulnerable to illness than other people.

14. For most people, the most significant sources of stress are _____ _____ . The stresses that accompany poverty and unemployment, for example, often compounded by _____ , may account for the higher rates of _____ among residents of impoverished areas.

Objective 14: Discuss the role of stress in causing coronary heart disease, and contrast Type A and Type B personalities.

15. The leading cause of death in North America is _____ _____ _____ . List several risk factors for developing this condition: _____ _____ _____ .

16. Friedman and Rosenman discovered that tax accountants experience an increase in blood _____ level and blood-_____ speed during tax season. This showed there was a link between coronary warning indicators and _____ .

Friedman and Rosenman, in a subsequent study, grouped people into Type A and Type B personalities. Characterize these types, and indicate the difference that emerged between them over the course of this nine-year study.

17. The Type A characteristic that is most strongly linked with coronary heart disease is

    _____ _____ ,

    especially _____

    _____ .

18. When a _____ (Type A/Type B) person is angered, bloodflow is diverted away from the internal organs, including the liver, which is responsible for removing _____ and fat from the blood. Thus, such people have elevated levels of these substances in the blood.

19. Another toxic emotion is _____ ; researchers have found that _____ are more than twice as likely to develop heart disease as _____ .

20. Depression _____ (increases/has no effect on) one's risk of having a heart attack or developing other heart problems.

Objective 15: Define *psychophysiological illness*, and describe the effect of stress on immune system functioning, including its role in the progression of AIDS and cancer.

21. In _____ illnesses, physical symptoms are produced by psychological causes.

22. Examples of such illnesses are certain types of _____ and some _____ . Such illnesses appear to be linked to _____ .

23. The term _____ was once used to describe such illness. However, this term implied that symptoms were _____ .

24. The new field of _____ investigates how psychological, neural, and endocrine systems together affect the immune system and health.

25. The body's system of fighting disease is the _____ system. This system includes two types of white blood cells, called _____ : the _____ _____ , which fight bacterial infections, and the _____ _____ , which form in the _____ and attack viruses, cancer cells, and foreign substances.

26. Two other immune agents are the _____ , which pursues and ingests foreign substances, and _____ _____ cells, which pursue diseased cells.

27. Responding too strongly, the immune system may attack the body's tissues and cause _____ or an _____ reaction. Or it may _____ , allowing a dormant herpes virus to erupt or _____ cells to multiply.

28. _____ (Women/Men) are the immunologically stronger gender. This makes them less susceptible to _____ but more susceptible to _____ diseases such as _____ and _____ _____ .

29. Stress can suppress the lymphocyte cells, resulting in a(n) _____ (increase/decrease) in disease resistance. Stress diverts energy from the _____ _____ to the _____ and _____ , mobilizing the body for action and making us more vulnerable to disease.

30. The world's fourth leading cause of death and the number one killer in _____ is _____ , which is caused by the _____ _____ _____ , which is spread primarily through the exchange of _____ and _____ .

31. Stressful life circumstances _____ (have/have not) been shown to accelerate the progression of this chronic disease.

32. Educational initiatives, support groups, and other efforts to control stress _____ (have/have not) been shown to have positive consequences on HIV-positive individuals.

33. Stress and _____ emotions _____ (have/have not) been linked to cancer's rate of progression.

34. When rodents were inoculated with _____ cells or given _____ , tumors developed sooner in those that were also exposed to _____ stress.

35. Stress _____ (does/does not) create cancer cells.

PROGRESS TEST 1

Multiple-Choice Questions

Circle your answers to the following questions and check them with the answers beginning on page 225. If your answer is incorrect, read the explanation for why it is incorrect and then consult the appropriate pages of the text (in parentheses following the correct answer).

1. Researchers Friedman and Rosenman refer to individuals who are very time-conscious, super-motivated, verbally aggressive, and easily angered as
   a. ulcer-prone personalities.
   b. cancer-prone personalities.
   c. Type A.
   d. Type B.

2. Which division of the nervous system is especially involved in bringing about emotional arousal?
   a. somatic nervous system
   b. peripheral nervous system
   c. sympathetic nervous system
   d. parasympathetic nervous system

3. Concerning emotions and their accompanying body responses, which of the following appears to be true?
   a. Each emotion has its own body response and underlying brain circuit.
   b. All emotions involve the same body response as a result of the same underlying brain circuit.
   c. Many emotions involve similar body responses but have different underlying brain circuits.
   d. All emotions have the same underlying brain circuits but different body responses.

4. The Cannon-Bard theory of emotion states that
   a. emotions have two ingredients: physical arousal and a cognitive label.
   b. the conscious experience of an emotion occurs at the same time as the body's physical reaction.
   c. emotional experiences are based on an awareness of the body's responses to an emotion-arousing stimulus.
   d. emotional ups and downs tend to balance in the long run.

5. During which stage of the general adaptation syndrome is a person especially vulnerable to disease?
   a. alarm reaction   c. stage of exhaustion
   b. stage of resistance   d. stage of adaptation

6. The leading cause of death in North America is
   a. lung cancer.
   b. AIDS.
   c. coronary heart disease.
   d. alcohol-related accidents.

7. Which of the following was NOT raised as a criticism of the James-Lange theory of emotion?
   a. The body's responses are too similar to trigger the various emotions.
   b. Emotional reactions occur before the body's responses can take place.
   c. The cognitive activity of the cortex plays a role in the emotions we experience.
   d. People with spinal cord injuries at the neck typically experience less emotion.

8. (Thinking Critically) Current estimates are that the polygraph is inaccurate approximately _____ of the time.
   a. three-fourths   c. one-third
   b. one-half   d. one-fourth

9. In the Schachter-Singer experiment, which college men reported feeling an emotional change in the presence of the experimenter's highly emotional confederate?
   a. those receiving epinephrine and expecting to feel physical arousal
   b. those receiving a placebo and expecting to feel physical arousal
   c. those receiving epinephrine but not expecting to feel physical arousal
   d. those receiving a placebo and not expecting to feel physical arousal

10. Which of the following is true regarding happiness?
    a. People with more education tend to be happier.
    b. Beautiful people tend to be happier than plain people.
    c. Women tend to be happier than men.
    d. People who are socially outgoing or who exercise regularly tend to be happier.

11. Catharsis will be most effective in reducing anger toward another person if
    a. you wait until you are no longer angry before confronting the person.
    b. the target of your anger is someone you feel has power over you.
    c. your anger is directed specifically toward the person who angered you.
    d. the other person is able to retaliate by also expressing anger.

12. Emotions consist of which of the following components?
    a. physiological reactions
    b. behavioral expressions
    c. conscious feelings
    d. all of these components

13. Law enforcement officials sometimes use a lie detector to assess a suspect's responses to details of the crime believed to be known only to the perpetrator. This is known as the
    a. inductive approach.
    b. deductive approach.
    c. guilty knowledge test.
    d. screening examination.

14. Research on nonverbal communication has revealed that
    a. it is easy to hide your emotions by controlling your facial expressions.
    b. facial expressions tend to be the same the world over, while gestures vary from culture to culture.
    c. most authentic expressions last between 7 and 10 seconds.
    d. most gestures have universal meanings; facial expressions vary from culture to culture.

15. In laboratory experiments, fear and joy
    a. result in an increase in heart rate.
    b. stimulate different facial muscles.
    c. increase heart rate and stimulate different facial muscles.
    d. result in a decrease in heart rate.

16. Research suggests that people generally experience the greatest well-being when they strive for
    a. wealth.
    b. modest income increases from year to year.
    c. slightly higher status than their friends, neighbors, and co-workers.
    d. intimacy and personal growth.

17. Research indicates that a person is most likely to be helpful to others if he or she
    a. is feeling guilty about something.
    b. is happy.
    c. recently received help from another person.
    d. recently offered help to another person.

18. With regard to emotions, Darwin believed that
    a. the expression of emotions helped our ancestors to survive.
    b. all humans express basic emotions using similar facial expressions.
    c. human facial expressions of emotion retain elements of animals' emotional displays.
    d. all of these statements are true.

19. A graph depicting the course of positive emotions over the hours of the day since waking would
    a. start low and rise steadily until bedtime.
    b. start high and decrease steadily until bedtime.
    c. remain at a stable, moderate level throughout the day.
    d. rise over the early hours and fall during the day's last several hours.

20. Research with subliminally flashed stimuli supports Robert Zajonc's view that
    a. the heart is always subject to the mind.
    b. emotional reactions involve deliberate rational thinking.
    c. cognition is not necessary for emotion.
    d. responding to a subliminal stimulus is a learned skill.

21. Genuine illnesses that are caused by stress are called _____ illnesses.

   a. psychophysiological c. psychogenic
   b. cathartic   d. psychotropic

22. Stress has been demonstrated to place a person at increased risk of

   a. cancer.
   b. progressing from HIV infection to AIDS.
   c. bacterial infections.
   d. all of these conditions.

23. *Stress* is defined as

   a. unpleasant or aversive events that cannot be controlled.
   b. situations that threaten health.
   c. the process by which we perceive and respond to challenging or threatening events.
   d. anything that decreases immune responses.

24. Research studies demonstrate that after a catastrophe rates of _____ often increase.

   a. depression
   b. anxiety
   c. sleeplessness
   d. all of these problems

25. Behavioral and medical knowledge about factors influencing health form the basis of the field of

   a. health psychology.
   b. holistic medicine.
   c. behavioral medicine.
   d. osteopathic medicine.

26. The stress hormones epinephrine and norepinephrine are released by the _____ gland(s) in response to stimulation by the _____ branch of the nervous system.

   a. pituitary; sympathetic
   b. pituitary; parasympathetic
   c. adrenal; sympathetic
   d. adrenal; parasympathetic

Matching Items

Match each definition or description with the appropriate term.

Definitions or Descriptions

_____ 1. the tendency to react to changes on the basis of recent experience
_____ 2. an individual's self-perceived happiness
_____ 3. emotional release
_____ 4. the tendency to evaluate our situation negatively against that of other people
_____ 5. emotions consist of physical arousal *and* a cognitive label
_____ 6. an emotion-arousing stimulus triggers cognitive and body responses simultaneously
_____ 7. the division of the nervous system that calms the body following arousal
_____ 8. the division of the nervous system that activates arousal
_____ 9. a device that measures the physiological correlates of emotion
_____ 10. the tendency of people to be helpful when they are in a good mood
_____ 11. we are sad because we cry

Terms

   a. adaptation-level phenomenon
   b. two-factor theory
   c. catharsis
   d. sympathetic nervous system
   e. James-Lange theory
   f. polygraph
   g. Cannon-Bard theory
   h. parasympathetic nervous system
   i. relative deprivation principle
   j. feel-good, do-good phenomenon
   k. well-being

PROGRESS TEST 2

Progress Test 2 should be completed during a final unit review. Answer the following questions after you thoroughly understand the correct answers for the section reviews and Progress Test 1.

Multiple-Choice Questions

1. Which of the following most accurately describes emotional arousal?
   a. Emotions prepare the body to fight or flee.
   b. Emotions are voluntary reactions to emotion-arousing stimuli.
   c. Because all emotions have the same physiological basis, emotions are primarily psychological events.
   d. Emotional arousal is always accompanied by cognition.

2. Schachter's and Singer's two-factor theory emphasizes that emotion involves both
   a. the sympathetic and parasympathetic divisions of the nervous system.
   b. verbal and nonverbal expression.
   c. physical arousal and a cognitive label.
   d. universal and culture-specific aspects.

3. When students studied others who were worse off than themselves, they felt greater satisfaction with their own lives. This is an example of the principle of
   a. relative deprivation.
   b. adaptation level.
   c. behavioral contrast.
   d. opponent processes.

4. Which theory of emotion emphasizes the simultaneous experience of the body's response and emotional feeling?
   a. James-Lange theory
   b. Cannon-Bard theory
   c. two-factor theory
   d. catharsis theory

5. Izard believes that there are _____ basic emotions.
   a. 3   c. 7
   b. 5   d. 10

6. (Thinking Critically) The polygraph measures
   a. lying.
   b. brain rhythms.
   c. chemical changes in the body.
   d. physiological indexes of arousal.

7. People who are exuberant and persistently cheerful show increased activity in the brain's _____, which is rich in receptors for the neurotransmitter _____ .
   a. right frontal lobe; dopamine
   b. left frontal lobe; dopamine
   c. amygdala; serotonin
   d. thalamus; serotonin

8. Which of the following is true regarding gestures and facial expressions?
   a. Gestures are universal; facial expressions, culture-specific.
   b. Facial expressions are universal; gestures, culture-specific.
   c. Both gestures and facial expressions are universal.
   d. Both gestures and facial expressions are culture-specific.

9. Which theory of emotion implies that every emotion is associated with a unique physiological reaction?
   a. James-Lange theory
   b. Cannon-Bard theory
   c. two-factor theory
   d. catharsis theory

10. In order, the sequence of stages in the general adaptation syndrome is
    a. alarm reaction, stage of resistance, stage of exhaustion.
    b. stage of resistance, alarm reaction, stage of exhaustion.
    c. stage of exhaustion, stage of resistance, alarm reaction.
    d. alarm reaction, stage of exhaustion, stage of resistance.

11. Which of the following was NOT presented in the text as evidence that some emotional reactions involve no deliberate, rational thinking?
    a. Some of the neural pathways involved in emotion are separate from those involved in thinking and memory.
    b. Emotional reactions are sometimes quicker than our interpretations of a situation.
    c. People can develop an emotional preference for visual stimuli to which they have been unknowingly exposed.
    d. Arousal of the sympathetic nervous system will trigger an emotional reaction even when artificially induced by an injection of epinephrine.

12. Concerning the catharsis hypothesis, which of the following is true?
    a. Expressing anger can be temporarily calming if it does not leave one feeling guilty or anxious.
    b. The arousal that accompanies unexpressed anger never dissipates.
    c. Expressing one's anger always calms one down.
    d. Psychologists agree that under no circumstances is catharsis beneficial.

13. In an emergency situation, emotional arousal will result in
    a. increased rate of respiration.
    b. increased blood sugar.
    c. a slowing of digestion.
    d. all of these events.

14. AIDS is a disorder that causes a breakdown in the body's
    a. endocrine system.
    b. circulatory system.
    c. immune system.
    d. respiratory system.

15. Several studies have shown that physical arousal can intensify just about any emotion. For example, when people who have been physically aroused by exercise are insulted, they often misattribute their arousal to the insult. This finding illustrates the importance of
    a. cognitive labels of arousal in the conscious experience of emotions.
    b. a minimum level of arousal in triggering emotional experiences.
    c. the simultaneous occurrence of physical arousal and cognitive labeling in emotional experience.
    d. all of these things.

16. (Thinking Critically) Many psychologists are opposed to the use of lie detectors because
    a. they represent an invasion of a person's privacy and could easily be used for unethical purposes.
    b. there are often serious discrepancies among the various indicators such as perspiration and heart rate.
    c. polygraphs cannot distinguish the various possible causes of arousal.
    d. they are accurate only about 50 percent of the time.

17. "Tend and befriend" refers to
    a. the final stage of the general adaptation syndrome.
    b. the health-promoting impact of having a strong system of social support.
    c. an alternative to the "fight-or-flight" response that may be more common in women.
    d. the fact that spiritual people typically are not socially isolated.

18. When asked how they handled anger, most people responded that they often recalled
    a. reacting hurtfully.
    b. walking away from the situation.
    c. reacting assertively.
    d. internalizing the anger.

19. Which of these factors have researchers NOT found to correlate with happiness?
    a. a satisfying marriage or close friendship
    b. high self-esteem
    c. religious faith
    d. education

20. In cultures that emphasize social interdependence
    a. emotional displays are typically intense.
    b. emotional displays are typically prolonged.
    c. personal emotions are displayed less visibly.
    d. only anger is displayed visibly.

21. Which of the following statements concerning Type A and B persons is true?
    a. Even when relaxed, Type A persons have higher blood pressure than Type B persons.
    b. When stressed, Type A persons redistribute bloodflow to the muscles and away from internal organs.
    c. Type B persons tend to suppress anger more than Type A persons.
    d. Type A persons tend to be more outgoing than Type B persons.

22. The disease- and infection-fighting cells of the immune system are
    a. B lymphocytes.
    b. T lymphocytes.
    c. macrophages.
    d. all of these types of cells.

23. One effect of stress on the body is to
    a. suppress the immune system.
    b. facilitate the immune system response.
    c. increase disease resistance.
    d. increase the growth of B and T lymphocytes.

24. Compared with men, women
    a. have weaker immune systems.
    b. are more susceptible to infections.
    c. are more susceptible to self-attacking diseases such as multiple sclerosis.
    d. are more likely to develop cancer.

25. Allergic reactions and arthritis are caused by
    a. an overreactive immune system.
    b. an underreactive immune system.
    c. the presence of B lymphocytes.
    d. the presence of T lymphocytes.

26. Research on cancer patients reveals that
    a. stress affects the growth of cancer cells by weakening the body's natural resources.
    b. patients' attitudes can influence their rate of recovery.
    c. cancer occurs slightly more often than usual among those widowed, divorced, or separated.
    d. all of these statements are true.

27. The component of Type A behavior that is the most predictive of coronary disease is
    a. time urgency.   c. high motivation.
    b. competitiveness.   d. anger.

28. The field of health psychology is concerned with
    a. the prevention of illness.
    b. the promotion of health.
    c. the treatment of illness.
    d. all of these things.

True–False Items

Indicate whether each statement is true or false by placing *T* or *F* in the blank next to the item.

_____ 1. Stressors tend to increase activity in the immune system and in this way make people more vulnerable to illness.
_____ 2. Men are generally better than women at detecting nonverbal emotional expression.
_____ 3. The sympathetic nervous system triggers physiological arousal during an emotion.
_____ 4. When one imitates an emotional facial expression, the body may experience physiological changes characteristic of that emotion.
_____ 5. The immune system is influenced by age, nutrition, genetics, body temperature, and stress.
_____ 6. Wealthy people tend to be much happier than middle-income people.
_____ 7. Physical arousal can intensify emotion.
_____ 8. All emotions involve conscious thought.
_____ 9. The two-factor theory states that emotions are given a cognitive label before physical arousal occurs.
_____ 10. Type A persons are more physiologically reactive to stress than are Type B persons.

PSYCHOLOGY APPLIED

Answer these questions the day before a test as a final check on your understanding of the unit's terms and concepts.

Multiple-Choice Questions

1. You are on your way to school to take a big exam. Suddenly, on noticing that your pulse is racing and that you are sweating, you feel nervous. With which theory of emotion is this experience most consistent?
   a. Cannon-Bard theory
   b. James-Lange theory
   c. relative deprivation theory
   d. adaptation-level theory

2. When Albert Simon acquired a spacious new office, he was overjoyed. Six months later, however, he was taking the office for granted. His behavior illustrates the
   a. relative deprivation principle.
   b. adaptation-level phenomenon.
   c. two-factor theory.
   d. optimum arousal principle.

3. After Brenda scolded her brother for forgetting to pick her up from school, the physical arousal that had accompanied her anger diminished. Which division of her nervous system mediated her physical *relaxation*?
   a. sympathetic division
   b. parasympathetic division
   c. somatic division
   d. peripheral nervous system

4. Two years ago, Maria was in an automobile accident in which her spinal cord was severed, leaving her paralyzed from her neck down. Today, Maria finds that she experiences emotions less intensely than she did before her accident. This tends to support which theory of emotion?
   a. James-Lange theory
   b. Cannon-Bard theory
   c. adaptation-level theory
   d. relative deprivation theory

5. The candidate stepped before the hostile audience, panic written all over his face. It is likely that the candidate's facial expression caused him to experience
   a. a lessening of his fear.
   b. an intensification of his fear.
   c. a surge of digestive enzymes in his body.
   d. increased body temperature.

6. Jane was so mad at her brother that she exploded at him when he entered her room. That she felt less angry afterward is best explained by the principle of
   a. adaptation level.
   b. physiological arousal.
   c. relative deprivation.
   d. catharsis.

7. After hitting a grand-slam home run, Mike noticed that his heart was pounding. Later that evening, after nearly having a collision while driving on the freeway, Mike again noticed that his heart was pounding. That he interpreted this reaction as fear, rather than as ecstasy, can best be explained by the
   a. James-Lange theory.
   b. Cannon-Bard theory.
   c. two-factor theory.
   d. adaptation-level theory.

8. As part of her job interview, Jan is asked to take a lie-detector test. Jan politely refuses and points out that
   a. a guilty person can be found innocent by the polygraph.
   b. an innocent person can be found guilty.
   c. these tests err one-third of the time.
   d. all of these statements are true.

9. A student participating in an experiment concerned with physical responses that accompany emotions reports that her mouth is dry, her heart is racing, and she feels flushed. Can the emotion she is experiencing be determined?

   a. Yes, it is anger.
   b. Yes, it is fear.
   c. Yes, it is ecstasy.
   d. No, it cannot be determined from the information given.

10. Who will probably be angrier after getting a parking ticket?
    a. Bob, who has just awakened from a nap
    b. Veronica, who has just finished eating a big lunch
    c. Dan, who has just completed a tennis match
    d. Alicia, who has been reading a romantic novel

11. Children in New York, Nigeria, and New Zealand smile when they are happy and frown when they are sad. This suggests that
    a. the Cannon-Bard theory is correct.
    b. some emotional expressions are learned at a very early age.
    c. the two-factor theory is correct.
    d. facial expressions of emotion are universal and biologically determined.

12. Who is the LEAST likely to display personal emotions openly?
    a. Paul, a game warden in Australia
    b. Niles, a stockbroker in Belgium
    c. Deborah, a physicist in Toronto
    d. Yoko, a dentist in Japan

13. Nine-month-old Nicole's left frontal lobe is more active than her right frontal lobe. We can expect that, all other things being equal, Nicole
    a. may suffer from mild depression for most of her life.
    b. may have trouble "turning off" upsetting feelings later in her life.
    c. may be more cheerful than those with more active right frontal lobes.
    d. may have trouble expressing feelings later in her life.

14. Julio was extremely angry when he came in for a routine EEG of his brain activity. When he later told this to the doctor, she was no longer concerned about the
    a. increased electrical activity in Julio's right hemisphere.
    b. increased electrical activity in Julio's left hemisphere.
    c. decreased electrical activity in Julio's amygdala.
    d. increased electrical activity in Julio's amygdala.

15. As elderly Mr. Hooper crosses the busy intersection, he stumbles and drops the packages he is carrying. Which passerby is most likely to help Mr. Hooper?
    a. Drew, who has been laid off from work for three months
    b. Leon, who is on his way to work
    c. Bonnie, who earned her doctoral degree the day before
    d. Nancy, whose father recently passed away

16. Expressing anger can be adaptive when you
    a. retaliate immediately.
    b. have mentally rehearsed all the reasons for your anger.
    c. count to 10, then blow off steam.
    d. first wait until the anger subsides, then deal with the situation in a civil manner.

17. Cindy was happy with her promotion until she found out that Janice, who has the same amount of experience, receives a higher salary. Cindy's feelings are *best* explained according to the
    a. adaptation-level phenomenon.
    b. two-factor theory.
    c. catharsis hypothesis.
    d. principle of relative deprivation.

18. I am an emotionally literate person who is very accurate at reading others' nonverbal behavior, detecting lies, and describing my feelings. Who am I?
    a. an introvert
    b. an extravert
    c. a woman
    d. a man

19. Every year, Bob does not start studying until just before final exams. Then he is forced to work around the clock until he takes the last final, which makes him sick, probably because he is in the _____ phase of the _____ .
    a. alarm; post-traumatic stress syndrome
    b. resistance; general adaptation syndrome
    c. exhaustion; general adaptation syndrome
    d. depletion; post-traumatic stress syndrome

20. Connie complains to the school counselor that she has too much stress in her life. The counselor tells her that the level of stress people experience depends primarily on
    a. how many activities they are trying to do at the same time.
    b. how they appraise the events of life.
    c. their physical hardiness.
    d. how predictable stressful events are.

21. Jill is an easygoing, noncompetitive person who is happy in her job and enjoys her leisure time. She would *probably* be classified as
    a. Type A.
    b. Type B.
    c. Type C.
    d. There is too little information to tell.

22. A white blood cell that is formed in the thymus and that attacks cancer cells is
    a. a macrophage.   c. a T lymphocyte.
    b. a B lymphocyte.   d. any of these cells.

23. When would you expect that your immune responses would be WEAKEST?
    a. during summer vacation
    b. during final exams week
    c. just after receiving good news
    d. Immune activity would probably remain constant during these times.

24. Frank is a hard-driving, competitive person who always feels pressured for time and somewhat hostile toward others, especially those who keep him from getting things done at work. He would probably be classified as
    a. Type A.
    b. Type B.
    c. Type C.
    d. none of these types; there is too little information to tell.

25. Brenda became very angry with her brother for forgetting to pick her up from school. Which division of her nervous system mediated the physical arousal that accompanied her anger?
    a. sympathetic division
    b. parasympathetic division
    c. somatic division
    d. peripheral nervous system

Essay Question

Discuss biological and cultural influences on emotions. (Use the space below to list the points you want to make, and organize them. Then write the essay on a separate sheet of paper.)

KEY TERMS

Using your own words, on a separate piece of paper write a brief definition or explanation of each of the following terms.

1. emotion
2. James-Lange theory
3. Cannon-Bard theory
4. two-factor theory
5. polygraph
6. facial feedback
7. catharsis
8. feel-good, do-good phenomenon
9. well-being
10. adaptation-level phenomenon
11. relative deprivation
12. behavioral medicine
13. health psychology
14. stress
15. general adaptation syndrome (GAS)
16. coronary heart disease
17. Type A
18. Type B
19. psychophysiological illness
20. psychoneuroimmunology
21. lymphocytes

ANSWERS

Unit Review

Theories of Emotion

1. physiological arousal; expressive behaviors; conscious experience

2. follow
Cannon argued that the body's responses were not sufficiently distinct to trigger the different emotions and, furthermore, that physiological changes occur too slowly to trigger sudden emotion.

3. cortex; sympathetic; Cannon-Bard

4. physiological; cognitive; Stanley Schachter; Jerome Singer

Embodied Emotion

1. a. Heart rate increases.
   b. Muscles become tense.
   c. The liver pours extra sugar into the bloodstream.
   d. Breathing rate increases.
   e. Digestion slows.
   f. Pupils dilate.
   g. Blood tends to clot more rapidly.
   h. Skin perspires.

2. sympathetic; adrenal; epinephrine (adrenaline); norepinephrine (noradrenaline)

3. parasympathetic

4. similar; fear; anger; sexual arousal

5. fear; rage; finger; hormone

6. fear; joy

7. are; amygdala; angry; depression; right frontal

8. left frontal lobe

9. left; frontal; nucleus accumbens

10. polygraph
The polygraph measures several of the physiological responses that accompany emotion, such as changes in breathing, pulse rate, blood pressure, and perspiration. The assumption is that lying is stressful, so a person who is lying will become physiologically aroused.

11. anxiety

12. innocent; emotions; arousal

13. do not agree

14. guilty knowledge test

15. arousal
16. did not; did
17. fuels; channels
18. can

First, experiments on subliminal perception indicate that although stimuli are not consciously perceived, people later prefer these stimuli to others they have never been exposed to. Second, there is some separation of the neural pathways involved in emotion and cognition.

19. eye or ear; thalamus; amygdala; cognition; cortex
20. Richard Lazarus; appraise
21. interpretations; expectations; memories

It seems that some emotional responses—especially simple likes, dislikes, and fears—involve no conscious thinking. Other emotions are greatly affected by our interpretations and expectations.

Expressed Emotion

1. threats; anger; eyes; mouth; deceiving
2. better; easier
3. e-mail
4. better; lies; literacy; simpler; responsiveness
5. more; smaller; more
6. different
7. the same; display rules; does not vary; are
8. Darwin; interpret; contexts
9. individuality; hide their emotions; social-cultural
10. intensified
11. found
12. facial feedback
13. leads
14. behavior feedback

Experienced Emotion

1. 10; are; combinations
2. valence; pleasant (positive valence); unpleasant (negative valence); arousal
3. adaptive
4. learning (conditioning)
5. observing

The fact that humans quickly learn and slowly unlearn to fear snakes, spiders, and cliffs—fears that were presumably very useful to our ancestors—suggests that these are biologically predisposed fears that develop with little or no learning.

6. amygdala; limbic; remember; emotional
7. hippocampus; emotional reaction; will not
8. amygdala
9. phobias; experience; genes

10. willful; unjustified; avoidable
11. individuality; catharsis; interdependence; Tahiti; Japan
12. a. Retaliation must be directed against the person who provoked the anger.
    b. Retaliation must be justifiable.
    c. The target of the retaliation must not be someone who is intimidating.

One problem with expressing anger is that it breeds more anger, in part because it may trigger retaliation. Expressing anger can also magnify anger and reinforce its occurrence.

13. a. Wait to calm down.
    b. Deal with anger in a way that involves neither chronic anger nor sulking.
14. forgave
15. safer; healthier
16. more; feel-good, do-good
17. well-being
18. rise; is gone by
19. regain
20. overestimate; underestimate
21. do not
22. remained almost unchanged
23. intimacy, personal growth, and contribution to the community; wealth
24. adaptation-level

If we acquire new possessions, we feel an initial surge of pleasure. But we then adapt to having these new possessions, come to see them as normal, and require other things to give us another surge of happiness.

Realize that happiness doesn't come from financial success. Take control of your time. Act happy. Seek work and leisure that engage your skills. Engage in regular aerobic exercise. Get plenty of sleep. Give priority to close relationships. Focus beyond self. Be grateful. Nurture your spiritual self.

25. relative deprivation; slightly more
26. high self-esteem; satisfying marriage or close friendships; meaningful religious faith; optimistic outgoing personality; good sleeping habits and regular exercise; having work and leisure that engage our skills
27. age; gender; parenthood; physical attractiveness
28. 50

Stress and Health

1. behavioral medicine; health
2. stimulus; response; process
3. appraise; both positive and negative

4. Cannon; epinephrine (adrenaline); norepineph- rine (noradrenaline); sympathetic; fight or flight

5. hypothalamus; pituitary; adrenal glands; gluco- corticoid; cortisol

6. tend and befriend; seek and give support

7. general adaptation syndrome

8. alarm; sympathetic

9. resistance

10. exhaustion; more

11. telomeres; DNA; chromosomes; divide

12. psychological disorders such as depression and anxiety

13. more

14. daily hassles; racism; hypertension

15. coronary heart disease; smoking, obesity, high-fat diet, physical inactivity, elevated cholesterol level

16. cholesterol; clotting; stress

Type A people are competitive, hard-driving, super- motivated, impatient, time-conscious, verbally aggressive, and easily angered. Type B people are more relaxed and easygoing. In the Friedman and Rosenman study, heart attack victims came over- whelmingly from the Type A group.

17. negative emotions; the anger associated with an aggressively reactive temperament

18. Type A; cholesterol

19. pessimism; pessimists; optimists

20. increases

21. psychophysiological

22. hypertension; headaches; stress

23. psychosomatic; unreal

24. psychoneuroimmunology

25. immune; lymphocytes; B lymphocytes; T lym- phocytes; thymus

26. macrophage; natural killer (NK)

27. arthritis; allergic; underreact; cancer

28. Women; infections; self-attacking; lupus; multiple sclerosis

29. decrease; immune system; brain; muscles

30. Africa; AIDS; human immunodeficiency virus (HIV); blood; semen

31. have

32. have

33. negative; have

34. tumor; carcinogens; uncontrollable

35. does not

Progress Test 1

Multiple-Choice Questions

1. **c.** is the answer. (p. 402)
   a. & b. Researchers have not identified such per- sonality types.
   d. Individuals who are more easygoing are labeled Type B.

2. **c.** is the answer. (p. 369)
   a. The somatic division of the peripheral nervous system carries sensory and motor signals to and from the central nervous system.
   b. The peripheral nervous system is too general an answer, since it includes the sympathetic and parasympathetic divisions, as well as the somatic division.
   d. The parasympathetic nervous system restores the body to its unaroused state.

3. **c.** is the answer. Although many emotions have the same general body arousal, resulting from activation of the sympathetic nervous system, they appear to be associated with different brain circuits. (p. 370)

4. **b.** is the answer. (p. 367)
   a. This expresses the two-factor theory.
   c. This expresses the James-Lange theory.
   d. This theory was not discussed.

5. **c.** is the answer. (p. 399)
   a. & b. During these stages, the body's defensive mechanisms are at peak function.
   d. This is not a stage of the GAS.

6. **c.** is the answer. Coronary heart disease is fol- lowed by cancer, stroke, and chronic lung dis- ease. AIDS has not yet become one of the four leading causes of death in North America among the general population. (p. 401)

7. **d.** is the answer. The finding that people whose brains can't sense the body's responses experi- ence considerably less emotion in fact supports the James-Lange theory, which claims that experienced emotion follows from the body's responses. (p. 371)
   a., b., & c. All these statements go counter to the theory's claim that experienced emotion is essen- tially just an awareness of the body's response.

8. **c.** is the answer. (p. 372)

9. **c.** is the answer. The men who received epineph- rine without an explanation felt arousal and expe- rienced this arousal as whatever emotion the experimental confederate in the room with them was displaying. (p. 374)

a. Epinephrine recipients who expected arousal attributed their arousal to the drug and reported no emotional change in reaction to the confederate's behavior.
b. & d. In addition to the two groups discussed in the text, the experiment involved placebo recipients; these subjects were not physically aroused and did not experience an emotional change.

10. **d.** is the answer. Education level, parenthood, gender, and physical attractiveness seem unrelated to happiness. (p. 396)

11. **c.** is the answer. (p. 388)
    a. This would not be an example of catharsis because catharsis involves releasing, rather than suppressing, aggressive energy.
    b. Expressions of anger in such a situation tend to cause the person anxiety and thus tend not to be effective.
    d. One danger of expressing anger is that it will lead to retaliation and an escalation of anger.

12. **d.** is the answer. These are the three components of emotions identified in the text. (p. 366)

13. **c.** is the answer. If the suspect becomes physically aroused while answering questions about details only the perpetrator of the crime could know, it is presumed that he or she committed the crime. (p. 372)

14. **b.** is the answer. (p. 381)
    a. The opposite is true; relevant facial muscles are hard to control voluntarily.
    c. Authentic facial expressions tend to fade within 4 or 5 seconds.
    d. Facial expressions are generally universal; many gestures vary from culture to culture.

15. **c.** is the answer. Both fear and joy increase heart rate but stimulate different facial muscles. (p. 370)

16. **d.** is the answer. (p. 393)

17. **b.** is the answer. (p. 390)
    a., c., & d. Research studies have not found these factors to be related to altruistic behavior.

18. **d.** is the answer. (p. 382)

19. **d.** is the answer. (p. 390)

20. **c.** is the answer. (p. 374)
    a. & b. These answers imply that cognition *always* precedes emotion.
    d. These responses are unconscious and automatic and so are not learned.

21. **a.** is the answer. (p. 403)
    b. Catharsis refers to the release of emotion.
    c. *Psychogenic* means "originating in the mind." One's reaction to stress is partially psychological,

but this term is not used to refer to stress-related illness.
    d. There is no such term in psychology.

22. **d.** is the answer. Because stress depresses the immune system, stressed individuals are prone to all of these conditions. (pp. 403–405)

23. **c.** is the answer. (p. 397)
    a., b., & d. Whether an event is stressful or not depends on how it is appraised.

24. **d.** is the answer. (p. 400)

25. **c.** is the answer. (p. 397)
    a. Health psychology is a subfield of behavioral medicine.
    b. Holistic medicine is an older term that refers to medical practitioners who take more of an interdisciplinary approach to treating disorders.
    d. Osteopathy is a medical therapy that emphasizes manipulative techniques for correcting physical problems.

26. **c.** is the answer. (p. 369)
    a., b., & d. The pituitary does not produce stress hormones nor is the parasympathetic division involved in arousal.

Matching Items

1. a (p. 394)   5. b (p. 394)   9. f (p. 372)
2. k (p. 390)   6. g (p. 367)   10. j (p. 390)
3. c (p. 388)   7. h (p. 369)   11. e (p. 367)
4. i (p. 394)   8. d (p. 369)

Progress Test 2

Multiple-Choice Questions

1. **a.** is the answer. Emotional arousal activates the sympathetic nervous system, causing the release of sugar into the blood for energy, pupil dilation, and the diverting of blood from the internal organs to the muscles, all of which help prepare the body to meet an emergency. (p. 369)
    b. Being autonomic responses, most emotions are *involuntary* reactions.
    c. All emotions do *not* have the same physiological basis.
    d. Some emotions occur without cognitive awareness.

2. **c.** is the answer. According to Schachter and Singer, the two factors in emotion are (1) physical arousal and (2) conscious interpretation of the arousal. (p. 367)

3. **a.** is the answer. The principle of relative deprivation states that happiness is relative to others' attainments. This helps explain why those who

are relatively well off tend to be slightly more satisfied than the relatively poor, with whom the better-off can compare themselves. (p. 394)
b. Adaptation level is the tendency for our judgments to be relative to our prior experience.
c. This phenomenon has nothing to do with the interpretation of emotion.
d. Opponent processes are not discussed in the text in relation to emotion.

4. **b.** is the answer. (p. 367)
a. The James-Lange theory states that the experience of an emotion is an awareness of one's physical response to an emotion-arousing stimulus.
c. The two-factor theory states that to experience emotion one must be physically aroused and attribute the arousal to an emotional cause.
d. There is no such theory; catharsis refers to the release of emotion.

5. **d.** is the answer. (p. 384)

6. **d.** is the answer. No device can literally measure lying. The polygraph measures breathing, pulse rate, blood pressure, and perspiration for changes indicative of physiological arousal. (p. 372)

7. **b.** is the answer. (p. 371)

8. **b.** is the answer. Whereas the meanings of gestures vary from culture to culture, facial expressions seem to have the same meanings around the world. (pp. 380–381)

9. **a.** is the answer. If, as the theory claims, emotions are triggered by physiological reactions, then each emotion must be associated with a unique physiological reaction. (p. 367)
b. According to the Cannon-Bard theory, the same general body response accompanies many emotions.
c. The two-factor theory states that the cognitive interpretation of a general state of physical arousal determines different emotions.
d. There is no such theory; catharsis refers to the release of emotion.

10. **a.** is the answer. (p. 399)

11. **d.** is the answer. As the Schachter-Singer study indicated, physical arousal is not always accompanied by an emotional reaction. Only when arousal was attributed to an emotion was it experienced as such. The results of this experiment, therefore, support the viewpoint that conscious interpretation of arousal must precede emotion. (pp. 373–374)
a., b., & c. Each of these was presented as a supporting argument in the text.

12. **a.** is the answer. (p. 388)

b. The opposite is true. Any emotional arousal will simmer down if you wait long enough.
c. Catharsis often magnifies anger, escalates arguments, and leads to retaliation.
d. When counterattack is justified and can be directed at the offender, catharsis may be helpful.

13. **d.** is the answer. (p. 369)

14. **c.** is the answer. (p. 405)

15. **a.** is the answer. That physical arousal can be misattributed demonstrates that it is the cognitive interpretation of arousal, rather than the intensity or specific nature of the body's arousal, that determines the conscious experience of emotions. (pp. 373–374)
b. & c. The findings of these studies do not indicate that a minimum level of arousal is necessary for an emotional experience nor that applying a cognitive label must be simultaneous with the arousal.

16. **c.** is the answer. As heightened arousal may reflect feelings of anxiety or irritation rather than of guilt, the polygraph, which simply measures arousal, may easily err. (p. 372)
a. Misuse and invasion of privacy are valid issues, but Lykken primarily objects to the use of lie detectors because of their inaccuracy.
b. Although there are discrepancies among the various measures of arousal, this was not what Lykken objected to.
d. The lie detector errs about one-third of the time.

17. **c.** is the answer. (p. 399)
a. The final stage of the general adaptation syndrome is exhaustion.
b. & d. Although both of these are true, neither has anything to do with "tend and befriend."

18. **c.** is the answer. (p. 387)

19. **d.** is the answer. (p. 396)

20. **c.** is the answer. (p. 382)
a. & b. These are true of cultures that emphasize individuality rather than interdependence.

21. **b.** is the answer. The result is that their blood may contain excess cholesterol and fat. (p. 402)
a. Under relaxed situations, there is no difference in blood pressure.
c. Anger, both expressed and suppressed, is more characteristic of Type A people.
d. The text doesn't indicate that Type A persons are more outgoing than Type B persons.

22. **d.** is the answer. B lymphocytes fight bacterial infections; T lymphocytes attack cancer cells,

viruses, and foreign substances; and macrophages ingest harmful invaders. (p. 403)

23. **a.** is the answer. A variety of studies have shown that stress depresses the immune system, increasing the risk and potential severity of many diseases. (p. 403)

24. **c.** is the answer. (p. 403)

25. **a.** is the answer. (p. 403)
    b. An *under*reactive immune system would make an individual more susceptible to infectious diseases or the proliferation of cancer cells.
    c. & d. Lymphocytes are disease- and infection-fighting white blood cells in the immune system.

26. **d.** is the answer. (p. 405)

27. **d.** is the answer. The crucial characteristic of Type A behavior seems to be a tendency to react with negative emotions, especially anger; other aspects of Type A behavior appear not to predict heart disease, and some appear to be helpful to the individual. (p. 402)

28. **d.** is the answer. This unit deals with the topics of health psychology, namely, preventing illness, by developing better ways to cope with stress; treating illness, by improving the ways in which people notice and explain symptoms; and promoting health, for example, through nutrition and weight control. (p. 397)

True–False Items

1. F (p. 403) 5. T (p. 403)   9. F (p. 367)
2. F (p. 378) 6. F (p. 392)   10. T (p. 402)
3. T (p. 369) 7. T (p. 374)
4. T (p. 383) 8. F (p. 374)

Psychology Applied

Multiple-Choice Questions

1. **b.** is the answer. The James-Lange theory proposes that the experienced emotion is an awareness of a prior body response: Your pulse races, and so you feel nervous. (p. 367)
    a. According to the Cannon-Bard theory, your body's reaction would occur simultaneously with, rather than before, your experience of the emotion.
    c. Relative deprivation refers to our sense that we are worse off than others with whom we compare ourselves.
    d. The adaptation-level phenomenon concerns our tendency to judge stimuli on the basis of recent experience.

2. **b.** is the answer. Professor Simon's judgment of his office is affected by his recent experience: When that experience was of a smaller office, his new office seemed terrific; now, however, it is commonplace. (p. 394)
    a. Relative deprivation is the sense that one is worse off than those with whom one compares oneself.
    c. The two-factor theory has to do with the cognitive labeling of physical arousal.
    d. This is the idea that there is an inverse relationship between the difficulty of a task and the optimum level of arousal. It is not discussed in this unit.

3. **b.** is the answer. The parasympathetic division is involved in calming arousal. (p. 369)
    a. The sympathetic division is active during states of arousal and hence would not be active in the situation described.
    c. The somatic division is involved in transmitting sensory information and controlling skeletal muscles; it is not involved in arousing and calming the body.
    d. This answer is too general, since the peripheral nervous system includes not only the parasympathetic division but also the sympathetic division and the somatic division.

4. **a.** is the answer. According to the James-Lange theory, Maria's emotions should be greatly diminished since her brain is unable to sense physical arousal. (p. 371)
    b. Cannon and Bard would have expected Maria to experience emotions normally because they believed that the experiencing of emotions occurs separately from the body's responses.
    c. & d. These theories and principles make no particular prediction regarding the importance of physical arousal in the conscious experience of emotion.

5. **b.** is the answer. Expressions may amplify the associated emotions. (p. 383)
    a. Laboratory studies have shown that facial expressions *intensify* emotions.
    c. Arousal of the sympathetic nervous system, such as occurs when one is afraid, slows digestive function.
    d. Increased body temperature accompanies anger but not fear.

6. **d.** is the answer. In keeping with the catharsis hypothesis, Jane feels less angry after releasing her aggression. (p. 388)
    a. Adaptation level is our tendency to judge things relative to our experiences.

b. This is not a specific theory.

c. Relative deprivation is the sense that one is worse off relative to those with whom one compares oneself.

7. **c.** is the answer. According to the two-factor theory, it is cognitive interpretation of the same general physiological arousal that distinguishes the two emotions. (p. 367)

a. According to the James-Lange theory, if the same physical arousal occurred in the two instances, the same emotions should result.

b. The Cannon-Bard theory argues that conscious awareness of an emotion and body reaction occur at the same time.

d. Adaptation level concerns our tendency to judge things relative to our experiences.

8. **d.** is the answer. (p. 372)

9. **d.** is the answer. (p. 370)

10. **c.** is the answer. Because physical arousal tends to intensify emotions, Dan (who is likely to be physically aroused after playing tennis) will probably be angrier than Bob or Veronica, who are in more relaxed states. (pp. 373–374)

11. **d.** is the answer. (p. 381)

a. & c. The Cannon-Bard and two-factor theories of emotion do not address the universality of emotional expressions.

b. Even if it is true that emotional expressions are acquired at an early age, this would not necessarily account for the common facial expressions of children from around the world. If anything, the different cultural experiences of the children might lead them to express their feelings in very *different* ways.

12. **d.** is the answer. In Japan and China, cultures that emphasize human connections and interdependence, personal emotional displays are rare. (p. 382)

a., b., & c. In cultures that encourage individuality, as in Western Europe, Australia, and North America, personal emotions are displayed openly.

13. **c.** is the answer. (p. 371)

a. Individuals with more active right frontal lobes tend to be less cheerful and are more likely to be depressed.

b. In fact, just the opposite is true: People with greater left frontal activity tend to be better able to turn off upsetting feelings.

d. The text does not suggest that greater left or right frontal activity influences a person's ability to express his or her feelings.

14. **a.** is the answer. As people experience negative emotions, such as anger, the right hemisphere becomes more electrically active. (p. 371)

c. & d. The EEG measures electrical activity on the surface of the cortex, not at the level of structures deep within the brain, such as the amygdala.

15. **c.** is the answer. People who are in a good mood are more likely to help others. Bonnie, who is probably pleased with herself for earning a Ph.D., is likely to be in a better mood than Drew, Leon, or Nancy. (p. 390)

16. **d.** is the answer. (p. 388)

a. Venting anger immediately may lead you to say things you later regret and/or may lead to retaliation by the other person.

b. Going over the reasons for your anger merely prolongs the emotion.

c. Counting to 10 may give you a chance to calm down, but "blowing off steam" may rekindle your anger.

17. **d.** is the answer. Cindy is unhappy with her promotion because she feels deprived relative to Janice. (p. 394)

a. The adaptation-level phenomenon would predict that Cindy's raise would cause an increase in her happiness, since her most recent experience was to earn a lower salary.

b. The two-factor theory has to do with the cognitive labeling of physical arousal.

c. The catharsis hypothesis maintains that venting one's anger may relieve aggressive urges.

18. **c.** is the answer. (p. 379)

19. **c.** is the answer. According to Selye's general adaptation syndrome, diseases are most likely to occur in this final stage. (p. 399)

a. & b. Resistance to disease is greater during the alarm and resistance phases because the body's mobilized resources are not yet depleted.

d. There is no such thing as the "depletion phase." Moreover, the post-traumatic stress syndrome refers to the haunting nightmares and anxiety of those who have suffered extreme stress, such as that associated with combat.

20. **b.** is the answer. (pp. 397–398)

a., c., & d. Each of these is a factor in stress, but it is how an event is *perceived* that determines whether it is stressful or not.

21. **b.** is the answer. (p. 402)

a. Type A persons are hard-driving and competitive.

c. There is no such thing as a "Type C" person.

22. **c.** is the answer. (p. 403)

a. Macrophages are immune agents that search for and ingest harmful invaders.

b. B lymphocytes form in the bone marrow and release antibodies that fight bacterial infections.

23. **b.** is the answer. Stressful situations, such as final exams, decrease immune responses. (pp. 403–404)

24. **a.** is the answer. (p. 402)

   b. Type B is relaxed and easygoing.

   c. There is no such thing as Type C.

25. **a.** is the answer. (p. 369)

   b. The parasympathetic division would calm her down.

   c. The somatic division enables voluntary control of our skeletal muscles.

   d. The peripheral nervous system is too general an answer.

Essay Question

All emotions involve some degree of physiological arousal of the sympathetic nervous system. Although the arousal that occurs with different emotions is in most ways undifferentiated, there may be subtle differences in the brain pathways and hormones associated with different emotions. Other examples of the influence of biological factors on emotion are the universality of facial expressions of emotion.

Unlike facial expressions of emotion, the meaning of many gestures is culturally determined. Culture also influences how people express their feelings. In cultures that encourage individuality, for example, personal emotions are displayed openly. In cultures that emphasize human interdependence, the display of personal emotions is discouraged.

Key Terms

1. **Emotion** is a response of the whole organism involving three components: (1) physiological arousal, (2) expressive behaviors, and (3) conscious experience. (p. 366)

2. The **James-Lange theory** states that emotional experiences are based on an awareness of the body's responses to emotion-arousing stimuli: A stimulus triggers the body's responses that in turn trigger the experienced emotion. (p. 367)

3. The **Cannon-Bard theory** states that the subjective experience of an emotion occurs at the same time as the body's physical reaction. (p. 367)

4. The **two-factor theory** of emotion proposes that emotions have two ingredients: physical arousal and a cognitive label. Thus, physical arousal is a

necessary, but not a sufficient, component of emotional change. For an emotion to be experienced, arousal must be attributed to an emotional cause. (p. 367)

5. The **polygraph**, or lie detector, is a device that measures several of the physiological responses accompanying emotion. (p. 372)

6. **Facial feedback** is the effect of facial expressions on experienced emotions, often intensifying them. (p. 383)

7. **Catharsis** is emotional release; according to the catharsis hypothesis, by expressing our anger, we can reduce it. (p. 388)

8. The **feel-good, do-good phenomenon** is the tendency of people to be helpful when they are in a good mood. (p. 390)

9. **Well-being** refers to a person's sense of satisfaction with his or her life. (p. 390)

10. The **adaptation-level phenomenon** refers to our tendency to judge things relative to a neutral level defined by our prior experience. (p. 394)

11. The principle of **relative deprivation** is the perception that we are worse off relative to those with whom we compare ourselves. (p. 394)

12. **Behavioral medicine** is the interdisciplinary field that applies behavioral and medical knowledge to the treatment of disease and the promotion of health. (p. 397)

13. **Health psychology** is a subfield of psychology that studies how health and illness are influenced by emotions, stress, personality, life-style, and other psychological factors. (p. 397)

14. **Stress** refers to the process by which we perceive and respond to events, called *stressors*, that we perceive as threatening or challenging. (p. 397)

15. The **general adaptation syndrome (GAS)** is the three-stage sequence of bodily reaction to stress outlined by Hans Selye. (p. 399)

16. The leading cause of death in North America today, **coronary heart disease** results from the clogging of the vessels that nourish the heart muscle. (p. 401)

17. **Type A** personality is Friedman and Rosenman's term for the coronary-prone behavior pattern of competitive, hard-driving, impatient, verbally aggressive, and anger-prone people. (p. 402)

18. **Type B** personality is Friedman and Rosenman's term for the coronary-resistant behavior pattern of easygoing, relaxed people. (p. 402)

19. A **psychophysiological illness** is any genuine illness such as hypertension and some headaches that is apparently linked to stress rather than caused by a physical disorder. (p. 403)

    Memory aid: Psycho- refers to mind; *physio-* refers to body; a **psychophysiological illness** is a mind-body disorder.

20. **Psychoneuroimmunology (PNI)** is the study of how psychological, neural, and endocrine processes affect the immune system and resulting health. (p. 403)

21. **Lymphocytes** are the two types of white blood cells of the immune system that fight bacterial infections (B lymphocytes) and viruses, cancer cells, and foreign substances in the body (T lymphocytes). (p. 403)

Developmental Psychology

UNIT OVERVIEW

Developmental psychologists study the life cycle, from conception to death. Unit 9 covers physical, cognitive, and social development over the life span and introduces two major issues in developmental psychology: (1) whether development is best described as gradual and continuous or as a discontinuous sequence of stages and (2) whether the individual's personality remains stable or changes over the life span. The issue of the relative impact of genes and experience on behavior is the subject of Unit 3C. This unit also explores how genes and environment interact to shape both the biological and social aspects of our gender.

There is a great deal of inforation to learn in this unit, including many terms and a number of important research findings. Pay particular attention to the stage theories of Jean Piaget, Lawrence Kohlberg, and Erik Erikson, as well as to the discussion regarding intellectual stability during adulthood.

NOTE: Answer guidelines for all Unit 9 questions begin on page 253.

UNIT REVIEW

First, skim this section, noting headings and boldface items. After you have read the section, review each objective by completing the sentences and answering the questions that follow it. As you proceed, evaluate your performance by consulting the answers beginning on page 253. Do not continue with the next section until you understand each answer. If you need to, review or reread the section in the textbook before continuing.

Introduction (p. 411)

Objective 1: State three areas of change that developmental psychologists study, and identify the three major issues in developmental psychology.

1. Scientists who study physical, cognitive, and social changes throughout the life cycle are called
_____ _____ .

2. One of the major issues in developmental psychology concerns the relative importance of genetic inheritance and experience in determining behavior; this is called the
_____ and _____
issue.

3. A second developmental issue concerns whether developmental changes are gradual or abrupt; this is called the _____ and
_____ issue.

4. A third controversial issue concerns the consistency of personality and whether development is characterized more by _____
over time or by change.

Prenatal Development and the Newborn
(pp. 411–415)

Objective 2: Discuss the course of prenatal development and the destructive impact of teratogens, and describe some abilities of the newborn.

1. Conception begins when a woman's
_____ releases a mature
_____ .

2. The few _____ from the man that reach the egg release digestive _____
that eat away the egg's protective covering. As soon as one sperm penetrates the egg, the egg's surface _____ all other sperm.

3. The egg and sperm _____ fuse and become one.

4. Fertilized human eggs are called
_____ . During the first week, the
cells in this cluster begin to specialize in structure
and function, that is, they begin to
_____ . The outer part of the fertilized egg attaches to the _____ wall.

5. From about 2 until 8 weeks of age the developing
human, formed from the inner cells of the fertilized egg, is called a(n) _____ .
During the final stage of prenatal development,
the developing human is called a(n)
_____ .

6. Formed as the zygote attached to the uterus, the
_____ transfers _____
and _____ from mother to fetus.
Along with nutrients, a range of harmful substances known as _____ can pass
through the placenta.

7. Moderate consumption of alcohol during pregnancy _____ (usually does not
affect/can affect) the fetal brain. If a mother
drinks heavily, her baby is at risk for the birth
defects and intellectual disability that
accompany _____
_____ _____ .

8. When an infant's cheek is touched, it will vigorously _____ for a nipple. Other
infant reflexes include _____ ,
_____ , _____ , and
_____ .

9. American psychologist _____
believed that the newborn experiences a "bloom-
ing, buzzing confusion." This belief is
_____ (correct/incorrect).

Give some evidence supporting the claim that a newborn's sensory equipment is biologically prewired to
facilitate social responsiveness.

10. To study infants' thinking, developmental
researchers have focused on a simple form of
learning called _____ , which
involves a _____ in responding
with repeated stimulation. Using the
_____-_____
procedure, researchers have found that infants
prefer sights, such as faces, that facilitate
_____ responsiveness.

Infancy and Childhood (pp. 415–441)

Objective 3: Describe some developmental changes
in brain and motor abilities during infancy and childhood, and explain why our earliest memories rarely
predate our third birthdays.

1. The developing brain _____
(over/under)produces neurons. At birth, the
human nervous system
_____ (is/is not) fully mature.

2. Between 3 and 6 years of age, the brain is developing most rapidly in the _____
lobes, which enable _____
_____ . The last cortical areas of the
brain to develop are the _____
_____ linked with _____ ,
_____ , and _____ .

3. After puberty, a process of _____
shuts down some neural connections and
strengthens others.

4. Biological growth processes that enable orderly
changes in behavior and are relatively uninfluenced by experience are called
_____ .

5. Infants pass the milestones of _____
development at different rates, but the basic
_____ of stages is fixed. Infants sit
before they _____ and walk before
they _____ .

6. Genes play a _____ (major/minor)
role in motor development.

7. Until the necessary muscular and neural maturation is complete, including the rapid develop-

ment of the brain's _____ ,
experience has a _____ (large/
small) effect on learning to walk, for example.

8. Our earliest memories generally do not occur
   before age _____ .

9. This phenomenon has been called

   _____ _____ .

Objective 4: State Piaget's understanding of how the
mind develops, and outline Piaget's four stages of
cognitive development, noting current thinking
regarding cognitive stages.

10. *Cognition* refers to all the mental activities associ-
    ated with _____ , _____ ,
    _____ , and _____ .

11. The first researcher to show that the thought
    processes of adults and children are very
    different was _____ .

12. To organize and interpret his or her experiences,
    the developing child constructs cognitive
    concepts called _____ .

13. The interpretation of new experiences in terms of
    existing ideas is called _____ . The
    adaptation of existing ideas to fit new experiences
    is called _____ .

14. In Piaget's first stage of development, the
    _____ stage, children experience the
    world through their motor and sensory interac-
    tions with objects. This stage occurs between
    infancy and nearly age _____ .

15. The awareness that things continue to exist even
    when they are removed from view is called
    _____ _____ . This
    awareness begins to develop at about
    _____ months of age.

16. Developmental researchers have found that
    Piaget and his followers _____
    (overestimated/underestimated) young
    children's competence. For instance, babies have
    an intuitive grasp of simple laws of
    _____ , as Sarah Shuwairi showed,

and an understanding of _____ , as
Karen Wynn demonstrated.

17. According to Piaget, during the preschool years
    and up to age _____ , children are
    in the _____ stage.

18. The principle that the quantity of a substance
    remains the same even when the shape of its con-
    tainer changes is called _____ .
    Piaget believed that preschoolers
    _____ (have/have not) developed
    this concept.

19. Preschoolers have difficulty perceiving things
    from another person's point of view. This inabili-
    ty is called _____ .

20. The child's growing ability to take another's per-
    spective is evidence that the child is acquiring a

    _____ _____

    _____ . Between about 3½ and 4½,
    children come to realize that others may hold

    _____ _____ .

21. (Close-Up) The disorder characterized by defi-
    cient _____ and _____
    interaction and an impaired _____

    _____ _____ is

    _____ . This disorder is related to
    malfunctions of brain areas that allow us to take
    another's _____ . The "high-
    functioning" form of this disorder is called

    _____ _____ .

22. (Close-Up) Baron-Cohen's theory proposes that
    autism represents an "extreme _____
    brain." According to this theory, girls tend to be
    _____ , who are better than boys at
    reading facial expressions and gestures, which is
    a challenging task for those with autism. Boys
    tend to be _____ , who understand
    things in terms of rules or laws. Because of
    _____ mating, two
    _____ are likely to mate and have a
    child, which increases the risk of the child having
    autism.

23. In contrast to Piaget's findings, researchers have discovered that the abilities to perform mental _____ , to think _____ , and to take another's _____ begin to show up early and continue to develop _____ (abruptly/gradually).

24. Russian psychologist _____ noted that by age _____ children stop thinking aloud and instead rely on _____ _____ . Talking to themselves helps children control their _____ and _____ and master new skills.

25. Piaget believed that children acquire the mental abilities needed to comprehend mathematical transformations and conservation by about _____ years of age. At this time, they enter the _____ _____ stage.

26. In Piaget's final stage, the _____ _____ stage, reasoning expands from the purely concrete to encompass _____ thinking. Piaget believed most children begin to enter this stage by age _____ .

Explain briefly how contemporary researchers view Piaget's theory.

27. Complementing Piaget's emphasis on interaction with the _____ environment is Vygotsky's emphasis on interaction with the _____ environment. When parents mentor children and give them new words, they provide, according to Vygotsky, a _____ upon which the child can build higher-level thinking.

Objective 5: Discuss the effects of nourishment, body contact, and familiarity on infant social attachment.

28. Soon after _____ _____ emerges and children become mobile, a new fear, called _____ _____ , emerges.

29. This fear emerges at about age _____ .

30. The development of a strong emotional bond between infant and parent is called _____ .

31. The Harlows' studies of monkeys have shown that mother-infant attachment does not depend on the mother providing nourishment as much as it does on her providing the comfort of _____ _____ . Another key to attachment is _____ .

32. Human attachment involves one person providing another with a _____ _____ when distressed and a _____ _____ from which to explore.

33. In some animals, attachment will occur only during a restricted time called a _____ _____ .

    Konrad Lorenz discovered that young birds would follow almost any object if it were the first moving thing they observed. This phenomenon is called _____ .

34. Human infants _____ (do/do not) have a precise critical period for becoming attached. However, because of _____ _____ , they attach to what they know.

Objective 6: Contrast secure and insecure attachment, and discuss the roles of parents' and infants' temperaments in the development of attachment and an infant's feelings of basic trust.

35. Placed in a research setting called the _____ _____ , children show one of two patterns of attachment: _____ attachment or _____ attachment.

Contrast the responses of securely and insecurely attached infants to strange situations.

_____

_____

Discuss the impact of responsive parenting on infant attachment.

_____

_____

36. The term that refers to the a person's characteristic emotional reactivity and intensity is
_____ , which
_____ (does/does not) endure over time.

37. From the first weeks of life, _____ babies are more _____ ,
_____ , and _____ . In contrast, _____ babies are
_____ , _____ , and
_____ in feeding and sleeping.
_____-_____-
_____-_____ babies tend to resist or withdraw from new people or situations. _____ predisposes these characteristic differences.

38. A father's love and acceptance for his children are
_____ (comparable to/less important than) a mother's love in predicting their children's health and well-being.

39. Separation anxiety peaks in infants around
_____ months, then
_____ (gradually declines/remains constant for about a year). This is true of children
_____ (in North America/throughout the world).

40. According to Erikson, securely attached infants approach life with a sense of

_____ _____ .

41. Most researchers now believe that early attachments _____ (do/do not) form the basis of adult attachments. Attachment style is also associated with _____ :
Securely attached people exhibit greater drive to achieve.

Objective 7: Assess the impact of parental neglect, family disruption, and day care on attachment patterns and development.

42. The Harlows found that when monkeys reared in social isolation were placed with other monkeys, they reacted with either fear or _____ .

43. Most abused children _____ (do/do not) later become abusive parents.

44. Although most children who grow up under adversity are _____ and become normal adults, early abuse and excessive exposure to _____ _____ may alter the development of the brain chemical
_____ .

45. When placed in a more positive and stable environment, most infants _____ (recover/do not recover) from disruptions in attachment.

46. Experts agree that child care per se
_____ (does/does not) constitute a risk factor in children's development. High-quality child care consists of warm, supportive interactions with adults in an environment that is
_____ , _____ , and
_____ . More important than time spent in day care in influencing a child's development are _____
_____ .

Objective 8: Trace the onset and development of children's self-concept.

47. The primary social achievement of childhood is the development of a _____ , which occurs in most children by age
_____ .

48. A child's self-image generally becomes stable between the ages of _____ and _____ , when children begin to describe themselves in terms of gender, group memberships, and psychological _____ , and they _____ themselves with other children.

Identify several characteristics of children who have formed a positive self-image.

Objective 9: Describe three parenting styles, and explain why authoritative parenting is considered most effective.

49. Parents who impose rules and expect obedience are exhibiting a(n) _____ style of parenting.

50. Parents who make few demands of their children and tend to submit to their children's desires are identified as _____ parents.

51. Setting and enforcing standards after discussion with their children is the approach taken by _____ parents.

52. Studies have shown that children with the highest self-esteem, self-reliance, and social competence usually have _____ parents.

Explain why the correlation between authoritative parenting and social competence does not necessarily reveal cause and effect.

Objective 10: Identify some ways in which culture affects child-rearing practices.

53. Whereas most Western parents place more emphasis on _____ (emotional closeness/independence) in their children, many Asian and African parents focus on cultivating _____ (emotional closeness/independence).

54. Children in collectivist cultures grow up with a strong sense of _____ _____ , a sense that what shames or honors the person also shames or honors the family.

Objective 11: Discuss gender similarities and differences in psychological traits such as aggression, social power, and social connectedness.

55. The biological and socially influenced characteristics by which people define *male* or *female* is our _____ .

56. Compared with the average man, an average woman has more _____ , less _____ , and is a few inches _____ . Women are more likely than men to suffer from _____ , _____ , and _____ _____ .

57. Compared with women, men are more likely to commit _____ and to suffer _____ _____ . They are also more likely to be diagnosed with _____ , _____ - _____ , _____ - _____ _____ _____ , and _____ _____ _____ .

58. *Aggression* is defined as _____ or _____ behavior that is _____ to hurt someone.

59. Throughout the world, men are more likely than women to engage in _____ , _____ , and _____ .

60. The aggression gender gap pertains to _____ rather than _____ aggression.

61. Compared with women, men are perceived as being more _____ , _____ , and _____ . As leaders, they tend to be more _____ , while women are more _____ .

62. Compared with men, women are perceived as being more _____ , _____ , and _____ .

63. These perceived differences occur _____ (throughout the world/only in certain cultures).

64. According to Carol Gilligan, women are more concerned than men in making _____ with others.

65. This difference is noticeable in how children _____ , and it continues throughout the teen and adult years. Girls play in groups that are _____ and less _____ than boys' groups.

66. Because they are more _____ , women are likely to use conversation to _____ _____ , while men are likely to use conversation to _____ _____ .

67. Women tend and befriend—for example, they turn to others for _____ , especially when coping with _____ .

68. Gender differences in power, connectedness, and other traits peak in late _____ and early _____ . By age 50, the differences have _____ (decreased/increased).

Objective 12: Explain how biological sex is determined, and describe the role of sex hormones in biological development and gender differences.

69. The twenty-third pair of chromosomes determines the developing person's _____ . The mother always contributes a(n) _____ chromosome. When the father contributes a(n) _____ chromosome, the testes begin producing the hormone

_____ . In about the _____ (what week?), this hormone initiates the development of external male sex organs.

70. Sex chromosomes control _____ that influence the brain's wiring. In adulthood, part of the _____ lobe, an area involved in _____ fluency, is thicker in women. Part of the brain's _____ cortex, a key area for _____ perception, is thicker in men.

Objective 13: Discuss the importance of gender roles in development, and describe the relationship between gender and child-rearing.

71. Our expectations about the way men and women behave define our culture's _____ _____ .

72. Gender roles _____ (are/are not) rigidly fixed by evolution, as evidenced by the fact that they vary across _____ and over _____ . For instance, in _____ societies there tends to be minimal division of labor by sex; by contrast, in _____ societies, women remain close to home while men roam freely, herding cattle or sheep.

73. Our individual sense of being male or female is called our _____ _____ . The degree to which we exhibit traditionally male or female traits and interests is called _____ _____ .

74. According to _____ _____ theory, children learn gender-linked behaviors by observing and imitating others and being rewarded or punished. When their families discourage traditional gender typing, children _____ (do/do not) organize themselves into "boy worlds" and "girl worlds."

75. Children also learn from their _____ _____ what it means to be male or female and adjust their behavior accordingly, thereby demonstrating that _____ is important in the formation of gender identity.

Parents and Peers (pp. 441–445)

Objective 14: Describe how experience can modify the brain.

1. Environmental influences begin during the period of _____ development.

2. Rosenzweig and Krech discovered that rats raised from a young age in enriched environments had _____ (thicker/thinner) brain cortexes than animals raised in isolation.

Describe the effects of sensory stimulation on neural development.

3. Experience shapes the brain by preserving activated _____ connections and allowing unused connections to _____ . This _____ process results in a massive loss of unused connections by _____ .

Objective 15: Explain why we should be careful about attributing children's successes and failures to their parents' influence, and evaluate the importance of peer influence on development.

4. The idea that parents shape their children's futures came from _____ _____ and _____ .

5. Parents do influence some areas of their children's lives, such as their _____ _____ , _____ _____ , and _____ _____ .

6. In areas such as _____ , the environment siblings share at home accounts for less than _____ percent of their differences.

7. Experiences with _____ have a powerful effect on how children develop, partly as a result of a _____ effect by which kids seek out others with similar attitudes and interests.

Adolescence (pp. 445–455)

Objective 16: Define *adolescence*, and identify the major physical changes during this period.

1. *Adolescence* is defined as the transition period between _____ and _____ .

2. The "storm and stress" view of adolescence is credited to _____ , one of the first American psychologists to describe adolescence.

3. Adolescence begins with the time of developing sexual maturity known as _____ . A two-year period of rapid physical development begins in girls at about the age of _____ and in boys at about the age of _____ . This growth spurt is marked by the development of the reproductive organs and external genitalia, or _____ _____ characteristics, as well as by the development of traits such as pubic hair and enlarged breasts in females and facial hair in males. These nonreproductive traits are known as _____ _____ characteristics.

4. The first menstrual period is called _____ . In boys, the first ejaculation is called _____ .

5. The _____ (timing/sequence) of pubertal changes is more predictable than their _____ (timing/sequence).

6. Boys who mature _____ (early/late) tend to be more popular, self-assured, and independent; they also are at increased risk for _____ _____ .

For girls, _____ (early/late) maturation can be stressful, especially when their bodies are out of sync with their _____ _____ . This reminds us that

_____ and _____ interact.

7. The adolescent brain undergoes a selective _____ of unused neurons and connections. Also, teens' occasional impulsiveness and risky behaviors may be due, in part, to the fact that development in the brain's _____ _____ lags behind that of the _____ _____ .

Objective 17: Describe adolescents' reasoning abilities and moral development, according to Piaget and Kohlberg, and note the impact of emotional intuitions on our moral judgments.

8. Adolescents' developing cognitive ability enables them to think about what is _____ possible and _____ that with imperfect reality.

9. During the early teen years, reasoning is often _____ , as adolescents often feel their experiences are unique.

10. Piaget's final stage of cognitive development is the stage of _____ _____ . Adolescents in this stage are capable of thinking logically about _____ as well as concrete propositions. This enables them to detect _____ in others' reasoning and to spot hypocrisy.

11. The theorist who proposed that moral thought progresses through stages is _____ . These stages are divided into three basic levels: _____ , _____ , and _____ .

12. In the preconventional stages of morality, characteristic of children, the emphasis is on obeying rules in order to avoid _____ or gain _____ .

13. Conventional morality usually emerges by early _____ . The emphasis is on gaining social _____ or upholding the social _____ .

14. Individuals who base moral judgments on their own perceptions of basic ethical principles are said by Kohlberg to employ _____ morality.

Summarize the criticisms of Kohlberg's theory of moral development.

15. The idea that moral feelings precede moral reasoning is expressed in the _____ _____ explanation of morality. Research studies using _____ _____ support the idea that moral judgment involves more than merely thinking; it is also gut-level feeling.

16. Morality involves doing the right thing, and what we do depends on _____ influences. Today's _____ _____ _____ focus on moral issues and doing the right thing. They teach children _____ for others' feelings.

17. Children who learn to delay _____ become more socially responsible, often engaging in responsible action through _____ learning. They also become more _____ successful and more productive.

18. Moral ideas grow _____ (stronger/ weaker) when acted on.

Objective 18: Identify Erikson's eight stages of psychosocial development and their accompanying issues, and discuss how forming an identity prepares us for intimacy.

Complete the missing information in the following table of Erikson's stages of psychosocial development.

Group Age	Psychosocial Stage
Infancy	_____
_____	Autonomy vs. shame and doubt
Preschooler	_____
_____	Competence vs. inferiority
Adolescence	_____
_____	Intimacy vs. isolation
Middle adulthood	_____
_____	Integrity vs. despair

19. To refine their sense of identity, adolescents in individualistic cultures experiment with different _____ in different situations. The result may be role _____ , which is resolved by forming a self-definition, or _____ .

20. Some adolescents forge their identity early, simply by _____ their parents' values and expectations. Others may assume an identity _____ that of their parents.

21. During the early to mid-teen years, self-esteem generally _____ (rises/falls/remains stable). During the late teens and twenties, self-esteem generally _____ (rises/falls/remains stable) and identity beomes more _____ .

22. Erikson saw the formation of identity as a prerequisite for the development of _____ in young adulthood.

Objective 19: Contrast parental and peer influences during adolescence, and discuss the characteristics of emerging adulthood.

23. Adolescence is typically a time of increasing influence from one's _____ and decreasing influence from _____ .

24. Most adolescents report that they _____ (do/do not) get along with their parents. They see their parents as having the most influence in shaping their _____ _____ , for example.

25. When rejected adolescents withdraw, they are vulnerable to _____ , low _____ , and _____ .

26. As a result of increased _____ _____ and weakened _____-_____ bonds, sexual maturity is beginning _____ (earlier/later) than in the past.

27. Because the time from 18 to the mid-twenties is increasingly a not-yet-settled phase of life, some psychologists refer to this period as a time of _____ _____ .

Adulthood (pp. 455–471)

Objective 20: Identify the major changes in physical and sensory abilities that occur in middle adulthood and later life.

1. During adulthood, age _____ (is/is not) a very good predictor of people's traits.

2. The mid-twenties are the peak years for _____ _____ , _____ _____ , _____ _____ , and _____ _____ . Because they mature earlier, _____ (women/men) also peak earlier.

3. During early and middle adulthood, physical vigor has less to do with _____ than with a person's _____ and _____ habits.

4. The cessation of the menstrual cycle, known as _____ , occurs within a few years of _____ . This biological change results from lowered levels of the hormone _____ . A woman's emotional experience during this time depends largely on her _____ and _____ .

5. Although men experience no equivalent to menopause, they do experience a more gradual decline in _____ count, level of the hormone _____ , and speed of erection and ejaculation during later life.

6. Worldwide, life expectancy at birth increased from 49 years in 1950 to _____ years and beyond in 2004 in some developed countries. Women outlive men by nearly _____ years worldwide and by _____ years in Canada, the United States, and Australia. With age, the tips of our chromosomes, called _____ , shorten.

7. According to one evolutionary theory, our bodies age and wear out because once we've completed our _____-_____ and nurturing task, there are no _____ pressures against genes that cause degeneration in later life.

8. The human spirit also affects life expectancy. The death rate increases when people reach their birthdays, a finding referred to as the _____-_____ phenomenon.

9. With age, the eye's pupil _____ (shrinks/enlarges) and its lens becomes _____ (more/less) transparent. As a result, the amount of light that reaches the retina is _____ (increased/reduced).

10. Although older adults are _____ (more/less) susceptible to life-threatening ailments, they suffer from short-term ailments such as flu _____ (more/less) often than younger adults.

11. Aging _____ (slows/speeds/has no effect on) neural processing and causes a gradual loss of _____ _____ .

12. Physical exercise stimulates _____ _____ development and _____ connections, thanks perhaps to increased _____ and nutrient flow.

13. The mental erosion that results from progressive damage to the brain is called _____ .

14. The irreversible disorder that causes progressive brain deterioration is _____ disease. This disease has been linked to a deterioration of neurons that produce the neurotransmitter _____ .

Objective 21: Assess the impact of aging on memory and intelligence.

15. Studies of developmental changes in learning and memory show that during adulthood there is a decline in the ability to _____ (recall/recognize) new information but not in the ability to _____ (recall/recognize) such information. One factor that influences memory in older people is the _____ of material.

16. Adults' _____ memory remains strong when events help trigger recall.

17. Cognitive abilities among 70-year-olds are _____ (less/more) varied than among 20-year-olds.

18. A research study in which people of various ages are compared with one another is called a _____-_____ study. This kind of study found evidence of intellectual _____ during adulthood.

19. A research study in which the same people are retested over a period of years is called a _____ study. This kind of study found evidence of intellectual _____ during adulthood.

Explain why studies of intellectual decline and aging yielded conflicting results.

20. The accumulation of stored information that comes with education and experience is called _____ intelligence, which tends to _____ with age.

21. The ability to reason abstractly is referred to as _____ intelligence, which tends to _____ with age.

Objective 22: Explain why the path of adult development need not be tightly linked to chronological age, and discuss the importance of love, marriage, children, and work in adulthood.

22. Contrary to popular opinion, job and marital dissatisfaction do not surge during the forties, thus suggesting that a midlife _____ need not occur.

23. The term used to refer to the culturally preferred timing for leaving home, getting a job, marrying, and so on is the _____ _____ . Today, the timing of such life events is becoming _____ (more/less) predictable. More important than age are _____ _____ and chance encounters.

24. According to Erikson, the two basic tasks of adulthood are achieving _____ and _____ . According to Freud, the healthy adult is one who can _____ and _____ .

25. Human societies have nearly always included a relatively _____ bond. Marriage bonds are usually lasting when couples marry after age _____ and are _____ _____ .

26. Marriages today are _____ (half/twice) as likely to end in divorce as they were 40 years ago. Couples who live together before marrying have a _____ (higher/ lower) divorce rate than those who do not.

27. Marriage is a predictor of _____ , _____ _____ , _____ , and _____ . Lesbian couples report _____ (greater/less) well-being than those who are alone.

28. As children begin to absorb time and energy, satisfaction with the marriage itself _____ (increases/decreases). This is particularly true among _____ women, who shoulder most of the burden.

29. For most couples, the children's leaving home produces a(n) _____ (increase/ decrease) in marital satisfaction.

30. During the first two years of college or university, most students _____ (can/cannot) predict their later careers. Most _____ (do/do not) shift from their original major.

Objective 23: Describe trends in people's life satisfaction across the life span, and describe the range of reactions to the death of a loved one.

31. From early adulthood to midlife, people typically experience a strengthening sense of _____ , _____ , and _____ .

32. According to studies, older people _____ (do/do not) report as much happiness and satisfaction with life as younger people do. In addition, their feelings _____ (do/do not) mellow.

33. As we age, the brain area called the _____ shows _____ (increased/decreased) activity in response to negative events.

34. More and more people flourish into later life, thanks to _____ influences.

35. Grief over a loved one's death is especially severe when it comes _____ _____ .

36. Reactions to a loved one's death _____ (do/do not) vary according to cultural norms. Those who express the strongest grief immediately _____ (do/do not) purge their grief more quickly.

37. Terminally ill and bereaved people _____ (do/do not) go through predictable stages.

38. According to Erikson, the final task of adulthood is to achieve a sense of _____ .

Reflections on Three Major Developmental Issues (pp. 471–473)

Objective 24: Summarize current views on continuity versus stages and stability versus change in lifelong development.

1. Our life courses are directed by the interaction of _____ and _____ .

2. Stage theories that have been considered include the theory of cognitive development proposed by _____ , the theory of moral development proposed by _____ , and the theory of psychosocial development proposed by _____ .

3. Although research casts doubt on the idea that life proceeds through age-linked _____ , there are spurts of _____ growth during childhood and puberty that correspond roughly to the stages proposed by _____ .

4. The first two years of life _____ (do/do not) provide a good basis for predicting a person's eventual traits.

5. Research on the consistency of personality shows that some traits, such as those related to _____ , are more stable than others, such as social attitudes.

PROGRESS TEST 1

Multiple-Choice Questions

Circle your answers to the following questions and check them with the answers beginning on page 256. If your answer is incorrect, read the explanation for why it is incorrect and then consult the appropriate pages of the text (in parentheses following the correct answer).

1. Dr. Joan Goodman is studying how memory changes as people get older. She is most likely a(n) _____ psychologist.
   a. social   c. developmental
   b. cognitive   d. experimental

2. In Piaget's stage of concrete operational intelligence, the child acquires an understanding of the principle of
   a. conservation.   c. attachment.
   b. deduction.   d. object permanence.

3. Piaget held that egocentrism is characteristic of the
   a. sensorimotor stage.
   b. preoperational stage.
   c. concrete operational stage.
   d. formal operational stage.

4. During which stage of cognitive development do children acquire object permanence?
   a. sensorimotor   c. concrete operational
   b. preoperational d. formal operational

5. Newborns vigorously root for a nipple when
   a. their foot is tickled.
   b. their cheek is touched.
   c. they hear a loud noise.
   d. they make eye contact with their caregiver.

6. The Harlows' studies of attachment in monkeys showed that
   a. provision of nourishment was the single most important factor motivating attachment.
   b. a cloth mother produced the greatest attachment response.
   c. whether a cloth or wire mother was present mattered less than the presence or absence of other infants.
   d. attachment in monkeys is based on imprinting.

7. When psychologists discuss maturation, they are referring to stages of growth that are NOT influenced by

   a. conservation.   c. nurture.
   b. nature.   d. continuity.

8. The developmental theorist who suggested that securely attached children develop an attitude of basic trust is

   a. Jean Piaget.   c. Lev Vygotsky.
   b. Harry Harlow.   d. Erik Erikson.

9. Research findings on infant motor development are consistent with the idea that

   a. cognitive development lags significantly behind motor skills development.
   b. maturation of physical skills is relatively unaffected by experience.
   c. in the absence of relevant earlier learning experiences, the emergence of motor skills will be slowed.
   d. in humans, the process of maturation may be significantly altered by cultural factors.

10. Temperament refers to a person's characteristic

    a. emotional reactivity and intensity.
    b. attitudes.
    c. behaviors.
    d. role-related traits.

11. Which of the following most accurately expresses the extent of parental influence on personality?

    a. It is more extensive than most people believe.
    b. It is weaker today than in the past.
    c. It is more limited than popular psychology supposes.
    d. It is almost completely unpredictable.

12. Gender refers to

    a. the biological and social definition of male and female.
    b. the biological definition of male and female.
    c. one's sense of being male or female.
    d. the extent to which one exhibits traditionally male or female traits.

13. The fertilized egg will develop into a boy if, at conception,

    a. the sperm contributes an X chromosome.
    b. the sperm contributes a Y chromosome.
    c. the egg contributes an X chromosome.
    d. the egg contributes a Y chromosome.

14. The hormone testosterone

    a. is found only in females.
    b. determines the sex of the developing person.

c. stimulates growth of the female sex organs.
d. stimulates growth of the male sex organs.

15. Research studies have found that when infant rats and premature human babies are regularly touched or massaged, they

    a. become attached to the person doing the massaging.
    b. develop faster neurologically.
    c. have more agreeable temperaments.
    d. do none of these things.

16. According to Erikson, the central psychological challenges pertaining to adolescence, young adulthood, and middle age, respectively, are

    a. identity formation; intimacy; generativity.
    b. intimacy; identity formation; generativity.
    c. generativity; intimacy; identity formation.
    d. intimacy; generativity; identity formation.

17. In preconventional morality, the person

    a. obeys out of a sense of social duty.
    b. conforms to gain social approval.
    c. obeys to avoid punishment or to gain concrete rewards.
    d. follows the dictates of his or her conscience.

18. Which of the following is correct?

    a. Early maturation places both boys and girls at a distinct social advantage.
    b. Early maturing girls are more popular and self-assured than girls who mature late.
    c. Early maturation places both boys and girls at a distinct social disadvantage.
    d. Early maturing boys are more popular and self-assured than boys who mature late.

19. A person's general ability to think abstractly is called _____ intelligence. This ability generally _____ with age.

    a. fluid; increases
    b. fluid; decreases
    c. crystallized; decreases
    d. crystallized; increases

20. Among the hallmarks of growing up are a boy's first ejaculation and a girl's first menstrual period, which also is called

    a. puberty.   c. menarche.
    b. menopause.   d. generativity.

21. An older person who can look back on life with satisfaction and reminisce with a sense of completion has attained Erikson's stage of
    a. generativity.   c. isolation.
    b. intimacy.   d. integrity.

22. According to Piaget, the ability to think logically about abstract propositions is indicative of the stage of
    a. preoperational thought.
    b. concrete operations.
    c. formal operations.
    d. fluid intelligence.

23. The cognitive ability that has been shown to decline during adulthood is the ability to
    a. recall new information.
    b. recognize new information.
    c. learn meaningful new material.
    d. use judgment in dealing with daily life problems.

24. Which of the following statements concerning the effects of aging is true?
    a. Aging almost inevitably leads to total memory failure if the individual lives long enough.
    b. Aging increases susceptibility to short-term ailments such as the flu.
    c. Significant increases in life satisfaction are associated with aging.
    d. The aging process can be significantly affected by the individual's activity patterns.

25. Longitudinal research
    a. compares people of different ages.
    b. studies the same people at different times.
    c. usually involves a larger sample than does cross-sectional research.
    d. usually involves a smaller sample than does cross-sectional research.

26. The average age at which puberty begins is _____ in boys; in girls, it is _____ .
    a. 14; 13   c. 11; 10
    b. 13; 11   d. 10; 9

27. After puberty, the self-concept usually becomes
    a. more positive in boys.
    b. more positive in girls.
    c. more positive in both boys and girls.
    d. more negative in both boys and girls.

28. Adolescence is marked by the onset of
    a. an identity crisis.
    b. parent-child conflict.
    c. the concrete operational stage.
    d. puberty.

29. Of the following, which is a possible cause of dementia?
    a. stroke
    b. brain tumor
    c. alcohol dependence
    d. All of these are possible causes.

30. The end of menstruation is called
    a. menarche.
    b. menopause.
    c. the midlife crisis.
    d. generativity.

True–False Items

Indicate whether each statement is true or false by placing *T* or *F* in the blank next to the item.

_____ 1. Most abused children later become abusive parents.

_____ 2. At birth, the brain and nervous system of a healthy child are fully developed.

_____ 3. The sequence in which children develop motor skills varies from one culture to another.

_____ 4. Current research shows that young children are more capable and development is more continuous than Piaget believed.

_____ 5. The process of grieving is much the same throughout the world.

_____ 6. The impact of day care on child development, even if it is high quality, remains controversial.

_____ 7. During adulthood, age only moderately correlates with people's traits.

_____ 8. Intelligence declines throughout adulthood.

_____ 9. By age 50, most adults have experienced a "midlife crisis."

_____ 10. Compared with those who are younger, older people are more susceptible to short-term ailments such as flu and cold viruses.

_____ 11. The symptoms of Alzheimer's disease are simply an intensified version of normal aging.

PROGRESS TEST 2

Progress Test 2 should be completed during a final unit review. Answer the following questions after you thoroughly understand the correct answers for the section reviews and Progress Test 1.

1. Stranger anxiety develops soon after
   a. the concept of conservation.
   b. egocentrism.
   c. a theory of mind.
   d. the concept of object permanence.

2. Before Piaget, people were more likely to believe that
   a. the child's mind is a miniature model of the adult's.
   b. children think about the world in radically different ways from adults.
   c. the child's mind develops through a series of stages.
   d. children interpret their experiences in terms of their current understandings.

3. Which is the correct sequence of stages in Piaget's theory of cognitive development?
   a. sensorimotor, preoperational, concrete operational, formal operational
   b. sensorimotor, preoperational, formal operational, concrete operational
   c. preoperational, sensorimotor, concrete operational, formal operational
   d. preoperational, sensorimotor, formal operational, concrete operational

4. A child can be born a drug addict because
   a. drugs used by the mother will pass into the child's bloodstream.
   b. addiction is an inherited personality trait.
   c. drugs used by the mother create genetic defects in her chromosomes.
   d. the fetus' blood has not yet developed a resistance to drugs.

5. A child whose mother drank heavily when she was pregnant is at heightened risk of
   a. being emotionally excitable during childhood.
   b. becoming insecurely attached.
   c. being born with the physical and cognitive abnormalities of fetal alcohol syndrome.
   d. addiction to a range of drugs throughout life.

6. Which is the correct order of stages of prenatal development?
   a. zygote, fetus, embryo
   b. zygote, embryo, fetus
   c. embryo, zygote, fetus
   d. embryo, fetus, zygote

7. The term *critical period* refers to
   a. prenatal development.
   b. the initial 2 hours after a child's birth.
   c. the preoperational stage.
   d. a restricted time for learning.

8. Which of the following was NOT found by the Harlows in socially deprived monkeys?
   a. They had difficulty mating.
   b. They showed extreme fear or aggression when first seeing other monkeys.
   c. They showed abnormal physical development.
   d. The females were abusive mothers.

9. Most people's earliest memories do not predate _____ of age.
   a. 6 months   c. 2 years
   b. 1 year   d. 3 years

10. Insecurely attached infants who are left by their mothers in an unfamiliar setting often will
    a. hold fast to their mothers on their return.
    b. explore the new surroundings confidently.
    c. be indifferent toward their mothers on their return.
    d. display little emotion at any time.

11. Of the following, parents are most likely to influence their children's
    a. temperament.
    b. personality.
    c. faith.
    d. emotional reactivity.

12. The selection effect in peer influence refers to the tendency of children and youth to
    a. naturally separate into same-sex playgroups.
    b. establish large, fluid circles of friends.
    c. seek out friends with similar interests and attitudes.
    d. choose friends their parents like.

13. Children who are raised by parents who discourage traditional gender typing
    a. are less likely to display gender-typed behaviors themselves.
    b. often become confused and develop an ambiguous gender identity.
    c. nevertheless organize themselves into "girl worlds" and "boy worlds."

d. display excessively masculine and feminine traits as adults.

14. Providing a child with a stimulating educational environment during early childhood is likely to
   a. ensure the formation of a strong attachment with parents.
   b. foster the development of a calm, easygoing temperament.
   c. prevent neural connections from degenerating.
   d. enable the child to develop motor skills at an earlier age.

15. Whose stage theory of moral development was based on how people reasoned about ethical dilemmas?
   a. Erik Erikson
   b. Jean Piaget
   c. Harry Harlow
   d. Lawrence Kohlberg

16. Cross-sectional research
   a. compares people of different ages with one another.
   b. studies the same group of people at different times.
   c. tends to paint too favorable a picture of the effects of aging on intelligence.
   d. is more appropriate than longitudinal research for studying intellectual change over the life span.

17. The social clock refers to
   a. an individual or society's distribution of work and leisure time.
   b. adulthood responsibilities.
   c. typical ages for starting a career, marrying, and so on.
   d. age-related changes in one's circle of friends.

18. To which of Kohlberg's levels would moral reasoning based on the existence of fundamental human rights pertain?
   a. preconventional morality
   b. conventional morality
   c. postconventional morality
   d. generative morality

19. In Erikson's theory, individuals generally focus on developing _____ during adolescence and then _____ during young adulthood.
   a. identity; intimacy
   b. intimacy; identity
   c. basic trust; identity
   d. identity; basic trust

20. Teratogens are
   a. physical abnormalities in the developing fetus.
   b. cognitive abnormalities in the developing fetus.
   c. chemicals and viruses that cross the placenta and may harm the developing fetus.
   d. fertilized eggs.

21. Notable achievements in fields such as _____ are often made by younger adults in their late twenties or early thirties, when _____ intelligence is at its peak.
   a. mathematics; fluid
   b. philosophy; fluid
   c. science; crystallized
   d. literature; crystallized

22. After their grown children have left home, most couples experience
   a. the distress of the empty nest syndrome.
   b. increased strain in their marital relationship.
   c. the need to have their children visit often.
   d. greater happiness and enjoyment in their relationship.

23. Underlying Alzheimer's disease is a deterioration in neurons that produce
   a. epinephrine.
   b. norepinephrine.
   c. serotonin.
   d. acetylcholine.

24. A person's accumulation of stored information, called _____ intelligence, generally _____ with age.
   a. fluid; decreases
   b. fluid; increases
   c. crystallized; decreases
   d. crystallized; increases

25. In terms of incidence, susceptibility to short-term illnesses _____ with age and susceptibility to long-term ailments _____ with age.
   a. decreases; increases
   b. increases; decreases
   c. increases; increases
   d. decreases; decreases

26. Research on the American family indicates that
    a. fewer than 23 percent of unmarried adults, but nearly 40 percent of married adults, report being "very happy" with life.
    b. the divorce rate is now one-half the marriage rate.
    c. children born to cohabiting parents are five times more likely to experience their parents' separation.
    d. all of these statements are true.

27. The popular idea that terminally ill and bereaved people go through predictable stages, such as denial, anger, and so forth
    a. is widely supported by research.
    b. more accurately describes grieving in some cultures than others.
    c. is true of women but not men.
    d. is not supported by research studies.

PSYCHOLOGY APPLIED

Answer these questions the day before an exam as a final check on your understanding of the unit's terms and concepts.

Multiple-Choice Questions

1. Compared to when he was younger, 4-year-old Antonio is better able to empathize with his friend's feelings. This growing ability to take another's perspective indicates that Antonio is acquiring a
   a. self-concept.   c. temperament.
   b. schema.   d. theory of mind.

2. Calvin, who is trying to impress his psychology professor with his knowledge of infant motor development, asks why some infants learn to roll over before they lift their heads from a prone position, while others develop these skills in the opposite order. What should Calvin's professor conclude from this question?
   a. Calvin clearly understands that the sequence of motor development is not the same for all infants.
   b. Calvin doesn't know what he's talking about. Although some infants reach these developmental milestones ahead of others, the order is the same for all infants.
   c. Calvin needs to be reminded that rolling over is an inherited reflex, not a learned skill.
   d. Calvin understands an important principle: Motor development is unpredictable.

3. Deborah is a mathematician and Willie is a philosopher. Considering their professions
   a. Deborah will make her most significant career accomplishments at an earlier age than Willie will.
   b. Deborah will make her most significant career accomplishments at a later age than Willie will.
   c. Deborah will make her most significant career accomplishments at about the same time as Willie.
   d. there is still not enough information for predicting such accomplishments.

4. Based on the text discussion of maturation and popularity, who among the following is probably the most popular sixth grader?
   a. Jessica, the most physically mature girl in the class
   b. Roger, the most intellectually mature boy in the class
   c. Rob, the tallest, most physically mature boy in the class
   d. Cindy, who is average in physical development and is on the school debating team

5. As a child observes, liquid is transferred from a tall, thin tube into a short, wide jar. The child is asked if there is now less liquid in order to determine if she has mastered
   a. the schema for liquids.
   b. the concept of object permanence.
   c. the concept of conservation.
   d. the ability to reason abstractly.

6. I am 14 months old and fearful of strangers. I am in Piaget's _____ stage of cognitive development.
   a. sensorimotor   c. concrete operational
   b. preoperational   d. formal operational

7. I am 3 years old, can use language, and have trouble taking another person's perspective. I am in Piaget's _____ stage of cognitive development.
   a. sensorimotor   c. concrete operational
   b. preoperational   d. formal operational

8. In Piaget's theory, conservation is to egocentrism as the _____ stage is to the _____ stage.
   a. sensorimotor; formal operational
   b. formal operational; sensorimotor
   c. preoperational; sensorimotor
   d. concrete operational; preoperational

9. Four-year-old Jamail has a younger sister. When asked if he has a sister, he is likely to answer _____ ; when asked if his sister has a brother, Jamail is likely to answer _____ .

   a. yes; yes
   b. no; no
   c. yes; no
   d. no; yes

10. In one movie, a young girl finds that a flock of geese follows her wherever she goes because she was the first "object" they saw after they were born. This is an example of

    a. conservation.
    b. imprinting.
    c. egocentrism.
    d. basic trust.

11. Joshua and Ann Bishop have a 13-month-old boy. According to Erikson, the Bishops' sensitive, loving care of their child contributes to

    a. the child's sense of basic trust.
    b. the child's secure attachment.
    c. the child's sense of control.
    d. the child's egocentrism.

12. I am a rat whose cortex is lighter and thinner than my littermates. What happened to me?

    a. You were born prematurely.
    b. You suffer from fetal alcohol syndrome.
    c. You were raised in an enriched environment.
    d. You were raised in a deprived environment.

13. Chad, who grew up in the United States, is more likely to encourage _____ in his future children than Asian-born Hidiyaki, who is more likely to encourage _____ in his future children.

    a. obedience; independence
    b. independence; emotional closeness
    c. emotional closeness; obedience
    d. loyalty; emotional closeness

14. Rod has always felt pressure to be the driver when traveling in a car with Sue because he learned that this was expected of men. Rod's feelings illustrate the influence of

    a. temperament.
    b. gender roles.
    c. the selection effect.
    d. maturation.

15. Compared with men, women

    a. use conversation to communicate solutions.
    b. emphasize freedom and self-reliance.
    c. talk more openly.
    d. do all of these things.

16. When his son cries because another child has taken his favorite toy, Brandon admonishes him by saying, "Big boys don't cry." Evidently, Brandon is an advocate of _____ in accounting for the development of gender-linked behaviors.

    a. Freudian theory
    b. gender identity theory
    c. gender-typing theory
    d. social learning theory

17. Four-year-old Sarah, who has very specific ideas about what it means to be female and frequently adjusts her behavior accordingly, is demonstrating the importance of _____ in the formation of gender identity.

    a. gender schemas
    b. norms
    c. genes
    d. behavior genetics

18. Three-year-old Jack is inhibited and shy. As an adult, Jack is likely to be

    a. cautious and unassertive.
    b. spontaneous and fearless.
    c. socially assertive.
    d. Who knows? This aspect of personality is not very stable over the life span.

19. Fourteen-year-old Cassandra feels freer and more open with her friends than with her family. Knowing this is the case, Cassandra's parents should

    a. be concerned, because deteriorating parent-teen relationships, such as this one, are often followed by a range of problem behaviors.
    b. encourage Cassandra to find new friends.
    c. seek family counseling.
    d. not worry, since adolescence is typically a time of growing peer influence and diminishing parental influence.

20. Thirteen-year-old Irene has no trouble defeating her 11-year-old brother at a detective game that requires following clues in order to deduce the perpetrator of a crime. How might Piaget explain Irene's superiority at the game?

    a. Being older, Irene has had more years of schooling.
    b. Girls develop intellectually at a faster rate than boys.
    c. Being an adolescent, Irene is beginning to develop abstract reasoning skills.
    d. Girls typically have more experience than boys at playing games.

21. Sixty-five-year-old Calvin cannot reason as well as he could when he was younger. More than likely, Calvin's _____ intelligence has declined.
    a. analytic
    b. crystallized
    c. fluid
    d. preoperational

22. Cross-sectional studies of intelligence are potentially misleading because
    a. they are typically based on a very small and unrepresentative sample of people.
    b. retesting the same people over a period of years allows test performance to be influenced by practice.
    c. they compare people who are not only different in age, but of different eras, education levels, and affluence.
    d. of all these reasons.

23. Which statement illustrates cognitive development during the course of adult life?
    a. Adults in their forties have better recognition memory than do adults in their seventies.
    b. Recall and recognition memory both remain strong throughout life.
    c. Recognition memory decreases sharply at midlife.
    d. Adults in their forties have better recall memory than adults in their seventies.

24. Given the text discussion of life satisfaction patterns, which of the following people is likely to report the greatest life satisfaction?
    a. Billy, a 7-year-old second-grader
    b. Kathy, a 17-year-old high-school senior
    c. Mildred, a 70-year-old retired teacher
    d. too little information to tell

25. Which of the following statements is consistent with the current thinking of developmental psychologists?
    a. Development occurs in a series of sharply defined stages.
    b. The first two years are the most crucial in determining the individual's personality.
    c. The stability of personality in most people tends to increase over the life span.
    d. Social and emotional style are among the characteristics that show the least stability over the life span.

26. Sam, a junior in high school, regularly attends church because his family and friends think he should. Which stage of moral reasoning is Sam in?
    a. preconventional
    b. conventional
    c. postconventional
    d. too little information to tell

27. Research on social relationships between parents and their adolescent children shows that
    a. parental influence on children increases during adolescence.
    b. high school girls who have the most affectionate relationships with their mothers tend to enjoy the most intimate friendships with girlfriends.
    c. high school boys who have the most affectionate relationships with their fathers tend to enjoy the most intimate friendships with friends.
    d. most teens are strongly influenced by parents in matters of personal taste.

28. After a series of unfulfilling relationships, 30-year-old Carlos tells a friend that he doesn't want to marry because he is afraid of losing his freedom and independence. Erikson would say that Carlos is having difficulty with the psychosocial task of
    a. trust versus mistrust.
    b. autonomy versus doubt.
    c. intimacy versus isolation.
    d. identity versus role confusion.

Essay Question

Sheryl is 12 years old and in the sixth grade. Describe the developmental changes she is likely to be experiencing according to Piaget, Kohlberg, and Erikson. (Use the space below to list the points you want to make, and organize them. Then write the essay on a separate sheet of paper.)

KEY TERMS

Using your own words, on a piece of paper write a brief definition or explanation of each of the following terms.

1. developmental psychology
2. zygote
3. embryo
4. fetus
5. teratogens
6. fetal alcohol syndrome (FAS)
7. habituation
8. maturation
9. cognition
10. schema
11. assimilation
12. accommodation
13. sensorimotor stage
14. object permanence
15. preoperational stage
16. conservation
17. egocentrism
18. theory of mind
19. concrete operational stage
20. formal operational stage
21. autism
22. stranger anxiety
23. attachment
24. critical period
25. imprinting
26. temperament
27. basic trust
28. self-concept
29. gender
30. aggression
31. X chromosome
32. Y chromosome
33. testosterone
34. role
35. gender role
36. gender identity
37. gender typing
38. social learning theory
39. adolescence
40. puberty
41. primary sex characteristics
42. secondary sex characteristics
43. menarche
44. identity
45. social identity
46. intimacy
47. emerging adulthood
48. menopause
49. cross-sectional study
50. longitudinal study
51. crystallized intelligence
52. fluid intelligence
53. social clock

ANSWERS

Unit Review

Introduction

1. developmental psychologists
2. nature; nurture
3. continuity; stages
4. stability

Prenatal Development and the Newborn

1. ovary; egg
2. sperm; enzymes; blocks
3. nuclei
4. zygotes; differentiate; uterine
5. embryo; fetus
6. placenta; nutrients; oxygen; teratogens
7. can affect; fetal alcohol syndrome
8. root; sucking; swallowing; tonguing; breathing
9. William James; incorrect

Newborns reflexively turn their heads in the direction of human voices. They gaze longer at a drawing of a facelike image than at a bull's-eye pattern. They focus best on objects about 8 to 12 inches away, which is about the distance between a nursing infant's eyes and the mother's. Within days, they recognize their mother's smell and voice.

10. habituation; decrease; novelty-preference; social

Infancy and Childhood

1. over; is not
2. frontal; rational planning; association areas; thinking; memory; language
3. pruning
4. maturation
5. motor; sequence; crawl; run
6. major
7. cerebellum; small
8. 3
9. infantile amnesia
10. thinking; knowing; remembering; communicating
11. Jean Piaget
12. schemas
13. assimilation; accommodation
14. sensorimotor; 2
15. object permanence; 8
16. underestimated; physics; numbers
17. 6 or 7; preoperational
18. conservation; have not
19. egocentrism
20. theory of mind; false beliefs
21. communication; social; theory of mind; autism; viewpoint; Asperger syndrome
22. male; empathizers; systemizers; assortative; systemizers
23. operations; symbolically; perspective; gradually
24. Lev Vygotsky; 7; inner speech; behavior; emotions
25. 6 or 7; concrete operational
26. formal operational; abstract; 12

Contemporary researchers see development as more continuous than did Piaget. By detecting the beginnings of each type of thinking at earlier ages, they have revealed conceptual abilities that Piaget missed. They also see formal logic as a smaller part of cognition than Piaget did. Despite these revisions to Piaget's theory, studies support the basic idea that cognitive development unfolds in the sequence Piaget described.

27. physical; social; scaffold
28. object permanence; stranger anxiety
29. 8 months
30. attachment
31. body contact; familiarity
32. safe haven; secure base
33. critical period; imprinting
34. do not; mere exposure
35. strange situation; secure; insecure

Placed in a strange situation, securely attached infants play comfortably, happily exploring their new environment. In contrast, insecurely attached infants are less likely to explore their surroundings and may even cling to their mothers. When separated from their mothers, insecurely attached infants are much more distressed than securely attached infants. When reunited with their mothers, insecurely attached infants may be indifferent.

Research studies conducted by Mary Ainsworth have revealed that sensitive, responsive mothers tend to have securely attached infants, whereas insensitive, unresponsive mothers often have insecurely attached infants. Other studies have found that temperamentally difficult infants whose mothers receive training in responsive parenting are more likely to become securely attached than are control infants. This points to the importance of considering the infant's temperament in studying attachment.

36. temperament; does
37. difficult; irritable; intense; unpredictable; easy; cheerful; relaxed; predictable; slow-to-warm-up; Heredity
38. comparable to
39. 13; gradually declines; throughout the world
40. basic trust
41. do; motivation
42. aggression
43. do not
44. resilient; stress hormones; serotonin
45. recover
46. does not; safe; healthy; stimulating; the mother's sensitivity, the child's temperament, and the family's economic and educational level
47. self-concept; 12
48. 8; 10; traits; compare

Children who have formed a positive self-concept tend to be more confident, independent, optimistic, assertive, and sociable.

49. authoritarian
50. permissive
51. authoritative
52. authoritative

There are at least three possible explanations for the correlation between authoritative parenting and social competence in children. (1) Parenting may foster children's competence. (2) Children's competence may promote authoritative parenting. (3) A third factor, such as heredity, may foster both authoritative parenting and child competence.

53. independence; emotional closeness
54. family self

55. gender
56. fat; muscle; shorter; depression; anxiety; eating disorders
57. suicide; alcohol dependence; autism; color-blindness; attention-deficit hyperactivity disorder (as children); antisocial personality disorder (as adults)
58. physical; verbal; intended
59. hunting; fighting; warring
60. physical; verbal
61. dominant; forceful; independent; directive (or autocratic); democratic
62. deferential; nurturant; affiliative
63. throughout the world
64. connections
65. play; smaller; competitive
66. interdependent; explore relationships; communicate solutions
67. support; stress
68. adolescence; adulthood; decreased
69. sex; X; Y; testosterone; seventh
70. hormones; frontal; verbal; parietal; space
71. gender roles
72. are not; cultures; time; nomadic; agricultural
73. gender identity; gender typing
74. social learning; do
75. gender schemas; cognition

Parents and Peers

1. prenatal
2. thicker

Research has shown that human and animal infants given extra sensory stimulation develop faster neurologically. Throughout life, sensory stimulation activates and strengthens particular neural connections, while other connections weaken with disuse. In this way, our experiences shape the very structure of the neural pathways that process those experiences.

3. neural; degenerate; pruning; puberty
4. Freudian psychiatry; psychology
5. political attitudes; personal manners; religious beliefs

6. personality; 10
7. peers; selection

Adolescence

1. childhood; adulthood
2. G. Stanley Hall
3. puberty; 11; 13; primary sex; secondary sex
4. menarche; spermarche
5. sequence; timing
6. early; alcohol use, delinquency, and premature sexual activity; early; emotional maturity; heredity; environment
7. pruning; frontal lobe; limbic system
8. ideally; compare
9. self-focused
10. formal operations; abstract; inconsistencies
11. Lawrence Kohlberg; preconventional; conventional; postconventional
12. punishment; rewards
13. adolescence; approval; order
14. postconventional

Critics of Kohlberg's theory argue that the perception of postconventional moral reasoning as the highest level of moral development reflects a European and North American educated middle-class bias. Others have argued that people's thinking about real-world issues also engages their emotions, and moral feeling doesn't fit neatly into Kohlberg's stages.

15. social intuitionist; moral paradoxes
16. social; character education programs; empathy
17. gratification; service; academically
18. stronger

Erikson's stages of psychosocial development

Group Age	Psychosocial Stage
Infancy	Trust vs. mistrust
Toddlerhood	Autonomy vs. shame and doubt
Preschooler	Initiative vs. guilt
Elementary school	Competence vs. inferiority
Adolescence	Identity vs. role confusion
Young adulthood	Intimacy vs. isolation
Middle adulthood	Generativity vs. stagnation
Late adulthood	Integrity vs. despair

19. selves; confusion; identity
20. adopting; opposing

21. falls; rises; personalized
22. intimacy
23. peers; parents
24. do; religious faith
25. loneliness; self-esteem; depression
26. body fat; parent-child; earlier
27. emerging adulthood

Adulthood

1. is not
2. muscular strength, reaction time, sensory keenness, cardiac output; women
3. age; health; exercise
4. menopause; 50; estrogen; expectations; attitude
5. sperm; testosterone
6. 80; 4; 5 to 6; telomeres
7. gene-reproducing; natural selection
8. death-deferral
9. shrinks; less; reduced
10. more; less
11. slows; brain cells
12. brain cell; neural; oxygen
13. dementia
14. Alzheimer's; acetylcholine
15. recall; recognize; meaningfulness
16. prospective
17. more
18. cross-sectional; decline
19. longitudinal; stability

Because cross-sectional studies compare people not only of different ages but also of different eras, education levels, family size, and affluence, it is not surprising that such studies reveal cognitive decline with age. In contrast, longitudinal studies test one group over a span of years. However, because those who survive to the end of longitudinal studies may be the brightest and healthiest, these studies may underestimate the average decline in intelligence. Research is also complicated by the fact that certain tests measure only one type of intelligence. Tests that measure fluid intelligence reveal decline with age; tests that measure crystallized intelligence reveal just the opposite.

20. crystallized; increase
21. fluid; decrease
22. transition (crisis)
23. social clock; less; life events
24. intimacy; generativity; love; work
25. monogamous; 20; well educated

26. twice; higher
27. happiness; sexual satisfaction; health; income; greater
28. decreases; employed
29. increase
30. cannot; do
31. identity; confidence; self-esteem
32. do; do
33. amygdala; decreased
34. biopsychosocial
35. suddenly and before its expected time on the social clock
36. do; do not
37. do not
38. integrity

Reflections on Three Major Developmental Issues

1. genes; environment
2. Piaget; Kohlberg; Erikson
3. stages; brain; Piaget
4. do not
5. temperament

Progress Test 1

Multiple-Choice Questions

1. **c.** is the answer. Developmental psychologists study physical, cognitive (memory, in this example), and social change throughout the life span. (p. 411)
   a. Social psychologists study how people influence and are influenced by others.
   b. Cognitive psychologists *do* study memory; because Dr. Goodman is interested in life-span *changes* in memory, she is more likely a developmental psychologist.
   d. Experimental psychologists study physiology, sensation, perception, learning, and other aspects of behavior. Only developmental psychologists focus on developmental changes in behavior and mental processes.

2. **a.** is the answer. (p. 423)
   b. Deduction, or deductive reasoning, is a formal operational ability.
   c. Piaget's theory is not concerned with attachment.
   d. Attaining object permanence is the hallmark of sensorimotor thought.

3. **b.** is the answer. The preoperational child sees the world from his or her own vantage point. (p. 421)

a. As immature as egocentrism is, it represents a significant cognitive advance over the sensorimotor child, who knows the world only through senses and actions. Even simple self-awareness takes a while to develop.
c. & d. As children attain the operational stages, they become more able to see the world through the eyes of others.

4. **a.** is the answer. Before object permanence is attained, "out of sight" is truly "out of mind." (p. 419)
b., c., & d. Developments during the preoperational, concrete operational, and formal operational stages include the use of language, conservation, and abstract reasoning, respectively.

5. **b.** is the answer. The infant turns its head and begins sucking when its cheek is stroked. (p. 413)
a., c., & d. These stimuli produce other reflexes in the newborn.

6. **b.** is the answer. (p. 426)
a. When given the choice between a wire mother with a bottle and a cloth mother without, the monkeys preferred the cloth mother.
c. The presence of other infants made no difference.
d. Imprinting plays no role in the attachment of higher primates.

7. **c.** is the answer. Through maturation—an orderly sequence of biological growth processes that are relatively unaffected by experience—all humans develop. (p. 416)
a. Conservation is the cognitive awareness that objects do not change with changes in shape.
b. The forces of nature *are* those that direct maturation.
d. The continuity/stages debate has to do with whether development is a gradual and continuous process or a discontinuous, stagelike process. Those who emphasize maturation see development as occurring in stages, not continuously.

8. **d.** is the answer. Erikson proposed that development occurs in a series of stages, in the first of which the child develops an attitude of either basic trust or mistrust. (p. 429)
a. Piaget's theory is concerned with cognitive development.
b. Harlow conducted research on attachment and deprivation.
c. Vygotsky focused on the influence of social factors on cognitive development.

9. **b.** is the answer. (p. 416)

10. **a.** is the answer. (p. 428)

11. **c.** is the answer. (pp. 443–444)

12. **a.** is the answer. (p. 435)
b. This definition is incomplete.
c. This defines gender identity.
d. This defines gender typing.

13. **b.** is the answer. (p. 438)
a. In this case, a female would develop.
c. & d. The egg can contribute only an X chromosome. Thus, the sex of the child is determined by which chromosome the sperm contributes.

14. **d.** is the answer. (p. 438)
a. Although testosterone is the principal male hormone, it is present in both females and males.
b. This is determined by the sex chromosomes.
c. In the absence of testosterone, female sex organs will develop.

15. **d.** is the answer. (p. 442)

16. **a.** is the answer. (p. 451)

17. **c.** is the answer. At the preconventional level, moral reasoning centers on self-interest, whether this means obtaining rewards or avoiding punishment. (p. 449)
a. & b. Moral reasoning based on a sense of social duty or a desire to gain social approval is associated with the conventional level of moral development.
d. Reasoning based on ethical principles is characteristic of the postconventional level of moral development.

18. **d.** is the answer. Boys who show early physical maturation are generally stronger and more athletic than boys who mature late; these qualities may lead to greater popularity and self-assurance. (p. 447)
a. & c. Early maturation tends to be socially advantageous for boys but not for girls.
b. Early maturing girls often suffer embarrassment and are objects of teasing.

19. **b.** is the answer. (p. 464)
a. Fluid intelligence tends to decrease with age.
c. & d. Crystallized intelligence refers to the accumulation of facts and general knowledge that takes place during a person's life. Crystallized intelligence generally *increases* with age.

20. **c.** is the answer. (p. 447)
a. Puberty refers to the early adolescent period during which accelerated growth and sexual maturation occur, not to the first menstrual period.
b. Menopause is the cessation of menstruation, which typically occurs in the early fifties.
d. In Erikson's theory, generativity, or the sense of contributing and being productive, is the task of middle adulthood.

21. d. is the answer. (p. 471)
a. Generativity is associated with middle adulthood.
b. & c. Intimacy and isolation are associated with young adulthood.

22. c. is the answer. Once formal operational thought has been attained, thinking is no longer limited to concrete propositions. (p. 423)
a. & b. Preoperational thought and concrete operational thought emerge before, and do not include, the ability to think logically about abstract propositions.
d. Fluid intelligence refers to abstract reasoning abilities; however, it is unrelated to Piaget's theory and stages.

23. a. is the answer. (p. 464)
b., c., & d. These cognitive abilities remain essentially unchanged as the person ages.

24. d. is the answer. "Use it or lose it" seems to be the rule: Often, changes in activity patterns contribute significantly to problems regarded as being part of usual aging. (pp. 460–461)
a. Most older people suffer some memory loss but remember some events very well.
b. Although older people are more subject to long-term ailments than younger adults, they actually suffer fewer short-term ailments.
c. People of all ages report equal happiness or satisfaction with life.

25. b. is the answer. (p. 463)

26. b. is the answer. (pp. 445–446)

27. c. is the answer. Because the late teen years provide many new opportunities for trying out possible roles, adolescents' identities typically incorporate an increasingly positive self-concept. (p. 452)

28. d. is the answer. The physical changes of puberty mark the onset of adolescence. (p. 445)
a. & b. An identity crisis or parent-child conflict may or may not occur during adolescence; neither of these formally marks its onset.
c. Formal operational thought, rather than concrete reasoning, typically develops in adolescence.

29. d. is the answer. (p. 460)

30. b. is the answer. (p. 456)
a. Menarche refers to the onset of menstruation.
c. When it does occur, the midlife crisis is a psychological, rather than biological, phenomenon.
d. Generativity is Erikson's term for productivity during middle adulthood.

True–False Items

1. F (p. 430)	**5.** F (p. 471)	**9.** F (p. 465)
2. F (p. 415)	**6.** F (p. 431)	**10.** F (p. 459)
3. F (p. 416)	**7.** T (p. 455)	**11.** F (p. 460)
4. T (p. 424)	**8.** F (p. 463)	

Progress Test 2

1. d. is the answer. With object permanence, a child develops schemas for familiar objects, including faces, and may become upset by a stranger who does not fit any of these schemas. (p. 426)
a. The concept of conservation develops during the concrete operational stage, whereas stranger anxiety develops during the sensorimotor stage.
b. & c. Egocentrism and a theory of mind both develop during the preoperational stage. This follows the sensorimotor stage, during which stranger anxiety develops.

2. a. is the answer. (p. 418)
b., c., & d. Each of these is an understanding developed by Piaget.

3. a. is the answer. (p. 420)

4. a. is the answer. Any drug taken by the mother passes through the placenta and enters the child's bloodstream. (p. 413)
b. Addiction cannot be inherited; it requires exposure to an addictive drug.
c. Drugs may disrupt the mechanisms of heredity, but there is no evidence that such changes promote addiction.
d. This answer is incorrect because at no age does the blood "resist" drugs.

5. c. is the answer. (p. 413)
a., b., & d. A child's emotional temperament, attachment, and addiction have not been linked to the mother's drinking while pregnant.

6. b. is the answer. (p. 412)

7. d. is the answer. A critical period is a restricted time during which an organism must be exposed to certain influences or experiences for a particular kind of learning to occur. (p. 427)
a. Critical periods refer to developmental periods after birth.
b. Critical periods vary from behavior to behavior, but they are not confined to the hours following birth.
c. Critical periods are not specifically associated with the preoperational period.

8. c. is the answer. Deprived monkeys were impaired in their social behaviors but not in their physical development. (p. 430)

a., b., & d. Each of these was found in socially deprived monkeys.

9. **d.** is the answer. This is because of a lack of neural connections before that age. (p. 417)

10. **c.** is the answer. (p. 428)
a. Insecurely attached infants often cling to their mothers when placed in a new situation; yet, when the mother returns after an absence, the infant's reaction tends to be one of indifference.
b. These behaviors are characteristic of securely attached infants.
d. Insecurely attached infants in unfamiliar surroundings will often exhibit a range of emotional behaviors.

11. **c.** is the answer. (p. 444)
a. & d. Temperament, which refers to a person's emotional reactivity, is determined primarily by genes.
b. Genes limit parents' influence on their children's personalities.

12. **c.** is the answer. (p. 444)

13. **c.** is the answer. (p. 440)
b. & d. There is no evidence that being raised in a "gender neutral" home confuses children or fosters a backlash of excessive gender typing.

14. **c.** is the answer. (pp. 441–442)
a. Although early experiences are a factor in the development of attachment, educational stimulation is probably less important than warmth and nurturance.
b. Because temperament appears to be a strongly genetic trait, it is unlikely that early educational experiences would affect its nature.

15. **d.** is the answer. (p. 449)
a. Erik Erikson is known for his theory of psychosocial development.
b. Jean Piaget is known for his theory of cognitive development.
c. Harry Harlow is known for his studies of attachment in infant monkeys.

16. **a.** is the answer. (p. 463)
b. This answer describes the longitudinal research method.
c. & d. Cross-sectional studies have tended to exaggerate the negative effects of aging on intellectual functioning; for this reason they may not be the most appropriate method for studying life-span development.

17. **c.** is the answer. Different societies and eras have somewhat different ideas about the age at which major life events should ideally occur. (p. 465)

18. **c.** is the answer. (p. 449)

a. Preconventional morality is based on avoiding punishment and obtaining rewards.
b. Conventional morality is based on gaining the approval of others and/or on following the law and social convention.
d. There is no such thing as generative morality.

19. **a.** is the answer. (pp. 451, 452)
b. According to Erikson, identity develops before intimacy.
c. & d. The formation of basic trust is the task of infancy.

20. **c.** is the answer. (p. 413)
a. & b. Physical and cognitive abnormalities usually result from teratogens, but that's not a definition of a teratogen.
d. A fertilized egg is a zygote.

21. **a.** is the answer. A mathematician's skills are likely to reflect abstract reasoning, or fluid intelligence, which declines with age. (p. 464)
b. & d. Philosophy and literature are fields in which individuals often do their most notable work later in life, after more experiential knowledge (crystallized intelligence) has accumulated.
c. Scientific achievements generally reflect fluid, rather than crystallized, intelligence.

22. **d.** is the answer. (p. 468)
a., b., & c. Most couples do not feel a loss of purpose or marital strain following the departure of grown children.

23. **d.** is the answer. Significantly, drugs that block the activity of the neurotransmitter acetylcholine produce Alzheimer's-like symptoms. (p. 460)
a. & b. Epinephrine and norepinephrine are hormones produced by the adrenal glands of the endocrine system.
c. Serotonin is a neurotransmitter and hence is produced by neurons, but it has not been implicated in Alzheimer's disease.

24. **d.** is the answer. (p. 464)
a. & b. Fluid intelligence, which decreases with age, refers to the ability to reason abstractly.
c. Crystallized intelligence increases with age.

25. **a.** is the answer. (p. 459)

26. **d.** is the answer. (pp. 466–467)

27. **d.** is the answer. (p. 471)

Psychology Applied

Multiple-Choice Questions

1. **d.** is the answer. (p. 422)

2. **b.** is the answer. (p. 416)

a. & d. Although the rate of motor development varies from child to child, the basic sequence is universal and, therefore, predictable.

c. Rolling over and head lifting are both learned.

3. **a.** is the answer. Mathematical and philosophical reasoning involve fluid and crystallized intelligence, respectively. Because fluid intelligence generally declines with age while crystallized intelligence increases, it is likely that significant mathematical accomplishments will occur at an earlier age than philosophical accomplishments. (p. 464)

4. **c.** is the answer. Early maturing boys tend to be more popular. (p. 447)

    a. Early maturing girls may temporarily suffer embarrassment and be the objects of teasing.

    b. & d. The social benefits of early or late maturation are based on physical development, not on cognitive skills.

5. **c.** is the answer. This test is designed to determine if the child understands that the quantity of liquid is conserved, despite the shift to a container that is different in shape. (p. 421)

    a. These are general processes related to concept building.

    b. Object permanence is the concept that an object continues to exist even when not perceived; in this case, the water is perceived throughout the experiment.

    d. This experiment does not require abstract reasoning, only the ability to reason logically about the concrete.

6. **a.** is the answer. This child's age and stranger anxiety clearly place him within Piaget's sensorimotor stage. (pp. 419, 426)

7. **b.** is the answer. This child's age, ability to use language, and egocentrism clearly place her within Piaget's preoperational stage. (p. 421)

8. **d.** is the answer. Conservation is a hallmark of the concrete operational stage; egocentrism is a hallmark of the preoperational stage. (pp. 421, 423)

9. **c.** is the answer. Being 4 years old, Jamail would be in Piaget's preoperational stage. Preoperational thinking is egocentric, which means Jamail would find it difficult to "put himself in his sister's shoes" and perceive that she has a brother. (p. 421)

10. **b.** is the answer. (p. 427)

    a. Conservation is the ability to realize that the amount of an object does not change even if its shape changes.

    c. Egocentrism is having difficulty perceiving things from another's perspective.

d. According to Erikson, basic trust is feeling that the world is safe as a result of sensitive, loving caregivers.

11. **a.** is the answer. Although loving parents will also produce securely attached children, Erikson's theory deals with trust or mistrust. (p. 429)

    c. Control is not a factor in this stage of Erikson's theory.

    d. Egocentrism is an aspect of Piaget's cognitive theory.

12. **d.** is the answer. (pp. 441–442)

    a. & b. Premature birth and fetal alcohol syndrome usually do not have this effect on the developing brain.

    c. If the question had stated, "I have a heavier and thicker cortex," this answer would be correct.

13. **b.** is the answer. Although parental values differ from one time and place to another, studies reveal that Western parents today want their children to think for themselves, while Asian and African parents place greater value on emotional closeness. (p. 434)

    d. Both of these values are more typical of Asian than Western cultures.

14. **b.** is the answer. (p. 439)

15. **c.** is the answer. (p. 437)

16. **d.** is the answer. Following social learning theory, Brandon is using verbal punishment to discourage what he believes to be an inappropriate gender-linked behavior in his son. (p. 440)

    a. Freudian theory does not deal with gender-typed behaviors.

    b. & c. No such theories were discussed.

17. **a.** is the answer. (p. 440)

    b. Norms are cultural standards of behavior unrelated to the person's gender.

    c. & d. Genes and behavior genetics apply to inherited characteristics. Here, we are talking about learned behavior.

18. **a.** is the answer. (p. 473)

    b., c., & d. Temperament is one of the most stable personality traits.

19. **d.** is the answer. (p. 452)

    a. This description of Cassandra's feelings does not suggest that her relationship with her parents is deteriorating. Cassandra's social development, like that of most adolescents, is coming under increasing peer influence and diminishing parental influence.

    b. & c. Because Cassandra's feelings are normal, there is no reason for her to change her circle of friends or for her parents to seek counseling.

20. **c.** is the answer. (p. 448)
a., b., & d. Piaget did not link cognitive ability to amount of schooling, gender, or differences in how boys and girls are socialized.

21. **c.** is the answer. Reasoning is based on fluid intelligence. (p. 464)
a. There is no "analytic" intelligence.
b. Crystallized intelligence increases up to old age.
d. Preoperational refers to the thinking of young children before they are capable of reasoning.

22. **c.** is the answer. Because several variables (education, affluence, etc.) generally distinguish the various groups in a cross-sectional study, it is impossible to rule out that one or more of these, rather than aging, is the cause of the measured intellectual decrease. (p. 463)
a. Small sample size and unrepresentativeness generally are not limitations of cross-sectional research.
b. This refers to longitudinal research.

23. **d.** is the answer. (p. 461)
a. & c. In tests of recognition memory, the performance of older persons shows little decline.
b. The ability to recall material, especially meaningless material, declines with age.

24. **d.** is the answer. Research has not uncovered a tendency for people of any particular age group to report greater feelings of satisfaction or well-being. (pp. 468–469)

25. **c.** is the answer. Although some researchers emphasize stability and others emphasize potential for change, they all agree that stability increases over the life span. (p. 473)
a. One criticism of stage theories is that development does not occur in sharply defined stages.
b. Research has shown that individuals' adult personalities cannot be predicted from their first two years.
d. Social and emotional style are two of the most stable traits.

26. **b.** is the answer. Conventional morality is based in part on a desire to gain others' approval. (p. 449)
a. Preconventional reasoning is based on external incentives such as gaining a reward or avoiding punishment.
c. Postconventional morality reflects an affirmation of agreed-upon rights or universal ethical principles.
d. Fear of others' disapproval is one of the bases of conventional moral reasoning.

27. **b.** is the answer. (p. 453)

a. In fact, just the opposite is true: Parental influence on children decreases during adolescence.
d. Teens reflect their parents' social, political, and religious views, but rely on peers for matters of personal taste.

28. **c.** is the answer. Carlos' age and struggle to form a close relationship place him squarely in this stage. (p. 452)
a. Trust versus mistrust is the psychosocial task of infancy.
b. Autonomy versus doubt is the psychosocial task of toddlerhood.
d. Identity versus role confusion is the psychosocial task of adolescence.

Essay Question

Sheryl's age would place her at the threshold of Piaget's stage of formal operations. Although her thinking is probably still somewhat self-focused, Sheryl is becoming capable of abstract, logical thought. This will increasingly allow her to reason hypothetically and deductively. Because her logical thinking also enables her to detect inconsistencies in others' reasoning and between their ideals and actions, Sheryl and her parents may be having some heated debates about now.

According to Kohlberg, Sheryl is probably at the threshold of postconventional morality. When she was younger, Sheryl probably abided by rules in order to gain social approval, or simply because "rules are rules" (conventional morality). Now that she is older, Sheryl's moral reasoning will increasingly be based on her own personal code of ethics and an affirmation of people's agreed-upon rights.

According to Erikson, psychosocial development occurs in eight stages, each of which focuses on a particular task. As an adolescent, Sheryl's psychosocial task is to develop a sense of self by testing roles, then integrating them to form a single identity. Erikson called this stage *identity versus role confusion*.

Key Terms

1. **Developmental psychology** is the branch of psychology concerned with physical, cognitive, and social change throughout the life span. (p. 411)

2. The **zygote** (a term derived from the Greek word for "joint") is the fertilized egg, that is, the cluster of cells formed during conception by the union of sperm and egg. (p. 412)

3. The **embryo** is the developing prenatal organism from about 2 weeks through 2 months after conception; formed from the inner cells of the zygote. (p. 412)

4. The **fetus** is the developing prenatal human from 9 weeks after conception to birth. (p. 412)

5. **Teratogens** (literally, poisons) are any chemicals and viruses that cross the mother's placenta and can harm the developing embryo or fetus. (p. 413)

6. **Fetal alcohol syndrome (FAS)** refers to the physical and cognitive abnormalities that heavy drinking by a pregnant woman may cause in the developing child. (p. 413)

7. A simple form of learning used to study infant cognition, **habituation** is decreasing responsiveness to a stimulus that is repeatedly presented. (p. 414)

8. **Maturation** refers to the biological growth processes that enable orderly changes in behavior, relatively uninfluenced by experience or other environmental factors. (p. 416)

   Example: The ability to walk depends on a certain level of neural and muscular **maturation**. For this reason, until the toddler's body is physically ready to walk, practice "walking" has little effect.

9. **Cognition** refers to all the mental processes associated with thinking, knowing, remembering, and communicating. (p. 417)

10. In Piaget's theory of cognitive development, **schemas** are mental concepts or frameworks that organize and interpret information. (p. 418)

11. In Piaget's theory, **assimilation** refers to interpreting a new experience in terms of an existing schema. (p. 418)

12. In Piaget's theory, **accommodation** refers to changing an existing schema to incorporate new information that cannot be assimilated. (p. 418)

13. In Piaget's theory of cognitive stages, the **sensorimotor stage** lasts from birth to nearly age 2. During this stage, infants gain knowledge of the world through their senses and their motor activities. (p. 419)

14. **Object permanence,** which develops during the sensorimotor stage, is the awareness that things do not cease to exist when not perceived. (p. 419)

15. In Piaget's theory, the **preoperational stage** lasts from about 2 to 6 or 7 years of age. During this stage, language development is rapid, but the child is unable to understand the mental operations of concrete logic. (p. 421)

16. **Conservation** is the principle that properties such as number, volume, and mass remain constant despite changes in the forms of objects; it is acquired during the concrete operational stage. (p. 421)

17. In Piaget's theory, **egocentrism** refers to the difficulty that preoperational children have in considering another's viewpoint. *Ego* means "self," and *centrism* indicates "in the center"; the preoperational child is "self-centered." (p. 421)

18. Our ideas about our own and others' thoughts, feelings, and perceptions and the behaviors these might predict constitute our **theory of mind.** (p. 422)

19. During the **concrete operational stage,** lasting from about ages 6 or 7 to 11, children can think logically about concrete events and objects. (p. 423)

20. In Piaget's theory, the **formal operational stage** normally begins about age 12. During this stage people begin to think logically about abstract concepts. (p. 423)

   Memory aid: To help differentiate Piaget's stages remember that "operations" are mental transformations. *Pre*operational children, who lack the ability to perform transformations, are "before" this developmental milestone. Concrete operational children can operate on real, or concrete, objects. Formal operational children can perform logical transformations on abstract concepts.

21. **Autism** is a disorder that appears in childhood and is marked by deficient communication, social interaction, and understanding of others' states of mind. (p. 424)

22. **Stranger anxiety** is the fear of strangers that infants begin to display by about 8 months of age. (p. 426)

23. **Attachment** is an emotional tie with another person, shown in young children by their seeking closeness to a caregiver and showing distress on separation. (p. 426)

24. A **critical period** is a limited time shortly after birth during which an organism must be exposed to certain stimuli or experiences if it is to develop properly. (p. 427)

25. **Imprinting** is the process by which certain animals form attachments during a limited critical period early in life. (p. 427)

26. **Temperament** is a person's characteristic emotional reactivity and intensity. (p. 428)

27. According to Erikson, **basic trust** is a sense that the world is predictable and trustworthy, a concept that infants form if their needs are met by responsive caregiving. (p. 429)

28. **Self-concept** is our understanding and evaluation of who we are. (p. 432)

29. **Gender** refers to the biological and social characteristics by which people define *male* and *female*. (p. 435)

30. **Aggression** is physical or verbal behavior intended to hurt someone. (p. 436)

31. The **X chromosome** is the sex chromosome found in both men and women. Females inherit an X chromosome from each parent. (p. 438)

32. The **Y chromosome** is the sex chromosome found only in men. Males inherit an X chromosome from their mothers and a Y chromosome from their fathers. (p. 438)

33. **Testosterone** is the principal male sex hormone. During prenatal development, testosterone stimulates the development of the external male sex organs. (p. 438)

34. A **role** is a cluster of prescribed behaviors expected of those who occupy a particular social position. (p. 439)

35. A **gender role** is a set of expected behaviors for males and females. (p. 439)

36. **Gender identity** is one's sense of being male or female. (p. 440)

37. **Gender typing** is the acquisition of a traditional feminine or masculine role. (p. 440)

38. According to **social learning theory**, people learn social behavior (such as gender roles) by observing and imitating and by being rewarded or punished. (p. 440)

39. **Adolescence** refers to the life stage from puberty to independent adulthood, denoted physically by a growth spurt and maturation of primary and secondary sex characteristics, cognitively by the onset of formal operational thought, and socially by the formation of identity. (p. 445)

40. **Puberty** is the early adolescent period of sexual maturation, during which a person becomes capable of reproducing. (p. 445)

41. The **primary sex characteristics** are the body structures (ovaries, testes, and external genitalia) that enable reproduction. (p. 446)

42. The **secondary sex characteristics** are the nonreproductive sexual characteristics, for example, female breasts, male voice quality, and body hair. (p. 446)

43. **Menarche** is the first menstrual period. (p. 447)

44. In Erikson's theory, establishing an **identity**, or one's sense of self, is the primary task of adolescence. (p. 451)

45. **Social identity** refers to person's self-concept as defined by the groups to which he or she belongs. (p. 451)

46. In Erikson's theory, **intimacy**, or the ability to establish close, loving relationships, is the primary task of late adolescence and early adulthood. (p. 452)

47. **Emerging adulthood** is the period from age 18 to the mid-twenties, when many young people are not yet fully independent. (p. 454)

48. **Menopause** is the cessation of menstruation and typically occurs in the early fifties. It also refers to the biological changes experienced during a woman's years of declining ability to reproduce. (p. 456)

49. In a **cross-sectional study,** people of different ages are compared with one another. (p. 463)

50. In a **longitudinal study,** the same people are tested and retested over a period of years. (p. 463)

51. **Crystallized intelligence** refers to those aspects of intellectual ability, such as vocabulary and general knowledge, that reflect accumulated learning. Crystallized intelligence tends to increase with age. (p. 464)

52. **Fluid intelligence** refers to a person's ability to reason speedily and abstractly. Fluid intelligence tends to decline with age. (p. 464)

53. The **social clock** refers to the culturally preferred timing of social events, such as leaving home, marrying, having children, and retiring. (p. 465)

Personality

UNIT OVERVIEW

Personality refers to each individual's characteristic pattern of thinking, feeling, and acting. Unit 10 examines four perspectives on personality. Psychoanalytic theory emphasizes the unconscious and irrational aspects of personality. Humanistic theory draws attention to the concept of self and to the human potential for healthy growth. Trait theory led to advances in techniques for evaluating and describing personality. The social-cognitive perspective emphasizes the effects of our interactions with the environment. The text first describes and then evaluates the contributions, shortcomings, and historical significance of the psychoanalytic and humanistic perspectives. Next, the text turns to contemporary research on personality, focusing on how the trait and social-cognitive perspectives explore and assess traits and the focus of many of today's researchers on the concept of self.

NOTE: Answer guidelines for all Unit 10 questions begin on page 281.

UNIT REVIEW

First, skim each section, noting headings and boldface items. After you have read the section, review each objective by answering the fill-in and essay-type questions that follow it. As you proceed, evaluate your performance by consulting the answers beginning on page 281. Do not continue with the next section until you understand each answer. If you need to, review or reread the section in the textbook before continuing.

Introducing Personality and The Psychoanalytic Perspective (pp. 479–490)

Objective 1: Define *personality*, and explain how Freud's treatment of psychological disorders led to his study of the unconscious mind.

1. Personality is defined as an individual's characteristic pattern of _____ , _____ , and _____ .

2. The psychoanalytic perspective on personality was proposed by _____ . A second, historically significant perspective was the _____ approach, which focused on people's capacities for _____ and _____ .

3. Today's theories are more _____ and down-to-earth than these classic theories.

4. Sigmund Freud was a medical doctor who specialized in _____ disorders.

5. Freud developed his theory in response to his observation that many patients had disorders that did not make _____ sense.

Objective 2: Describe Freud's view of personality structure in terms of the id, ego, and superego.

6. At first, Freud thought _____ would unlock the door to the unconscious.

7. The technique later used by Freud, in which the patient relaxes and says whatever comes to mind, is called _____ _____ .

8. Freud called his theory and associated techniques, whereby painful unconscious memories are exposed, _____ .

9. According to this theory, many of a person's thoughts, wishes, and feelings are hidden in a large _____ region. Some of the thoughts in this region can be retrieved at will into consciousness; these thoughts are said to be _____ . Many of the memories of this region, however, are blocked, or _____ , from consciousness.

10. Freud believed that a person's _____ wishes are often reflected in his or her beliefs, habits, symptoms, and _____ of the tongue or pen. Freud called the remembered content of dreams the _____ _____ , which he believed to be a censored version of the dream's true _____ _____ .

11. Freud believed that all facets of personality arise from conflict between our _____ impulses and the _____ restraints against them.

12. According to Freud, personality consists of three interacting structures: the _____ , the _____ , and the _____ .

13. The id is a reservoir of psychic energy that is primarily _____ (conscious/ unconscious) and operates according to the _____ principle.

14. The ego develops _____ (before/after) the id and consists of perceptions, thoughts, and memories that are mostly _____ (conscious/unconscious). The ego operates according to the _____ principle.

Explain why the ego is considered the "executive" of personality.

15. The personality structure that reflects moral values is the _____ , which Freud believed began emerging at about age _____ .

16. A person with a _____ (strong/ weak) superego may be self-indulgent; one with an unusually _____ (strong/ weak) superego may be virtuous but guilt-ridden.

Objective 3: Identify Freud's psychosexual stages of development, and describe the effects of fixation on behavior.

17. According to Freud, personality is formed as the child passes through a series of _____ stages, each of which is focused on a distinct body area called an _____ _____ .

18. The first stage is the _____ stage, which takes place during the first 18 months of life. During this stage, the id's energies are focused on behaviors such as _____ .

19. The second stage is the _____ stage, which lasts from about age _____ months to _____ months.

20. The third stage is the _____ stage, which lasts roughly from ages _____ to _____ years. During this stage, the id's energies are focused on the _____ . Freud also believed that during this stage children develop sexual desires for the _____ (same/opposite)-sex parent. Freud referred to these feelings as the _____ _____ in boys. Some psychoanalysts in Freud's era believed that girls experience a parallel _____ _____ .

21. Freud believed that _____ with the same-sex parent is the basis for what psychologists now call _____ _____ .

Explain how this complex of feelings is resolved through the process of identification.

22. During the next stage, sexual feelings are repressed: this phase is called the _____ stage and lasts until puberty.

23. The final stage of development is called the _____ stage.

24. According to Freud, it is possible for a person's development to become blocked in any of the stages; in such an instance, the person is said to be _____ .

Objective 4: Discuss how defense mechanisms serve to protect the individual from anxiety.

25. The ego attempts to protect itself against anxiety through the use of _____ _____ . The process underlying each of these mechanisms is _____ .

26. Dealing with anxiety by returning to an earlier stage of development is called _____ .

27. When a person reacts in a manner opposite that of his or her true feelings, _____ _____ is said to have occurred.

28. When a person attributes his or her own feelings to another person, _____ has occurred.

29. When a person offers a false, self-justifying explanation for his or her actions, _____ has occurred.

30. When impulses are directed toward an object other than the one that caused arousal, _____ has occurred.

31. When a person refuses to believe or even perceive a painful reality, he or she is experiencing _____ .

Matching Items

Match each defense mechanism in the following list with the proper example of its manifestation.

Defense Mechanisms

_____ 1. displacement
_____ 2. projection
_____ 3. reaction formation
_____ 4. rationalization
_____ 5. regression
_____ 6. denial

Manifestations

a. nail biting or thumb sucking in an anxiety-producing situation
b. overzealous crusaders against "immoral behaviors" who don't want to acknowledge their own sexual desires
c. saying you drink "just to be sociable" when in reality you have a drinking problem
d. thinking your child could not possibly be taking drugs
e. thinking someone hates you when in reality you hate that person
f. a child who is angry at his parents and vents this anger on the family pet, a less threatening target

32. Defense mechanisms are _____ (conscious/unconscious) processes.

Objective 5: Contrast the views of the neo-Freudians and psychodynamic theorists with Freud's original theory.

33. The theorists who established their own, modified versions of psychoanalytic theory are called

_____-_____ .

These theorists typically place _____ (more/less) emphasis on the conscious mind than Freud did and _____ (more/less) emphasis on sex and aggression.

Briefly summarize how each of the following theorists departed from Freud.

a. Alfred Adler _____

_____

b. Karen Horney _____

_____

_____

c. Carl Jung _____

_____

34. Today's psychologists _____ (accept/reject) the idea of inherited experiences, which _____ (which theorist?) called a _____

_____ .

35. More recently, some of Freud's ideas have been incorporated into _____ theory. Unlike Freud, the theorists advocating this perspective do not believe that _____ is the basis of personality. They do agree, however, that much of mental life is _____ , that _____ shapes personality, and that we often struggle with

_____ _____ .

Objective 6: Describe two projective tests used to assess personality, and discuss some criticisms of them.

36. Tests that provide people with ambiguous stimuli for interpretation are called _____ tests. Henry Murray

introduced the personality assessment technique called the _____

_____ Test.

37. The most widely used projective test is the _____ , in which people are shown a series of _____ . Critics contend that these tests have _____ (little/significant) validity and reliability.

Objective 7: Summarize psychology's current assessment of Freud's theory of psychoanalysis, including its portrayal of the unconscious.

38. Contrary to Freud's theory, research indicates that human development is _____ (fixed in childhood/lifelong), children gain their gender identity at a(n) _____ (earlier/later) age, and the presence of a same-sex parent _____ (is/is not) necessary for the child to become strongly masculine or feminine.

39. Research also disputes Freud's belief that dreams disguise _____ and that defense mechanisms disguise _____ and _____ impulses. Another Freudian idea that is no longer widely accepted is that psychological disorders are caused by

_____ _____ .

40. Psychoanalytic theory rests on the assumption that the human mind often _____ painful experiences. Many of today's researchers think that this process is much _____ (more common/rarer) than Freud believed. They also believe that when it does occur, it is a reaction to terrible _____ .

41. Today's psychologists agree with Freud that we have limited access to all that goes on in our minds. Research confirms the reality of

_____ _____ learning.

42. An example of the defense mechanism that Freud called _____ is what researchers

today call the _____
_____ effect. This refers to our
tendency to _____ the extent to
which others share our beliefs and behaviors.

43. Another Freudian idea that has received support
is that people defend themselves against
_____ . According to
_____-_____
theory, when people are faced with a threatening
world, they act to enhance their
_____ and may adhere more
strongly to the _____ that create
meaning in their lives.

44. Criticism of psychoanalysis as a scientific theory
centers on the fact that it provides
_____-_____-
_____ explanations and does not
offer _____ _____ .

State several of Freud's ideas that have endured.

The Humanistic Perspective (pp. 490–493)

Objective 8: Describe the humanistic perspective on
personality in terms of Maslow's focus on self-
actualization and Rogers' emphasis on people's
potential for growth.

1. Two influential theories of humanistic psychology were proposed by _____ and
_____ . These theorists offered a
_____-_____
perspective that emphasized human
_____ .

2. According to Maslow, humans are motivated by
needs that are organized into a
_____ . Maslow refers to the

process of fulfilling one's potential as
_____ and the process of find-
ing meaning, purpose, and communion beyond
the self as _____ . Many people
who fulfill their potential have been moved by
_____ _____
that surpass ordinary consciousness.

List some of the characteristics Maslow associated
with those who fulfilled their potential.

3. According to Rogers, a person nurtures growth in
a relationship by being _____ ,
_____ , and _____ .

4. People who are accepting of others offer them
_____ _____
_____ . By so doing, they enable
others to be _____ without fearing the loss of their esteem.

5. For both Maslow and Rogers, an important feature of personality is how an individual perceives
himself or herself; this is the person's
_____ .

Objective 9: Explain how humanistic psychologists
assessed personality, and discuss the major criticisms
of the humanistic perspective on personality.

6. Humanistic psychologists sometimes use
_____ to assess personality, that
is, to evaluate the _____ .

7. One questionnaire, inspired by Carl Rogers,
asked people to describe themselves both as they
would _____ like to be and as
they _____ are. When these two
selves are alike, the self-concept is
_____ .

8. Some humanistic psychologists feel that questionnaires are _____ and prefer to
use _____ to assess personality.

9. Humanistic psychologists have influenced such diverse areas as _____ , _____ , _____-_____ , and _____ . They have also had a major impact on today's _____ psychology.

State three criticisms of humanistic psychology.

The Trait Perspective (pp. 493–503)

Objective 10: Discuss psychologists' interest in personality types, and describe research efforts to identify fundamental personality traits.

1. Gordon Allport developed trait theory, which defines personality in terms of people's characteristic _____ and conscious _____ . Unlike Freud, he was generally less interested in _____ individual traits than in _____ them.

2. The _____-_____ _____ _____ classifies people according to Carl Jung's personality types. Although recently criticized for its lack of predictive value, this test has been widely used in _____ and _____ counseling.

3. To reduce the number of traits to a few basic ones, psychologists use the statistical procedure of _____ _____ . Hans and Sybil Eysenck think that two or three genetically influenced personality dimensions are sufficient; these include _____– _____ and emotional _____–_____ .

4. Some researchers believe that extraverts seek stimulation because their level of _____ _____ is relatively low. PET scans reveal an area of the brain's _____ lobe that is less active in _____ (extraverts/introverts) than in _____ (extraverts/introverts). Dopamine and dopamine-related neural activity tend to be higher in _____ (extraverts/introverts).

5. Research increasingly reveals that our _____ play an important role in defining our _____ and _____ style.

6. Jerome Kagan attributes differences in children's _____ and _____ to autonomic nervous system reactivity.

7. Personality differences among dogs, birds, and other animals _____ (are/are not) stable.

Objective 11: Discuss the value of using personality inventories to assess traits, and identify the Big Five trait dimensions.

8. Questionnaires that categorize personality traits are called _____ _____ .

9. The most widely used of all such personality tests is the _____ _____ _____ _____ ; its questions are grouped into _____ (how many?) clinical scales.

10. This test was developed by testing a large pool of items and selecting those that differentiated particular individuals; in other words, the test was _____ derived.

11. Researchers have arrived at a cluster of five factors that seem to describe the major features of personality. List and briefly describe the Big Five.

   a. _____
   b. _____
   c. _____
   d. _____
   e. _____

12. While some traits wane a bit during early and middle adulthood, others increase. For example, as young adults mature and learn to manage their commitments, _____ increases. From the thirties through the sixties, _____ increases.

13. In adulthood, the Big Five are quite _____ (stable/variable), with heritability estimated at _____ percent or more for each dimension. Moreover, these traits _____ (do/do not) predict other attributes.

Objective 12: Summarize the person-situation controversy, and explain its importance as a commentary on the trait perspective.

14. Human behavior is influenced both by our inner _____ and by the external _____ . The issue of which of these is the more important influence on personality is called the _____- _____ controversy.

15. To be considered a personality trait, a characteristic must persist over _____ and across _____ . Research studies reveal that personality trait scores _____ (correlate/do not correlate) with scores obtained seven years later. The consistency of specific behaviors from one situation to the next is _____ (predictably consistent/not predictably consistent).

16. An individual's score on a personality test _____ (is/is not) very predictive of his or her behavior in any given situation.

Explain the apparent contradiction between behavior in specific situations and average behavior patterns.

17. People's expressive styles, which include their _____ , manner of _____ , and _____ , are quite _____ (consistent/inconsistent), which _____ (does/does not) reveal distinct personality traits.

(Thinking Critically About) Explain several techniques used by astrologers to persuade people to accept their advice.

The Social-Cognitive Perspective
(pp. 503–510)

Objective 13: Describe the social-cognitive perspective, and discuss the important consequences of personal control and optimism.

1. Social-cognitive theory, which focuses on how the individual and the _____ interact, was proposed by _____ .

2. Social-cognitive theorists propose that personality is shaped by the mutual influence of our internal _____ , _____ factors, and _____ factors. This is the principle of _____ _____ .

Describe three different ways in which the environment and personality interact.

3. In studying how we interact with our environment, social-cognitive theorists point to the importance of our sense of _____ _____ . Individuals who believe that they control their own destinies are said to perceive an _____

_____ _____

_____ . Individuals who believe that their fate is determined by outside forces are said to perceive an _____

_____ _____

_____ . Self-control, which is the ability to control _____ and _____ gratification, predicts good _____ , better _____ , and _____ success.

4. People who feel helpless and oppressed often perceive control as _____ and may develop

.

5. People become happier when they are given _____ (more/less) control over what happens to them.

6. One measure of a person's feelings of effectiveness is his or her degree of _____ . Our characteristic manner of explaining negative and positive events is called our

_____ _____ .

7. (Close-Up) During its first century, psychology focused primarily on understanding and alleviating _____ _____ . Today, however, thriving Western cultures have an opportunity to create a more _____ psychology, focused on three pillars:

   a. _____

   b. _____

   c. _____

8. Our natural positive-thinking bias can sometimes promote an _____ _____ about future life events that can be unhealthy.

9. People tend to be most overconfident of their abilities in areas where they are, in fact, most _____ (competent/incompetent).

Objective 14: Explain why social-cognitive researchers assess behavior in realistic situations, and state the major criticism of the social-cognitive perspective.

10. It follows from the social-cognitive perspective that the best means of predicting people's future behavior is their _____

_____ .

11. The major criticism of the social-cognitive perspective is that it fails to appreciate a person's

_____ _____ .

Exploring the Self (pp. 511–518)

Objective 15: Explain why psychology has generated so much research on the self, and discuss the importance of self-esteem to human well-being.

1. One of Western psychology's most vigorously researched topics today is the _____ .

2. Hazel Markus and colleagues introduced the concept of an individual's _____

_____ to emphasize how our aspirations motivate us through specific goals.

3. Our tendency to overestimate the extent to which others are noticing and evaluating us is called the

_____ _____ .

4. According to self theorists, personality development hinges on our feelings of self-worth, or _____ . People who feel good about themselves are relatively _____ (dependent on/independent of) outside pressures.

5. In a series of experiments, researchers found that people who were made to feel insecure were _____ (more/less) critical of other persons or tended to express heightened

_____ _____ .

Objective 16: Discuss some evidence for self-serving bias, and contrast defensive and secure self-esteem.

6. Research has shown that most people tend to have _____ (low/high) self-esteem.

7. The tendency of people to judge themselves favorably is called the _____ bias.

8. Responsibility for success is generally accepted _____ (more/less) readily than responsibility for failure.

9. Most people perceive their own behavior and traits as being _____ (above/below) average.

10. Bushman and Baumeister found that students with unrealistically _____ (low/high) self-esteem were most likely to become exceptionally aggressive after criticism.

11. Some researchers distinguish _____ self-esteem, which is fragile and sensitive to _____ , from _____ self-esteem, which is less focused on _____ evaluations.

Objective 17: Identify some ways a primarily individualist culture differs from a primarily collectivist culture.

12. Cultures based on _____ value personal _____ and individual _____ . Examples of such cultures occur in _____ _____ , _____ _____ , _____ , and _____ _____ .

13. In contrast, cultures based on _____ value _____ , _____ , and _____ . Examples of such cultures occur in _____ _____ , _____ , and _____ .

14. Whereas people in _____ cultures value freedom, they suffer more _____ , divorce, _____ and _____-related disease.

PROGRESS TEST 1

Multiple-Choice Questions

Circle your answers to the following questions and check them with the answers beginning on page 283. If your answer is incorrect, read the explanation for

why it is incorrect and then consult the appropriate pages of the text (in parentheses following the correct answer).

1. The text defines *personality* as
   a. the set of personal attitudes that characterizes a person.
   b. an individual's characteristic pattern of thinking, feeling, and acting.
   c. a predictable set of responses to environmental stimuli.
   d. an unpredictable set of responses to environmental stimuli.

2. Which of the following places the greatest emphasis on the unconscious mind?
   a. the humanistic perspective
   b. the social-cognitive perspective
   c. the trait perspective
   d. the psychoanalytic perspective

3. Which of the following is the correct order of psychosexual stages proposed by Freud?
   a. oral; anal; phallic; latency; genital
   b. anal; oral; phallic; latency; genital
   c. oral; anal; genital; latency; phallic
   d. anal; oral; genital; latency; phallic

4. According to Freud, defense mechanisms are methods of reducing
   a. anger.   c. anxiety.
   b. fear.   d. lust.

5. Neo-Freudians such as Adler and Horney believed that
   a. Freud placed too great an emphasis on the conscious mind.
   b. Freud placed too great an emphasis on sexual and aggressive instincts.
   c. the years of childhood were more important in the formation of personality than Freud had indicated.
   d. Freud's ideas about the id, ego, and superego as personality structures were incorrect.

6. Research on locus of control indicates that internals are _____ than externals.
   a. more dependent
   b. more intelligent
   c. better able to cope with stress
   d. more sociable

7. Which two dimensions of personality have the Eysencks emphasized?

   a. extraversion–introversion and emotional stability–instability

   b. internal–external locus of control and extraversion–introversion

   c. internal–external locus of control and emotional stability–instability

   d. melancholic–phlegmatic and choleric–sanguine

8. With regard to personality, it appears that

   a. there is little consistency of behavior from one situation to the next and little consistency of traits over the life span.

   b. there is little consistency of behavior from one situation to the next but significant consistency of traits over the life span.

   c. there is significant consistency of behavior from one situation to the next but little consistency of traits over the life span.

   d. there is significant consistency of behavior from one situation to the next and significant consistency of traits over the life span.

9. The humanistic perspective on personality

   a. emphasizes the driving force of unconscious motivations in personality.

   b. emphasizes the growth potential of "healthy" individuals.

   c. emphasizes the importance of interaction with the environment in shaping personality.

   d. describes personality in terms of scores on various personality scales.

10. According to Rogers, three conditions are necessary to promote growth in personality. These are

   a. honesty, sincerity, and empathy.

   b. high self-esteem, honesty, and empathy.

   c. high self-esteem, genuineness, and acceptance.

   d. genuineness, acceptance, and empathy.

11. Regarding self-serving bias, psychologists who study the self have found that self-affirming thinking

   a. is generally maladaptive to the individual because it distorts reality by overinflating self-esteem.

   b. is generally adaptive to the individual because it reduces shyness, anxiety, and loneliness.

   c. tends to prevent the individual from viewing others with compassion and understanding.

   d. tends *not* to characterize people who have experienced unconditional positive regard.

12. Which of Freud's ideas would NOT be accepted by most contemporary psychologists?

   a. Development is essentially fixed in childhood.

   b. Sexuality is a potent drive in humans.

   c. The mind is an iceberg with consciousness being only the tip.

   d. Repression can be the cause of forgetting.

13. Projective tests such as the Rorschach inkblot test have been criticized because

   a. their scoring system is too rigid and leads to unfair labeling.

   b. they were standardized with unrepresentative samples.

   c. they have low reliability and low validity.

   d. it is easy for people to fake answers in order to appear healthy.

14. A major criticism of trait theory is that it

   a. places too great an emphasis on early childhood experiences.

   b. overestimates the consistency of behavior in different situations.

   c. underestimates the importance of heredity in personality development.

   d. places too great an emphasis on positive traits.

15. For humanistic psychologists, many of our behaviors and perceptions are ultimately shaped by whether our _____ is _____ or _____ .

   a. ego; strong; weak

   b. locus of control; internal; external

   c. personality structure; introverted; extraverted

   d. self-concept; positive; negative

16. In studying personality, a trait theorist would MOST LIKELY

   a. use a projective test.

   b. observe a person in a variety of situations.

   c. use a personality inventory.

   d. use the method of free association.

17. Id is to ego as _____ is to _____ .

   a. reality principle; pleasure principle

   b. pleasure principle; reality principle

   c. conscious forces; unconscious forces

   d. conscience; "personality executive"

18. Which of the following is the major criticism of the social-cognitive perspective?
    a. It focuses too much on early childhood experiences.
    b. It focuses too little on the inner traits of a person.
    c. It provides descriptions but not explanations.
    d. It lacks appropriate assessment techniques.

19. Recent research has provided more support for defense mechanisms such as _____ than for defense mechanisms such as _____ .
    a. displacement; reaction formation
    b. reaction formation; displacement
    c. displacement; regression
    d. displacement; projection

20. Some contemporary researchers are focusing their work on
    a. basic dimensions of personality.
    b. promoting positive aspects of life.
    c. classic theories of behavior.
    d. negative states.

21. Collectivist cultures
    a. give priority to the goals of their groups.
    b. value the maintenance of social harmony.
    c. foster social interdependence.
    d. have all of these characteristics.

Matching Items

Match each definition or description with the appropriate term.

Definitions or Descriptions

_____ 1. redirecting impulses to a less threatening object
_____ 2. test consisting of a series of inkblots
_____ 3. the conscious executive of personality
_____ 4. personality inventory
_____ 5. disguising an impulse by imputing it to another person
_____ 6. switching an unacceptable impulse into its opposite
_____ 7. the unconscious repository of instinctual drives
_____ 8. a statistical technique that identifies clusters of personality traits
_____ 9. personality structure that corresponds to a person's conscience
_____ 10. providing self-justifying explanations for an action
_____ 11. a projective test consisting of a set of ambiguous pictures

Terms

a. id
b. ego
c. superego
d. reaction formation
e. rationalization
f. displacement
g. factor analysis
h. projection
i. TAT
j. Rorschach
k. MMPI

PROGRESS TEST 2

Progress Test 2 should be completed during a final unit review. Answer the following questions after you thoroughly understand the correct answers for the section reviews and Progress Test 1.

Multiple-Choice Questions

1. Which perspective on personality emphasizes the interaction between the individual and the environment in shaping personality?
   a. psychoanalytic
   b. trait
   c. humanistic
   d. social-cognitive

2. According to Freud's theory, personality arises in response to conflicts between
   a. our unacceptable urges and our tendency to become self-actualized.
   b. the process of identification and the ego's defense mechanisms.
   c. the collective unconscious and our individual desires.
   d. our biological impulses and the social restraints against them.

3. The _____ classifies people according to Carl Jung's personality types.
   a. Myers-Briggs Type Indicator
   b. MMPI
   c. Locus of Control Scale
   d. Kagan Temperament Scale

4. People who feel oppressed and so perceive control as external may develop
   a. an internal locus of control.
   b. a reaction formation.
   c. learned helplessness.
   d. self-serving bias.

5. Research has shown that individuals who are made to feel insecure are subsequently
   a. more critical of others.
   b. less critical of others.
   c. more likely to display self-serving bias.
   d. less likely to display self-serving bias.

6. An example of self-serving bias described in the text is the tendency of people to
   a. see themselves as average on nearly any desirable dimension.
   b. accept more responsibility for successes than for failures.
   c. be overly critical of other people.
   d. exhibit heightened racial prejudice.

7. The Minnesota Multiphasic Personality Inventory (MMPI) is a(n)
   a. projective personality test.
   b. empirically derived and objective personality test.
   c. personality test developed mainly to assess job applicants.
   d. personality test used primarily to assess locus of control.

8. Trait theory attempts to
   a. show how development of personality is a lifelong process.
   b. describe and classify people in terms of their predispositions to behave in certain ways.
   c. determine which traits are most conducive to individual self-actualization.
   d. explain how behavior is shaped by the interaction between traits, behavior, and the environment.

9. With which of the following statements would a social-cognitive psychologist agree?
   a. People with an internal locus of control achieve more in school.
   b. "Externals" are better able to cope with stress than "internals."
   c. "Internals" are less independent than "externals."
   d. A social-cognitive psychologist would agree with all of these statements.

10. Which of the following statements about self-esteem is NOT correct?
    a. People with low self-esteem tend to be negative about others.
    b. People with high self-esteem are less prone to drug addiction.
    c. People with low self-esteem tend to be non-conformists.
    d. People with high self-esteem suffer less from insomnia.

11. The Oedipus and Electra complexes have their roots in the
    a. anal stage.
    b. oral stage.
    c. latency stage.
    d. phallic stage.

12. Which of the following is a common criticism of the humanistic perspective?
    a. Its concepts are vague and subjective.
    b. The emphasis on the self encourages selfishness in individuals.
    c. Humanism fails to appreciate the reality of evil in human behavior.
    d. All of these are common criticisms.

13. In studying personality, a social-cognitive theorist would MOST LIKELY make use of
    a. personality inventories.
    b. projective tests.
    c. observing behavior in different situations.
    d. factor analyses.

14. A major difference between the psychoanalytic and trait perspectives is that
    a. trait theory defines personality in terms of behavior; psychoanalytic theory, in terms of its underlying dynamics.
    b. trait theory describes behavior but does not attempt to explain it.
    c. psychoanalytic theory emphasizes the origins of personality in childhood sexuality.
    d. all of these are differences.

15. The Big Five personality factors are
    a. emotional stability, openness, introversion, sociability, locus of control.
    b. neuroticism, extraversion, openness, emotional stability, sensitivity.
    c. neuroticism, gregariousness, extraversion, impulsiveness, conscientiousness.
    d. emotional stability, extraversion, openness, agreeableness, conscientiousness.

16. Which of the following was NOT mentioned in the text as a criticism of Freud's theory?
    a. The theory is sexist.
    b. It offers few testable hypotheses.
    c. There is no evidence of anything like an "unconscious."
    d. The theory ignores the fact that human development is lifelong.

17. According to Freud, _____ is the process by which children incorporate their parents' values into their _____ .
    a. reaction formation; superegos
    b. reaction formation; egos
    c. identification; superegos
    d. identification; egos

18. Which of the following refers to the tendency to overestimate the extent to which others share our beliefs?
    a. the spotlight effect
    b. projection
    c. rationalization
    d. the false consensus effect

19. In promoting personality growth, the person-centered perspective emphasizes all but
    a. empathy.   c. genuineness.
    b. acceptance.   d. altruism.

20. Research on the Big Five personality factors provides evidence that
    a. some tendencies decrease during adulthood, while others increase.
    b. these traits only describe personality in Western, individualist cultures.
    c. the heritability of individual differences in these traits generally runs about 25 percent or less.
    d. all of these statements are true.

Matching Items

Match each term with the appropriate definition or description.

Terms

_____ 1. projective test
_____ 2. identification
_____ 3. collective unconscious
_____ 4. reality principle
_____ 5. psychosexual stages
_____ 6. pleasure principle
_____ 7. empirically derived test
_____ 8. reciprocal determinism
_____ 9. personality inventory
_____ 10. Oedipus complex
_____ 11. preconscious

Definitions or Descriptions

a. the id's demand for immediate gratification
b. a boy's sexual desires toward the opposite-sex parent
c. information that is retrievable but currently not in conscious awareness
d. stages of development proposed by Freud
e. questionnaire used to assess personality traits
f. the two-way interactions of behavior with personal and environmental factors
g. personality test that provides ambiguous stimuli
h. the repository of universal memories proposed by Jung
i. the process by which children incorporate their parents' values into their developing superegos
j. the process by which the ego seeks to gratify impulses of the id in nondestructive ways
k. developed by testing a pool of items and then selecting those that discriminate the group of interest

PSYCHOLOGY APPLIED

Answer these questions the day before an exam as a final check on your understanding of the unit's terms and concepts.

Multiple-Choice Questions

1. Darrell Minton believes that people are basically good and are endowed with self-actualizing tendencies. Evidently, Mr. Minton is a proponent of
   a. trait theory.
   b. psychodynamic theory.
   c. the humanistic perspective.
   d. the social-cognitive perspective.

2. A psychoanalyst would characterize a person who is impulsive and self-indulgent as possessing a strong _____ and a weak _____ .
   a. id and ego; superego   c. ego; superego
   b. id; ego and superego   d. id; superego

3. Because Ramona identifies with her politically conservative parents, she chose to enroll in a conservative school. After four years in this environment, Ramona's politics have become even more conservative. Which perspective best accounts for the mutual influences of Ramona's upbringing, choice of school, and political viewpoint?
   a. psychoanalytic   c. humanistic
   b. trait   d. social-cognitive

4. Jill has a biting, sarcastic manner. According to Freud, she is
   a. projecting her anxiety onto others.
   b. fixated in the oral stage of development.
   c. fixated in the anal stage of development.
   d. displacing her anxiety onto others.

5. James attributes his failing grade in chemistry to an unfair final exam. His attitude exemplifies
   a. internal locus of control.
   b. unconditional positive regard.
   c. self-serving bias.
   d. reciprocal determinism.

6. The behavior of many people has been described in terms of a *spotlight effect*. This means that they
   a. tend to see themselves as being above average in ability.
   b. perceive that their fate is determined by forces not under their personal control.
   c. overestimate the extent to which other people are noticing them.
   d. accept more responsibility for successes than for failures.

7. Because you have a relatively low level of brain arousal, a trait theorist would suggest that you are an _____ who would naturally seek _____ .
   a. introvert; stimulation
   b. introvert; isolation
   c. extravert; stimulation
   d. extravert; isolation

8. A psychologist at the local mental health center administered an empirically derived personality test to diagnose an emotionally troubled student. Which test did the psychologist MOST LIKELY administer?
   a. the MMPI
   b. the TAT
   c. the Rorschach
   d. the Locus of Control Scale

9. The personality test Teresa is taking involves her describing random patterns of dots. What type of test is she taking?
   a. an empirically derived test
   b. the MMPI
   c. a personality inventory
   d. a projective test

10. Mr. Gonzalez believes that most students can be classified as "Type A" or "Type B" according to the intensities of their personalities and competitiveness. Evidently, Mr. Gonzalez is working within the _____ perspective.
   a. psychoanalytic
   b. trait
   c. humanistic
   d. social-cognitive

11. According to the psychoanalytic perspective, a child who frequently "slips" and calls her teacher "mom" PROBABLY
   a. has some unresolved conflicts concerning her mother.
   b. is fixated in the oral stage of development.
   c. did not receive unconditional positive regard from her mother.
   d. can be classified as having a weak sense of personal control.

12. Isaiah is sober and reserved; Rashid is fun-loving and affectionate. The Eysencks would say that Isaiah _____ and Rashid _____ .
   a. has an internal locus of control; has an external locus of control
   b. has an external locus of control; has an internal locus of control
   c. is an extravert; is an introvert
   d. is an introvert; is an extravert

13. In high school, Britta and Debbie were best friends. They thought they were a lot alike, as did everyone else who knew them. After high school, they went on to very different colleges, careers, and life courses. Now, at their twenty-fifth reunion, they are shocked at how little they have in common. Bandura would suggest that their differences reflect the interactive effects of environment, personality, and behavior, which he refers to as
   a. reciprocal determinism.
   b. personal control.
   c. identification.
   d. self-serving bias.

14. For his class presentation, Bruce plans to discuss the Big Five personality factors used by people throughout the world to describe others or themselves. Which of the following is NOT a factor that Bruce will discuss?
   a. extraversion
   b. openness
   c. independence
   d. conscientiousness

15. Dayna is not very consistent in showing up for class and turning in assignments when they are due. Research studies would suggest that Dayna's inconsistent behavior
   a. indicates that she is emotionally troubled and may need professional counseling.
   b. is a sign of learned helplessness.
   c. is not necessarily unusual.
   d. probably reflects a temporary problem in another area of her life.

16. Andrew's grandfather, who has lived a rich and productive life, is a spontaneous, loving, and self-accepting person. Maslow might say that he
   a. has an internal locus of control.
   b. is an extravert.
   c. has resolved all the conflicts of the psychosexual stages.
   d. is a self-actualizing person.

17. The school psychologist believes that having a positive self-concept is necessary before students can achieve their potential. Evidently, the school psychologist is working within the _____ perspective.
   a. psychoanalytic
   b. trait
   c. humanistic
   d. social-cognitive

18. Wanda wishes to instill in her children an accepting attitude toward other people. Maslow and Rogers would probably recommend that she
    a. teach her children first to accept themselves.
    b. use discipline sparingly.
    c. be affectionate with her children only when they behave as she wishes.
    d. help them to understand their unconscious desires.

19. Suzy bought a used, high-mileage automobile because it was all she could afford. Attempting to justify her purchase, she raves to her friends about the car's attractiveness, good acceleration, and stereo. According to Freud, Suzy is using the defense mechanism of
    a. displacement.   c. rationalization.
    b. reaction formation.   d. projection.

20. (Close-Up) During a class discussion, Trevor argues that positive psychology is sure to wane in popularity because it suffers from the same criticisms as humanistic psychology. You counter his argument by pointing out that, unlike humanistic psychology, positive psychology
    a. focuses on advancing human fulfillment.
    b. is rooted in science.
    c. is not based on the study of individual characteristics.
    d. does not advocate social responsibility.

21. Chad, who grew up in the United States, is more likely to encourage _____ in his future children than Asian-born Hidiyaki, who is more likely to encourage _____ in his future children.
    a. obedience; independence
    b. independence; emotional closeness
    c. emotional closeness; obedience
    d. loyalty; emotional closeness

Essay Question

You are an honest, open, and responsible person. Discuss how these characteristics would be explained according to the major perspectives on personality. (Use the space below to list points you want to make, and organize them. Then write the essay on a separate piece of paper.)

KEY TERMS

Using your own words, on a separate piece of paper write a brief definition or explanation of each of the following terms.

1. personality
2. free association
3. psychoanalysis
4. unconscious
5. id
6. ego
7. superego
8. psychosexual stages
9. Oedipus complex
10. identification
11. fixation
12. defense mechanisms
13. repression
14. regression
15. reaction formation
16. projection
17. rationalization
18. displacement
19. denial
20. collective unconscious
21. projective tests
22. Thematic Apperception Test (TAT)
23. Rorschach inkblot test
24. terror-management theory
25. self-actualization
26. unconditional positive regard
27. self-concept
28. trait
29. personality inventory
30. Minnesota Multiphasic Personality Inventory (MMPI)
31. empirically derived test
32. social-cognitive perspective

33. reciprocal determinism

34. personal control

35. external locus of control

36. internal locus of control

37. positive psychology

38. self

39. spotlight effect

40. self-esteem

41. self-serving bias

42. individualism

43. collectivism

ANSWERS

Unit Review

Introducing Personality and *The Psychoanalytic Perspective*

1. thinking; feeling; acting
2. Sigmund Freud; humanistic; growth; self-fulfillment
3. focused
4. nervous
5. neurological
6. hypnosis
7. free association
8. psychoanalysis
9. unconscious; preconscious; repressed
10. unconscious; slips; manifest content; latent content
11. biological; social
12. id; ego; superego
13. unconscious; pleasure
14. after; conscious; reality

The ego is considered the executive of personality because it directs our actions as it intervenes among the impulsive demands of the id, the reality of the external world, and the ideals of the superego.

15. superego; 4 or 5
16. weak; strong
17. psychosexual; erogenous zone
18. oral; sucking (also biting, chewing)
19. anal; 18; 36

20. phallic; 3; 6; genitals; opposite; Oedipus complex; Electra complex
21. identification; gender identity

Children eventually cope with their feelings for the opposite-sex parent by repressing them and by identifying with the rival (same-sex) parent. Through this process children incorporate many of their parents' values, thereby strengthening the superego.

22. latency
23. genital
24. fixated
25. defense mechanisms; repression
26. regression
27. reaction formation
28. projection
29. rationalization
30. displacement
31. denial

Matching Items

1. f
2. e
3. b
4. c
5. a
6. d

32. unconscious
33. neo-Freudians; more; less

   a. Adler emphasized the social, rather than the sexual, tensions of childhood and said that much of behavior is driven by the need to overcome feelings of inferiority.

   b. Horney questioned the male bias in Freud's theory, such as the assumptions that women have weak egos and suffer "penis envy." Like Adler, she emphasized social tensions.

   c. Jung emphasized an inherited collective unconscious.

34. reject; Jung; collective unconscious
35. psychodynamic; sex; unconscious; childhood; inner conflicts
36. projective; Thematic Apperception
37. Rorschach; inkblots; little
38. lifelong; earlier; is not
39. wishes; sexual; aggressive; sexual suppression
40. represses; rarer; trauma
41. unconscious implicit

42. projection; false consensus; overestimate
43. anxiety; terror-management; self-esteem; worldviews
44. after-the-fact; testable predictions

Freud drew attention to the unconscious and the irrational, to human defenses against anxiety, to the importance of human sexuality, to the tension between our biological impulses and our social well-being, and to our potential for evil.

The Humanistic Perspective

1. Abraham Maslow; Carl Rogers; third-force; potential
2. hierarchy; self-actualization; self-transcendence; peak experiences

For Maslow, such people were self-aware, open, self-accepting, spontaneous, loving, caring, not paralyzed by others' opinions, secure, and problem-centered rather than self-centered.

3. genuine; accepting; empathic
4. unconditional positive regard; spontaneous
5. self-concept
6. questionnaires; self-concept
7. ideally; actually; positive
8. depersonalizing; interviews
9. counseling; education; child-rearing; management; popular

Three criticisms of humanistic psychology are that its concepts are vague and subjective; the individualism it encourages can lead to self-indulgence, selfishness, and an erosion of moral restraints; and it fails to appreciate the human capacity for evil.

The Trait Perspective

1. behaviors; motives; explaining; describing
2. Myers-Briggs Type Indicator; business; career
3. factor analysis; extraversion–introversion; stability–instability
4. brain arousal; frontal; extraverts; introverts; extraverts
5. genes; temperament; behavioral
6. shyness; inhibition
7. are
8. personality inventories
9. Minnesota Multiphasic Personality Inventory; 10
10. empirically
11. a. Emotional stability: on a continuum from calm to anxious; secure to insecure

    b. Extraversion: from sociable to retiring
    c. Openness: from preference for variety to routine
    d. Agreeableness: from soft-hearted to ruthless
    e. Conscientiousness: from disciplined to impulsive
12. conscientiousness; agreeableness
13. stable; 50; do
14. traits (or dispositions); situation (or environment); person-situation
15. time; situations; correlate; not predictably consistent
16. is not

At any given moment a person's behavior is powerfully influenced by the immediate situation, so that it may appear that the person does not have a consistent personality. But averaged over many situations a person's outgoingness, happiness, and carelessness, for instance, are more predictable.

17. animation; speaking; gestures; consistent; does

Astrologers use a "stock spiel" that includes information that is generally true of almost everyone. The willingness of people to accept this type of phony information is called the "Barnum effect." A second technique used by astrologers is to "read" a person's clothing, features, reactions, etc. and build their advice from these observations.

The Social-Cognitive Perspective

1. environment; Albert Bandura
2. behaviors; personal; environmental; reciprocal determinism

Different people choose different environments partly on the basis of their dispositions. Our personality shapes how we interpret and react to events. It also helps create the situations to which we react.

3. personal control; internal locus of control; external locus of control; impulses; delay; adjustment; grades; social
4. external; learned helplessness
5. more
6. optimism; attributional style
7. negative states; positive
    a. positive emotions
    b. positive character
    c. positive groups, communities, and cultures
8. unrealistic (illusory) optimism
9. incompetent
10. past behavior in similar situations
11. inner traits

Exploring the Self

1. self

2. possible selves

3. spotlight effect

4. self-esteem; independent of

5. more; racial prejudice

6. high

7. self-serving

8. more

9. above

10. high

11. defensive; criticism; secure; external

12. individualism; independence (or control); achievement; North America; Western Europe; Australia; New Zealand

13. collectivism; interdependence; tradition; harmony; South Korea; Japan; China

14. individualist; loneliness; homicide; stress

Progress Test 1

Multiple-Choice Questions

1. **b.** is the answer. Personality is defined as patterns of response—of thinking, feeling, and acting— that are relatively consistent across a variety of situations. (p. 479)

2. **d.** is the answer. (p. 480)
   a. & b. Conscious processes are the focus of these perspectives.
   c. The trait perspective focuses on the description of behaviors.

3. **a.** is the answer. (p. 482)

4. **c.** is the answer. According to Freud, defense mechanisms reduce anxiety unconsciously, by disguising one's threatening impulses. (p. 483)
   a., b., & d. Unlike these specific emotions, anxiety need not be focused. Defense mechanisms help us cope when we are unsettled but are not sure why.

5. **b.** is the answer. (p. 484)
   a. According to most neo-Freudians, Freud placed too great an emphasis on the *unconscious* mind.
   c. Freud placed great emphasis on early childhood, and the neo-Freudians basically agreed with him.
   d. The neo-Freudians accepted Freud's ideas about the basic personality structures.

6. **c.** is the answer. (p. 505)
   a. & d. In fact, just the opposite is true.
   b. Locus of control is not related to intelligence.

7. **a.** is the answer. (p. 495)
   b. & c. Locus of control is emphasized by the social-cognitive perspective.
   d. This is how the ancient Greeks described personality.

8. **b.** is the answer. Studies have shown that people do not act with predictable consistency from one situation to the next. But, over a number of situations, consistent patterns emerge, and this basic consistency of traits persists over the life span. (p. 501)

9. **b.** is the answer. (p. 490)
   a. This is true of the psychoanalytic perspective.
   c. This is true of the social-cognitive perspective.
   d. This is true of the trait perspective.

10. **d.** is the answer. (p. 491)

11. **b.** is the answer. Psychologists who study the self emphasize that for the individual, self-affirming thinking is generally adaptive. People with high self-esteem have fewer sleepless nights, succumb less easily to pressures to conform, and are just plain happier. (p. 515)

12. **a.** is the answer. Developmental research indicates that development is lifelong. (p. 487)
    b., c., & d. To varying degrees, research has partially supported these Freudian ideas.

13. **c.** is the answer. As scoring is largely subjective and the tests have not been very successful in predicting behavior, their reliability and validity have been called into question. (p. 486)
    a. This is untrue.
    b. Unlike empirically derived personality tests, projective tests are not standardized.
    d. Although this may be true, it was not mentioned as a criticism of projective tests.

14. **b.** is the answer. In doing so, it underestimates the influence of the environment. (pp. 500–501)
    a. The trait perspective does not emphasize early childhood experiences.
    c. This criticism is unlikely since trait theory does not seek to explain personality development.
    d. Trait theory does not look on traits as being "positive" or "negative."

15. **d.** is the answer. (p. 492)
    a. & c. Personality structure is a concern of the psychoanalytic perspective.
    b. Locus of control is a major focus of the social-cognitive perspective.

16. **c.** is the answer. (p. 496)
    a. & d. A psychoanalytic theorist would be most likely to use a projective test or free association.

b. This would most likely be the approach taken by a social-cognitive theorist.

17. **b.** is the answer. In Freud's theory, the id operates according to the pleasure principle; the ego operates according to the reality principle. (p. 481)

c. The id is presumed to be unconscious.

d. The superego is, according to Freud, the equivalent of a conscience; the ego is the "personality executive."

18. **b.** is the answer. The social-cognitive theory has been accused of putting so much emphasis on the situation that inner traits are neglected. (p. 510)

a. Such a criticism has been made of the psychoanalytic perspective but is not relevant to the social-cognitive perspective.

c. Such a criticism might be more relevant to the trait perspective; the social-cognitive perspective offers an explanation in the form of reciprocal determinism.

d. There are assessment techniques appropriate to the theory, namely, questionnaires and observations of behavior in situations.

19. **b.** is the answer. (p. 489)

a., c., & d. The evidence supports defenses that defend self-esteem, rather than those that are tied to instinctual energy.

20. **b.** is the answer. (p. 508)

21. **d.** is the answer. (p. 517)

Matching Items

1. f (p. 483)	**5.** h (p. 483)	**9.** c (p. 482)
2. j (p. 486)	**6.** d (p. 483)	**10.** e (p. 483)
3. b (p. 481)	**7.** a (p. 481)	**11.** i (p. 486)
4. k (p. 496)	**8.** g (p. 495)	

Progress Test 2

Multiple-Choice Questions

1. **d.** is the answer. (p. 503)

a. This perspective emphasizes unconscious dynamics in personality.

b. This perspective is more concerned with *describing* than *explaining* personality.

c. This perspective emphasizes the healthy, self-actualizing tendencies of personality.

2. **d.** is the answer. (p. 481)

a. Self-actualization is a concept of the humanistic perspective.

b. Through identification, children *reduce* conflicting feelings as they incorporate their parents' values.

c. Jung, rather than Freud, proposed the concept of the collective unconscious.

3. **a.** is the answer. (p. 494)

4. **c.** is the answer. In such situations, passive resignation, called learned helplessness, develops. (p. 506)

a. This refers to the belief that one controls one's fate; the circumstances described lead to precisely the opposite belief.

b. Reaction formation is a defense mechanism in which unacceptable impulses are channeled into their opposites.

d. Just the opposite would be true.

5. **a.** is the answer. Feelings of insecurity reduce self-esteem, and those who feel negative about themselves tend to feel negative about others as well. (p. 512)

6. **a.** is the answer. (p. 513)

7. **b.** is the answer. The MMPI was developed by selecting from many items those that differentiated between the groups of interest; hence, it was empirically derived. That it is an objective test is shown by the fact that it can be scored by computer. (p. 496)

a. Projective tests present ambiguous stimuli for people to interpret; the MMPI is a questionnaire.

c. Although sometimes used to assess job applicants, the MMPI was developed to assess emotionally troubled people.

d. The MMPI does not focus on control but, rather, measures various aspects of personality.

8. **b.** is the answer. Trait theory attempts to describe behavior and not to develop explanations or applications. The emphasis is more on consistency than on change. (p. 494)

9. **a.** is the answer. "Internals," or those who have a sense of personal control, have been shown to achieve more in school. Relative to externals, they also cope better with stress and are more independent. (p. 505)

10. **c.** is the answer. In actuality, people with *high* self-esteem are generally more independent of pressures to conform. (p. 512)

11. **d.** is the answer. (p. 482)

12. **d.** is the answer. (p. 493)

13. **c.** is the answer. In keeping with their emphasis on interactions between people and situations, social-cognitive theorists would most likely make use of observations of behavior in relevant situations. (p. 509)

a. & d. Personality inventories and factor analyses would more likely be used by a trait theorist. **b.** Projective tests would more likely be used by a psychologist working within the psychoanalytic perspective.

14. **d.** is the answer. Trait theory defines personality in terms of behavior and is therefore interested in describing behavior; psychoanalytic theory defines personality as dynamics underlying behavior and therefore is interested in explaining behavior in terms of these dynamics. (pp. 480, 494)

15. **d.** is the answer. (p. 497)

16. **c.** is the answer. Although many researchers think of the unconscious as information processing without awareness rather than as a reservoir of repressed information, they agree with Freud that we do indeed have limited access to all that goes on in our minds. (p. 488)

17. **c.** is the answer. (p. 482)
    a. & b. Reaction formation is the defense mechanism by which people transform unacceptable impulses into their opposites.
    d. It is the superego, rather than the ego, that represents parental values.

18. **d.** is the answer. (pp. 488–489)

19. **d.** is the answer. (p. 491)

20. **a.** is the answer. Neuroticism, extraversion, and openness tend to decrease, while agreeableness and conscientiousness tend to increase. (p. 498)

    b. The Big Five dimensions describe personality in various cultures reasonably well.

    c. Heritability generally runs 50 percent or more for each dimension.

Matching Items

1. g (p. 486)	**5.** d (p. 482)	**9.** e (p. 496)
2. i (p. 482)	**6.** a (p. 481)	**10.** b (p. 482)
3. h (p. 485)	**7.** k (p. 496)	**11.** c (p. 480)
4. j (p. 481)	**8.** f (p. 503)	

Psychology Applied

Multiple-Choice Questions

1. **c.** is the answer. (p. 491)
   b., c., & d. None of these theories or perspectives offers any particular explanation of this tendency.

2. **d.** is the answer. Impulsiveness is the mark of a strong id; self-indulgence is the mark of a weak superego. Because the ego serves to mediate the demands of the id, the superego, and the outside world, its strength or weakness is judged by its decision-making ability, not by the character of the decision—so the ego is not relevant to the question asked. (pp. 481–482)

3. **d.** is the answer. The social-cognitive perspective emphasizes the reciprocal influences between people and their situations. In this example, Ramona's parents (situational factor) helped shape her political beliefs (internal factor), which influenced her choice of colleges (situational factor) and created an environment that fostered her predisposed political attitudes. (p. 503)

4. **b.** is the answer. Sarcasm is said to be an attempt to deny the passive dependence characteristic of the oral stage. (p. 483)
   a. A person who is projecting attributes his or her own feelings to others.
   c. Such a person might be either messy and disorganized or highly controlled and compulsively neat.
   d. Displacement involves diverting aggressive or sexual impulses onto a more acceptable object than that which aroused them.

5. **c.** is the answer. (p. 513)
   a. A person with an internal locus of control would be likely to *accept* responsibility for a failing grade.
   b. Unconditional positive regard is an attitude of total acceptance directed toward others.
   d. Reciprocal determinism refers to the mutual influences among personality, environment, and behavior.

6. **c.** is the answer. (pp. 511–512)
   a. This describes self-serving bias.
   b. This describes external locus of control.

7. **c.** is the answer. (p. 495)
   a. & b. According to this theory, introverts have relatively *high* levels of arousal, causing them to crave solitude.
   d. Isolation might lower arousal level even further.

8. **a.** is the answer. (p. 496)
   b. & c. The TAT and Rorschach are projective tests that were not empirically derived.
   d. A personality test that measures locus of control would not be helpful in identifying troubled behaviors.

9. **d.** is the answer. Projective tests provide ambiguous stimuli, such as random dot patterns, in an attempt to trigger in the test-taker projection of his or her personality. (p. 486)

10. **b.** is the answer. (p. 494)
   a. The psychoanalytic perspective emphasizes unconscious processes in personality dynamics.
   c. The humanistic perspective emphasizes each person's potential for healthy growth and self-actualization.
   d. The social-cognitive perspective emphasizes the reciprocal influences of personality and environment.

11. **a.** is the answer. Freud believed that dreams and such slips of the tongue reveal unconscious conflicts. (p. 481)
   b. A person fixated in the oral stage might have a sarcastic personality; this child's slip of the tongue reveals nothing about her psychosexual development.
   c. & d. Unconditional positive regard and personal control are not psychoanalytic concepts.

12. **d.** is the answer. (p. 495)
   a. & b. The traits of Isaiah and Rashid reveal nothing about their sense of personal control.

13. **a.** is the answer. Reciprocal determinism refers to the mutual influences among personal factors, environmental factors, and behavior. (p. 503)
   b. Personal control is one's sense of controlling, or being controlled by, the environment.
   c. In Freud's theory, identification is the process by which children incorporate parental values into their developing superegos.
   d. Self-serving bias describes our readiness to perceive ourselves favorably.

14. **c.** is the answer. (p. 497)

15. **c.** is the answer. (pp. 500–501)

16. **d.** is the answer. (p. 491)
   a. & b. These are concepts used by trait theorists rather than humanistic theorists such as Maslow.
   c. This reflects Freud's viewpoint.

17. **c.** is the answer. (p. 492)
   a., b., & d. The self-concept is not relevant to the psychoanalytic, trait, or social-cognitive perspectives.

18. **a.** is the answer. (p. 491)
   b. The text does not discuss the impact of discipline on personality.
   c. This would constitute *conditional*, rather than unconditional, positive regard and would likely cause the children to be *less* accepting of themselves and others.

19. **c.** is the answer. Suzy is trying to justify her purchase by generating (inaccurate) explanations for her behavior. (p. 483)

a. Displacement is the redirecting of impulses toward an object other than the one responsible for them.
b. Reaction formation is the transformation of unacceptable impulses into their opposites.
d. Projection is the attribution of one's own unacceptable thoughts and feelings to others.

20. **b.** is the answer. (p. 508)
   a. Both positive psychology and humanistic psychology focus on advancing human fulfillment.
   c. Both perspectives focus, at least partly, on individual characteristics.

21. **b.** is the answer. Although parental values differ from one time and place to another, studies reveal that Western parents today want their children to think for themselves, while Asian and African parents place greater value on emotional closeness. (p. 517)
   d. Both of these values are more typical of Asian than Western cultures.

Essay Question

Because you are apparently in good psychological health, according to the psychoanalytic perspective you must have experienced a healthy childhood and successfully passed Freud's stages of psychosexual development. Freud would also say that your ego is functioning well in balancing the demands of your id with the restraining demands of your superego and reality. Freud might also say that your honest nature reflects a well-developed superego, while Jung might say it derives from a universal value found in our collective unconscious.

According to the humanistic perspective, your open and honest nature indicates that your basic needs have been met and you are in the process of self-actualization or even self-transcendence (Maslow). Furthermore, your openness indicates that you have a healthy self-concept and were likely nurtured by genuine, accepting, and empathic caregivers (Rogers). More recently, researchers who emphasize the self would also focus on the importance of a positive self-concept.

Trait theorists would be less concerned with explaining these specific characteristics than with describing them, determining their consistency, and classifying your personality type. Some trait theorists, such as Allport, Eysenck, and Kagan, attribute certain trait differences to biological factors such as autonomic reactivity and heredity.

According to the social-cognitive perspective, your personal factors, behavior, and environmental influences interacted in shaping your personality and behaviors. The fact that you are a responsible person indicates that you perceive yourself as controlling, rather than as controlled by, your environment.

Key Terms

1. **Personality** is an individual's characteristic pattern of thinking, feeling, and acting. (p. 479)

2. **Free association** is the Freudian technique in which the person is encouraged to say whatever comes to mind as a means of exploring the unconscious. (p. 480)

3. **Psychoanalysis** is Freud's theory of personality that attributes thoughts and actions to unconscious motives and conflicts; also, the techniques used in treating psychological disorders by seeking to expose and interpret the tensions within a patient's unconscious. (p. 480)

4. In Freud's theory, the **unconscious** is the reservoir of mostly unacceptable thoughts, wishes, feelings, and memories. According to contemporary psychologists, it is a level of information processing of which we are unaware. (p. 480)

5. In Freud's theory, the **id** is the unconscious system of personality, consisting of basic sexual and aggressive drives, that supplies psychic energy to personality. It operates on the *pleasure principle*. (p. 481)

6. In psychoanalytic theory, the **ego** is the conscious division of personality that attempts to mediate among the demands of the id, the superego, and reality. It operates on the *reality principle*. (p. 481)

7. In Freud's theory, the **superego** is the division of personality that contains the conscience and develops by incorporating the perceived moral standards of society. (p. 482)

8. Freud's **psychosexual stages** are developmental periods children pass through during which the id's pleasure-seeking energies are focused on different erogenous zones. (p. 482)

9. According to Freud, boys in the phallic stage develop a collection of feelings, known as the **Oedipus complex**, that center on sexual attraction to the mother and resentment of the father. Some psychologists believe girls have a parallel *Electra complex*. (p. 482)

10. In Freud's theory, **identification** is the process by which the child's superego develops and incorporates the parents' values. Freud saw identification as crucial, not only to resolution of the Oedipus complex, but also to the development of *gender identity*. (p. 482)

11. In Freud's theory, **fixation** occurs when development becomes arrested, due to unresolved conflicts, in an earlier psychosexual stage. (p. 483)

12. In Freud's theory, **defense mechanisms** are the ego's methods of unconsciously protecting itself against anxiety by distorting reality. (p. 483)

13. The basis of all defense mechanisms, **repression** is the unconscious exclusion of anxiety-arousing thoughts, feelings, and memories from the conscious mind. Repression is an example of motivated forgetting: One "forgets" what one really does not wish to remember. (p. 483)

14. **Regression** is the defense mechanism in which a person faced with anxiety reverts to a more infantile psychosexual stage. (p. 483)

15. **Reaction formation** is the defense mechanism in which the ego converts unacceptable impulses into their opposites. (p. 483)

16. In psychoanalytic theory, **projection** is the unconscious attribution of one's own unacceptable feelings, attitudes, or desires to others. (p. 483)

    Memory aid: To project is to thrust outward. **Projection** is an example of thrusting one's own feelings outward to another person.

17. **Rationalization** is the defense mechanism in which one devises self-justifying but incorrect reasons for one's behavior. (p. 483)

18. **Displacement** is the defense mechanism in which a sexual or aggressive impulse is shifted to a more acceptable or less threatening object other than the one that originally aroused the impulse. (p. 484)

19. **Denial** is the defense mechanism in which people refuse to believe or even perceive a painful reality. (p. 484)

20. The **collective unconscious** is Jung's concept of an inherited unconscious shared by all people and deriving from our species' history. (p. 485)

21. **Projective tests**, such as the TAT and Rorschach, present ambiguous stimuli onto which people supposedly *project* their own inner feelings. (p. 486)

22. The **Thematic Apperception Test (TAT)** is a projective test that consists of ambiguous pictures about which people are asked to make up stories, which are thought to reflect their inner feelings and interests. (p. 486)

23. The **Rorschach inkblot test**, the most widely used projective test, consists of 10 inkblots that people are asked to interpret; it seeks to identify people's inner feelings by analyzing their interpretations of the blots. (p. 486)

24. According to **terror-management theory,** thinking about one's mortality can provoke terror-management defenses such as prejudice. (p. 489)

25. In Maslow's theory, **self-actualization** describes the process of fulfilling one's potential and becoming spontaneous, loving, creative, and self-accepting. Self-actualization becomes active only after the more basic physical and psychological needs have been met. (p. 491)

26. According to Rogers, **unconditional positive regard** is an attitude of total acceptance toward another person. (p. 491)

27. **Self-concept** refers to one's personal awareness of "who I am." In the humanistic perspective, the self-concept is a central feature of personality; life happiness is significantly affected by whether the self-concept is positive or negative. (p. 492)

28. **Traits** are people's characteristic patterns of behavior. (p. 494)

29. **Personality inventories,** associated with the trait perspective, are questionnaires used to assess personality traits. (p. 496)

30. Consisting of 10 clinical scales, the **Minnesota Multiphasic Personality Inventory (MMPI)** is the most widely researched and clinically used personality inventory. (p. 496)

31. An **empirically derived test** is one developed by testing many items to see which best distinguish between groups of interest. (p. 496)

32. According to the **social-cognitive perspective,** behavior is the result of interactions between people (and their thinking) and their social context. (p. 503)

33. According to the social-cognitive perspective, personality is shaped through **reciprocal deter-** **minism,** or the interacting influences of behavior, internal cognition, and environment. (p. 503)

34. **Personal control** refers to the extent to which people perceive control over their environment. (p. 505)

35. **External locus of control** is the perception that your fate is determined by forces not under personal control. (p. 505)

36. **Internal locus of control** is the perception that, to a great extent, you control your own destiny. (p. 505)

37. Focusing on positive emotions, character virtues such as creativity and compassion, and healthy families and neighborhoods, **positive psychology** is the scientific study of optimal human functioning. (p. 508)

38. In contemporary psychology, the **self** is the organizer of our thoughts, feelings, and actions. (p. 511)

39. The **spotlight effect** is the tendency of people to overestimate the extent to which other people are noticing and evaluating them. (p. 512)

40. **Self-esteem** refers to an individual's sense of self-worth. (p. 512)

41. **Self-serving bias** is the tendency to perceive oneself favorably. (p. 513)

42. **Individualism** is giving priority to personal goals over group goals and defining one's identity in terms of personal attributes rather than group identification. (p. 516)

43. **Collectivism** is giving priority to the goals of one's group and defining one's identity accordingly. (p. 516)

Testing and Individual Differences

UNIT OVERVIEW

An enduring controversy in psychology involves attempts to define and measure intelligence. Unit 11 discusses whether intelligence is a single general ability or several specific ones as well as research that attempts to assess the neurological basis of intelligence. It also describes the historical origins of intelligence tests and discusses several important issues concerning their use. These include the methods by which intelligence tests are constructed and whether such tests are valid, reliable, and free of bias. The unit also explores the stability of intelligence and the extent of genetic and environmental influences on intelligence.

NOTE: Answer guidelines for all Unit 11 questions begin on page 301.

UNIT REVIEW

First, skim each section, noting headings and boldface items. After you have read the section, review each objective by answering the fill-in and essay-type questions that follow it. As you proceed, evaluate your performance by consulting the answers beginning on page 301. Do not continue with the next section until you understand each answer. If you need to, review or reread the section in the textbook before continuing.

What Is Intelligence? (pp. 524–532)

Objective 1: Discuss the difficulty of defining *intelligence*, and explain what it means to reify intelligence.

1. Psychologists _____ (do/do not) agree on a definition of intelligence.

2. To regard an abstract concept as a concrete entity is to commit the error known as _____ . By doing this, we are viewing intelligence as something a person has, rather than a score obtained on an _____ _____ .

3. Intelligence is a _____ constructed concept.

4. In any context, intelligence can be defined as ____ _____ .

5. One controversy regarding the nature of intelligence centers on whether intelligence is one _____ ability or several _____ abilities.

Objective 2: Present arguments for and against considering intelligence as one general mental ability.

6. The statistical procedure used to identify groups of items that appear to measure a common ability is called _____ _____ .

7. Charles Spearman, one of the developers of this technique, believed that a factor called *g*, or _____ _____ , runs through the more specific aspects of intelligence.

8. Opposing Spearman, _____ identified seven clusters of _____ _____ .

9. One psychologist believes that general intelligence evolved as a means of helping people solve _____ _____ .

Objective 3: Compare Gardner's and Sternberg's theories of intelligence.

10. People with _____ _____ score at the low end of intelligence tests but possess extraordinary specific skills.

11. Howard Gardner proposes that there are _____ _____ , each independent of the others. However, critics point out that the world is not so just: General intelligence scores _____ (do/do not) predict performance on various complex tasks and in various jobs.

12. Sternberg's _____ theory distinguishes three types of intelligence: _____ intelligence, _____ intelligence, and _____ intelligence.

Objective 4: Describe the three aspects of emotional intelligence, and discuss criticisms of this concept.

13. A critical part of social intelligence is _____ _____ —the ability to _____ , _____ , _____ , and _____ emotions.

14. More specifically, the four components of emotional intelligence are as follows: the ability to _____ emotions in faces, the ability to _____ them and how they change and blend, the ability to _____ them correctly in varied situations, and the ability to use them to enable _____ or creative thinking.

Briefly describe emotionally intelligent people.

15. Some scholars believe that the concept of _____ intelligence stretches the idea of multiple intelligences too far.

Objective 5: Describe the relationship between intelligence and brain anatomy.

16. Earlier studies _____ (did/did not) reveal a clear-cut correlation between head size (relative to body size) and intelligence score.

17. Newer studies that measure brain _____ using _____ scans reveal a _____ (more/less) significant correlation between brain size (adjusted for body size) and intelligence score. The cause of this could be differing _____ , nutrition, _____ _____ , or some combination of these.

18. A study of Einstein's brain revealed that it was 15 percent larger in the lower _____ lobe—known to be an important neural center for processing _____ and _____ information.

19. Postmortem analyses reveal that the brains of highly educated people have more _____ than do those of people with less education. Other evidence suggests that highly intelligent people differ in their neural _____ . Higher intelligence scores have also been linked with more _____ _____ in brain areas known to be involved in _____ , _____ , and _____ .

Objective 6: Discuss findings on the correlations among perceptual speed, neural processing speed, and intelligence.

20. When people ponder intelligence test questions, for example, an area in the brain's _____ _____ becomes especially active in the _____ (left/right) brain for verbal questions and _____ (in the right brain/in the left brain/on both sides of the brain) for spatial questions. People who are able to more quickly retrieve information from memory tend to score high in _____ ability.

21. Studies looking at a range of tasks have found that people with high intelligence scores tend to

take in perceptual information _____ (faster/more slowly) than people with low intelligence scores.

22. Other studies have found that the brain waves of highly intelligent people register simple stimuli more _____ and with greater _____ .

Assessing Intelligence (pp. 532–539)

Objective 7: Discuss the history of intelligence testing.

1. The early Greek philosopher _____ concluded that individuals differed in their natural endowments.

2. Although Francis Galton's search for a simple intelligence measure failed, he gave us some _____ techniques that we still use, as well as the terms _____ and _____ .

3. The French psychologist who devised a test to predict the success of children in school was _____ . Predictions were made by comparing children's chronological ages with their _____ ages, which were determined by the test. This test _____ (was/was not) designed to measure inborn intelligence; Binet leaned toward an _____ explanation of intelligence.

4. Lewis Terman's revision of Binet's test is referred to as the _____ - _____ . This test enables one to derive a(n) _____ _____ for an individual.

Give the original formula for computing IQ, and explain any items used in the formula.

5. Today's tests compute _____ (IQ/an intelligence test score) by comparing the individual's performance to the average performance of people of _____ (the same/different) age(s). These tests are designed so that a score of _____ is considered average.

6. The misguided movement called _____ proposed measuring human traits and using the results to determine who should be allowed to reproduce.

7. When given intelligence tests in the early 1900s, immigrants arriving in the United States often scored _____ (above/below) average. This is because the tests were based on a particular _____ background.

Objective 8: Distinguish between aptitude and achievement tests, and describe modern tests of mental abilities such as the WAIS.

8. Tests designed to measure what you already have learned are called _____ tests. Tests designed to predict your ability to learn something new are called _____ tests.

9. The most widely used intelligence test is the _____ _____ _____ _____ . Consisting of 11 subtests, it provides not only a general intelligence score but also separate scores for _____ _____ , _____ _____ , _____ _____ , and _____ _____ .

Objective 9: Discuss the importance of standardizing psychological tests, and describe the distribution of scores in a normal curve.

10. One requirement of a good test is the process of defining meaningful scores relative to a pretested comparison group, which is called _____ .

11. When scores on a test are compiled, they generally result in a bell-shaped pattern, or _____ distribution.

Describe the normal curve, and explain its significance in the standardization process.

12. The Stanford-Binet and the Wechsler Scales _____ (are/are not) periodically restandardized, thereby keeping the average score near _____ .

13. During the 1960s and 1970s, college entrance aptitude scores showed a steady _____ (increase/decline). At the same time, intelligence test performance _____ (improved/decreased). This phenomenon is called the _____ _____ .

14. Although the actual cause of this effect is unknown, one explanation is that it is due to improved _____ . The recent performance gains on the WAIS are greatest among people at the lowest _____ levels.

Objective 10: Explain the meanings of reliability and validity in terms of test construction, and describe two types of validity.

15. If a test yields consistent results, it is said to be _____ .

16. When a test is administered more than once to the same people, the psychologist is determining its _____-_____ reliability.

17. When a person's scores for the odd- and even-numbered questions on a test are compared, _____-_____ reliability is being assessed.

18. The Stanford-Binet, WAIS, and WISC have reliabilities of about _____ .

19. The degree to which a test measures or predicts what it is supposed to is referred to as the test's _____ .

20. The degree to which a test measures the behavior it was designed to measure is referred to as the test's _____ _____ .

21. The degree to which a test predicts future performance of a particular behavior, called the test's _____ , is referred to as the test's _____ _____ .

Choose a specific example and use it to illustrate and explain the concept of criterion and its relationship to predictive validity.

22. Generally speaking, the predictive validity of general aptitude tests _____ (is/is not) as high as their reliability. The predictive validity of these tests _____ (increases/diminishes) as individuals move up the educational ladder.

The Dynamics of Intelligence (pp. 539–544)

Objective 11: Describe the stability of intelligence scores over the life span.

1. Some studies have found that infants who quickly become bored when looking at a picture score _____ (higher/lower) on tests of brain speed and intelligence up to 21 years later.

2. Traditional intelligence tests before age _____ predict future aptitudes only modestly.

3. During childhood, the stability of intelligence scores _____ (increases/ decreases) with age. After about age _____ ,

intelligence scores stabilize. A long-term study of mental ability in Scottish children revealed that this _____ (holds/does not hold) through late adulthood.

Objective 12: Describe the two extremes of the normal distribution of intelligence.

4. Individuals whose intelligence scores fall below 70 and who have difficulty adapting to life may be labeled _____ _____ . This label applies to approximately _____ percent of the population.

5. Intellectual disability sometimes has a physical basis, such as _____ _____ , a genetic disorder caused by an extra chromosome.

6. The current view is that children with mild intellectual disability should be integrated, or _____ , into regular classrooms.

7. At the high extreme, Lewis Terman's "gifted children" turned out to be _____ , well-_____ , and unusually successful _____ .

Discuss criticisms of programs that sort children into gifted and nongifted tracks.

Genetic and Environmental Influences on Intelligence (pp. 544–556)

Objective 13: Discuss the evidence for the genetic contribution to individual intelligence, and explain what psychologists mean by the heritability of intelligence.

1. The intelligence scores of identical twins reared together are _____ (more/no more) similar than those of fraternal twins. Brain scans also reveal that identical twins have similar volume to their brain's _____ _____ , and those areas associated with _____ and _____ intelligence.

2. Because intelligence is influenced by many genes, it is said to be _____ .

3. The intelligence test scores of fraternal twins are _____ (more alike/no more alike) than the intelligence test scores of other siblings. This provides evidence of a(n) _____ (genetic/environmental) effect because fraternal twins, being the same _____ , are treated more alike.

4. Studies of adopted children and their adoptive and biological families demonstrate that with age, genetic influences on intelligence become _____ (more/less) apparent. Thus, children's intelligence scores are more like those of their _____ (biological/adoptive) parents than their _____ (biological/adoptive) parents.

5. The amount of variation in a trait within a group that is attributed to genetic factors is called its _____ . For intelligence, this has been estimated at _____ percent.

6. If we know a trait has perfect heritability, this knowledge _____ (does/does not) enable us to rule out environmental factors in explaining differences between groups.

Objective 14: Discuss the evidence for environmental influences on individual intelligence.

7. Studies indicate that neglected children _____ (do/do not) show signs of recovery in intelligence and behavior when placed in more nurturing environments. Although normal brain development can be retarded by _____ , _____ deprivation, and _____ _____ , there is no sure environment that will transform a normal baby into a genius.

8. High-quality programs for disadvantaged children, such as the government-funded

   _____ _____ program, increase children's school readiness; that is, they increase their _____

   _____ , creating better attitudes toward learning.

Objective 15: Describe gender differences in abilities.

9. Girls tend to outscore boys on

   _____ tests and are more

   _____ fluent. They also have an

   edge in _____ and

   _____ objects, in sensation, and in

   _____-detecting ability.

10. Although girls have an edge in math

    _____ , boys score higher in math

    _____ _____ . Boys

    tend to outscore girls on tests of _____

    _____ .

11. Working from an _____ perspective, some theorists speculate that these gender differences in spatial manipulation helped our ancestors survive.

12. There is evidence that spatial abilities are enhanced by high levels of_____

    _____ _____

    during prenatal development.

13. According to many, boys' and girls' interests and abilities are shaped in large part by

    _____ _____

    and divergent opportunities. The mental ability scores of males tend to vary _____ (less/more) than those of females.

Objective 16: Describe ethnic similarities and differences in intelligence test scores, and discuss some genetic and environmental factors that might explain them.

14. Group differences in intelligence scores

    _____ (do/do not) provide an accurate basis for judging individuals. Individual differences within a race are

    _____ (greater than/less than) between-race differences.

Explain why heredity may contribute to individual differences in intelligence but not necessarily contribute to group differences.

15. Under the skin, the races _____ (are/are not) alike. Race _____ (is/is not) a neatly defined biological category.

16. Although Asian students on the average score _____ (higher/lower) than North American students on math tests, this difference may be due to the fact that _____

    _____

    _____ .

17. On an infant intelligence measure (preference for looking at novel stimuli), Black infants score _____ (lower than/higher than/as well as) White infants.

Objective 17: Discuss whether intelligence tests are biased, and describe the stereotype threat phenomenon.

18. In the sense that they detect differences caused by cultural experiences, intelligence tests probably _____ (are/are not) biased.

19. Most psychologists agree that, in terms of predictive validity, the major aptitude tests _____ (are/are not) racially biased.

20. When women and members of ethnic minorities are led to expect that they won't do well on a test, a _____ _____ may result, and their scores may actually be lower.

PROGRESS TEST 1

Multiple-Choice Questions

Circle your answers to the following questions and check them with the answers on page 303. If your answer is incorrect, read the explanation for why it is incorrect and then consult the appropriate pages of the text (in parentheses following the correct answer).

1. Studies of adopted children and their biological and adoptive families demonstrate that with age, genetic influences on intelligence
   a. become more apparent.
   b. become less apparent.
   c. become more difficult to disentangle from environmental influences.
   d. become easier to disentangle from environmental influences.

2. A 6-year-old child has a mental age of 9. The child's IQ is
   a. 96.
   b. 100.
   c. 125.
   d. 150.

3. Which of the following is NOT true?
   a. In math grades, the average girl typically equals or surpasses the average boy.
   b. The gender gap in math and science scores is increasing.
   c. Women are better than men at detecting emotions.
   d. Males score higher than females on tests of spatial abilities.

4. Most psychologists believe that racial gaps in test scores
   a. have been exaggerated when they are, in fact, insignificant.
   b. indicate that intelligence is in large measure inherited.
   c. are in large measure caused by environmental factors.
   d. are increasing.

5. Standardization refers to the process of
   a. determining the accuracy with which a test measures what it is supposed to.
   b. defining meaningful scores relative to a representative pretested group.
   c. determining the consistency of test scores obtained by retesting people.
   d. measuring the success with which a test predicts the behavior it is designed to predict.

6. Down syndrome is normally caused by
   a. an extra chromosome in the person's genetic makeup.
   b. a missing chromosome in the person's genetic makeup.
   c. malnutrition during the first few months of life.
   d. prenatal exposure to an addictive drug.

7. Which of the following is NOT a requirement of a good test?
   a. reliability
   b. standardization
   c. reification
   d. validity

8. First-time parents Geena and Brad want to give their baby's intellectual abilities a jump-start by providing a super enriched learning environment. Experts would suggest that the new parents should
   a. pipe stimulating classical music into the baby's room.
   b. hang colorful mobiles and artwork over the baby's crib.
   c. take the child to one of the new "superbaby" preschools that specialize in infant enrichment.
   d. relax, since there is no surefire environmental recipe for giving a child a superior intellect.

9. Which of the following statements is true?
   a. The predictive validity of intelligence tests is not as high as their reliability.
   b. The reliability of intelligence tests is not as high as their predictive validity.
   c. Modern intelligence tests have extremely high predictive validity and reliability.
   d. The predictive validity and reliability of most intelligence tests is very low.

10. Before about age _____ , intelligence tests generally do not predict future scores.
    a. 1
    b. 3
    c. 5
    d. 10

11. Sorting children into gifted and nongifted educational groups
    a. creates a self-fulfilling prophecy.
    b. increases social isolation between the groups.
    c. promotes racial segregation and prejudice.
    d. has all of these effects.

12. Studies of infants show that babies who quickly become bored with a picture
    a. often develop learning disabilities later on.
    b. score lower on infant intelligence tests.
    c. score higher on intelligence tests many years later.
    d. score very low on intelligence tests many years later.

13. The existence of _____ reinforces the generally accepted notion that intelligence is a multidimensional quality.
    a. adaptive skills
    b. intellectual disability
    c. general intelligence
    d. savant syndrome

14. Which of the following provides the strongest evidence of the role of heredity in determining intelligence?
    a. The IQ scores of identical twins raised separately are more similar than those of fraternal twins raised together.
    b. The intelligence scores of fraternal twins are more similar than those of ordinary siblings.
    c. The intelligence scores of identical twins raised together are more similar than those of identical twins raised apart.
    d. The intelligence scores of adopted children show relatively weak correlations with scores of adoptive as well as biological parents.

15. Current estimates are that _____ percent of the total variation among intelligence scores can be attributed to genetic factors.
    a. less than 10
    b. approximately 25
    c. about 50
    d. 75 and over

16. Since 1910, college aptitude test scores have _____ and WAIS scores have _____ .
    a. declined; remained stable
    b. remained stable; declined
    c. risen; declined
    d. declined; risen

17. The bell-shaped distribution of intelligence scores in the general population is called a
    a. *g* distribution.
    b. standardization curve.
    c. bimodal distribution.
    d. normal curve.

18. Research on the effectiveness of Head Start suggests that enrichment programs
    a. produce permanent gains in intelligence scores.
    b. improve school readiness and may provide a small boost to emotional intelligence.
    c. improve intelligence scores but not school readiness.
    d. produce temporary gains in intelligence scores.

Matching Items

Match each term with its definition or description.

Terms

_____ 1. intelligence test score
_____ 2. *g*
_____ 3. eugenics
_____ 4. savant syndrome
_____ 5. factor analysis
_____ 6. aptitude test
_____ 7. achievement test
_____ 8. Stanford-Binet
_____ 9. criterion
_____ 10. content validity
_____ 11. reliability

Definitions or Descriptions

a. a test designed to predict a person's ability to learn something new
b. a test designed to measure current knowledge
c. the consistency with which a test measures performance
d. the degree to which a test measures what it is designed to measure
e. Terman's revision of Binet's original intelligence test
f. the behavior that a test is designed to predict
g. an underlying, general intelligence factor
h. a person's score on an intelligence test based on performance relative to the average performance of people the same age
i. a very low intelligence score accompanied by one extraordinary skill
j. a program for the selective breeding of the most intelligent individuals
k. a statistical technique that identifies related items on a test

PROGRESS TEST 2

Progress Test 2 should be completed during a final unit review. Answer the following questions after you thoroughly understand the correct answers for the section reviews and Progress Test 1.

Multiple-Choice Questions

1. The test created by Alfred Binet was designed specifically to
   a. measure inborn intelligence in adults.
   b. measure inborn intelligence in children.
   c. predict school performance in children.
   d. identify mentally retarded children so that they could be institutionalized.

2. Which of the following provides the strongest evidence of environment's role in intelligence?
   a. Adopted children's intelligence scores are more like their adoptive parents' scores than their biological parents'.
   b. Children's intelligence scores are more strongly related to their mothers' scores than to their fathers'.
   c. Children moved from a deprived environment into an intellectually enriched one show gains in intellectual development.
   d. The intelligence scores of identical twins raised separately are no more alike than those of siblings.

3. If a test designed to indicate which applicants are likely to perform the best on the job fails to do so, the test has
   a. low reliability.
   b. low content validity.
   c. low predictive validity.
   d. not been standardized.

4. By creating a label such as "gifted," we begin to act as if all children are naturally divided into two categories, gifted and nongifted. This logical error is referred to as
   a. rationalization.
   b. nominalizing.
   c. factor analysis.
   d. reification.

5. The formula for the intelligence quotient was devised by
   a. Sternberg.   c. Terman.
   b. Binet.   d. Stern.

6. Current intelligence tests compute an individual's intelligence score as
   a. the ratio of mental age to chronological age multiplied by 100.
   b. the ratio of chronological age to mental age multiplied by 100.
   c. the amount by which the test-taker's performance deviates from the average performance of others the same age.
   d. the ratio of the test-taker's verbal intelligence score to his or her nonverbal intelligence score.

7. J. McVicker Hunt found that institutionalized children given "tutored human enrichment"
   a. showed no change in intelligence test performance compared with institutionalized children who did not receive such enrichment.
   b. responded so negatively as a result of their impoverished early experiences that he felt it necessary to disband the program.
   c. thrived intellectually and socially on the benefits of positive caregiving.
   d. actually developed greater intelligence than control subjects who had lived in foster homes since birth.

8. The concept of a *g* factor implies that intelligence
   a. is a single overall ability.
   b. is several specific abilities.
   c. cannot be defined or measured.
   d. is a reified concept.

9. Gerardeen has superb social skills, manages conflicts well, and has great empathy for her friends and co-workers. John Mayer, Peter Salovey, and David Caruso would probably say that Gerardeen possesses a high degree of
   a. *g.*
   b. social intelligence.
   c. practical intelligence.
   d. emotional intelligence.

10. By what age does a child's performance on an intelligence test stabilize?
    a. 2   c. 6
    b. 3   d. 7

11. The Flynn effect refers to the fact that
  a. White and Black infants score equally well on measures of infant intelligence.
  b. Asian students outperform North American students on math achievement tests.
  c. The IQ scores of today's better-fed and educated population exceed that of the 1930s population.
  d. Individual differences within a race are much greater than between-race differences.

12. In his study of children with high intelligence scores, Terman found that
  a. the children were more emotional and less healthy than a control group.
  b. the children were ostracized by classmates.
  c. the children were healthy and well-adjusted, and did well academically.
  d. later, as adults, they nearly all achieved great vocational success.

13. When highly skilled people are performing a task, their brains
  a. retrieve information from memory more quickly.
  b. register simple stimuli more quickly.
  c. demonstrate a more complex brain-wave response to stimuli.
  d. do all of these things.

14. Most experts view intelligence as a person's
  a. ability to perform well on intelligence tests.
  b. innate mental capacity.
  c. ability to learn from experience, solve problems, and adapt to new situations.
  d. diverse skills acquired throughout life.

15. Which of the following statements is true?
  a. About 1 percent of the population is intellectually disabled.
  b. More males than females are intellectually disabled.
  c. A majority of the intellectually disabled can learn academic skills.
  d. All of these statements are true.

16. Prenatal hormones have an influence on
  a. verbal reasoning.
  b. spatial abilities.
  c. overall intelligence.
  d. emotional perception.

17. Which of the following is NOT cited as evidence of the reciprocal relationship between schooling and intelligence?

  a. Neither education level nor intelligence scores accurately predict income.
  b. Intelligence scores tend to rise during the school year.
  c. High school graduates have higher intelligence scores than do those who drop out early.
  d. High intelligence scores correlate with prolonged schooling.

18. Originally, IQ was defined as
  a. mental age divided by chronological age and multiplied by 100.
  b. chronological age divided by mental age and multiplied by 100.
  c. mental age subtracted from chronological age and multiplied by 100.
  d. chronological age subtracted from mental age and multiplied by 100.

19. Tests of _____ measure what an individual can do now, whereas tests of _____ predict what an individual will be able to do later.
  a. aptitude; achievement
  b. achievement; aptitude
  c. reliability; validity
  d. validity; reliability

20. Which of the following statements most accurately reflects the text's position regarding the relative contribution of genes and environment in determining intelligence?
  a. Except in cases of a neglectful early environment, each individual's basic intelligence is largely the product of heredity.
  b. Except in those with genetic disorders such as Down syndrome, intelligence results primarily from environmental experiences.
  c. Both genes and life experiences significantly influence performance on intelligence tests.
  d. Because intelligence tests have such low predictive validity, the question cannot be addressed until psychologists agree on a more valid test of intelligence.

True–False Items

Indicate whether each statement is true or false by placing *T* or *F* in the blank next to the item.

_____ **1.** In the current version of the Stanford-Binet intelligence test, one's performance is compared only with the performance of others the same age.

_____ 2. Intelligence scores in the United States have been dropping over the past 50 years.

_____ 3. Most of the major aptitude tests have higher validity than reliability.

_____ 4. People with high intelligence scores tend to process sensory information more quickly.

_____ 5. The gap in intelligence scores between Black and White children is increasing.

_____ 6. The intelligence scores of adopted children are more similar to those of their adoptive parents than their biological parents.

_____ 7. The consensus among psychologists is that most intelligence tests are extremely biased.

_____ 8. Most psychologists agree that intelligence is mainly determined by heredity.

_____ 9. The Stanford-Binet test and the Wechsler scales are periodically restandardized.

_____ 10. The variation in intelligence scores within a racial group is much larger than that between racial groups.

_____ 11. Telling students they are unlikely to succeed often erodes their performance on aptitude tests.

PSYCHOLOGY APPLIED

Answer these questions the day before a test as a final check on your understanding of the unit's terms and concepts.

Multiple-Choice Questions

1. To say that the heritability of a trait is approximately 50 percent means
   a. that genes are responsible for 50 percent of the trait in an individual, and the environment is responsible for the rest.
   b. that the trait's appearance in a person will reflect approximately equal genetic contributions from both parents.
   c. that of the variation in the trait within a group of people, 50 percent can be attributed to heredity.
   d. all of these things.

2. Twenty-two-year-old Dan has an intelligence score of 63 and the academic skills of a fourth-grader, and he is unable to live independently. Dan PROBABLY
   a. has Down syndrome.
   b. has savant syndrome.
   c. is intellectually disabled.
   d. will eventually achieve self-supporting social and vocational skills.

3. At age 16, Angel's intelligence score was 110. What will her score probably be at age 32?
   a. 125
   b. 110
   c. 115
   d. There is no basis for predicting an individual's future IQ.

4. A school psychologist found that 85 percent of those who scored above 115 on an aptitude test were A students and 75 percent of those who scored below 85 on the test were D students. The psychologist concluded that the test had high
   a. content validity because scores on it correlated highly with the criterion behavior.
   b. predictive validity because scores on it correlated highly with the criterion behavior.
   c. content validity because scores on it correlated highly with the target behavior.
   d. predictive validity because scores on it correlated highly with the target behavior.

5. Benito was born in 1937. In 1947, he scored 130 on an intelligence test. What was Benito's mental age when he took the test?
   a. 9   c. 11
   b. 10   d. 13

6. Melvin has been diagnosed as having savant syndrome, which means that he
   a. has an IQ of 120 or higher.
   b. would score high on a test of analytical intelligence.
   c. is limited in mental ability but has one exceptional ability.
   d. was exposed to high levels of testosterone during prenatal development.

7. The contribution of environmental factors to racial gaps in intelligence scores is indicated by
   a. evidence that individual differences within a race are much greater than differences between races.
   b. evidence that White and Black infants score equally well on certain measures of infant intelligence.
   c. the fact that Asian students outperform North American students on math achievement and aptitude tests.
   d. all of this evidence.

8. Hiroko's math achievement score is considerably higher than that of most American students her age. Which of the following is true regarding this difference between Asian and North American students?
   a. It is not a recent phenomenon.
   b. It may be due to the fact that Asian students have a longer school year.
   c. It holds only for girls.
   d. It holds only for boys.

9. Jack takes the same test of mechanical reasoning on several different days and gets virtually identical scores. This suggests that the test has
   a. high content validity.
   b. high reliability.
   c. high predictive validity.
   d. been standardized.

10. You would not use a test of hearing acuity as an intelligence test because it would lack
    a. content reliability.
    b. predictive reliability.
    c. predictive validity.
    d. content validity.

11. Before becoming attorneys, law students must pass a special licensing exam, which is an _____ test. Before entering college, high school students must take the SAT, which is an _____ test.
    a. achievement; aptitude
    b. aptitude; achievement
    c. achievement; achievement
    d. aptitude; aptitude

12. If you compare the same trait in people of similar heredity who live in very different environments, heritability for that trait will be _____ ; heritability for the trait is most likely to be _____ among people of very different heredities who live in similar environments.
    a. low; high
    b. high; low
    c. environmental; genetic
    d. genetic; environmental

13. A psychologist who is looking at a student's intelligence score finds a jump of 30 points between the earliest score at age 2 and the most recent at age 17. The psychologist's knowledge of testing would probably lead her to conclude that such a jump
    a. indicates that different tests were used, creating an apparent change in intelligence level, although it actually remained stable.
    b. signals a significant improvement in the child's environment over this period.
    c. is unsurprising, since intelligence scores do not become stable until late adolescence.
    d. is mainly the result of the age at which the first test was taken.

14. If you wanted to develop a test of musical aptitude in North American children, which would be the appropriate standardization group?
    a. children all over the world
    b. North American children
    c. children of musical parents
    d. children with known musical ability

15. Don's intelligence scores were only average, but he has been enormously successful as a corporate manager. Psychologists Sternberg and Wagner would probably suggest that
    a. Don's verbal intelligence exceeds his performance intelligence.
    b. Don's performance intelligence exceeds his verbal intelligence.
    c. Don's academic intelligence exceeds his practical intelligence.
    d. Don's practical intelligence exceeds his academic intelligence.

16. According to the text, what can be concluded from early intelligence testing in the United States?
    a. Most European immigrants were "feeble-minded."
    b. Army recruits of other than West European heritage were intellectually deficient.

c. The tests were biased against people who did not share the culture assumed by the test.

d. None of these things could be concluded.

17. If asked to guess the intelligence score of a stranger, your best guess would be
    a. 75.
    b. 100.
    c. 125.
    d. "I don't know, intelligence scores vary too widely."

18. Which of the following is true of people who score high on aptitude tests?
    a. They achieve greater career success.
    b. They are likely to be happier.
    c. They always do well in school.
    d. None of these statements are true.

Essay Question

You have been asked to devise a Psychology Achievement Test (PAT) that will be administered to freshmen who declare psychology as their major. What steps will you take to ensure that the PAT is a good intelligence test? (Use the space below to list the points you want to make, and organize them. Then write the essay on a separate sheet of paper.)

KEY TERMS

Using your own words, write on a separate piece of paper a brief definition or explanation of each of the following terms.

1. intelligence test
2. intelligence
3. general intelligence (*g*)
4. factor analysis
5. savant syndrome

6. emotional intelligence
7. mental age
8. Stanford-Binet
9. intelligence quotient (IQ)
10. achievement tests
11. aptitude tests
12. Wechsler Adult Intelligence Scale (WAIS)
13. standardization
14. normal curve (normal distribution)
15. reliability
16. validity
17. content validity
18. predictive validity
19. intellectual disability
20. Down syndrome
21. stereotype threat

ANSWERS

Unit Review

What Is Intelligence?

1. do not
2. reification; intelligence test
3. socially
4. a mental quality consisting of the ability to learn from experience, solve problems, and use knowledge to adapt to new situations
5. overall (general); specific
6. factor analysis
7. general intelligence
8. L. L. Thurstone; primary mental abilities
9. novel problems
10. savant syndrome
11. multiple intelligences; do
12. triarchic; analytical (academic problem solving); practical; creative
13. emotional intelligence; perceive; understand; manage; use
14. recognize; predict; express; adaptive

Emotionally intelligent people are self-aware. They can manage their emotions and they can delay gratification. They handle others' emotions skillfully. They also exhibit modestly better job performance.

15. emotional

16. did not

17. volume; MRI; more; genes; environmental stimulation

18. parietal; mathematical; spatial

19. synapses; plasticity; gray matter; memory; attention; language

20. frontal lobe; left; on both sides of the brain; verbal

21. faster

22. quickly; complexity

Assessing Intelligence

1. Plato

2. statistical; nature; nurture

3. Alfred Binet; mental; was not; environmental

4. Stanford-Binet; intelligence quotient

In the original formula for IQ, measured mental age is divided by chronological age and multiplied by 100. "Mental age" refers to the chronological age that most typically corresponds to a given level of performance.

5. an intelligence test score; the same; 100

6. eugenics

7. below; cultural

8. achievement; aptitude

9. Wechsler Adult Intelligence Scale; verbal comprehension; perceptual organization; working memory; processing speed

10. standardization

11. normal

The normal curve describes the distribution of many physical phenomena and psychological attributes (including intelligence test scores), with most scores falling near the average and fewer near the extremes. When a test is standardized on a normal curve, individual scores are assigned according to how much they deviate above or below the distribution's average.

12. are; 100

13. decline; improved; Flynn effect

14. nutrition; economic

15. reliable

16. test-retest

17. split-half

18. +.9

19. validity

20. content validity

21. criterion; predictive validity

The criterion is the particular behavior a predictive test, such as an aptitude test, is intended to predict. For example, performance in a relevant job situation would be the criterion for a test measuring managerial aptitude. The criterion determines whether a test has predictive validity. For example, the on-the-job success of those who do well on a job aptitude test would indicate the test has predictive validity.

22. is not; diminishes

The Dynamics of Intelligence

1. higher

2. 3

3. increases; 7; holds

4. intellectually disabled; 1

5. Down syndrome

6. mainstreamed

7. healthy; adjusted; academically

Critics of ability tracking contend that it sometimes creates self-fulfilling prophecies and that it promotes racial segregation and prejudice. Denying lower-ability students opportunities for enriched education widens the achievement gap between ability groups.

Genetic and Environmental Influences on Intelligence

1. more; gray matter; verbal; spatial

2. polygenetic

3. more alike; environmental; age

4. more; biological; adoptive

5. heritability; 50

6. does not

7. do; malnutrition; sensory; social isolation

8. Head Start; emotional intelligence

9. spelling; verbally; remembering; locating; emotion

10. computation; problem solving; mental rotation

11. evolutionary

12. male sex hormones

13. social expectations; more

14. do not; greater than

Because of the impact of environmental factors such as education and nutrition on intelligence test performance, even if the heritability of intelligence is high within a particular group, differences in intelligence among groups may be environmentally caused. One group may, for example, thrive in an enriched environment while another of the same genetic predisposition may falter in an impoverished one.

15. are; is not

16. higher; Asian students have a longer school year and spend more time studying math

17. as well as

18. are

19. are not

20. stereotype threat

Progress Test 1

Multiple-Choice Questions

1. **a.** is the answer. (p. 545)

   c. & d. Separating genetic from environmental influences is difficult *at any age.*

2. **d.** is the answer. If we divide 9, the measured mental age, by 6, the chronological age, and multiply the result by 100, we obtain 150. (p. 534)

3. **b.** is the answer. As social expectations have changed, the gender gap in math and science scores is narrowing. (p. 551)

4. **c.** is the answer. (pp. 552–553)

   a. On the contrary, many *group* differences are highly significant, even though they tell us nothing about specific *individuals.*

   b. Although heredity contributes to individual differences in intelligence, it does not necessarily contribute to group differences.

   d. In fact, the difference has diminished somewhat in recent years.

5. **b.** is the answer. (p. 536)

   a. This answer refers to a test's content validity.

   c. This answer refers to test-retest reliability.

   d. This answer refers to predictive validity.

6. **a.** is the answer. (p. 542)

   b. Down syndrome is normally caused by an extra, rather than a missing, chromosome.

   c. & d. Down syndrome is a genetic disorder that is manifest during the earliest stages of prenatal development, well before malnutrition and exposure to drugs would produce their harmful effects on the developing fetus.

7. **c.** is the answer. Reification is a reasoning error, in which an abstract concept such as IQ is regarded as though it were real. (pp. 524, 536–538)

8. **d.** is the answer. (p. 547)

9. **a.** is the answer. (p. 538)

   c. & d. Most modern tests have high reliabilities of about +.9; their validity scores are much lower.

10. **b.** is the answer. (p. 540)

11. **d.** is the answer. (p. 543)

12. **c.** is the answer. (p. 540)

13. **d.** is the answer. That people with savant syndrome excel in one area but are intellectually disabled in others suggests that there are multiple intelligences. (p. 525)

    a. The ability to adapt defines the capacity we call intelligence.

    b. Intellectual disability is at the lower end of the range of human intelligence.

    c. A general intelligence factor was hypothesized by Spearman to underlie each specific factor of intelligent behavior, but its existence is controversial and remains to be proved.

14. **a.** is the answer. Identical twins who live apart have the same genetic makeup but different environments; if their scores are similar, this is evidence for the role of heredity. (p. 544)

    b. Because fraternal twins are no more genetically alike than ordinary siblings, this could not provide evidence for the role of heredity.

    c. That twins raised together have more similar scores than twins raised apart provides evidence for the role of the environment.

    d. As both sets of correlations are weak, little evidence is provided either for or against the role of heredity.

15. **c.** is the answer. (p. 546)

16. **d.** is the answer. College aptitude tests are complex tests that are not periodically restandardized. The WAIS, a more basic test that is periodically restandardized so that the average is always 100, also reflects the performance of a more diverse group. (p. 537)

17. **d.** is the answer. (p. 537)

    a. *g* is Spearman's term for "general intelligence"; there is no such thing as a "*g* distribution."

    b. There is no such thing.

    c. A bimodal distribution is one having two (bi-) modes, or averages. The normal distribution has only one mode.

18. **b.** is the answer. Enrichment programs do improve school readiness, create better attitudes toward learning, and reduce school dropouts and criminality. (p. 548)

Matching Items

1. h (p. 534)	5. k (p. 524)	9. f (p. 538)
2. g (p. 524)	6. a (p. 535)	10. d (p. 538)
3. j (p. 534)	7. b (p. 536)	11. c (p. 538)
4. i (p. 525)	8. e (p. 534)	

Progress Test 2

Multiple-Choice Questions

1. **c.** is the answer. French compulsory education laws brought more children into the school system, and the government didn't want to rely on teachers' subjective judgments to determine which children would require special help. (p. 533)
   a. & b. Binet's test was intended for children, and Binet specifically rejected the idea that his test measured inborn intelligence, which is an abstract capacity that cannot be quantified.
   d. This was not a purpose of the test, which dealt with children in the school system.

2. **c.** is the answer. (p. 547)
   a., b., & d. None of these is true.

3. **c.** is the answer. Predictive validity is the extent to which tests predict what they are intended to predict. (p. 538)
   a. Reliability is the consistency with which a test samples the particular behavior of interest.
   b. Content validity is the degree to which a test measures what it is designed to measure.
   d. Standardization is the process of defining meaningful test scores based on the performance of a representative group.

4. **d.** is the answer. Reification is the error of creating a concept and then assuming the created concept has a concrete reality. (p. 524)
   a. To rationalize is to develop self-satisfying explanations of one's behavior.
   b. The term "nominalizing" has no relevance to psychology.
   c. Factor analysis is a statistical procedure that identifies clusters of related items, or factors, on a test.

5. **d.** is the answer. (p. 534)

6. **c.** is the answer. (p. 534)
   a. This is William Stern's original formula for the intelligence quotient.
   b. & d. Neither of these formulas is used to compute the score on current intelligence tests.

7. **c.** is the answer. Enrichment led to dramatic results and thereby testified to the importance of environmental factors. (p. 547)
   a. & d. The study involved neither intelligence tests nor comparisons with control groups.
   b. The children showed a dramatic positive response.

8. **a.** is the answer. (p. 524)

9. **d.** is the answer. (p. 528)
   a. The concept of general intelligence pertains more to academic skills.
   b. Although emotional intelligence *is* a key component of social intelligence, Salovey and Mayer coined the newer term "emotional intelligence" to refer to skills such as Gerardeen's.
   c. Practical intelligence is that which is required for everyday tasks, not all of which involve emotions.

10. **d.** is the answer. Intelligence test performances begin to become predictive at about age 4 and become stable by about age 7. (p. 548)

11. **c.** is the answer. (p. 537)

12. **c.** is the answer. (p. 543)
    a. & b. There was no evidence of either in the individuals studied by Terman.
    d. Vocational success in adulthood varied.

13. **d.** is the answer. (pp. 530–531)

14. **c.** is the answer. (p. 524)
    a. Performance ability and intellectual ability are separate traits.
    b. This has been argued by some, but certainly not most, experts.
    d. Although many experts believe that there are multiple intelligences, this would not be the same thing as diverse acquired skills.

15. **d.** is the answer. (p. 543)

16. **b.** is the answer. (p. 550)

17. **a.** is the answer. Both schooling and intelligence enhance later income. (p. 548)

18. **a.** is the answer. (p. 534)

19. **b.** is the answer. (p. 535)
    c. & d. Reliability and validity are characteristics of good tests.

20. **c.** is the answer. (p. 548)
    a. & b. Studies of twins, family members, and adopted children point to a significant hereditary contribution to intelligence scores. These same studies, plus others comparing children reared in neglectful or enriched environments, indicate that life experiences also significantly influence test performance.
    d. Although the issue of how intelligence should be defined is controversial, intelligence tests generally have predictive validity, especially in the early years.

True–False Items

1. T (p. 534)   6. F (p. 545)   11. T (p. 555)
2. F (p. 537)   7. F (p. 556)
3. F (p. 538)   8. F (p. 548)
4. T (p. 531)   9. T (p. 537)
5. F (p. 532)   10. T (p. 553)

Psychology Applied

Multiple-Choice Questions

1. **c.** is the answer. Heritability is a measure of the extent to which a trait's variation within a group of people can be attributed to heredity. (p. 546)
   a. & b. Heritability is *not* a measure of how much of an *individual's* behavior is inherited, nor of the relative contribution of genes from that person's mother and father. Further, the heritability of any trait depends on the context, or environment, in which that trait is being studied.

2. **c.** is the answer. To be labeled intellectually disabled a person must have a test score below 70 and experience difficulty adapting to the normal demands of living independently. (p. 542)
   a. Down syndrome is a common cause of *severe* intellectual disability; Dan's test score places him in the range of mild disability.
   b. There is no indication that Dan possesses one extraordinary skill, as do people with savant syndrome.
   d. The text does not suggest that people with intellectual disability eventually become self-supporting.

3. **b.** is the answer. Intelligence scores become quite stable during adolescence. (p. 534)

4. **b.** is the answer. (p. 538)
   a., c., & d. Content validity is the degree to which a test measures what it claims to measure. Furthermore, "target behavior" is not a term used by intelligence researchers.

5. **d.** is the answer. At the time he took the test, Benito's chronological age (CA) was 10. Knowing that IQ = 130 and CA = 10, solving the equation for mental age yields a value of 13. (p. 534)

6. **c.** is the answer. People with savant syndrome tend to score low on intelligence tests but have one exceptional ability. (p. 525)

7. **d.** is the answer. These reasons, along with other historical and cross-cultural reasons, all argue for the role of environment in creating and perpetuating the gap. (pp. 552–553)

8. **b.** is the answer. (p. 553)
   a. It is a recent phenomenon.
   c. The gap is found in both girls and boys.

9. **b.** is the answer. (p. 538)

10. **d.** is the answer. Because the hearing acuity test would in no way sample behaviors relevant to intelligence, it would not have content validity as a test of intelligence. (p. 538)
    a. & b. There is no such thing as content reliability or predictive reliability.
    c. There is nothing to indicate that, used to test hearing, this test would lack predictive validity.

11. **a.** is the answer. An exam for a professional license is intended to measure whether you have gained the overall knowledge and skill to practice the profession. The SAT is designed to predict ability, or aptitude, for learning a new skill. (p. 535)

12. **a.** is the answer. If everyone has nearly the same heredity, then heritability—the variation in a trait attributed to heredity—must be low. If individuals within a group come from very similar environments, environmental differences cannot account for variation in a trait; heritability, therefore, must be high. (p. 546)

13. **d.** is the answer. It is not until after age 4 that intelligence-test performance begins to predict adult scores. (p. 540)
    a. Such a conclusion is unlikely, given the high validity of the commonly used intelligence tests.
    b. No such conclusion is possible, because intelligence-test performance before age 4 does not predict later aptitude.
    c. Stability in intelligence scores is generally established by age 7—long before adulthood.

14. **b.** is the answer. A standardization group provides a representative comparison for the trait being measured by a test. Because this test will measure musical aptitude in North American children, the standardization group should be limited to North American children but should include children of all degrees of musical aptitude. (p. 536)

15. **d.** is the answer. Sternberg and Wagner distinguish among *academic* intelligence, as measured by intelligence tests; *practical* intelligence, which is involved in everyday life and tasks, such as managerial work; and *creative* intelligence. (p. 527)
    a. & b. Verbal and performance intelligence are both measured by standard intelligence tests such as the WAIS and would be included in Sternberg and Wagner's academic intelligence.

c. Academic intelligence refers to skills assessed by intelligence tests; practical intelligence applies to skills required for everyday tasks and, often, for occupational success.

16. **c.** is the answer. (p. 534)
    a. & b. Although at the time the tests were administered some individuals reached these conclusions, they were, of course, misled.

17. **b.** is the answer. Modern intelligence tests are periodically restandardized so that the average remains near 100. (p. 537)

18. **d.** is the answer. As we move up the educational ladder, the predictive validity of aptitude tests diminishes. The narrower the range, the less predictive the test. Also, intelligence tests have nothing to do with happiness. (pp. 538–539)

Essay Question

The first step in constructing the test is to create a valid set of questions that measure psychological knowledge and therefore give the test content validity. If your objective is to predict students' future achievement in psychology courses, the test questions should be selected to measure a criterion, such as information faculty members expect all psychology majors to master before they graduate.

To enable meaningful comparisons, the test must be standardized. That is, the test should be administered to a representative sample of incoming freshmen at the time they declare psychology to be their major. From the scores of your pretested sample you will then be able to assign an average score and evaluate any individual score according to how much it deviates above or below the average.

To check your test's reliability you might retest a sample of people using the same test or another version of it. If the two scores are correlated, your test is reliable. Alternatively, you might split the test in half and determine whether scores on the two halves are correlated.

Key Terms

1. **Intelligence tests** measure people's mental aptitudes and compare them with those of others, using numerical scores. (p. 524)

2. Most experts define **intelligence** as a mental quality consisting of the ability to learn from experience, solve problems, and use knowledge to adapt to new situations. (p. 524)

3. **General intelligence (g)**, according to Spearman and others, is a general intelligence factor that underlies each of the more specific mental abilities identified through factor analysis. (p. 524)

4. **Factor analysis** is a statistical procedure that identifies factors, or clusters of related items, that seem to define a common ability. Using this procedure, psychologists have identified several clusters, including verbal intelligence, spatial ability, and reasoning ability factors. (p. 524)

5. A person with **savant syndrome** has a very low intelligence score, yet possesses one exceptional ability, for example, in music or drawing. (p. 525)

6. **Emotional intelligence** is the ability to perceive, manage, understand, and use emotions. (p. 528)

7. A concept introduced by Binet, **mental age** is the chronological age that most typically corresponds to a given level of performance. (p. 533)

8. The **Stanford-Binet** is Lewis Terman's widely used revision of Binet's original intelligence test. (p. 534)

9. The **intelligence quotient (IQ)** was defined originally as the ratio of mental age to chronological age multiplied by 100. Contemporary tests of intelligence assign a score of 100 to the average performance for a given age and define other scores as deviations from this average. (p. 534)

10. **Achievement tests** measure a person's current knowledge. (p. 535)

11. **Aptitude tests** are designed to predict future performance. They measure your capacity to learn new information, rather than measuring what you already know. (p. 535)

12. The **Wechsler Adult Intelligence Scale (WAIS)** is the most widely used intelligence test. It is individually administered, contains 11 subtests, and yields separate verbal and performance intelligence scores, as well as an overall intelligence score. (p. 535)

13. **Standardization** is the process of defining meaningful scores by comparison with a pretested standardization group. (p. 536)

14. The **normal curve** is a bell-shaped curve that represents the distribution (frequency of occurrence) of many physical and psychological attributes. The curve is symmetrical, with most scores near the average and fewer near the extremes. (p. 536)

15. **Reliability** is the extent to which a test produces consistent results. (p. 538)

16. **Validity** is the degree to which a test measures or predicts what it is supposed to. (p. 538)

17. The **content validity** of a test is the extent to which it samples the behavior that is of interest. (p. 538)

18. **Predictive validity** is the extent to which a test predicts the behavior it is designed to predict; also called *criterion-related validity*. (p. 538)

19. The two criteria that designate **intellectual disability** (formerly called *mental retardation*) are an IQ below 70 and difficulty adapting to the normal demands of independent living. (p. 542)

20. A common cause of severe retardation and associated physical disorders, **Down syndrome** is usually the result of an extra chromosome in the person's genetic makeup. (p. 542)

21. **Stereotype threat** is the phenomenon in which a person's concern that he or she will be evaluated based on a negative stereotype (as on an aptitude test, for example) is actually followed by lower performance. (p. 555)

Abnormal Psychology

UNIT OVERVIEW

Although there is no clear-cut line between normal and abnormal behavior, we can characterize as abnormal those behaviors that are deviant, distressful, and dysfunctional. Unit 12 discusses types of anxiety disorders, somatoform disorders, dissociative disorders, mood disorders, schizophrenia, and personality disorders, as classified by the *Diagnostic and Statistical Manual of Mental Disorders* (DSM-IV-TR). Although this classification system follows a medical model, in which disorders are viewed as illnesses, the unit discusses psychological as well as physiological factors, as advocated by the current biopsychosocial approach. Thus, psychoanalytic theory, learning theory, social-cognitive theory, and other psychological perspectives are drawn on when relevant. The unit concludes with a discussion of the incidence of serious psychological disorders in society today.

Your major task in this chapter is to learn about psychological disorders, their various subtypes and characteristics, and their possible causes. Since the material to be learned is extensive, it may be helpful to rehearse it by mentally completing the Unit Review several times.

NOTE: Answer guidelines for all Unit 12 questions begin on page 324.

UNIT REVIEW

First, skim each section, noting headings and boldface items. After you have read the section, review each objective by answering the fill-in and essay-type questions that follow it. As you proceed, evaluate your performance by consulting the answers beginning on page 324. Do not continue with the next section until you understand each answer. If you need to, review or reread the section in the textbook before continuing.

Perspectives on Psychological Disorders
(pp. 562–569)

Objective 1: Identify the criteria for judging whether behavior is psychologically disordered, and discuss the controversy over the diagnosis of attention-deficit hyperactivity disorder.

1. Mental health workers label thoughts, feelings, and actions disordered when they are

   _____ , _____ ,

   and _____ .

2. This definition emphasizes that standards of acceptability for behavior are

   _____ (constant/variable).

3. (Thinking Critically) ADHD, or

   _____-_____

   _____ _____ ,

   plagues children who display one or more of three key symptoms:

   _____ , _____ ,

   and _____ .

4. (Thinking Critically) ADHD is diagnosed more often in _____
   (boys/girls). In the past three decades, the proportion of American children being treated for this disorder _____
   (increased/decreased) dramatically. Experts _____ (agree/do not agree) that ADHD is a real disorder.

5. (Thinking Critically) ADHD _____
   (is/is not) thought by some to be heritable, and it _____ (is/is not) caused by eating too much sugar or poor schools.

ADHD is often accompanied by a _____ disorder or with behavior that is _____ or temper-prone.

Objective 2: Contrast the medical model of psychological disorders with the biopsychosocial approach to disordered behavior.

6. The view that psychological disorders are sicknesses is the basis of the _____ model. According to this view, psychological disorders are viewed as mental _____, or _____, diagnosed on the basis of _____ and cured through _____.

7. One of the first reformers to advocate this position and call for providing more humane living conditions for the mentally ill was

   _____.

8. Today's psychologists recognize that all behavior arises from the interaction of _____ and _____. To presume that a person is "mentally ill" attributes the condition solely to an _____ problem.

9. Major psychological disorders such as _____ and _____ are universal; others, such as _____ _____ and _____ _____, are culture-bound. These culture-bound disorders may share an underlying _____, such as _____, yet differ in their _____.

10. Most mental health workers today take a _____ approach, whereby they assume that disorders are influenced by

    _____ _____ and _____ _____, inner _____ _____, and _____ and _____ circumstances.

Objective 3: Describe the goals and content of the DSM-IV-TR, and discuss the potential dangers and benefits of using diagnostic labels.

11. The most widely used system for classifying psychological disorders is the American Psychiatric Association manual, commonly known by its abbreviation, _____. It was developed in coordination with the World Health Organization's _____ _____ of _____. This manual _____ (does/does not) explain the cause of a disorder; rather, it _____ the disorder.

12. Independent diagnoses made with the current manual generally _____ (show/do not show) agreement.

13. One criticism of DSM-IV is that as the number of disorder categories has _____ (increased/decreased), and the number of adults who meet the criteria for at least one psychiatric ailment has _____ (increased/decreased).

(Close-Up) Briefly describe the "unDSM."

14. Studies have shown that labeling has _____ (little/a significant) effect on our interpretation of individuals and their behavior.

Outline the pros and cons of labeling psychological disorders.

15. (Thinking Critically) Most people with psychological disorders _____ (are/are not) violent. A 1999 study found that 16 percent of U.S. prison inmates had severe

    _____ _____.

Anxiety Disorders (pp. 569–576)

Objective 4: Define *anxiety disorders,* and contrast the symptoms of generalized anxiety disorder and panic disorder.

1. Anxiety disorders are psychological disorders characterized by _____

_____ .

2. Five anxiety disorders discussed in the text are

_____ _____

_____ , _____

_____ , _____ ,

_____-_____

_____ , and _____-

_____ _____

_____ .

3. When a person is continually tense, apprehensive, and physiologically aroused for no apparent reason, he or she is diagnosed as suffering from a

_____ _____

disorder. In Freud's term, the anxiety is

_____-_____ .

4. Generalized anxiety disorder can lead to physical problems, such as _____

_____ _____ .

In some instances, anxiety may intensify dramatically and unpredictably and be accompanied by heart palpitations or choking, for example; people with these symptoms are said to have

_____ _____ . This anxiety may escalate into a minutes-long episode of intense fear, or a _____

_____ .

5. People who _____ have an increased risk of a first-time _____

_____ because _____ is a stimulant.

Objective 5: Explain how a phobia differs from the fears we all experience.

6. When a person has an irrational fear of a specific object, activity, or situation, the diagnosis is a _____ . Although in many situations, the person can live with the problem, some

_____ _____ , such as a fear of thunderstorms, are incapacitating.

7. When a person has an intense fear of being scrutinized by others, the diagnosis is a

_____ _____ .

People who fear situations in which escape or help might not be possible when panic strikes suffer from _____ .

Objective 6: Describe the symptoms of obsessive-compulsive disorder.

8. When a person cannot control repetitive thoughts and actions, an _____-

_____ disorder is diagnosed.

9. Older people are _____ (more/less) likely than teens and young adults to suffer from this disorder.

Objective 7: Describe the symptoms of post-traumatic stress disorder, and discuss survivor resiliency.

10. Traumatic stress, such as that associated with witnessing atrocities or combat, can produce

_____-_____

_____ disorder. The symptoms of this disorder include _____

_____ , _____ ,

_____ _____ ,

_____ _____ ,

and _____ . People who have a sensitive _____

_____ are more vulnerable to this disorder. Research with identical twins indicates that _____ may also play a role.

11. Researchers who believe this disorder may be overdiagnosed point to the _____

_____ of most people who suffer trauma. Also, suffering can lead to

_____-_____

_____ , in which people experience an increased appreciation for life.

Objective 8: Discuss the contributions of the learning and biological perspectives to our understanding of the development of anxiety disorders.

12. Freud assumed that anxiety disorders are symptoms of submerged mental energy that derives from intolerable impulses that were _____ during childhood.

13. Learning theorists, drawing on research in which rats are given unpredictable electric shocks, link general anxiety with _____ conditioning of _____ .

14. Some fears arise from _____ _____ , such as when a person who fears heights after a fall also comes to fear airplanes.

15. Phobias and compulsive behaviors reduce anxiety and thereby are _____ . Through _____ learning, someone might also learn fear by seeing others display their own fears.

16. Humans probably _____ (are/are not) biologically prepared to develop certain fears. Compulsive acts typically are exaggerations of behaviors that contributed to our species' _____ .

17. The anxiety response probably _____ (is/is not) genetically influenced. There may be anxiety _____ that affect brain levels of the neurotransmitter _____ , which influences mood, as well as the neurotransmitter _____ , which regulates the brain's alarm centers.

18. fMRI scans of persons with obsessive-compulsive disorder reveal excessive activity in a brain region called the _____ _____ cortex. Some antidepressant drugs dampen fear-circuit activity in the _____ , thus reducing this behavior.

Somatoform Disorders (pp. 576–577)

Objective 9: Describe somatoform disorders, and explain how the symptoms differ from other physical symptoms.

1. In somatoform disorders, symptoms take a _____ form without having an apparent _____ cause.

2. One type of this disorder is _____ _____ , in which _____ is presumably converted into a physical symptom. This disorder is _____ (more/less) common today than in Freud's time.

3. People suffering from _____ interpret normal sensations as symptoms of serious disease.

Dissociative Disorders (pp. 577–579)

Objective 10: Describe the symptoms of dissociative disorders.

1. In _____ disorders, a person experiences a sudden loss of _____ or change in _____ .

2. Dissociation means to become _____ from painful memories, thoughts, and feelings.

3. Dissociation itself _____ (is/is not so) rare.

Objective 11: Define *dissociative identity disorder,* and discuss the controversy regarding its diagnosis.

4. A person who develops two or more distinct personalities is suffering from _____ _____ disorder.

5. Nicholas Spanos has argued that such people may merely be playing different _____ .

6. Those who accept this as a genuine disorder point to evidence that differing personalities may be associated with distinct _____ and _____ states.

Identify two pieces of evidence brought forth by those who do not accept dissociative identity disorder as a genuine disorder.

7. The psychoanalytic and learning perspectives view dissociative disorders as ways of dealing with _____ . Others view them as a protective response to histories of

_____ _____

and so include them under the umbrella of

_____-_____

_____ _____ .

Skeptics claim these disorders are sometimes contrived by _____-_____ people and sometimes constructed out of the _____-_____ interaction.

Mood Disorders (pp. 579–589)

Objective 12: Define *mood disorders,* and contrast major depressive disorder and bipolar disorder.

1. Mood disorders are psychological disorders characterized by _____ _____ . They come in two forms: The experience of prolonged depression with no discernible cause is called _____ _____ disorder. When a person's mood alternates between depression and the hyperactive state of _____ , a _____ disorder is diagnosed.

2. Although _____ are more common, _____ is the number one

reason that people seek mental health services. It is also the leading cause of disability worldwide.

3. The possible signs of depression include

_____

_____ .

4. Major depression occurs when its signs last _____ _____ or more with no apparent cause.

5. Depressed persons usually _____ (can/cannot) recover without therapy.

6. Symptoms of mania include _____

_____ .

7. Bipolar disorder is less common among creative professionals who rely on _____ and _____ than among those who rely on _____ expression and vivid _____ .

Objective 13: Explain the development of mood disorders, paying special attention to the biological and social-cognitive perspectives.

8. The commonality of depression suggests that its _____ must also be common.

9. Compared with men, women are _____ (more/less) vulnerable to major depression. In general, women are most vulnerable to disorders involving _____ states, such as

_____

_____ .

10. Men's disorders tend to be more _____ and include _____

_____ .

11. It usually _____ (is/is not) the case that a depressive episode has been triggered by a stressful event. An individual's vulnerability to depression also increases following, for example, _____ .

12. With each new generation, the rate of depression is _____ (increasing/decreasing) and the disorder is striking _____ (earlier/later). In North America today, young adults are _____ times (how many?) more likely than their grandparents to suffer depression.

State the psychoanalytic explanation of depression.

13. Mood disorders _____
    (tend/do not tend) to run in families. Studies of
    _____ also reveal that genetic
    influences on mood disorders are
    _____ (weak/strong).

14. To determine which genes are involved in
    depression, researchers use
    _____ _____ , in
    which they examine the _____
    of both affected and unaffected family members.

(Close-Up) Identify several group differences in
suicide rates.

15. The brains of depressed people tend to be
    _____ (more/less) active, espe-
    cially in an area of the _____
    _____ lobe. In severely
    depressed patients, this brain area may also be
    _____ (smaller/larger) in size.
    The brain's _____ , which is
    important in processing _____ , is
    vulnerable to stress-related damage. Most people
    with a history of depression also were habitual
    _____ .

16. Depression may also be caused by
    _____ (high/low) levels of two
    neurotransmitters, _____ and
    _____ .

17. Drugs that alleviate mania reduce
    _____ ; drugs that relieve
    depression increase _____ or
    _____ supplies by blocking

either their _____ or their
chemical _____ .

18. According to the social-cognitive perspective,
    depression may be linked with
    _____ beliefs and a
    _____ _____
    style.

19. Such beliefs may arise from _____
    _____ , the feeling that can arise
    when the individual repeatedly experiences
    uncontrollable, painful events.

20. Gender differences in responding to
    _____ help explain why women
    have been twice as vulnerable to depression.

21. According to Susan Nolen-Hoeksema, when trou-
    ble strikes, men tend to _____
    and women tend to _____ .

Describe how depressed people differ from others in
their explanations of failure and how such explanations tend to feed depression.

22. According to Martin Seligman, depression is
    more common in Western cultures that empha-
    size _____ and that have shown
    a decline in commitment to _____
    and family.

23. Depression-prone people respond to bad events
    in an especially _____ way.

24. Being withdrawn, self-focused, and complaining
    tends to elicit social _____
    (empathy/rejection).

Outline the vicious cycle of depression.

Schizophrenia (pp. 589–596)

Objective 14: Describe the symptoms of schizophrenia, and differentiate delusions and hallucinations.

1. Schizophrenia, or "split mind," refers not to a split personality but rather to a split from _____ .

2. Three manifestations of schizophrenia are disorganized _____ , disturbed _____ , and inappropriate _____ and _____ .

3. The distorted, false beliefs of schizophrenia patients are called _____ .

4. Many psychologists attribute the disorganized thinking of schizophrenia to a breakdown in the capacity for _____ _____ .

5. The disturbed perceptions of people suffering from schizophrenia may take the form of _____ , which usually are _____ (visual/auditory).

6. Some victims of schizophrenia lapse into a zombielike state of apparent apathy, or _____ _____ ; others, who exhibit _____ , may remain motionless for hours and then become agitated.

Objective 15: Distinguish the five subtypes of schizophrenia, and contrast chronic and acute schizophrenia.

7. People with schizophrenia who display inappropriate behavior are said to have _____ _____ , while those with toneless voices and expressionless faces are said to have _____ _____ .

8. Schizophrenia is a cluster of disorders, including five subtypes: preoccupation with delusions or hallucinations, or _____ ; disordered speech or behavior, or _____ ; immobility, or _____ ; many and varied symptoms, or _____ ; and withdrawal, or _____ .

9. When schizophrenia develops slowly (called _____ schizophrenia), recovery is _____ (more/less) likely than when it develops rapidly in reaction to particular life stresses (called _____ schizophrenia).

Objective 16: Outline some abnormal brain chemistry, functions, and structures associated with schizophrenia, and discuss the possible link between prenatal viral infections and schizophrenia.

10. The brain tissue of schizophrenia patients has been found to have an excess of receptors for the neurotransmitter _____ . Drugs that block these receptors have been found to _____ (increase/decrease) schizophrenia symptoms.

11. Brain scans have shown that many people suffering from schizophrenia have abnormally _____ (high/low) brain activity in the _____ lobes.

12. Enlarged, _____-filled areas and a corresponding _____ of cerebral tissue is also characteristic of schizophrenia. Schizophrenia patients also have a smaller-than-normal _____ , which may account for their difficulty in filtering _____ _____ and focusing _____ .

13. Some scientists contend that the brain abnormalities of schizophrenia may be caused by a prenatal problem, such as _____ _____ ; birth complications, such as _____ _____ ; or a _____ _____ contracted by the mother.

List several pieces of evidence for the fetal-virus idea.

Objective 17: Discuss the evidence for a genetic contribution to the development of schizophrenia, and describe some psychological factors that may be early warning signs of schizophrenia in children.

14. Twin studies _____ (support/do not support) the contention that heredity plays a role in schizophrenia.

15. The role of the prenatal environment in schizophrenia is demonstrated by the fact that identical twins who share the same _____, and are therefore more likely to experience the same prenatal _____, are more likely to share the disorder.

16. Adoption studies _____ (confirm/do not confirm) a genetic link in the development of schizophrenia.

17. It appears that for schizophrenia to develop there must be both a _____ predisposition and other factors such as those listed earlier that "_____ _____" the _____ that predispose this disease.

Personality Disorders (pp. 596–599)

Objective 18: Contrast the three clusters of personality disorders, and describe the behaviors and brain activity associated with the antisocial personality disorder.

1. Personality disorders exist when an individual has character traits that are enduring and impair _____ _____ .

2. A fearful sensitivity to rejection may predispose the _____ personality disorder. Eccentric behaviors, such as emotionless disengagement, are characteristic of the _____ personality disorder. The third cluster exhibits dramatic or _____ behaviors, such as the _____ or _____ personality disorders.

3. An individual who seems to have no conscience, lies, steals, is generally irresponsible, and may be criminal is said to have an _____ personality. Previously, this person was labeled a _____ .

4. Studies of biological relatives of those with antisocial and unemotional tendencies suggest that there _____ (is/is not) a biological predisposition to such traits.

5. Some studies have detected early signs of antisocial behavior in children as young as _____ . Antisocial adolescents tended to have been _____ , _____ , unconcerned with _____ _____ , and low in _____ .

6. PET scans of murderers' brains reveal reduced activity in the _____ _____ , an area of the cortex that helps control _____ .

7. As in other disorders, in antisocial personality, genetics _____ (is/is not) the whole story. In one study, two combined factors—_____ _____ and a gene that altered neurotransmitter balance—predicted antisocial behavior.

Rates of Psychological Disorders (pp. 599–600)

Objective 19: Discuss the prevalence of psychological disorders, and summarize the findings on the link between poverty and serious psychological disorders.

1. Research reveals that approximately _____ percent of adult Americans suffered a clinically significant mental disorder during the prior year.

2. The incidence of serious psychological disorders is _____ (higher/lower) among those below the poverty line.

3. In terms of age of onset, most psychological disorders appear by _____ (early/middle/late) adulthood. Some, such as the _____ _____ and _____ , appear during childhood.

PROGRESS TEST 1

Multiple-Choice Questions

Circle your answers to the following questions and check them with the answers on page 326. If your answer is incorrect, read the explanation for why it is incorrect and then consult the appropriate pages of the text (in parentheses following the correct answer).

1. Gender differences in the prevalence of depression may be partly due to the fact that when stressful experiences occur
   a. women tend to act, while men tend to think.
   b. women tend to think, while men tend to act.
   c. women tend to distract themselves by drinking, while men tend to delve into their work.
   d. women tend to delve into their work, while men tend to distract themselves by drinking.

2. The criteria for classifying behavior as psychologically disordered
   a. vary from culture to culture.
   b. vary from time to time.
   c. vary by culture and with time.
   d. have remained largely unchanged over the course of history.

3. Most mental health workers today take the view that disordered behaviors
   a. are usually genetically triggered.
   b. are organic diseases.
   c. arise from the interaction of nature and nurture.
   d. are the product of learning.

4. The view that all behavior arises from the interaction of heredity and environment is referred to as the _____ approach.
   a. biopsychosocial
   b. psychoanalytic
   c. medical
   d. conditioning

5. Which of the following is the most pervasive of the psychological disorders?
   a. depression
   b. schizophrenia
   c. bipolar disorder
   d. generalized anxiety disorder

6. Which of the following is NOT true concerning depression?
   a. Depression is more common in females than in males.
   b. Most depressive episodes appear not to be preceded by any particular factor or event.
   c. Most depressive episodes last less than 3 months.
   d. Most people recover from depression without professional therapy.

7. Which of the following is NOT true regarding schizophrenia?
   a. It occurs more frequently in people born in winter and spring months.
   b. It occurs less frequently as infectious disease rates have declined.
   c. It occurs more frequently in lightly populated areas.
   d. It usually appears during adolescence or early adulthood.

8. Evidence of environmental effects on psychological disorders is seen in the fact that certain disorders, such as _____ , are universal, whereas others, such as _____ , are culture-bound.
   a. schizophrenia; depression
   b. depression; schizophrenia
   c. antisocial personality; neurosis
   d. depression; anorexia nervosa

9. The effect of drugs that block receptors for dopamine is to
   a. alleviate schizophrenia symptoms.
   b. alleviate depression.
   c. increase schizophrenia symptoms.
   d. increase depression.

10. The diagnostic reliability of DSM-IV-TR
   a. is unknown.
   b. depends on the age of the patient.
   c. is very low.
   d. is relatively high.

11. Because of some troubling thoughts, Carl recently had a PET scan of his brain that revealed excessive activity in the anterior cingulate area. Carl's psychiatrist believes that Carl suffers from
    a. schizophrenia.
    b. a mood disorder.
    c. a personality disorder.
    d. obsessive-compulsive disorder.

12. (Thinking Critically) The term *insanity* refers to
    a. legal definitions.
    b. psychotic disorders only.
    c. personality disorders only.
    d. both psychotic disorders and personality disorders.

13. Phobias and obsessive-compulsive behaviors are classified as
    a. anxiety disorders.
    b. mood disorders.
    c. dissociative disorders.
    d. personality disorders.

14. According to the social-cognitive perspective, a person who experiences unexpected aversive events may develop helplessness and manifest a(n)
    a. obsessive-compulsive disorder.
    b. dissociative disorder.
    c. personality disorder.
    d. mood disorder.

15. Which of the following was presented in the text as evidence of biological influences on anxiety disorders?
    a. Identical twins often develop similar phobias.
    b. Brain scans of persons with obsessive-compulsive disorder reveal unusually high activity in the anterior cingulate cortex.

    c. Drugs that dampen fear-circuit activity in the amygdala also alleviate OCD.
    d. All of these findings were presented.

16. Most of the hallucinations of schizophrenia patients involve the sense of
    a. smell.   c. hearing.
    b. vision.   d. touch.

17. When expecting to be electrically shocked, people with an antisocial personality disorder, as compared with normal people, show
    a. less fear and greater arousal of the autonomic nervous system.
    b. less fear and less autonomic arousal.
    c. greater fear and greater autonomic arousal.
    d. greater fear and less autonomic arousal.

18. Hearing voices would be a(n) _____ ; believing that you are Napoleon would be a(n)

    _____ .
    a. obsession; compulsion
    b. compulsion; obsession
    c. delusion; hallucination
    d. hallucination; delusion

19. In treating depression, a psychiatrist would probably prescribe a drug that would
    a. increase levels of acetylcholine.
    b. decrease levels of dopamine.
    c. increase levels of norepinephrine.
    d. decrease levels of serotonin.

20. When schizophrenia is slow to develop, called _____ schizophrenia, recovery is _____ .
    a. reactive; unlikely   c. process; unlikely
    b. process; likely   d. reactive; likely

Matching Items

Match each term with the appropriate definition or description.

Terms

_____ 1. dissociative disorder
_____ 2. medical model
_____ 3. mood disorders
_____ 4. social phobia
_____ 5. biopsychosocial approach
_____ 6. mania
_____ 7. obsessive-compulsive disorder
_____ 8. schizophrenia
_____ 9. hallucination
_____ 10. panic attack
_____ 11. post-traumatic growth
_____ 12. conversion disorder

Definitions or Descriptions

a. psychological disorders marked by emotional extremes
b. an extremely elevated mood
c. a false sensory experience
d. approach that considers behavior disorders as illnesses that can be diagnosed, treated, and, in most cases, cured
e. a sudden escalation of anxiety often accompanied by a sensation of choking or other physical symptoms
f. a disorder in which conscious awareness becomes separated from previous memories, feelings, and thoughts
g. approach that considers behavior disorders to be the result of biological, psychological, and social-cultural influences
h. intense fear of being scrutinized by others
i. a group of disorders marked by disorganized thinking, disturbed perceptions, and inappropriate emotions and actions
j. a disorder characterized by repetitive thoughts and actions
k. a rare somatoform disorder
l. positive psychological changes stemming from dealing with an extreme crisis

PROGRESS TEST 2

Progress Test 2 should be completed during a final unit review. Answer the following questions after you thoroughly understand the correct answers for the Unit Review and Progress Test 1.

Multiple-Choice Questions

1. Which of the following is true concerning abnormal behavior?
   a. Definitions of abnormal behavior are culture-dependent.
   b. A behavior cannot be defined as abnormal unless it is considered harmful to society.
   c. Abnormal behavior can be defined as any behavior that is distressful.
   d. Definitions of abnormal behavior are based on physiological factors.

2. The psychoanalytic perspective would most likely view phobias as
   a. conditioned fears.
   b. displaced responses to incompletely repressed impulses.
   c. biological predispositions.
   d. manifestations of self-defeating thoughts.

3. Many psychologists believe the disorganized thoughts of people with schizophrenia result from a breakdown in
   a. selective attention.   c. motivation.
   b. memory storage.   d. memory retrieval.

4. Research evidence links the brain abnormalities of schizophrenia to _____ during prenatal development.
   a. maternal stress
   b. a viral infection contracted
   c. abnormal levels of certain hormones
   d. the weight of the unborn child

5. The fact that disorders such as schizophrenia are universal and influenced by heredity, whereas other disorders such as anorexia nervosa are culture-bound provides evidence for the _____ model of psychological disorders.
   a. medical
   b. biopsychosocial
   c. social-cultural
   d. psychoanalytic

6. Our early ancestors commonly attributed disordered behavior to
   a. "bad blood."
   b. evil spirits.
   c. brain injury.
   d. laziness.

7. In general, women are more vulnerable than men to
   a. external disorders such as anxiety.
   b. internal disorders such as depression.
   c. external disorders such as antisocial conduct.
   d. internal disorders such as alcohol dependence.

8. Which of the following statements concerning the labeling of disordered behaviors is NOT true?
   a. Labels interfere with effective treatment of psychological disorders.
   b. Labels promote research studies of psychological disorders.
   c. Labels may create preconceptions that bias people's perceptions.
   d. Labels may influence behavior by creating self-fulfilling prophecies.

9. Nicholas Spanos considers dissociative identity disorder to be
   a. a genuine disorder.
   b. merely role-playing.
   c. a disorder that cannot be explained according to the learning perspective.
   d. a biological phenomenon.

10. Which neurotransmitter is present in overabundant amounts during the manic phase of bipolar disorder?
   a. dopamine
   b. serotonin
   c. epinephrine
   d. norepinephrine

11. After falling from a ladder, Joseph is afraid of airplanes, although he has never flown. This demonstrates that some fears arise from
   a. observational learning.
   b. reinforcement.
   c. stimulus generalization.
   d. stimulus discrimination.

12. Which of the following provides evidence that human fears have been subjected to the evolutionary process?
   a. Compulsive acts typically exaggerate behaviors that contributed to our species' survival.
   b. Most phobias focus on objects that our ancestors also feared.
   c. It is easier to condition some fears than others.
   d. All of these provide evidence.

13. Which of the following is true of the medical model?
   a. In recent years, it has been in large part discredited.
   b. It views psychological disorders as sicknesses that are diagnosable and treatable.
   c. It emphasizes the role of psychological factors in disorders over that of physiological factors.
   d. It focuses on cognitive factors.

14. Psychoanalytic and learning theorists both agree that dissociative and anxiety disorders are symptoms that represent the person's attempt to deal with
   a. unconscious conflicts.
   b. anxiety.
   c. unfulfilled wishes.
   d. unpleasant responsibilities.

15. Behavior is classified as disordered when it
   a. is deviant.
   b. is distressful.
   c. is dysfunctional.
   d. has all of these characteristics.

16. Most practitioners find the DSM-IV-TR a helpful and practical tool despite its
   a. failure to emphasize observable behaviors in the diagnostic process.
   b. learning theory bias.
   c. medical model bias.
   d. psychoanalytic bias.

17. Which of the following is NOT a symptom of schizophrenia?
   a. inappropriate emotions
   b. disturbed perceptions
   c. panic attacks
   d. disorganized thinking

18. Social-cognitive theorists contend that depression is linked with
   a. negative moods.
   b. maladaptive explanations of failure.
   c. self-defeating beliefs.
   d. all of these characteristics.

19. According to psychoanalytic theory, memory of losses, especially in combination with internalized anger, is likely to result in
   a. learned helplessness.
   b. self-serving bias.
   c. weak ego defense mechanisms.
   d. depression.

20. Among the following, which is generally accepted as a possible cause of schizophrenia?
   a. an excess of endorphins in the brain
   b. being a twin
   c. extensive learned helplessness
   d. a genetic predisposition

Matching Items

Match each term with the appropriate definition or description.

Terms

_____ **1.** dissociative identity disorder
_____ **2.** phobia
_____ **3.** dopamine
_____ **4.** panic disorder
_____ **5.** antisocial personality
_____ **6.** norepinephrine
_____ **7.** serotonin
_____ **8.** bipolar disorder
_____ **9.** delusions
_____ **10.** agoraphobia
_____ **11.** somatoform disorder
_____ **12.** hypochondriasis

Definitions or Descriptions

a. a neurotransmitter for which there are excess receptors in some schizophrenia patients
b. a neurotransmitter that is overabundant during mania and scarce during depression
c. an individual who seems to have no conscience
d. false beliefs that may accompany psychological disorders
e. an anxiety disorder marked by a persistent, irrational fear of a specific object or situation
f. a disorder formerly called multiple personality disorder
g. a neurotransmitter possibly linked to obsessive-compulsive behavior
h. a type of mood disorder
i. an anxiety disorder marked by episodes of intense dread
j. a fear of situations in which help might not be available during a panic attack
k. disorder in which bodily symptoms occur without an apparent physical cause
l. misinterpreting normal physical sensations as disease

PSYCHOLOGY APPLIED

Answer these questions the day before an exam as a final check on your understanding of the unit's terms and concepts.

Multiple-Choice Questions

1. Joe has an intense, irrational fear of snakes. He is suffering from a(n)
   a. generalized anxiety disorder.
   b. obsessive-compulsive disorder.
   c. phobia.
   d. mood disorder.

2. As a child, Monica was criticized severely by her mother for not living up to her expectations. This criticism was always followed by a beating with a whip. As an adult, Monica is generally introverted and extremely shy. Sometimes, however, she acts more like a young child, throwing tantrums if she doesn't get her way. At other times, she is a flirting, happy-go-lucky young lady. Most likely, Monica is suffering from
   a. a phobia.
   b. dissociative schizophrenia.
   c. dissociative identity disorder.
   d. bipolar disorder.

3. Bob has never been able to keep a job. He's been in and out of jail for charges such as theft, sexual assault, and spousal abuse. Bob would most likely be diagnosed as having
   a. a dissociative identity disorder.
   b. major depressive disorder.
   c. schizophrenia.
   d. an antisocial personality.

4. Julia's psychologist believes that Julia's fear of heights can be traced to a conditioned fear she developed after falling from a ladder. This explanation reflects a _____ perspective.
   a. medical   c. social-cognitive
   b. psychoanalytic d. learning

5. Before he can study, Rashid must arrange his books, pencils, paper, and other items on his desk so that they are "just so." The campus counselor suggests that Rashid's compulsive behavior may help alleviate his anxiety about failing in school, which reinforces the compulsive actions. This explanation of obsessive-compulsive behavior is most consistent with which perspective?
   a. learning   c. humanistic
   b. psychoanalytic   d. social-cognitive

6. Sharon is continually tense, jittery, and apprehensive for no specific reason. She would probably be diagnosed as suffering a(n)
   a. phobia.
   b. major depressive disorder.
   c. obsessive-compulsive disorder.
   d. generalized anxiety disorder.

7. Jason is so preoccupied with staying clean that he showers as many as 10 times each day. Jason would be diagnosed as suffering from a(n)
   a. dissociative disorder.
   b. generalized anxiety disorder.
   c. personality disorder.
   d. obsessive-compulsive disorder.

8. Although she escaped from war-torn Bosnia several years ago, Zheina still has haunting memories and nightmares. Because she is also severely depressed, her therapist diagnoses her condition as
   a. dissociative identity disorder.
   b. bipolar disorder.
   c. schizophrenia.
   d. post-traumatic stress disorder.

9. Claiming that she heard a voice commanding her to warn other people that eating is harmful, Sandy attempts to convince others in a restaurant not to eat. The psychiatrist to whom she is referred finds that Sandy's thinking and speech are often fragmented and incoherent. In addition, Sandy has an unreasonable fear that someone is "out to get her" and consequently trusts no one. Her condition is most indicative of
   a. schizophrenia.
   b. generalized anxiety disorder.
   c. a phobia.
   d. obsessive-compulsive disorder.

10. Irene occasionally experiences unpredictable episodes of intense dread accompanied by heart palpitations and a sensation of smothering. Since her symptoms have no apparent cause, they would probably be classified as indicative of
    a. schizophrenia.
    b. bipolar disorder.
    c. post-traumatic stress disorder.
    d. panic attack.

11. To which of the following is a person MOST likely to acquire a phobia?
    a. heights
    b. being in public
    c. being dirty
    d. cars.

12. Dr. Jekyll, whose second personality was Mr. Hyde, had a(n) _____ disorder.
    a. anxiety   c. mood
    b. dissociative   d. personality

13. For the past six months, a woman has complained of feeling isolated from others, dissatisfied with life, and discouraged about the future. This woman could be diagnosed as suffering from
    a. bipolar disorder.
    b. major depressive disorder.
    c. generalized anxiety disorder.
    d. a dissociative disorder.

14. On Monday, Matt felt optimistic, energetic, and on top of the world. On Tuesday, he felt hopeless and lethargic, and thought that the future looked very grim. Matt would *most* likely be diagnosed as having
    a. bipolar disorder.
    b. major depressive disorder.
    c. schizophrenia.
    d. panic disorder.

15. Connie's therapist has suggested that her depression stems from unresolved anger toward her parents. Evidently, Connie's therapist is working within the _____ perspective.
    a. learning
    b. social-cognitive
    c. biological
    d. psychoanalytic

16. Ken's therapist suggested that his depression is a result of his self-defeating thoughts and negative assumptions about himself, his situation, and his future. Evidently, Ken's therapist is working within the _____ perspective.
    a. learning
    b. social-cognitive
    c. biological
    d. psychoanalytic

17. Alicia's doctor, who thinks that Alicia's depression has a biochemical cause, prescribes a drug that
    a. reduces norepinephrine.
    b. increases norepinephrine.
    c. reduces serotonin.
    d. increases acetylcholine.

18. Wayne's doctor attempts to help Wayne by prescribing a drug that blocks receptors for dopamine. Wayne has apparently been diagnosed with
    a. a mood disorder.
    b. an anxiety disorder.
    c. a personality disorder.
    d. schizophrenia.

19. (Thinking Critically) Thirteen-year-old Ronald constantly fidgets in his seat at school, frequently blurts out answers without being called, and is extremely distractible. A psychiatrist might diagnose Ronald with
    a. bipolar disorder.
    b. panic disorder.
    c. attention-deficit hyperactivity disorder.
    d. obsessive-compulsive disorder.

20. Janet, whose class presentation is titled "Current Views on the Causes of Schizophrenia," concludes her talk with the statement
    a. "Schizophrenia is caused by intolerable stress."
    b. "Schizophrenia is inherited."
    c. "Genes may predispose some people to react to particular experiences by developing schizophrenia."
    d. "As of this date, schizophrenia is completely unpredictable and its causes are unknown."

Essay Question

Clinical psychologists label people disordered if their behavior is (1) deviant, (2) distressful, and (3) dysfunctional. Demonstrate your understanding of the classification process by giving examples of behaviors that might be considered deviant, distressful, or dysfunctional but, because they do not fit all three criteria, would not necessarily be labeled disordered. (Use the space below to list the points you want to make, and organize them. Then write the essay on a separate piece of paper.)

KEY TERMS

Using your own words, on a separate piece of paper write a brief definition or explanation of each of the following terms.

1. psychological disorder

2. attention-deficit hyperactivity disorder (ADHD)

3. medical model

4. DSM-IV-TR

5. anxiety disorders

6. generalized anxiety disorder

7. panic disorder

8. phobia

9. obsessive-compulsive disorder (OCD)

10. post-traumatic stress disorder (PTSD)

11. post-traumatic growth

12. somatoform disorder

13. conversion disorder

14. hypochondriasis

15. dissociative disorders

16. dissociative identity disorder (DID)

17. mood disorders

18. major depressive disorder

19. mania

20. bipolar disorder

21. schizophrenia

22. delusions

23. personality disorders

24. antisocial personality disorder

ANSWERS

Unit Review

Perspectives on Psychological Disorders

1. deviant; distressful; dysfunctional

2. variable

3. attention-deficit hyperactivity disorder; inattention; hyperactivity; impulsivity

4. boys; increased; agree

5. is; is not; learning; defiant

6. medical; sickness; psychopathology; symptoms; therapy

7. Philippe Pinel

8. nature; nurture; internal

9. depression; schizophrenia; anorexia nervosa; bulimia nervosa; dynamic; anxiety; symptoms

10. biopsychosocial; genetic predispositions; physiological states; psychological dynamics; social; cultural

11. DSM-IV-TR; Internal Classification; Diseases; does not; describes

12. show

13. increased; increased

The "unDSM" is a new classification system that identifies 24 human strengths and virtues grouped into six clusters: wisdom and knowledge, courage, love, justice, temperance, and transcendence.

14. a significant

Psychological labels may be arbitrary. They can create preconceptions that bias our perceptions and interpretations and they can affect people's self-images. Moreover, labels can change reality, by serving as self-fulfilling prophecies. Despite these drawbacks, labels are useful in describing, treating, and researching the causes of psychological disorders.

15. are not; mental disorders

Anxiety Disorders

1. distressing, persistent anxiety or maladaptive behaviors that reduce anxiety

2. generalized anxiety disorder; panic disorder; phobias; obsessive-compulsive disorder; post-traumatic stress disorder

3. generalized anxiety; free-floating

4. high blood pressure; panic disorder; panic attack

5. smoke; panic attack; nicotine

6. phobia; specific phobias

7. social phobia; agoraphobia

8. obsessive-compulsive

9. less

10. post-traumatic stress; haunting memories; nightmares; social withdrawal; jumpy anxiety; insomnia; limbic system; genes

11. survivor resiliency; post-traumatic growth

12. repressed

13. classical; fears

14. stimulus generalization

15. reinforced; observational

16. are; survival

17. is; genes; serotonin; glutamate

18. anterior cingulate; amygdala

Somatoform Disorders

1. bodily (somatic); physical

2. conversion disorder; anxiety; less

3. hypochondriasis

Dissociative Disorders

1. dissociative; memory; identity

2. separated

3. is not so

4. dissociative identity

5. roles

6. brain; body

Skeptics point out that the recent increase in the number of reported cases of dissociative identity disorder indicates that it has become a fad. The fact that the disorder is much less prevalent outside North America also causes skeptics to doubt the disorder's genuineness.

7. anxiety; childhood trauma; post-traumatic stress disorder; fantasy-prone; therapist-patient

Mood Disorders

1. emotional extremes; major depressive; mania; bipolar

2. phobias; depression

3. lethargy, feelings of worthlessness, and loss of interest in family, friends, and activities

4. two weeks

5. can

6. euphoria, hyperactivity, and a wildly optimistic state

7. precision; logic; emotional; imagery

8. causes

9. more; internal; depression, anxiety, and inhibited sexual desire

10. external; alcohol abuse, antisocial conduct, and lack of impulse control

11. is; a family member's death, loss of a job, a marital crisis, or a physical assault

12. increasing; earlier; three

The psychoanalytic perspective suggests that adulthood depression can be triggered by losses that evoke feelings associated with earlier childhood losses. Alternatively, unresolved anger toward one's parents is turned inward and takes the form of depression.

13. tend; twins; strong

14. linkage analysis; DNA

Suicide rates are higher among White Americans, the rich, older men, the nonreligious, and those who are single, widowed, or divorced. Although women more often attempt suicide, men are more likely to succeed. Suicide rates also vary widely around the world.

15. less; left frontal; smaller; hippocampus; memories; smokers

16. low; norepinephrine; serotonin

17. norepinephrine; norepinephrine; serotonin; reuptake; breakdown

18. self-defeating; negative explanatory

19. learned helplessness

20. stress

21. act; think (or overthink)

Depressed people are more likely than others to explain failures or bad events in terms that are stable (it's going to last forever), global (it will affect everything), and internal (it's my fault). Such explanations lead to feelings of hopelessness, which in turn feed depression.

22. individualism; religion

23. self-blaming

24. rejection

Depression is often brought on by stressful experiences. Depressed people brood over such experiences with maladaptive explanations that produce self-blame and amplify their depression, which in turn triggers other symptoms of depression. In addition, being withdrawn and complaining tends to elicit social rejection and other negative experiences.

Schizophrenia

1. reality

2. thinking; perceptions; emotions; actions

3. delusions

4. selective attention

5. hallucinations; auditory

6. flat affect; catatonia

7. positive symptoms; negative symptoms

8. paranoid; disorganized; catatonic; undifferentiated; residual

9. chronic (or process); less; acute (or reactive)

10. dopamine; decrease

11. low; frontal

12. fluid; shrinkage; thalamus; sensory input; attention

13. low birth weight; oxygen deprivation; viral infection

Risk of schizophrenia increases for those who undergo fetal development during a flu epidemic, or simply during the flu season. People born in densely populated areas and those born during winter and spring months are at increased risk. The months of excess schizophrenia births are reversed in the Southern Hemisphere, where the seasons are the reverse of the Northern Hemisphere's. Mothers who were sick with influenza during their pregnancy may be more likely to have children who develop schizophrenia. Blood drawn from pregnant women whose children develop schizophrenia have higher-than-normal levels of viral infection antibodies.

14. support

15. placenta; viruses

16. confirm

17. genetic; turn on; genes

Personality Disorders

1. social functioning

2. avoidant; schizoid; impulsive; histrionic; narcissistic

3. antisocial; psychopath or sociopath

4. is

5. 3 to 6; impulsive; uninhibited; social rewards; anxiety

6. frontal lobe; impulses

7. is not; childhood maltreatment

Rates of Psychological Disorders

1. 26

2. higher

3. early; antisocial personality; phobias

Progress Test 1

Multiple-Choice Questions

1. **b.** is the answer. (p. 587)
   c. & d. Men are more likely than women to cope with stress in these ways.

2. **c.** is the answer. (p. 562)

3. **c.** is the answer. Most clinicians agree that psychological disorders may be caused by both psychological (d.) and physical (a. and b.) factors. (p. 565)

4. **a.** is the answer. (p. 565)

5. **a.** is the answer. (p. 580)

6. **b.** is the answer. Depression is often preceded by a stressful event related to work, marriage, or a close relationship. (p. 583)

7. **c.** is the answer. (p. 593)

8. **d.** is the answer. Although depression is universal, anorexia nervosa and bulimia are rare outside of Western culture. (pp. 564–565)
   a. & b. Schizophrenia and depression are both universal.
   c. The text mentions only schizophrenia and depression as universal disorders. Furthermore, neurosis is no longer utilized as a category of diagnosis.

9. **a.** is the answer. (p. 592)

b. & d. Thus far, only norepinephrine and serotonin have been implicated in depression and bipolar disorder.
c. Schizophrenia has been associated with an excess of dopamine receptors. Blocking them alleviates, rather than increases, schizophrenia symptoms.

10. **d.** is the answer. (p. 565)
    b. The text does not mention DSM-IV-TR's reliability in terms of a person's age.

11. **d.** is the answer. These areas show increased activity during compulsive behaviors. (pp. 575–576)

12. **a.** is the answer. (p. 569)

13. **a.** is the answer. (p. 570)
    b. The mood disorders include major depressive disorder and bipolar disorder.
    c. Dissociative identity disorder is the only dissociative disorder discussed in the text.
    d. The personality disorders include the antisocial and schizoid personalities.

14. **d.** is the answer. Learned helplessness may lead to self-defeating beliefs, which in turn are linked with depression, a mood disorder. (pp. 586–587)

15. **d.** is the answer. (pp. 575–576)

16. **c.** is the answer. (p. 590)

17. **b.** is the answer. Those with antisocial personality disorders show less autonomic arousal in such situations, and emotions, such as fear, are tied to arousal. (p. 597)

18. **d.** is the answer. Hallucinations are false sensory experiences; delusions are false beliefs. (p. 590)
    a. & b. Obsessions are repetitive and unwanted thoughts. Compulsions are repetitive behaviors.

19. **c.** is the answer. Drugs that relieve depression tend to increase levels of norepinephrine. (p. 586)
    a. Acetylcholine is a neurotransmitter involved in muscle contractions.
    b. It is in certain types of schizophrenia that decreasing dopamine levels is known to be helpful.
    d. On the contrary, it appears that a particular type of depression may be related to *low* levels of serotonin.

20. **c.** is the answer. (p. 592)

Matching Items

1. f (p. 577)   5. g (p. 565)   9. c (p. 590)
2. d (p. 564)   6. b (p. 581)   10. e (p. 570)
3. a (p. 579)   7. j (p. 571)   11. l (pp. 573–574)
4. h (p. 571)   8. i (p. 590)   12. k (p. 577)

Progress Test 2

Multiple-Choice Questions

1. **a.** is the answer. Different cultures have different standards for behaviors that are considered acceptable and normal. (p. 562)
   b. Some abnormal behaviors are simply maladaptive for the individual.
   c. Many individuals who are deviant, such as Olympic gold medalists, are not considered abnormal. There are other criteria that must be met in order for behavior to be considered abnormal.
   d. Although physiological factors play a role in the various disorders, they do not define abnormal behavior. Rather, behavior is said to be abnormal if it is deviant, distressful, and dysfunctional.

2. **b.** is the answer. (p. 574)
   a. This answer reflects the learning perspective.
   c. Although certain phobias are biologically predisposed, this could not fully explain phobias, nor is it the explanation offered by psychoanalytic theory.
   d. Social-cognitive theorists propose self-defeating thoughts as a cause of depression.

3. **a.** is the answer. Schizophrenia sufferers are easily distracted by irrelevant stimuli, evidently because of a breakdown in the capacity for selective attention. (p. 590)

4. **b.** is the answer. (p. 593)

5. **b.** is the answer. The fact that some disorders are universal and at least partly genetic in origin implicates biological factors in their origin. The fact that other disorders appear only in certain parts of the world implicates sociocultural and psychological factors in their origin. (pp. 564–565)

6. **b.** is the answer. (p. 564)

7. **b.** is the answer. (p. 582)
   a. Anxiety is an internal disorder.
   d. Alcohol dependency is an external disorder.

8. **a.** is the answer. In fact, just the opposite is true. Labels are useful in promoting effective treatment of psychological disorders. (p. 568)

9. **b.** is the answer. (p. 578)
   c. Playing a role is most definitely a learned skill.
   d. Role-playing, being completely learned, is not biologically based.

10. **d.** is the answer. In bipolar disorder, norepinephrine appears to be overabundant during mania and in short supply during depression. (p. 586)

a. There is an overabundance of dopamine receptors in some schizophrenia patients.
b. Serotonin sometimes appears to be scarce during depression.
c. Epinephrine has not been implicated in psychological disorders.

11. **c.** is the answer. Joseph's fear has generalized from ladders to airplanes. (p. 574)
    a. Had Joseph acquired his fear after seeing someone *else* fall, observational learning would be implicated. This process would not, however, explain how his fear was transferred to airplanes.
    b. There is no indication that Joseph's phobia was acquired through reinforcement.
    d. Through stimulus discrimination, Joseph's fear would *not* have generalized from ladders to airplanes.

12. **d.** is the answer. (p. 575)

13. **b.** is the answer. (p. 564)
    a. This isn't the case; in fact, the medical model has gained credibility from recent discoveries of genetic and biochemical links to some disorders.
    c. & d. The medical perspective tends to place more emphasis on physiological factors.

14. **b.** is the answer. The psychoanalytic explanation is that these disorders are a manifestation of incompletely repressed impulses over which the person is anxious. According to the learning perspective, the troubled behaviors that result from these disorders have been reinforced by anxiety reduction. (pp. 574, 579)
    a. & c. These are true of the psychoanalytic, but not the learning, perspective.

15. **d.** is the answer. (pp. 562–563)

16. **c.** is the answer. DSM-IV-TR was shaped by the medical model. (pp. 565–566)
    a. In fact, just the opposite is true. DSM-IV-TR was revised to improve reliability by basing diagnoses on observable behaviors.
    b. & d. DSM-IV-TR does not reflect a learning or a psychoanalytic bias.

17. **c.** is the answer. Panic attacks are characteristic of certain anxiety disorders, not of schizophrenia. (pp. 590–591)

18. **d.** is the answer. (pp. 586–588)

19. **d.** is the answer. A loss may evoke feelings of anger associated with an earlier loss. Such anger is turned against the self. This internalized anger results in depression. (p. 583)
    a. Learned helplessness would be an explanation offered by the social-cognitive perspective.
    b. Self-serving bias is not discussed in terms of its relationship to depression.

c. This is the psychoanalytic explanation of anxiety.

20. **d.** is the answer. Risk for schizophrenia increases for individuals who are related to a schizophrenia victim, and the greater the genetic relatedness, the greater the risk. (pp. 594–595)
    a. Schizophrenia victims have an overabundance of the neurotransmitter dopamine, not endorphins.
    b. Being a twin is, in itself, irrelevant to developing schizophrenia.

    c. Although learned helplessness has been suggested by social-cognitive theorists as a cause of self-defeating depressive behaviors, it has not been suggested as a cause of schizophrenia.

Matching Items

1. f (p. 578)	**5.** c (p. 597)	**9.** d (p. 590)
2. e (p. 571)	**6.** b (p. 586)	**10.** j (p. 571)
3. a (p. 592)	**7.** g (p. 586)	**11.** k (p. 576)
4. i (p. 570)	**8.** h (p. 581)	**12.** l (p. 577)

Psychology Applied

Multiple-Choice Questions

1. **c.** is the answer. An intense fear of a specific object is a phobia. (p. 571)
   a. His fear is focused on a specific object, not generalized.
   b. In this disorder a person is troubled by repetitive thoughts and actions.
   d. Conditioned fears form the basis for anxiety rather than mood disorders.

2. **c.** is the answer. (p. 579)
   a. Phobias focus anxiety on a specific object, activity, or situation.
   b. There is no such disorder.
   d. In this mood disorder, a person alternates between feelings of hopeless depression and overexcited mania.

3. **d.** is the answer. Repeated wrongdoing and aggressive behavior are part of the pattern associated with the antisocial personality disorder, which may also include marital problems and an inability to keep a job. (p. 597)
   a. Although dissociative identity disorder may involve an aggressive personality, there is nothing in the example to indicate a dissociation.
   b. Nothing in the question indicates that Bob is passive and resigned and having the self-defeating thoughts characteristic of depression.

c. Bob's behavior does not include the disorganized thinking and disturbed perceptions typical of schizophrenia.

4. **d.** is the answer. In the learning perspective, a phobia, such as Julia's, is seen as a conditioned fear. (p. 574)
   a. Because the fear is focused on a specific stimulus, the medical model does not easily account for the phobia. In any event, it would presumably offer an internal, biological explanation.
   b. The psychoanalytic view of phobias would be that they represent incompletely repressed anxieties that are displaced onto the feared object.
   c. The social-cognitive perspective would emphasize a person's conscious, cognitive processes, not reflexive conditioned responses.

5. **a.** is the answer. According to the learning view, compulsive behaviors are reinforced because they reduce the anxiety created by obsessive thoughts. Rashid's obsession concerns failing, and his desk-arranging compulsive behaviors apparently help him control these thoughts. (p. 574)
   b. The psychoanalytic perspective would view obsessive thoughts as a symbolic representation of forbidden impulses. These thoughts may prompt the person to perform compulsive acts that counter these impulses.
   c. & d. The text does not offer explanations of obsessive-compulsive behavior based on the humanistic or social-cognitive perspectives. Presumably, however, these explanations would emphasize growth-blocking difficulties in the person's environment (humanistic perspective) and the reciprocal influences of personality and environment (social-cognitive perspective), rather than symbolic expressions of forbidden impulses.

6. **d.** is the answer. (p. 570)
   a. In phobias, anxiety is focused on a specific object.
   b. Major depressive disorder does not manifest these symptoms.
   c. The obsessive-compulsive disorder is characterized by repetitive and unwanted thoughts and/or actions.

7. **d.** is the answer. Jason is obsessed with cleanliness; as a result, he has developed a compulsion to shower. (p. 571)
   a. Dissociative disorders involve a separation of conscious awareness from previous memories and thoughts.
   b. Generalized anxiety disorder does not have a specific focus.
   c. This disorder is characterized by maladaptive character traits.

8. **d.** is the answer. (p. 572)
   a. There is no evidence that Zheina has *lost* either her memory or her identity, as would occur in dissociative disorders.
   b. Although she has symptoms of depression, Zheina does not show signs of mania, which occurs in bipolar disorder.
   c. Zheina shows no signs of disorganized thinking or disturbed perceptions.

9. **a.** is the answer. Because Sandy experiences hallucinations (hearing voices), delusions (fearing someone is "out to get her"), and incoherence, she would most likely be diagnosed as suffering from schizophrenia. (p. 590)
   b., c., & d. These disorders are not characterized by disorganized thoughts and perceptions.

10. **d.** is the answer. (p. 570)
    a. Baseless physical symptoms rarely play a role in schizophrenia.
    b. There is no indication that she is exhibiting euphoric behavior.
    c. There is no indication that she has suffered a trauma.

11. **a.** is the answer. Humans seem biologically prepared to develop a fear of heights and other dangers that our ancestors faced. (p. 575)

12. **b.** is the answer. (p. 577)

13. **b.** is the answer. The fact that this woman has had these symptoms for more than two weeks indicates that she is suffering from major depressive disorder. (p. 580)

14. **a.** is the answer. Matt's alternating states of the hopelessness and lethargy of depression and the energetic, optimistic state of mania are characteristic of bipolar disorder. (p. 581)
    b. Although he was depressed on Tuesday, Matt's manic state on Monday indicates that he is not suffering from major depressive disorder.
    c. Matt was depressed, not detached from reality.
    d. That Matt is not exhibiting episodes of intense dread indicates that he is not suffering from panic disorder.

15. **d.** is the answer. Freud believed that the anger once felt toward parents was internalized and would produce depression. (p. 583)
    a. & b. The learning and social-cognitive perspectives focus on environmental experiences, conditioning, and self-defeating attitudes in explaining depression.
    c. The biological perspective focuses on genetic predispositions and biochemical imbalances in explaining depression.

16. **b.** is the answer. (pp. 586–587)

17. **b.** is the answer. Norepinephrine, which increases arousal and boosts mood, is scarce during depression. Drugs that relieve depression tend to increase norepinephrine. (p. 588)
    c. Increasing serotonin, which is sometimes scarce during depression, might relieve depression.
    d. This neurotransmitter is involved in motor responses but has not been linked to psychological disorders.

18. **d.** is the answer. Schizophrenia patients sometimes have an excess of receptors for dopamine. Drugs that block these receptors can therefore reduce symptoms of schizophrenia. (p. 592)
    a., b., & c. Dopamine receptors have not been implicated in these psychological disorders.

19. **c.** is the answer. (p. 563)

20. **c.** is the answer. (pp. 594–595)

Essay Question

There is more to a psychological disorder than being different from other people. Gifted artists, athletes, and scientists have deviant capabilities, yet are not considered psychologically disordered. Also, what is deviant in one culture may not be in another, or at another time. Homosexuality, for example, was once classified as a psychological disorder, but it is no longer. Similarly, nudity is common in some cultures and disturbing in others. Deviant behaviors are more likely to be considered disordered when judged as distressful and dysfunctional to the individual. Prolonged feelings of depression or the use of drugs to avoid dealing with problems are examples of deviant behaviors that may signal a psychological disorder if the person is unable to function, to perform routine behaviors (becomes dysfunctional).

Key Terms

1. To be classified as a **psychological disorder**, behavior must be deviant, distressful, and dysfunctional. (p. 562)

2. **Attention-deficit hyperactivity disorder (ADHD)** is a psychological disorder characterized by the appearance by age 7 of one or more of three symptoms: extreme inattention, hyperactivity, and impulsivity. (p. 563)

3. The **medical model** holds that psychological disorders are illnesses that can be diagnosed, treated, and, in most cases, cured, often through treatment in a psychiatric hospital. (p. 564)

4. **DSM-IV-TR** is a short name for the American Psychiatric Association's *Diagnostic and Statistical Manual of Mental Disorders* (*Fourth Edition, Text Revision*), which provides a widely used system of classifying psychological disorders. (p. 565)

5. **Anxiety disorders** involve distressing, persistent anxiety or maladaptive behaviors that reduce anxiety. (p. 569)

6. In the **generalized anxiety disorder**, the person is continually tense, apprehensive, and in a state of autonomic nervous system arousal for no apparent reason. (p. 570)

7. A **panic disorder** is an episode of intense dread accompanied by chest pain, dizziness, or choking. It is essentially an escalation of the anxiety associated with generalized anxiety disorder. (p. 570)

8. A **phobia** is an anxiety disorder in which a person has a persistent, irrational fear and avoidance of a specific object or situation. (p. 571)

9. **Obsessive-compulsive disorder (OCD)** is an anxiety disorder in which the person experiences uncontrollable and repetitive thoughts (obsessions) and actions (compulsions). (p. 571)

10. **Post-traumatic stress disorder (PTSD)** is an anxiety disorder characterized by haunting memories, nightmares, social withdrawal, jumpy anxiety, and/or insomnia lasting four weeks or more following a traumatic experience. (p. 572)

11. **Post-traumatic growth** refers to positive psychological changes that may result from dealing with extremely challenging circumstances. (pp. 573–574)

12. **Somatoform disorders** are psychological disorders in which bodily symptoms occur without apparent physical cause. (p. 576)

13. **Conversion disorder** is a rare somatoform disorder in which anxiety presumably is converted into a physical symptom such as blindness or paralysis. (p. 577)

14. **Hypochondriasis** is a somatoform disorder in which a person interprets normal physical sensations as symptoms of a disease. (p. 577)

15. **Dissociative disorders** involve a separation of conscious awareness from one's previous memories, thoughts, and feelings. (p. 577)

Memory aid: To *dissociate* is to separate or pull apart. In the **dissociative disorders** a person becomes dissociated from his or her memories and identity.

16. The **dissociative identity disorder (DID)** is a dissociative disorder in which a person exhibits two or more distinct and alternating personalities; formerly called *multiple personality disorder*. (p. 578)

17. **Mood disorders** are characterized by emotional extremes. (p. 579)

18. **Major depressive disorder** is the mood disorder that occurs when a person exhibits the lethargy, feelings of worthlessness, or loss of interest in family, friends, and activities characteristic of depression for more than a two-week period and for no discernible reason. Because of its relative frequency, depression has been called the "common cold" of psychological disorders. (p. 580)

19. **Mania** is the wildly optimistic, euphoric, hyperactive state that alternates with depression in the bipolar disorder. (p. 581)

20. **Bipolar disorder** is the mood disorder in which a person alternates between depression and the euphoria of a manic state. (p. 581)

Memory aid: *Bipolar* means having two poles, that is, two opposite qualities. In **bipolar disorder,** the opposing states are mania and depression.

21. **Schizophrenia** refers to the group of severe disorders whose symptoms may include disorganized and delusional thinking, inappropriate emotions and actions, and disturbed perceptions. (p. 590)

22. **Delusions** are false beliefs that often are symptoms of psychotic disorders. (p. 590)

23. **Personality disorders** are characterized by inflexible and enduring maladaptive character traits that impair social functioning. (p. 596)

24. The **antisocial personality disorder** is a personality disorder in which the person is aggressive, is ruthless, and shows no sign of a conscience that would inhibit wrongdoing. (p. 597)

Treatment of Psychological Disorders

UNIT OVERVIEW

Unit 13 discusses the major psychotherapies and biomedical therapies for maladaptive behaviors. The various psychotherapies all derive from the personality theories discussed earlier, namely, the psychoanalytic, humanistic, behavioral, and cognitive theories. The unit groups the therapies by perspective but also emphasizes the common threads that run through them. In evaluating the therapies, the unit points out that, although people who are untreated often improve, those receiving psychotherapy tend to improve somewhat more, regardless of the type of therapy they receive. This section also includes a discussion of several popular alternative therapies.

The biomedical therapies discussed are drug therapies, electroconvulsive therapy and other forms of brain stimulation, and psychosurgery, which is seldom used. By far the most important of these, drug therapies are being used in the treatment of psychotic, anxiety, and mood disorders.

Because the origins of problems often lie beyond the individual, the unit concludes with approaches that aim at preventing psychological disorders by focusing on the family or on the larger social environment as possible contributors to psychological disorders.

NOTE: Answer guidelines for all Unit 13 questions begin on page 345.

UNIT REVIEW

First, skim each section, noting headings and boldface items. After you have read the section, review each objective by answering the fill-in and essay-type questions that follow it. As you proceed, evaluate your performance by consulting the answers beginning on page 345. Do not continue with the next section until you understand each answer. If you need to, review or reread the section in the textbook before continuing.

Introducing Treatment of Psychological Disorders (pp. 605–606)

Objective 1: Discuss how psychotherapy, biomedical therapy, and an eclectic approach to therapy differ.

1. Mental health therapies are classified as either _____therapies or _____therapies.

2. Psychological therapy is more commonly called _____ . This type of therapy is appropriate for disorders that are _____ .

3. Biomedical therapies include the use of _____ _____ and medical procedures that act directly on the patient's _____ _____ .

4. Some therapists blend several psychotherapy techniques and so are said to take an _____ approach. Closely related to this approach is _____ _____ , which attempts to combine methods into a single, coherent system.

The Psychological Therapies (pp. 606–618)

Objective 2: Define *psychoanalysis,* and discuss the aims, methods, and criticisms of this form of therapy.

1. The goal of Freud's psychoanalysis, which is based on his personality theory, is to help the patient gain _____ .

2. Freud assumed that many psychological problems originate in childhood impulses and conflicts that have been _____ .

3. Psychoanalysts attempt to bring _____ feelings into _____ awareness where they can be dealt with.

4. Freud's technique in which a patient says whatever comes to mind is called _____ _____ .

5. When, in the course of therapy, a person omits shameful or embarrassing material, _____ is occurring. Insight is facilitated by the analyst's _____ of the meaning of such omissions, of dreams, and of other information revealed during therapy sessions.

6. Freud referred to the hidden meaning of a dream as its _____ _____ .

7. When strong feelings, similar to those experienced in other important relationships, are developed toward the therapist, _____ has occurred.

8. Critics point out that psychoanalysts' interpretations are hard to _____ and that therapy takes a long time and is very _____ .

Objective 3: Contrast psychodynamic therapy and interpersonal therapy with traditional psychoanalysis.

9. Therapists who are influenced by Freud's psychoanalysis but who talk to the patient face to face are _____ therapists. In addition, they work with patients only _____ (how long?) and for only a few weeks or months. These therapists focus on _____ across important relationships.

10. A brief alternative to psychodynamic therapy that has proven effective with _____ patients is _____ .

11. While this approach aims to help people gain _____ into the roots of their difficulties, it focuses on _____ _____ rather than on past hurts.

Objective 4: Identify the basic characteristics of the humanistic therapies, and describe the specific goals and techniques of Carl Rogers' client-centered therapy.

12. Humanistic therapies attempt to help people meet their potential for _____ .

List several ways that humanistic therapy differs from psychoanalysis.

13. The humanistic therapy based on Rogers' theory is called _____-_____ therapy, which is described as _____ therapy because the therapist _____ (interprets/does not interpret) the person's problems.

14. To promote growth in clients, Rogerian therapists exhibit _____ , _____ , and _____ .

15. Rogers' technique of restating and clarifying what a person is saying is called _____ _____ .

Given a nonjudgmental environment that provides _____ _____ _____ , patients are better able to accept themselves as they are and to feel valued and whole.

16. Three tips for listening more actively in your own relationships are to _____ , _____ _____ , and _____ _____ .

Objective 5: Explain how the basic assumption of behavior therapy differs from those of traditional psychoanalytic and humanistic therapies, and describe the techniques used in exposure therapies and aversive conditioning.

17. Behavior therapy applies principles of _____ to eliminate troubling behaviors.

Contrast the assumptions of the behavior therapies with those of psychoanalysis and humanistic therapy.

18. One cluster of behavior therapies is based on the principles of _____
_____ , as developed in Pavlov's experiments. This technique, in which a new, incompatible response is substituted for a maladaptive one, is called _____ .
Two examples of this technique are

_____ _____

and _____ _____ .

19. One widely used technique of behavior therapy is the _____ _____ .
The technique of systematic desensitization has been most fully developed by the therapist _____ . The assumption behind this technique is that one cannot simultaneously be _____ and relaxed.

20. The first step in systematic desensitization is the construction of a _____ of anxiety-arousing stimuli. The second step involves training in _____
_____ . In the final step, the person is trained to associate the
_____ state with the
_____-arousing stimuli.

21. For those who are unable to visually imagine an anxiety-arousing situation, or too afraid or embarrassed to do so, _____

_____ _____

therapy offers a promising alternative.

22. In aversive conditioning, the therapist attempts to substitute a _____ (positive/negative) response for one that is currently _____ (positive/negative) to a harmful stimulus. In this technique, a person's unwanted behaviors become associated with _____ feelings. In the long run, aversive conditioning _____ (does/does not) work.

Objective 6: State the main premise of therapy based on operant conditioning principles, and describe the views of proponents and critics of behavior modification.

23. Reinforcing desired behaviors and withholding reinforcement for undesired behaviors are key aspects of _____

_____ .

24. Therapies that influence behavior by controlling its consequences are based on principles of _____ conditioning. One application of this form of therapy to institutional settings is the _____
_____ , in which desired behaviors are rewarded.

State two criticisms of behavior modification.

State some responses of proponents of behavior modification.

Objective 7: Contrast cognitive therapy and cognitive-behavioral therapy, and give some examples of cognitive therapy for depression.

25. Therapists who teach people new, more constructive ways of thinking are using _____ therapy.

26. One variety of cognitive therapy attempts to reverse the _____ beliefs often associated with _____ by helping clients see their irrationalities. This therapy was developed by _____ .

27. Training people to restructure their thinking in stressful situations is the goal of _____ _____ training. Students trained to _____ their negative thoughts are less likely to experience future depression.

28. Treatment that combines an attack on negative thinking with efforts to modify behavior is known as _____-_____ therapy.

Objective 8: Discuss the rationale and benefits of group therapy, including family therapy.

List several advantages of group therapy.

29. The type of group interaction that focuses on the fact that we live and grow in relation to others is _____ _____ .

30. In this type of group, therapists focus on improving _____ within the family.

Evaluating Psychotherapies (pp. 619–628)

Objective 9: Explain why clients and clinicians tend to overestimate the effectiveness of psychotherapy, and describe two phenomena that contribute to clients' and clinicians' misperceptions in this area.

1. In contrast to earlier times, most therapy today _____ (is/is not) provided by psychiatrists.

2. A majority of psychotherapy clients express _____ (satisfaction/dissatisfaction) with their therapy.

Give three reasons that client testimonials are not persuasive evidence for psychotherapy's effectiveness.

3. Clinicians tend to _____ (overestimate/underestimate) the effectiveness of psychotherapy.

4. One reason clinicians' perceptions of the effectiveness of psychotherapy are inaccurate is that clients justify entering therapy by emphasizing their _____ and justify leaving therapy by emphasizing their _____ .

5. (Thinking Critically) Clients' and therapists' perceptions of therapy's effectiveness may be inflated by their _____ that a treatment works. This phenomenon is called the _____ _____ . Another phenomenon that may inflate their perceptions of therapy's effectiveness is the phenomenon called _____ _____ _____ _____ , which is the tendency for _____ events or emotions to return to their _____ state.

Objective 10: Discuss some of the findings of outcome studies in judging the effectiveness of psychotherapies, and describe which psychotherapies are most effective for specific disorders.

6. In hopes of better assessing psychotherapy's effectiveness, psychologists have turned to _____ research studies.

7. The debate over the effectiveness of psychotherapy began with a study by _____ ;

it showed that the rate of improvement for those who received therapy _____ (was/was not) higher than the rate for those who did not.

8. In the best studies of the effectiveness of therapy, researchers randomly assign people on a waiting list to therapy or no therapy and later evaluate everyone. These are _____ _____ trials.

9. A statistical technique that makes it possible to combine the results of many different psychotherapy outcome studies is called _____ . Overall, the results of such analyses indicate that psychotherapy is _____ (somewhat effective/ineffective).

10. Comparisons of the effectiveness of different forms of therapy reveal _____ (clear/no clear) differences, that the type of therapy provider _____ (matters greatly/does not matter), and that whether therapy is provided by an individual therapist or within a group _____ (makes a difference/does not make a difference).

11. With phobias, compulsions, and other specific behavior problems, _____ _____ therapies have been the most effective. Other studies have demonstrated that depression may be effectively treated with _____ therapy. As a rule, psychotherapy is most effective with problems that are _____ (specific/nonspecific).

12. Therapies that are not supported by scientific evidence should be avoided. These include _____ , _____ -_____ , and _____ therapies, as well as _____ _____ and _____ _____ .

13. Clinical decision making that integrates research with clinical expertise and patient preferences is called _____-_____ _____ .

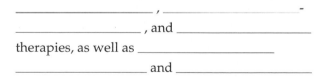

Objective 11: Evaluate the effectiveness of eye movement desensitization and reprocessing (EMDR) and light exposure therapies.

14. Today, many forms of _____ _____ are touted as effective treatments for a variety of complaints.

15. Aside from testimonials, there is very little evidence based on _____ research for such therapies.

16. In one popular alternative therapy, a therapist triggers eye movements in patients while they imagine _____ _____ . This therapy, called _____ _____ _____ _____ _____ , has proven _____ (completely ineffective/somewhat effective) as a treatment for nonmilitary _____- _____ _____ _____ . However, skeptics point to evidence that _____ _____ is just as effective as triggered eye movements in producing beneficial results. The key seems to be in the person's _____ traumatic memories and in a _____ effect.

17. For people who suffer from the wintertime form of depression called _____ _____ _____ , timed _____-_____ therapy may be beneficial.

Objective 12: Describe the three benefits attributed to all psychotherapies.

18. All forms of psychotherapy offer three benefits: _____ for demoralized people; a new _____ on oneself; and a relationship that is _____ , _____ , and _____ .

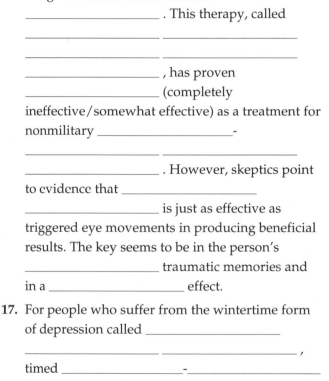

19. The emotional bond between therapist and client—the _____ _____—is a key aspect of effective therapy. In one study of depression treatment, the most effective therapists were those who were perceived as most _____ and _____ .

Objective 13: Discuss the role of values and cultural differences in the therapeutic process, and identify some guidelines for selecting a therapist.

20. Generally speaking, psychotherapists' personal values _____ (do/do not) influence their therapy. This is particularly significant when the therapist and client are from different _____ . Another area of potential value conflict is _____ .

21. In North America, Europe, and Australia, most therapists reflect their culture's _____ .

22. Differences in values may help explain the reluctance of some _____ populations to use mental health services.

23. (Close-Up) The American Psychological Association suggests that a person should seek help when he or she has feelings of _____ , a deep and lasting _____ , disruptive _____ , sudden _____ shifts, and _____ rituals, for example.

The Biomedical Therapies (pp. 628–637)

Objective 14: Define *psychopharmacology*, and explain how double-blind studies help researchers evaluate a drug's effectiveness.

1. As noted earlier, therapy involving changing the brain's functioning is referred to as _____ therapy. The most widely used biomedical treatments are the _____ therapies. Thanks to these therapies, the number of residents in mental hospitals has _____ (increased/ decreased) sharply.

2. The field that studies the effects of drugs on the mind and behavior is _____ .

3. To guard against the _____ effect and normal _____ , neither the patients nor the staff involved in a study may be aware of which condition a given individual is in; this is called a _____-_____ study.

Objective 15: Describe the characteristics of antipsychotic, antianxiety, antidepressant, and mood-stabilizing drugs, and discuss their use in treating psychological disorders.

4. One effect of _____ drugs such as _____ is to help those experiencing _____ (positive/ negative) symptoms of schizophrenia by decreasing their responsiveness to irrelevant stimuli. Schizophrenia patients who are apathetic and withdrawn may be more effectively treated with atypical antipsychotics such as _____ .

5. The antipsychotic drugs work by blocking the receptor sites for the neurotransmitter _____ . The atypical antipsychotics also target _____ receptors.

6. Long-term use of antipsychotic drugs can produce _____ _____ , which involves involuntary movements of the muscles of the _____ , _____ , and _____ .

7. Xanax and Ativan are classified as _____ drugs.

8. These drugs depress activity in the _____ _____ .

9. When used in combination with _____ _____ , these drugs can help people cope with frightening situations.

10. Antianxiety drugs have been criticized for merely reducing _____ , rather than resolving underlying _____ . These drugs can also cause _____ .

11. Drugs that are prescribed to alleviate depression are called _____ drugs. They are increasingly being used to treat _____ disorders. These drugs work by increasing levels of the neurotransmitters _____ or _____ .

12. One example of this type of drug is _____ , which works by blocking the reabsorption and removal of _____ from synapses and is therefore called a _____-_____-_____ drug. Increased serotonin promotes _____ , the development of new brain cells.

13. Equally effective in calming anxious people and energizing depressed people is _____ _____ , which has positive side effects. Even better is to use drugs, which work _____ (bottom-up/top-down), in conjunction with _____-_____ therapy, which works _____ (bottom-up/top-down).

14. Although people with depression often improve after one month on antidepressants, studies demonstrate that a large percentage of the effectiveness is due to _____ _____ or a _____ _____ .

15. To stabilize the mood swings of a bipolar disorder, the simple salt _____ is often prescribed.

16. Another effective drug in the control of mania was originally used to treat epilepsy; it is _____ .

Objective 16: Describe the use of brain stimulation techniques and psychosurgery in treating specific disorders.

17. The therapeutic technique in which the patient receives an electric shock to the brain is referred to as _____ therapy, abbreviated as _____ .

18. ECT is most often used with patients suffering from severe _____ . Research evidence _____ (confirms/does not confirm) ECT's effectiveness with such patients.

19. The mechanism by which ECT works is _____ .

20. A gentler alternative is a chest _____ that intermittently stimulates the _____ nerve.

21. Another gentler procedure called _____ _____ _____ aims to treat depression by presenting pulses through a magnetic coil held close to a person's skull above the right eyebrow. Unlike ECT, this procedure produces no _____ , _____ loss, or other side effects. This procedure may work by energizing the brain's left _____ _____ , which is relatively inactive in depressed patients.

22. The biomedical therapy in which a portion of brain tissue is removed or destroyed is called _____ .

23. In the 1930s, Moniz developed an operation called the _____ . In this procedure, the _____ lobe of the brain is disconnected from the rest of the brain.

24. Today, most psychosurgery has been replaced by the use of _____ or some other form of treatment.

Objective 17: Explain how therapeutic life-style change reflects the idea that humans are integrated biopsychosocial systems.

25. A recent approach to therapy promotes _____ _____-_____ change, which includes regular aerobic exercise, adequate sleep, light exposure, social connection, anti-rumination, and nutritional supplementation.

26. The relative success of this _____ approach seems to confirm that everything psychological is also biological and that we are all social creatures.

Preventing Psychological Disorders
(pp. 637–638)

Objective 16: Explain the rationale of preventive mental health programs.

1. Faced with unforeseen trauma, most adults exhibit _____ .

2. Psychotherapies and biomedical therapies locate the cause of psychological disorders within the _____ . An alternative viewpoint is that many psychological disorders are responses to _____ _____ .

3. According to this viewpoint, it is not just the _____ who needs treatment but also the person's _____ _____ .

4. One advocate of _____ mental health, George Albee, believes that many social stresses undermine people's sense of _____ , _____ _____ , and _____ . These stresses include _____ , work that is _____ , constant _____ , _____ , _____ , and _____ .

5. Albee's views remind us that disorders are not just biological and not just environmental or psychological because we are all an _____ _____ system.

PROGRESS TEST 1

Multiple-Choice Questions

Circle your answers to the following questions and check them with the answers beginning on page 346. If your answer is incorrect, read the explanation for why it is incorrect and then consult the appropriate pages of the text (in parentheses following the correct answer).

1. Electroconvulsive therapy is most useful in the treatment of
   a. schizophrenia.
   b. depression.
   c. personality disorders.
   d. anxiety disorders.

2. The technique in which a person is asked to report everything that comes to his or her mind is called _____ ; it is favored by_____ therapists.
   a. active listening; cognitive
   b. spontaneous remission; humanistic
   c. free association; psychoanalytic
   d. systematic desensitization; behavior

3. Of the following categories of psychotherapy, which is known for its nondirective nature?
   a. psychoanalysis
   c. behavior therapy
   b. humanistic therapy
   d. cognitive therapy

4. Which of the following is NOT a common criticism of psychoanalysis?
   a. It emphasizes the existence of repressed memories.
   b. It provides interpretations that are hard to disprove.
   c. It is generally a very expensive process.
   d. It gives therapists too much control over patients.

5. Which of the following types of therapy does NOT belong with the others?
   a. cognitive therapy
   b. family therapy
   c. behavior therapy
   d. psychosurgery

6. Which of the following is NOT necessarily an advantage of group therapies over individual therapies?
   a. They tend to take less time for the therapist.
   b. They tend to cost less money for the client.
   c. They are more effective.
   d. They allow the client to test new behaviors in a social context.

7. Which biomedical therapy is MOST likely to be practiced today?
   a. psychosurgery
   b. electroconvulsive therapy
   c. drug therapy
   d. counterconditioning

8. The effectiveness of psychotherapy has been assessed both through clients' perspectives and through controlled research studies. What have such assessments found?
   a. Clients' perceptions and controlled studies alike strongly affirm the effectiveness of psychotherapy.
   b. Whereas clients' perceptions strongly affirm the effectiveness of psychotherapy, studies point to more modest results.

c. Whereas studies strongly affirm the effectiveness of psychotherapy, many clients feel dissatisfied with their progress.

d. Clients' perceptions and controlled studies alike paint a very mixed picture of the effectiveness of psychotherapy.

9. Cognitive-behavioral therapy aims to
   a. alter the way people act.
   b. make people more aware of their irrational negative thinking.
   c. alter the way people think and act.
   d. countercondition anxiety-provoking stimuli.

10. The results of outcome research on the effectiveness of different psychotherapies reveal that
    a. no single type of therapy is consistently superior.
    b. behavior therapies are most effective in treating specific problems, such as phobias.
    c. cognitive therapies are most effective in treating depressed emotions.
    d. all of these statements are true.

11. The antipsychotic drugs appear to produce their effects by blocking the receptor sites for
    a. dopamine.   c. norepinephrine.
    b. epinephrine.   d. serotonin.

12. Psychologists who advocate a _____ approach to mental health contend that many psychological disorders could be prevented by changing the disturbed individual's _____ .
    a. biomedical; diet
    b. family; behavior
    c. humanistic; feelings
    d. preventive; environment

13. An eclectic psychotherapist is one who
    a. takes a nondirective approach in helping clients solve their problems.
    b. views psychological disorders as usually stemming from one cause, such as a biological abnormality.
    c. uses one particular technique, such as psychoanalysis or counterconditioning, in treating disorders.
    d. uses a variety of techniques, depending on the client and the problem.

14. The technique in which a therapist echoes and restates what a person says in a nondirective manner is called
    a. active listening.
    b. free association.
    c. systematic desensitization.
    d. transference.

15. Unlike traditional psychoanalytic therapy, interpersonal psychotherapy
    a. helps people gain insight into the roots of their problems.
    b. offers interpretations of patients' feelings.
    c. focuses on current relationships.
    d. does all of these things.

16. The technique of systematic desensitization is based on the premise that maladaptive symptoms are
    a. a reflection of irrational thinking.
    b. conditioned responses.
    c. expressions of unfulfilled wishes.
    d. inner conflicts.

17. The operant conditioning technique in which desired behaviors are rewarded with points or poker chips that can later be exchanged for various rewards is called
    a. counterconditioning.
    b. systematic desensitization.
    c. a token economy.
    d. exposure therapy.

18. One variety of _____ therapy is based on the finding that depressed people often attribute their failures to _____ .
    a. humanistic; themselves
    b. behavior; external circumstances
    c. cognitive; external circumstances
    d. cognitive; themselves

19. A person can derive benefits from psychotherapy simply by believing in it. This illustrates the importance of
    a. spontaneous recovery.
    b. the placebo effect.
    c. the transference effect.
    d. interpretation.

20. Before 1950, the main mental health providers were
    a. psychologists.   c. psychiatrists.
    b. paraprofessionals. d. the clergy.

Matching Items

Match each term with the appropriate definition or description.

Terms

_____   1. cognitive therapy
_____   2. behavior therapy
_____   3. systematic desensitization
_____   4. cognitive-behavioral therapy
_____   5. client-centered therapy
_____   6. exposure therapy
_____   7. aversive conditioning
_____   8. psychoanalysis
_____   9. preventive mental health
_____   10. biomedical therapy
_____   11. counterconditioning
_____   12. insight therapy

Definitions or Descriptions

a. associates unwanted behavior with unpleasant experiences
b. associates a relaxed state with anxiety-arousing stimuli
c. emphasizes the social context of psychological disorders
d. integrated therapy that focuses on changing self-defeating thinking and unwanted behavior
e. category of therapies that teach people more adaptive ways of thinking and acting
f. the most widely used method of behavior therapy
g. therapy developed by Carl Rogers
h. therapy based on Sigmund Freud's theory of personality
i. treatment with psychosurgery, electroconvulsive therapy, or drugs
j. classical conditioning procedure in which new responses are conditioned to stimuli that trigger unwanted behaviors
k. category of therapies based on learning principles derived from classical and operant conditioning
l. therapies that aim to increase the client's awareness of underlying motives and defenses

PROGRESS TEST 2

Progress Test 2 should be completed during a final unit review. Answer the following questions after you thoroughly understand the correct answers for the section reviews and Progress Test 1.

Multiple-Choice Questions

1. Carl Rogers was a _____ therapist who was the creator of _____ .
   a. behavior; systematic desensitization
   b. psychoanalytic; insight therapy
   c. humanistic; client-centered therapy
   d. cognitive; cognitive therapy for depression

2. Using techniques of classical conditioning to develop an association between unwanted behavior and an unpleasant experience is known as
   a. aversive conditioning.
   b. systematic desensitization.
   c. transference.
   d. electroconvulsive therapy.

3. Which type of psychotherapy emphasizes the individual's inherent potential for self-fulfillment?
   a. behavior therapy   c. humanistic therapy
   b. psychoanalysis   d. biomedical therapy

4. Light-exposure therapy has proven useful as a form of treatment for people suffering from
   a. bulimia.
   b. seasonal affective disorder.
   c. schizophrenia.
   d. dissociative identity disorder.

5. Which type of psychotherapy focuses on changing unwanted behaviors rather than on discovering their underlying causes?
   a. behavior therapy
   b. cognitive therapy
   c. humanistic therapy
   d. psychoanalysis

6. The techniques of counterconditioning are based on principles of
   a. observational learning.
   b. classical conditioning.
   c. operant conditioning.
   d. behavior modification.

7. In which of the following does the client learn to associate a relaxed state with a hierarchy of anxiety-arousing situations?
   a. cognitive therapy
   b. aversive conditioning
   c. counterconditioning
   d. systematic desensitization

8. Principles of operant conditioning underlie which of the following techniques?
   a. counterconditioning
   b. systematic desensitization
   c. stress inoculation training
   d. the token economy

9. Which of these therapies emphasizes that we are all integrated biopsychosocial systems?
   a. interpersonal psychotherapy
   b. cognitive therapy
   c. therapeutic life-style change
   d. eye movement desensitization and reprocessing

10. Which type of therapy focuses on eliminating irrational thinking?
    a. EMDR
    b. client-centered therapy
    c. cognitive therapy
    d. behavior therapy

11. Antidepressant drugs are believed to work by affecting serotonin or
    a. dopamine.   c. norepinephrine.
    b. lithium.   d. acetylcholine.

12. After many years of taking antipsychotic drugs, Greg's facial muscles sometimes twitch involuntarily. This behavior is called
    a. tardive dyskinesia.
    b. spontaneous recovery.
    c. repetitive transcranial magnetic stimulation.
    d. EMDR.

13. Which of the following is the mood-stabilizing drug most commonly used to treat bipolar disorder?
    a. Ativan   c. Xanax
    b. chlorpromazine   d. lithium

14. The type of drugs criticized for reducing symptoms without resolving underlying problems are the
    a. antianxiety drugs.
    b. antipsychotic drugs.
    c. antidepressant drugs.
    d. amphetamines.

15. Which form of therapy is *most* likely to be successful in treating depression?
    a. behavior modification   c. cognitive therapy
    b. psychoanalysis   d. humanistic therapy

16. Although Moniz won the Nobel Prize for developing the lobotomy procedure, the technique is not widely used today because
    a. it produces a lethargic, immature personality.
    b. it is irreversible.
    c. calming drugs became available in the 1950s.
    d. of all of these reasons.

17. Unusual emotions tend to return to their average state. This phenomenon is called
    a. regression toward the mean.
    b. resistance.
    c. counterconditioning.
    d. systematic desensitization.

18. Among the common ingredients of the psychotherapies is
    a. the offer of a therapeutic relationship.
    b. the expectation among clients that the therapy will prove helpful.
    c. the chance to develop a fresh perspective on oneself and the world.
    d. all of these are common ingredients.

19. Family therapy differs from other forms of psychotherapy because it focuses on
    a. using a variety of treatment techniques.
    b. conscious rather than unconscious processes.
    c. the present instead of the past.
    d. how family tensions may cause individual problems.

20. One reason that aversive conditioning may only be temporarily effective is that
   a. for ethical reasons, therapists cannot use sufficiently intense unconditioned stimuli to sustain classical conditioning.
   b. patients are often unable to become sufficiently relaxed for conditioning to take place.
   c. patients know that outside the therapist's office they can engage in the undesirable behavior without fear of aversive consequences.
   d. most conditioned responses are elicited by many nonspecific stimuli and it is impossible to countercondition them all.

Matching Items

Match each term with the appropriate definition or description.

Terms

_____ 1. active listening
_____ 2. token economy
_____ 3. placebo effect
_____ 4. lobotomy
_____ 5. lithium
_____ 6. psychopharmacology
_____ 7. double-blind procedure
_____ 8. Xanax
_____ 9. free association
_____ 10. stress inoculation training
_____ 11. evidence-based practice
_____ 12. regression toward the mean
_____ 13. meta-analysis

Definitions or Descriptions

a. type of psychosurgery
b. mood-stabilizing drug
c. clinical decision making that integrates research, clinical expertise, and patient characteristics
d. empathic technique used in person-centered therapy
e. the beneficial effect of a person's expecting that treatment will be effective
f. antianxiety drug
g. the tendency for unusual emotions to return toward their average state
h. technique of psychoanalytic therapy
i. an operant conditioning procedure
j. the study of the effects of drugs on the mind and behavior
k. a procedure for statistically combining the results of many research studies
l. experimental procedure in which both the patient and staff are unaware of a patient's treatment condition
m. cognitive-behavior therapy in which people are trained to restructure their thinking in stressful situations

PSYCHOLOGY APPLIED

Answer these questions the day before a test as a final check on your understanding of the unit's terms and concepts.

Multiple-Choice Questions

1. During a session with his psychoanalyst, Jamal hesitates while describing a highly embarrassing thought. In the psychoanalytic framework, this is an example of
   a. transference.
   b. insight.
   c. mental repression.
   d. resistance.

2. During psychoanalysis, Jane has developed strong feelings of hatred for her therapist. The analyst interprets Jane's behavior in terms of a _____ of her feelings toward her father.
   a. projection
   b. resistance
   c. regression
   d. transference

3. Given that Jim's therapist attempts to help him by offering genuineness, acceptance, and empathy, she is probably practicing
   a. psychoanalysis.
   b. behavior therapy.
   c. cognitive therapy.
   d. client-centered therapy.

4. To help Sam quit smoking, his therapist blew a blast of smoke into Sam's face each time Sam inhaled. Which technique is the therapist using?

   a. exposure therapy
   b. behavior modification
   c. systematic desensitization
   d. aversive conditioning

5. After Darnel dropped a pass in an important football game, he became depressed and vowed to quit the team because of his athletic incompetence. The campus psychologist used gentle questioning to reveal to Darnel that his thinking was irrational: His "incompetence" had earned him an athletic scholarship. The psychologist's response was most typical of a _____ therapist.

   a. behavior   c. client-centered
   b. psychoanalytic   d. cognitive

6. Seth enters therapy to talk about some issues that have been upsetting him. The therapist prescribes some medication to help him. The therapist is MOST likely a

   a. clinical psychologist.
   b. psychiatrist.
   c. psychiatric social worker.
   d. clinical social worker.

7. In an experiment testing the effects of a new antipsychotic drug, neither Dr. Cunningham nor her patients know whether the patients are in the experimental or the control group. This is an example of

   a. meta-analysis.
   b. within-subjects research.
   c. the double-blind technique.
   d. the single-blind technique.

8. A close friend who for years has suffered from wintertime depression is seeking your advice regarding the effectiveness of light-exposure therapy. What should you tell your friend?

   a. "Don't waste your time and money. It doesn't work."
   b. "A more effective treatment for seasonal affective disorder is eye movement desensitization and reprocessing."
   c. "You'd be better off with a prescription for lithium."
   d. "It might be worth a try. There is some evidence that morning light exposure produces relief."

9. A relative wants to know which type of therapy works best. You should tell your relative that

   a. psychotherapy does not work.
   b. behavior therapy is the most effective.
   c. cognitive therapy is the most effective.
   d. no one type of therapy is consistently the most successful.

10. Leota is startled when her therapist says that she needs to focus on eliminating her problem behavior rather than gaining insight into its underlying cause. Most likely, Leota has consulted a _____ therapist.

    a. behavior   c. cognitive
    b. humanistic   d. psychoanalytic

11. To help him overcome his fear of flying, Duane's therapist has him construct a hierarchy of anxiety-triggering stimuli and then learn to associate each with a state of deep relaxation. Duane's therapist is using the technique called

    a. systematic desensitization.
    b. aversive conditioning.
    c. shaping.
    d. free association.

12. A patient in a hospital receives poker chips for making her bed, being punctual at meal times, and maintaining her physical appearance. The poker chips can be exchanged for privileges, such as television viewing, snacks, and magazines. This is an example of the

    a. psychodynamic therapy technique called systematic desensitization.
    b. behavior therapy technique called token economy.
    c. cognitive therapy technique called token economy.
    d. humanistic therapy technique called systematic desensitization.

13. Ben is a cognitive-behavioral therapist. Compared with Rachel, who is a behavior therapist, Ben is more likely to

    a. base his therapy on principles of operant conditioning.
    b. base his therapy on principles of classical conditioning.
    c. address clients' attitudes as well as behaviors.
    d. focus on clients' unconscious urges.

14. A psychotherapist who believes that the best way to treat psychological disorders is to prevent them from developing would be MOST likely to view disordered behavior as
    a. maladaptive thoughts and actions.
    b. expressions of unconscious conflicts.
    c. conditioned responses.
    d. an understandable response to stressful social conditions.

15. Linda's doctor prescribes medication that blocks the activity of dopamine in her nervous system. Evidently, Linda is being treated with an _____ drug.
    a. antipsychotic   c. antidepressant
    b. antianxiety   d. anticonvulsive

16. Abraham's doctor prescribes medication that increases the availability of norepinephrine or serotonin in his nervous system. Evidently, Abraham is being treated with an _____ drug.
    a. antipsychotic
    b. mood-stabilizing
    c. antidepressant
    d. anticonvulsive

17. In concluding her talk titled "Psychosurgery Today," Ashley states that
    a. "Psychosurgery is still widely used throughout the world."
    b. "Electroconvulsive therapy is the only remaining psychosurgical technique that is widely practiced."
    c. "With advances in psychopharmacology, psychosurgery has largely been abandoned."
    d. "Although lobotomies remain popular, other psychosurgical techniques have been abandoned."

18. A psychiatrist has diagnosed a patient as having bipolar disorder. It is likely that she will prescribe
    a. an antipsychotic drug.
    b. lithium.
    c. an antianxiety drug.
    d. a drug that blocks receptor sites for serotonin.

19. Which type of psychotherapy would be most likely to use the interpretation of dreams as a technique for bringing unconscious feelings into awareness?
    a. client-centered therapy
    b. psychodynamic therapy
    c. cognitive therapy
    d. behavior therapy

20. Of the following therapists, who would be most likely to interpret a person's psychological problems in terms of repressed impulses?
    a. a behavior therapist
    b. a cognitive therapist
    c. a humanistic therapist
    d. a psychoanalyst

Essay Question

Willie has been diagnosed as suffering from major depressive disorder. Describe the treatment he might receive from a psychoanalyst, a cognitive therapist, and a biomedical therapist. (Use the space below to list points you want to make, and organize them. Then write the essay on a separate sheet of paper.)

KEY TERMS

Using your own words, on a separate piece of paper write a brief definition or explanation of each of the following terms.

1. eclectic approach
2. psychotherapy
3. psychoanalysis
4. resistance
5. interpretation
6. transference
7. psychodynamic therapy
8. insight therapies
9. client-centered therapy
10. active listening
11. unconditional positive regard
12. behavior therapy

13. counterconditioning

14. exposure therapies

15. systematic desensitization

16. virtual reality exposure therapy

17. aversive conditioning

18. token economy

19. cognitive therapy

20. cognitive-behavioral therapy

21. family therapy

22. regression toward the mean

23. meta-analysis

24. evidence-based practice

25. biomedical therapy

26. psychopharmacology

27. antipsychotic drugs

28. tardive dyskinesia

29. antianxiety drugs

30. antidepressant drugs

31. electroconvulsive therapy (ECT)

32. repetitive transcranial magnetic stimulation (rTMS)

33. psychosurgery

34. lobotomy

35. resilience

ANSWERS

Unit Review

Introducing Treatment of Psychological Disorders

1. psychological; biomedical

2. psychotherapy; learned

3. prescribed medications; nervous system

4. eclectic; psychotherapy integration

The Psychological Therapies

1. insight

2. repressed

3. repressed; conscious

4. free association

5. resistance; interpretation

6. latent content

7. transference

8. prove or disprove; expensive

9. psychodynamic; once a week; themes

10. depressed; interpersonal psychotherapy

11. insight; current relationships

12. self-fulfillment

Unlike psychoanalysis, humanistic therapy is focused on the present and future instead of the past, on conscious rather than unconscious processes, on promoting growth and fulfillment instead of curing illness, and on helping clients take immediate responsibility for their feelings and actions rather than on uncovering the obstacles to doing so.

13. client-centered; nondirective; does not interpret

14. genuineness; acceptance; empathy

15. active listening; unconditional positive regard

16. paraphrase; invite clarification; reflect feelings

17. learning

Whereas psychoanalysis and humanistic therapies assume that problems diminish as self-awareness grows, behavior therapists doubt that self-awareness is the key. Instead of looking for the inner cause of unwanted behavior, behavior therapy applies learning principles to directly attack the unwanted behavior itself.

18. classical conditioning; counterconditioning; exposure therapy; aversive conditioning

19. exposure therapies; Joseph Wolpe; anxious

20. hierarchy; progressive relaxation; relaxed; anxiety

21. virtual reality exposure

22. negative; positive; unpleasant; does not

23. behavior modification

24. operant; token economy

Behavior modification is criticized because the desired behavior may stop when the rewards are stopped. Also, critics contend that one person should not be allowed to control another.

Proponents of behavior modification contend that some clients request this therapy and that the behaviors will persist if patients are properly weaned from the tokens. Also, control already exists.

25. cognitive

26. catastrophizing; depression; Aaron Beck

27. stress inoculation; dispute

28. cognitive-behavioral

Group therapy saves therapists time and clients money. The social context of group therapy allows people to discover that others have similar problems and to try out new ways of behaving.

29. family therapy
30. communication

Evaluating Psychotherapies

1. is not
2. satisfaction

   People often enter therapy in crisis. When the crisis passes, they may attribute their improvement to the therapy. Clients, who may need to believe the therapy was worth the effort, may overestimate its effectiveness. Clients generally find positive things to say about their therapists, even if their problems remain.

3. overestimate
4. unhappiness; well-being
5. belief; placebo effect; regression toward the mean; unusual; average
6. controlled
7. Hans Eysenck; was not
8. randomized clinical
9. meta-analysis; somewhat effective
10. no clear; does not matter; does not make a difference
11. behavioral conditioning; cognitive; specific
12. energy; recovered-memory; rebirthing; facilitated communication; crisis debriefing
13. evidence-based practice
14. alternative therapy
15. controlled
16. traumatic events; eye movement desensitization and reprocessing (EMDR); somewhat effective; post-traumatic stress disorder; finger tapping; reliving; placebo
17. seasonal affective disorder; light-exposure
18. hope; perspective; caring; trusting; empathic
19. therapeutic alliance; empathic; caring
20. do; cultures; religion
21. individualism
22. minority
23. hopelessness; depression; fears; mood; compulsive

The Biomedical Therapies

1. biomedical; drug; decreased
2. psychopharmacology
3. placebo; recovery; double-blind
4. antipsychotic; chlorpromazine (Thorazine); positive; clozapine (Clozaril)
5. dopamine; serotonin
6. tardive dyskinesia; face; tongue; limbs
7. antianxiety
8. central nervous system
9. psychological therapy
10. symptoms; problems; physiological dependence
11. antidepressant; anxiety; norepinephrine; serotonin
12. fluoxetine (Prozac); serotonin; selective-serotonin-reuptake-inhibitor; neurogenesis
13. aerobic exercise; bottom-up; cognitive-behavioral; top-down
14. spontaneous recovery; placebo effect
15. lithium
16. Depakote
17. electroconvulsive; ECT
18. depression; confirms
19. unknown
20. implant; vagus
21. repetitive transcranial magnetic stimulation (rTMS); seizures; memory; frontal lobe
22. psychosurgery
23. lobotomy; frontal
24. drugs
25. therapeutic life-style
26. biopsychosocial

Preventing Psychological Disorders

1. resilience
2. person; a disturbing and stressful society
3. person; social context
4. preventive; competence; personal control; self-esteem; poverty; meaningless; criticism; unemployment; racism; sexism
5. integrated biopsychosocial

Progress Test 1

Multiple-Choice Questions

1. **b.** is the answer. Although no one is sure how ECT works, one possible explanation is that it increases release of norepinephrine, the neurotransmitter that elevates mood. (p. 632)
2. **c.** is the answer. (p. 607)
   a. Active listening is a Rogerian technique in which the therapist echoes, restates, and seeks clarification of the client's statements.

b. Spontaneous recovery refers to improvement without treatment.

d. Systematic desensitization is a process in which a person is conditioned to associate a relaxed state with anxiety-triggering stimuli.

3. **b.** is the answer. (p. 609)

4. **d.** is the answer. This is not among the criticisms commonly made of psychoanalysis. (It would more likely be made of behavior therapies.) (pp. 607–608)

5. **d.** is the answer. (p. 635)
   a., b., & c. Each of these is a type of psychological therapy.

6. **c.** is the answer. Outcome research on the relative effectiveness of different therapies reveals no clear winner; the other factors mentioned are advantages of group therapies. (pp. 617, 622)

7. **c.** is the answer. (p. 628)
   a. The fact that its effects are irreversible makes psychosurgery a drastic procedure, and with advances in psychopharmacology, psychosurgery was largely abandoned.
   b. ECT is still widely used as a treatment of severe depression, but in general it is not used as frequently as drug therapy.
   d. Counterconditioning is not a biomedical therapy.

8. **b.** is the answer. Clients' testimonials regarding psychotherapy are generally very positive. The research, in contrast, seems to show that therapy is only *somewhat* effective. (pp. 619, 620–621)

9. **c.** is the answer. (p. 616)

10. **d.** is the answer. (p. 622)

11. **a.** is the answer. By occupying receptor sites for dopamine, these drugs block its activity and reduce its production. (p. 629)

12. **d.** is the answer. (p. 638)

13. **d.** is the answer. Today, half of all psychotherapists describe themselves as eclectic—as using a blend of therapies. (p. 606)
    a. An eclectic therapist may use a nondirective approach with certain behaviors; however, a more directive approach might be chosen for other clients and problems.
    b. In fact, just the opposite is true. Eclectic therapists generally view disorders as stemming from many influences.
    c. Eclectic therapists, in contrast to this example, use a combination of treatments.

14. **a.** is the answer. (p. 609)

15. **c.** is the answer. (p. 608)

16. **b.** is the answer. (pp. 611–612)

a. This reflects a cognitive perspective.
c. This reflects a psychoanalytic perspective.

17. **c.** is the answer. (p. 614)
    a. & b. Counterconditioning is the replacement of an undesired response with a desired one by means of aversive conditioning or systematic desensitization.
    d. Exposure therapy exposes a person, in imagination or in actuality, to a feared situation.

18. **d.** is the answer. (p. 615)

19. **b.** is the answer. (p. 621)
    a. Spontaneous recovery refers to improvement without any treatment.
    c. Transference is the psychoanalytic phenomenon in which a client transfers feelings from other relationships onto his or her analyst.
    d. Interpretation is the psychoanalytic procedure through which the analyst helps the client become aware of resistances and understand their meaning.

20. **c.** is the answer. (p. 619)

Matching Items

1. e (p. 614)	5. g (p. 609)	9. c (p. 638)
2. k (pp. 610–611)	6. f (p. 611)	10. i (p. 628)
3. b (p. 611)	7. a (p. 613)	11. j (p. 611)
4. d (p. 616)	8. h (p. 606)	12. l (p. 609)

Progress Test 2

Multiple-Choice Questions

1. **c.** is the answer. (p. 609)
   a. This answer would be a correct description of Joseph Wolpe.
   b. There is no such thing as insight therapy.
   d. This answer would be a correct description of Aaron Beck.

2. **a.** is the answer. (p. 613)
   b. In systematic desensitization, a hierarchy of anxiety-provoking stimuli is gradually associated with a relaxed state.
   c. Transference refers to a patient's transferring of feelings from other relationships onto his or her psychoanalyst.
   d. Electroconvulsive therapy is a biomedical shock treatment.

3. **c.** is the answer. (p. 609)
   a. Behavior therapy focuses on behavior, not self-awareness.
   b. Psychoanalysis focuses on bringing repressed feelings into awareness.

d. Biomedical therapy focuses on physical treatment through drugs, ECT, or psychosurgery.

4. **b.** is the answer. (pp. 624–625)

5. **a.** is the answer. For behavior therapy, the problem behaviors *are* the problems. (p. 611)
b. Cognitive therapy teaches people to think and act in more adaptive ways.
c. Humanistic therapy promotes growth and self-fulfillment by providing an empathic, genuine, and accepting environment.
d. Psychoanalytic therapy focuses on uncovering and interpreting repressed feelings.

6. **b.** is the answer. Counterconditioning techniques involve taking an established stimulus, which triggers an undesirable response, and pairing it with a new stimulus in order to condition a new, and more adaptive, response. (p. 611)
a. As indicated by the name, counterconditioning techniques are a form of conditioning; they do not involve learning by observation.
c. & d. The principles of operant conditioning are the basis of behavior modification, which, in contrast to counterconditioning techniques, involves use of reinforcement.

7. **d.** is the answer. (pp. 611–612)
a. This is a confrontational therapy, which is aimed at teaching people to think and act in more adaptive ways.
b. Aversive conditioning is a form of counterconditioning in which unwanted behavior is associated with unpleasant feelings.
c. Counterconditioning is a general term, including not only systematic desensitization, in which a hierarchy of fears is desensitized, but also other techniques, such as aversive conditioning.

8. **d.** is the answer. (p. 614)
a. & b. These techniques are based on classical conditioning.
c. This is a type of cognitive therapy.

9. **c.** is the answer. (p. 636)
a. Interpersonal psychotherapy, like psychoanalysis, emphasizes inner conflicts.
b. Cognitive therapies focus on how our thinking colors our feelings.
d. Eye movement desensitization and reprocessing is an alternative therapy that combines the basic premise of exposure therapy with a placebo effect.

10. **c.** is the answer. (pp. 614–615)
a. This is an alternative therapy in which the practitioner triggers eye movements in patients who are imagining traumatic events.

b. In this humanistic therapy, the therapist facilitates the client's growth by offering a genuine, accepting, and empathic environment.
d. Behavior therapy concentrates on modifying the actual symptoms of psychological problems.

11. **c.** is the answer. (p. 630)

12. **a.** is the answer. (p. 629)

13. **d.** is the answer. Lithium works as a mood stabilizer. (p. 632)
a. & c. Ativan and Xanax are antianxiety drugs.
b. Chlorpromazine is an antipsychotic drug.

14. **a.** is the answer. (p. 630)

15. **c.** is the answer. (p. 622)
a. Behavior modification is most likely to be successful in treating specific behavior problems, such as bed wetting.
b. & d. The text does not single out particular disorders for which these therapies tend to be most effective.

16. **d.** is the answer. (pp. 635–636)

17. **a.** is the answer. (p. 621)

18. **d.** is the answer. (pp. 625–626)

19. **d.** is the answer. (p. 617)
a. This is true of most forms of psychotherapy.
b. & c. This is true of humanistic, cognitive, and behavior therapies.

20. **c.** is the answer. Although aversive conditioning may work in the short run, the person's ability to discriminate between the situation in which the aversive conditioning occurs and other situations can limit the treatment's effectiveness. (p. 613)
a., b., & d. These were not offered in the text as limitations of the effectiveness of aversive conditioning.

Matching Items

1. d (p. 609)	6. j (p. 628)	10. m (p. 616)
2. i (p. 614)	7. l (p. 629)	11. c (p. 623)
3. e (p. 621)	8. f (p. 630)	12. g (p. 621)
4. a (p. 635)	9. h (p. 607)	13. k (p. 621)
5. b (p. 632)		

Psychology Applied

Multiple-Choice Questions

1. **d.** is the answer. Resistances are blocks in the flow of free association that hint at underlying anxiety. (p. 607)
a. In transference, a patient redirects feelings from other relationships to his or her analyst.

b. The goal of psychoanalysis is for patients to gain insight into their feelings.

c. Although such hesitation may well involve material that has been repressed, the hesitation itself is a resistance.

2. **d.** is the answer. In transference, the patient develops feelings toward the therapist that were experienced in important early relationships but were repressed. (p. 607)
a. Projection is a defense mechanism in which a person imputes his or her own feelings to someone else.
b. Resistances are blocks in the flow of free association that indicate repressed material.
c. Regression is a defense mechanism in which a person retreats to an earlier form of behavior.

3. **d.** is the answer. According to Rogers' client-centered therapy, the therapist must exhibit genuineness, acceptance, and empathy if the client is to move toward self-fulfillment. (p. 609)
a. Psychoanalysts are much more directive in providing interpretations of clients' problems than are humanistic therapists.
b. Behavior therapists focus on modifying the behavioral symptoms of psychological problems.
c. Cognitive therapists teach people to think and act in new, more adaptive ways.

4. **d.** is the answer. Aversive conditioning is the classical conditioning technique in which a positive response is replaced by a negative response. (In this example, the US is the blast of smoke, the CS is the taste of the cigarette as it is inhaled, and the intended CR is aversion to cigarettes.) (p. 613)
a. Exposure therapy exposes someone, in imagination (virtual reality exposure therapy) or actuality, to a feared situation.
b. Behavior modification applies the principles of operant conditioning and thus, in contrast to the example, uses reinforcement.
c. Systematic desensitization is used to help people overcome specific anxieties.

5. **d.** is the answer. Because the psychologist is focusing on Darnel's irrational thinking, this response is most typical of Beck's cognitive therapy for depression. (pp. 615–616)
a. Behavior therapists treat behaviors rather than thoughts.
b. Psychoanalysts focus on helping patients gain insight into previously repressed feelings.
c. Client-centered therapists attempt to facilitate clients' growth by offering a genuine, accepting, empathic environment.

6. **b.** is the answer. Psychiatrists are physicians who specialize in treating psychological disorders. As doctors they can prescribe medications. (p. 627)
a., c., & d. These professionals cannot prescribe drugs.

7. **c.** is the answer. (p. 629)
a. This is a statistical technique used to combine the results of many different research studies.
b. In this design, which is not mentioned in the text, there is only a single research group.
d. This answer would be correct if the experimenter, but not the research participants, knew which condition was in effect.

8. **d.** is the answer. (pp. 624–625)
a. In fact, there is evidence that light-exposure therapy can be effective in treating SAD.
b. There is no evidence that EMDR is effective as a treatment for SAD.
c. Lithium is a mood-stabilizing drug that is often used to treat bipolar disorder.

9. **d.** is the answer. (p. 622)
a. Psychotherapy has proven "somewhat effective" and more cost-effective than physician care for psychological disorders.
b. & c. Behavior and cognitive therapies are both effective in treating depression, and behavior therapy is effective in treating specific problems such as phobias.

10. **a.** is the answer. (p. 611)
b. & c. These types of therapists are more concerned with promoting self-fulfillment (humanistic) and healthy patterns of thinking (cognitive) than with correcting specific problem behaviors.
d. Psychoanalysts see the behavior merely as a symptom and focus their treatment on its presumed underlying cause.

11. **a.** is the answer. (pp. 611–612)
b. Aversive conditioning associates unpleasant states with unwanted behaviors.
c. Shaping is an operant conditioning technique in which successive approximations of a desired behavior are reinforced.
d. Free association is a psychoanalytic technique in which a patient says whatever comes to mind.

12. **b.** is the answer. (p. 614)

13. **c.** is the answer. (p. 616)
a. & b. Behavior therapists make extensive use of techniques based on both operant and classical conditioning.
d. Neither behavior therapists nor cognitive-behavioral therapists focus on clients' unconscious urges.

14. **d.** is the answer. (p. 638)
   a. This would be the perspective of a cognitive-behavioral therapist.
   b. This would be the perspective of a psychoanalyst.
   c. This would be the perspective of a behavior therapist.

15. **a.** is the answer. (p. 629)

16. **c.** is the answer. (p. 630)

17. **c.** is the answer. (p. 636)
   b. Although still practiced, electroconvulsive therapy is not a form of psychosurgery.

18. **b.** is the answer. (p. 632)

19. **b.** is the answer. Like psychoanalysis, psychodynamic therapy seeks insight into a patient's unconscious feelings. The analysis of dreams, slips of the tongue, and resistances are considered a window into these feelings. (p. 608)
   a. Client-centered therapy focuses on the conscious mind and on the present and future.
   c. Cognitive therapists avoid reference to unconscious feelings and would therefore be uninterested in interpreting dreams.
   d. Behavior therapy is not concerned with unconscious feelings.

20. **d.** is the answer. A key aim of psychoanalysis is to unearth and understand repressed impulses. (p. 607)
   a., b., & c. Behavior and cognitive therapists avoid concepts such as "repression" and "unconscious"; behavior and humanistic therapists focus on the present rather than the past.

Essay Question

Psychoanalysts assume that psychological problems such as depression are caused by unresolved, repressed, and unconscious impulses and conflicts from childhood. A psychoanalyst would probably attempt to bring these repressed feelings into Willie's conscious awareness and help him gain insight into them. He or she would likely try to interpret Willie's resistance during free association, the latent content of his dreams, and any emotional feelings he might transfer to the analyst.

   Cognitive therapists assume that a person's emotional reactions are influenced by the person's thoughts in response to the event in question. A cognitive therapist would probably try to teach Willie new and more constructive ways of thinking in order to reverse his catastrophizing beliefs about himself, his situation, and his future.

   Biomedical therapists attempt to treat disorders by altering the functioning of the patient's brain. A biomedical therapist would probably prescribe an antidepressant drug such as fluoxetine to increase the availability of norepinephrine and serotonin in Willie's nervous system. If Willie's depression is especially severe, a *psychiatrist* might treat it with several sessions of electroconvulsive therapy.

Key Terms

1. With an **eclectic approach**, therapists are not locked into one form of psychotherapy, but draw on whatever combination seems best suited to a client's problems. (p. 606)

2. **Psychotherapy** is an interaction between a trained therapist and someone who suffers from psychological difficulties or wants to achieve personal growth. (p. 606)

3. **Psychoanalysis**, the therapy developed by Sigmund Freud, attempts to give clients self-insight by bringing into awareness and interpreting previously repressed feelings. (p. 606)
   Example: The tools of the **psychoanalyst** include free association, the analysis of dreams and transferences, and the interpretation of repressed impulses.

4. **Resistance** is the psychoanalytic term for the blocking from consciousness of anxiety-laden memories. Hesitation during free association may reflect resistance. (p. 607)

5. **Interpretation** is the psychoanalytic term for the analyst's helping the client to understand resistances and other aspects of behavior, so that the client may gain deeper insights. (p. 607)

6. **Transference** is the psychoanalytic term for a patient's redirecting to the analyst emotions from other relationships. (p. 607)

7. Derived from the psychoanalytic tradition, **psychodynamic therapy** seeks to enhance patients' self-insight into their symptoms by focusing on childhood experiences and important relationships in addition to unconscious forces. (p. 608)

8. **Insight therapies** such as psychoanalysis and humanistic therapy aim to increase the client's awareness of underlying motives and defenses. (p. 609)

9. **Client-centered therapy** is a humanistic nondirective therapy developed by Carl Rogers, in which growth and self-awareness are facilitated in an environment that offers genuineness, acceptance, and empathy. (p. 609)

10. **Active listening** is a nondirective technique of Rogers' client-centered therapy, in which the lis-

tener echoes, restates, and seeks clarification of, but does not interpret, clients' remarks. (p. 609)

11. **Unconditional positive regard** refers to the accepting, nonjudgmental attitude that is the basis of client-centered therapy. (p. 610)

12. **Behavior therapy** is therapy that applies learning principles to the elimination of problem behaviors. (pp. 610–611)

13. **Counterconditioning** is a category of behavior therapy in which new responses are classically conditioned to stimuli that trigger unwanted behaviors. (p. 611)

14. **Exposure therapies** treat anxiety by exposing people to things they normally fear and avoid. Among these therapies are systematic desensitization and virtual reality exposure therapy. (p. 611)

15. **Systematic desensitization** is a type of exposure therapy in which a state of relaxation is classically conditioned to a hierarchy of gradually increasing anxiety-provoking stimuli. (p. 611)

    Memory aid: This is a form of **counterconditioning** in which sensitive, anxiety-triggering stimuli are *desensitized* in a progressive, or **systematic**, fashion.

16. **Virtual reality exposure therapy** progressively exposes people to simulations of feared situations to treat their anxiety. (p. 612)

17. **Aversive conditioning** is a form of counterconditioning in which an unpleasant state becomes associated with an unwanted behavior. (p. 613)

18. A **token economy** is an operant conditioning procedure in which desirable behaviors are promoted in people by rewarding them with tokens, or positive reinforcers, which can be exchanged for privileges or treats. For the most part, token economies are used in hospitals, schools, and other institutional settings. (p. 614)

19. **Cognitive therapy** focuses on teaching people new and more adaptive ways of thinking and acting. The therapy is based on the idea that our feelings and responses to events are strongly influenced by our thinking, or cognition. (p. 614)

20. **Cognitive-behavioral therapy** is an integrated therapy that focuses on changing self-defeating thinking (cognitive therapy) and unwanted behaviors (behavior therapy). (p. 616)

21. **Family therapy** views problem behavior as influenced by, or directed at, other members of the client's family. Therapy therefore focuses on relationships and problems among the various members of the family. (p. 617)

22. **Regression toward the mean** is the tendency for unusual events (or emotions) to return toward their average state. (p. 621)

23. **Meta-analysis** is a procedure for statistically combining the results of many different research studies. (p. 621)

24. **Evidence-based practice** is clinical decision making that integrates the best available research with clinical expertise and patient characteristics and preferences. (p. 623)

25. **Biomedical therapy** is the use of prescribed medications or medical procedures that act on a patient's nervous system to treat psychological disorders. (p. 628)

26. **Psychopharmacology** is the study of the effects of drugs on mind and behavior. (p. 628)

    Memory aid: Pharmacology is the science of the uses and effects of drugs. *Psycho*pharmacology is the science that studies the psychological effects of drugs.

27. **Antipsychotic drugs** are used to treat schizophrenia and other severe thought disorders. (p. 629)

28. **Tardive dyskinesia** is an involuntary movement of the muscles of the face, tongue, and limbs that sometimes accompanies the long-term use of certain antipsychotic drugs. (p. 629)

29. **Antianxiety drugs** help control anxiety and agitation by depressing activity in the central nervous system. (p. 630)

30. **Antidepressant drugs** treat depression by altering the availability of various neurotransmitters. Also increasingly prescribed for anxiety. (p. 630)

31. In **electroconvulsive therapy (ECT)**, a biomedical therapy often used to treat severe depression, a brief electric shock is passed through the brain. (p. 632)

32. **Repetitive transcranial magnetic stimulation (rTMS)** is the delivery of repeated pulses of magnetic energy to stimulate or suppress brain activity. (p. 634)

33. **Psychosurgery** is a biomedical therapy that attempts to change behavior by removing or destroying brain tissue. Since drug therapy became widely available in the 1950s, psychosurgery has been infrequently used. (p. 635)

34. Once used to control violent patients, the **lobotomy** is a form of psychosurgery in which the nerves linking the emotion centers of the brain to the frontal lobes are severed. (p. 635)

35. **Resilience** is personal strength that helps people cope with stress, adversity, and trauma. (p. 637)

Social Psychology

UNIT OVERVIEW

Unit 14 demonstrates the powerful influences of social situations on the behavior of individuals. Central to this topic are research studies on attitudes and actions, conformity, compliance, and group and cultural influences. The social principles that emerge help us to understand how individuals are influenced by advertising, political candidates, and the various groups to which they belong. Although social influences are powerful, it is important to remember the significant role of individuals in choosing and creating the social situations that influence them.

The unit also discusses how people relate to one another, from the negative—developing prejudice and behaving aggressively—to the positive—being attracted to people who are nearby and/or similar and behaving altruistically.

The unit concludes with a discussion of situations that provoke conflict and techniques that have been shown to promote conflict resolution.

Although there is some terminology for you to learn in this unit, your primary task is to absorb the findings of the many research studies discussed. The unit headings, which organize the findings, should prove especially useful to you here. In addition, you might, for each main topic (conformity, group influence, aggression, etc.), ask yourself the question, "What situational factors promote this phenomenon?" The research findings can then form the basis for your answers.

NOTE: Answer guidelines for all Unit 14 questions begin on page 368.

UNIT REVIEW

First, skim each section, noting headings and boldface items. After you have read the section, review each objective by answering the fill-in and essay-type questions that follow it. As you proceed, evaluate your performance by consulting the answers beginning on page 368. Do not continue with the next section until you understand each answer. If you need to, review or reread the section in the textbook before continuing.

Social Thinking (pp. 643–650)

Objective 1: Describe the three main focuses of social psychology, and explain how the fundamental attribution error affects our judgments of others.

1. Psychologists who study how we think about, influence, and relate to one another are called

   _____ _____

2. Heider's theory of how we explain others' behavior is the _____ theory. According to this theory, we attribute behavior either to an internal cause, which is called a

   _____ _____ ,

   or to an external cause, which is called a

   _____ _____ .

3. Most people tend to_____ (overestimate/underestimate) the extent to which people's actions are influenced by social situations because their _____ is focused on the person. This tendency is called the

   _____ _____
   _____ . When explaining our own behavior, or that of someone we know well, this tendency is _____ (stronger/weaker). When observers view the world from others' perspectives, attributions are _____ (the same/reversed).

Give an example of the practical consequences of attributions.

Objective 2: Define *attitude*, and explain how attitudes and actions affect each other.

4. Feelings, often based on our beliefs, that predispose our responses are called

   _____ . When people focus on an issue and respond favorably to an argument,

   _____ _____

   _____ has occurred. Persuasion may also occur through the _____ (slower/faster) _____

   _____ as people respond to incidental cues such as a speaker's appearance.

5. Many research studies demonstrate that our attitudes are strongly influenced by our

   _____ . One example of this is the tendency for people who agree to a small request to comply later with a larger one. This is the _____-_____-

   _____-_____

   phenomenon.

6. When you follow the social prescriptions for how you should act as, say, a college student, you are adopting a _____ .

7. Taking on a set of behaviors, or acting in a certain way, generally _____ (changes/does not change) people's attitudes.

8. According to _____

   _____ theory, thoughts and feelings change because people are motivated to justify actions that would otherwise seem hypocritical. This theory was proposed by

   _____ .

9. Dissonance theory predicts that people induced (without coercion) to behave contrary to their true attitudes will be motivated to reduce the resulting _____ by changing their _____ .

Social Influence (pp. 650–664)

Objective 3: Describe the chameleon effect, and discuss Asch's experiments on conformity, noting the difference between normative and informational social influence.

1. The *chameleon effect* refers to our natural tendency to unconsciously _____ others' expressions, postures, and voice tones. This helps us to feel what they are feeling, referred to as _____

   _____ .

2. Copycat violence is a serious example of the effects of _____ on behavior.

3. Sociologists have found that suicides sometimes increase following a _____

   _____ suicide.

4. The term that refers to the tendency to adjust one's behavior to coincide with an assumed group standard is _____ .

5. The psychologist who first studied the effects of group pressure on conformity is

   _____ .

6. In this study, when the opinion of other group members was contradicted by objective evidence, research participants _____ (were/were not) willing to conform to the group opinion.

7. One reason that people comply with social pressure is to gain approval or avoid rejection; this is called _____

   _____ _____ .

8. Another reason people comply is that they have genuinely been influenced by what they have learned from others; this type of influence is called _____

   _____ _____ .

Objective 4: Describe Milgram's experiments on obedience, and explain how the conformity and obedience studies can help us understand our susceptibility to social influence.

9. The classic social psychology studies of obedience were conducted by _____ . When ordered by the experimenter to electrically shock the "learner," the majority of participants (the "teachers") in these studies _____ (complied/refused). More recent studies have found that women's compliance rates in similar situations were _____ (higher than/lower than/similar to) men's.

List the conditions under which obedience was highest in Milgram's studies.

10. In getting people to administer increasingly larger shocks, Milgram was in effect applying the _____-_____-_____-_____ technique.

11. The Asch and Milgram studies demonstrate that strong _____ influences can make _____ people _____ to falsehoods and _____ orders to commit cruel acts.

Objective 5: Describe conditions in which the presence of others is likely to result in social facilitation, social loafing, or deindividuation.

12. The tendency to perform a task better when other people are present is called _____ _____ . In general, people become aroused in the presence of others, and arousal enhances the correct response on a(n) _____ (easy/difficult) task. Later

research revealed that arousal strengthens the response that is most _____ in a given situation.

13. Researchers have found that the reactions of people in crowded situations are often _____ (lessened/amplified).

14. Ingham found that people worked _____ (harder/less hard) in a team tug-of-war than they had in an individual contest. This phenomenon has been called _____ _____ .

15. The feeling of anonymity and loss of self-restraint that an individual may develop when in a group is called _____ .

Objective 6: Discuss how group interaction can facilitate group polarization and groupthink.

16. Over time, the initial differences between groups usually _____ (increase/ decrease).

17. The enhancement of each group's prevailing tendency over time is called _____ _____ . Electronic discussions on the _____ provide a medium for this tendency.

18. When the desire for group harmony overrides realistic thinking in individuals, the phenomenon known as _____ has occurred.

Objective 7: Describe how behavior is influenced by cultural norms.

19. The enduring behaviors, ideas, attitudes, values, and traditions of a group of people and transmitted from one generation to the next defines the group's _____ .

20. One landmark of human culture is the preservation of _____ , which is derived from our mastery of _____ , so that we can pass it on to future generations. Culture also enables an efficient division of _____ .

21. All cultural groups evolve their own rules for expected behavior, called _____ .

22. One such rule involves the buffer zone that people maintain around their bodies, called

_____ _____ .

Identify several cultural differences in personal space, expressiveness, and pace of life.

23. The speed at which culture changes is much _____ (faster/slower) than the pace of evolutionary changes in the human

_____ _____ .

Objective 8: Identify the characteristic common to minority positions that successfully sway majorities.

24. In considering the power of social influence, we cannot overlook the interaction of

_____ _____

(the power of the situation) and

_____ _____

(the power of the individual).

25. The power of one or two individuals to sway the opinion of the majority is called

_____ _____ .

26. A minority opinion will have the most success in swaying the majority if it takes a stance that is _____ (unswerving/flexible).

Social Relations (pp. 664–692)

Objective 9: Identify the three components of prejudice, and contrast overt and subtle forms of prejudice.

1. Prejudice is an _____ (and usually _____) attitude toward a group that involves overgeneralized beliefs known as _____ .

2. Like all attitudes, prejudice is a mixture of

_____ , _____ ,

and predispositions to _____ .

3. Prejudice is a negative _____ ,
and _____ is a negative

_____ .

4. Americans today express _____ (less/the same/more) racial and gender prejudice than they did 50 years ago.

5. (text and Close-Up) Blatant forms of prejudice _____ (have/have not) diminished. However, even people who deny holding prejudiced attitudes may carry negative _____ about race.

6. (Close-Up) Studies of prejudice indicate that it is often unconscious, or _____ . Several studies have shown that the more a person's features are perceived as typical of their

_____ _____ ,

the more likely they are to elicit

_____ - _____

responding.

7. (Close-Up) Today's biopsychosocial approach has stimulated neuroscience studies that have detected implicit prejudice in people's

_____ -muscle responses and in the activation of their brain's

_____ .

8. Worldwide, _____ (women/men) are more likely to live in poverty. People tend to perceive women as being more

_____ and _____

and less _____ than men.

Objective 10: Discuss the social factors that contribute to prejudice, and explain how scapegoating illustrates the emotional component of prejudice.

9. For those with money, power, and prestige, prejudice often serves as a means of _____ social inequalities.

10. Discrimination increases prejudice through the tendency of people to _____ victims for their plight.

11. Through our _____

_____ , we associate ourselves with certain groups.

12. Prejudice is also fostered by the

_____ _____ , a
tendency to favor groups to which one belongs—
called the _____—while exclud-
ing others, or the _____ .

13. Research studies also reveal that the terror of facing _____ tends to heighten
patriotism and produce loathing and aggression
toward people who threaten one's

_____ .

14. That prejudice derives from attempts to blame
others for one's frustration is proposed by the
_____ theory.

15. People who feel loved and supported become
more _____ to and
_____ of those who differ from
them.

Objective 11: Cite three ways that cognitive processes
help create and maintain prejudice.

16. Research suggests that prejudice may also derive
from _____ , the process by
which we attempt to simplify our world by classifying people into groups. One by-product of this
process is that people tend to
_____ the similarity of those
within a group. One manifestation of this is the
_____-_____
_____ , the tendency to recall
faces of one's own race more accurately than
those of other races.

17. Another factor that fosters the formation of group
stereotypes and prejudice is the tendency to
_____ from vivid or memorable
cases.

18. The belief that people get what they deserve—
that the good are rewarded and the bad punished—is expressed in the _____ -
_____ phenomenon. This phenomenon is based in part on _____
_____ , the tendency to believe
that one would have foreseen how something
turned out.

Objective 12: Explain how psychology's definition of
aggression differs from everyday usage, and describe
various biological influences on aggression.

19. Aggressive behavior is defined by psychologists
as _____

_____ .
Thus, psychologists _____ (do/
do not) consider assertive salespeople to be
aggressive.

20. Like other behaviors, aggression emerges from
the interaction of _____ and

_____ .

21. Today, most psychologists _____
(do/do not) consider human aggression to be
instinctive.

22. In humans, aggressiveness _____
(varies/does not vary) greatly from culture to
culture, era to era, and person to person.

23. That there are genetic influences on aggression
can be shown by the fact that many species of
animals have been _____ for
aggressiveness.

24. Twin studies suggest that genes
_____ (do/do not) influence
human aggression. One genetic marker of those
who commit the most violence is the
_____ chromosome. Studies of
violent criminals reveal diminished activity in the
brain's _____ _____ ,
which play an important role in controlling

_____ .

25. In humans and animals, aggression is facilitated
by _____ systems, which are in
turn influenced by _____ , alcohol, and other substances in the blood.

26. The aggressive behavior of animals can be manipulated by altering the levels of the hormone
_____ . When this level is
_____ (increased/decreased),
aggressive tendencies are reduced.

27. High levels of testosterone correlate with
_____ , low tolerance for

_____ , _____ ,
and _____ . Among teenage

boys and adult men, high testosterone also correlates with _____, hard _____ _____, and aggressive-bullying responses to _____ . With age, testosterone levels—and aggressiveness— _____ (increase/decrease). Although testosterone heightens aggressiveness, aggression _____ (increases/ decreases) testosterone level.

28. One drug that unleashes aggressive responses to provocation is _____ .

Objective 13: Outline psychological and social-cultural triggers of aggression, noting the relationship between violent video games and aggressive behavior.

29. According to the _____- _____ principle, inability to achieve a goal leads to anger, which may generate aggression.

30. Other aversive stimuli can provoke hostility, including _____ _____ .

31. Aggressive behavior can be learned through _____ , as shown by the fact that people use aggression where they've found it pays, and through _____ of others. Also, those who have been socially rejected, or _____ , are more likely to respond aggressively to insults.

32. Crime rates are higher in countries in which there is a large disparity between those who are _____ and those who are _____ . High violence rates also are typical of cultures and families in which there is minimal _____ _____ .

33. Once established, aggressive behavior patterns are _____ (difficult/not difficult) to change. However, _____- _____ programs have been successful in bringing down re-arrest rates of juvenile offenders and gang members.

34. Violence on television tends to _____ people to cruelty and

_____ them to respond aggressively when they are provoked.

35. The "rape myth" is the mistaken idea that _____ . Most rapists _____ (accept/do not accept) this myth.

Comment on the impression of women that pornography frequently conveys and the effects this impression has on attitudes and behavior.

Summarize the findings of the Zillmann and Bryant study on the effects of pornography on attitudes toward rape.

36. Experiments have shown that, among other factors, depictions by the media of _____ _____ most directly affect men's acceptance and performance of aggression against women. Such depictions may create _____ _____ to which people respond when they are in new situations or are uncertain how to act.

37. Kids who play a lot of violent video games see the world as more _____ , get into more _____ and _____ , and get worse _____ .

38. Research studies of the impact of violent video games _____ (confirm/disconfirm) the idea that we feel better if we "blow off steam" by venting our emotions. This idea is the _____ _____ . Expressing anger breeds _____ (more/less) anger.

39. Many factors contribute to aggression, including _____ factors, such as an increase in testosterone; _____ factors, such as frustration; and _____-_____ factors, such as deindividuation.

Objective 14: Describe the influence of proximity, physical attractiveness, and similarity on interpersonal attraction.

40. A prerequisite for, and perhaps the most powerful predictor of, attraction is _____ .

41. When people are repeatedly exposed to unfamiliar stimuli, their liking of the stimuli _____ (increases/decreases). This phenomenon is the _____ _____ effect. For our ancestors, for whom the unfamiliar was often dangerous, this effect was _____ . One implication of this is that _____ against those who are culturally different may be a primitive, _____ emotional response.

42. Our first impression of another person is most influenced by the person's _____ .

43. In a sentence, list several of the characteristics that physically attractive people are judged to possess: _____ _____ .

44. A person's attractiveness _____ (is/is not) strongly related to his or her self-esteem or happiness.

45. Cross-cultural research reveals that men judge women as more attractive if they have a _____ appearance, whereas women judge men who appear _____ , _____ , and _____ as more attractive. People also seem to prefer physical features that are neither unusually _____ nor _____ . Average faces, which tend to be _____ , are judged to be more sexually attractive.

46. Compared with strangers, friends and couples are more likely to be similar in terms of _____ _____ .

Explain what a reward theory of attraction is and how it can account for the three predictors of liking—proximity, attractiveness, and similarity.

Objective 15: Describe the effect of physical arousal on passionate love, and identify two predictors of enduring companionate love.

47. Elaine Hatfield has distinguished two types of love: _____ love and _____ love.

48. According to the two-factor theory, emotions have two components: physical _____ and a _____ label.

49. When college men were placed in an aroused state, their feelings toward an attractive woman _____ (were/were not) more positive than those of men who had not been aroused.

50. Companionate love is promoted by _____—mutual sharing and giving by both partners. Another key ingredient of loving relationships is the revealing of intimate aspects of ourselves through _____ .

Objective 16: Define *altruism*, and describe the steps in the decision-making process involved in bystander intervention.

51. An unselfish regard for the welfare of others is called _____ .

Give an example of altruism.

52. According to John Darley and Bibb Latané, people will help only if a three-stage decision-making process is completed: Bystanders must first _____ the incident, then _____ it as an emergency, and finally _____ _____ for helping.

53. When people who overheard a seizure victim calling for help thought others were hearing the same plea, they were _____ (more/less) likely to go to his aid than when they thought no one else was aware of the emergency.

54. In a series of staged accidents, Latané and Darley found that a bystander was _____ (more/less) likely to help if other bystanders were present. This phenomenon has been called the _____ _____ .

Identify the circumstances in which a person is most likely to offer help during an emergency.

Objective 17: Explain altruism from the perspectives of social exchange theory and social norms.

55. The idea that social behavior aims to maximize rewards and minimize costs is proposed by _____ _____ theory.

56. One rule of social behavior tells us to return help to those who have helped us; this is the _____ norm.

57. Another rule tells us to help those who need our help; this is the _____-_____ norm.

Objective 18: Explain how social traps and mirror-image perceptions fuel social conflict, and discuss effective ways of encouraging peaceful cooperation and reducing conflict.

58. A perceived incompatibility of actions, goals, or ideas is called _____ . This perception can take place between individuals, _____ , or _____ .

59. Situations in which conflicting parties become caught in mutually destructive behavior by pursuing their own self-interests are called _____ _____ .

60. The distorted images people in conflict form of each other are called _____-_____ perceptions. These perceptions may become _____-_____ that confirm themselves by influencing others to react in ways that seem to justify them.

61. In most situations, establishing contact between two conflicting groups _____ (is/is not) sufficient to resolve conflict.

62. In Muzafer Sherif's study, two conflicting groups of campers were able to resolve their conflicts by working together on projects in which they shared _____ goals. Shared _____ breed solidarity, as demonstrated by a surge in use of the word _____ in the weeks after 9/11.

63. When conflicts arise, a third-party _____ may facilitate communication and promote understanding.

64. Charles Osgood has advanced a strategy of conciliation called GRIT, which stands for _____ and _____ _____ in _____-_____ . The key to this method is each side's offering of a small _____ gesture in order to increase mutual trust and cooperation.

PROGRESS TEST 1

Multiple-Choice Questions

Circle your answers to the following questions and check them with the answers beginning on page 370. If your answer is incorrect, read the explanation for why it is incorrect and then consult the appropriate pages of the text (in parentheses following the correct answer).

1. In his study of obedience, Stanley Milgram found that the majority of participants
   a. refused to shock the learner even once.
   b. complied with the experiment until the "learner" first indicated pain.
   c. complied with the experiment until the "learner" began screaming in agony.
   d. complied with all the demands of the experiment.

2. According to cognitive dissonance theory, dissonance is most likely to occur when
   a. a person's behavior is not based on strongly held attitudes.
   b. two people have conflicting attitudes and find themselves in disagreement.
   c. an individual does something that is personally disagreeable.
   d. an individual is coerced into doing something that he or she does not want to do.

3. Which of the following statements is true?
   a. Groups are almost never swayed by minority opinions.
   b. Group polarization is most likely to occur when group members frequently disagree with one another.
   c. Groupthink provides the consensus needed for effective decision making.
   d. A group that is like-minded will probably not change its opinions through discussion.

4. Conformity increased under which of the following conditions in Solomon Asch's studies of conformity?
   a. The group had more males than females.
   b. The group's status was equal to that of the participant.
   c. Individuals were made to feel insecure.
   d. The participant had made a prior commitment to a particular response.

5. Violent criminals often have diminished activity in the _____ of the brain, which play(s) an important role in _____ .
   a. occipital lobes; aggression
   b. hypothalamus; hostility
   c. frontal lobes; controlling impulses
   d. temporal lobes; patience

6. The phenomenon in which individuals lose their identity and relinquish normal restraints when they are part of a group is called
   a. groupthink.   c. empathy.
   b. cognitive dissonance. d. deindividuation.

7. Subjects in Solomon Asch's line-judgment experiment conformed to the group standard when their judgments were observed by others but not when they were made in private. This tendency to conform in public demonstrates
   a. social facilitation.
   b. overjustification.
   c. informational social influence.
   d. normative social influence.

8. Based on findings from Stanley Milgram's obedience studies, participants would be LESS likely to follow the experimenter's orders when
   a. they hear the "learner" cry out in pain.
   b. they merely administer the test while someone else delivers the shocks.
   c. the "learner" is an older person or mentions having some physical problem.
   d. they see another participant disobey instructions.

9. *Aggression* is defined as behavior that
   a. hurts another person.
   b. is intended to hurt another person.
   c. is hostile, passionate, and produces physical injury.
   d. has all of these characteristics.

10. Which of the following is true about aggression?
    a. It varies too much to be instinctive in humans.
    b. It is just one instinct among many.
    c. It is instinctive but shaped by learning.
    d. It is the most important human instinct.

11. Research studies have found a positive correlation between aggressive tendencies in animals and levels of the hormone
    a. estrogen.   c. noradrenaline.
    b. adrenaline.   d. testosterone.

12. Research studies have indicated that the tendency of viewers to misperceive normal sexuality, devalue their partners, and trivialize rape is
   a. increased by exposure to pornography.
   b. not changed after exposure to pornography.
   c. decreased in men by exposure to pornography.
   d. decreased in both men and women by exposure to pornography.

13. Increasing the number of people that are present during an emergency tends to
   a. increase the likelihood that people will cooperate in rendering assistance.
   b. decrease the empathy that people feel for the victim.
   c. increase the role that social norms governing helping will play.
   d. decrease the likelihood that anyone will help.

14. Which of the following was NOT mentioned in the text discussion of the roots of prejudice?
   a. people's tendency to overestimate the similarity of people within groups
   b. people's tendency to assume that exceptional, or especially memorable, individuals are unlike the majority of members of a group
   c. people's tendency to assume that the world is just and that people get what they deserve
   d. people's tendency to discriminate against those they view as "outsiders"

15. The mere exposure effect demonstrates that
   a. familiarity breeds contempt.
   b. opposites attract.
   c. birds of a feather flock together.
   d. familiarity breeds fondness.

16. In one experiment, college men were physically aroused and then introduced to an attractive woman. Compared with men who had not been aroused, these men
   a. reported more positive feelings toward the woman.
   b. reported more negative feelings toward the woman.
   c. were ambiguous about their feelings toward the woman.
   d. were more likely to feel that the woman was "out of their league" in terms of attractiveness.

17. The deep affection that is felt in long-lasting relationships is called _____ love; this feeling is fostered in relationships in which _____ .
   a. passionate; there is equity between the partners
   b. passionate; traditional roles are maintained
   c. companionate; there is equity between the partners
   d. companionate; traditional roles are maintained

18. Which of the following is associated with an increased tendency on the part of a bystander to offer help in an emergency situation?
   a. being in a good mood
   b. having recently needed help and not received it
   c. observing someone as he or she refuses to offer help
   d. being a female

19. The belief that those who suffer deserve their fate is expressed in the
   a. just-world phenomenon.
   b. phenomenon of ingroup bias.
   c. fundamental attribution error.
   d. mirror-image perception principle.

20. Which of the following phenomena is best explained by cognitive dissonance theory?
   a. group polarization
   b. the foot-in-the-door phenomenon
   c. normative social influence
   d. informational social influence

21. The traditions of a culture are passed from one generation to the next by means of
   a. norms.
   b. temperaments.
   c. genes.
   d. chromosomes.

Matching Items

Match each term with the appropriate definition or description.

Terms

_____ 1. social facilitation
_____ 2. social loafing
_____ 3. bystander effect
_____ 4. conformity
_____ 5. ingroup bias
_____ 6. normative social influence
_____ 7. informational social influence
_____ 8. group polarization
_____ 9. stereotype
_____ 10. attribution
_____ 11. altruism
_____ 12. mere exposure effect
_____ 13. central route persuasion
_____ 14. norm

Definitions or Descriptions

a. a causal explanation for someone's behavior
b. a generalized belief about a group of people
c. people work less hard in a group
d. performance is improved by an audience
e. the tendency to favor one's own group
f. the effect of social approval or disapproval
g. adjusting one's behavior to coincide with a group standard
h. group discussion enhances prevailing tendencies
i. the effect of accepting others' opinions about something
j. unselfish regard for others
k. the tendency that a person is less likely to help someone in need when others are present
l. the increased liking of a stimulus that results from repeated exposure to it
m. responding favorably to arguments as a result of systematic thinking about an issue
n. an understood rule for accepted and expected behavior

PROGRESS TEST 2

Progress Test 2 should be completed during a final unit review. Answer the following questions after you thoroughly understand the correct answers for the section reviews and Progress Test 1.

Multiple-Choice Questions

1. (Close-Up) Which of the following is an example of implicit prejudice?
   a. Jake, who is White, gives higher evaluations to essays he believes to be written by Blacks than to White-authored essays.
   b. Carol believes that White people are arrogant.
   c. Brad earns more than Jane, despite having the same job skills, performance level, and seniority.
   d. In certain countries, women are not allowed to drive.

2. We tend to perceive the members of an ingroup as _____ and the members of an outgroup as _____ .
   a. similar to one another; different from one another
   b. different from one another; similar to one another
   c. above average in ability; below average in ability
   d. below average in ability; above average in ability

3. Regarding the influence of alcohol and testosterone on aggressive behavior, which of the following is true?
   a. Consumption of alcohol increases aggressive behavior; injections of testosterone reduce aggressive behavior.
   b. Consumption of alcohol reduces aggressive behavior; injections of testosterone increase aggressive behavior.
   c. Consumption of alcohol and injections of testosterone both promote aggressive behavior.
   d. Consumption of alcohol and injections of testosterone both reduce aggressive behavior.

4. Most people prefer mirror-image photographs of their faces. This is best explained by
   a. the principle of equity.
   b. the principle of self-disclosure.
   c. the mere exposure effect.
   d. mirror-image perceptions.

5. Research studies have shown that frequent exposure to sexually explicit films
   a. makes a woman's friendliness seem more sexual.
   b. diminishes the attitude that rape is a serious crime.
   c. may lead individuals to devalue their partners.
   d. may produce all of these effects.

6. Research studies indicate that in an emergency situation, the presence of others often
   a. prevents people from even noticing the situation.
   b. prevents people from interpreting an unusual event as an emergency.
   c. prevents people from assuming responsibility for assisting.
   d. leads to all of these behaviors.

7. Two neighboring nations are each stockpiling weapons. Each sees its neighbor's actions as an act of aggression and its own actions as self-defense. Evidently, these nations are victims of
   a. prejudice.
   b. groupthink.
   c. self-serving bias.
   d. the fundamental attribution error.

8. Which of the following factors is the MOST powerful predictor of friendship?
   a. similarity in age
   b. common racial and religious background
   c. similarity in physical attractiveness
   d. physical proximity

9. Most researchers agree that
   a. media violence is a factor in aggression.
   b. there is a negative correlation between media violence and aggressiveness.
   c. paradoxically, watching excessive pornography ultimately diminishes an individual's aggressive tendencies.
   d. media violence is too unreal to promote aggression in viewers.

10. When male students in an experiment were told that a woman to whom they would be speaking had been instructed to act in a friendly or unfriendly way, most of them subsequently attributed her behavior to
    a. the situation.
    b. the situation *and* her personal disposition.
    c. her personal disposition.
    d. their own skill or lack of skill in a social situation.

11. Which of the following is true?
    a. Attitudes and actions rarely correspond.
    b. Attitudes predict behavior about half the time.
    c. Attitudes are excellent predictors of behavior.
    d. Attitudes predict behavior under certain conditions.

12. People with power and status may become prejudiced because
    a. they tend to justify the social inequalities between themselves and others.
    b. those with less status and power tend to resent them.
    c. those with less status and power appear less capable.
    d. they feel proud and are boastful of their achievements.

13. Which of the following most accurately states the effects of crowding on behavior?
    a. Crowding makes people irritable.
    b. Crowding sometimes intensifies people's reactions.
    c. Crowding promotes altruistic behavior.
    d. Crowding usually weakens the intensity of people's reactions.

14. Research has found that for a minority to succeed in swaying a majority, the minority must
    a. make up a sizable portion of the group.
    b. express its position as consistently as possible.
    c. express its position in the most extreme terms possible.
    d. be able to convince a key majority leader.

15. Which of the following conclusions did Stanley Milgram derive from his studies of obedience?
    a. Even ordinary people, without any particular hostility, can become agents in a destructive process.
    b. Most people are able, under the proper circumstances, to suppress their natural aggressiveness.
    c. The need to be accepted by others is a powerful motivating force.
    d. He reached all of these conclusions.

16. Which of the following best summarizes the relative importance of personal control and social control of our behavior?
    a. Situational influences on behavior generally are much greater than personal influences.
    b. Situational influences on behavior generally are slightly greater than personal influences.

c. Personal influences on behavior generally are much greater than situational influences.

d. Situational and personal influences interact in determining our behavior.

17. Which of the following best describes how GRIT works?

a. The fact that two sides in a conflict have great respect for the other's strengths prevents further escalation of the problem.

b. The two sides engage in a series of reciprocated conciliatory acts.

c. The two sides agree to have their differences settled by a neutral, third-party mediator.

d. The two sides engage in cooperation in those areas in which shared goals are possible.

18. Which of the following is important in promoting conformity in individuals?

a. whether an individual's behavior will be observed by others in the group

b. whether the individual is male or female

c. the size of the room in which a group is meeting

d. whether the individual is of a higher status than other group members

19. Which theory describes how we explain others' behavior as being due to internal dispositions or external situations?

a. cognitive dissonance theory

b. reward theory

c. two-factor theory

d. attribution theory

20. Which of the following is most likely to promote groupthink?

a. The group's leader fails to take a firm stance on an issue.

b. A minority faction holds to its position.

c. The group consults with various experts.

d. Group polarization is evident.

21. Which of the following is NOT true regarding cultural diversity?

a. Culture influences emotional expressiveness.

b. Culture influences personal space.

c. Culture does not have a strong influence on how strictly social roles are defined.

d. All cultures evolve their own norms.

True–False Items

Indicate whether each statement is true or false by placing *T* or *F* in the blank next to the item.

_____ 1. When explaining another's behavior, we tend to underestimate situational influences.

_____ 2. When explaining our own behavior, we tend to underestimate situational influences.

_____ 3. An individual is more likely to conform when the rest of the group is unanimous.

_____ 4. The tendency of people to conform is influenced by the culture in which they were socialized.

_____ 5. A bystander is more likely to offer help in an emergency if other bystanders are present.

_____ 6. Counterattitudinal behavior (acting contrary to our beliefs) often leads to attitude change.

_____ 7. Human aggression is instinctual.

_____ 8. Group polarization tends to prevent groupthink from occurring.

_____ 9. Crowded conditions usually subdue people's reactions.

_____ 10. When individuals lose their sense of identity in a group, they often become more uninhibited.

_____ 11. Peripheral route persuasion allows for fast responding to an issue.

_____ 12. In our relations with others of similar status, we tend to give more than we receive.

_____ 13. North Americans prefer more personal space than do Latin Americans.

PSYCHOLOGY APPLIED

Answer these questions the day before an exam as a final check on your understanding of the unit's terms and concepts.

Multiple-Choice Questions

1. After waiting in line for an hour to buy concert tickets, Teresa is told that the concert is sold out. In her anger she pounds her fist on the ticket counter, frightening the clerk. Teresa's behavior is best explained by

a. evolutionary psychology.

b. deindividuation.

c. reward theory.

d. the frustration-aggression principle.

2. Before she gave a class presentation favoring gun control legislation, Wanda opposed it. Her present attitude favoring such legislation can best be explained by
   a. attribution theory.
   b. cognitive dissonance theory.
   c. reward theory.
   d. evolutionary psychology.

3. Which of the following would most likely be subject to social facilitation?
   a. proofreading a page for spelling errors
   b. typing a letter with accuracy
   c. playing a difficult piece on a musical instrument
   d. running quickly around a track

4. Jane and Sandy were best friends in their first year of university. Jane joined a sorority; Sandy didn't. By the end of their last year, they found that they had less in common with each other than with the other members of their respective circles of friends. Which of the following phenomena most likely explains their feelings?
   a. group polarization   c. deindividuation
   b. groupthink   d. social facilitation

5. Which of the following strategies would be MOST likely to foster positive feelings between two conflicting groups?
   a. Take steps to reduce the likelihood of mirror-image perceptions.
   b. Separate the groups so that tensions diminish.
   c. Increase the amount of contact between the two conflicting groups.
   d. Have the groups work on a superordinate goal.

6. José is the one student member on his school's board of trustees. At the board's first meeting, José wants to disagree with the others on several issues but in each case decides to say nothing. Studies on conformity suggest all except one of the following are factors in José's not speaking up. Which one is NOT a factor?
   a. The board is a large group.
   b. The board is prestigious and most of its members are well known.
   c. The board members are already aware that José and the student body disagree with them on these issues.
   d. Because this is the first meeting José has attended, he feels insecure and not fully competent.

7. Given the tendency of people to categorize information according to preformed schemas, which of the following stereotypes would Juan, a 65-year-old political liberal and fitness enthusiast, be most likely to have?
   a. "People who exercise regularly are very extraverted."
   b. "All political liberals are advocates of a reduced defense budget."
   c. "Young people today have no sense of responsibility."
   d. "Older people are lazy."

8. Ever since their cabin lost the camp softball competition, the campers have become increasingly hostile toward one camper in their cabin, blaming her for every problem in the cabin. This behavior is best explained in terms of
   a. the ingroup bias.
   b. prejudice.
   c. the scapegoat theory.
   d. catharsis.

9. Maria recently heard a speech calling for a ban on aerosol sprays that endanger the earth's ozone layer. Maria's subsequent decision to stop using aerosol sprays is an example of
   a. informational social influence.
   b. normative social influence.
   c. deindividuation.
   d. social facilitation.

10. Mr. and Mrs. Samuels are constantly fighting, and each perceives the other as hard-headed and insensitive. Their conflict is being fueled by
    a. self-disclosure.
    b. stereotypes.
    c. a social norm.
    d. mirror-image perceptions.

11. Which of the following situations should produce the GREATEST cognitive dissonance?
    a. A soldier is forced to carry out orders he finds disagreeable.
    b. A student who loves animals has to dissect a cat in order to pass biology.
    c. As part of an experiment, a subject is directed to deliver electric shocks to another person.
    d. A student volunteers to debate an issue, taking the side he personally disagrees with.

12. Professor Washington's students did very poorly on the last exam. The tendency to make the fundamental attribution error might lead her to conclude that the class did poorly because
    a. the test was unfair.
    b. not enough time was given for students to complete the test.
    c. students were distracted by some social function on campus.
    d. students were unmotivated.

13. Students at Metropolitan High School are convinced that their school is better than any other; this most directly illustrates
    a. an ingroup bias.
    b. prejudice and discrimination.
    c. the scapegoat effect.
    d. the just-world phenomenon.

14. Concluding her presentation on deindividuation, Renée notes that deindividuation is less likely in situations that promote
    a. anonymity.
    b. decreased self-awareness.
    c. increased self-awareness.
    d. the fundamental attribution error.

15. Ahmed and Monique are on a blind date. Which of the following will probably be *most* influential in determining whether they like each other?
    a. their personalities
    b. their beliefs
    c. their social skills
    d. their physical attractiveness

16. Opening her mail, Joan discovers a romantic greeting card from her boyfriend. According to the two-factor theory, she is likely to feel the most intense romantic feelings if, prior to reading the card, she has just
    a. completed her daily run.
    b. finished reading a unit in her psychology textbook.
    c. awakened from a nap.
    d. finished eating lunch.

17. Summarizing his report on the biology of aggression, Sam notes that
    a. biology does not significantly influence aggression.
    b. when one identical twin has a violent temperament, the other member of the twin pair rarely does.
    c. hormones and alcohol influence the neural systems that control aggression.
    d. testosterone reduces dominance behaviors in animals.

18. Having read the unit, which of the following is best borne out by research on attraction?
    a. Birds of a feather flock together.
    b. Opposites attract.
    c. Familiarity breeds contempt.
    d. Absence makes the heart grow fonder.

19. Alexis believes that all male athletes are self-centered and sexist. Her beliefs are an example of
    a. in-group bias.
    b. groupthink.
    c. stereotypes.
    d. the fundamental attribution error.

20. Which of the following is an example of the foot-in-the-door phenomenon?
    a. To persuade a customer to buy a product a store owner offers a small gift.
    b. After agreeing to wear a small "Enforce Recycling" lapel pin, a woman agrees to collect signatures on a petition to make recycling required by law.
    c. After offering to sell a car at a ridiculously low price, a car salesperson is forced to tell the customer the car will cost $1000 more.
    d. After running a race, a young man develops very strong feelings for the woman he's been dating.

21. Although the fitness center has many unused lockers, Rabab picks a locker right next to Chalina's, who feels uncomfortable because Rabab has intruded into her
    a. social trap.
    b. personal space.
    c. role.
    d. culture.

Essay Question

The Panhellenic Council on your campus has asked you to make a presentation on the topic "Social Psychology" to all freshmen who have signed up to "rush" a fraternity or sorority. In a fit of cynicism following your rejection last year by a prestigious fraternity or sorority, you decide to speak on the negative influences of groups on the behavior of individuals. What will you discuss? (Use the space below to list the points you want to make, and organize them. Then write the essay on a separate sheet of paper.)

KEY TERMS

Using your own words, on a separate piece of paper write a brief definition or explanation of each of the following terms.

1. social psychology
2. attribution theory
3. fundamental attribution error
4. attitudes
5. central route persuasion
6. peripheral route persuasion
7. foot-in-the-door phenomenon
8. role
9. cognitive dissonance theory
10. conformity
11. normative social influence
12. informational social influence
13. social facilitation
14. social loafing
15. deindividuation

16. group polarization
17. groupthink
18. culture
19. norm
20. personal space
21. prejudice
22. stereotype
23. discrimination
24. ingroup
25. outgroup
26. ingroup bias
27. scapegoat theory
28. other-race effect
29. just-world phenomenon
30. aggression
31. frustration-aggression principle
32. mere exposure effect
33. passionate love
34. companionate love
35. equity
36. self-disclosure
37. altruism
38. bystander effect
39. social exchange theory
40. reciprocity norm
41. social-responsibility norm
42. conflict
43. social trap
44. mirror-image perceptions
45. self-fulfilling prophecy
46. superordinate goals
47. GRIT

ANSWERS

Unit Review

Social Thinking

1. social psychologists
2. attribution; dispositional attribution; situational attribution
3. underestimate; attention; fundamental attribution error; weaker; reversed

Our attributions—to individuals' dispositions or to situations—have important practical consequences. A hurtful remark from an acquaintance, for example, is more likely to be forgiven if it is attributed to a temporary situation than to a mean disposition.

4. attitudes; central route persuasion; faster; peripheral route
5. actions (or behavior); foot-in-the-door
6. role
7. changes
8. cognitive dissonance; Leon Festinger
9. dissonance; attitudes

Social Influence

1. mimic; mood linkage
2. suggestibility
3. highly publicized
4. conformity
5. Solomon Asch
6. were
7. normative social influence
8. informational social influence
9. Stanley Milgram; complied; similar to

Obedience was highest when the person giving the orders was close at hand and perceived to be a legitimate authority figure, the authority figure was supported by a prestigious institution, the victim was depersonalized or at a distance, and when there were no role models for defiance.

10. foot-in-the-door
11. social; ordinary; conform; obey
12. social facilitation; easy; likely
13. amplified
14. less hard; social loafing
15. deindividuation
16. increase
17. group polarization; Internet
18. groupthink
19. culture
20. innovation; language; labor
21. norms
22. personal space

Most North Americans, the British, and Scandinavians prefer more personal space than do Latin Americans, Arabs, and the French. Cultural differences in expressiveness and the pace of life often create misunderstandings. For example, people with

northern European roots may perceive people from Mediterranean cultures as warm and charming but inefficient, while Mediterraneans may see the northern Europeans as efficient but emotionally cold.

23. faster; gene pool
24. social control; personal control
25. minority influence
26. unswerving

Social Relations

1. unjustifiable; negative; stereotypes
2. beliefs; emotions; action
3. attitude; discrimination; behavior
4. less
5. have; associations
6. implicit; racial category; race-based
7. facial; amygdala
8. women; nurturant; sensitive; aggressive
9. justifying
10. blame
11. social identities
12. ingroup bias; ingroup; outgroup
13. death; world
14. scapegoat
15. open; accepting
16. categorization; overestimate; other-race effect
17. overgeneralize
18. just-world; hindsight bias
19. any physical or verbal behavior intended to hurt or destroy; do not
20. biology; experience
21. do not
22. varies
23. bred
24. do; Y; frontal lobes; impulses
25. neural; hormones
26. testosterone; decreased
27. irritability; frustration; assertiveness; impulsiveness; delinquency; drug use; frustration; decrease; increases
28. alcohol
29. frustration-aggression
30. physical pain, personal insults, foul odors, hot temperatures, cigarette smoke
31. rewards; observation (or imitation); ostracized
32. rich; poor; father care

33. difficult; aggression-replacement

34. desensitize; prime

35. some women invite or enjoy rape; accept

Pornography tends to portray women as enjoying being the victims of sexual aggression, and this perception increases the acceptance of coercion in sexual relationships. Repeatedly watching X-rated films also makes one's partner seem less attractive, makes a woman's friendliness seem more sexual, and makes sexual aggression seem less serious.

The study by Dolf Zillman and Jennings Bryant found that after viewing sexually explicit films for several weeks, undergraduates were more likely to recommend a lighter prison sentence for a convicted rapist than were those who viewed nonerotic films.

36. sexual violence; social scripts

37. hostile; arguments; fights; grades

38. disconfirm; catharsis hypothesis; more

39. biological; psychological; social-cultural

40. proximity

41. increases; mere exposure; adaptive; prejudice; automatic

42. appearance

43. Attractive people are perceived as happier, more sensitive, more successful, and more socially skilled.

44. is not

45. youthful; mature; dominant; affluent; large; small; symmetrical

46. attitudes, beliefs, interests, religion, race, education, intelligence, smoking behavior, economic status, age

A reward theory of attraction says that we are attracted to, and continue relationships with, those people whose behavior provides us with more benefits than costs. Proximity makes it easy to enjoy the benefits of friendship at little cost, attractiveness is pleasing, and similarity is reinforcing to us.

47. passionate; companionate

48. arousal; cognitive

49. were

50. equity; self-disclosure

51. altruism

An example of altruism is giving food and shelter to people displaced by an earthquake, hurricane, or other major disaster without expectation of reward.

52. notice; interpret; assume responsibility

53. less

54. less; bystander effect

People are most likely to help someone when they have just observed someone else being helpful; when they are not in a hurry; when the victim appears to need and deserve help; when they are in some way similar to the victim; when in a small town or rural area; when feeling guilty; when not preoccupied; and when in a good mood.

55. social exchange

56. reciprocity

57. social-responsibility

58. conflict; groups; nations

59. social traps

60. mirror-image; self-fulfilling prophecies

61. is not

62. superordinate; predicaments; "we"

63. mediator

64. Graduated; Reciprocated Initiatives; Tension-Reduction; conciliatory

Progress Test 1

Multiple-Choice Questions

1. **d.** is the answer. In Milgram's initial experiments, 63 percent of the subjects complied fully with the experiment. (p. 654)

2. **c.** is the answer. Cognitive dissonance is the tension we feel when we are aware of a discrepancy between our thoughts and actions, as would occur when we do something we find distasteful. (p. 648)
   a. Dissonance requires strongly held attitudes, which must be perceived as not fitting behavior.
   b. Dissonance is a personal cognitive process.
   d. In such a situation the person is less likely to experience dissonance, since the action can be attributed to "having no choice."

3. **d.** is the answer. In such groups, discussion usually strengthens prevailing opinion; this phenomenon is known as group polarization. (p. 659)
   a. Minority opinions, especially if consistently and firmly stated, can sway the majority in a group.
   b. Group polarization, or the strengthening of a group's prevailing tendencies, is most likely in groups where members agree.
   c. When groupthink occurs, there is so much consensus that decision making becomes less effective.

4. **c.** is the answer. (p. 652)

5. **c.** is the answer. (p. 671)

6. **d.** is the answer. (p. 659)

a. Groupthink refers to the mode of thinking that occurs when the desire for group harmony overrides realistic and critical thinking.
b. Cognitive dissonance refers to the discomfort we feel when two thoughts (which include the knowledge of our *behavior*) are inconsistent.
c. Empathy is feeling what another person feels.

7. **d.** is the answer. Normative social influence refers to influence on behavior that comes from a desire to look good to others. Subjects who were observed conformed because they didn't want to look like oddballs. (p. 653)
a. Social facilitation involves performing tasks better or faster in the presence of others.
b. Overjustification occurs when a person is rewarded for doing something that is already enjoyable.
c. Informational social influence is the tendency of individuals to accept the opinions of others, especially in situations where they themselves are unsure.

8. **d.** is the answer. Role models for defiance reduce levels of obedience. (p. 655)
a. & c. These did not result in diminished obedience.
b. This "depersonalization" of the victim resulted in increased obedience.

9. **b.** is the answer. Aggression is any behavior, physical or verbal, that is intended to hurt or destroy. (p. 670)
a. A person may accidentally be hurt in a nonaggressive incident; aggression does not necessarily prove hurtful.
c. Verbal behavior, which does not result in physical injury, may also be aggressive. Moreover, acts of aggression may be cool and calculated, rather than hostile and passionate.

10. **a.** is the answer. The very wide variations in aggressiveness from culture to culture indicate that aggression cannot be considered an unlearned instinct. (p. 671)

11. **d.** is the answer. (p. 672)

12. **a.** is the answer. (p. 674)

13. **d.** is the answer. This phenomenon is known as the bystander effect. (p. 685)
a. This answer is incorrect because individuals are less likely to render assistance at all if others are present.
b. Although people are less likely to assume responsibility for helping, this does not mean that they are less empathic.

c. This answer is incorrect because norms such as the social responsibility norm encourage helping others, yet people are less likely to help with others around.

14. **b.** is the answer. In fact, people tend to overgeneralize from vivid cases, rather than assume that they are unusual. (p. 669)
a., c., & d. Each of these is an example of a cognitive (a. & c.) or a social (d.) root of prejudice.

15. **d.** is the answer. Being repeatedly exposed to novel stimuli increases our liking for them. (p. 678)
a. For the most part, the opposite is true.
b. & c. The mere exposure effect concerns our tendency to develop likings on the basis, not of similarities or differences, but simply of familiarity, or repeated exposure.

16. **a.** is the answer. This result supports the two-factor theory of emotion and passionate attraction, according to which arousal from any source can facilitate an emotion, depending on how we label the arousal. (p. 683)

17. **c.** is the answer. Deep affection is typical of companionate love, rather than passionate love, and is promoted by equity, whereas traditional roles may be characterized by the dominance of one sex. (p. 684)

18. **a.** is the answer. (p. 686)
b. & c. These factors would most likely decrease a person's altruistic tendencies.
d. There is no evidence that one sex is more altruistic than the other.

19. **a.** is the answer. (p. 670)
b. Ingroup bias is the tendency of people to favor their own group.
c. The fundamental attribution error is the tendency of people to underestimate situational influences when observing the behavior of other people.
d. The mirror-image perception principle is the tendency of conflicting parties to form similar, diabolical images of each other.

20. **b.** is the answer. (p. 648)
a. Group polarization involves group opinions.
c. Normative and informational social influence have to do with reasons for influence.

21. **a.** is the answer. (p. 662)

Matching Items

1. d (p. 657)   **6.** f (p. 653)   **11.** j (p. 685)
2. c (p. 658)   **7.** i (p. 653)   **12.** l (p. 678)
3. k (p. 686)   **8.** h (p. 659)   **13.** m (p. 646)
4. g (p. 651)   **9.** b (p. 664)   **14.** n (p. 662)
5. e (p. 668)   **10.** a (p. 644)

Progress Test 2

Multiple-Choice Questions

1. a. is the answer. (p. 666)
 b. This is an example of overt prejudice.
 c. & d. These are examples of discrimination.

2. b. is the answer. (p. 668)
 a. We are keenly sensitive to differences within our group, less so to differences within other groups.
 c. & d. Although we tend to look more favorably on members of the ingroup, the text does not suggest that ingroup bias extends to evaluations of abilities.

3. c. is the answer. (pp. 671–672)

4. c. is the answer. The mere exposure effect refers to our tendency to like what we're used to, and we're used to seeing mirror images of ourselves. (p. 678)
 a. Equity refers to equality in giving and taking between the partners in a relationship.
 b. Self-disclosure is the sharing of intimate feelings with a partner in a loving relationship.
 d. Although people prefer mirror images of their faces, mirror-image perceptions are often held by parties in conflict. Each party views itself favorably and the other negatively.

5. d. is the answer. (pp. 674–675)

6. d. is the answer. (p. 685)

7. d. is the answer. In this case, each nation has mistakenly attributed the other's action to a *dispositional* trait, whereas its own action is viewed as a *situational* response. (p. 644)

8. d. is the answer. Because it provides people with an opportunity to meet, proximity is the most powerful predictor of friendship, even though, once a friendship is established, the other factors mentioned become more important. (p. 678)

9. a. is the answer. (p. 674)

10. c. is the answer. In this example of the fundamental attribution error, even when given the situational explanation for the woman's behavior, students ignored it and attributed her behavior to her personal disposition. (p. 644)

11. d. is the answer. Our attitudes are more likely to guide our actions when other influences are minimal, especially when the attitude is stable, specific to the behavior, and easily recalled. The presence of other people would more likely be an outside factor that would lessen the likelihood of actions being guided by attitude. (p. 646)

12. a. is the answer. Such justifications arise as a way to preserve inequalities. The just-world phenomenon presumes that people get what they deserve. According to this view, someone who has less must deserve less. (pp. 667, 670)

13. b. is the answer. (p. 658)
 a. & c. Crowding may amplify irritability or altruistic tendencies that are already present. Crowding does not, however, produce these reactions as a general effect.
 d. In fact, just the opposite is true. Crowding often intensifies people's reactions.

14. b. is the answer. (p. 663)
 a. Even if they made up a sizable portion of the group, although still a minority, their numbers would not be as important as their consistency.
 c. & d. These aspects of minority influence were not discussed in the text; however, they are not likely to help a minority sway a majority.

15. a. is the answer. (p. 656)

16. d. is the answer. The text emphasizes the ways in which personal and social controls interact in influencing behavior. It does not suggest that one factor is more influential than the other. (p. 663)

17. b. is the answer. (p. 692)
 a. GRIT is a technique for reducing conflict through a series of conciliatory gestures, not for maintaining the status quo.
 c. & d. These measures may help reduce conflict but they are not aspects of GRIT.

18. a. is the answer. As Solomon Asch's experiments demonstrated, individuals are more likely to conform when they are being observed by others in the group. The other factors were not discussed in the text and probably would not promote conformity. (p. 652)

19. d. is the answer. (p. 644)

20. d. is the answer. Group polarization, or the enhancement of a group's prevailing attitudes, promotes groupthink, which leads to the disintegration of critical thinking. (p. 660)
 a. Groupthink is more likely when a leader highly favors an idea, which may make members reluctant to disagree.

b. A strong minority faction would probably have the opposite effect: It would diminish group harmony while promoting critical thinking.
c. Consulting experts would discourage groupthink by exposing the group to other opinions.

21. **c.** is the answer. (p. 662)

True–False Items

1. T (p. 644)	**6.** T (p. 648)	**11.** T (p. 646)
2. F (p. 644)	**7.** F (p. 671)	**12.** F (p. 687)
3. T (p. 652)	**8.** F (p. 669)	**13.** T (p. 662)
4. T (p. 652)	**9.** F (p. 658)	
5. F (p. 685)	**10.** T (p. 659)	

Psychology Applied

1. **d.** is the answer. According to the frustration-aggression principle, the blocking of an attempt to achieve some goal—in Teresa's case, buying concert tickets—creates anger and can generate aggression. (p. 672)
   a. Evolutionary psychology maintains that aggressive behavior is a genetically based drive. Teresa's behavior clearly was a reaction to a specific situation.
   b. Deindividuation refers to loss of self-restraint in group situations that foster arousal. Teresa's action has only to do with her frustration.
   c. Reward theory views behavior as an exchange process in which people try to maximize the benefits of their behavior by minimizing the costs. Teresa's behavior likely brought her few benefits while exacting some costs, including potential injury, embarrassment, and retaliation by the clerk.

2. **b.** is the answer. Dissonance theory focuses on what happens when our actions contradict our attitudes. (p. 648)
   a. Attribution theory holds that we give causal explanations for others' behavior, often by crediting either the situation or people's dispositions.
   c. Reward theory maintains that we continue relationships that maximize benefits and minimize costs. This has nothing to do with relationships.
   d. This is not a theory of social influence.

3. **d.** is the answer. Social facilitation, or better performance in the presence of others, occurs for easy tasks but not for more difficult ones. For tasks such as proofreading, typing, playing an instrument, or giving a speech, the arousal resulting from the presence of others can lead to mistakes. (p. 657)

4. **a.** is the answer. Group polarization means that the tendencies within a group—and therefore the differences among groups—grow stronger over time. Thus, because the differences between the sorority and nonsorority students have increased, Jane and Sandy are likely to have little in common. (p. 659)
   b. Groupthink is the tendency for realistic decision making to disintegrate when the desire for group harmony is strong.
   c. Deindividuation is the loss of self-restraint and self-awareness that sometimes occurs when one is part of a group.
   d. Social facilitation refers to improved performance of a task in the presence of others.

5. **d.** is the answer. Sherif found that hostility between two groups could be dispelled by giving the groups superordinate, or shared, goals. (p. 690)
   a. Although reducing the likelihood of mirror-image perceptions might reduce mutually destructive behavior, it would not lead to positive feelings between the groups.
   b. Such segregation would likely increase in-group bias and group polarization, resulting in further group conflict.
   c. Contact by itself is not likely to reduce conflict.

6. **c.** is the answer. Prior commitment to an opposing view generally tends to work against conformity. In contrast, large group size, prestigiousness of a group, and an individual's feelings of incompetence and insecurity all strengthen the tendency to conform. (p. 652)

7. **c.** is the answer. People tend to overestimate the similarity of people within groups other than their own. Thus, Juan is not likely to form stereotypes of fitness enthusiasts (a.), political liberals (b.), or older adults (d.) because these are groups to which he belongs. (p. 664)

8. **c.** is the answer. According to the scapegoat theory, when things go wrong, people look for someone on whom to take out their anger and frustration. (p. 669)
   a. These campers are venting their frustration on a member of their *own* cabin group (although this is not always the case with scapegoats).
   b. Prejudice refers to an unjustifiable and usually negative attitude toward another group.
   d. Catharsis is the idea that releasing aggressive energy relieves aggressive urges.

9. **a.** is the answer. As illustrated by Maria's decision to stop buying aerosol products, informational social influence occurs when people have

genuinely been influenced by what they have learned from others. (p. 653)

b. Had Maria's behavior been motivated by the desire to avoid rejection or to gain social approval (which we have no reason to suspect is the case), it would have been an example of normative social influence.

c. Deindividuation refers to the sense of anonymity a person may feel as part of a group.

d. Social facilitation is the improvement in performance of well-learned tasks that may result when one is observed by others.

10. **d.** is the answer. The couple's similar, and presumably distorted, feelings toward each other fuel their conflict. (p. 689)

a. Self-disclosure, or the sharing of intimate feelings, fosters love.

b. Stereotypes are overgeneralized ideas about groups.

c. A social norm is an understood rule for expected and accepted behavior.

11. **d.** is the answer. In this situation, the counterattitudinal behavior is performed voluntarily and cannot be attributed to the demands of the situation. (p. 648)

a., b., & c. In all of these situations, the counterattitudinal behaviors should not arouse much dissonance because they can be attributed to the demands of the situation.

12. **d.** is the answer. The fundamental attribution error refers to the tendency to underestimate situational influences in favor of this type of dispositional attribution when explaining the behavior of other people. (p. 644)

a., b., & c. These are situational attributions.

13. **a.** is the answer. (p. 668)

b. Prejudices are unjustifiable and usually negative attitudes toward other groups. They may result from an ingroup bias, but they are probably not why students favor their own school.

c. Scapegoats are individuals or groups toward which prejudice is directed as an outlet for the anger of frustrated individuals or groups.

d. The just-world phenomenon is the tendency for people to believe others "get what they deserve."

14. **c.** is the answer. Deindividuation involves the loss of self-awareness and self-restraint in group situations that involve arousal and anonymity, so (a.) and (c.) cannot be right. (p. 659)

15. **d.** is the answer. Hundreds of experiments indicate that first impressions are most influenced by physical appearance. (p. 680)

16. **a.** is the answer. According to the two-factor theory, physical arousal can intensify whatever emotion is currently felt. Only in the situation described in a. is Joan likely to be physically aroused. (p. 683)

17. **c.** is the answer. (pp. 671–672)

a. & b. Biology is an important factor in aggressive behavior. This includes genetics, which means identical twins would have similar temperaments.

d. Just the opposite is true.

18. **a.** is the answer. Friends and couples are much more likely than randomly paired people to be similar in views, interests, and a range of other factors. (p. 682)

b. The opposite is true.

c. The mere exposure effect demonstrates that familiarity tends to breed fondness.

d. This is unlikely, given the positive effects of proximity and intimacy.

19. **c.** is the answer. (p. 664)

a. The ingroup bias is the tendency to favor one's own group.

b. Groupthink refers to the unrealistic thought processes and decision making that occur within groups when the desire for group harmony becomes paramount.

d. The fundamental attribution error is our tendency to underestimate the impact of situations and to overestimate the impact of personal dispositions on the behavior of others.

20. **b.** is the answer. In the foot-in-the-door phenomenon, compliance with a small initial request, such as wearing a lapel pin, later is followed by compliance with a much larger request, such as collecting petition signatures. (p. 647)

21. **b.** is the answer. (p. 662)

Essay Question

Your discussion might focus on some of the following topics: normative social influence; conformity, which includes suggestibility; obedience; group polarization; and groupthink.

As a member of any group with established social norms, individuals will often act in ways that enable them to avoid rejection or gain social approval. Thus, a fraternity or sorority pledge would probably be very suggestible and likely to eventually conform to the attitudes and norms projected by the group—or be rejected socially. In extreme cases of pledge hazing, acute social pressures may lead to atypical and antisocial individual behaviors—for example, on the part of pledges complying with the demands of senior members of the fraternity or sorority. Over time, meetings and discussions will probably enhance the group's prevailing attitudes (group polarization). This may lead to the unrealistic and irrational decision making that is groupthink. The potentially negative consequences of groupthink depend on the issues being discussed, but may include a variety of socially destructive behaviors.

Key Terms

1. **Social psychology** is the scientific study of how we think about, influence, and relate to one another. (p. 643)

2. **Attribution theory** deals with our causal explanations of behavior. We attribute behavior to the individual's disposition or to the situation. (p. 644)

3. The **fundamental attribution error** is our tendency to underestimate the impact of situations and to overestimate the impact of personal dispositions upon the behavior of others. (p. 644)

4. **Attitudes** are feelings, often influenced by our beliefs, that may predispose us to respond in particular ways to objects, people, and events. (p. 646)

5. **Central route persuasion** occurs when people respond favorably to arguments as a result of engaging in systematic thinking about an issue. (p. 646)

6. **Peripheral route persuasion** occurs when people are influenced by more superficial and incidental cues, such as a speaker's reputation or appearance. (p. 646)

7. The **foot-in-the-door phenomenon** is the tendency for people who agree to a small request to comply later with a larger request. (p. 647)

8. A **role** is a set of expectations (norms) about how people in a specific social position ought to behave. (p. 647)

9. **Cognitive dissonance theory** refers to the theory that we act to reduce the psychological discomfort we experience when our behavior conflicts with what we think and feel or, more generally, when two of our thoughts are inconsistent. This is frequently accomplished by changing our attitude rather than our behavior. (p. 648)

   Memory aid: *Dissonance* means "lack of harmony." **Cognitive dissonance** occurs when two thoughts, or cognitions, are at variance with one another.

10. **Conformity** is the tendency to change one's thinking or behavior to coincide with a group standard. (p. 651)

11. **Normative social influence** refers to influence that results from a person's desire to avoid rejection or gain social approval. (p. 653)

    Memory aid: *Normative* means "based on a norm, or pattern, regarded as typical for a specific group." **Normative social influence** is the pressure groups exert on the individual to behave in ways acceptable to the group standard.

12. **Informational social influence** results when a person is willing to accept others' opinions about reality. (p. 653)

13. **Social facilitation** is stronger performance of simple or well-learned tasks that occurs when other people are present. (p. 657)

14. **Social loafing** is the tendency for individual effort to be diminished when one is part of a group working toward a common goal. (p. 658)

15. **Deindividuation** refers to the loss of self-restraint and self-awareness that sometimes occurs in group situations that foster arousal and anonymity. (p. 659)

    Memory aid: As a prefix, *de-* indicates reversal or undoing. To *de*individuate is to undo one's individuality.

16. **Group polarization** refers to the enhancement of a group's prevailing tendencies through discussion, which often has the effect of accentuating the group's differences from other groups. (p. 659)

    Memory aid: To *polarize* is to "cause thinking to concentrate about two poles, or contrasting positions."

17. **Groupthink** refers to the unrealistic thought processes and decision making that occur within groups when the desire for group harmony overrides a realistic appraisal of alternatives. (p. 660)

    Example: The psychological tendencies of self-justification, conformity, and group polarization foster the development of the "team spirit" mentality known as **groupthink**.

18. A **culture** is the enduring behaviors, ideas, attitudes, values, and traditions shared by a group of people and transmitted from one generation to the next. (p. 661)

19. **Norms** are understood rules for accepted and expected behavior. (p. 662)

20. **Personal space** refers to the buffer zone that people like to maintain around their bodies. (p. 662)

21. **Prejudice** is an unjustifiable (and usually negative) attitude toward a group and its members. (p. 664)

22. A **stereotype** is a generalized (sometimes accurate but often overgeneralized) belief about a group of people. (p. 664)

23. **Discrimination** is unjustifiable negative behavior toward a group or its members (p. 664)

24. The **ingroup** refers to the people and groups with whom we share a common identity. (p. 668)

25. The **outgroup** refers to the people and groups that are excluded from our ingroup. (p. 668)

26. The **ingroup bias** is the tendency to favor our own group. (p. 668)

27. The **scapegoat theory** proposes that prejudice provides an outlet for anger by finding someone to blame. (p. 669)

28. The **other-race effect** is our tendency to recall the faces of our own race more accurately than those of other races. (p. 669)

29. The **just-world phenomenon** is a manifestation of the commonly held belief that good is rewarded and evil is punished. The logic is indisputable: "If I am rewarded, I must be good." (p. 670)

30. **Aggression** is any physical or verbal behavior intended to hurt or destroy. (p. 670)

31. The **frustration-aggression principle** states that aggression is triggered when people become angry because their efforts to achieve a goal have been blocked. (p. 672)

32. The **mere exposure effect** refers to the fact that repeated exposure to an unfamiliar stimulus increases our liking of it. (p. 678)

33. **Passionate love** refers to an aroused state of intense positive absorption in another person, especially at the beginning of a relationship. (p. 683)

34. **Companionate love** refers to a deep, affectionate attachment to those with whom we share our lives. (p. 684)

35. **Equity** refers to the condition in which there is mutual giving and receiving between the partners in a relationship. (p. 684)

36. **Self-disclosure** refers to a person's sharing intimate feelings with another. (p. 684)

37. **Altruism** is unselfish regard for the welfare of others. (p. 685)

38. The **bystander effect** is the tendency of a person to be less likely to offer help to someone if there are other people present. (p. 686)

39. **Social exchange theory** states that our social behavior revolves around exchanges, in which we try to minimize our costs and maximize our benefits. (p. 687)

40. The **reciprocity norm** is the expectation that people will help those who have helped them. (p. 687)

41. The **social-responsibility norm** is the expectation that people will help those who depend on them. (p. 687)

42. **Conflict** is a perceived incompatibility of actions, goals, or ideas between individuals or groups. (p. 688)

43. A **social trap** is a situation in which conflicting parties become caught in mutually destructive behaviors because each persists in pursuing its own self-interest. (p. 688)

44. **Mirror-image perceptions** are the negative, mutual views that conflicting people often hold about one another. (p. 689)

44. A **self-fulfilling prophecy** is a belief that leads to its own fulfillment. (p. 689)

45. **Superordinate goals** are mutual goals that require the cooperation of individuals or groups otherwise in conflict. (p. 690)

46. **GRIT** (Graduated and Reciprocated Initiatives in Tension-Reduction) is a strategy of conflict resolution based on the defusing effect that conciliatory gestures can have on parties in conflict. (p. 692)

Psychology at Work

APPENDIX OVERVIEW

Appendix B discusses work motivation. People who view their work as a meaningful calling, those working in jobs that optimize their skills, and those who become absorbed in activities that result in flow find work satisfying and enriching. Effective leaders recognize this and develop management styles that focus on workers' strengths and adapt their leadership style to the situation. Research on achievement motivation underscores the importance of self-discipline and persistence in achieving one's goals.

In demonstrating how psychology is applied in the workplace, this appendix describes the specific functions of the major subfields of industrial-organizational psychology, including personnel psychology, organizational psychology, and human factors psychology.

NOTE: Answer guidelines for all Appendix B questions begin on page 381.

UNIT REVIEW

First, skim each section, noting headings and boldface items. After you have read the section, review each objective by answering the fill-in and essay-type questions that follow it. As you proceed, evaluate your performance by consulting the answers beginning on page 381. Do not continue with the next section until you understand each answer. If you need to, review or reread the section in the textbook before continuing.

The Nature of Work (pp. B-1–B-2)

Objective 1: Explain the concept of flow, and identify three subfields of industrial-organizational psychology.

1. According to Freud, the healthy life is filled with _____ and _____ .

2. Most people _____ (have/do not have) a predictable career path, which is one reason that many colleges and universities focus less on _____ and more on _____ .

3. People who view their work as a _____ report the greatest satisfaction.

4. Psychologist Mihaly Csikszentmihalyi formulated the concept of _____ , which is defined as a focused state of _____ and diminished awareness of _____ and time. People who experience this state also experience increased feelings of _____ , _____ , and _____ .

5. People who are unemployed _____ (report/do not report) lower well-being.

6. In industrialized nations, the nature of work has changed, from _____ to _____ to _____ . More and more work is _____ to temporary employees and consultants.

7. The field of _____-_____ psychology applies psychology's principles to the workplace. The subfield of _____ _____ focuses on employee recruitment, training, appraisal, and development. Another subfield, _____ _____ , examines how work environments and _____ styles influence worker motivation, satisfaction,

and productivity. A third subfield,

_____ _____

psychology, focuses on the design of appliances, machines, and work environments.

Personnel Psychology (pp. B-2–B-7)

Objective 2: Describe how personnel psychologists help organizations with employee selection, work placement, and performance appraisal.

1. Researchers note that the first step to a stronger organization is to institute a

   _____-_____

   selection system, which matches strengths to work.

2. (Close-Up) Satisfied and successful people devote less time to _____

   _____ than to

   _____ _____ .

3. Interviewers tend to _____ (feel confident/lack confidence) in their ability to predict job performance from unstructured interviews. These impressions tend to be highly

   _____ (accurate/error-prone).

4. The best predictor of long-term job performance for most jobs is _____

   _____ _____ .

   Interviewers tend to _____ (over/under)estimate their interviewing skills and intuition—a phenomenon labeled the

   _____ _____ .

State four effects that fuel this phenomenon.

5. A more disciplined method of collecting information from job applicants is the

   _____ _____ , which

   asks the same questions of all applicants. This method enhances the _____

accuracy and _____ of the interview process.

6. Performance appraisal has several purposes, including helping organizations decide

   _____ ,

   how to appropriately _____

   _____ ,

   and how to better harness employees'

   _____ . Performance appraisal methods include _____ ,

   _____ _____ scales,

   and _____ _____ scales.

7. Some organizations practice _____-

   _____ feedback, in which employees not only rate themselves but are also rated by their supervisors and other colleagues.

8. Performance appraisal is subject to bias. When the overall evaluation of an employee biases ratings of work-related behaviors, a

   _____ _____

   has occurred. The tendency to be too easy or too harsh results in _____ and

   _____ errors, respectively. When raters focus on easily remembered recent behavior, they are committing the

   _____ error.

Organizational Psychology: Motivating Achievement (pp. B-7–B-13)

Objective 3: Define *achievement motivation*, and explain why organizations would employ an I/O psychologist to help motivate employees and foster employee satisfaction.

1. Psychologists refer to the desire for significant accomplishments, for mastering skills or ideas, for control, and for attaining a high standard as

   _____ _____ .

2. Research has shown that _____ is a better predictor of school performance than

   _____ _____

   have been. Extremely successful individuals differ from equally talented peers in their

   _____ , their passionate dedication to a long-term goal.

3. Positive moods at work contribute to worker

_____ , _____ , and

_____ . Researchers have also

found a positive correlation between measures of

organizational success and employee

_____ , or the extent of workers'

involvement, satisfaction, and enthusiasm.

Objective 4: Describe some effective management techniques.

4. The best managers help people to

_____ , match

tasks to _____ , care how their peo-

ple feel about their work, and

_____ positive behaviors.

5. Higher worker achievement is motivated by a

leader who sets _____ ,

_____ goals.

6. Managers who are directive, set clear standards, organize work, and focus attention on specific goals are said to employ

_____ _____ . More

democratic managers who aim to build team-

work and mediate conflicts in the work force

employ _____ _____ .

7. Effective leaders tend to exude a self-confident

_____ that is a mix of a

_____ of some goal, an ability to

_____ the goal clearly, and enough

optimism to _____ others to fol-

low. Leadership that inspires others to transcend

their own self-interests for the sake of the group

is called _____ leadership.

8. The most effective style of leadership

_____ (varies/does not vary) with

the situation and/or the person.

9. Effective managers _____

(rarely/often) exhibit a high degree of both task

and social leadership. The _____

effect occurs when people respond more positive-

ly to managerial decisions on which they have

voiced an opinion.

Human Factors Psychology (pp. B-13–B-15)

Objective 5: Describe the role human factors psychologists play in creating user-friendly machines and
physical environments.

1. Psychologists who study the importance of con-

sidering perceptual principles in the design of

machines, appliances, and work settings are

called _____

_____ psychologists.

2. Victims of the "curse of knowledge," technology

developers who assume that others share their

_____ may create designs that are

unclear to others.

3. Another example of failure to consider the

human factor in design is the

"_____ _____"

technology that provides embarrassing headsets

that amplify sound for people with hearing loss.

PROGRESS TEST

Multiple-Choice Questions

Circle your answers to the following questions and
check them with the answers on page 382. If your
answer is incorrect, read the explanation for why it is
incorrect and then consult the appropriate pages of
the text (in parentheses following the correct answer).

1. The best predictor of on-the-job performance for
   all but less-skilled jobs is
   a. age.
   b. general mental ability.
   c. motivation.
   d. stated intentions.

2. In almost every industrialized nation, unemployed people report
   a. better health.
   b. lower well-being.
   c. being bored.
   d. enjoying time to travel.

3. To increase employee productivity, industrial-
   organizational psychologists advise managers to
   a. adopt a directive leadership style.
   b. adopt a democratic leadership style.
   c. instill competitiveness in each employee.
   d. deal with employees according to their
      individual motives.

4. Which of the following is NOT an aspect of Henry Murray's definition of achievement motivation?
   a. the desire to master skills
   b. the desire for control
   c. the desire to gain approval
   d. the desire to attain a high standard

5. Which of the following was NOT identified as a contributing factor in the interviewer illusion?
   a. The fact that interviews reveal applicants' intentions but not necessarily their habitual behaviors.
   b. The tendency of interviewers to think that interview behavior only reflects applicants' enduring traits.
   c. The tendency of interviewers to more often follow the successful careers of applicants they hired rather than those who were not hired.
   d. The tendency of most interviewers to rely on unstructured rather than structured interviews.

6. Munson is conducting his annual appraisal of employees' performance. Which of the following is NOT a type of appraisal method?
   a. graphic rating
   b. behavior rating
   c. checklist
   d. unstructured interview

7. Because Brent believes that his employees are intrinsically motivated to work for reasons beyond money, Brent would be described as a(n) _____ manager.
   a. directive   c. task-oriented
   b. social-oriented   d. charismatic

8. Jack works for a company that requires employees to periodically rate their own performance and to be rated by their managers, other colleagues, and customers. This type of assessment is called
   a. 360-degree feedback.
   b. multifactorial evaluation.
   c. analytical performance review.
   d. human resource management.

9. During a meeting with the parents of a struggling high school student, the guidance counselor notes which of the following as the best predictor of school performance?
   a. attendance   c. talent
   b. intelligence scores d. self-discipline

10. Which of the following individuals would be characterized as experiencing flow?
    a. Sheila, who, despite viewing her work as merely a job, performs her work conscientiously
    b. Larry, who sees his work as an artist as a calling
    c. Arnie, who views his present job as merely a stepping stone in his career
    d. Montel, who often becomes so immersed in his writing that he loses all sense of self and time

11. Darren, a sales clerk at a tire store, enjoys his job, not so much for the money as for its challenge and the opportunity to interact with a variety of people. The store manager asks you to recommend a strategy for increasing Darren's motivation. Which of the following is most likely to be effective?
    a. Create a competition among the salespeople so that whoever has the highest sales each week receives a bonus.
    b. Put Darren on a week-by-week employment contract, promising him continued employment only if his sales increase each week.
    c. Leave Darren alone unless his sales drop and then threaten to fire him if his performance doesn't improve.
    d. Involve Darren as much as possible in company decision making and use rewards to inform him of his successful performance.

12. For as long as she has been the plant manager, Juanita has welcomed input from employees and has delegated authority. Bill, in managing his department, takes a more authoritarian, iron-fisted approach. Juanita's style is one of _____ leadership, whereas Bill's is one of _____ leadership.
    a. task; social
    b. social; task
    c. directive; democratic
    d. democratic; participative

13. Dr. Iverson conducts research focusing on how management styles influence worker motivation. Dr. Iverson would most accurately be described as a(n)
    a. motivation psychologist.
    b. personnel psychologist.
    c. organizational psychologist.
    d. human factors psychologist.

14. Dr. Martin is using natural mapping to redesign the instrument gauges of automobiles to be more user-friendly. Dr. Martin is evidently a(n)
    a. psychophysicist.
    b. cognitive psychologist.
    c. human factors psychologist.
    d. experimental psychologist.

15. Thanks to _____ , TiVo and DVR have solved the TV recording problem caused by the complexity of VCRs.
    a. personnel psychologists
    b. human factors psychologists
    c. industrial psychologists
    d. organizational psychologists

Matching Items

Match each term with its definition or description.

Terms

_____ 1. personnel psychology
_____ 2. flow
_____ 3. task leadership
_____ 4. social leadership
_____ 5. industrial-organizational (I/O) psychology
_____ 6. organizational psychology

Definitions or Descriptions

a. state of focused consciousness
b. studies issues related to optimizing behavior in the workplace
c. applies psychological methods and principles to the selection and evaluation of workers
d. goal-oriented leadership that sets standards, organizes work, and focuses attention on goals
e. group-oriented leadership that builds teamwork, mediates conflict, and offers support
f. examines organizational influences on worker satisfaction and productivity

KEY TERMS

Using your own words, write on a separate piece of paper a brief definition or explanation of each of the following terms.

1. flow
2. industrial-organizational (I/O) psychology
3. personnel psychology
4. organizational psychology
5. human factors psychology
6. structured interview
7. achievement motivation
8. task leadership
9. social leadership

ANSWERS
Appendix Review

The Nature of Work

1. work; love

2. do not have; training job skills; enlarging capacities for understanding, thinking, and communicating in any work environment
3. calling
4. flow; consciousness; self; self-esteem, competence, well-being
5. report
6. farming; manufacturing; knowledge work; outsourced
7. industrial-organizational; personnel psychology; organizational psychology; management; human factors

Personnel Psychology

1. strengths-based
2. correcting deficiencies; accentuating strengths
3. feel confident; error-prone
4. general mental ability; over; interviewer illusion
    a. Interviews disclose the interviewee's good intentions, which are less revealing than their typical behaviors.
    b. Interviewers tend to follow the successful careers of people they hired and lose track of those they did not hire.

c. Interviewers mistakenly presume that *how* interviewees present themselves reflects only their enduring traits.

d. Interviewers' preconceptions and moods influence their perceptions of job applicants.

5. structured interview; predictive; reliability

6. who to retain; reward and pay workers; strengths; checklists; graphic rating; behavior rating

7. 360-degree

8. halo error; leniency; severity; recency

Organizational Psychology

1. achievement motivation

2. self-discipline; intelligence scores; grit

3. creativity; persistence; helpfulness; engagement

4. identify and measure their talents; talent; reinforce

5. specific; challenging

6. task leadership; social leadership

7. charisma; vision; communicate; inspire; transformational

8. varies

9. often; voice

Human Factors Psychology

1. human factors

2. expertise

3. assistive listening

Progress Test

Multiple-Choice Questions

1. **b.** is the answer. (p. B-4)

2. **b.** is the answer. (p. B-2)

3. **d.** is the answer. As different people are motivated by different things, to increase motivation and thus productivity, managers are advised to learn what motivates individual employees and to challenge and reward them accordingly. (p. B-10–B-11)
a. & b. The most effective management style will depend on the situation.
c. This might be an effective strategy with some, but not all, employees.

4. **c.** is the answer. (p. B-7)

5. **d.** is the answer. Although unstructured interviews *are* more prone to bias than structured

interviews, the text does not suggest that they are used more often. (p. B-5)

6. **d.** is the answer. (p. B-6)
a., b., & c. These are all performance appraisal methods used by supervisors.

7. **b.** is the answer. (p. B-12)
a. & c. Directive, or task-oriented, managers are likely to assume that worker motivation is low.
d. The most effective leaders are generally charismatic, which has nothing to do with whether they are directive or democratic leaders.

8. **a.** is the answer. (p. B-6–B-7)

9. **d.** is the answer. (p. B-7)

10. **d.** is the answer. (p. B-1)

11. **d.** is the answer. Because Darren appears to resonate with the principle that people are intrinsically motivated to work for reasons beyond money, giving him feedback about his work and involving him in decision making are probably all he needs to be very satisfied with his situation. (pp. B-10–B-11)
a., b., & c. Creating competitions and using controlling, rather than informing, rewards may have the opposite effect and actually undermine Darren's motivation.

12. **b.** is the answer. (p. B-12)
a. Bill's style is one of task leadership, whereas Juanita's is one of social leadership.
c. Juanita's style is democratic, whereas Bill's is directive.
d. Participative is another term used to refer to the social or group-oriented style of leadership.

13. **c.** is the answer. (p. B-2)

14. **c.** is the answer. (p. B-2)

15. **b.** is the answer. (p. B-13)

Matching Items

1. c (p. B-2)
2. a (p. B-1)
3. d (p. B-12)
4. e (p. B-12)
5. b (p. B-2)
6. f (p. B-2)

Key Terms

1. **Flow** is a completely involved, focused state of consciousness on a task that optimally engages a person's skills, often accompanied by a diminished awareness of self and time. (p. B-1)

2. **Industrial-organizational (I/O) psychology** is a profession that applies psychological principles

to optimizing human behavior in workplaces. (p. B-2)

3. **Personnel psychology** is a subfield of I/O psychology that applies psychological methods and principles to the selection and evaluation of workers. (p. B-2)

4. **Organizational psychology** is a subfield of I/O psychology that explores how work environments and management styles affect worker motivation, satisfaction, and productivity. (p. B-2)

5. **Human factors psychology** explores how people and machines interact and how machines and physical environments can be made safe and easy to use. (p. B-2)

6. A **structured interview** is one in which an interviewer asks the same job-relevant questions of all interviewees, who are then rated on established evaluation scales. (p. B-5)

7. **Achievement motivation** is a desire for significant accomplishment; for mastery of things, people, or ideas; and for attaining a high standard. (p. B-7)

8. **Task leadership** is goal-oriented leadership that sets standards, organizes work, and focuses attention on goals. (p. B-12)

9. **Social leadership** is group-oriented leadership that builds teamwork, mediates conflict, and offers support. (p. B-12)

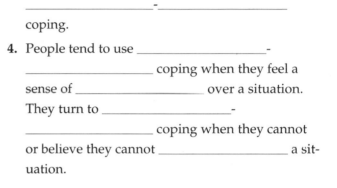

Promoting Health

APPENDIX OVERVIEW

Appendix C addresses important issues related to the ways in which we cope with and manage stress. Important to our ability to cope is a sense of control over the situation, our outlook on life, and the amount of social support we receive from friends and relatives. Managing stress may be accomplished through aerobic exercise, biofeedback, or other relaxation techniques. Research has shown that there is a positive correlation between religiosity and longevity.

NOTE: Answer guidelines for all Appendix C questions begin on page 388.

APPENDIX REVIEW

First, skim each section, noting headings and boldface items. After you have read the section, review each objective by answering the fill-in and essay-type questions that follow it. As you proceed, evaluate your performance by consulting the answers beginning on page 388. Do not continue with the next section until you understand each answer. If you need to, review or reread the section in the textbook before continuing.

Coping With Stress (pp. C-1–C-6)

Objective 1: Identify two ways people cope with stress.

1. People learn to _____ with stress by finding emotional, cognitive, or behavioral ways to alleviate it.

2. When we cope directly with a stressor, we are using _____-_____ coping.

3. When we attempt to alleviate stress by avoiding it and attending to emotional needs, we are using

   _____-_____

   coping.

4. People tend to use _____-

   _____ coping when they feel a

   sense of _____ over a situation.

   They turn to _____-

   _____ coping when they cannot

   or believe they cannot _____ a situation.

Objective 2: Discuss the links among perceived control, outlook on life, social support, stress, and health.

5. Negative situations are especially stressful when they are appraised as _____ .

6. With higher economic status comes lower risks of infant _____ , a low

   _____ _____ ,

   smoking, and _____ .

7. In animals and humans, sudden lack of control is followed by a drop in immune responses, a(n) _____ (increase/decrease) in blood pressure, and a rise in the levels of

   _____ _____ .

8. People who have an _____ outlook on life are less likely than others to suffer ill health.

9. Researchers have found that life events may be less stressful for people who have a good sense of

   _____ .

10. One study found that laughter caused improved _____ and increased
_____ .

11. Another buffer against the effects of stress is _____ support.

12. Longitudinal research reveals that a
_____ _____ at age 50 predicts healthy aging better than
_____ _____ at the same age.

State some possible reasons for the link between health and social support.

13. James Pennebaker has found that emotional _____ can adversely affect our physical health.

14. Health can also be improved by _____ about personal traumas in a diary.

15. Another way to reduce stress is to talk about it. In another study by Pennebaker, Holocaust survivors who were the most _____ had the most improved health.

Manging Stress (pp. C-6–C-12)

Objective 3: Discuss the advantages of aerobic exercise as a technique for managing stress and fostering well-being.

1. Sustained exercise that increases heart and lung fitness is known as _____ exercise.

2. Experiments _____ (have/have not) been able to demonstrate conclusively that such exercise reduces anxiety, depression, and stress.

3. Exercise increases the body's production of mood-boosting neurotransmitters such as
_____ , _____ , and the _____ . It also strengthens the heart, increases _____ , keeps blood vessels open, and lowers
_____ _____ .

And, it predicts better _____ functioning and reduced risk of _____ and Alzheimer's disease.

4. By one estimate, moderate exercise adds, on average, _____ (how many?) years to one's life expectancy.

Objective 4: Compare the benefits of biofeedback and relaxation training as stress-management techniques, and discuss meditation as a relaxation technique.

5. A system for recording a physiological response and providing information concerning it is called _____ . The instruments used in this system _____ (provide/do not provide) the individual with a means of monitoring physiological responses.

6. (text and Close-Up) Simple relaxation procedures have been shown to help alleviate
_____ , _____ , _____ , and _____ . Lowered blood pressure, heart rate, and oxygen consumption have been found to be characteristic of people who regularly practice
_____ . The _____ response is a state of calm resulting from sitting quietly, with closed eyes, while breathing deeply.

7. Brain scans of experienced meditators reveal decreased activity in the _____ lobe and increased activity in the _____ lobe.

Objective 5: Discuss the controversy over complementary and alternative medicine, and explain how it is best resolved through scientific research.

8. (Thinking Critically) Acupuncture, massage therapy, homeopathy, and similar treatments comprise the growing health care market called

_____ _____

_____ _____ . In

China, _____ therapies have

flourished for centuries, as have acupuncture and

acupressure therapies that claim to correct imbal-

ances in the flow of the energy called

_____ .

9. (Thinking Critically) Critics of alternative medi-

cine point out that such treatments seem especial-

ly effective with _____

diseases such as arthritis and _____ ,

as well as with diseases that disappear

naturally—a phenomenon called

_____ _____ .

Critics also argue that the seeming effectiveness

of alternative medicine is due to a

_____ effect.

Objective 6: Discuss the correlation between
religiosity and longevity, and offer some possible
explanations for this link.

10. Until fairly recently in history, the healing tradi-

tions of _____ and

_____ have worked

_____ (together/separately).

11. Several recent studies demonstrate that religious

involvement _____ (predicts/

does not predict) health and longevity.

State two possible intervening variables that might
account for the "faith factor" in health.

PROGRESS TEST

Circle your answers to the following questions and
check them with the answers on page 389. If your
answer is incorrect, read the explanation for why it is
incorrect and then consult the appropriate pages of
the text (in parentheses following the correct answer).

1. Attempting to alleviate stress directly by changing a stressor or how we interact with it is an
example of
   a. problem-focused coping.
   b. emotion-focused coping.
   c. managing rather than coping with stress.
   d. catharsis.

2. Which of the following was NOT mentioned in
the text as a potential health benefit of exercise?
   a. Exercise can increase ability to cope with
      stress.
   b. Exercise can lower blood pressure.
   c. Exercise can reduce stress, depression, and
      anxiety.
   d. Exercise improves functioning of the immune
      system.

3. Social support _____ our ability to cope with
stressful events.
   a. has no effect on
   b. usually increases
   c. usually decreases
   d. has an unpredictable effect on

4. Research has demonstrated that as a predictor of
health and longevity, religious involvement
   a. has a small, insignificant effect.
   b. is more accurate for women than men.
   c. is more accurate for men than women.
   d. rivals nonsmoking and exercise.

5. Which of the following is true of biofeedback
training?
   a. A person is given sensory feedback for a sub-
      tle body response.
   b. Biological functions controlled by the auto-
      nomic nervous system may come under con-
      scious control.
   c. The accompanying relaxation is much the
      same as that produced by other, simpler
      methods of relaxation.
   d. All of these statements are true.

6. Which of the following was NOT suggested as a
possible explanation of the "faith factor" in
health?
   a. Having a coherent worldview is a buffer
      against stress.
   b. Religious people tend to have healthier life-
      styles.
   c. Those who are religious have stronger net-
      works of social support.
   d. Because they are more affluent, religiously
      active people receive better health care.

7. (Thinking Critically) Acupuncture, aromatherapy, and homeopathy are forms of
   a. psychophysiological medicine.
   b. complementary and alternative medicine.
   c. *Chi* therapy.
   d. psychosomatic medicine.

8. Ricardo has been unable to resolve a stressful relationship with a family member. To cope, he turns to a close friend for social support. Ricardo's coping strategy is an example of
   a. problem-focused coping.
   b. emotion-focused coping.
   c. managing rather than coping.
   d. general adaptation.

9. To help him deal with a stressful schedule of classes, work, and studying, Randy turns to a regular program of exercise and relaxation training. Randy's strategy is an example of
   a. problem-focused coping.
   b. emotion-focused coping.
   c. managing rather than coping.
   d. general adaptation.

10. Which of the following would be the BEST piece of advice to offer a person who is trying to minimize the adverse effects of stress on his or her health?
    a. "Avoid challenging situations that may prove stressful."
    b. "Learn to play as hard as you work."
    c. "Maintain a sense of control and a positive approach to life."
    d. "Keep your emotional responses in check by keeping your feelings to yourself."

11. You have just transferred to a new school and find yourself in a potentially stressful environment. According to the text, which of the following would help you cope with the stress?
    a. believing that you have some control over your environment
    b. having a friend to confide in
    c. feeling optimistic that you will eventually adjust to your new surroundings
    d. All of these things would help.

12. (Thinking Critically) Andrew, who is convinced that an expensive herbal remedy "cured" his arthritis, has decided to turn to homeopathy and herbal medicine for all of his health care. You caution him by pointing out that
    a. arthritis is a cyclical disease that often

improves on its own.
    b. botanical herbs have never been proven effective in controlled experiments.
    c. alternative medicine is a recent fad in this country that has few proponents in other parts of the world.
    d. all of these statements are true.

Essay Question

Discuss several factors that enhance a person's ability to cope with stress. (Use the space below to list the points you want to make, and organize them. Then write the essay on a separate sheet of paper.)

KEY TERMS

Using your own words, on a separate piece of paper write a brief definition or explanation of each of the following terms.

1. coping
2. problem-focused coping
3. emotion-focused coping
4. aerobic exercise
5. biofeedback
6. complementary and alternative medicine (CAM)

ANSWERS

Unit Review

Coping With Stress
1. cope
2. problem-focused
3. emotion-focused
4. problem-focused; control; emotion-focused; change
5. uncontrollable

6. mortality; birth weight; violence

7. increase; stress hormones

8. optimistic

9. humor

10. tone; bloodflow

11. social

12. good marriage; low cholesterol

Close relationships provide the opportunity to confide painful feelings, which may mitigate physical reactions to stressful events. Environments that foster our need to belong also foster stronger immune functioning.

13. suppression

14. writing

15. self-disclosing

Managing Stress

1. aerobic

2. have

3. norepinephrine; serotonin; endorphins; bloodflow; blood pressure; cognitive; dementia

4. two

5. biofeedback; provide

6. headaches; hypertension; anxiety; insomnia; meditation; relaxation

7. parietal; frontal

8. complementary and alternative medicine; herbal; *Qi* or *Chi*

9. cyclical; allergies, spontaneous remission; placebo

10. religion; medicine; together

11. predicts

Religiously active people have healthier life-styles. They also tend to have stronger networks of social support and are more likely to be married.

Progress Test

Multiple-Choice Questions

1. **a.** is the answer. (p. C-1)
   b. In emotion-focused coping, we attempt to alleviate stress by avoiding or ignoring it.
   c. This is an example of coping rather than managing stress because it involves an attempt to actually alleviate a stressor.
   d. Catharsis refers to the release of emotion.

2. **d.** is the answer. Regular aerobic exercise has been shown to increase ability to cope with stress, lower blood pressure, and reduce depression and anxiety. The text does not cite evidence that exercise enhances immune function. (pp. C-6–C-7)

3. **b.** is the answer. (p. C-4)

4. **d.** is the answer. (p. C-11)
   b. & c. The text does not indicate that a gender difference exists in the "faith factor" in health.

5. **d.** is the answer. In biofeedback training, people are given sensory feedback about subtle physiological responses. Although biofeedback may promote relaxation, its benefits may be no greater than those produced by simpler, and less expensive, methods. (p. C-8)

6. **d.** is the answer. As a group, religiously active people are no more affluent than other people. (pp. C-11–C-12)

7. **b.** is the answer. (p. C-9)
   a. There is no such subfield of medicine.
   c. *Chi* is an alleged form of energy, imbalances of which Chinese herbal therapies and acupuncture are intended to treat.
   d. The term "psychosomatic" was once used to describe psychologically caused symptoms. Many forms of alternative medicine, including acupuncture, are intended to treat a full range of symptoms and diseases.

8. **b.** is the answer. Ricardo is attempting to address his emotional needs, since he has been unable to alleviate stress directly. (p. C-1)

9. **c.** is the answer. (pp. C-6, C-8)

10. **c.** is the answer. (pp. C-2, C-3)
    a. This is not realistic.
    b. & d. These might actually *increase* the health consequences of potential stressors.

11. **d.** is the answer. (pp. C-2–C-4)

12. **a.** is the answer. (p. C-9)
    b. In fact, botanical herbs have given us many widely used drugs, including morphine and penicillin, each of which was proven to be useful in controlled research studies.
    c. Herbal remedies and acupuncture—to name two forms of complementary and alternative medicine—have a long tradition in other parts of the world and remain enormously popular today.

Essay Question

When potentially stressful events occur, a person's appraisal is a major determinant of their impact. Events are especially stressful when appraised as negative and uncontrollable and when the person has a pessimistic outlook on life. Under these circumstances, stressful events may suppress immune responses and make the person more vulnerable to disease. If stressors cannot be eliminated, aerobic exercise, biofeedback, relaxation, and spirituality can help the person cope. Aerobic exercise can reduce stress, depression, and anxiety, perhaps by increasing production of mood-boosting neurotransmitters.

During biofeedback training, people enjoy a calm, relaxing experience that can be helpful in reducing stress. Research demonstrates that people who regularly practice relaxation techniques enjoy a greater sense of tranquility and have lower blood pressure and stronger immune responses. People with strong social ties eat better, exercise more, and smoke and drink less. Social support may also help people evaluate and overcome stressful events. In addition, confiding painful feelings to others has been demonstrated to improve health.

Key Terms

1. **Coping** refers to any effort to alleviate stress using emotional, cognitive, or behavioral methods. (p. C-1)

2. **Problem-focused coping** involves reducing stress by directly changing a stressor or how we interact with it. (p. C-1)

3. **Emotion-focused coping** involves reducing stress by avoiding or ignoring a stressor and attending to the emotional reactions it triggers. (p. C-1)

4. **Aerobic exercise** is any sustained activity such as running, swimming, or cycling that promotes heart and lung fitness and may help alleviate depression and anxiety. (p. C-6)

5. **Biofeedback** refers to a system for electronically recording, amplifying, and feeding back information regarding a subtle physiological state. (p. C-8)

   Memory aid: A **biofeedback** device, such as a brain-wave trainer, provides auditory or visual feedback about biological responses.

6. **Complementary and alternative medicine (CAM)** is a collection of health care remedies and treatments that have not been accepted by medical science or verified by controlled research trials. (p. C-9)

Animal Thinking and Language

APPENDIX OVERVIEW

Appendix D is concerned with thinking and language use by animals. Both humans and animals such as the great apes form concepts, display insight, use tools, demonstrate an understanding of numbers, and transmit cultural innovations.

NOTE: Answer guidelines for all Appendix D questions appear on page 392.

APPENDIX REVIEW

First, skim each section, noting headings and boldface items. After you have read the section, review each objective by answering the fill-in and essay-type questions that follow it. As you proceed, evaluate your performance by consulting the answers on page 392. Do not continue with the next section until you understand each answer. If you need to, review or reread the section in the textbook before continuing.

What Do Animals Think? (pp. D-1–D-2)

Objective 1: Identify some of the cognitive skills shared by the great apes and humans.

1. Animals are capable of forming

   _____ .

2. Forest-dwelling chimpanzees learn to use different sticks as _____ . These behaviors, along with behaviors related to grooming and courtship, _____ (vary/do not vary) from one group of chimpanzees to another, suggesting the transmission of _____ customs.

3. Some animals also display an amazing _____ ability; for example, Alex the parrot could say how many objects were in a group.

Do Animals Exhibit Language? and The Case of the Apes (pp. D-3–D-6)

Objective 2: Outline the arguments for and against the idea that animals and humans share the capacity for language.

1. Animals definitely _____ (do/do not) communicate. For example, honeybees do so by means of a _____ .

2. Allen and Beatrix Gardner attempted to communicate with the chimpanzee Washoe by teaching her _____ _____ .

3. Skeptics believe that some chimpanzee trainers may be overgenerous in interpreting ambiguous animal signing, thanks to their

   _____ _____ , the tendency to see what they want or expect to see.

4. Most now agree that humans _____ (alone/along with primates) possess language that involves complex grammar.

5. The philosopher _____ believed that animals were living robots that could not think.

Summarize some of the arguments of skeptics of the "talking apes" research and some responses of believers.

PROGRESS TEST

Multiple-Choice Questions

Circle your answers to the following questions and check them with the answers on this page. If your answer is incorrect, read the explanation for why it is incorrect and then consult the appropriate pages of the text (in parentheses following the correct answer).

1. Which of the following has been argued by critics of ape language research?
   a. Ape language is merely imitation of the trainer's behavior.
   b. There is little evidence that apes can equal even a 3-year-old's ability to order words with proper syntax.
   c. By seeing what they wish to see, trainers attribute greater linguistic ability to apes than actually exists.
   d. All of these are arguments by critics.

2. Researchers who are convinced that animals can think point to evidence that
   a. chimpanzees demonstrate the ability to "count" by learning to touch pictures of objects in ascending numerical order.
   b. chimpanzees regularly use sticks as tools in their natural habitats.
   c. chimps invent grooming and courtship customs and pass them on to their peers.
   d. they exhibit all of these skills

3. Researchers who believe that some primates can read intent point to evidence that
   a. chimpanzees have recognized themselves in a mirror.
   b. marmosets can learn from and imitate others.
   c. chimpanzees in the wild use sticks as tools.
   d. honeybees communicate the direction and distance of a food source by performing a dance.

4. Researchers taught the chimpanzee Washoe and the gorilla Koko to communicate by using
   a. various sounds.
   b. plastic symbols of various shapes and colors.
   c. sign language.
   d. lifelike dolls and other toys.

ANSWERS
Appendix Review

What Do Animals Think?

1. concepts
2. tools; vary; cultural
3. numerical

Do Animals Exhibit Language? and *The Case of the Apes*

1. do; dance
2. sign language
3. perceptual set
4. alone
5. René Descartes

Chimps have acquired only limited vocabularies and—in contrast to children—have acquired these vocabularies only with great difficulty. Also in contrast to children, it's unclear that chimps can use syntax to express meaning. The signing of chimps is often nothing more than imitation of the trainer's actions. People tend to interpret such ambiguous behavior in terms of what they want to see. Believers contend that although animals do not have our facility for language, they have the abilities to communicate. For example, Washoe and Loulis sign spontaneously. Also, pygmy chimps can learn to comprehend the nuances of spoken English.

Progress Test

1. d. is the answer. (p. D-4)
2. d. is the answer. (pp. D-1–D-2)
3. a. is the answer. (p. D-2)
   b. & c. Imitation and tool use are clear indicators of animal communication and thinking, respectively. However, they reveal nothing about the ability to read intent in another.
   d. Honeybees are insects, not primates!
4. c. is the answer. (p. D-3)